Reading Victorian Literature

Reading Victorian Literature

Essays in Honour of J. Hillis Miller

Edited by Julian Wolfreys
and Monika Szuba

EDINBURGH
University Press

Edinburgh University Press is one of the leading university presses in the UK. We publish academic books and journals in our selected subject areas across the humanities and social sciences, combining cutting-edge scholarship with high editorial and production values to produce academic works of lasting importance. For more information visit our website: edinburghuniversitypress.com

© editorial matter and organisation Julian Wolfreys and Monika Szuba, 2019, 2021
© the chapters their several authors, 2019, 2021

Edinburgh University Press Ltd
The Tun – Holyrood Road, 12(2f) Jackson's Entry, Edinburgh EH8 8PJ

First published in hardback by Edinburgh University Press 2019

Typeset in 10.5/13 Adobe Sabon by
Servis Filmsetting Ltd, Stockport, Cheshire

A CIP record for this book is available from the British Library

ISBN 978 1 4744 4797 3 (hardback)
ISBN 978 1 4744 4798 0 (paperback)
ISBN 978 1 4744 4799 7 (webready PDF)
ISBN 978 1 4744 4800 0 (epub)

The right of Julian Wolfreys and Monika Szuba to be identified as the Editor of this work has been asserted in accordance with the Copyright, Designs and Patents Act 1988, and the Copyright and Related Rights Regulations 2003 (SI No. 2498).

Contents

Notes on Contributors viii
Acknowledgements xiv

Foreword xv
Monika Szuba and Julian Wolfreys

Introduction: There Can Be No Doubt – The Reading of
J. Hillis Miller 1
Monika Szuba and Julian Wolfreys

I Singular Hardy

1. Varieties of Rural Experience: Country Communities in
   Virginia and Wessex 13
   J. Hillis Miller
2. 'There were three men came out of the west': Experiencing
   the Rural or, the Ghosts of Community – a 'Response' for
   J. Hillis Miller 52
   Julian Wolfreys
3. 'What consciousness grasps': 'silent knowing' and the
   Natural World in Hardy's Poetry 83
   Monika Szuba
4. The Hills Have Eyes 100
   Éamonn Dunne

II Self and World

5. J. Hillis Miller's Hopkins: Poet of the Anthropocene 117
   Claire Colebrook

6. Walter Pater in the Wilderness — 135
   Megan Becker-Leckrone
7. 'This world is now thy pilgrimage': William Michael Rossetti's Cognitive Maps of France and Italy — 170
   Eleonora Sasso
8. Personal and Political Fainéance in George Gissing's *Veranilda* — 184
   Tom Ue
9. *Great Expectations*: Narration, Cognition, Possibility — 202
   Dianne F. Sadoff

III Histories, Historicities

10. How Not to Historicise a Poem: On McGann's 'Light Brigade' — 223
    Henry Staten
11. Hellenising the Roman Past: Walter Pater's *Marius the Epicurean* and Anthony Trollope's *Life of Cicero* — 239
    Frederik Van Dam and Melanie Hacke
12. The Ghost in the Machinal: De-/Re-contextualising *Daniel Deronda* — 254
    Sundeep Bisla
13. J. Hillis Miller's All Souls' Day: Formalism and Historicism in Victorian and Modern Fiction Studies — 284
    Perry Meisel

IV Strange Pleasures

14. The Comedian as the Letter C: Wit in *Martin Chuzzlewit* — 299
    Robert Douglas-Fairhurst
15. Dickens's Theatre of Shame — 316
    James Eli Adams
16. Critical Listening and Rhetorical Reading: Performative Utterance in George Eliot's *Felix Holt* — 332
    Helen Groth
17. Repetition and/of/in Victorian Pleasures — 346
    John Maynard
18. Philanthropic Rot in Print Run for Profit: The *Tu-Quoque*-Time-Bomb in Conrad's *Heart of Darkness* — 358
    Ortwin de Graef

V Interviews

19. *The Pleasure of That Obstinacy*: An Interview with J. Hillis Miller 387
    Frederik Van Dam
20. Toward an Appreciation of the Victorian *Umwelt*: An Interview with J. Hillis Miller 400
    Monika Szuba and Julian Wolfreys

Afterword

Dickens in My Life 409
J. Hillis Miller

Bibliography 418
Index 441

Notes on Contributors

James Eli Adams is Professor and Director of Graduate Studies in English and Comparative Literature at Columbia University. He is the author of *Dandies and Desert Saints: Styles of Victorian Masculinity* (Cornell, 1995) and *A History of Victorian Literature* (Wiley-Blackwell, 2009), as well as the co-editor, with Andrew Miller, of *Sexualities in Victorian Britain* (Indiana, 1996) and the general editor of *The Encyclopedia of the Victorian Era* (Grolier, 2004). From 1993 until 2000 he co-edited *Victorian Studies*, where he remains a member of the Advisory Board. He is also the author of numerous articles and chapters on Victorian literature and culture, most recently 'The Trouble with Angels: Dickens, Gender, and Sexuality', in *The Oxford Companion to Charles Dickens* (2018).

Megan Becker-Leckrone is Associate Professor of English at the University of Nevada, Las Vegas, where she specializes in critical theory, late-Victorian studies, and medical humanities. J. Hillis Miller served as her doctoral advisor at the University of California, Irvine, from which she received her PhD in 1996. Becker-Leckrone is the author of *Julia Kristeva and Literary Theory* (Palgrave, 2005), the former editor of *The Pater Newsletter* (2007–11), and a former book review editor for *Victoriographies*. She has contributed to *The Bloomsbury Handbook of Literary and Cultural Theory* (2019) and other guides to theory. Her essay 'Wilde's Cosmos: Language, Citation, and Aesthetic Communities' was recently published in *Wilde's Other Worlds* (Routledge, 2018), edited by Michael Davis and Petra Dierkes-Thrun. Forthcoming publications include 'Max Beerbohm's "Improved" *Intentions* and the Aesthetics of *Cosmesis*', in *Extraordinary Aesthetes* (University of Toronto, 2019), edited by Joseph Bristow, and a related article on a species of eighteenth-

and nineteenth-century extra-illustration called 'Grangerism' is included in *Microgenres: A Quick Survey* (Bloomsbury, 2019), edited by Anne Stevens and Molly O'Donnell. Her current research in medical humanities is centred around a book-length study called 'The Materiality of Migraine'; a selection from this work appears in the Winter 2018 issue of *Narrative Inquiry in Bioethics: A Journal of Qualitative Bioethics*.

Deep Bisla is Associate Professor of Victorian Literature in the English Department of York College/CUNY. From 1993 to 1995 he was a graduate student in the Department of English and Comparative Literature at the University of California at Irvine. While there, he took a graduate course with J. Hillis Miller entitled 'Proust and Others'. His term paper for this class became his first published essay, 'Reading the Native Informant Reading: The Art of Passing on Empathy in *Beloved*' (1999). He has since published a deconstructive analysis of the major works of Wilkie Collins: *Wilkie Collins and Copyright* (2013).

Claire Colebrook is author of *New Literary Histories* (Manchester University Press, 1997), *Ethics and Representation* (Edinburgh University Press, 1999), *Deleuze: A Guide for the Perplexed* (Continuum, 1997), *Gilles Deleuze* (Routledge, 2002), *Understanding Deleuze* (Allen and Unwin, 2002), *Irony in the Work of Philosophy* (Nebraska University Press, 2002), *Gender* (Palgrave, 2003), *Irony* (Routledge, 2004), *Milton, Evil and Literary History* (Continuum, 2008), *Deleuze and the Meaning of Life* (Continuum, 2010), and *William Blake and Digital Aesthetics* (Continuum, 2011). She co-authored *Theory and the Disappearing Future* with Tom Cohen and J. Hillis Miller (Routledge, 2011), and co-edited *Deleuze and Feminist Theory* with Ian Buchanan (Edinburgh University Press, 2000), *Deleuze and History* with Jeff Bell (Edinburgh University Press, 2008), *Deleuze and Gender* with Jami Weinstein (Edinburgh University Press, 2009) and *Deleuze and Law* (Palgrave) with Rosi Braidotti and Patrick Hanafin. She is the co-editor, with Tom Cohen, of a series of monographs for Open Humanities Press: Critical Climate Change. She has written articles on visual culture, poetry, literary theory, queer theory and contemporary culture. She recently completed two books on Extinction for Open Humanities Press, *The Death of the Posthuman* and *Sex After Life*, and has co-authored (with Jason Maxwell) *Agamben* (Polity, 2015) and (with Tom Cohen and J. Hillis Miller) *Twilight of the Anthropocene Idols* (Open Humanities Press, 2016). She is now completing a book on fragility (of the species, the archive and the earth).

Robert Douglas-Fairhurst is Professor of English Literature at the University of Oxford and a Fellow and Tutor at Magdalen College. He is the author of *Victorian Afterlives* (Oxford University Press, 2002), *Becoming Dickens: The Invention of a Novelist* (Harvard University Press, 2011), which was awarded the 2011 Duff Cooper Prize, and *The Story of Alice: Lewis Carroll and the Secret History of Wonderland* (Harvill Secker and Harvard University Press), which was shortlisted for the 2015 Costa Prize. He has also produced editions of Dickens's *Christmas Stories* and *Great Expectations*, Kingsley's *The Water-Babies*, and Henry Mayhew's *London Labour and the London Poor*, all for Oxford World's Classics, and is currently completing editions of *The Collected Peter Pan* for Oxford University Press and *A Tale of Two Cities* for Norton. He writes regularly for publications including the *Guardian*, *TLS*, *Times*, *Spectator*, *Literary Review* and *New Statesman*. Radio and television appearances include *Start the Week*, *BBC Breakfast* and *The Culture Show*, and he has also acted as the historical consultant on BBC productions of *Jane Eyre*, *Emma*, *Great Expectations* and *Dickensian*. In 2013 he was a judge of the Man Booker Prize, and in 2015 he was made a Fellow of the Royal Society of Literature.

Éamonn Dunne is a researcher in the School of Education, Trinity College Dublin, Ireland, where he is writing on the limits of understanding, pervo-pedagogics, unlearning and reading. He holds a doctorate in modern English and contemporary literature from University College Dublin and is also at work researching a new book on radical pedagogy and the philosophy of unlearning. He is the author of *J. Hillis Miller and the Possibilities of Reading: Literature after Deconstruction* (Continuum, 2010), *Reading Theory Now* (Bloomsbury, 2013) and, with Aidan Seery, *The Pedagogics of Unlearning* (Punctum, 2016). Research interests include philosophies of the event, radical pedagogies, Holocaust studies, and literature and trauma.

Ortwin de Graef, professor of English Literature at Katholieke Universiteit Leuven, is the author of two books on Paul de Man and has published widely on Romantic and post-Romantic writing ranging from Wordsworth, Tennyson, Browning, Arnold and George Eliot through Isaac Rosenberg, Virginia Woolf and Pearl S. Buck to Hafid Bouazza, David Grossman, Alan Warner and A. L. Kennedy. He has also co-produced the documentary *The Pleasure of that Obstinacy: J. Hillis Miller on Anthony Trollope, Reading, and Technology* (2015). His principal research interests are the Very-Long-Nineteenth-Century ideologies of sympathy, science and the State reflected and refracted through the transmission technologies of the literary.

Helen Groth is Professor of English and Associate Dean of Arts and Social Sciences, University of New South Wales. Her publications include *Victorian Photography and Literary Nostalgia* (Oxford University Press, 2003), *Moving Images: Nineteenth-Century Reading and Screen Practices* (Edinburgh University Press, 2013), and with Natalya Lusty, *Dreams and Modernity: A Cultural History* (Routledge, 2013). She has recently co-edited two collections, *Sounding Modernism* (Edinburgh University Press, 2017), and *Mindful Aesthetics: Literature and the Science of Mind* (Bloomsbury, 2014), and has published on Victorian visual culture, literature and dreams, and more recently, sound and literature. Forthcoming are a chapter on 'Charlotte Brontë and the Listening Reader' in *The Brontës and the Idea of the Human*, edited by Alexandra Lewis, with Cambridge University Press, 2019 and, also with Cambridge and forthcoming in 2019, a chapter on 'Literary Soundscapes' in *Literature and Sound*, edited by Anna Snaith. She has two current book projects, one on 'The Listening Reader' and another on rioting in the literary archive from 1780 to the present.

Melanie Hacke graduated as Master of Western Literature (English and Latin) at the University of Leuven in 2015, and as Master in Victorian Studies at the University of Exeter in 2016. Since 2016, she has been a PhD candidate at the Centre for Reception Studies (University of Leuven, Brussels campus), where she is preparing a dissertation on the reception and translation of foreign cultures in British Romantic periodicals.

John Maynard is Emeritus Professor of English at New York University. He has written on biography, especially of Robert Browning, on Victorian sexuality, especially in the work of Charlotte Brontë, on various Victorian discourses on sexuality and religion, and on theory of interpretation, especially the issues around literary intentionality and readers. He served as chair of his department for six years and as co-editor of *Victorian Literature and Culture* for twenty-six years.

Perry Meisel's books include *The Myth of the Modern*, *The Literary Freud* and *The Myth of Popular Culture*. He is also co-editor of Ferdinand de Saussure's *Course in General Linguistics* and co-editor of *Bloomsbury/Freud: The Letters of James and Alix Strachey, 1934–25*.

J. Hillis Miller is UCI Distinguished Research Professor of Comparative Literature and English Emeritus at the University of California at Irvine. He has published many books and essays on nineteenth- and twentieth-century literature and on literary theory: *Communities in Fiction* appeared in 2015 from Fordham University Press, *Twilight of the Anthropocene Idols*, co-authored with Tom Cohen and Claire Colebrook, appeared in 2016 from Open Humanities Press and *An Innocent Abroad: Lectures in China*, which gathers fifteen of the more than thirty lectures Miller gave at various universities in China between 1988 and 2012, appeared in late 2015 from Northwestern University Press. Miller is a Fellow of the American Academy of the Arts and Sciences and a member of the American Philosophical Society.

Dianne F. Sadoff is professor emerita of English and former Director of the Program in Cinema Studies at Rutgers University, New Brunswick. She has published *Victorian Vogue: British Novels on Screen* (Minnesota, 2010), *Sciences of the Flesh: Representing Subject and Body in Psychoanalysis* (Stanford, 1998) and *Monsters of Affection: Dickens, Brontë, and Eliot on Fatherhood* (Johns Hopkins, 1982). She has co-edited *Victorian Afterlife: Postmodernism Rewrites the Nineteenth Century* (Minnesota, 2000) and *Teaching Theory to Undergraduates* (MLA, 1994). Her current project interrogates nineteenth-century novelistic genres, subgenres and hybridizations.

Eleonora Sasso is Senior Lecturer in English at the 'G. d'Annunzio' University of Chieti-Pescara (Italy). Her major research fields include Victorian literature, the Pre-Raphaelites, cognitive linguistics, inter-semiotic and audio-visual translation, and Canadian studies. She has translated into Italian W. M. Rossetti's *Some Reminiscences* and is author of four monographs, the most recent being *The Pre-Raphaelites and Orientalism: Language and Cognition in Remediations of the East* (Edinburgh University Press).

Henry Staten is Professor of English and Lockwood Professor in the Humanities at the University of Washington. He is most recently the author of *Spirit Becomes Matter: the Brontës, George Eliot, Nietzsche* and, with Derek Attridge, *The Craft of Poetry: Dialogues on Minimal Interpretation*. He is currently at work on *Techne Theory: A New Language for Art*.

Monika Szuba is Lecturer in English Literature at the University of Gdańsk. Her research covers twentieth- and twenty-first-century Scottish and English poetry and prose, with a particular interest in ecocriticism informed by Environmental Humanities and phenomenological perspectives. She is co-editor with Julian Wolfreys of *The Poetics and Politics of Space and Place in Scottish Literature* (Palgrave, 2019). She is the author of *Contemporary Scottish Poetry and the Natural World: Burnside, Jamie, Robertson and White* (Edinburgh University Press, 2019).

Tom Ue is Assistant Professor of English at Dalhousie University and an Honorary Research Associate at University College London. He is the author of *Gissing, Shakespeare, and the Life of Writing* (Edinburgh University Press) and *George Gissing* (Northcote House Publishers/British Council) and the editor of *George Gissing, The Private Papers of Henry Ryecroft* (Edinburgh University Press). Ue has held a Frederick Banting Postdoctoral Fellowship at the University of Toronto Scarborough.

Frederik Van Dam is Assistant Professor of European Literature at Radboud University Nijmegen. He is the author of *Anthony Trollope's Late Style: Victorian Liberalism and Literary Form* (2016) and has recently co-edited a special issue on literature and economics of the *European Journal of English Studies* (2017). He is currently working on the *Edinburgh Companion to Anthony Trollope* (2019) and a literary history of diplomacy from the Congress of Vienna up to the present.

Julian Wolfreys is author and editor of numerous books, including *Haunted Selves, Haunting Places in English Literature and Culture* (Palgrave, 2018), *New Critical Thinking: Criticism to Come* (Edinburgh University Press, 2018), *Key Concepts in Literary Theory*, with Kenneth Womack and Ruth Robbins (Edinburgh University Press, 2017), *Dickens's London* (Edinburgh University Press, 2015), *Literature in Theory: Tropes, Subjectivities, Responses and Responsibilities* (Bloomsbury, 2010) and *Thomas Hardy* (Palgrave, 2009). His most recent publications are a scholarly edition of *The Silence of Dean Maitland* by Maxwell Gray (Edinburgh University Press, 2019) and, as co-editor with Monika Szuba, *The Poetics and Politics of Space and Place in Scottish Literature* (Palgrave, 2019).

Acknowledgements

The editors would like to thank in the first instance J. Hillis Miller, for his generosity of vision, spirit and time, regarding first of all, this volume, but also, literature, without whom this book would not exist, obviously, but also without whom many critical voices and good readers might never have taken their particular paths.

We would also like to thank all the contributors for being so willing, ready and more than able to contribute in so generous a fashion to the present volume, both those who first appeared in the journal *Victoriographies*, and return again here, revenants all, in altered form, and those who did not hesitate in responding to the call. And of course, we must thank the Journals Division of Edinburgh University Press for permission to reproduce the material from the journal.

Many thanks to Michelle Houston, whose unwavering championing of and enthusiasm for this project has spurred us on and kept us going, and to Ersev Ersoy, who is as enthusiastic as she is efficient and professional.

Special thanks must also go to Malcolm Andrews, Editor of *The Dickensian*, for permission to reprint from *The Dickensian*, 'Dickens in My Life'.

Foreword

Monika Szuba and Julian Wolfreys

Reading Victorian Literature: Essays in Honour of J. Hillis Miller is, simply put, a *Festschrift*, a collection of writings published in recognition of, and dedicated to, J. Hillis Miller. It contains essays by James Eli Adams, Megan Becker-Leckrone, Deep Bisla, Claire Colebrook, Ortwin de Graef, Éamonn Dunne, Robert Douglas-Fairhurst, Helen Groth, Melanie Hacke, John Maynard, Perry Meisel, Dianne F. Sadoff, Eleonora Sasso, Henry Staten, Monika Szuba, Tom Ue, Frederik Van Dam and Julian Wolfreys. And there is also an essay by J. Hillis Miller, and an interview with him. This is a celebration in writing, as the appropriately nineteenth-century German term announces in all its portmanteau directness; but it is also, very much, a celebration *of* writing, of the writing of J. Hillis Miller, specifically the vast, and always significant and timely criticism produced by Miller of nineteenth-century texts. In recognition of Miller's work, the virtual 'community' of this volume, in speaking of J. Hillis Miller, speaks, writes as if with one voice on authors, themes, subjects, topics, tropes, novels, poems which Miller has already considered, responded to, written upon, determined with an unparalleled insight, originality and acuity.

Whether we do justice to J. Hillis Miller is not for us to say – we can only hope for this. That we seek to honour him is undeniable, but again we remain to be judged. A fact that is indisputable is that we all write, and speak, as critics of nineteenth-century literature, and so *read* after Miller. What this means (to borrow from one of our contributors, Éamonn Dunne, who has been writing and reading after Miller since his doctoral thesis, and quite possibly before) is that we are obliged to countersign Miller's work in our own names, and so to 'take responsibility for engaging with his writings and for putting them to work in a different context'. That responsibility, again as Dunne notes – in a sense all of us are, in writing *after* Miller, writing *after* Dunne, who has, in writing after Miller, said everything already, everything and all the rest – comes in responding to something we find in texts by acknowledging those places where texts go against the grain of what they seem to be saying, or what we think they should be saying. There is, then, an irresponsibility, as all the contributors know, in the response, and the responsibility. In being faithful to Miller, we have all been unfaithful.

This is the ineluctable double bind of good reading and writing, and it is what J. Hillis Miller has taught, or sought to teach, from the 1950s with *Charles Dickens: The World of His Novels* (1958) to the present day with, as we write, *What Happens When I Read, Watch, or Listen* (2019) shortly to be published by Routledge. Of course, no amount of teaching can make someone learn, and what they learn is not in the control of the teacher; which is why it were better, as Miller says in the interview included in this volume, not to use the word 'deconstruction' ever again, since the misprision and just plain 'false understanding . . . has won the day'. Like Julian Barnes's narrator in *Flaubert's Parrot*, Miller desires the possibility of a moratorium on the word 'in any context that involves literary study' – and we would add philosophy, cultural studies and just about everything else, but above all, journalism. Yet though he says this, J. Hillis Miller knows that, particular words excepted, one never gives up on the responsibility despite that with which one is faced, all those places where reading and writing fail to take place, where teaching goes awry. Cats starve constantly even though we feed those we call ours, and even though we all know it feels on occasion as if we can't go on, yet we do. And so, countersigning collectively and individually the collaborators here continue, to read, to write, to teach nineteenth-century literature in honour of J. Hillis Miller, hoping that one day, we each of us may have learned from him how to read well, to be the good readers J. Hillis Miller has always sought those he teaches to become.

Introduction: There Can Be No Doubt – The Reading of J. Hillis Miller

Monika Szuba and Julian Wolfreys

> Sometimes, however, the longest way round is the shortest way home.
> J. Hillis Miller, *Literature as Conduct*

Of Roger Laporte and the act of reading, Jacques Derrida attempts to take the measure. Specifically, the measure is, Derrida remarks, 'of this force of fascination', which 'would thus be of a gap. Gap between, on the one hand, *all* the schemas of criticism, all the codes of theory, all the programs of reading that are available today for constructing a metalanguage that comes to speak *on* this text and, on the other hand, this text, *itself*, if one can still say that.'[1] If indeed, one can still say that; if one can speak, can allow oneself permission to speak of the text *itself* any longer; after these long years of 'theory', years that are too long to count given all the war economies mobilised in or against this impossible, ugly name, and years that have passed far too swiftly, where reading has remained to come for the most part, without ever having arrived. But we are getting ahead of ourselves, even as we arrive at the party too late, unlooked for and unbidden. How could we not recognise, supposing we know how to read or believing ourselves that we can indeed read, and so speak *on* this or that text, our own belatedness, given that Derrida acknowledges, around a too hasty, too late reading of 'force' in Laporte, that he is hasty and yet tardy, 'lagging behind', as he puts it (81). He is, he says, commenting, designating 'in an inadequate manner' (82), while delivering that which he calls, but that which he also stages even as he calls, as he responds, a 'measured *àpres coup* ... in the readable or writable ... recognizable as a law' (82). Indeed, this too, too tardy haste remarks – stages, performs itself with an admirable irony – in the crude exercise of speed, of velocity that accrues, in that iteration and supplement of the 'all' in Derrida's remark, between two hands, first once, then twice, then a third time, as if, by, as it were, a Dickensian analogue, Derrida were finding himself hurried down a street only to arrive at that doubt, the 'itself', the sign not of certainty, but an impassable sign of the 'no thoroughfare': *itself. The text, itself.* If one can still say that. If one can, indeed. Belatedly arriving at a *cul de sac*, Derrida reads after, in the wake of Laporte, forcing his rhetoric in a measured manner to perform the force of Laporte's own acts of reading, doing so in such a manner that we read Derrida observing himself reading improperly: 'one tenses up, defends onself against a *mise en abyme* that has already been done. The already is more important than the operation, and the enigma of all this work is perhaps, as we will see in a moment, that of the *already*. So, one defends oneself after the fact and too late' (83).

Those who have at least made the effort however haltingly, stumblingly, displayed the good will, to read, *to begin to read* Derrida carefully, time and again, will know this dilemma, this impasse. For every time reading assumes itself to have begun – as if there were a reading *itself*, a single reading that was not always already countersigned by all the other readings, each and every other reading, readings of the other, that remain as traces and remain to come – it finds 'itself' in this network of barely discernible readings; if you don't know they're there, at work, their force pressing in on you, no amount of erudition will illuminate them; if you do, no amount of erudition is necessary. Of this, there can be, to luxuriate momentarily, and so as to apply the brakes to our own act of too precipitate and ill-tempered force, in an erstwhile favoured locution of J. Hillis Miller's, no doubt. Or can there? How could you tell? How would you know? Take that remark of Derrida's on Laporte first cited. Is the former too precipitate himself? Is he in too much of a hurry, while being already late, and mistaking a blind alley for a rabbit hole? Or is there a measure of force at work? Is there the deployment of a reflexive force in the measure, the tempo, the counterpoint and syncopation of the measure in Derrida's statement, which gives us, so generously – if we can stop to read it – a performative analogy of the very force of fascination of which he speaks, that force that opens a gap as much as it causes one to find oneself struck by an *après-coup* as if one stood before the law of the text; which is to say before the fathomless law of the *mise en abyme*. There can be no doubt, as we shall, perhaps, in a moment come to see, apropos the reading of J. Hillis Miller, in whose name this book arrives, and for whom it is countersigned by divers hands. In the face of the reading of J. Hillis Miller, one tenses up, defends oneself against a *mise en abyme* that has already been done.

What though is meant by this seemingly unapologetic phrase, *the reading of J. Hillis Miller*? On the face of things, it seems to say on the one hand too much, and on the other hand not enough. It appears too rapid, too forceful, extravagant; it seems too recalcitrant, too tight-lipped, hesitant. It gives everything away, and nothing. For, on the one hand, it refers to those acts on the part of those gathered here, and many others elsewhere who have read, well or poorly, with care, rigour and faithfulness or otherwise misread (and these are not mutually exclusive, one may be rigorous or faithful and yet still betray, of this there can be no doubt) J. Hillis Miller, the texts 'in themselves' that are signed in his name. On the other hand, *the reading of J. Hillis Miller* signifies more than one reading: those readings, those acts of critical interpretation, exposition and intervention that he has tirelessly and ceaselessly engaged in since the 1950s; and also, by a certain looseness in the English language, all the reading, all the taking up of books and other matter, all those journals, monographs and other publications, that J. Hillis Miller has read since a child, from *The Swiss Family Robinson* onward; all the matter filling shelves in offices in Baltimore, Yale, Irvine and in two houses in Sedgwick and Deer Isle, Maine. All this reading. And all the rest. To speak thus of the *mise en abyme* that reading, however you read it, might be read as naming, which we provisionally gather under the name 'J. Hillis Miller', is to speak of reading as if it were a figure that approaches, as it were, and indirectly, 'a series of metaphors not destined to be replaced one day by a direct language' but which rather is 'with neither beginning nor end' (Derrida 85).

This might all seem too much play, too playful, a mere messing around in words, with words, a game of language. But we insist, on this let there be no doubt, on approaching – not yet reading – the figure of 'the reading of J. Hillis Miller' (in italics, without, with or without quotation marks, render it as you will) as a figure of the *mise en abyme* that just is reading itself, and this '*mise en abyme* is *practical* – and more than practical' (Derrida 87). This *mise en abyme* – that goes here by the turn of the phrase, *the reading of J. Hillis Miller*, seeks to recognise and so respond to, albeit belatedly and in far too much of a hurry, however tardy its arrival may be – does not 'proceed to a thesis on a thesis, a theorization of a theory, a representation of a representation' (Derrida 87). The *mise en abyme* figured as it is here is a 'topos' for all that J. Hillis Miller has pursued across more publications than Éamonn Dunne can count, and which can be perceived, as Derrida says of Laporte, as 'this self-defence of the text, which, by explaining, teaching, and posing itself, by installing itself complacently . . . in the infinite representation of self' thereby announces reading as 'an agonistic field that exceeds it', and so transforms all reading in a 'counterwriting' that by virtue of close reading produces an always political act of reading (beyond, as Derrida would have it, 'the depoliticizing codes and stereotypings' [Derrida 87] of the wilful mis-readers and non-readers of J. Hillis Miller, theory, deconstruction and so on and so forth, etc.), which 'regularly and irregularly introduces a dysfunctioning and certain gaps in the working of the [institutional, pedagogical, business as usual] working of the machine' (Derrida 87).

All of which is to say that the reading of J. Hillis Miller, make of that what you will, reinscribes the writing read as remaining to be read, as a writing for which reading remains to come. Miller presents us, again and again, with the event of reading, a 'having-happened' that 'tears off this strange remainder', that reminds us – those of us who try to read rather than resisting the reading of J. Hillis Miller – why 'there is reading to be done' (Derrida 89). This is for Miller unconditional. To read, to want to read, to be the good reader – or at least aspire to that impossible goal – is to accept the unconditional in reading. One cannot just impose one's will or a form of thought on reading, in order to keep it in good order. This is not reading. It is a grim calculated determinism, a restricted economy institutionally imposed. Reading is for Miller, unconditionally, like democracy; it remains to come. Reading has to proceed *as if* it were always a response, however unprepared – and part of unconditionality is that one must be open, utterly, impossible as that is – to respond 'to the call of what Derrida calls *le tout autre*, the wholly other'.[2] Reading, to paraphrase Miller on Derrida, breaks with any 'predetermined course ... it is always an uncertain matter' (Miller 5). Reading, Miller has taught us, or sought to teach us over the years, is the name for the bleak, weak hope that something will come, something will arrive, appearing 'of its own accord and in its own time ... We cannot call it. It calls us' (Miller 6). Wouldn't it be nice if we could just ask our students to accept this, and they did? That we could say to them, 'look here; I can't promise you'll get anything from this class, I can't tell you there are aims and objectives, goals, that there is knowledge at which you will arrive; I cannot even assume we will read at all, let alone properly, each and every set book (let's not get into talking about what constitutes a text)'? And wouldn't it be nice, if the students did accept this and we just moved along, or not, paragraph by paragraph, a page here, a chapter there – perhaps – never knowing if we would reach any conclusion or end, much less complete the assigned syllabus?

Each time a reading has a chance of happening, it does so only on the condition of literature's unconditional alterity; this is something the institution of Higher Education cannot countenance. Yet reading has very little to do with education, at the risk of scandalising someone out there; for every 'literary work is entirely singular, "counter, original, spare, strange"', as Gerard Manley Hopkins puts it. 'Each work', Miller continues,

> is as different from every other work as each person differs from all the others, or as each leaf differs from all the others. When I as a reader or teacher respond to the wholly other as embodied in a literary work and try to mediate it to my students or to readers of what I write, I am, perhaps, just 'perhaps', fulfilling my professional duty to put everything in question and to help make or keep my university 'without condition'. (Miller 8)

You, the reader, whoever you are, whether or not you believe yourself to be a good reader – and who would admit to being a bad reader, who would confess even to themselves that they have engaged in an act of misreading, accidental or wilful? – might wish to pause here, reflecting on this statement, this declaration of reading's independence.

But what of Gerard Manley Hopkins, this 'counter, original, spare, strange' figure of Victorian literature (the focus of this volume in honour of Miller's work on the nineteenth century)? The phrase quoted by Miller – 'counter, original, spare, strange' – comes from 'Pied Beauty'. The poem is worth citing in full for its strange, its terrible beauty:

Glory be to God for dappled things –
    For skies of couple-colour as a brinded cow;
        For rose-moles all in stipple upon trout that swim;
Fresh-firecoal chestnut-falls; finches' wings;
    Landscape plotted and pieced – fold, fallow, and plough;
        And áll trades, their gear and tackle and trim.

All things counter, original, spáre, strange;
    Whatever is fickle, frecklèd (who knows how?)
        With swíft, slów; sweet, sóur; adázzle, dím;
He fathers-forth whose beauty is pást change:
                Práise him.

Here is a poem that many a reader would not associate with reading. It is about those strange ideas 'God' and 'Nature', each as equally self-evident and 'other' as one another. On the surface, 'Pied Beauty', a poem written in 1877 (for the historicists among you), is ostensibly a paean in honour of the 'god-made world', that not created by humans. Except that it is, and Miller knows this. For the so-called natural world is not separate from the language that signifies it; and, as Hopkins would have us see, through his use of accents and stresses, his diacritical marks and his insistence on the materiality of language – a materiality arguably different in degree rather than kind from all those other things 'counter, original, spáre, strange' – the world remains before us, like the language of the poem to be read, and read well. The poem is thus about poetry, about the reading of poetry and about reading in general. Language, and the good reader knows this, is a 'dappled thing', it is 'plotted and pieced', its motions fickle, freckled, its rhythms 'swift, slów; sweet, sóur; adázzle, dím'. Such a sketchy commentary, we will not call it a reading, might appear perverse; but as Miller argues elsewhere, Hopkins's theory of language 'in "The Wreck of the Deutschland" and in other writings is not compatible with this theological overthought'.[3] The matter, the question of language is what Miller calls the 'underthought' to the theological overthought, and while 'it would be a mistake to make too much of its presence in Hopkins ... it is indubitably there'. There can be no doubt.

Another way of understanding this – and to return briefly to Derrida's discussion of the gap in Laporte and literature – is to understand, as Miller does, in referring to Hopkins elsewhere, that there are antitheses in literature and criticism that overlap, but 'do not form a neat continuum. There are breaks and contradictions between any one opposition and some of the others. ... To borrow a word from Gerard Manley Hopkins, the oppositions might better be thought of as so many topographical "cleaves" of the landscape,'[4] a landscape 'plotted and pieced – fold, fallow, and plough' (Miller 1991: 3). The problem with Hopkins, of course, which is not exclusive to him but one that reading Hopkins makes especially acute, it would seem, in the 'introit' of 'Pied Beauty' is how the reader addresses the 'religious meanings' (Miller 1991: 71). Hence, one must understand that 'there are echoes, resemblances, fraternal similarities [across texts, poetry or prose] ... Each poem lives in a context which includes everything' (Miller 1991: 71) That everything – and all the rest – is not restricted, in any context, least of all the religious one, merely to Hopkins's own writings, but also *the reading of Gerard Manley Hopkins*: Scotus, Ignatus, Suárez, the Bible, Catholic liturgy, Walter Pater, Greek philosophy, the Oxford Movement, and, as Miller avers, 'the general history of Victorian religious experience' (Miller 1991: 71). And so it is, we rush in haste, belatedly, in the name of reading, after the reading of the other – and there's a phrase that can be read in at least two different ways! – in the face of the *mise en abyme*. Such is, there can be no doubt, the force of fascination, a force that Miller makes evident on every page, whether writing about Jacques Derrida, Gerard Manley Hopkins, the Anthropocene, or – *even* – the Republicans. Gerard Manley Hopkins might be said, however, to be that singular figure for J. Hillis Miller[5] – along with all those other singular figures of the nineteenth, twentieth and twenty-first centuries that figure the complex web, the mesh, with all its interconnections and gaps, that is being called the reading of J. Hillis Miller. If Hopkins is one of those writers who for Edward Said exemplifies what Said, citing D. H. Lawrence, describes as 'the unceasing struggle to be a writer',[6] then we might well argue – as indeed we do – Hopkins is the name that countersigns the unceasing struggle to be a reader, a good reader.

The difficulty that haunts the phrase *the reading of J. Hillis Miller*, a difficulty that is at once hidden and in plain sight – an over- and an underthought simultaneously interwoven before or beyond that double genitive already considered – is that one might not unreasonably assume 'J. Hillis Miller' as the goal, the teleological endpoint. If this is the overthought, the underthought is that this signature names good reading as such – whatever that is, hence the unceasing struggle. For if 'J. Hillis Miller' exhorts or persuades us to be good readers, or seduces us into good reading by force of his own example, then in that name we also set off toward readings to come, readings that remain. The reading of 'J. Hillis Miller' is an act of reading that folds back on itself to begin again, the scales of trajectory having fallen from our eyes. The goal – that which 'Miller' is taken to name, to signify, for both the editors and the contributors of this volume – of reading is analogous to the 'goal of poetry for Hopkins', or 'the goal of narrative for Proust', which 'is to find some way to speak this unspeakable, the wholly other of . . . private emotions'.[7] Reading, J. Hillis Miller teaches us, can touch 'an "it", that is wholly alien to me, wholly "other", and yet that is more myself than I am. (I borrow that phrase from Gerard Manley Hopkins . . .)'.[8] This may never arrive, but there is always the chance – this is the chance by which all good reading takes place – that it can 'come unbidden', to cite another phrase of Hopkins, cited by Miller (Miller 2015: 141).

Gerard Manley Hopkins is just one Victorian writer among many on whom Miller has written, whom Miller has read tirelessly, persuasively, entrancingly, on several occasions. Were the reader of this introduction desirous of reading more, the editors would direct them to three chapters in particular: 'Naming, Doing, Placing: Hopkins' in *Topographies*; 'Gerard Manley Hopkins' in *The Disappearance of God*; and from *The Linguistic Moment*, 'Hopkins'.[9] In the end, or from the beginning, though – and of course, with reading, *good* reading, we end up where we began, albeit with a difference, and so have to start again, wherever you are, this is where you start with reading – literary works have special *force*, as Miller argues. They have moments of 'unlocking the door. . . All it takes is a few words, and I become a believer, a seer. I become a fascinated witness of a new virtual reality. . . . "I caught this morning morning's minion, king- /dom of daylight's dauphin, dapple-drawn-dawn Falcon," does it for me with Gerard Manley Hopkins's "The Windhover."'[10] And who wouldn't this line do it for? This 'fictional community' gathered for the purpose of celebrating the work, the life, the person of J. Hillis Miller in this volume, can all attest to their own personal 'Open Sesame' moments, even as all of them, directly or indirectly, through an overthought or underthought, a direct statement or countersignature buried and yet, at the same time, in full view, bear witness in their contributions to the fact that J. Hillis Miller, and the reading of J. Hillis Miller, however you may now wish to take that impossible phrase, figure innumerable moments of turning the key, opening the door, turning on the light. And he has done this for countless students, several generations of readers, and as we write continues so to do – indeed, will continue so to do, as long as there are those out there who desire to be the good reader. To paraphrase a remark of Miller's from a source neither of the editors can remember, you can learn quite a lot about reading from J. Hillis Miller. Or to put this another way, if, as Miller asserts with that disarmingly straightforward manner of expression beneath which there remains to be encountered the unspeakable toward which speech strives, Gerard Manley Hopkins 'is one of the great English landscape poets, not only in his poems but also in his journal', then, there can be no doubt, J. Hillis Miller is one of the great critics in the English language of the landscape of literature.

We began this Introduction with a reading of Jacques Derrida reading Roger Laporte. It seems fitting – and we hope Hillis will not object – to return to Jacques Derrida, in an essay presented first in honour of J. Hillis Miller and published in *Provocations of Reading: J. Hillis Miller and the Democracy to Come*.[11] Beginning by drawing the reader's attention to the untranslatable *J* that he and Miller share, which letter in French says 'I', Derrida wonders about the alterity of Miller in a friendship wherein, nevertheless, 'J. Hillis Miller [is], *himself*, the other, the wholly other that he remains for me' (Derrida 2005: 229). Perhaps, as Derrida continues, 'it is a matter here of what Gerard Manley Hopkins, in the great texts that J. Hillis Miller has taught me to read, called "selftaste". Selftaste', Derrida continues, acknowledging the reading of J. Hillis Miller, 'constitutes all "selfbeing", all "selving", Hopkins tells us, "my selfbeing, my consciousness, and feeling of myself, that taste of myself, of *I* and *me* above and in all things"' (Derrida 2005: 229–30). Pondering the imponderable, seeking a way to speak the unspeakable, Jacques Derrida wonders how one might get that 'taste of myself' of a very close friend. Resigning himself to the 'specter of Gerard Manley Hopkins', Derrida announces how, on two occasions, Hopkins 'names the *just*'. And this becomes the 'name' Derrida grants to Miller, recognising also in his reading of Miller that justice, the just, belongs to Miller, as a 'gift that cannot be acquired' (2005: 230). This collection of essays seeks to do justice to J. Hillis Miller, to the justice he brings to reading, to the justice that is tirelessly, vigilantly at work in *the reading of J. Hillis Miller*. We cannot acquire the gift of justice that Miller gives us in each and every reading, any more than we can hope to do justice to Miller for all he has given us, as readers. As Derrida puts it with reference to Miller's *The Ethics of Reading*, doing justice to his close friend in a manner we cannot hope to match, Miller exceeds the 'ethics of reading'; his reading 'overflows both mere reading and morality' (2005: 260). Twice, Derrida gives way to Miller in the conclusion of his essay, allowing Miller's voice to arrive, as the other who steps forward, and we can do no more than reiterate this step. In the words of J. Hillis Miller,

> By 'ethics' of reading', the reader will remember, I mean that aspect of the act of reading in which there is a response to the text that is both necessitated, in the sense of an irresistible demand, and free, in the sense that I must take responsibility for my response, and for the further effects, 'interpersonal', institutional, political, historical, of my act of reading.[12]

Notes

1. Derrida, 'What Remains by Force of Music', p. 82. Any further references are given parenthetically.
2. Miller, 'A Profession of Faith', in *For Derrida*, p. 5. Further references are given parenthetically.
3. Miller, *Fiction and Repetition: Seven English Novels*, p. 16. Miller is here referring to his reading of Hopkins in 'The Linguistic Moment in "The Wreck of the Deutschland"'.
4. Miller, *Theory Now and Then*, p. 3. Further references are given parenthetically.
5. The reader is directed to Miller's reading of Geoffrey Hartman's reading of Gerard Manley Hopkins in *Theory Now and Then* (p. 125).
6. Said, *Beginnings: Intentions and Method*, p. 233.
7. Miller, *Speech Acts in Literature*, p. 161.
8. Miller, *Communities in Fiction*, p. 14. Further references are given parenthetically.
9. Miller, *Topographies*, pp. 150–69; *The Disappearance of God*, pp. 270–361; *The Linguistic Moment*, pp. 229–67.
10. Miller, *On Literature*, p. 24.
11. Derrida, 'Justices', in *Provocations to Reading*, pp. 228–61. Further references are given parenthetically.
12. Miller, *The Ethics of Reading*, p. 43.

I
Singular Hardy

Chapter 1

Varieties of Rural Experience: Country Communities in Virginia and Wessex

J. Hillis Miller

Rural? Experience?

The two words in the title of the conference where the Hardy part of this essay was first presented, 'rural' and 'experience', are both problematic and complex. This is true in spite of the fact that we use these words all the time without thinking much about them. They become problems when you hesitate in that using and interrogate them: 'Come forth and tell me what you mean!'

The *American Heritage Dictionary* defines 'rural' as 'pertaining to the country as opposed to the city; rustic' (Morris 1136b). *The Country and the City* is of course the name of a well-known book by Raymond Williams (1973). The *AHD* goes on to say that rural and its many synonyms ('arcadian, bucolic, rustic, pastoral, sylvan') 'are all descriptive of existence or environment which is close to nature ... *Rural* applies to sparsely settled or agricultural country, as distinct from settled communities.' Really? Does that mean even a very small town is no longer rural? Just how sparsely settled does a piece of country need to be in order to remain rural? All the rural areas I know or have lived in in the United States differ in many ways from one another, though all are unmistakably rural. The Township of Sedgwick, Maine, where I now live in the winter, is certainly rural. It is, however, dotted with small agglomerations of houses, a church, and even shops. These have distinct names and are small towns or villages: Sargentville, North Sedgwick, Sedgwick Village. Villages shade off into less populated areas, but the whole of Sedgwick Township looks pretty rural to me. The same thing can be said of Thomas Hardy's Mellstock (based on Hardy's birth-village of Upper Bockhampton) in *Under the Greenwood Tree/or/The*

Mellstock Choir (1872) (Hardy, *Writings* vol. 7). This novel, Hardy's second to be published, is my chief example in this essay of rural experience as represented in British fiction.

An admirably specific passage near the beginning of Hardy's *The Mayor of Casterbridge* describes Casterbridge (modelled on Dorchester, the big town near Upper Bockhampton) as a place where the town shades off so imperceptibly into agricultural country that bees and butterflies in the summer fly right down the main street on their way from one part of rural country to another. It's all rural to them: 'Casterbridge was the complement of the rural life around; not its urban opposite. Bees and butterflies in the cornfields at the top of the town, who desired to get to the meads at the bottom, took no circuitous course, but flew straight down High Street without any apparent consciousness that they were traversing strange latitudes' (Hardy, *Writings* 5, 65). A passage in *Far From the Madding Crowd* (1874) specifies in a different way what is unique about rural Wessex:

> This picture of to-day in its frame of four hundred years ago did not produce that marked contrast between ancient and modern which is implied by the contrast of date. In comparison with cities, Weatherbury was immutable. The citizen's *Then* is the rustic's *Now*. In London, twenty or thirty years ago are old times; in Paris ten years, or five; in Weatherbury three or four score years were included in the mere present, and nothing less than a century set a mark on its face or tone . . . In these Wessex nooks the busy outsider's ancient times are only old; his old times are still new; his present is futurity. (Hardy, *Writings* 2: 166; original emphasis)

If town and country are not easily distinguished, at least by bees and butterflies, what about rural land as against wilderness? Little remains of wilderness in Britain. Almost all the land has been inhabited and cultivated for millennia. The woods of birches, beeches and elms through which Dick Dewey walks on Christmas Eve at the opening of *Under the Greenwood Tree* is not a remnant of wilderness. It is defined as a 'plantation' (1). It is as much a product of cultivation as cornfields and orchards. Much genuine wilderness, on the contrary, still remains in the United States, for example the deserts in Southern California. About a hundred miles from the coast of Maine, where I write this, is something called 'The Hundred Mile Wilderness'. The Appalachian Trail runs through it from west to east. Until recently not even logging roads went into it. It was notorious to through-hikers on the Appalachian Trail because you had to carry food enough for the whole hundred miles, there are rivers to ford, and the terrain is quite rough. It is not rural, but is a genuine wilderness. Henry David Thoreau, in his *The Maine Woods* (1864), describes his experience as he climbed Mt Katahdin by the trail that is now the northernmost bit of the Appalachian Trail. The rocks around him, wrote Thoreau, seemed to have no sympathy with mankind, but to be completely indifferent. I have descended from Mt Katahdin by that trail. It is indifferent all right, a steep granite hillside. No Wordsworthian 'something far more deeply interfused' for Thoreau (l. 97), just an experience of inhuman wilderness, as opposed to humanised rural landscape such as he describes in *A Week on the Concord and Merrimack Rivers* (1849).

The complexities of the word 'rural' can be defined as arising from the way 'rural' is usually one half of a binary opposition (rural as against urban; rural as against wilderness). Any clear line of opposition in either direction breaks down, however. 'Rural' shades off into being experienced as the complement of its apparent opposites, urban in one direction and wilderness in the other. As Hardy puts this breakdown of clear alternatives, 'Casterbridge was the complement of the rural life around; not its urban opposite.'

*

'Experience', as in 'rural experience', is also, like 'rural', an ambiguous or complex word, though in a different way. We all know what 'experience' is. It differs from knowledge or perception in being more bodily and more a matter of something taken in by all the senses. The *American Heritage Dictionary* catches these features of the word's usages in all five of its definitions, particularly the first two: '1. The apprehension of an object, thought, or emotion through the senses or mind . . . 2. Active participation in events or activities, leading to the accumulation of knowledge or skill' (Morris 462a), as in 'She was an experienced mountain-climber and bicyclist' (my example). The word 'experience' comes from the Latin *expiriri*, meaning to 'try, test'. In the great British empirical tradition from Locke on down, to experience something means to test it on all the senses. You learn how to ride a bicycle by riding a bicycle.

We use the word 'experience' in all sorts of ways, however, from the title of William James's *Varieties of Religious Experience*, to 'sexual experience', to the title of a recent presentation at the University of California at Irvine's School of Education: 'Children's Experiences of and Reasoning about Poverty' (5 February 2013 email announcement), to the title of one of Julian Wolfreys' admirable music albums *The Cheeseboard Experience*, all the way down to an advertisement for a painkiller that might say 'Experience the Relief', or one for water-skiing that might say 'Experience the Thrill'. 'Rural Experience' is in resonance with all these uses. It focuses, I am assuming, on what it is really like to live in the country. That is something knowable only through intimate experience. Anthropologists call this 'local knowledge', including in the case of 'rural experience' close familiarity with the topography, the smell and look of the vegetation, the sound of the wind in the trees, the taste of the local food, what houses, roads, and schools there are like, local accents and idioms (like 'eyah' for 'yes' in rural Maine), habits of church-going or not going, courtship and marriage habits or rituals, and all the complex traditions and conventions of social intercourse in a given setting.

As with the word 'rural', the word 'experience', however, is a matter of shades rather than of unequivocal delimitation. In the case of 'experience', as my examples of usage suggest, the nuances go all the way from the sublime ('religious experience') to the ridiculous ('experience the thrill'), with 'cheeseboard experience' a deliberately comic and witty locution somewhere in middle of the spectrum. In spite of these shades, a somewhat fuzzy opposition between abstract knowledge and the local knowledge born of intimate experience 'on the ground', as we say, always hovers behind uses of the word. Anthropologists get local knowledge by living with those 'native' to the culture they study, but they then turn that bodily knowledge, for example, into the conceptual knowledge of 'kinship systems', with charts and abstract analyses. In a similar way, Thomas Hardy bases *Under the Greenwood Tree* on his childhood experience of growing up in Upper Bockhampton. Nevertheless, the narrator of that novel to a considerable degree sees the characters, their environment and all their ways and doings from the outside, from the perspective of the sophisticated person with urban experience Hardy had become by 1872, when the novel was first published. The narrator is both inside, enjoying qualified telepathic knowledge of the characters' thoughts and feelings, and outside, a spectator of a way of life that he has left forever and that indeed no longer exists in 1872.

The novel's emblem of that vanishing is the substitution in the early nineteenth century of the solo organ for the traditional 'choir' of stringed instruments and singing voices that had provided the music at church services. *The Mellstock Quire* was Hardy's original name for the novel. *Under the Greenwood Tree*, the final name, with *The Mellstock Quire* as a subtitle, is a sophisticated and learned allusion to the title and first line of one of Shakespeare's most beautiful songs in *As You Like It* (Act 2, scene 5):

Under the greenwood tree
Who loves to lie with me,

And tune his merry note
Unto the sweet bird's throat –
Come hither, come hither, come hither!

Lord Amiens, one of the courtiers who has gone into exile in the Forest of Arden, sings the song. It is then ironically parodied by the melancholy Jacques. Alluding to this song locates Hardy and his delegate the narrator outside the culture he dramatises so intimately. It asks for sympathy from that sort of reader who will have read Shakespeare, unlike the rural characters in the novel. The sub-sub-title, 'A Rural Painting of the Dutch School', distances the novel even further by comparing it to something else of which the characters in the novel would never have heard. They could not imagine themselves as characters in a painting by Breughel or some other Dutch genre painter.

In an analogous way, what I shall have to say about rural life in Virginia in the 1930s is based on my own personal experience, but even then, as a small child, I was to a considerable degree an outsider. I was a visitor to my grandparents' farm, but had lived most of my life in the North. Though I was born in Virginia, it was in the seaport city of Newport News, not in the country. My parents, in any case, took me away from Virginia when I was a few months old. I am not really a native son, not a real Southerner. My Grandmother Critzer (pronounced 'Cry-zer'; my mother's mother) once said to me, 'You talk like a Yankee.' That was not praise. Quite the contrary. On the one hand, I was a wide-eyed child spectator, watching in amazement the behaviour of a family group doing things and speaking in a way unlike anything I had ever seen or heard before. On the other hand, I was inducted into that family as the honoured oldest grandchild, shown everything, given chores to do (fetching water in a bucket from the spring, turning the butter churn, helping to bring the cows back from pasture, learning how to feed them and how to milk them [not all that easy; there's a trick to it], assisting in raking and bringing in the hay in the horse-drawn wagon, and so on). I can still remember the sharp feel of hay stubble on my bare feet and how hot it was in the hayfield. I was inside and outside rural Virginia culture at once – like an anthropologist, and like Hardy and his narrator.

*

I turn now to a comparison of rural life as I experienced it in Afton, Virginia, in the 1930s with rural experience in Mellstock, Wessex, as registered by Thomas Hardy in *Under the Greenwood Tree*. My readers may think it is absurd to set real experience against fictional experience. It is common knowledge, however, that *Under the Greenwood Tree* is a fictional transformation of Hardy's childhood experience in his birthplace, Upper Bockhampton, in Dorsetshire, three miles from Dorchester, while my memories are a reconstruction of childhood rural experiences I had eighty years ago in Afton, Virginia. Like autobiographical accounts generally, however, mine is, as Paul de Man said of all autobiographical texts, an example of 'Autobiography as De-facement', not least in constructing a unified selfhood for myself by a species of prosopopoeia. My account is a selective fictional confabulation. As de Man says in 'The Resistance to Theory', 'it is very difficult not to conceive the pattern of one's past and future existence as in accordance with temporal and spatial schemes that belong to fictional narratives and not to the world' (de Man 11).

My account will not have escaped such fictionality, however hard I try to bear true witness and to 'tell it like it was'. So I am setting two fictional narratives side by side. I begin with rural Afton, Virginia. I do that because my way of reading *Under the Greenwood Tree* is, I suspect, to a considerable degree determined, however unconsciously, by my own childhood rural experience. I see one in terms of the other. I read *Under the Greenwood Tree* to some extent as someone who as a child knew farm life in Albemarle and Nelson Counties, Virginia, in the 1930s. As in Hardy's case, many other rural and urban experiences have intervened for me since my childhood, not to speak of all those disillusioning books and essays I have read.

The Critzers at Afton

'Pour la commodité du récit', as Proust somewhere puts it, for economy of narration and in order not to get too lost in details, I have focused on the question of community in both my examples of rural experience. The term 'rural community' is perhaps even more common than 'rural experience'. I live in the winters now in the 'rural community' of Sedgwick, Maine. Were either Hardy's Mellstock or my Afton communities? If so, of what sort? Is it, as we are likely to assume, entirely a good thing that they were communities, if indeed they were?

An enormous (and contradictory) literature on the question of community exists, from Aristotle, Plato, and Augustine through the Scholastics to Hobbes, Rousseau, Hegel, Marx, Tönnies, and Nietzsche, down to Heidegger, Blanchot, Bataille, Foucault, Deleuze and Guattari, Nancy, Rorty, Laclau, Mouffe, Agamben, Williams, Derrida, Esposito, Hägglund, Van Den Abbeele, and many others in our own day. Almost every philosophical, theological or political thinker in western culture has had a go at the topic of community.

The embarrassment, complexity, and somewhat desperate apodictic pronouncements that characterise these attempts to define 'community' indicate the difficulties this topic presents. Each learned writer has a tendency to say or to imply, 'I have got community right at last, whereas all the others so far have got it wrong.' That does not keep the next in line from having yet another go and making the same claim. To untangle these ideas of community in any detail would be a long work. This is not the place to do that. I have made a partial foray in 'Part One: Theories of Community, Nancy Contra Stevens' of my *The Conflagration of Community*. That essay sets Nancy's '*communauté désoeuvrée*', awkwardly translated as 'inoperative community', against Wallace Stevens's ironically nostalgic celebration of organic community in a segment of 'The Auroras of Autumn': 'We were as Danes in Denmark all day long/And knew each other well, hale-hearted landsmen,/For whom the outlandish was another day/Of the week, queerer than Sunday' (Stevens 418). The issue of communities in fiction also comes up in my book on Henry James, *Literature as Conduct: Speech Acts in Henry James* (2005). Julián Jiménez Heffernan has presented a much more inclusive account than mine of western ideas of community. He does this in a long, brilliant and learned introduction to a collection of fourteen essays by various scholars from Córdoba and Granada in Spain entitled *Into Separate Worlds* (2013). The essays are about community in late twentieth- and early twenty-first-century fiction in English. One valuable point they demonstrate is that in the novels they discuss, characters are sometimes shown as belonging to multiple communities at the same time. Heffernan's admirable essay is called 'Togetherness and Its Discontents' (Heffernan 1–47).

Though untangling the tangled skein of what theorists have said about community would be a difficult task, one major opposition, treated in many ways, tends to run through most concepts of community. As in the case of 'rural' and 'experience', this doublet tends to be expressed as a binary opposition that breaks down into a matter of shades and into a matter of the impossibility of deciding which is the good member of the pair, which the bad. In all these writers, in a seemingly inexhaustible number of ways and valences, an organic, immanent community of individual egos that know each other well is set against a non-community or 'unworked' community of disaggregated disunified subjectivities. Perhaps the most famous and influential expression of this opposition is Ferdinand Tönnies's distinction between *Gemeinschaft* (the organic community) and *Gesellschaft* (a mechanical assemblage of persons) in *Community and Civil Society* (2001), but Marx and Engels were already, in *The German Ideology* (1846), expressing their version of this opposition:

The first case presupposes individuals united by some kind of bond, be it family, tribe, the soil itself, etc.; the second case presupposes that they are independent of one another and are held together only by exchange. In the first case, exchange is mainly an exchange between man and nature, an exchange in which the labour of the one is exchanged for the products of the other; in the second case, it is predominantly an exchange of men among themselves. In the first case, average human understanding suffices, and physical and mental labour are not yet divided; in the second case, the separation between intellectual and physical labour must already be completed in practice. In the first case, the dominance of the property owner over the non-owner rests on personal relationships, on a form of community; in the second case, this dominance must have taken on the form of a third element, the form of a thing, money. (154)

Generally speaking, thinkers of community have tended to favour *Gemeinschaft* over *Gesellschaft*. Their ideal is the 'primitive' community of a small group of people bound by family ties and living together in the same place according to the same customs, courtship and marriage conventions, religion, language, eating habits, and so on, like 'Danes in Denmark', as Wallace Stevens puts it. Such a community is, in the words of Marx and Engels, 'based on the real ties present in every familial and tribal conglomeration, as consanguinity, language, division of labour in its larger dimensions' (131). Such a community, we are inclined to believe, is better, more natural, than a mere assemblage of separate people brought together by accident or by business or technological relations. Such a model of community tends to assume a fair amount of telepathic communication among its members. Each member knows what the others are thinking, as in the novels by Anthony Trollope.

Both my childhood community in rural Virginia and Hardy's Mellstock seem to be clear examples of organic communities that display the right way to live. This, however, has to be explored later in a little more detail and with a little more sceptical interrogation.

Matters are not quite so simple, even for Marx and Engels. He sees primitive organic communities superseded by capitalism, and capitalism in turn by a new kind of communist community, the dictatorship of the proletariat. Marx and Engels, however, had no way of foreseeing twentieth-century technological revolutions, nor the concomitant globalisation, nor the rise of totalitarian states that appealed to precisely the basic ideas of the organic community. A notorious example is the Nazis' appeal to blood and soil and to the oneness of the Aryan race. These historical developments, in part, led Jean-Luc Nancy to develop the positive counter-idea of an 'unworked community' of singularities that are each divided within themselves, that are each open to others, and that can never come together except in a mystified fashion in anything like the old 'operative' community. The primitive organic community never existed in any case, according to Nancy. Thinking it did is a mystification. Belonging to a *Gemeinschaft*, moreover, is, as Nancy argues, an exceedingly dangerous political ideal, as witness the Holocaust and the self-destruction of the Nazi regime, not to speak of racism in the United States.

*

With these somewhat perplexing notations in mind, I ask whether Afton and Mellstock were or were not communities. If so, of what sort? Is it unequivocally a good thing in either case? What does being or not being a *Gemeinschaft* have to do with 'rural experience'? I discuss Afton first, partly because I read Hardy's account of Dorsetshire rural experience in *Under the Greenwood Tree* from the perspective of my childhood rural experience in Afton.

It would appear that my Afton fully satisfies the criteria for being a happy *Gemeinschaft*. In this section I assemble childhood memories of my mother's birthplace: a farm in rural Virginia in the southern United States. My first cousin Ann Critzer Gaynor, youngest daughter of my Uncle Jack, my mother's brother, lived until recently a few miles from the Afton farm, but has now joined her son in Illinois. Her account is called *Three Families Come to America*. It traces the interconnected lineages of the Critzer, Schultz and Rodes families. It also contains many informative and, to me, touching photographs of the farm and of my immediate family, some of which I use in this text. Here is the first: it is a photograph of my grandparents, my mother and her siblings, with assorted aunts, all in their Sunday best clothes (Fig. 1.1). It was taken about 1907 on the front porch of the old farmhouse in Afton. The Nellie Martin Critzer in the photo is my mother, aged ten. I shall say more later about the apparently anomalous African American woman in the back row. What is she doing there?

The Afton farm was at the centre of a close-knit community consisting almost entirely of members of the Critzer family: my grandparents, my great-uncles, who farmed nearby, my uncles, aunts and cousins, plus a few other nearby families. All had shared the experience of the Civil War, at least as a memory by way of their parents or grandparents. All spoke the same Virginia country dialect. All went to the same church close by, a tiny Presbyterian church hardly bigger than a living room. My Grandfather Critzer ('Chet', short for his grand first name of 'Chesterfield'), taught Men's Bible Class weekly at that church for forty or fifty years. He really knew the Bible – much more intimately than my

Figure 1.1 Photograph taken at the Old House at Critzer Home, Afton, Virginia, c.1907. References to relatives are from Nellie Martin Critzer: Back row, beginning far left: Unknown – maybe Aunt Emma Schulz (Minnie Hopkins Shultz's sister), Minnie Hopkins Schultz Critzer (mother), likely the daughter of a former slave who lived in a small house off the path that led to the Spring house, Aunt Josephine Rodes Fox, Mrs James Iverson Critzer (Elisabeth C. McCue) or Great Grandmother Schultz (if the baby in Aunt Carrie Schultz's lap is Filmore Critzer, who was born in 1906 or 1907, then Mrs James Iverson would not have been alive since she died in 1904), and Chesterfield Critzer (father). Front row, beginning far left: Nellie Martin Critzer Miller (age 10), Aunt Carrie Schultz with Filmore (born 1906 or 1907, who died in 1916), Bessie Hopkins Critzer Brooks (age 4, Nellie's younger sister), Adele Schultz (Hall, daughter of Letitia Catherine 'Lettie' Critzer Shultz, Chesterfield Critzer's younger sister who died in 1901 and who married Charles Rodes 'Charlie' Schultz, brother of Minnie Hopkins Schultz Critzer), Frank James Critzer (age 8, Nellie's younger brother), and Jack Caldwell Critzer (age 6, Nellie's younger brother).

Baptist minister father. About a third of the churchyard now consists of my dead relatives. My father, mother, maternal grandparents, uncles, great-aunts and so on, are buried there. See Figure 1.2 for a photo of my grandfather, Chesterfield ('Chet') Critzer, with his brother, my Uncle Everett.

Thinking of the family churchyard reminds me of a wonderful poem by Thomas Hardy. This is one of several poems linked to the people and events of his second novel, *Under the Greenwood Tree*. Hardy mentions these poems in the 1912 preface to the novel. Here are three verses of one such poem, 'The Dead Quire', from *Time's Laughingstocks*:

II
'Twas the Birth-tide Eve, and the hamleteers
Made merry with ancient Mellstock zest,
But the Mellstock quire of former years
    Had entered into rest.

Figure 1.2 Photograph of my grandfather, Chesterfield ('Chet') Critzer, with his brother, my Uncle Everett.

> III
> Old Dewy lay by the gaunt yew tree,
> And Reuben and Michael a pace behind,
> And Bowman with his family
>   By the wall that the ivies bind.
>
> IV
> The singers had followed one by one,
> Treble, and tenor, and thorough-bass;
> And the worm that wasteth had begun
>   To mine their mouldering place. (*Complete Poems* 256)

Just as Hardy here sees the vitally alive personages in his novel from the perspective of their deaths, so I do the same with those relatives in Afton I knew as very much alive eighty years ago. It was only in Afton, for the most part, that I got to see my various boy and girl cousins, children of my mother's siblings. It was a living community that brought three generations together in different mixtures at Christmas and during the summers when I visited there with my parents for some weeks. Now almost all are in the Afton churchyard.

To tell over all my memories of those days and weeks would take more space than I have in this essay. I focus on some details that will indicate what kind of community Afton was during the 1930s.

Unlike Hardy's Mellstock, Afton consisted of dispersed farms with no discernible village. Mellstock is a 'parish', whereas Afton is a secular rather than religious topographical unit. Except at church I remember no gatherings beyond those of my immediate family at Christmas and in the summer. Hardy's Mellstock has, on the contrary, community dances that bring many families with different surnames together. The Quire circulates from house to house throughout Mellstock on Christmas Eve to play and sing at each doorstep. Hardy describes the gathering of the Quire for practice or for performing in church. The Afton family community had nothing like that. We in Afton had a decorated family Christmas tree, presents to open on Christmas morning and Christmas carols to sing at the small grand piano in the living room. None of that happens in *Under the Greenwood Tree*. Nevertheless, the endless murmur of the adults talking and telling stories late into the night that I remember at Afton is echoed by the talk of Hardy's Mellstock folk. An odd sort of non-division of labour characterised Afton, whereas Mellstock has a shoemaker, farmers, dairymen, a 'tranter' or deliverer of goods by wagon, a games-keeper/timberman – a separate profession and division of labour for each, as Marx and Engels specify.

My grandparents did it all themselves. They grew all of their own food, vegetables, and fruit. They ate pigs and chickens they had grown and killed themselves. Hams were cured according to a recipe handed down from generation to generation. That recipe differed from the one used by my other grandfather in northern Virginia. The latter had more black pepper. Honey was collected at the Afton farm from hives near the house in a way not unlike the honey-gathering described in *Under the Greenwood Tree*. My grandfather took care of the pigs, cows, and horses, while my grandmother fed the chickens, gathered the eggs, and tended the vegetable garden. She 'put up' vegetables and fruits – peaches, string beans or, in Virginia terminology, 'snaps', and so on. She 'canned' them, that is, in Mason jars for use in the winter. My grandfather killed the chickens for our suppers by beheading them with an ax. I remember one running around the lawn with its head cut off. They had a small dairy herd, which produced almost the only cash product: milk.

My Grandfather Critzer milked the cows by hand at three or four in the morning, then separated the cream from the milk in a noisy mechanical separator. I can remember being wakened by the sound in the early morning. The milk was then left in shiny metal jugs by the side of the dirt road to be picked up and sold in town. 'Chet' had crippled fingers in his right hand, caused by catching his hand in some piece of farm machinery, or perhaps in some other farm activity. Flour was little used, since it had to be bought. Cornmeal was the staple. It was made from corn, that is, maize, grown on the farm. My grandmother got up very early for fifty years to make and then cook cornbread in the wood-fired cook-stove in the lowest level of the house. The newly baked cornbread was sent up from the basement kitchen by dumbwaiter to the dining room above, along with ham and fried eggs for a huge farm breakfast. They churned their own butter. I remember being given the task of turning the butter churn and being taught just when to stop churning so the fresh butter could be separated at the right moment from the whey and shaped in a mould.

My grandmother also cooked a less complicated cornmeal cake (just cornmeal and water) to feed the dogs and the barn-cats outside the kitchen door. The cats were kept not as pets but to kill mice. The dogs also were not pets. They were kept for hunting 'birds', that is, quail, and even rabbits and squirrels, all important parts of the food supply. I remember one setter named 'Hitler'. He was kept on a chain attached to a long wire down below the old farmhouse, so he could run back and forth but not get loose. 'Hitler' was pronounced 'Hitlah': 'Heah Hitlah! You come heah, Hitlah!' There was later another dog named 'Stalin', but he was not so expert a hunter.

I witnessed what became a family story: the gift from my Grandfather Miller up north near Front Royal, Virginia, to my Grandfather Critzer of a big awkward young hunting dog named 'Bozo'. Bozo was transported by car by my father along with the whole family from one farm to the other at Christmas time. We used to spend part of Christmas at each farm. Bozo kept getting carsick on that trip and throwing up in the car. It was almost the only time I ever heard my father, ordained as a Baptist minister, swear. He said, euphemistically but forcefully: 'Horses!' Bozo turned out to be pretty useless as a hunting dog after all that trouble. But I forbear from telling that story in all its details.

Pigeons lived in a pigeon loft in the peak of the barn across the road from the main house. They were occasionally killed for food by my grandfather with a shotgun after they were scared into making the big mistake of flying out of the pigeon loft. The dinners at Afton were impressively abundant: four or five different vegetables, fried chicken, strawberries in season, and so on. I remember especially a Sunday treat, in season, of homemade peach ice cream made in one of those now obsolete ice cream makers with a container put in iced brine and turned with a crank handle, another task I helped perform.

The farmhouse was a large Victorian-style house built around 1900. Here are two photographs of it, from different angles (Figs 1.3 and 1.4). That dog might even be 'Hitlah'. This house still stands, so far as I know. It has a good many bedrooms, one downstairs for my grandparents, a big one upstairs that had been slept in by my three uncles when they were children and three more smaller bedrooms, two for the girls when they were growing up (my mother and my Aunt Bess) and one for guests, in one of which my brother and I slept when we were visiting. An older, much smaller farm house adjacent to the big one (and visible in the background of the first photo) was not torn down, but was used for storage, the front porch for the cream separator, the old basement for

Figure 1.3 The farmhouse, built around 1900. The dog might even be 'Hitlah'.

Figure 1.4 Another view of the farmhouse.

the dogs. The porch is the stage for the first photo I showed. My mother was born in that house, in 1898, but her siblings were all born in the grand new house.

A front parlour of the new house (to the right and downstairs in the first photo) was never used or heated except for weddings and funerals. I do not remember ever being there when it was used by the family. I used to retreat there to be alone to read. That is where I taught myself to read *Alice in Wonderland* so I would no longer need my mother to read it to me. A small organ powered by foot-pedals stood in that room. I gather that such an organ stood in practically every farmhouse parlour in Virginia. Ours was never used, but I was allowed to 'play with it'. My Grandfather Miller had a similar organ in his also unheated and unused front parlour. Some itinerant entrepreneur probably went from farm to farm selling them all over rural Virginia. Such organs were, I suppose, a sign of prestige.

No central heating, of course, in the Afton farmhouse. Separate wood stoves heated each room. I can remember the cold wood floor on my bare feet when I got out of bed in the morning to start up the stove in the bedroom I shared with my brother. No electricity until my grandfather installed a generator that made a great racket under the front porch every Saturday afternoon charging a large rank of batteries for the week. Later, Franklin Roosevelt's rural electrification and the Tennessee Valley Authority changed all that, just as the two dirt roads that crossed at one corner of the front yard have long since been paved with asphalt. We in the United States today should have something like the TVA for distributing wind-power and universal broadband internet connectivity, but the United States seems determined to fall behind such countries as Finland or China in such technologies. The TVA transformed rural America, as Roosevelt knew it would.

No telephone service existed at Afton until the community of local farm families installed a private system. It was later bought by the statewide system and joined to it. I can remember that you indicated whom you were calling by cranking two longs, or a long and a short, or whatever the code was for a given farm. You answered when you heard your own code ring. I think the Afton farm had a radio by the 1930s, but I don't remember it as looming large in my experience there. Mail was delivered to a mailbox beside the road. Hardy's narrator in *Under the Greenwood Tree* mentions the way the local vicar, Mr Maybold, intends to walk to Casterbridge from Mellstock (Bockhampton to Dorcester – three miles, in 'real life') to post a letter in order to avoid the delay of the local 'footpost'. Rural mail was already in 1930's Afton delivered by automobile to rural mailboxes, just as it still is today in Deer Isle, Maine, or in Sedgwick, Maine, where I now live in the summer and winter respectively.

At first, in the late 1800s, no school existed at Afton, until the small community of farmers banded together, built a tiny schoolhouse, and hired a teacher (see Fig. 1.5).

I remember it still standing derelict beside the road some distance from my grandparents' farm. It was pointed out to me by my mother, who went to school there. When my mother was a child, so she told me, a woman used to come once a year and stay a month, sewing new clothes for all the family. The seamstress would then move on to the next farm. Montgomery Ward and Sears Roebuck catalogues changed all that as a source of good, inexpensive clothes. At one point you could even order a house from Sears Roebuck. The few that remain, for example in Santa Barbara, California, are now valuable antiques. Catalogues changed lots of things in American rural experience.

Figure 1.5 Schoolhouse built by Afton's small community of farmers.

At first there was an outhouse at Afton a hundred and fifty feet up the hill, with an old Montgomery Ward catalogue for toilet paper. Later a regular bathroom was installed downstairs in the main house – a big improvement. The beehives were up near the outhouse and provided wonderful honey for the family. Though rain-water was collected in a cistern next to the house, the drinking water was carried up in a tin pail from a spring a hundred yards down hill. That was another of my chores when I was there. No alcohol was consumed that I remember, a big difference from Hardy's Mellstock, where much cider and mead are drunk. No electric refrigerator at Afton, of course. Ice for the icebox was provided from a nearby ice-pond. The ice was cut in cakes in the winter and stored in sawdust in an icehouse up the hill on the other side of the spring. The spring was a tiny pool in the 'branch'. 'Branch' is the local dialect word for a little stream. The word was used in this case for the small stream that flowed through the property down toward the road across which were all the farm outbuildings. I remember a splendid black walnut tree between the barn and the road. It produced abundant walnuts that fell to the ground in their big black husks.

Three features that might interest anthropologists characterised my grandparents' farm life:

1. Their total self-sufficiency, even in relation to the other farms around that were owned by relatives. Not only did they produce all their own food, and in abundance, but my grandfather had in a row along the road to the right of the barn, the blacksmith shop, a sawmill, a woodworking shop, and the gristmill for grinding corn. See Figure 1.6 for a picture of what they called 'the shop'. Note the telephone on the wall.

A belt attached to a small tractor powered machines in all these shops and mills. My grandfather was an expert cabinet-maker. We own now two beautiful and professionally finished small walnut side-tables that

Figure 1.6 'The shop' on my grandparents' farm.

he made and gave to my mother. One is a drop-leaf table. Though my grandfather served all our community with these mills and shops, for example grinding other people's corn, or shoeing horses for others with horseshoes made in the forge, the shops and mills were used especially for keeping his own farm going and that of my Great Uncle Everett. I was allowed to help by working the bellows in the forge, a great treat.

2. As opposed to Hardy's Mellstock, which is presented as a community made up of many families bound together by place and shared culture rather than by consanguinity, my Afton rural experience was primarily of a single family living in one house, with cordial relations but not much visiting back and forth with adjacent farms owned mostly by close relatives. No dances or big extended family get-togethers that I remember, even though the schoolhouse and the shop were joint ventures of the two adjacent Critzer families.

3. When I knew it in the 1930s, this small Afton community of one extended family was in the process of destroying itself or being destroyed. This was happening partly through rural electrification and other new technologies, partly through my grandfather's admirable desire to give his children a better life than his own. All his five children married people outside the neighbourhood and moved away to distant cities. My Uncle Jack eventually enacted the return of the native. He retired to a house he built on a piece of Critzer farmland after an urban life of several decades in Baltimore working for the telephone company. The peach orchard became no longer economically viable and was cut down. Bit by bit, in a short time, the old rural experience that I briefly shared disappeared. My celebration of it by describing it for you only

completes the work, since its existence as rural experience depended on being unselfconscious and taken for granted. I report it now from the perspective of its death and of the death of almost all the participants, just as Hardy does for Mellstock rural life.

*

I return in conclusion to my initial questions: Was Afton a genuine organic community of shared rural experience, a special kind of *Gemeinschaft*? If so, is that altogether a good thing?

I answer first that the Afton of my childhood eighty years ago seems to have been a rural *Gemeinschaft* if there ever was one. The Critzers formed a group living together according to the same rules, conventions, and culture. They shared language and religion, and had close family ties. They were not Stevens's 'Danes in Denmark', but 'Critzers in Afton', who, in Stevens's phrase, 'knew each other well, hale-hearted landsmen' (and landswomen!).

Matters were not quite so simple, however. The very success of this family community meant its imminent dissolution. This dissolution was caused in part by the technological advances that brought indoor plumbing, electricity from the grid, worldwide telephone access, television and so on. Television, even more rapidly than radio, tends to destroy a local accent as much in Virginia as in Maine. I live now in Maine and have learned that a genuine 'Maine accent' is harder and harder to find. Hardly anyone in Maine says 'Eyah!' for 'Yes' anymore. Nor do Virginians any longer say 'thang' for 'thing', as I still do after eighty-five years living in the North. I learned that pronunciation from my Critzer mother.

The energy of my Grandfather Critzer's work to give his five children a better life than he had led to the dissolution of the rural community in which they were brought up and which they had as a birthright. Only one of those five children remained on the farm, my mother's youngest brother Sheild; and even he went to college and worked for years as a young man not on the farm, but by commuting from the farm to a Dupont rayon factory located over the mountain in Waynesboro, Virginia. My Grandfather Critzer's income never exceeded a couple of thousand dollars a year, but somehow he sent all five of his children to college in the 1920s, the first children ever in the family to have a higher education. That was typical in rural America for the generation born around 1900. All in that generation in my family married people from outside the community and moved away to practise professions in urban places, only one of which was in Virginia, or to marry men whose work was not rural. Uncle Sheild's wife, Aunt Jean, who was from outside

Afton, has outlived all the others and was, until recently, living as a widow in extreme old age in the Afton Critzer farmhouse I remember. She was still alive in March 2014, but she passed away that June. It is many years since it was an active farm. Even when I knew that family community eighty years ago, it contained the seeds of its dissolution.

*

The apparent *Gemeinschaft* at Afton was, moreover, marked by fissures of several sorts inherited from the past. My mother brought me up to believe that I was 'Scotch-Irish and English, with a small admixture of German'. It is true that we were allied to the Martin, McCue and Rodes families, and that an ancestor of mine, Stephen Hopkins from Rhode Island, signed the Declaration of Independence. Part of the Hopkins family moved south and one member was a wealthy Maryland merchant, Johns Hopkins, who gave the money to found the great university that bears his name. We derived from the poor Virginia Hopkinses. Nevertheless, my maternal family (and my paternal family too) were overwhelmingly German. 'Critzer' is a German name, an Anglicisation of 'Kreitzer', just as my surname, 'Miller', was perhaps originally 'Müller'. My maternal grandmother's maiden name was 'Minta Hopkins Schultz', 'Minnie' for short. That is hardly a Scotch-Irish or English name. We were, in short, mostly what is called 'Pennsylvania Dutch', with 'Dutch' deriving from 'Deutsch'. It has nothing to do with the Netherlands.

My mother was ashamed of that heritage, probably in part because Germany was our enemy in WWI. A many times 'great' grandfather on my father's side was an impressed Hessian soldier in the British Army, sent to America during the War of Revolution. Like many other Hessian soldiers, he had sense enough to surrender at the Battle of Saratoga. As freed prisoners of war they were allowed to marry Americans and settle in the new United States, 'on condition that they never again bear arms'. That ancestor moved to join other German immigrants in Pennsylvania. He or his family, like many other Pennsylvania Dutch families, presumably including also the Critzer family, moved south into Virginia to become farmers on one side or the other of the Blue Ridge Mountains. The Critzers and Schultzes then intermarried with Martins, Hopkinses, McCues and Rodeses – to simplify the genealogy a little. The Critzer farm was on the east side of the Blue Ridge Mountains. My Grandfather Miller's small chicken farm was further north in the Shenandoah Valley, west of the Blue Ridge Mountains and across the South Fork of the Shenandoah River from Front Royal, Virginia.

Though the Critzer family was fissured in its forebears and not quite what my mother said it was, that would not seem to preclude its evolving in Afton into an organic *Gemeinschaft*, a genuine community. Things ('thangs'!) were not quite so simple at Afton, however. There was, as we say, a large elephant in the room. This beast was what C. Vann Woodward calls, in the title of a distinguished book, *The Burden of Southern History* (1968): that is, the horrible crime of slavery and its still-persisting aftermath of racism today. Read Toni Morrison's *Beloved* if you want a circumstantial account of what the South was like before the Civil War, with beatings, burnings alive, rapes of slave women by white slave owners, deliberate separation of families through sales of slaves, and so on.

My mother tried to teach me to believe in the Southern ideology about the Civil War. This was a set of beliefs that must have been taught all over in Southern schools, and probably is still taught. The Civil War was not about slavery, she told me, but about economic issues. That is at least partially true. She told me further that the South, given time, would have solved the problem of slavery on its own. Not all that likely in any immediate future in 1860! Slaves were needed for the cotton and tobacco plantations (the economic aspect!). Maybe emancipation after another hundred years or so! Maybe always 'not quite yet'. Most Southern cities, Atlanta for example, or Baltimore, or New Orleans, are still to a large degree segregated, as Martin Luther King and Rosa Parks experienced in the flesh. The eighteenth-century idea in the American south that African Americans should count as three-fifths of a white person has recently resurfaced in one Southern state. This is primarily a despicable scheme to dilute the Black vote, since African Americans mostly vote Democratic, overwhelmingly so for Barack Obama.

Wars that you have lost are remembered more vividly than wars you have won. To many Southerners even today, the Civil War seems like yesterday. I once in Atlanta heard a distinguished white businessman at a 'Friends of the Emory Library' meeting speak without a smile of 'the late unpleasantness'. It took me a minute or two to realise he was talking about the Civil War, and in particular about the burning of Atlanta. He spoke as if it had just happened yesterday. I was brought up to be proud of the fact that a great-uncle of mine was killed as a Confederate soldier in one of the worst mass slaughter battles of the Civil War: 'The Second Battle of Bull Run' or 'Second Manassas'. It was fought 28–30 August 1862, near the beginning of the war. The battle took place not all that many miles away from Afton, halfway toward Washington, and just fifty miles east of my Grandfather Miller's farm in Front Royal. One or more of the encounters took place in fairly flat fields without cover where both sides just mass-murdered one another. Approximately ten thousand Union soldiers were killed and wounded in the three-day battle, while approximately thirteen hundred Confederate soldiers were killed and seven thousand wounded.[1] The Confederate Army under General Robert E. Lee is said to have 'won' the battle.

During my childhood visits to the Afton farm, I was allowed to 'play with' a box of Civil War stereopticon photographs by Mathew Brady. These were slightly different photos side by side on cards that give the illusion of three-dimensionality when looked at through the stereopticon viewer. Horrible photos of dozens and dozens of dead soldiers on battlefields, along with dead horses. I especially pitied the latter for not being at fault, only unlucky enough to be in the wrong place at the wrong time. Fairly recently I learned that two of my great-grandfathers, both paternal and maternal, also served in the Confederate Army, though they survived. That was a remarkable piece of good luck for what were I assume enlisted men, not officers.

You will remember that the Southern states went to war to preserve slavery, whatever my mother said. That wrongful war caused immense loss of life for both sides. Slaves were only emancipated when the South lost the war and when Abraham Lincoln issued the Emancipation Proclamation.

No African American was included in the Critzer family community when I knew it, nor allowed in the church. I remember only one African American from my visits there, an old man named 'Pres' who did odd jobs around the farm. He must have been the grandson or great grandson of slaves. My mother showed me once the foundation of a small house she said was still inhabited when she was a child by an old African American woman who had been born a slave. She had remained in that little house after Emancipation until she died, still doing the same housework she had done before the war, as did many freed slaves. I have no reason to believe she was mistreated, but please remember that she was in her early life a slave, an object to be bought and sold as well as ordered around on pain of beatings or worse, if the owner so decided. The woman in the photograph I began by showing is said by my cousin Ann probably to be the daughter of that slave woman who lived in the little house I have mentioned, so maybe my mother got the generations wrong, or maybe I remember wrongly what she told me. In any case, an African American woman is included as a member of the household in that photograph. She is dressed, for example, in the same sort of clothes the other women wear.

My Afton relatives would have denied that they were racist. They just took for granted segregation and the superiority of the white race over the black race. I remember being even as a child troubled by the term my Grandfather Critzer and my uncles so casually used for African

Americans: 'nigra', halfway between 'Negro' and the 'n—' word my Virginian father taught me never to pronounce. The latter word they would have said they did not utter, but they did not clearly say 'Negro' either, much less 'African American', a term that so far as I know did not yet exist.

I conclude that the Afton Critzer family community I visited as a child was still, in the 1930s, thoroughly segregated. It was a *Gemeinschaft* that depended on the almost complete exclusion of African Americans. It was a rural experience that seemed idyllic but that was shadowed by the more or less suppressed memory of slavery and of the Civil War, the burden of Southern history. It is a burden I also carry. It was also secretly fissured by its denial of its German roots, as in what my mother told me.

It is important to remember, however, that slavery in the United States was by no means limited to the South. I was brought up to be proud of that distinguished Rhode Island ancestor of mine who signed the Declaration of Independence, Stephen Hopkins (1707–85). Hopkins, however, owned five slaves, one of whom he manumitted, while in his will he divided the others among his children, with instructions that they be treated with kindness. He also introduced in 1774 into the Rhode Island Assembly a bill prohibiting the importation of slaves into the colony ('Stephen Hopkins' n.pag.).

I would not, because of the slavery at Afton before the Civil War and because of continued racism there, propose the collection of Critzer farms as a good model of community life. New technologies, higher education and emigration were in any case rapidly destroying that particular form of rural experience. A dark past and an annihilating future hovered over what seemed to me as a child perdurable and even idyllic. Afton seemed an endless poise of midsummer farm life or of Christmas ritual festivities. Neither was altogether different from the ones described with such loving nostalgia in Hardy's *Under the Greenwood Tree*.

Hardy at Mellstock

My questions in this section are the same as for my questions about the Afton of my childhood. What is the nature of Thomas Hardy's Mellstock as he represents rural experience there in his novel of 1872, *Under the Greenwood Tree*? Is Hardy's Mellstock an organic community? Is it, in Ferdinand Tönnies's terms, a true *Gemeinschaft*, as opposed to a disaggregated *Gesellschaft*? If it is the former, is it wholly good that it should be so?

Hardy in *Under the Greenwood Tree* celebrates his imaginary Mellstock, based closely on his birthplace, the small Dorsetshire village called Bockhampton. This celebration is like the combination of closeness and distance in my description of the Afton farm. Hardy minutely describes details of weather, landscape, houses and gardens, domestic habits, behaviour, customs and ways of speech. Examples are the distinctions he makes in the opening scene among the sounds various trees make in the night-time wind. An adept can tell it is a beech without seeing it. Other examples are the description of the sanded floor in Tranter Dewy's kitchen, or of the hams hanging in the chimney there being smoked, or of the bacon being cooked over the chimney fire, hanging down on the gridiron 'like a cat in a child's arms' (Hardy, *Writings* 7:36, henceforth just page numbers), or of the cider barrel's broaching, or of honey-gathering, or of nutting (151), or of the various country dances that begin just after midnight Christmas day at the Dewys' party, or of the Mellstock Quire playing music for the dance, or for the Christmas eve carolling the night before, or for church services. The novel presents, moreover, wonderful renditions of the seemingly aimless repetitive conversations among Mellstockians.

A long example of this circumstantial 'realism' is the climactic description of the preparations for the wedding of Dick Dewy and Fancy Day at the end of the novel. This is followed by an account of outdoor dances literally 'under the greenwood tree', followed by the wedding supper indoors, and then by the traditional 'Walking' of the whole wedding party with the bride and bridegroom around the two parishes that are joined by the wedding. It is characteristic of Hardy's circumstantiality in *Under the Greenwood Tree* that he specifies just what dances were performed: 'five country dances, including "Haste to the Wedding", two reels, and three fragments of hornpipes' (208). All these details are represented lovingly from the inside by Hardy as if by a knowing participant and at the same time from the distancing-annihilating outside perspective of a professional city-dwelling novelist. This is like the combination of closeness and distance in my description of the Afton farm, or like an anthropologist's report made for sophisticated urban dwellers. The latter were the primary readers of Hardy's novels.

One recurrent demonstration of this inside/outside placement of the narrator is the use of 'poetic' comparisons, such as the simile already cited juxtaposing cooking bacon hanging on a gridiron and a cat in a child's arms. By 'poetic' I mean the sort of wry ironic figurative displacements that figure in Hardy's poetry. An example is a remarkable line from 'Wessex Heights': 'But mind-chains do not clank where one's next neighbour is the sky' (Hardy, *Complete Poems* 319). Hardy's mind-chains definitely clank in the complex alliterations in this sentence and in the harsh almost unpronounceable consonantal grating of 'next neighbour', as well as in the figure itself of the chained mind. The comparison of bacon to a cat in *Under the Greenwood Tree* is, surprisingly, ascribed to the lovesick Dick Dewy in a rare example of indirect discourse in this novel: 'but there was nothing in similes unless She [Fancy Day] uttered them' (36).

Most such comparisons seem to belong exclusively to the narrator as a somewhat detached spectator and subtle wry commenter. They tend to imply, but not directly state, some ironic comment on Mellstock life or on the main characters. Their function is not simply to make the reader imagine Mellstock life more vividly. Here are three examples: Fancy's 'womanly' anxiety about what she should wear on the next Sunday, her first appearance as organ-player in the church, is interrupted by an apparent irrelevance. She is 'looking at a group of hollyhocks in flower, round which a crowd of butterflies had gathered like female idlers round a bonnet-shop' (142). Fancy's vanity is as natural as the behaviour of butterflies. That is a pretty misogynist narrator's comment. A little later in the novel, when Dick Dewy is about to ask Geoffrey Day for Fancy's hand and be rejected, the narrator reports the apparently irrelevant fact that an owl is killing a little bird nearby: 'the stillness [of Geoffrey Day's silence] was disturbed only by some small bird that was being killed by an owl in the adjoining wood, whose cry passed into the silence without mingling with it' (162). The reader is left to infer the connection: Geoffrey Day is like the cruel owl in refusing happiness to Dick and Fancy. The owl is not a 'symbol'. It is an accidental ironic juxtaposition, it is, in Hardy's own phrase used as the title of one of his books of poems, a 'satire of circumstance' that makes human behaviour distressingly inhuman. In a final example, folk too old for dancing watch the youthful dancers under the greenwood tree after Fancy and Dick's wedding, 'as people on shore might be supposed to survey a naval engagement in the bay beyond' (207). Courtship or sex, which dancing figuratively mimes, is, at a double remove, as dangerous and violent as a naval engagement. In none of these cases except the bacon/cat one are the characters shown as aware of the comparison. The figures express rather the narrator's detached and ironic spectatorship.

Hardy's circumstantiality of description is reinforced by the way both the Wessex Edition of his works and the United States version with the same pagination, the Anniversary Edition (Hardy *Writings*), are 'illustrated' with photographs of the 'originals' of scenes and houses in each novel. I own a set of the Anniversary Edition and am citing it

Figure 1.7 The Mellstock Bridge and Farmer Shiner's House. The Bridge and Riverside House, Lower Bockhampton. Thomas Hardy's *Under the Greenwood Tree*, in *Writings in Prose and Verse*, Anniversary Edition, volume 7 (Harper & Brothers Publishers, 1920). Photographer: Hermann Lea.

Figure 1.8 Upper Mellstock (Upper Bockhampton). Thomas Hardy's *Under the Greenwood Tree*, in *Writings in Prose and Verse*, Anniversary Edition, volume 7 (Harper & Brothers Publishers, 1920). Photographer: Hermann Lea.

in this essay. The photographs are not the same in the two editions. The 1920 Anniversary Edition version of *Under the Greenwood Tree* contains four tipped-in photogravures, distributed throughout the novel and guarded by tissue papers with elaborate printed captions on them. The first is of 'The Bridge and Riverside House, Lower Bockhampton'. This is said to be the 'prototype' of 'The Mellstock Bridge and Farmer Shiner's House'. Other photogravures are of the 'prototypes' of 'Upper Mellstock', 'Mellstock Vicarage' and 'Yalbury Hill' (actually photos of Upper Bockhampton, the Bockhampton Vicarage and Yellowham Hill). The houses in these photographs, by the way, are much grander than any houses in the Afton, Virginia, of my early childhood, or even now, so far as I know (Figs 1.7, 1.8, 1.9 and 1.10).

Figure 1.9 Mellstock Vicarage (Stinsford Vicarage). Thomas Hardy's *Under the Greenwood Tree*, in *Writings in Prose and Verse*, Anniversary Edition, volume 7 (Harper & Brothers Publishers, 1920). Photographer: Hermann Lea.

Figure 1.10 Yalbury Hill (Yellowham). Thomas Hardy's *Under the Grenwood Tree*, in *Writings in Prose and Verse*, Anniversary Edition, volume 7 (Harper & Brothers Publishers, 1920). Photographer: Hermann Lea.

Much could be said about these photogravures. Their effect on the reader, at least on me, is extremely odd. On the one hand they persuade me that the novel is based on 'reality'. The use of fictitious names reminds the reader that the novel is a transposition into a realm in which Hardy can make up whatever story he likes to take place within this now fictitious scene. The photographs, moreover, were taken long after the story is supposed to have happened and use what seems now a manifestly antiquated technology. No million-pixelled digital colour photos taken with an iPhone such as might be used now! Of the first photo, tipped in, facing the title page, and protected by a sheet of tissue on which the caption is printed, Hardy, writing presumably at the time the Anniversary Edition was being prepared, observes that the village of Lower Bockhampton is 'nowadays more enclosed than formerly'.

The superimposition of different times (the time of the action, 1836 or 1846 [Hardy says 'fifty or sixty years ago' in the 1896 preface]; the time of publication, 1872; the time of the first preface, 1896, the time of the added preface for the Wessex Edition, 1912; the time of the Anniversary Edition, 1920, with its photos; the time of my first reading, about 1969; the time of my recent rereading, 2013), and the oscillation between fiction and reality has an extraordinarily complex effect on me. This effect is not to be reduced to saying that the photos reinforce the verisimilitude. They work rather to make reality less substantial, to turn it into poignantly fleeting images in an outmoded photographic technology that echo over the decades. This effect is reinforced by the sub-sub-title on the title page facing the first photo. The full title is *Under the Greenwood Tree/Or/The Mellstock Quire: A Rural Painting of the Dutch School*. Note our key word: 'rural'! Genre painting, photograph and fictitious story all work together to dissolve the 'original Bockhampton'. They may also remind the thoughtful reader how different these scenes must be today and by how different a technology they would be photographically recorded today.

*

Here is one example of Mellstockian conversation, as registered in Hardy's orthography. 'Reading' it, that is, interpreting it, will allow me to be a little more specific about rural experience in Mellstock. The Quire has finished drinking cider, lots of it, and is preparing to go out all around the parish to sing and play Christmas carols on their violins and other instruments:

> 'Better try over number seventy-eight before we start, I suppose?' said William, pointing to a heap of old Christmas-carol books on a side table.
> 'Wi' all my heart,' said the choir generally.
> 'Number seventy-eight was always a teaser – always. I can mind him ever since I was growing up a hard boy-chap.'
> 'But he's a good tune, and worth a mint o' practice,' said Michael.
> 'He is; though I've been mad enough wi' that tune at times to seize and tear en all to linnit. Ay, he's a splendid carrel – there's no denying that.'
> 'The first line is well enough,' said Mr Spinks; 'but when you come to "O, thou man", you make a mess o't.'
> 'We'll have another go into en, and see what we can make of the martel ["mortal"]. Half-an-hour's hammering at en will conquer the toughness of en; I'll warn it [short, I assume, for 'warrant it'].'
> ''Od rabbit it all!' said Mr Penny, interrupting with a flash of his spectacles, and at the same time clawing at something in the depths of a large side-pocket. 'If so be I hadn't been as scatter-brained and thirtingill as a chiel I should have called at the schoolhouse wi' a boot as I cam up along. Whatever is coming to me I really can't estimate at all!'

'The brain has its weaknesses,' murmured Mr Spinks, waving his head ominously. Mr Spinks was considered to be a scholar, having once kept a night-school, and always spoke up to that level. (16–17)[2]

This passage registers not so much intersubjectivity as interlinguality, if I may be permitted to use that neologism. Intersubjectivity in the usual sense of the word is for the most part missing in *Under the Greenwood Tree*. Anything like spontaneous telepathic insight into what the other person is thinking is absent. Even the conventionally telepathic or 'omniscient' narrator of the novel has only partial and intermittent access to what this or that character is thinking or feeling. The happy ending, as I shall show, is undermined by a lifelong secret Fancy Day, now Fancy Dewy, will keep from her husband.

In *Under the Greenwood Tree* it is as if there were some all-encompassing ubiquitous continuous village discourse in which all the inhabitants participate. That discourse seems to speak through them. They are spoken by it, rather than speaking it. Hardy often does not indicate just which person is speaking, as in the example I have cited. *Die Sprache spricht*, as Heidegger puts this, in a famous passage parodied and subverted by Paul de Man. *Die Sprache verspricht (sich)*, says de Man, which means not 'Language speaks', as Heidegger portentously says, but both 'Language promises' and 'Language misspeaks', or 'Language makes a slip of the tongue' ('Promises' 277). Some *versprechen* as well as *sprechen* characterises the speech of Hardy's Mellstockians, as I shall show.

A long interchange follows the passage cited above, as Mr Penny, the village boot-maker, explains how he can tell from a last whose 'voot' will fit into a boot made to a given pattern. Mr Spinks claims to go beyond that and to know the temperament and way of life of any person by his or her foot: 'I know little, 'tis true – I say no more; but show *me* a man's foot, and I'll tell you that man's heart' (20).

Much can be deduced about rural experience in Mellstock, as well as about Hardy's way of recording it, from the excerpt cited above. I claim it is a valid synecdoche, a fair sample of the whole. All participants in the interchange are men, though the wives also have their say in other conversations, for example in Mrs Dewy's often-repeated complaint that her husband, the tranter, is, like all the Dewys, a 'sweater'. He breaks out into perspiration at the slightest inspiration. Nevertheless, the men do most of the talking. The narrator specifies with exactitude that each of these represents a different rural profession: Old James, the maternal grandfather, was a mason, like Thomas Hardy's own father, while others are tranter, shoemaker, farmer, sometime keeper of a night-school, gamekeeper and so on. A 'tranter' is someone who transports goods in a horse-drawn wagon from one place to another. My Grandfather Critzer, in Afton, Virginia, on the contrary, practised many professions. He was farmer, Bible teacher, blacksmith, cabinet-maker, sawyer, gristmill operator, bee-keeper. That is a big difference in division of labour.

The characters in *Under the Greenwood Tree* are all more or less of the same 'class', except for the vicar, Mr Maybold, and Fancy Day herself, the heroine. Maybold and Fancy interrupt what would otherwise exemplify, for Hardy's Wessex rather than for Wales, Raymond Williams's celebration in *The Country and the City* (1973) of Welsh border classless village life before a vicar from away came and before the building of aristocratic manor houses. No manor house is mentioned in *Under the Greenwood Tree*, though Geoffrey Day, the heroine's father, lives deep in Yalbury Wood in a neighbouring parish. 'Yalbury Wood' is one of many redolent but fictitious place names that Hardy delights in substituting for the real Bockhampton ones, just as he renames the personages borrowed presumably from the real Bockhampton people Hardy knew as a child. Yalbury Wood is part of the Earl of Wessex's 'outlying estates'. Day is 'head game-keeper, timber-steward, and general overlooker for this district' of the Earl's estates (95–6). Day definitely has a higher-class status than does Dick Dewy's tranter father.

As opposed to the Earl of Wessex's estates as a remnant of English feudalism, my Grandfather Critzer's farm was part of what had been a much larger farm. It had been subdivided from generation to generation amongst various children of the original presumably early nineteenth-century owner. No law of primogeniture in the United States. No Earl of Afton and no big manor house either. Mr Maybold, the new vicar of the Mellstock church, is the destructive interloper in Mellstock Parish, as is to some degree Fancy Day. All the speakers in my extract have been intimately acquainted with one another since childhood. They appear to form a genuine *Gemeinschaft*, an organic rural community. What Tranter Reuben Dewy says at one point sums it up: 'We all know one another very well, don't we, neighbours?' to which all give assent (75).

Recurrent notations throughout the novel show that these rural folk seem at all times to have a total recall of their entire lives back to childhood. They live the present in terms of a panoramic simultaneous memory of their own lives and those of their neighbours. ('I can mind him [the Christmas carol] ever since I was growing up a hard boy-chap.') All speak unselfconsciously, in Hardy's rendition, with a heavy Dorset accent. Their speech is rich and eloquent. It is spontaneously 'poetic', for example in the personification of carol 'number seventy-eight' ('But he's a good tune . . .'), or in the multitude of pithy local idioms they use, often euphemistic curses ("Od rabbit it all!'). The next in line in each stichomythic give and take tends first explicitly and courteously to agree with what the previous speaker has said and then to modify it: 'But he's a good tune . . .'; 'He is; though I've been mad enough wi' that tune at times . . .'. What these folk say is often unintentionally comic, as in the long discussion of the relations among feet, boots, personality and family lineage. Nevertheless, the narrator reports this rural speech with respect for its eloquence, honesty and insight rather than with condescension.

Curiously enough, as I have said, given the cosiness of this organic community, Hardy grants neither the narrator nor the characters anything like spontaneous telepathic insight into what the other person is thinking and feeling. You must know the inner nature of another person indirectly, as Mr Penny knows people by their feet and by the boots that fit those feet, and as Mr Spinks knows a man's heart by his foot, at least so he says. The characters in *Under the Greenwood Tree* habitually just talk back and forth, each new speaker responding to what the previous speaker has said and to her or his gestures and facial expressions. The narrator often elaborately reports the latter: '"Yes, yes; too common it is!" said Spinks with an inward sigh, whilst his eyes seemed to be looking at the world in an abstract form rather than at the scene before him' (9); 'all the new arrivals reseated themselves with widespread knees, their eyes meditatively seeking out any speck or knot in the board upon which the gaze might precipitate itself' (13). This 'polite' looking anywhere but at the person to whom you are talking recurs frequently in the novel. It is a leitmotif of rural experience in Mellstock, as when Geoffrey Day first looks fixedly on his plate and spoon while he is eating, and later, still at table, looks out of the window before speaking, 'as if he read the words on a board at the further end of the vista' (101, 103).

The narrator rarely uses indirect discourse, as I have said, whereas it is, for example, the staple of narration in Anthony Trollope's novels or in George Eliot's novels. In Eliot's or Trollope's fictions indirect discourse is evidence of the narrator's ability to enter telepathically into the minds and hearts of the characters, unbeknownst to them. In Hardy's novels the narrator (he, she or it – we should not assume the narrator is straightforwardly male or an avatar of Thomas Hardy) is for the most part limited to reporting what any spectator would have seen or heard. I was limited as a child, in a similar way, in my grandparents' living room of an evening at the Afton farm, hearing the adults talk. I had no direct access to what was going on in their minds. I had only their speech, gestures and facial expressions on the basis of which to make inferences.

Tranter Dewy, Dick's father, expresses this as a general law of Mellstock rural experience: 'if you can't read a maid's mind by her motions, nature d'seem to say thou'st ought to be a bachelor' (116). Good luck with that attempt at mind-reading, as Dick Dewy's ignorance attests! Though it seems to the feeble-minded Leaf that Geoffrey Day 'do look at me as if 'a could see my thoughts running round like the works of a clock' (93), this may be a baseless inference by Leaf, just as it seems to Fancy, though without much objective confirmation, that the supposed witch, Mrs Endorfield, 'seemed to be watching her thoughts. Really one would almost think she must have the powers people ascribed to her' (167). That last sentence, by the way, is one of the rare examples in *Under the Greenwood Tree* of direct reporting of a character's inner speech. Mrs Endorfield does know that Fancy is unhappy, and she knows why, but this is an unusual clairvoyance in this novel. It supports her reputation as a witch.

The narrator does, however, frequently report objectively a given character's opinions, thoughts or moods. An example is the following notation about Tranter Dewy: 'He preferred to let such delicate affairs [as the fact that both Shiner and Dick Dewy are smitten with Fancy Day] right themselves; experience having taught him that the uncertain phenomenon of love, as it existed in other people, was not a groundwork upon which a single action of his own life could be founded' (95). The narrator here speaks as if Reuben Dewy's conviction about love were a more or less external fact about him, like the cut of his hair. What experience has taught him, moreover, is that love is an 'uncertain phenomenon' as it exists in other people, that is, something hidden and unpredictable. You can know your own love but not, except indirectly, the love others feel.

I have been 'reading', that is, interpreting, my initial long citation for its tacit phenomenological assumptions about rural experience. The passage ends with a cool, distancing remark by the narrator: 'Mr Spinks was considered to be a scholar, having once kept a night-school and always spoke up to that level.' This remark is like that of an anthropologist explaining to westerners some mystifying aspect of speech or behaviour in an alien culture. Hardy's narrator here speaks directly to sophisticated urban readers of *Under the Greenwood Tree*. He says something no Mellstockian would need to hear, nor would have expressed in those terms. This mixture of distance and closeness is the consistent stance and placement of the narrator throughout the novel. The discourse of this novel is made up of objective description of details of nature and dwellings in Mellstock; word-for-word report of the give and take of conversation in discrete scenes that bring this or that set of characters together indoors or out and advance the action; descriptions of the gestures and facial expressions of the characters; sparse objective notations by an unobtrusively and only partially telepathic narrator of the characters' thoughts and feelings. Even the narrator is sometimes wholly excluded, as when he, she or it says Fancy's thoughts are unknown: 'Sitting here and thinking again – of her lover, or of the sensation she had created at church that day? – well, it is unknown' (180).

Two stories are told by way of this narrative technique. They go in opposite directions, one toward the dissolution of community (the story of the replacement of the Mellstock Quire by an organ for music at church services in the parish church), the other toward the reaffirmation of community in the climactic marriage of Fancy Day and Dick Dewy. This marriage renews community bonds between family and family, parish and parish. It will prolong the community in their children and their children's children down through the generations.

*

It would seem that the community of Hardy's Mellstock is quite different in various ways from the Afton, Virginia, community of my childhood. Nevertheless, Mellstockian rural experience, like Afton's, was about to vanish. It is presented as already inhabited by the seeds of its self-destruction. This is embodied in the replacement of the Church Quire by the organ for church services. Nevertheless, Mellstock appears to have been a happy *Gemeinschaft* while it lasted. It was a functioning almost classless community where labour was diversified and where, as Marx and Engels put it, 'individuals are united by some bond: family, tribe, the land itself, etc.', 'what is involved is chiefly an exchange between men and nature in which the labour of the former is exchanged for the products of the latter' and 'the domination of the proprietor over the propertyless may be based on personal relations, on a kind of community' (63). This community is renewed from generation to generation by courtships and marriages such as the one between Dick Dewy and Fancy Day in *Under the Greenwood Tree*.

The Mellstockian community, moreover, is not shadowed by anything so dark as the slavery that is still the burden of Southern history, nor by a problematic heritage such as my mixture of British and German blood, nor by the effaced presence of a whole race, African Americans, that could not share as equals in the Afton white rural *Gemeinschaft*. In Hardy's case the much less disastrous (for England) Napoleonic Wars, marked by the acute fear in Napoleon's time, especially in southern England, of invasion by 'Bony', is the closest thing to the memory of the Civil War and of slavery by Southern Americans even today. Many a Confederate flag still today hides in Southern people's attics. Hardy's novel of 1880, *The Trumpet Major*, is set in the time of the Napoleonic Wars.

Hardy and Hardy's narrators and characters have, moreover, no reason to feel guilty about the Napoleonic Wars. Hardy was somewhat absurdly proud of being (so he believed) descended from the aristocratic Norman 'Le Hardies', just as Tess of the d'Urbervilles believes she belongs to a decayed aristocratic Norman family. The Norman Conquest was by the nineteenth century a distant memory of something that had happened seven hundred years before. It was a matter for pride and curiosity rather than of present anxiety, as was the Roman occupation many centuries before the Normans invaded.

*

Nevertheless, Hardy's Mellstock of the 1840s is not quite the happy egalitarian community Marx and Engels, and Raymond Williams after Marx and Engels, celebrate as an ideal they presuppose has existed and might exist again.

For one thing, *Gemeinschaft*, at least tacitly, presupposes a spontaneous insight among all its members into what the other person is thinking and feeling. The narrator of *Under the Greenwood Tree* affirms repeatedly that this is not the case in Mellstock, as I have already shown, even though the narrator has some insight into the hidden thoughts and feelings of the characters. No spontaneous intersubjectivity in Mellstock. Each character has to guess at the interiority of his or her fellow Mellstockians on the basis of speech, gestures, facial expressions, and the like, none of which is an infallible way of knowing the other.

The big example of this non-knowledge in *Under the Greenwood Tree* is Fancy's momentary betrayal of her betrothal to Dick when she promises to marry the richer and more highly educated vicar of the local church, the Reverend Maybold. Though she retracts the next day her promise to marry Maybold on the grounds that she is already affianced to Dick Dewy and loves him still, and though Maybold urges her to confess the episode to Dick, she refuses to do so. Their marriage, happy though it seems destined to be, will be perpetually shadowed by the dark secret of her infidelity. This makes *Under the Greenwood Tree* not the idyllic pastoral love story it might appear to be and is sometimes said to be, but rather an early example of Hardy's perpetual ironic themes in his poems, short stories, and novels of 'time's laughingstocks', 'satires of circumstance' (the titles of two of his books of poems) and secret infidelities.

Just one among many examples is 'The Workbox', from 'Satires of Circumstance'. Years ago I heard Dylan Thomas read this poem with great gusto and great admiration. He said, 'I like the bus that Hardy misses better than the buses that other poets catch.' In 'The Workbox' the young wife turns white when her husband, 'a joiner', or cabinet maker, tells her that the workbox he has made for her has come from a 'scantling' of the wood that was used to make 'poor John Wayward's coffin, who/Died of they knew not what' (Hardy, *Complete Poems* 398). John Wayward has died for love of her, as the young wife knows. She will use for her lifetime a workbox made for faithful love of her that is constructed of the leftover coffin wood for Wayward's coffin. As the husband says: 'The shingled pattern that seems to cease/Against your box's rim/Continues right on in the piece/That's underground with him' (398).

Almost against his will, Hardy could not resist, it seems, ending *Under the Greenwood Tree* not with an echo of the four happy love stories in Shakespeare's *As You Like It*, but with something much darker and more ironic, Fancy's secret infidelity. The marriages at the end of *As You Like It* are themselves shadowed by the dramatisation of the incompatibility between love and lust. A famous song from *As You Like It* is echoed in Hardy's title, as I earlier demonstrated. The ending of *Under the Greenwood Tree* depends on Hardy's assumption that we cannot see into one another's hearts and that this may be a good thing. Ignorance is bliss, the happiness of being well deceived.

*

The ending of *Under the Greenwood Tree* presents the last example in the novel of one of its leitmotifs: the wryly incongruent correspondence between events in non-human nature and human doings. Dick and Fancy, now happily married, are going in his 'new spring-cart' to their new cottage home after the wedding dance and feast:

> 'Ever since that time you confessed to that little flirtation with Shiner by the river (which was really no flirtation at all), I have thought how artless and good you must be to tell o' such a trifling thing, and to be so frightened about it as you were. It has won me to tell you my every deed and word since then. We'll have no secrets from each other, darling, will we ever? – no secret at all'.
> 'None from to-day,' said Fancy. 'Hark! what's that?'
> From a neighbouring thicket was suddenly heard to issue in a loud, musical, and liquid voice –
> 'Tippiwit! swe-e-et! ki-ki-ki! Come hither, come hither, come hither!'
> 'O, 'tis the nightingale,' murmured she, and thought of a secret she would never tell. (211)

'Come hither, come hither, come hither' is the refrain of Shakespeare's song, 'Under the Greenwood Tree', in *As You Like It*, as in my citation of part of the song near the beginning of this essay. In Shakespeare's song, the bird's cry, not identified by Shakespeare as a nightingale, is rendered in human language as an invitation to join it in the Forest of Arden, just as the Duke of Amiens invites the sophisticated courtiers to lie with him under the greenwood tree. It is characteristic of Hardy that he would do his best to represent on the page an actual nightingale's cry, whereas Keats does no such thing in the 'Ode to a Nightingale', a poem Hardy may also have had in mind. The nightingale's happy song makes Keats think of earthly sorrows. In this sad world, 'Beauty cannot keep her lustrous eyes,/Or new Love pine at them beyond to-morrow' (ll. 29–30). In lines that are hauntingly beautiful, Keats asserts that 'Perhaps the self-same song ... found a path/Through the sad heart of Ruth, when, sick for home,/She stood in tears among the alien corn' (ll. 65–7).

Some reference to Bockhamptonian folk beliefs may also lie behind the sudden voice of the nightingale just after Fancy lies without actually lying by promising to keep no secrets from Dick 'from to-day'. A Wikipedia search uncovers several folksongs that relate the nightingale's song to infidelity, to illicit love that crosses class lines, or to sexual jealousy, for example 'The Twa Sisters' (Wikipedia 2014) or 'Sweet Nightingale' (Wikipedia 2014). Hardy, who quotes numerous folksongs here and there in *Under the Greenwood Tree*, for example 'King Arthur he had three sons' (159), may have known one or another of these nightingale folksongs. In any case, the nightingale's cry acts as a reproach to Fancy for her infidelity. It also suggests that thus was it always. Life is like a timeless folksong, or like the endlessly repeated nightingale's song all over Europe. I heard that song once in Italy, in the country outside Florence, a memorable 'rural experience' for me. People, the nightingale's song is taken to imply, always keep secrets from one another. Even faithful young wives keep secrets from their husbands. What happens to Tess when she reveals her past to the abominably priggish Angel Clare on their wedding night, in *Tess of the d'Urbervilles*, suggests that Fancy was right to decide not to tell Dick the truth. The haunting 'Come hither, come hither, come hither!' that turns the inarticulate bird call into human language, adds one more distancing perspective to the troubling, even somewhat chilling, happy ending. Fancy hears perhaps the same song that the homesick Ruth heard. She will have to live out her married life keeping a shameful secret from her husband.

One final irony in the marriage that seems to go in the opposite direction from the abolishment of the Mellstock Quire must be mentioned in conclusion. It is one more element going against the idea that Mellstock is presented as a pastoral happy community. Fancy Day is after all the actual agent of the displacement of the Quire by the organ. She accepts Parson Maybold's request that she start playing the organ every Sunday in church. She shows up to do that with curls, wearing a hat with a feather and a splendid dress. Maybold thinks the Mellstock Quire is outmoded, low-class and quaint, while organ music is more refined and high-class. My opinion today is just the reverse. I know what a church organ sounds like, but I have never heard a country Quire. I much regret that it was impossible in 1845 to make recordings of the Mellstock Quire. It must have been really something to hear. It sounds from Hardy's description as if it must have been a wonderful example of sophisticated folk art passed down through the decades like the country dances for which the stringed instruments of the Quire also played. Hardy discusses country music both sacred and secular in the *Life* (see F. E. Hardy) when relating his father's and grandfather's musical gifts and performances. He also reports that as a small child he used to dance when his father played in order to hide the way that playing moved him to tears:

> He was of ecstatic temperament, extraordinarily sensitive to music, and among the endless jigs, hornpipes, reels, waltzes, and country-dances that his father played of an evening in his early married years, and to which the boy danced a *pas seul* in the middle of the room, there were three or four that always moved the child to tears, though he strenuously tried to hide them. (F. E. Hardy, *Life* 15)

The *Life*, though ostensibly by Hardy's second wife, Florence Emily Hardy, is almost all by Thomas Hardy himself, though of course he could not recount his own death.

Fancy contributes in other ways to the dissolution of the Mellstock *Gemeinschaft*. She is like a dangerous virus or 'bug' in a computer program. The program would otherwise work well, but the bug interferes with that smooth working. Or, to look at it another way, Fancy is a 'fix' that ensures the community program will go on working, though somewhat differently. Like Ruth, the Moabite who marries a man from Judea, and thereby ensures the continuation of the House of David even down to Jesus of Nazareth, Fancy Day comes from a neighbouring parish, not from Mellstock. Her father, Geoffrey Day, gamekeeper for the Earl of Wessex, is richer and of a slightly higher class than Dick Dewy, as I have said. Dick will carry on the family business of local transportation of goods. Day has high aspirations for his daughter. He educates her so that she might marry above her station. When he refuses Dick Dewy's request for her hand, he gives details about her upbringing.

After her mother's death, Fancy lived with an aunt who kept a boarding school and then went to a teachers' training school where 'her name stood first among the Queen's scholars of her year' (164). Training to be a teacher was still in the Virginia of my mother's youth in the early 1900s the way for a young farm woman to rise in the world and marry well. That is what my mother did. Geoffrey Day wants his daughter Fancy to work as a schoolmistress in Mellstock so 'that if any gentleman who sees her to be his equal in polish, should want to marry her, and she want to marry him, he shan't be superior to him in pocket' (164). Day has his eye on rich Farmer Shiner as a possible husband for Fancy. A marriage to a mere tranter's son would be a disaster to his plan.

The courtship of Dick and Fancy brings in issues involving both class and money, the 'cash nexus', those two solvents of traditional rural community life. As Marx and Engels put this, in a passage already cited in part: 'In the first case, the domination of the proprietor over the propertyless may be based on personal relations, on a kind of community; in the second, it must have taken on a material shape in a third party – money' (63). Money is no more than 'a material shape'. It turns personal relations, as in the original more or less classless community of Mellstock, into something abstract and disembodied.

Fancy is able to get her father eventually to agree to her marriage to Dick Dewy only by taking the advice of Mrs Endorfield of Higher Mellstock. The latter is reputed to be a witch. (Think 'Witch of Endor'.) Following Mrs Endorfield's advice, Fancy pretends to be dying of a broken heart, refuses to eat and eventually takes to her bed. Geoffrey Day gives in. What else could a fond father do? Fancy Day is a determined young woman, as in her handling of her false promise to marry Parson Maybold. She is someone likely to get her way with her husband Dick. She is also likely to make changes in the *Gemeinschaft* of Mellstock.

What these changes may well be is suggested in the culminating scenes of her wedding day. Fancy has all sorts of objections to the immemorial customs of a Mellstock wedding, though she agrees to go along with them in this case, as a way of honouring the memory of her dead mother. An example is her objection to the custom of a 'Walking' of the wedding party around both parishes after the wedding, which all the married members of the wedding party remember doing at their own weddings: '"Respectable people don't nowadays," said Fancy. "Still, since poor mother did, I will"' (202). She also instructs her father and the tranter, Dick's father, 'to carefully avoid saying "thee" and "thou" in their conversation, on the plea that those ancient words sounded so very humiliating to persons of newer taste' (206). She thinks the bridesmaids should walk together in the Walking procession, whereas the Mellstock custom is 'always young man and young woman, arm in crook' (204). The old custom hinted at the future marriages of the bridesmaids. The new way hides that desired future. Fancy gives in once more, in order to honour her dead mother, but the reader suspects she will not always be so amenable. Her agreement to play the organ in church is, one guesses, just the first of the changes she will bring over the years to the Mellstock community. She is an agent of the dissolution of that community as the reader encounters it at the beginning of *Under the Greenwood Tree*.

Mellstock, my second example of the varieties of rural experience, does not constitute an unequivocal organic community. It exemplifies, rather, what Jean-Luc Nancy calls an 'inoperative community', *'une communauté désoeuvrée'*. That kind of community, as Nancy explains in detail, resists the 'fusion' that seems to be promised for lovers and replaces it with a perpetual division between 'singularities' that can never fully understand one another.[3]

*

I conclude that neither Afton nor Mellstock, my examples in this essay of the varieties of rural experience, constitutes an unequivocal organic community. Both are, though in quite different ways, examples, rather, of Nancy's *'communauté désoeuvrée'*.

Notes

1. See Wikipedia, 'The Second Battle of Bull Run', for a detailed account of this deplorable slaughter.
2. I cannot forbear to give another splendid example of this kind of talk. Such interchanges permeate the novel. Hardy appears to have taken an exuberant pleasure in recording what he remembered from his childhood of the way his neighbours talked:

> 'That's a thing we shall never know. I can't unriddle her [Fancy Day], nohow.'
> 'Thou'st ought to be able to onriddle such a little chiel as she,' the tranter observed.
> 'The littler the maid, the bigger the riddle, to my mind. And coming of such stock, too, she may well be a twister.'
> 'Yes; Geoffrey Day is a clever man if ever there was one. Never says anything: not he.'
> 'Never.'
> 'You might live wi' that man, my sonnies, a hundred years, and never know there was anything in him.'
> 'Ay; one o' these up-country London ink-bottle chaps [as Hardy himself was at that time] would call Geoffrey a fool.' [Hardy's narrator is not so stupid as to do that.]
> 'Ye never find out what's in that man: never,' said Spinks. 'Close? Ah, he is close! He can hold his tongue well. That man's dumbness is wonderful to listen to.'

'There's so much sense in it. Every moment of it is brimmen over wi' sound understanding.'
''A can hold his tongue very clever – very clever truly,' echoed Leaf. ''A do look at me as if 'a could see my thoughts running round like the works of a clock.' (93)

3. See pp. 3–139 *passim* for 'fusion' and pp. 27–76 *passim* for 'singularities'.

Chapter 2

'There were three men came out of the west': Experiencing the Rural or, the Ghosts of Community – a 'response' for J. Hillis Miller

Julian Wolfreys

– . . . at this moment the landscape has just changed.
– But is there ever a natural landscape . . . ?
– No, rather what has just been disrupted would be the established scenery
. . .

Jacques Derrida[1]

. . . this pre-beginning does not come down . . . to the most originary . . . it is thus a question of thinking the before in the before, the abyss of antecedence . . . the process of the linearization of time . . . makes loss or the nonrestitution of the singular irreversible . . . the interpretation of *khōra* as memory, "the remembering force of representation", [is] an interpretation [that is] perilous".[2]

Jacques Derrida

Why bother chasing ghosts and trying to solve insoluble mysteries . . . ?
Patrick Modiano[3]

My title is complicated. Taking seriously the *pli* of 'complicate', it folds together, enfolds and entangles in a skein of discourses, cultures, histories even (about which I do not propose to go into detail just yet), a response for J. Hillis Miller's chapter in this volume, 'Varieties of Rural Experience in Virginia and Wessex'. That enfolding is merely the sketch of what is to follow. The sharp-eyed grammarian will cavil at the preposition *for* that unhinges the third part of my title, and which unhinging reiterates itself in the previous sentence. I have chosen that knowingly. For while I am responding to Miller, while this essay is something of an answer (not that a question was ever directly asked), this is also a response in its less familiar sense. Response comes into the English language from old French (*respuns, respons*), itself deriving genealogically from the Latin *responsum*: something offered in return. The Latin speaks also of a correspondence – in the sense of communication, mail, whether letters or postcards, email etc., but also in the sense of similarity, connection, equivalence and congruity. I am not suggesting that my correspondence is the equivalent of Miller's work, but merely signalling that there is agreement, connection through those shared concerns that a Venn diagram might map across, between our work, giving us as it were a common ground, a shared place. Something in the texts of J. Hillis Miller's work is of course already a response, in that sense of something given by the other, to which Miller responds. There is never a simple starting point, an origin or first time. This chapter is then something offered to J. Hillis Miller, a *response*, a *co-response*, something given in return for the incalculable debt gathered over the years for the gift of scholarship, the generosity of thought that he has given, to all that he has responded without condition.

*

There is nothing quite like confronting genealogical research and its numerous difficulties for reminding one that origins are myths, convenient markers to let one off the hook from the interminability of the search. The anxiety of the interminable is only assuaged, if at all, by the convenience of a fiction – J. Hillis Miller describes this accurately as 'a species of prosopopoeia', a 'selective fictional confabulation' (Miller, 'Varieties') – one might construct from the arrangements of the facts one garners.[4] Like history and psychology, genealogy is a 'science' of 'facts'. However, like those other sciences, genealogy can only be constituted in its meaning 'by something other than itself' involving an 'originarily temporal lived experience', a past or successive pasts apprehended, apperceived by a 'lived and experienced [*erlebte*][5] now'[6] that is not objective. Genealogical research is founded on the premise of becoming more oneself than one already is, while at the same time giving oneself place, becoming; it presupposes a form of appearance of the self as other, 'enframing' (*Gestell*) the subject, of giving place, 'emplacing' (*Gestell*) the subject.[7] *Gen*ealogy names the generation of the generations that generate, engender, give the *genre*, the *genus* to the subject, overwriting and countersigning the self. The subject searches for all that, retrospectively, produces the subject doing the searching in the first place. What is 'at stake' is not so much 'the placing of something' – although this is part of the motivating familial-historical installation – as it is 'the staking out of place as such'.[8] Wanting a greater sense of self through an assumption that self and family form two nodes, one monadic, one collective, which are interconnected, and possibly in some manner intersubjective, is what drives genealogical interests in the acts of emplacement. The researcher, professional or amateur, seeks out a 'community' of family, over successive generations, in order to 'experience'[9] that greater sense of self already mentioned through an informed apperceptive sense of belonging. Communing with a 'community' of one's own family ghosts, spectres and phantoms gives to the subject various pasts to which the subject can never belong as such, but which might perhaps be read or misread as informing the subject's consciousness, perception and experience in the given present, the temporal duration, of the research. Yet in the very effort in genealogy to give place, fix in place, emplace, there is also that manner of 'unsecuring, (and of disclosing). Emplacement, understood not only as a static state of affairs but as a dynamic process, can serve not just to close down but at the same time to open up.'[10] Emplacement is also, already, displacement.

*

A good deal of Thomas Hardy's fiction and his poetry concerns 'rural experience', and is informed by this search for belonging, this search for place, or alienation from that, especially in relation to the ideas of 'community', 'family' and location. His work is an exploration leading to the reading subject's 'experience' of the topology of subjectively perceived, largely rural topography, countersigned by spectral historicity. Hardy's writing foregrounds largely rural 'experience' through narratives and reflections on the secret of subjectivity in a given place, whether locally, in a specific town such as Casterbridge or Wessex, his poems and novels driven, sometimes relentlessly it appears, by the 'notion of emplacement, [which] collects and assembles the various ways in which everything, human beings included, is "cornered" (*Gestellt*) and set in place'.[11] Place, land, subjectivity in Hardy are inextricably and intimately enfolded, each in the other, and for the most part, there is no self in Hardy that is not gathered up into, or which does not desire a return to, the material and phenomenal specificities of place. Such searches, meditations, mediations are not only of a spatial, a phenomenal and psychological (attempted or sought-after) grasp of the individual's singular involvement in particular spaces; the involvement or desire for involvement, the perception or apperception are profoundly temporal. Hardy's writing presents predominantly if not completely a certain proto- or quasi-phenomenological turn in English literature; in its apprehension of space, place and temporality, as these haunt subjectivity and connect to or rupture that subjectivity from other subjectivities – through memory, perception, apperception, imagination and other forms of conscious 'experience' – it remarks itself as a form of phenomenological discourse that, attending to, being haunted by phenomena, pursues the worrying problematic of what it means to dwell, in a manner that, after the fact, we might read, however cautiously and with certain caveats, as Heideggerian. 'Dwelling', 'home', 'community' and the fraught relation of individual to these are Hardy's subject matter. Invariably, Hardy's subjects find that '"you" can't go home again' to quote J. Hillis Miller, referring to Michael Millgate's citation of Thomas Wolfe, in Miller's reading of *The Return of the Native*,[12] and this in turn makes the desire to belong, to return and to seek out origins all the more acute, unbearable and *unburiable*, as Tess Durbeyfield finds to her cost, as she is propelled by her father's economic (in all senses) desire for affiliation, family, 'community' and origin. *Tess of the d'Urbervilles* is nothing if not an entertainingly encrypted broadside against genealogy, a polemic that stages the deconstruction of the myth of communities, places and origins. Desiring the origin, the source, affiliation and the concomitant propriety – and property – of the proper name reconciled with its improper other that genealogical emplacement promises, Tess's father condemns Tess to an endless seriality of displacements, through the constancy of opening up, of disclosing.

The idea of 'origin', whether teleo-, bio-, or theological – other *logoi* are available – is of course merely a convenient fiction: the vessel or structure as root or foundation, *matrix* as *patrix*, *khora* as *logos*; the source *there*, never here, but for some comforting in its illusory power to promise, appearing to promise, the stability of *arkhe*. Root, source, telos as originary, trope misread as truth: all are phantoms, phantasms, spectres, ghosts, fantasies belonging to the 'experience' named nostalgia, *Sehnsucht, Saudade,* тоска (pronounced *toska*; Russian), the Galician *morriña*, or as the untranslatable Welsh has it, *Hiraeth*: that sense of a homesickness mixed with longing, yearning, grief or sadness over the departed, an earnest desire for the past. The word for the 'experience' – this haunting that is, or can be as cultural as it is personal, as political as it is poetic – in Ethopian refers to a specific form of expression, a genre of song, the equivalent of a ballad, and the musical mode employed for performing and composing such songs: *tizita* or *tezeta,* written in Amharic as ትዝታ. Western musicologists and musicoanthropologists are not immune from the cultural genea-teleological hunt in seeking comparisons and connections between *tizita* and the blues. Comparisons have been made with Portuguese *Saudade,* Tuareg *Assouf* and Romanian *Dor*.[13] Shared, yet ultimately irreconcilable, often untranslatable between tongues, individuals and the larger cultural identities to which they belong, this phantom or pseudo-family of terms points to the 'experience' of that longing or desire (these words feel woefully imprecise, vague, mere chimera for that which haunts and yet determines in no small measure the self, the culture, society, the nation) seeks a sense of belonging to or search for a selfhood, an identity greater than the subject. 'Experience' evokes in these many cases the search for 'community', for emplacement, rooted in the teleological striving after origin or source, and the concomitant impossibility of locating origin, source, community as such.

As J. Hillis Miller argues in 'Rural Experience in Virginia and Wessex', there is a vast, often contradictory literature devoted to the question of what 'community' is, how one defines it, what the ideal community might be. The longing for 'community' is entwined in that comparative work of musicologists and other commentators on the relation between western, northern hemispheric forms of music and particular African genres. Searching for roots, sources, origins, the commentator in his or her particular present determines a sense of that which is shared even as the teleological arc is traced, and so comforts him- or herself, and, importantly, the reader also, by positing implicitly or explicitly, a shared world, a sense of belonging, a fantasy or phantasmic 'community'. 'One world is enough for all of us,' sings Sting,[14] because then 'we' don't need to concern ourselves with the spectres of very real material, political, economic and other differences, if we can erase the cultural specificities and 'borrow', 'pay homage to' or 'acknowledge' all those cultural differences that are plundered by western thought, western thinkers or indeed, western musicians such as Sting.[15]

'Community' abides then, as a particularly desirable fiction; and as an ontological force also, erasing difference, silencing otherness, while 'experience' is at once individual, empirical, resistant for some to theorisation or simply mediated reflection, which tends toward an uncritical and 'common sense' appropriation. 'Experience' puts the 'common' in 'community', emphasising the shared, the habitual, the quotidian, as if 'we' were together a collective being-in-common. This is what Miller, in the interview with Frederik van Dam that is to be found in this volume, alerts us to, in commenting on the novels of Anthony Trollope, and in particular what Georges Poulet, Miller acknowledges, described as the 'collective consciousness of [the] community'.[16] More specifically yet, the 'narrator' – or, as I shall say from here on, the narrator-effect or narrator-machine in order to resist the anthropomorphising tendency in critical mimesis, a tendency that grounds as recording or trace of a phantom voice, and so privileges however implicitly or unthinkingly notions of origin, source, presence, and with that empirical 'experience' over carefully crafted rhetorical manipulation, mediation and a sleight of hand or feint in which subjectivity steps forward as a more or less objective 'omniscient' 'narrator'[17] – in the nineteenth-century novel stands in for, presents itself as 'collective consciousness',[18] as 'community voice'.[19] Among the shared narrator-functions of novelists in nineteenth-century fiction are those of acting, or standing in for, 'collective consciousness of the community', which serves to suggest a 'collective telepathic consciousness'[20] in the representation of events, encounters and 'experiences'.

*

The problems that terms like 'community' or 'experience' throw up for the good reader – and although Miller has already said all there is to say on the problematic of 'experience', I've yet to address the idea in any detail as it necessarily deserves here, as both a response to Miller's own work and also as it will inform this chapter – are all symptomatic of what by now (it should be apparent) are deeply ingrained, as many readers will doubtless be aware in metaphysical thinking in western civilisation from Plato (at least) onwards. The problem of collective consciousness serves merely to refocus the problem of 'experience' and 'community' in a different direction. It also, or I should say, Miller also opens for us a connection that is already in place – a connection that is also a rupture, the articulation of *anastomosis*[21] – a passage between the ontologies of 'fiction' on the one hand and 'reality' of the lived personal, cultural and historical varieties on the other. How might we provisionally adumbrate an approximation of that connection, that rupture? Miller himself acknowledges in *Communities in Fiction* how the question of the narrator effect, described variously as a question of consciousness at once omniscient, collective or telepathic, is, in its features a problem for phenomenology, found in the work of 'the distinguished phenomenological critic, or "critic of consciousness", Georges Poulet', and before him in the questions that 'obsessed Edmund Husserl in his later years'.[22] The phenomenology of Husserl was a study of consciousness and 'experience', particularly the structures of these. Husserl sought, as is well known, to apprehend our 'experience' of the world as a series of appearances, and how the phenomena of the world assume meaning. Included in the varieties of 'experience' are thoughts, memories, desires, emotions, perceptions and imagination, social activity, linguistic forms and so forth: in short, as the admirable entry in the *Stanford Encyclopedia of Philosophy* has it, all that makes up the 'directedness of experience toward things in the world, [revealing that] the property of consciousness [is] that it is a consciousness of or about something'. Our 'experience' is 'directed toward – represents or "intends" – things only through particular concepts, thoughts, ideas, images, etc. These make up the meaning or content of a given experience.'[23] While the central question for Husserl was not a matter of either origin, 'experience' or community, but rather solipsism; and while in his later writings he sought connections between the inference of isolated subjectivities that so troubled him, we see how the subject's longing/nostalgia/desire for 'community', like those for 'origins', 'beginnings' or 'sources', is found in the various revenant manifestations that haunt our 'experience' of such emotions or drives. Whether in the act of reading fiction, being involved in an event, the singularity of which I term 'experience', or pursuing research of the literary, philosophical or genealogical kind (to advert to the three most obvious areas of research I encounter as mapped by Miller and being mapped by him in 'Rural Experience in Virginia and Wessex') and trying to read, and so provide a counter-signature to that research, I find myself reflecting on, and inflected by an apperception. Apperception, the *Oxford English Dictionary* tells me, is the 'action or fact of becoming conscious by subsequent reflection of a perception already experienced; any act or process by which the mind unites or assimilates a particular idea (esp. one newly presented) to a larger set or mass of ideas (already possessed), so as to comprehend it as part of the whole'. As Miller remarks, 'the full awareness of the consciousness of another may be no more than the projection onto the face, speech, and behaviour of the other of my "past experience" of myself'.[24] Seeking a place for myself, I am emplaced and thus displaced.

*

Where then do I find myself in seeking to situate myself in this response to, for Miller's essay? Etymology, like genealogy, problematises the origins it proposes, opening up as much as it puts in place. Miller offers comprehensive commentaries on the problem-words 'rural' and 'experience', through complicating readings of the definitions provided by the *American Heritage Dictionary*. The *Oxford English Dictionary* is no more help in untangling the 'problematic and complex' nature of the terms (Miller, 'Varieties'). Of 'rural', the *OED* begins 'of multiple origins'. Signifying that which is the country as opposed to the town, 'rural' seems simple enough and yet, as Miller notices in his reading of Hardy, one cannot tell where the one ends or the other begins. At its seemingly most fundamental, 'rural' pertains to the country and to rustics, the inhabitants of the country, those, the dictionary would have it, lacking elegance or sophistication, peasants for example, though the classical Latin etymon *rūrālis* acknowledges the effect or spectral presence – the *genius loci*? – of a divinity presiding over, or inhabiting countryside, or place. Gabriel Oak is perhaps the archetypal rustic, though significantly, within his realist presentation, his *Gestell*, there is signalled also his other, his folkloric, pagan other, possible symbol of the green man. With his rural surname and peculiar appearance, of no particular time, but anachronistic in a number of ways, and orienting himself according to solar rather than clock time and the seasons, Oak on the one hand lacks urban elegance or sophistication while, on the other, presides over or inhabits, as the *OED* puts it, the countryside, being often in the narrative an inspiring force as if some minor pagan divinity or daemon.[25]

'Rural' equally in early as well as modern uses signifies agricultural activities and country pursuits (or matters, as Hamlet archly observes, being a little rustic himself in statement). 'Rural' therefore pertains not to the wilderness, but to managed, tended, and used – or exploited – landscape (again, Miller is before me in acknowledging this distinction). The *rūr* or *rūs* in the words 'rural' and 'rustic' place the subject in the countryside by signifying distinctly land or estate. Wilderness needs no humanity, it seems, while the rural cannot be defined without some human subject's perception, apperception, residence, usage or ownership. The rural therefore names the emplacement of place, enframing the subject and land (even as the subject can be instrumental in the act of enframing, an emplacement that also places the subject in turn, as just noted), dividing, parcelling up, naming. Hardy helpfully notes the distinction in passing in the opening sentence of *The Return of the Native*: 'A Saturday afternoon in November was approaching the time of twilight, and the vast tract of *unenclosed wild* known as Egdon Heath embrowned itself moment by moment.'[26] Enclosure, it would seem, transforms the wild into the rural, or at least this is one possible scene of the cultural transformation of the land into a landscape. A waste as well as a wild, there is a tension in the presentation of the land through the acknowledgement of its being known by the name Egdon Heath. Hardy's sentence enframes: it marks the place nominally, spatially and temporally, thereby supposing the framing subject. We are in the presence of the almost, but not quite rural in this installation of cultural *agon*. The heath however does not give up without a fight, a struggle that is never quite resolved. For 'it was a spot which returned upon the memory of those who loved it with an aspect of peculiar and kindly congruity'.[27] The decidedly rural, those '[s]miling champaigns of flowers and fruit hardly do this', hardly make the demand, call, haunt, as does the wild. And Hardy is quick to remind us, in a comment that seems consonant with Richard Jefferies' apocalyptic vision in *After London*, that '[t]he new Vale of Tempe may be a gaunt waste of Thule. . . . The time seems near, if it has not actually arrived, when the mournful sublimity of a moor, a sea, or a mountain will be all of nature that is absolutely in keeping with the moods of the more thinking of mankind.'[28] Despite naming and the various histories accompanying this, the place remains resistant to ruralisation, being and becoming periodically 'the home of strange phantoms' and being a template for 'wild regions of obscurity' as well as a 'heathy, furzy, briary wilderness'. Such details make up the 'intelligible facts regarding landscape'.[29] Far from being contained or framed by humanity, Hardy's installation of Egdon Heath frames the appearance of humanity on the scene, as the title of Chapter II has it.

What happens? What takes place when I am confronted with Hardy's presentation, representation, staging, installation, emplacing of the Heath? How and where am I, as a reader, placed? In short, what is my 'experience'? Hardy would have me – to draw again on the *OED*'s definitions of the verb – ascertain, to make trial and so prove, and thereby reveal, the heath through my 'experience' of his sustained, mutable and complex image, a figure that resists apprehension under the category 'rural'. The notion of experience implies, as Miller argues, 'on what it is really like' to be in a particular place, to live there, and which reveals its knowability 'only through intimate experience' (Miller, 'Varieties'). How then is it possible that I 'experience' that which is not before me, in which I stand, with which I am familiar? To say that Hardy's Wessex is *just* some fictional version of a 'real' Dorset (or other southwestern county, Hardy's map extending to the border between Devon and Cornwall, as far north as Oxfordshire, and including Somerset, Hampshire, Wiltshire and the Isle of Wight). My 'experience' is necessarily of a different order. It is, as Miller suggests, 'a matter of shades rather than unequivocal delimitation' (Miller, 'Varieties'). What should be obvious is that 'my experience' is that of the reader, the researcher. This constellation of questions moves in the orbit of appresentation rather than presentation, apperception rather than perception. Reading is always apperceptive for fiction, like the past, is a different, if not foreign country, to recall L. P. Hartley's novel of 'rural experiences', *The Go-Between*, a novel that, along with Laurie Lee's *Cider with Rosie* and Kenneth Grahame's *The Wind in the Willows*, has had an undoubtedly significant influence on my 'imaginary' sense of the rural. My use of 'experience' is at odds with that definition of 'intimate experience' or 'what something is really like'. It is not what the *OED* describes as the 'actual observation of facts or events, considered as a source of knowledge. It might be however – again the *OED* – a 'tentative procedure, an operation performed in order to ascertain or illustrate some truth'. The *Oxford English Dictionary* brings me a little closer to my sense of reading in its definition of 'experience' as the 'fact of being consciously the subject of a state or condition, or of being consciously affected by an event . . . a state or condition viewed subjectively'. Reading does not necessarily lead to me to answer the question proposed by Jimi Hendrix ('are you experienced?') but forms an experience through my always singular encounter with the event of reading, as the material of that reading is what has been 'experienced'.

Reading leads 'by analogical connection and repetition' to that which '*will have been* there'.[30] What we are dealing with here is a certain manifestation of the imagination, that which pertains to the phenomenological 'experience'. Hardy re-presents, and in turn our act of reading re-presents to us, that which is already re-presented as it is traced by Hardy, his imagination in conjunction with his memory. Hardy's play in the enframing, the installation, the *Ge-stell* of Egdon Heath with temporality 'begins' in this play by imagining the impossible, a time before time. There is no first time, no originary time for the Heath. Thus, its mere 'representation' in the first chapter of *The Return of the Native* is exceeded; in what is possibly the most audacious textual inauguration concerning place, the subject and temporality, the first chapter and the heath it presents, exceeds itself from within in the registration of that which lies at the edges of naming, of nomenclature, temporal determination, seasonal re-marking, and so forth. In placing representation, Hardy breaks open the frame in perilously allowing to emerge from within the place that narrating-machine the subject effect of narration creates, the 'abyss of antecedence'.[31] The frames proliferate, even as they open outward. Escaping at least partially the tyranny of the 'linearization of time' so beloved by evolutionists, biologists, geologists, theologians and novelists in the nineteenth century, Hardy's imagination returns what it is otherwise impossible to see. What one sees in the present is not the present but the 'disruption' of and from within 'any established scenery' called the 'natural landscape'.[32]

*

Imagination is, if not the opposite of 'experience', then its other, if I can put it this way. 'Experience' is taken to be empirical, imagination analogical; 'experience' is implicit in perception, imagination in apperception; 'experience' demands presence in its narrower definitions, while imagination frequently takes place, enframes, as a result of loss, absence, what haunts, what returns, what enframes the subject. Hardy's imagination, his 'power or capacity to form internal images or ideas of objects and situations not actually present to the senses, including remembered objects and situations, and . . . mentally combining or projecting images' (as the *OED* would have it of 'imagination') anticipates not only the promise of different phenomenological discourses, but also the work of deconstruction as the difference that makes any image, representation, text possible. 'Imagination', writes Jacques Derrida, 'is what *retraces*, what produces as reproduction the lost object of perception.' It is thus available only as apperception. I shall reproduce that which is already reproduced; let us retrace our steps:

> Imagination is what *retraces*, what produces as reproduction the lost object of perception, the moment attention (of which imagination is nevertheless only the first modification) no longer suffices to make the object of perception *subsist*, the moment the first modification of attention breaks with perception and regulates passing from weak presence to absence. Such is the case [*instance*] of the sign and then of the historic milieu in general . . .[33]

In his reading of Condillac's 1746 *Essay on the Origin of Human Knowledge*, Derrida essays, in what at first blush seems straightforwardly phenomenological, a retracing of the work of the imagination in its reproduction of that which is lost to, absent from perception. In this gesture he exceeds the purely phenomenological through the examples (the instances) on the one hand of language and signification in the broad sense and the 'historical milieu in general' on the other – that is to say, everything we describe and represent in too facile a manner as context, historicity, the materiality of experience as this is recuperated in the textuality of the historian, the novelist, the sociologist, the genealogist, the critic. Or some critics, certainly, as Henry Staten illustrates in his forceful reading of Tennyson, and Jerome McGann's misreading of that poet's 'The Charge of the Light Brigade'.

Derrida's gesture in passing is one that I read at work in J. Hillis Miller's 'Varieties of Rural Experience in Virginia and Wessex'. The Wessex of Miller's title refers, fairly obviously, to the landscapes and people of Thomas Hardy's novels. The Virginia is Miller's own, the Virginia of his family. Having discussed the problems of defining 'rural' and 'experience', Miller further complicates matters productively by considering phrases and passages from *Under the Greenwood Tree*, *The Mayor of Casterbridge* and *Far From the Madding Crowd*. In contrast, Miller says, there is the United States, in which wilderness, opposed to the rurality of Wessex, remains in evidence. The Maine woods of Henry David Thoreau are not the landscapes of Wordsworth's hedgerows, hardly hedgerows, the very phenomenon of which marks and serves to signify the 'historic milieu in general' of the effects of the Enclosure Acts. Wordsworth's perception and experience becomes the trace and expression for our apperception of the legislated transformation and cultural determination of a particular rural landscape in England.

Of course, as Miller says, with the 'rural' as much as 'experience', it 'is a matter of shades rather than of unequivocal delimitation'. The nuances of signification shade off, much like the line in genealogical research into silence, absence, that for which there is no definition, for which there are no supplementary words. Supplementarity always suggests that the text is never finished, but it leads through innumerable iterations to the analogical apperception of the abyssal. Miller hints at this process in noting the function of the continuator-effect in the titling, the enframing that a title enacts, in *Under the Greenwood Tree*, a novel that Hardy bases 'on his childhood experience of growing up in Upper Bockhampton . . . the narrator of that novel', Miller continues, 'to a considerable degree sees the characters, their environment, and all their ways and doings from the outside, from the perspective of the sophisticated person with urban experience Hardy had become in 1872, when the novel was first published' (Miller, 'Varieties'). Hardy is both 'inside' and 'outside', having a somewhat 'telepathic knowledge' but also seeing indirectly perforce a 'way of life that he has left forever and that indeed no longer exists' (Miller, 'Varieties') at the time of the novel's publication. The same is of course true of most of Hardy's novels, many being set a generation at least earlier than the time of composition or date of publication.

The shifts and supplements of title signal this becoming lost, the disappearance of 'experience', of ways of life, through successive replacements, substitutions, re-namings and displacements. As Miller says, the 'original name' for the novel was to have been *The Mellstock Quire*, which quire, or choir return as the dead quire of the poem of that name. 'Quire', now thought of, if thought at all – and even that cannot be certain – names four sheets of paper, or parchment, folded in two, so as to form eight leaves. Medieval French – *quaer, quair, quaier* – gives both the leaves folded, hence the name, and the modern French *cahier*, notebook. *Quire* on the other hand comes from Old French *cuer* (modern French *chœur*), becoming in Middle English *quēre*, then *quyer*, before becoming *quire*. If the *OED* examples are anything to go by, 'quire' (as in Hardy's usage) chiefly disappears by the early part of the eighteenth century, being replaced by 'choir'. Hardy's is a deliberate anachronism. It appears in what the imagination invents as the 'lost object of perception', signalling the almost always irreversible graphic transition from 'weak presence to absence', as Derrida says above. *Quire* appears to hover at the very limits between such weak presence and the magnetic demands of absence. What remains to be heard is of course the other within the one, the elder ghosting the younger, the graphic mark silently haunting that which is voiced, much as a ghost-quire 'returns' in the poem; there is a ghostly supplementarity at work. But equally important in Hardy's initial title is that estranging graphic quality, of the somewhat unfamiliar, yet uncannily familiar visitation. That first title became, to continue with Miller, the subtitle; having appeared without appearing first, the initial title becomes re-marked as the supplementary counter-signature, in something of a temporal reversal. The title now becomes *Under the Greenwood Tree: the Mellstock quire*, the new first part being, as Miller has it, a 'learned allusion to the title and first line of one of Shakespeare's most beautiful songs in *As You Like it* (Act 2, scene 5). And both are in turn supplemented with a tertiary framing title, 'A Rural Painting of the Dutch School', which 'distances the novel even further'. Hardy's imaginative apperception of an always already disappeared way of life and rural 'community' becomes one impossibly caught up in the tensions and meshes between various 'insides' and 'outsides', longings for revenance, if not presence, and confessions of immeasurable distances.

As much as there is a sense of knowing intimately the phantoms who appear briefly, Hardy nonetheless admits to his subjective 'experience' being one of apperception rather than the direct perception of 'experience'. In an analogous, though different way, Miller himself admits to the simultaneity of the phantasmic 'experience' of being 'inside' and 'outside' in the narrative he constructs of family memories. There is discernible here, it might be noted in passing, an analogical 'experience' of reading, and the 'experience' of reading and rereading fiction in general, one that Miller talks about in *On Literature*. In this, he addresses 'two ways of reading'. These are 'the innocent way and the demystified way', which, being contrary to one another, open the 'aporia of reading'.[34] Innocent reading is immersive, it is a reading that constructs the fiction of the inside, of being 'inside', of giving oneself up to the text. Being on the outside is to read in a demystified way, but the two do not remain separate, wholly separable entities or concepts either side of the binary divide. Hardy is too easily – and incorrectly – criticised for nostalgia and sentiment; rather one should see Hardy's narrator-machine or effect as struggling in that aporia, that tension between the inside and the outside, having a consciousness of the other, the one on the inside having access indirectly to the consciousness of the other on the outside, the one on the outside having consciousness of the other inside. This system of consciousness and conscious perception and apperception is not solely structural or spatial, it is also temporal. For the innocent reading is the 'experience' of reading as a child, while demystified reading is the critical reading of the professional reader; it is the 'rhetorical reading' that admits to the machinery of literary magic, as Miller puts it;[35] it is, or partakes of the 'selective fictional confabulation' of family memory and genealogical searches. Or rather, that 'selective fictional confabulation' is that machinery that drives memory, consciousness, phantasmic 'experience', negotiating in that no-man's-land of subjectivity between inside and outside. It is this profoundly unsettling play of multi-temporality and the Venn diagram that maps the overlap (the inside of the outside, the outside of the inside, and so on . . .) that Miller's reading of his memory of family, and the simultaneity of the inside/outside, enacts.

It is not my intention to work through a close reading of J. Hillis Miller's reading/s of 'rural experience' in Virginia. Good readers will be able to engage in this for themselves. Miller reads himself and his others as it is here, admitting all the while that his 'account will not have escaped fictionality however hard I try to bear true witness and "tell it like it was"' (Miller, 'Varieties'). Yet, however fictional the structure and rhetoric of the account might be, it is salutary to remind oneself of what a young Jacques Derrida observed in the preface to his 1953/4 dissertation: 'There is no consciousness that does not perceive every sense as a sense "for self" . . . Every sense being for a consciousness, by definition not being able to make itself a stranger to . . . an intentional ego, it always reveals itself as "already" present. At the limit, an invention without verification would deny the intentionality of consciousness.'[36] This is the 'paradox or strangeness of transcendental intentionality'.[37] However, Derrida continues, 'verification without invention is not verifying anything by anything'. It is 'a negation (of) consciousness, (of) world, (of) time, where every truth appears'.[38] For all that there is no escape from fiction, there is no fiction that is not at the same time the rhetorical articulation of the retracing of the 'experience' of truth, however phantasmic. Narrative serves the function of *Gestell*, enframing.

But I cannot narrate without installing myself, without my own subjectivity being enframed. Nothing is more immediately felt perhaps than in the phantom of 'community' that might be evoked in the appearance of the family name, for instance. The name is a hinge that gives access but which also reminds one of distances that one cannot cover, nor close up. While it is true, as Miller suggests, that the 'use of fictitious names [for the towns and villages of Wessex, for example] reminds the reader that the novel is a transposition into a realm in which Hardy can make up whatever story he likes to take place within this now fictitious scene' (Miller, 'Varieties'), the correspondences Hardy effects remind one that there is in his fiction and poetry always this problematising 'oscillation between fiction and reality [that] has an extraordinarily complex effect' (Miller, 'Varieties'). The proper name, the family name serves a double purpose. On the one hand, it jars to the extent that, when it is recognised, when there is a familiarity of the order of the 'family' resemblance calling up the ghost of a transhistorical 'community', then fiction can become disturbingly uncanny that ultimately serves to make one feel even more removed from the phantom phenomenological 'experience' that innocent reading engenders and encourages. On the other hand, reality becomes in the process 'less substantial', becoming a slide show of 'fleeting images' within which phantasmic spectral supplement I find myself enframed. An echo calls. A postcard is delivered to someone for whom it was never intended.

*

There were three men came out of the west, their fortunes for to try. At least, that's what the song 'John Barleycorn' tells us.[39] Hardy knew the song, and makes reference to it in his poem 'The Dead Quire' (l.40),[40] an uncanny phantasy and folkloric retracing, which through the entrance of the 'Mead of Memories' – a rural 'location' of sorts, but of no particular origin, and so the subject's imagination, a rural figure for imagination and apperception itself – return the phantasms of the quire of Mellstock to play various Christmas tunes and sing songs of the season. Dating back in various forms to the sixteenth century at least as far as records show, 'John Barleycorn' is, in the poem, both ballad and ale, the song telling the tale of the seasonal and cyclical 'life' and 'death' of barley, its contribution in the making of ale, and 'his' (or its) role in the seasonal life of the rural 'community'. The theme therefore is of the death and return of a corn divinity presiding (to recall the *OED*) or inhabiting (and so in part defining) the rural. This is Hardy's only mention of or allusion to 'John Barleycorn', but as a musician and collector of local songs, folklore[41] and regional 'facts', he would have been familiar with it. As Jacqueline Dillon remarks, the 'status of folkloric beliefs in Hardy's Wessex is frequently as uncertain for his characters as it is for the reader. His texts resist fixed or stable ways of viewing. . . . He creates a shifting world of varying beliefs, which reflects that of nineteenth-century Dorset.'[42] That brief allusion to 'Little Sir John', as the ballad names John Barleycorn on a couple of occasions, is perfectly in keeping with the poetic, phantastic rendering – in a deliberately wayward and distorted ballad form, which destabilises traditional structure, metre and prosody in general – of the phantasms of the Mellstock musicians in 'The Dead Quire', and indeed the very idea of Wessex itself.[43]

Who those three men coming out of the west, a west that is situated in overlapping spaces of a Venn diagram, might have been remains unknown (and, ultimately, is unimportant, of course), but it does allow for a certain imaginative turn, permitting me the possibility of invention, a strong reading at the least, or, as is more the case, a 'selective fictional confabulation', to recall Miller's happy phrase already employed near the beginning of this chapter. Venn is one possible name here to which I will return shortly, as is Turberville, d'Urberville, or Durbeyfield for that matter. Jack Durbeyfield walks 'out of the west' in the opening chapter of *Tess of the d'Urbervilles*, in 'the latter part of May' from 'Shaston to the village of Marlott, in the adjoining village of Blakemore or Blackmoor'.[44] Names are as shifting, unfixed or unstable as beliefs (recollect the various titular supplements to *Under the Greenwood Tree*), it would appear. Jack Durbeyfield is no exception to this mutability, being called on this occasion by the parson he happens to encounter 'Sir John', as he has been about a month before. Then of course, there is Diggory Venn, who is first named in the fourth chapter of *The Return of the Native*, but who appears anonymously as the unnamed reddleman: 'one of a class rapidly becoming extinct in Wessex, filling at present in the rural world the place which, during the last century, the dodo occupied in the world of animals . . . a curious, interesting, and nearly perished link between obsolete forms of life and those which generally prevail'.[45] The reddleman is first witnessed by an old man, who, like the reddleman, travels 'the great Western road of the Romans, the Via Iceniana, or Ikenild Street', a 'long laborious road, dry empty and white'.[46] As elsewhere, names are unstable, Hardy's iteration suggesting a destabilising supplementarity. Little can be said of place that cannot be undermined, transformed, translated. The subjects who do appear in this landscape are initially anonymous, their identities determined solely by this liminal and timeless place. The third name, the least significant of these appearances, comes briefly in Chapter 37 of *The Mayor of Casterbridge*, acknowledged when Elizabeth-Jane Henchard parts from her father, to witness the passage along Casterbridge (Dorchester) High Street of a 'Royal Personage', as Hardy has it near the beginning of the chapter:[47] 'As the appointed time drew near she got sight again of her stepfather. She thought he was going to the King of Prussia; but no, he elbowed his way through the gay throng to the shop of Woolfrey, the draper.'[48]

Woolfrey the draper is both a fiction and not a fiction. That is to say, he is a fictional draper with a shop in the high street of Casterbridge; but he is also a tailor from Broadmayne, a village just four miles from Lower Bockhampton, Hardy's childhood home and the Mellstock of *Under the Greenwood Tree*, and Dorchester, the 'reality' of *Casterbridge*. William Woolfrey – or Woolfreys, or Woolfries (the name was not standardised until the late nineteenth century)[49] – had a tailor's shop on Durngate Street, Dorchester, not on the high street and adjacent to what is now the Waitrose car park, near the dinosaur and teddy bear museums, just off the Icen Way and just a mile from Max Gate. Born in 1818, he died in 1864, and practised in the period in which *The Mayor of Casterbridge* is set. The surprise of seeing one's own name appear, however differently spelled, is a strange 'experience'. When the real figure shadowing the fictional character is found to be an ancestor, the strangeness becomes greater. That Hardy 'borrowed' from his immediate 'experience' and consciousness of Dorset in order to construct a fictional, sometimes more rural, sometimes more urban 'community' is hardly surprising. To think such an idea as a hypothesis is one thing, to find it to be the case with a small but personal referent is another, quite. The proper name has an enigmatic, not to say ambiguous quality, to say the least. Perhaps, Jean-Luc Nancy wonders, 'its nature is that of a *Wink*, of a gesture that invites or calls'.[50] The proper name must be judged not 'in relation to sense but in relation to gesture'.[51] The proper name makes a connection, a correspondence, it serves to propose in the imagination a community in death: for if I 'experience' my name as the name of another, as one who is to me always already dead, who does not exist as such; and if that name haunts all the more because of its fictional appropriation, in figure and form of someone who has never existed, my name, what I call 'my name', which, more than my name, is the name shared by an entire genealogy, calls to me and in so doing, inscribes me in this consciousness as belonging to a structure of meaning that finds itself in death, signifying nothing. The appearance of 'my name' as the name of the other countersigns the experience of my being of the essential mode of being-in-common, as if I were dead. There is a question of representation at work in reading. In reading 'Woolfrey, the draper', I 'experience' what Nancy elsewhere calls 'two logics: that of the subjectivity for which there is *phenomenon* and that of the *thing in itself* or "real presence". The one and the other must be the one for the other, even as they are shown to exclude one another. . . . [There is therefore the] double absence of/within presence that structures this double logic.'[52]

*

How should I feel about this chance discovery of a genetic-topographical association? There is, and has been since the chance discovery, a sense of 'so what'? That has been tempered however with a sense equally of curiosity. It is not that I 'recognize *myself* in the other: [Instead,] I experience the other's alterity . . . I experience alterity in the other with the alteration that "in me" sets my singularity outside me and indefinitely delimits it.'[53] Such an indefinite delimitation is a figure, again, of *memento mori*; there arrives from the disclosure of the other, as the gift of disclosure that the other delivers the realisation of a '*Being-toward-the-end* of this entity', as Heidegger argues.[54] This is the most phantasmal 'experience' and also the reproduction of the trace of that 'experience'. And this becomes intensified in the genealogical research, whereby comes the feeling that 'perception is not only present itself . . . it is also a making present',[55] a modality of *Gestell*, modification of perception being 'also a re-presentation of the perceived . . .'[56] The Wolfreys, however you spell it, go back quite a distance in Dorset, as do the Turbervilles. Hardy had an interest in his family tree and was, Miller tells us, 'somewhat absurdly proud of being (so he believed) descended from the aristocratic Norman "Le Hardies", just as Tess of the d'Urbervilles believes she belongs to a decayed aristocratic Norman family' (Miller, 'Varieties'). Whatever Hardy's investment, knowledge of the Wolfreys gives me no particular insight of any especial significance, much less about the rural, even though certain branches, and the families into which they married were populated with rural workers and belonged to a loose affiliation broadly described as a 'rural community', though of a more diffuse form than what appears to be the tight-knit family group, the Critzers. My knowledge is what Miller calls 'non-knowledge' (Miller, 'Varieties'). At best, I might describe this as a chance communication or correspondence between singularities, wherein might be read the 'communal fabric' that 'does not exist' and, as such is phantasmic. There is, Jean-Luc Nancy remarks in *The Inoperative Community*, 'no subject or substance of common being' to be noted.[57] Wherever there is 'community' in Hardy, communication is what rends that illusory fabric, inaugurating its dissolution, as I argue elsewhere.[58] Community exists if it exists at all in the silence (and at the other end, as it were, in death), the being-in-common that is assumed until someone communicates, and communication is an 'unworking',[59] the difference, that which deconstructs community from within.

The other communicates by chance. There is a contingency that cannot be anticipated in advance. Had Jack Durbeyfield not been walking along *that* road at *that* time, on *that* day, he would not have encountered the parson. Or if he had, the parson might not have said what he did. Or if he did, Tess's father might not have responded as he did, and so the entire chain of events would never have been set in motion in the manner that the fiction of *Tess* makes possible. The narrator-function is to introduce chance and genealogy as that impulse of 'unworking' that begins with the contingency of a conversation leading to the dissolution of the 'family community' through the ghost of family, of the familial other. The parson who delivers Tess's death sentence in conjuring the spectres of family is Parson Tringham, the self-styled 'antiquary of Stagfoot Lane'.[60] An antiquary was someone who collected folkloric knowledge, interested himself in local history and pursued genealogical research. As Tim Dolin clarifies in his note in the Penguin edition, 'the amateur antiquary was an often-scorned figure in the nineteenth century, despite the growing popularity of antiquarian clubs (Hardy was a member of the Dorset Natural History and Antiquarian Field Club)'.[61] Hardy's own interest in 'popular antiquities', as such studies were then called, gave him access to the history of the Turbervilles, or Turberviles, or Trubleviles. Tringham's brief commentary on Sir Pagan d'Urberville[62] had by chance caused him to make the connection with the Durbeyfield family, having seen the name on Durbeyfield's waggon the previous spring. Hardy 'derived' the narrative of the d'Urbervilles from 'his copy of the third edition of *The History and Antiquities of the County of Dorset* (1861–70) by John Hutchins', as Dolin points out in a subsequent detailed footnote.[63] Hardy had, Dolin notes, apparently considered calling the novel *Tess of the Hardys*, 'according to Sydney Cockerell's recollection of a conversation' with the author, who had a 'deep interest in his own fallen family'.[64]

The Turbervilles (to fix the spelling for the purposes of this chapter) have a family line in Britain, much of the family having been situated mostly in Bere Regis in Dorset, though having held the manor of South Molton in Devon and having also a branch in Glamorganshire. The family is traceable back to the Norman conquest, as Hardy knew and as is indicated in *The Histories*. While 'Pagon' or 'Payne' (Pagan) is the first to be acknowledged (he is mentioned in the Battel-Abby Roll according to Dolin, who cites *The Histories*), other Turbervilles are noted for their cultural or historical significance. Thomas de Turberville was executed in the thirteenth century for treason; Robert (1354–1420) served in the so-called Merciless Parliament (February–June 1388), which convicted many members of Richard II's court. Henry (d. 1239) was a notable soldier, as was Edward Turberville (1648–81), a member of the Glamorganshire branch. George Turberville's (*c*.1540 – *c*.1597) name is the one most likely to be known to literary scholars as a poet and translator of Ovid, Mantuanus, Boccaccio and Bandello.[65] There are though many Georges in the family, as there are Henrys and Williams. The proper name is a filiation, a textual and 'textile' thread intended in its iterable perpetuation to stitch the monadic and singular entity into the 'community fabric' of family, in the myth of endless narrative. None of which has anything to say to *Tess of the d'Urbervilles*, of course. Except that the function of context in literary study is nothing other than another form of 'selective fictional confabulation'. This is not to say that 'there is no such thing as history' or to make any other reductive and patently absurd affirmation. It is, though, to say that 'context' or 'history' in any commentary on or analysis of literary texts are narrative structures of meaning that aim to enframe and stage the work according to a metanarrative that foregrounds particular, privileged motifs valorised as truths, and with which, if the literary text is concerned, it is not primarily so.

Pausing at the Turberville proper name to reflect on what takes place in the reading of 'literature', it is necessary to reflect on why some critical discourses find a greater professional significance than others. Why, for example, should history, anthropology or sociology as disciplines have any greater validity in the rereading of literature than any other? Is it because they aspire to the condition of 'science', inasmuch as they rely upon and ground their discourses on a bedrock of 'facts'? How then is genealogy or biography any different? As soon as one is beyond the fact, one narrates. As soon as there is narration, there the fictive *Gestell* takes place. The privilege of 'context' in particular critical discourses, since the dismantling of the material/textual or textual/contextual divisions by strands of New Historicism (but exceeding this critical modality) effects a sleight of hand, or a pair of hands: on the one hand, it flattens distinctions and erases difference between the 'literary' and 'non-literary' text, as if 'literary' were understood, as if it were quite so easily apprehended; on the other hand, the contextual drive, privileging certain models of reading oriented around the political and ideological, strives to ignore or at least suppress the literary – or poetic – as such (not that we know with any surety of what this *as such* consists) in the name of a 'scientific' re-presentation of 'experience', however a discursive historicity is practised. 'Experience' as fact, as verifiable empirical event supported through textual supplement, is the implicit engine of particular readings that seeks to mute the rhetoric of reading in being implicitly positioned against imagination, perception, phantasy and other modalities of 'consciousness'. Yet it has to be said once again that it is only in narrating that a phantasmic 'experience' can become communicated in however fraught, fractured and fragmenting a manner. The 'rural' and 'historical experience' of communities perceived as such is only gathered in the narrative told.

*

As J. Hillis Miller remarks of his own narration of his memory of family, community, and rural Afton, Virginia:

> My celebration of it [the 'old rural experience' of the Critzer family community] by describing it for you ... completes the work, since its existence as rural experience depended on being unselfconscious and taken for granted. I report on it now from the perspective of its death and the death of almost all the participants, just as Hardy does for Mellstock rural life. (Miller, 'Varieties')

Narrative, and with it, the rhetoric of reading the life, biography, history, anthropology or genealogy of a family or community, a family community, a family within a community, forms a death sentence. Perception of the past arrives as the *Gestell* of the ghosts of community and the self's remembered experience. One's monadic consciousness folds itself into, as it opens, a sense of collective consciousness, and so inscribes the subject as belonging to communities of death, communities-in-death. That this takes place necessarily demands a rhetoric of presentation marked by a difference between the remembered reality of Afton, Virginia, and the imagination's translation of the traces of community in Mellstock, or the other hamlets, villages and towns of Wessex.

What Miller calls a celebration is also, importantly, an affirmation, a remembrance of things past, a search for lost time and an act of bearing witness. This is Miller's work here, but also this is Hardy's work everywhere, and the work of the literary. The literary stages a phantom experience, giving it an equally ghostly voice. The threads that good readers notice, and at which they pull, even as they seek to intertwine the filaments in order to supplement and sustain the text, serve the function of *khōra* in giving place to singular-collective perceptions in a provisional rhetorical apparition. Something other appears, comes to pass, giving the impression of being. Part of Miller's reading engages in tracing and pulling the threads; it contests the originary impulse, as he illustrates the ways in which the 'seeds of . . . dissolution' are already contained within 'family community' and the 'apparent *Gemeinschaft* [one of the two categories used by German sociologist Ferdinand Tönnies, the other being *Gesellschaft* and discussed by Miller in 'Varieties of Rural Experience'] of Afton was . . . marked by fissures of several sorts inherited from the past . . . fissured by its forebears' (Miller, 'Varieties'). Bearing this in mind, and in order to begin to conclude this response to J. Hillis Miller's reading that militates against any reductive or naïve model of, and longing for 'rural experience' and the idea of 'community', I want to pull at threads, fraying the fabric a little, while engaging in a highly adumbrated rhetorical ravelling, a ravelling up that is also, at the same time, an unravelling, a tangling that is also an untangling. Let us return to the 'community fabric' of the Turbervilles, an arbitrary departure point, as arbitrary, it might be said, as the chance encounter between Parson Tringham, the antiquary of Dorset and Jack – 'Sir John' – Durbeyfield.

The four-volume *Histories and Antiquities* of Dorset, published between 1861 and 1873, provides a family tree of the Turberville family, in the chapter on the town of Bere Regis (Hardy's Kingsbere). Poet and translator George Turberville and his wife Audrey (née Matthew) had a family of ten children: six daughters and four sons. The third of those sons, Thomas, of Woolbridge Manor (the ancestral home, called Wellbridge by Hardy, in which Tess and Angel Clare pass their 'honeymoon'), had five sons, John, Thomas, Matthew, William and George – again, the proper names thread themselves through the family text. George, grandson of George, married, on 6 June 1593, Avis Woolfry, or Woolfris, who died in 1610 and was buried at Holy Rood, Wool (being the village of Wellbridge in Hardy's Wessex). In his will, George Turberville left gifts to several Wolfreyes, Wolferys, or Wolfries (the will does not standardise the spelling): Henry, William, Dorothy – though the will lists Henry and William as 'gentlemen', so clearly the family had in part 'descended' by the time it reached Woolfrey, the draper. I find, in certain moments either whimsical or uncanny, that I am haunted by the passing and mostly silent weave of family lines in Hardy's writing, much as these families haunt Hardy's texts. This has on occasion less to do with the disclosure of the shared name than it does with the realisation of the extent to which Hardy frays the boundary between the real and the fictional, between fact and imagination. The Woolfrey textile, the family community, as it is perceived belatedly, is woven together in part through its being resolutely Catholic. However, it is not only fissured but frays continuously, certain threads leading to the draper, others to Robert Woolfrys, the gardener at Lulworth Manor, whose garden designs are still be be viewed in the Dorset Local History office, or to the brothers Odilo and Norbert Woolfrey, who helped found in Wool a short-lived Cistercian monastery.

Of the three names – Woolfrey, Turberville, Venn – and those who 'came out of the west', men and women, there remains just Venn. The unpropitious but necessary profession of reddleman seems wholly fictitious as far as the family goes, and there is no evidence that Thomas Hardy knew any of the Venns, who by Hardy's lifetime had largely left the West Country. One family member, John (1834–1923), gives the name to the Venn diagram, while another, Henry (1725–1797; John of the diagram was Henry's great-grandson), is a founding member of the Clapham Sect and, for those who care to know such things, played cricket for an All England team against Surrey. His son, John, and his grandson, Henry, both entered the church and were vicars of Holy Trinity Church, Clapham. Author of numerous works including *The Logic of Chance* (1866),[66] when not lecturing at Gonville and Caius, Cambridge, and inventing the earliest form of the bowling machine for batting practice in cricket, John Venn also wrote *Annals of a Clerical Family*,[67] a work of biographical genealogy, acknowledged by Venn as belonging to the genres of antiquary research and family pedigrees (his grandfather John, he notes, was 'somewhat of an antiquary'),[68] and having interest only to those with 'ties of consanguinity with the various persons mentioned' in the text.[69] In an uncanny echo of Miller's commentary on celebration, though with a different tone, Venn observes in his preface that his 'investigations' were 'deferred unfortunately until nearly all who belonged to the generations behind me were no longer present to assist'.[70] Venn begins the *Annals* with the forthright statement that '[t]here can be little or no doubt that our family name belongs to the class of *Place-names*, that is, that it originally indicated the district ... for which those who first obtained this surname sprang'.[71] Proper name and place name: the very interchangeability of the name, the one enfolding the other, unfolding so as to re*pli*cate, im*pli*cate and com*pli*-cate; the one bearing the trace of the other, the other in the one – such work figures both the imperative of the *Gestell*, while also adumbrating, intimating the topology of a phantasmic *Gemeinschaft*, an organic, if ghostly, community countersigned every time the proper name arrives, in both its singularity and iterability. This is, we might say, the law of the name, that it enframes, traces connections, and in maintaining this function both announces its own becoming-enframed, and its opening of that frame in other directions. John Venn's surmise, just cited, 'rests on the examination of contemporary records, in which the process of change can be observed'.[72] Thus, the source – not the origin – appears to consciousness as being of the rural, Venn being originarily Fen, the family name having been, depending on branch, '"atte Fenne" and "de la Fenne"'.[73] Venn is distinguished from Fenn in the two principal branches of the family – fraying and fissure are remarked as being *at* and *of* any discernible origin – the former being exclusively a West Country name, the latter appearing in Norfolk and Suffolk. Venn observes of the West Country families that '[t]hough not widely spread, the name is of frequent occurrence within a certain area.'[74] John Venn's 'line' belongs to Devon, deriving from the same family occupying in Devon 'the adjacent parishes of Broadhembury and Peyhembury'.[75]

Like that of Thomas Hardy in many of his novels and J. Hillis Miller in 'Varieties of Experience', John Venn figures the 'community' of family in 'the image of the "open chain"', a figure that 'does not exhaust the depth of ... communal subjectivity'.[76] The good reader, the novelist, the researcher, the logician; all express themselves through a 'collective consciousness', and 'tied to the others by the unity of an object or task';[77] though equally, 'the investigator's own subjectivity is constituted by the idea or horizon of ... subjectivity which is made responsible in and through him'.[78] The 'origin', then, if I can express it thus, is in the 'experience' of phantom 'community' that in reading rhetorically I perceive, which becomes the object of my perception; that I install and by which, in this process, reciprocally, I am enframed. The 'origin' that is consciousness constructs the open chain, weaving the threads in particular ways, so as to give meaning to the pattern. This is always a matter of contingency and narrative.

So far, so phallogocentric, even if paternity may be a legal fiction. Let me work backward and in a still sketchier fashion, my purpose being to thread the image of a phantom community, even as the thread frays more persistently. My mother's surname was Saintey, daughter of Sidney, granddaughter of Andrew. My mother's mother was Jessie Florence Venn. William Venn (1569–1621) of Broadhembury, Devon, had two sons, William and Richard. From Richard's line come Henry, John, Henry, and John, from William, Jessie Florence. Jane Catherine Venn (1793–1875), great-great-great-great-great-granddaughter of William Venn of Broadhembury, married Sir James Stephen and was the mother of Sir Leslie Stephen (1832–1904), whose first wife was Harriet Thackeray (mother of William Makepeace Thackeray) and whose second wife was Julia Prinsep Stephen (1846–1895). Julia's children included Thoby, Adrian, Vanessa and Adeline Virginia, making Virginia Woolf a distant cousin. As James Venn might (not) have said, what are the chances?

I have not finished quite, there remains another thread to work back. Julia Prinsep Stephen (née Jackson) was the daughter of Maria Jackson (1818–92), whose given name was Pattle. Maria Pattle's sister was Julia Margaret Pattle (1815–79) or, as she is now rather better known, Julia Margaret Cameron. Julia Prinsep Jackson – to return to her – had had a first husband before Stephen, Herbert Duckworth. Duckworth's father, Sir George Herbert Duckworth, had married Lady Leonora Evelyn Selina Howard Molyneux Herbert (what's in a name?); Eleonora's family line returns through the Walpole family to Calybutt Walpole, whose daughter was Anne, and who married Thomas Pettus (1591–1671). Thomas had a son, Thomas, who had a son, Thomas, who had a daughter, Elizabeth (1702–55). Elizabeth's son was John M. Hopkins; his daughter Jane had a son, Benjamin Franklin Rhodes. Rhodes's daughter Sarah Jane (1843–1924) married a Schultz, whose daughter was Minta Hopkins "Minnie" Schultz (1870–1951), whose daughter in turn was Nell Martin "Nellie" Schultz, who married a Critzer, and whose son is Joseph Hillis Miller. The more astute (or obsessive) reader may extrapolate at his or her leisure the however many degrees of separation there are between my cousin Hillis and me.

*

This chance, even random occurrence, taking as a starting point the arrival of a proper name in passing in the novels of a particular author, resists precisely the imposition of any meaning, first principle or teleological goal that might aspire to the name of a 'science'. It is precisely the random, the chance probability at any given moment from which Thomas Hardy's tales of 'rural experience' so often begin; and 'originate' not in the sole fact of the moment, but instead in the chance interaction between one moment and another. Hardy is not alone in this, of course, all narratives beginning *in medias res*, the start a fiction that refers back to the work of fiction, to all narrative. Hardy's chance encounters involve unexpected events of communication. Hardy states this as a principle from the outset of his very first novel, *Desperate Remedies*, which opens thus: 'the long and intricately inwrought chain of circumstance renders worthy of record some experiences of Cythera Graye, Edward Springrove, and others . . . '.[79] Gabriel Oak is found standing in a field, 'casually glancing over the hedge', when he sees a wagon on which rides 'a woman, young and attractive'.[80] Dick Dewey emerges from out a plantation on a dark night, interrupted in his passage and his song by a sound 'in the shape of "Ho-i-i-i-i-i!"'.[81]

Hardy assumes a more 'theoretical' tone in *A Pair of Blue Eyes*: 'Though people and places are here before us *in parvo* as the seed and vehicle of a history, who shall put limits to the possible extent of good, bad, or indifferent circumstance, that, in connection with these few agents and in this narrow scene, may have arisen, declined, and been finally deposited in the Past as valuable matter for inspection by eyes who know or care where to find it?'[82] As with other narratives, perception and sight are of significance for Hardy here, from that 'external' inspection to Elfride Swancourt's eyes, and the chance occurrence of a 'face to face with a man she had never seen before',[83] the result of her father happening to have gout and not being able to entertain the stranger as he would like. Michael Henchard, his wife and child might never have been noticed were it not for the 'peculiar' and 'perfect silence' in which they progressed, which hypothetically 'would have attracted the attention of any casual observer otherwise disposed to overlook them' as they passed along a rural lane '[o]ne evening of late summer'.[84] Hypothetical perception based on chance is a species of rhetoric favoured by Hardy and one which opens communication as part of the signalling system of Hardy's narrator-machine, serving to instal the sense of a random switch in directions. Were the countryside in Hardy not so haunted by so many hypothetical eyes (Fig. 2.1) chancing to notice, and so to open communication through the equally hypothetical perception of consciousness's reflection, then entire histories may never have happened; or had they, who could tell? At the beginning of *A Laodicean*, George Somerset pauses on a stile 'to imbibe the spirit of the scene and the hour'

Figure 2.1 Eweleaze near Wetherbury.

in a rural landscape, letting his mind wander and being surrounded by an evening 'so still that every trifling sound could be heard for miles'.[85] Lost in thought, he is communicated with by chance, his hearing singling out the sound of singing.[86] I have already noted the chance events of communication that take place at or very near the beginnings of *Tess* and *The Return of the Native*.

Hypothetical consciousness manifested as a rambler opens to the reader's consciousness a rural scene in *The Woodlanders* until through the narrative direction the reader's perception, a man is witnessed entering the scene 'temporarily influenced by some such feeling of being suddenly more alone than before he had emerged upon the highway'.[87] The encounter/perception/experience presented, staged and enframed for consciousness is aided in noting that the man is not rural, 'he did not belong to the country proper'.[88] Not knowing his way, by chance he is able to ask directions from the passengers of a coach that happens to be passing at that moment.[89] Of all these occurrences in Hardy, the observer, the reader might ask, hypothetically, what are the chances? After all, in Hardy's rural world, having a pizzle thrown at one leads to a marriage one regrets. What are the chances, given that one is 'surrounded by a world of objective phenomena extending indefinitely both ways in time, and in every direction in space'? Most are, 'and always will remain, unknown',[90] unless they 'come into being ... as contemplated possibilities whose correspondence with reality is [liable to be] either altogether disbelieved or regarded as entirely doubtful'.[91] As indeed were aspects of Hardy's fiction taken to be by certain contemporary reviewers. Perhaps though, chance and randomness, the improbable, are *just* that which might come to define 'rural experience'.[92]

*

If there exists some manifestation, some apparition of *Gemeinschaft* to be found; if there is some phenomenological apperception, an 'experience' or 'consciousness' (*Erlebnis*) of a ghostly kind of 'community', then it is of a fractured, self-fragmenting kind. The ghost of community is a community-in-ruins. There is perhaps in this, the slightest chance of passing correspondences, of communion. In the literary, in narrative, there is the possibility of a sharing, a momentary event of an alignment, the self recognising its mirror self in the other, or believing this to be so. The members of our respective families are, like Glenn Gould's fingers, 'long since turned to dust'.[93] And yet, like those recordings of Gould to which Miller admits to listening, or, in my case, the recordings of Bach by Keith Jarrett, the traces of family have revenant possibility as much as do the fictional figures of a novel, their thoughts and feelings. At the heart of these is the consciousness of the reader, the auditor, the narration-effect awaiting my 'experience of reading', my perception and consciousness, much as music on a CD or hard drive waits to be conjured. 'Community', if it exists at all, is in the 'experience' (that is to say the reflective consciousness) of what Edmund Husserl describes as an 'implicit *mutual being for one another*'. The other

> ... experiences me forthwith as an Other for him, just as I experience him as *my* Other. Likewise, I shall find that, in the case of a plurality of Others, they are experienced also by one another as Others, and consequently that I can experience any given Other not only as himself an Other but also as related in turn to *his* Others and perhaps – with a mediatedness that may be conceived as reiterable – related at the same time to me. It is also clear that men become apperceivable only as finding Others and still more Others, not just in the realm of actuality but likewise in the realm of possibility ... as subjects of possible intercommunion.[94]

'Literature' is the *Gestell* of such possible intercommunion. The 'discourse most preoccupied with the unknown',[95] literature remains 'an open underdetermined horizon'[96] – and it remains to come, as the chance, improbable possibility of experiencing the ghost of community, rural or otherwise.

Notes

1. Derrida, *Advances*, p. 5.
2. Ibid. p. 31.
3. Modiano, 'Flowers of Ruin', p. 180.
4. Going backwards one goes back until one can find no more, realising that all that remains is absence, loss, silence, the abyss of antecedence; going laterally promises little more relief, if any, for even if one continues onward the inexhaustibility of the tangential constitutes a matrix-abyss of its own.
5. While *Erlebnis* commonly translates as 'experience', Edmund Husserl also employs it to mean 'consciousness' in particular contexts.
6. Derrida, *The Problem of Genesis in Husserl's Philosophy*, p. 55.

7. 'Emplacing' or 'emplacement' are the translations of *Gestell* offered by Samuel Weber in *Mass Mediauras*, pp. 71–2.
8. Weber, *Mass Mediauras*, p. 71.
9. As J. Hillis Miller points out in his chapter in the present volume, the terms 'rural' and 'experience' are both problematic and complex, despite the widespread and common usage of such words. I begin here in my response to Miller by addressing such complexity and the attendant problems by speaking to particular words and the concept-ghosts they frame and make visible, without capturing fully. 'Experience' particularly is a phantom-word. It names a certain singularity of encounter within the self with the world and the other, as I shall go on to explore.
10. Weber, *Mass Mediauras*, p. 72.
11. Ibid.
12. Miller, *Communities in Fiction*, p. 93.
13. Definitions of *tizita* as 'memory', 'longing' or 'nostalgia' are given by Dag Woubshet in 'Tizita: A New World Interpretation' and Banning Eyre, 'Kay Kuafman Shelemay: Ethiopia: Empire and Revolution (interview)'. For comparisons with the blues, see also Eyre, 'Éthiopiques 10: Tezeta: Ethopian Blues and Ballad'.
14. The line comes from 'One World (Not Three)', on the Police album *Ghost in the Machine* (side two, track three), released 2 October 1981.
15. This is not to suggest that Gordon Sumner is such a plunderer, at least not to the extent that Led Zeppelin are known to have taken blues songs from African American blues musicians as their own. There might however be a case for a reading of the work of musicians such as Sting, analogous to Derrida's reading of Claude Lévi-Strauss's structuralist ethno-anthropology.
16. Miller talks also at length and in great detail about communities in fiction in the book of that name, in which the concept of 'the narrator as collective consciousness' is considered in a discussion of Trollope (pp. 39–43). The thinking of community in 'Rural Experience in Virginia and Wessex' works through similar and shared concerns.
17. As Miller says in *Communities in Fiction*, the idea of the 'omniscient narrator' 'has always been problematic. It carries with it, necessarily, a lot of theological baggage' (p. 40).
18. Miller, *Communities in Fiction*, p. 40.
19. Ibid.
20. Ibid. Miller acknowledges Nicholas Royle's marvellous figure of the 'telepathic narrator' as supplement for the 'omniscient narrator' (Miller, *Communities in Fiction*, p. 40). See Royle, '"The Telepathy Effect": Notes toward a Reconsideration of Narrative Fiction'.
21. On the subject of anastomosis and the reading of Thomas Hardy's poetry and Miller's use of the term, see Monika Szuba's essay in this collection.
22. Miller, *Communities in Fiction*, pp. 40–1.
23. Smith, 'Phenomenology'.
24. Miller, *Communities in Fiction*, p. 41.
25. Hardy, *Far from the Madding Crowd*, ed. and int. Rosemarie Morgan, pp. 3–5.
26. Hardy, *The Return of the Native*, ed. Tony Slade, int. Pamela Boumelha, p. 9.

27. Ibid. p. 10.
28. Ibid. pp. 10–11.
29. Ibid. p. 11.
30. Derrida, *The Archeology of the Frivolous*, p. 71.
31. Derrida, *Advances*, p. 31.
32. Ibid. p. 5.
33. Ibid. p. 73.
34. Miller, *On Literature*, p. 124.
35. Ibid. p. 125.
36. Derrida, *Problem of Genesis*, p. xxiii.
37. Ibid.
38. Ibid.
39. The English Broadside Ballad Archive at the University of California Santa Barbara lists 'A pleasant new Ballad to sing both Euen and Morne,/Of the bloody murther of Sir John Barley-corne', giving the publication date of this particular variant as 1601–40. A West Country version of the song was collected by Henry and Robert Hammond in 1904 and 1905, continuing the practice until 1907. During this time they collected over 900 songs across six south-western counties, most of which were from Dorset, Hardy's home county, and the centre of 'Wessex'.
40. Hardy, 'The Dead Quire'. As Tim Armstrong has argued in his hugely important study of Hardy's poetry, *Haunted Hardy: Poetry, History, Memory*, certain of Hardy's poems, particularly among the later works, engage in supplementarity, as an iterable phenomenon of their hauntological condition (pp. 1–30). Time for Hardy is 'a constant supplementarity, a meditation that exceeds its own forms as the poet writes on' (pp. 19–20). There are different modes of supplementarity, ghostly survivals and afterlives, a couple being, to use Hardy's own word to which Armstrong alerts the reader, figured by the tropes of 'after-writing' (in the form of subtitles) or the 'continuator', a human figure, sometimes the poet himself (Hardy used the word of himself in the poem 'Wessex Heights' [*Variorum Edition*, pp. 319–20], as Armstrong tells us), sometimes a character acting as a medium or mediator in the poetic text. There is in 'The Dead Quire' an example of the continuator. As Armstrong points out, there is a shift in tense on the part of the voice of the 'sad man [who] sighed his phantasies: He seems to sigh them still' (ll. 3–4). Expression, narrative, history, genealogy, all are incomplete, and the poem is no exception, being 'necessarily incomplete as a container for consciousness' (p. 19). Hardy's continuator is doomed to the role of the narrator of supplementarity, with its ever-opening framing and iterability in the form of bearing witness to the ghosts of the past, in a manner not dissimilar from Coleridge's Ancient Mariner.
41. In *Thomas Hardy: Folklore and Resistance*, Jacqueline Dillon opens her study by pointing out that the word 'Folk-Lore' was coined in 1846, when Hardy was six years old, but the interest in such country matters had been known since the eighteenth century as 'popular antiquities' (p. 1). Though the interest had been largely 'casual rather than systematic' (p. 1), as Dillon puts it, folkloric research nonetheless bore something of a resemblance to genealogical research in its tracing of lineages and the seeking out of origins.

42. Dillon, *Thomas Hardy: Folklore and Resistance*, p. 34.
43. There takes place in the act of naming that arrives through the medium of the 'continuator' and the ghostly voices of the quire a curious, uncanny border-crossing. The boundaries between poem and ballad, Hardy's poetic imagination and the worlds of Wessex and rural Dorset, past and present (already undone in that tense shift mentioned by Armstrong, between reader and poet, poet and unnamed mediator, phantasies and haunting voices) momentarily give way, in an example of the enframing that is an opening, of an installation that marks, traces and re-marks the abyss of antecedence.
44. Thomas Hardy, *Tess of the d'Urbervilles*, ed. Tim Dolin, int. Margaret R. Higgonet, p. 7. Shaston is Shaftesbury, Dorset, approximately 12 miles north of Blandford Forum (Shottsford Forum, in Hardy's Wessex); Marlott is the village of Marnhull, to the south-east of Shaftesbury, a distance of around eight miles. The Vale of Blackmoor or Blakemore covers three counties: Dorset, Somerset and Wiltshire. It becomes immediately obvious, if we take the journey literally, that Jack Durbeyfield is not coming 'out of the west', but he is of course an inhabitant of a rural west country, from out of which he appears.
45. Hardy, *The Return of the Native*, pp. 13–14.
46. Ibid. pp. 12, 13.
47. Hardy, *The Mayor of Casterbridge*, ed. and int. Keith Wilson, p. 259.
48. Ibid. p. 261.
49. Should one read such instability in the spelling of the name in the manner of the reading of the place name or proper name when the mutability is presented in a fictional context? There is here something quietly disturbing, I think, for any certainties concerning absolute distinctions between 'fiction' and 'reality'.
50. Nancy, *The Inoperative Community*, p. 116.
51. Ibid. p. 116.
52. Nancy, *The Ground of the Image*, p. 37.
53. Nancy, *The Inoperative Community*, p. 35.
54. Heidegger, *Being and Time*, ¶ 47.
55. Husserl, *On the Phenomenology of the Consciousness of Internal Time*, p. 94.
56. Ibid. p. 94.
57. Nancy, *The Inoperative Community*, p. 30.
58. Wolfreys, *Thomas Hardy*. The problematic status of communication in Hardy's work is explored throughout the book.
59. Nancy, *The Inoperative Community*, p. 31.
60. Hardy, *Tess*, p. 7. Stagfoot Lane is a small hamlet north of Puddletown, Dorset.
61. Tim Dolin in Hardy, *Tess*, p. 401 n. 1.
62. Hardy, *Tess*, pp. 8–9.
63. Dolin, *Tess*, pp. 401–2, n. 2.
64. Ibid.
65. Hankins, *The Life and Works of George Turbervile*, p. 25.
66. Venn, *The Logic of Chance*.
67. Venn, *Annals of a Clerical Family*, p. vii.

68. Ibid.
69. Ibid.
70. Ibid.
71. Ibid.
72. Ibid. p. 1.
73. Ibid.
74. Ibid. p. 2.
75. Ibid. p. 3.
76. Derrida, *Edmund Husserl's* Origin of Geometry: *An Introduction*, p. 61.
77. Ibid. p. 61.
78. Ibid.
79. Hardy, *Desperate Remedies*, ed. and int. Mary Rimmer, p. 7.
80. Hardy, *Madding Crowd*, p. 5.
81. Hardy, *Under the Greenwood Tree*, ed. and int. Tim Dolin, pp. 7–8.
82. Hardy, *A Pair of Blue Eyes*, p. 7.
83. Ibid. p. 9.
84. Hardy, *The Mayor of Casterbridge*, p. 3.
85. Hardy, *A Laodicean*, p. 6.
86. Ibid. pp. 7–8.
87. Hardy, *The Woodlanders*, p. 5.
88. Ibid.
89. Ibid. p. 6.
90. Venn, *Logic*, p. 274.
91. Venn, *Logic*, p. 275.
92. Thomas Hardy, sketch accompanying 'In a Ewleaze near Weatherbury', in *Wessex Poems and Other Verses*, repr. in Gibson, *Variorum Ed.*, pp. 70–1.
93. Miller, *On Literature*, p. 22.
94. Husserl, *The Essential Husserl*, pp. 157–8.
95. Johnson, *The Critical Difference*, p. xii.
96. Husserl, *The Essential Husserl*, p. 158.

Chapter 3

'What consciousness grasps': 'silent knowing' and the Natural World in Hardy's Poetry

Monika Szuba

> To dwellers in a wood almost every species of tree has its voice as well as its feature. At the passing of the breeze the fir-trees sob and moan no less distinctly than they rock; the holly whistles as it battles with itself; the ash hisses amid its quiverings; the beech rustles while its flat boughs rise and fall. And winter, which modifies the note of such trees as shed their leaves, does not destroy its individuality.
> Thomas Hardy, *Under the Greenwood Tree* (11)

Both visual perception and aural perception frequently serve as direct descriptions of experience. Replete with moments of vision, Hardy's poems approximate an immediate, unmediated experience of the landscape. The above passage evokes the musical Being of the world (and by extension, Being-in-the-world), where dwellers in the wood are also dwellers attuned to the world. The trees 'sob', 'moan' and 'whistle' as well as 'hiss' and 'rustle'; the anthropomorphic sounds blend with other voices of the earth. As Julian Wolfreys writes in 'The Idea of Wessex', '[e]ach voice carries in it, beyond and before any particular "saying", the meaning of Being itself' (842). In many of Hardy's poems, the self is immersed in the landscape, entwined in its voices, integrated into the environment, an unassuming presence which does not disturb the surroundings. The voices of the earth and their singular features are bodied forth in various forms as '[i]t is this "sympathy" that allows the poet to imagine the voices of inanimate objects, or nonhuman organisms' (Wolfreys 843). This sympathy exudes from the passage taken from *Under the Greenwood Tree* where collective and nameless 'dwellers' are juxtaposed with singular trees, each named and endowed with an individuality. As Tom Paulin writes, 'Reading Hardy, we are always listening to the unique, the inscaped cadences of individual voices' (Introduction xxii).

The self's intertwining with the flesh of the world in Hardy's sympathetic poems confirms Wolfreys' argument that Hardy may be read as a proto-phenomenologist ('Idea' 837). After all, Barbara Hardy reminds us that Hardy insists that his work 'records . . . impressions and appearances' (2). Things appear to us phenomenologically: their presence is seen, heard and felt. Immediate experience is evoked by variable sensations, particularly sight and sound. While sight may often constitute 'mindsight', as Hardy calls 'visual memory' (Paulin, *Poetry* 111), aurality involves the here and now (the now as opposed to the present). Birdsong is a recurrent motif in Hardy's poetry and birds appear more frequently than any other animals. Merleau-Pontyan phenomenological thought is employed by Marion Thain in her reading of Hardy's verse, which focuses on tactility. As she aptly notices, even if the term 'phenomenology' in its current philosophical understanding appeared at the beginning of the twentieth century and Merleau-Ponty's texts were published a few decades after Hardy's death, 'it is clearly the case that these poetic and philosophical works are both responding to the same problems, and both come out of the key conceptual and philosophical shifts that occurred across the course of the nineteenth century' (131). One of these shifts involves the 'notion of man as a spectator [which] gave way to a conception that gave man a more powerful and active relationship with the world' (132).

Discussion of Hardy's concern with landscape constitutes an important strand in criticism, for example in Andrew Enstice's *Thomas Hardy: Landscapes of the Mind* or Ralph Pite's *Hardy's Geography: Wessex and the Regional Novel*. Critics note that the representation of nature in Hardy's novels is similar to that of his poems. For instance, in reference to *The Mayor of Casterbridge*, Mark Asquith avers that it is 'a cosmic process indifferent to the plight of man' (14). Robert Langbaum writes about 'the cosmic indifference and blundering' and argues rather provocatively that 'Hardy gives less emphasis in his poems than in his novels to nature's beauty; although he does, when turning in later poems to realistic rendition, show in nature a hard-won beauty' (46). Langbaum perpetuates the commonly held view that nature represented in Hardy's writing is 'indifferent', arguing that Hardy's 'poems insist on nature's indifference. Here and elsewhere Hardy's blatant anthropomorphism, as compared to Wordsworth's gentle animation of nature, indicates how utterly non-anthropomorphic nature really is' (45). It is certainly difficult to draw conclusions pertaining to all the poems as there are so many and they are so varied. The editors of *Thomas Hardy's 'Poetical Matter' Notebooks*, Pamela Dalziel and Michael Millgate, notice that 'the astonishing creativity demonstrated by the sheer number of poems thus brought successfully to completion in his last few years and by the profusion of new poetic projects, [are] persistently inventive if often impossibly ambitious' (xxii). As Tom Paulin points out in *Thomas Hardy: The Poetry of Perception*, 'It's sometimes said that the reason why there are so few books about Hardy's poetry is that the poems are so various that no one has found a consistent way of approaching them – a lever to shift them with' (Preface ix). Over forty years later, there are still more books on Hardy's novels being produced than on his poetry. They defy the techniques of analysis or do not seem to need them', as J. Hillis Miller aptly writes (*Linguistic* 269). Some critics, such as Julian Wolfreys and Robert Langbaum, combine the discussion of novels and poetry, the latter distinguishing between major and minor works. Hopefully, the limiting claim made by some critics that Hardy's poetry is 'profoundly autobiographical' is no longer applicable (Gibson n.p.).

Hardy's work occupies a special place in J. Hillis Miller's writing, including a study devoted to *Thomas Hardy: Distance and Desire* (1970), as well as many other books of which Hardy is an important part, such as *The Form of Victorian Fiction: Thackeray, Dickens, Trollope, George Eliot, Meredith and Hardy* (1968), *Fiction and Repetition: Seven English Novels* (1982), *The Linguistic Moment: From Wordsworth to Stevens* (1985), *Communities in Fiction* (2015). Recurrently in his work, Miller considers the subtle thread joining consciousnesses: a thread running between the author and reader, between one character and another. In *Ariadne's Thread: Story Lines*, he employs the figure of anastomosis to depict the weft of relations in literary texts. This is an extraordinary image which transports us from the literary realm to the organic world. Originating from biology, anastomosis denotes the connection of two or more parts of a branching system, e.g. of blood vessels, leaf veins, stems of woody plants, or rivers. According to Miller, anastomosis introduces an 'image of a line joining two vessels or enclosures ... the line from person to person, like a telephone line' (*Ariadne's* 144), creating 'the topography of the self in various modes of intersection with others' (*Ariadne's* 145). Employing John Keats's figure, Miller writes that the soul 'spins an elaborate spider's web in its movement through time. This is the soul the self makes to dwell in. [...] Each man's web, however individual and private it may seem, a secret airy citadel, nevertheless overlaps here and there, in fact at innumerable points, with those of others' (145). For the purposes of this essay, I wish to expand the understanding of Miller's concept and suggest that it may also be applicable in poetry to denote a line joining the self with other consciousnesses, as in Hardy's poems, where the interconnection reaches beyond the human towards non-human beings and things.

I would therefore like to extend the possibilities for discussion of Hardy's poetic oeuvre and offer a reading of selected poems, which combines the phenomenological thought of Maurice Merleau-Ponty with J. Hillis Miller's figure of anastomosis. I shall focus on the relation of the self with the world, attempting to demonstrate that the 'cosmic indifference' is not only lacking from many of Hardy's poems, but also that they display a chiasmatic intertwining of beings. What follows is inevitably a deplorably unsuccessful reading of 'a handful of Hardy's poems'; as J. Hillis Miller rightly points out all 'attempts to survey the whole and organize it thematically, or phenomenologically, by noting similarities from poem to poem and generalizing on that basis' are necessarily 'unsatisfactory' (*Linguistic* 270). Fully aware of the doomed nature of my endeavour, I intend to undertake a tentative effort to offer a reading of handful of poems, appreciating the uniqueness of the moments of consciousness that they record.

Being and the World

Before turning to the poems, I wish to introduce some of Merleau-Ponty's concepts, focusing on his unfinished work, *Le visible et l'invisible* [*The Visible and the Invisible*]. His phenomenology of perception centres on a *corps-sujet*, the body-subject, immersed in a *Lebenswelt*, or lifeworld, which is irreducible to any representation, because the subject of the lifeworld is the experience of being alive, or the 'lived-through-world' (*Primacy* 71). The world is unknowable, as the self may only access reality after a reflective process. The perception of an object is always temporally dislocated. In *The Rhythm of Thought: Art, Literature, and Music after Merleau-Ponty*, Jessica Wiskus explains, 'What consciousness grasps ... is not the thing itself but the reflection – the image – of the initial perception of the thing. There exists always a lacuna, a gap, between reflection and the thing: consciousness does not obtain to the world directly' (4). However, as Merleau-Ponty argues, there exists an originary source of the sense, an 'ontology of brute Being' (*Visible* 165), where brute, or wild Being, is an attempt to access the infinity of lifeworld, through uncovering 'layers of wild being' (178), in the pre-reflective experience. Wild being is thus 'silent knowing', 'a pre-knowing' (178), which occurs at the level of the human body. The self is immersed in the 'environment of brute existence and essence is not something mysterious: we never quit it, we have no other environment' (117). It is hidden from us but the world invites us to see its things, its objects, and engage with them. Corporeal sensations bridge the gap of otherness as the becoming subject strives to transcend the fragmentation of experience. As Merleau-Ponty writes, 'The body unites us directly with the things through its own ontogenesis, by welding to one another the two outlines of which it is made' (*Visible* 136), where the two outlines are its sensible nature. Thus, the body is a thing among things, it is of things (137), as we are not separate from the world – we are *of* the world. What Merleau-Ponty calls the body's 'coupling with the flesh of the world' enriches the latter, while the 'floating in Being with another life . . . making itself the outside of its inside and the inside of its outside' immerses the self in intersubjectivity (144).

An important concept in Merleau-Pontyan phenomenology, reversibility suggests that the flesh of the world returns to itself (*Visible* 146): 'a reversibility of the seeing and the visible, of the touching and the touched' (147). There occurs the reversibility of the visible and the tangible for we see and are seen, we touch and are touched, which results in a creation of 'an intercorporeal being' (143). From *Phénoménologie de la perception* [*Phenomenology of Perception*] to *L'Œil et l'esprit* [*Eye and Mind*] to *Le Visible et l'invisible* [*The Visible and Invisible*], vision held a significant position in Merleau-Ponty's phenomenology. In his unfinished manuscript, he emphasises the interrelation of senses, suggesting that the gaze is endowed with tactile attributes, employing such terms as 'envelops' (*Visible* 131, 133) and 'palpates' (133) the visible things, 'cloth[ing] them with its own flesh' (131). There exists an intertwining between the embodied subject and the world; borders are crossed when 'encroachment, infringement' occurs between the touching and the touched (134).

The realisation of reversibility may take place in moments of vision which approximate wild Being. Many of Hardy's poems seem to approach an immediate response to such 'raw' or 'brute' experience. As P. N. Furbank points out, 'The key to Hardy's verse is authenticity. He was seized by a particular impulse – an immediate or recollected emotion combined with a particular rhythm – and would override ordinary proprieties of speech in his intense concern for faithfulness to it' (qtd in Cash 3). This authenticity lies in approximating the immediacy of the experience as seen in a number of Hardy's poems.

'That tiny pinch of priceless dust'

Moments of vision evoke the movement of time and its momentum. As J. Hillis Miller argues, '[t]here is only one realm, that of matter in motion', which reflects the Hardyesque conception of human life as dual, paired with consciousness (12). Both the material and non-material realms of dwelling are subject to temporality. Since Hardy wrote about dwellers in *Under the Greenwood Tree* in 1872, the word 'to dwell' has assumed another meaning, especially after Martin Heidegger who writes about 'our dwelling plight' (159). In his essay 'Building Dwelling Thinking' (1951), he emphasises the importance of learning how to dwell properly, which is about Being-in-the-world as to dwell is to maintain a relationship with the world. Situating Hardy's writing within the phenomenological heritage, Wolfreys explains that 'to dwell means to orient oneself with regard to one's being, and the historicity of being' (*Thomas Hardy* 5). 'Historicity' is one of the most important features of dwelling as it is provisory and temporary, given to time. The realisation of one's finitude is thus inscribed in dwelling. The sense of impermanence and provisionality pervading his work is combined with Hardy's insistence on vision characterised by its fleeting, impressionistic nature.

Tom McAlindon aptly remarks that even if numerous critics have noticed that 'Hardy's poetry manifests an almost obsessive preoccupation with time and change' (22), it has rarely been a serious consideration. As he argues,

> Hardy's obsession with time and mutability encompasses everything from the cosmic to the personal and finds expression in remarkably diverse ways. But although the cosmos, external nature, prehistory and history are often alluded to, being the great theatres of Time, mostly their function is to serve as a significant backdrop to his elegiac, ironic and bitter reflections on change in the personal domain: change from youth to age, innocence to experience, illusion to disillusion, bliss to blank desolation. (28)

Further, McAlindon cites Shelley's line, 'nought may endure but Mutability', which is fitting in the context of Hardy, who 'constantly seeks in the material world for signs of permanence that simultaneously defy and define it' (34). Barbara Hardy notices 'the rhetoric of provisionality' in his novels and poems, 'especially those in which he reaches out to comprehend otherness, in memories, ghosts, birds, beasts and flowers' (3). I shall return to this remark further on. Impermanence and transience constitute recurrent motifs in Hardy's poems, especially when geological permanence and the repeatability of life cycles are opposed to the impermanence of human achievement. Yet the moments of vision – those moments of being – are paradoxically timeless as the self becomes immersed in the experience, approaching a brute perception of the thing.

Inscribed in the living body of the world, transitoriness marks dwelling as it entails sharing the experience of death. In 'Afterwards' (*Complete Poems* 553), the speaker envisions his passing as leaving behind the world replete with 'green leaves like wings' (2), 'the dewfall-hawk' (6), 'the wind-warped upland thorn' (7), moths, and hedgehogs, travelling 'furtively over the lawn' (10). All of them constitute 'a familiar sight' (8). The poem relies heavily on vision, foregrounded in such words and expressions as 'he was a man who used to notice such things' (4), 'like an eyelid's soundless blink' (5), 'a gazer' (7), 'during some nocturnal blackness' (9), 'watching the full-starred heavens that winter sees' (14), and 'He was one who had an eye for such mysteries' (16). This last line suggests that the seen often remains undecipherable, 'an enigmatic world of which we catch a glimpse' (Merleau-Ponty, *World* 54). In the final stanza the sense of sight is joined by the sense of hearing, thus foregrounding aurality: 'And will any say when my bell of quittance is heard in the gloom . . .' (17); 'He hears it not now, but used to notice such things' (20). This reminds us that the Earth resounds in many voices.

The poetic subject in 'Afterwards' appears to be someone filled with sympathy for all beings. As he imagines, 'One may say, "He strove that such innocent creatures should come to no harm,/But he could do little for them; and now he is gone"' (11–12).

Recognising that they are at times treated instrumentally, Hardy rehabilitates such beings, pointing to the injustice and cruelty as in 'The Blinded Bird' or reminding us of the significance of their role as for instance in 'Shelley's Skylark (The neighbourhood of Leghorn: March 1887)':

Somewhere afield here something lies
In Earth's oblivious eyeless trust
That moved a poet to prophecies –
A pinch of unseen, unguarded dust

The dust of the lark that Shelley heard,
And made immortal through times to be; –
Though it only lived like another bird,
And knew not its immortality.

Lived its meek life; then, one day, fell –
A little ball of feather and bone;
And how it perished, when piped farewell,
And where it wastes, are alike unknown.

Maybe it rests in the loam I view,
Maybe it throbs in a myrtle's green,
Maybe it sleeps in the coming hue
Of a grape on the slopes of yon inland scene.

Go find it, faeries, go and find
That tiny pinch of priceless dust,
And bring a casket silver-lined,
And framed of gold that gems encrust;

> And we will lay it safe therein,
> And consecrate it to endless time;
> For it inspired a bard to win
> Ecstatic heights in thought and rhyme. (*Complete Poems* 101)

In dialogue with Romantic visions of 'nature', in which the natural world serves as auxiliary, a mere source of inspiration or as a surface reflecting the poet's ego, the poem reclaims the significance of a tiny being. In Hardy's poem, the personal pronoun 'I' appears only once, halfway through the poem, which offers an important shift of perspective from the self of the Romantic poet to something as unassuming as the skylark. Thus, Hardy offers a counter-romantic discourse that moves the ground of perception for the reader through an address that implicitly erases the limits of the Romantic vision. A poetic figure for Shelley, who denies its real existence – 'Bird thou never wert!' (Shelley 2) – for Hardy the skylark is fleshed out, still there, transfigured in another material form. In the first stanza, the bird is 'a pinch of unseen, unguarded dust' (Hardy 4), in the second 'the dust of the lark' (5), and in the fifth stanza it becomes 'that tiny pinch of priceless dust' (18). The shift between those descriptions is marked by the use of adjectives: first the skylark's remains are 'unseen, unguarded' (4), but fourteen lines later they are 'priceless' (18). The repeated negative adjectives are echoed in 'unknown' (12), all alluding to Shelley's negatives ('Thou art unseen' (20), 'unpremeditated' (5), 'unbodied' (15), 'unbeholden' (43)), which moved the skylark into a realm of a disembodied symbol. Hardy stresses the skylark's commonality, lifting the burden thrust on it by Shelley: 'it only lived like another bird,/And knew not its immortality' (7–8), emphasised by the next line describing the bird in corporeal terms as 'a little ball of feather and bone' (10). In Hardy's poem, the skylark is immortalised not in art but becomes transformed and lives in another form on the earth. The anaphora in the fourth stanza emphasises the existence of many possibilities. The repeated speculation of '[m]aybe it . . .' (13, 14, 15) reveals the speaker's belief in the return of living beings in another form, in the transformation of matter into another form. The bird may remain in the soil, dissolved, or its pulsating being may be in the evergreen bush or the ripening grape. The emphasis on grounding contrasts with Shelley's line 'thou scorner of the ground' (50). Hardy places the skylark 'somewhere afield here . . . In Earth's oblivious eyeless trust' (1–2): not in the sky but in a field, grounded. Being of the Earth, the bird may not possess awareness or knowledge but demonstrates 'eyeless trust' (2) in the ways of the world.

'And earth, and air, and rain'

Time and again, the question of changeability and transience returns in Hardy's poems, as for instance in 'Proud Songsters', where time cycles are foregrounded. Focusing on familiar garden birds – thrushes, finches and nightingales – which can be seen and heard in woods and gardens, the poem evokes a commonplace event:

> The thrushes sing as the sun is going,
> And the finches whistle in ones and pairs,
> And as it gets dark loud nightingales
> In bushes
> Pipe, as they can when April wears,
> As if all Time were theirs.
>
> These are brand new birds of twelvemonths' growing,
> Which a year ago, or less than twain,
> No finches were, nor nightingales,
> Nor thrushes,
> But only particles of grain,
> And earth, and air, and rain. (*Complete Poems* 816)

As the trees in the passage from *Under the Greenwood Tree*, the birds are all endowed with singularity and given individual features based on sound: the thrushes 'sing' (1), the finches 'whistle' (2) and nightingales 'pipe' (5). The singing, whistling and piping continues, oblivious to time. Paradoxically perhaps, because of the iterability of their song, birds mark time. They keep musical time of their own. In the space of the poem, which is given solely to birds and their world, birds are the creators of Time: it is made by and belongs to them. Ungoverned by necessity from the human perspective in the text, birdsong has no appreciable purpose fathomable to people, and so what they do is in essence all time. Because of this they are irreducible in their song and appearance to any anthropomorphism. Yet human assessment appears in the conjunction in the line 'As if all Time were theirs' (6), which highlights the improbability of owning time, stressed by the capital letter, and foregrounds transience and the fleeting nature of Being. The second stanza stresses this further, evoking a recent time without 'the brand new birds' (7; cf. 'At Day-Close in November', *Complete Poems* 334). Even if not stated explicitly in the poem, reaching towards the past is a reminder that something which 'a year ago or less than twain' (8) was inexistent, will cease to exist, given a limited life span: the mention of temporality stresses the finitude of every living being. The final two lines foreground the inanimate world which existed before and which will continue with 'the particles of grain,/And earth, and air, and rain' (11–12), where all the particles are interconnected, bound with the conjunction and the sound: all one-syllable words, combined by a liquid consonant. Here, as in the previous poem, Hardy demonstrates a predilection for nouns like 'a particle', 'grain', 'a pinch', and 'dust': small-scale fragments of the material world, which are volatile and given to dispersal.

At the same time there are more poems which focus on ethereal atmospheric conditions, foregrounding temporality through seasons. For instance, 'June Leaves and Autumn' (*Winter* 150) opens with a line – 'Lush summer lit the trees to green' (1) – focused on rhythm, containing mostly one-syllable words, a promise of the harmony that the season brings. The first stanza is devoid of human presence, even the line 'It seemed a melancholy fate' (6) evokes an impersonal impression. The self is manifest in the first line of the second stanza where the speaker returns to the same place after the summer. The joyous future perspective ending the first stanza – 'Still joyed aloft in pride of place/ With store of days to come' (10–11) – is replaced with the past tense when the speaker notices that those boughs which 'Had length of days in store' (22) during his early summer walk joined the ones which lay in the ditch then. The speaker's wanderings are both physical and metaphysical, the melancholy sight of the lush June leaves meeting the same end as the prematurely broken bough reminds him of the transient nature of Being.

In 'The Darkling Thrush', one of the most widely anthologised poems and 'Hardy's most imaginative bird lyric' (B. Hardy 199), the speaker's desolation is foregrounded by the words such as 'spectre-grey' (2), 'dregs' (3), 'broken' (6), 'weakening' (4), and 'haunted' (7):

> I leant upon a coppice gate
>   When Frost was spectre-grey,
> And Winter's dregs made desolate
>   The weakening eye of day.
> The tangled bine-stems scored the sky
>   Like strings of broken lyres,
> And all mankind that haunted nigh
>   Had sought their household fires.
>
> The land's sharp features seemed to be
>   The Century's corpse outleant,
> His crypt the cloudy canopy,
>   The wind his death-lament.
> The ancient pulse of germ and birth
>   Was shrunken hard and dry,
> And every spirit upon earth
>   Seemed fervourless as I.

> At once a voice arose among
>   The bleak twigs overhead
> In a full-hearted evensong
>   Of joy illimited;
> An aged thrush, frail, gaunt, and small,
>   In blast-beruffled plume,
> Had chosen thus to fling his soul
>   Upon the growing gloom.
>
> So little cause for carolings
>   Of such ecstatic sound
> Was written on terrestrial things
>   Afar or nigh around,
> That I could think there trembled through
>   His happy good-night air
> Some blessed Hope, whereof he knew
>   And I was unaware. (*Complete Poems* 119)

The landscape seems unwelcoming with its 'sharp features' (9), the whine of the wind like a 'death-lament' (12). The throbbing pulse of life is 'shrunken hard and dry' (14), barely audible 'among/The bleak twigs' (19–20). The land's features resemble 'the Century's corpse outleant' (10). It is a tomb-like winter landscape, where, as the speaker admits, 'every spirit upon earth/Seemed fervourless as I' (15–16), in which the adjective 'fervourless' further enhances the impression of coldness and desolation. The position of the burdened self, as if stooped under the weight of unhappiness, is demonstrated in the opening line: 'I leant upon a coppice gate' (1). The speaker listens for the voices, but the wintry land seems to be like a dead body, yielding a spectral vision that is mute until suddenly a song is heard, which renders the contrast between the dead silence and the thrilling trill all the more striking. The sound of the 'death-lament' (12) is juxtaposed with a rapturous song. After the first two stanzas focused on death and desolation, the effect of the sudden 'full-hearted evensong/Of joy illimited' (19–20) seems powerful. The sound is 'ecstatic' (26) as the bird transcends himself. The birdsong is doubly unseasonal as it is winter and the thrush is old and fragile. The thrush turns out to be 'aged' (21), 'frail, gaunt, and small' (21), his feathers 'blast-beruffled' (22), who chooses to 'fling his soul/Upon the growing gloom' (23). The bird knows hope, which, like his song, 'trembled through' (29), of which the speaker is 'unaware' (32), a mystery of Being that in that moment remains concealed.

The tone of the next poem, 'Weathers', differs considerably from the tone of 'The Darkling Thrush', as it is light and celebratory. The plural form of the title foregrounds the changeability of the weather-world, but here transience is approached in an upbeat, sing-song manner:

> This is the weather the cuckoo likes,
> And so do I;
> When showers betumble the chestnut spikes,
> And nestlings fly;
> And the little brown nightingale bills his best,
> And they sit outside at 'The Traveller's Rest',
> And maids come forth sprig-muslin drest,
> And citizens dream of the south and west,
> And so do I.
> This is the weather the shepherd shuns,
> And so do I;
> When beeches drip in browns and duns,
> And thresh and ply;
> And hill-hid tides throb, throe on throe,
> And meadow rivulets overflow,
> And drops on gate bars hang in a row,
> And rooks in families homeward go,
> And so do I. (*Complete Poems* 512)

Starting with the cuckoo and adding other elements one by one, the poem demonstrates an appreciation for the nonhuman beings celebrating the multiplicity of the world. The speaker and the shepherd mentioned in the tenth line are the only human presences. The pronoun 'This' in the line 'This is the weather' (10) foregrounds the self's immersion in the world, who is placed in it and experiences things happening here and now. 'I' becomes emphasised by the placement at the end of the line and the rhyming scheme, but it is soon decentred by a shift of rhymes for the next four lines, only to return at the end of the stanza as a musical refrain. The weather is not specified; it is merely impressionistically sketched. While the first stanza suggests spring showers and the air sufficiently warm to wear 'sprig-muslin' (7), the second stanza offers an autumnal image where the weather is 'shunned' (10), and it pours with rain: 'beeches drip browns and duns' (12), 'meadow rivulets overflow' (15), 'drops on gate bars hang in a row' (16). The voices of the natural world are echoed by the poetic sound effects in lines such as 'little brown nightingale bills his best' (5) and 'hill-hid tides throb, throe on throe' (14). Hardy makes use of sound, thus rendering the rhythms of the world in the rhythms of language. Regular rhymes reverberate throughout, stressing the speaker's attunement with the rhythms of the world. This is further emphasised by the employment of the anaphora 'And', which links the elements in a chain-like manner, and the speaker's enthusiastically repeated 'And so do I' (2, 9, 11, 18), demonstrating his alignment with the world, being in tune with all its forms.

Beginning and End

In 'Birds at Winter Nightfall', human perspective is absent altogether, the point of view belonging entirely to animals. Employing empathy for the nonhuman other, Hardy here offers a real bird's-eye view. A human hand (and perspective) is only visible in title of the poem:

> Around the house the flakes fly faster,
> And all the berries now are gone
> From holly and cotoneaster
> Around the house. The flakes fly! – faster
> Shutting indoors that crumb-outcaster
> We used to see upon the lawn
> Around the house. The flakes fly faster,
> And all the berries now are gone! (*Complete Poems* 115)

Employing the triolet, a form based on repetition and rhyme, Hardy foregrounds the unmistakeable rhythms of the earth. The alliterative phrase 'the flakes fly faster' (1) with a combination of the fricative sounds, like the flapping of small bird wings, is repeated three times, every time with altered punctuation. The exclamation mark appears twice in the poem: the first one in the middle of the phrase, the second one ending the poem, both seem to express astonishment. The inhabitant of the house is described as 'that crumb-outcaster' (5), which according to Barbara Hardy demonstrates a 'merely instrumental' attitude of the birds, 'simplifying the human being' (198). Limiting human beings to one function offers an ironic reversal of a common situation in which humans do the same to nonhuman animals. The phrase also demonstrates Hardy's playful suggestion that the birds possess poetic skills – even if Pinion thinks that '[t]he rhyming is not of the best, especially with "crumb-outcaster"' (52). Offering an imaginative vision of otherness, the poem is an attempt to experience the world of the other.

'A simple, much anthologised and mysterious poem' (200–1), as Barbara Hardy puts it, 'The Fallow Deer at the Lonely House' calls up an animal presence:

> One without looks in tonight
> Through the curtain-chink
> From the sheet of glistening white;
> One without looks in tonight
> As we sit and think
> By the fender-brink.
>
> We do not discern those eyes
> Watching in the snow;

> Lit by lamps of rosy dyes
> We do not discern those eyes
> Wandering, aglow
> Four-footed, tiptoe. (*Complete Poems* 551)

It seems intriguing that in the poem which relies so heavily on the sense of sight, no looks are exchanged; the animal seems to remain imagined yet unseen. The act of watching belongs to the fallow deer from the title, who 'looks in' (4), while the collective poetic subject 'we' does not 'discern' (7), its verbs are 'sit' and 'think' (5). Through the synecdoche the deer becomes the eyes which are 'watching' (8) and 'wandering' (11) on a winter's night. The deer looks in through the 'curtain-chink' (2), a border separating it from the inside, a fissure. In turn the 'we' of the poem sit by the 'fender-brink' (6), or something that protects, fends off, a threshold. Both words are joined by a hyphen, a combination of plosive and liquid consonants creating sound effects. While the curtain obscures the view, the fender defends, both seemingly separate, suggesting a division. In the second stanza the phrase 'we do not discern' is repeated twice, drawing attention to the verb 'discern', from Latin *discernere*, 'to perceive', 'to sift', 'to discriminate', but also 'to divide' and 'to separate'. Perhaps we do not discern between us and the creature, or cannot distinguish between 'we' and 'the one without', between the self and the world. And perhaps paradoxically this is what is offered in the moment of illumination which the poem calls up in phrases such as 'from the sheet of glistening white' (3), 'lit by lamps of rosy dyes' (9) and 'aglow' (11). The final lines – 'Wandering, aglow / Four-footed, tiptoe' (11–12) – succinctly capture the deer in four words, only one of which is exclusive to the nonhuman other, thus endowing it with shared features and making it less radically different. Another attempt to 'comprehend otherness in . . . birds, beasts and flowers' (B. Hardy 3), the poem imaginatively extends sympathy towards a nonhuman perspective, making possible the experience of a chiasmatic intertwining.

The last poem under discussion, 'I Am the One' combines the features in the poems above, such as animal presence, otherness, visibility/invisibility, intertwining and transience:

> I am the one whom ringdoves see
> Through chinks in boughs
> When they do not rouse
> In sudden dread,
> But stay on cooing, as if they said:
> 'Oh; it's only he.'
> I am the passer when up-eared hares,
> Stirred as they eat

The new-sprung wheat,
Their munch resume
As if they thought: 'He is one for whom
Nobody cares.'
Wet-eyed mourners glance at me
As in train they pass
Along the grass
To a hollowed spot,
And think: 'No matter; he quizzes not
Our misery.'
I hear above: 'We stars must lend
No fierce regard
To his gaze, so hard
Bent on us thus, –
Must scathe him not. He is one with us
Beginning and end.' (*Complete Poems* 818)

The poem relies on an exchange of looks between the speaker and other beings. Aware of the gaze of ringdoves, hares, mourners and stars, the speaker passes by, not disturbing their usual activity: the ringdoves 'do not rouse/In sudden dread' (3–4) and hares 'resume' (10) munching wheat. To them, he is 'the passer' (7) who appears in their field of vision for a brief moment, unthreatening, harmless. But what should be stressed is that he is of the world. Bodily there, the self is involved – incorporated in things – moving through the landscape. From a phenomenological perspective, the body and its movement are crucial elements of each visual experience. According to Merleau-Ponty, in the act of perception vision and the body become entangled, resulting in a 'folding back' or an 'invagination', revealing a possibility that is a principle of the actual that transcends duality (*Visible* 152). The repeated expression 'as if' – the ringdoves 'as if' say and the hares 'as if' think – highlights the self's sense of unimportance: 'Oh; it's only he' (6) and 'He is one for whom/Nobody cares' (11–12). The subject imagines that he is perceived as someone who does not matter. He is seen, but his visibility is inconsequential as it bears no relevance to the world. The conjunction 'as if' introduces an imaginary situation as the subject imagines voices and voiced thoughts of the inhabitants of the earth, but not until the final part of the poem does he actually hear. Merleau-Ponty writes, '[L]anguage is everything, since it is the voice of no one, since it is the very voice of the things, the waves, and the forests' (*Visible* 155). The speaker hears voices of the universe and through them sees himself through the eyes of the others, and in that moment the self is created as the visible constitutes the seer, the 'transfigured world' (Merleau-Ponty, *World* 54) becoming changed by gaze. The poem offers a self-effacing self-portrayal where the subject sees and is conscious of being seen, an experience which leads to a powerful sense of welding with the world.

Yet the situation is marked by temporality as the subject is 'the passer' (7) and the mourners 'pass' (14) on the train. The verb 'to pass' means at least two things here: 'to go past' but also 'to move past in time', 'to cease to exist', 'to die' (cf. 'Afterwards': 'If I pass during some nocturnal blackness, mothy and warm' [9]). The speaker, the mourners (and the one(s) they mourn) – they are all passers. So are ringdoves and hares, and even the stars, even if their time perspective is extended. Hardy's stars are not only endowed with agency and a voice but also sympathy as the speaker 'hears' (19) the stars say 'we' (19). They spare the stargazing speaker a 'fierce regard' (20) and scathing. The definite article in the opening phrase 'I am the one' is dropped in the penultimate line 'He is one with us' (23), which radically changes the meaning. The self is no longer singled out, separate from the world, but becomes one with it. The opening words undergo a change as does the self, having seen that he is accepted by the human and nonhuman inhabitants of the earth. The stars, which leave the man unscathed, add a cosmic perspective to the poem, far from being that of a 'cosmic indifference'. Inserted between the leaves of the world, the self lies 'in Earth's oblivious eyeless trust'. The final line in this form suggests an expression 'from beginning to end' (24), but it also leads to a reflection that a beginning inevitably entails an end, and things coming to pass. Yet it may also offer a perspective of continuity as '[t]he endless, iterable voice of the inhuman world is set in counterpoint to the merely material and transient' (Wolfreys, 'Idea' 843–4).

Conclusion

As Virginia Woolf writes, Hardy's 'is a vision of the world and of man's lot as they revealed themselves to a powerful imagination, a profound and poetic genius, a gentle and humane soul', thanks to which 'we have drunk deep of the beauty of the earth' (Woolf n.p.). Hardy's poetic self is a passer, 'a pinch of dust', temporally immersed in the landscape, experiencing the lifeworld. It dwells in 'a secret airy citadel' yet it intersects and overlaps with other consciousness 'at innumerable points', to cite J. Hillis Miller's words once again. Thus in 'a network of pathways', the self encounters 'the withinness of others' (*Ariadne's* 145). In his poetical matter, Hardy envisions and opens up the visible within the invisible, foregrounding, as Miller notices, 'the uniqueness of each moment of experience, as well as of each record in words of such a moment' (*Linguistic* 270–1). These moments of vision allow him to perceive directly, accessing the 'raw' or 'wild' Being. As Merleau-Ponty argues, 'the rediscovery of the world of perception' reveals 'the whole spectacle that is the world and human life takes on a new meaning' (*World* 54). Vacillating between the importance of all endeavours and the vanity of things, Hardy shows a variety of physical forms subject to change, offering a vision spread between desolation and wonder, imbued with an awareness of fragility and transience. His sympathetic approach and the appreciation of all beings make him attuned to the voices of the Earth, an approach that is visible in poems which propose two-way communication between the self and the world, constantly highlighting that the self is the world.

Chapter 4

The Hills Have Eyes

Éamonn Dunne

> Miller's Law: The greatest critics are those whose readings exceed their theoretical presuppositions
>
> J. Hillis Miller

In a most epigrammatic of epigrammatic sentences, Sylvia Plath opens one of her very last poems with this: 'Your clear eye is the one absolutely beautiful thing.'[1] The reader inevitably wonders why the speaker in this poem, 'Child', uses the singular 'eye' instead of the obvious descriptor for the young child. Shouldn't it be 'eyes'? Shouldn't we see the entire face in the image? Isn't it odd that the poet should refer to a mother gazing at a child in this manner? Concentrating, as it were, on this single focal point, the eye.

Here is the poem:

> Your clear eye is the one absolutely beautiful thing.
> I want to fill it with color and ducks,
> The zoo of the new
>
> Whose names you meditate —
> April snowdrop, Indian pipe,
> Little
>
> Stalk without wrinkle,
> Pool in which images
> Should be grand and classical
>
> Not this troublous
> Wringing of hands, this dark
> Ceiling without a star.[2]

So strange is the line in fact, if you really start to think about it, that the singular 'eye' begins to function like a Hitchcockian motif, a strange disembodied organ (a bit creepy); or it's like something from an Edgar

Allan Poe tale: 'I think it was his eye. Yes, that's it.' Odd. And why 'clear'? Why is the child's eye clear, one wonders: immaturity? naïvety? unworldliness? Or is it a formal figure working in apposition with 'absolute'? Perfect, pure, unequivocal, undiluted.

One reason we might conclude after having read the poem several times over is that there's a pun on the word 'eye' – an eye rhyme, if you will – which is also being used here as a pronoun. You read it again to mean that the child is an individual, that the speaker is homophonically celebrating the child's individuality and distinctiveness, its clear 'I' ('Your clear [I] is the one absolutely beautiful thing'). There's nobody and nothing like him in the world. His beauty, his singularity, is absolutely unique. She celebrates her son, Nicholas, by celebrating his difference and greets it with an appreciation for what she will later call 'the zoo of the new', the sense of pure possibility that the world outside holds in store for him.

Read this way, those lines open up to a series of double readings, wherein the ocular imagery becomes at once a carnal and an ontological landscape, a series of vacillations between the child as knowable and the individual as unknowable, a diverse range of singularities and alterities, the others within the one, so to speak, the being singular/plural, the uncanny otherness of each of us in a world of others. Every other is absolutely other, says the poem. That singularity is the beauty of the world entire. A mother looks at her child and sees pure, unlimited difference; and she memorialises it in words. In St Augustine's celebrated phrase, the poem could then be read to mean 'I love you. I want you to be' [*amo. volo ut sis*].

Miller's Theory

In case you haven't already guessed it, I'm thinking here about similar issues of seeing, knowing and understanding in J. Hillis Miller's work. Most particularly I'm thinking about what he refers to so often (and in so many essays and so many books) as prosopopoeia – giving a face or a voice to something absent or dead, 'the fundamental generative linguisitic act making a given story possible'.[3] Anyone who's read Miller, especially his *The Ethics of Reading* (1986), *Versions of Pygmalion* (1990), *Hawthorne and History* (1991), *Topographies* (1995), *Others* (2001) and *On Literature* (2002) will know how important this figure becomes to him and how central it is in all of the work. My title is therefore not just a bad orthographic or acoustic pun on his surname and a cult Wes Craven horror movie, although there may conceivably be a great deal more to that analogy than I have yet been able to adduce thus far. No. My claim is that reading Miller closely means confronting, at some point or other, the central importance of this trope in his writings. Reading Miller means reading prosopopoeia as an act and function of literature. It means asking yourself what it really means to *see* a character as a real person and thinking about what affects readers in the act and event of reading narratives, of bringing stories to life in the mind's eye. It simply means thinking about what stories do to us and why we need them and what responsibilities we have to them.

Facing up to a responsibility in reading – facing what confronts us as we read, seeing through it – means understanding that what happens to us in the stories we read is simultaneously free and not free. We are directed by a text to a point, but how we read is entirely unique to us. What happens in reading, when we really read, happens, with all the inaugural violence, Miller will tell us, of an event. *It is sheer unexpectedness.* No matter how many times you read the same book, no matter how many times those characters appear to us on the page, something fortuitous happens, something new. Miller's way of putting this is as follows:

> One way to define this quality of true acts of reading is to say that they never correspond exactly to what other readers tell me I am going to find when I read that book, however learned, expert, and authoritative those previous readers have been. Another way to describe what is unpredictable in a genuine act of reading is to say that reading is always the disconfirmation or modification of presupposed literary theory rather than its confirmation. What happens when I read a book never quite fits my theory (or anyone else's) of what is going to happen.[4]

However unpredictable or new the reading experience, however free it feels, however limitless, nonetheless there is a responsibility for seeing what happens, to follow a path; and the responsibility is the reader's own. How Miller sees this is infinitely fascinating to him and, I daresay, to his readers. This is Miller's absolute uniqueness. To see eye to eye with Miller is (however counterintuitively) not a process of clarity, therefore, rather it is a process of absolute submersion into a question of what it means to read well – to really read – with both eyes open. Not to be given over to what others think a novel or poem ought to mean (even him) but to begin to see it for what it is, an invitation to think beyond what others have said about it. The inaugural violence of reading – what Miller calls *good reading* – its eventness, its quality of infinite surprise and regress, is the absolute challenge to the theories we bring with us. If there *is* an ethics of reading, then it is an ethics based on the quality of honest and open disclosure of the event of reading itself, of seeing and saying what happens every time we encounter otherness in the texts we read, especially when that is a failure to comprehend what we are seeing or hearing therein. No theory absolves us from the risk of reading. No theorist comes before the event.

This is why calling Miller a literary theorist is actually a gross misnomer. Miller is *not* a literary theorist. He is not a theorist, that is, if by that you mean someone who sees through texts (the word 'theory', by the way, etymologically comes from the Greek word *theoria* meaning 'seeing'). He is not a literary theorist if you mean by that denomination someone who can tell you by way of didactic instruction and conclusion how to read literature, so that you might be able to say one fine day, 'now I am a good reader'. Just as one can never say 'I *am* just,' so can one never say 'I *am* a good reader.'

Miller's eyes/I(s) are deeper than that, full of blindness and insight, full of what happens in the incoming, inventive, event, with no end in sight (no sight in end). Miller cannot show us the way because the way does not exist. What Miller does is incite us to read better by showing us time and again that the fundamental vein of literature is that it remains always already open to reinterpretation. Thus his incite to insight. Miller's reading eye is unique. Absolute. Other. Though, let us call it what it is: it is distinctly unclear.

On First Looking into Miller's Prosopopoeias

Permit me to carry my seeing-eye analogy a little further before I perform a brief reading of Thomas Hardy's *Tess of the d'Urbervilles* as an example of prosopopoeia. One might say (with a grinning kind of paranoia) that readers of Miller's work often find themselves experiencing the unsettling feeling that they are being watched from afar, like the characters in Wes Craven's movie, that someone (or some thing) is quietly and furtively regarding them from some unseen location, tracking and predicting their steps in order to catch them out. Readers may also have the somewhat uncanny experience that in reading one of his many essays and books they are *themselves* being read, that their gaze is somehow being returned without them fully knowing it, or from where exactly. This is the experience you often get when you're reading Miller reading a book or essay you already know. He seems to know how to predict your reading. You think you've found something in it worth following, and lo and behold, he says it before you've even formulated it. Then what may have at first seemed the objective or epistemologically detached critical exercise of reading Miller discussing some literary work or other, turning an ignorance into a knowledge, learning something not previously known, exploring new worlds from the comfortable armchair of quotidian reality, often becomes a kind of performative unlearning, a way of experiencing the unknown, the absent, the radical otherness of the other inventively and catachrestically. You look at the work you know and it morphs a second time into something wholly new. You see it again for the first time.

There also seems to be a somewhat fortuitous echo of this kind of inventive (re)seeing in my title, which is another form of catachrestic positing, as prosopopoeias often are, anthropomorphic ascriptions to inanimate objects for which we have no other terms: for example, the hands of a clock, the legs of a chair or the eye of a storm. Though we do not of course generally speak of the *eye* of a hill, we do often think of them as a having a brow or a face, of their having the ability to stare down at us. In order for us to engage with this idea, there has to be a kind of unlearning or critical naïvety, a childlike innocence. Like looking at cloud patterns or stars and reading shapes, we need to suspend our disbelief in order to read. It's this kind of unlearning that I take to be fundamental to Miller's spectacularly peculiar idiom, and I will try to follow this up in what I say.

Prosopopoeia, for Miller, as we've seen, is the inaugural trope, our first step into the virtual dimension, and therefore essential to all acts of reading. Reading narratives are ways of breathing life into something inanimate or absent, of conjuring spirits, giving a name, a voice and a face to some absent and otherwise unreachable other. It is for this reason that reading literature is one of the greatest responsibilities we have to the dead, our way of mourning them, of not fully forgetting them or letting go of their memories and deeds. All reading is therefore bound to an Ariadnean umbilical cord, fastening us forever to our most distant ancestral lines. Hence Joyce's fantastically metafictive tele-techno-prosopopoeic joke:

> Have a gramophone in every grave or keep it in the house. After dinner on a Sunday. Put on dear old greatgrandfather kraahraak! Hellohellohello amawfullyglad kraak awfullygladaseeragain hellohello amarawf kopthsth. Remind you of the voice like the photograph reminds you of the face. Otherwise you couldn't remember the face after fifteen years, say.[5]

The odd thing here is of course that Joyce's joke is hyperbolic. I mean this in the sense that it exaggerates the everyday, the way in which reading and writing are avenues for switching on that gramophone, encountering otherness, letting it (or better them) come. How often do we really think about this? How often do we think about raising the spirit of George Eliot or Anthony Trollope? How often do we wonder about the sheer peculiar necromancy of it all?

The best place to see why all reading is a species of necromancy is probably Dickens's celebrated opening lines in *Great Expectations*, where the young Pip's burgeoning literacy manifests the letters as pure prosopopoepias:

> My father's family name being Pirrip, and my Christian name Philip, my infant tongue could make of both names nothing longer or more explicit than Pip. So, I called myself Pip, and came to be called Pip.
>
> I give Pirrip as my father's family name, on the authority of his tombstone and my sister – Mrs Joe Gargery, who married the blacksmith. As I never saw my father or my mother, and never saw any likeness of either of them (for their days were long before the days of photographs), my first fancies regarding what they were like, were unreasonably derived from their tombstones. The shape of the letters on my father's, gave me an odd idea that he was a square, stout, dark man, with curly black hair. From the character and turn of the inscription, 'Also Georgiana Wife of the Above', I drew a childish conclusion that my mother was freckled and sickly.[6]

Pip's reading of his parents' tombstones is an allegory of reading as prosopopoeial interjection, of seeing beyond the letter. It is one of the great moments in literature for seeing reading as symbolic action: that it sees through the word, relates it, and brings it back to itself. The joke is, of course, that Pip isn't really reading the names AND that he is doing precisely that, simultaneously, in a whirligig of wonderful little ironies. Pip is doing what all readers must do; he is seeing through the letters on the headstone in order to imagine his parents. But they are letters, not his parents. The boy reads by substituting the letters for images, thus falling in love with the inanimate, as does Pygmalion in Ovid's *Metamorphoses*, with Galatea's statue: perhaps the ur-allegory of characterisation. What Pip wants to do is to restore life into an inanimate text.

Without what Miller calls in *On Literature* those little 'Open Sesames' delivering us over to the wonder of a virtual reality, there is no reading and no responsibility.[7] There is no narrative without it, no poetry, no literature. This condition is also, therefore, what essentially makes the foundation of storytelling invulnerable to deconstruction. Any accounting for prosopopoeia as a critical exercise is bound to fail since by an ineluctable necessity the initial criticism must set this trope in motion before the analysis can even begin. In Paul de Man's odd formulation of this (de Man is never far from Miller on these issues): 'to read is to understand, to question, to know, to forget, to erase, to deface, to repeat

– that is to say, the endless prosopopoeia by which the dead are made to have a face and a voice which tells the allegory of their demise and allows us to apostrophise them in our turn'.[8]

That's a wonderful list of contradictions. But you really need to think about it and how you actually read a text. How can a reading be at the same time understanding *and* forgetting, knowing *and* erasure, prosopopoeia *and* defacement? Each term cancels out the other until we arrive at the last, *repetition*, meaning that this process begins again anew each time, however knowledgeable we think we have become. Thus we are destined to repeat the crimes we condemn – we are destined to read as children. Like Pip – like him or not. We read. We repeat. We envisage. We deface. We start again.

This is the aporia of reading: to be critical of the trope one has to learn to become a slow reader, but – and this is a very large *but* indeed – in order to become a critical reader you must first pass naïvely through this prejudice. You have to, in other words, learn to read at two speeds (*allegro* and *lento*) at once. Impossibly. A naïve reading is not necessarily replaced by a critical reading when the critical reading comes to pass, since the naïvety is the possibility of reading itself. You have to be naïve but you don't have to be critical. That's theory for you.[9]

Miller's hypothesis in his chapter on Plato in *Topographies*, I take it, is the best place to see this question really open up in his work.[10] Plato's *Protagoras* takes as its theme the idea that virtue can be taught. A young student, Hippocrates, wishes to have Socrates introduce him to the Sophist Protagoras in the hope that he might learn about virtue, for Protagoras proclaims that he can teach it. Socrates is of course sceptical and proceeds to question Protagoras on his teachings, creating a dialogue in which the two ultimately change their positions on the issue in a strange about-turn. For Miller, 'virtue has to be expressed in the figure fundamental to any allegory: prosopopoeia', and Plato uses the figure of the face to do it.

Virtue, he says, is like a face made up of its constituent parts: ears, eyes, nose and mouth.[11] We can talk about them and understand them as separate entities making a single whole. Therefore we can discuss virtue in terms of its constituent parts: wisdom, temperance, courage, justice and holiness, while also realising that they form a larger unity. The paradox is that the parts are singular, *sui generis*, and yet parts of a greater unity that can only be expressed laterally. This then points to the way in which ordinary language both coaxes us into believing in the connections between singularities, as in, say, the face of a mountain, or Pip's letters, while simultaneously exposing that notion as an error. 'The best and most successful teaching in the humanities', says Miller, 'is probably of this kind. Learning to be virtuous and learning to read a story both depend ... on the figure of prosopopoeia and on learning to be adept in manipulating this figure, no easy task. Stories function to teach virtue not because they mediate some abstract message, but because they are the best practical training in using and reading prosopopoeia, though perhaps also coaching us to take it for granted and to forget that it is a figure.'[12] This learning to be virtuous, I claim, is Miller's most resonant message because it may more exactly be termed an *unlearning*. It is an insight into responsibility, which resonates profoundly with a Levinasian kind of response to an infinitely foreign otherness, a responsibility that transcends knowledge.

In becoming a good reader, a virtuous or responsible reader, one must unlearn how to be critical over again each time in an endless process of reading again. If each act of reading is a singular response, situated at a single moment in time, *an event*, then it follows that that reading must necessarily have taken that figure for granted. Learning how to read Miller's way is not only to become aware that the hills have eyes but that it is necessary for us to believe it.

'Doomed to be seen'

As promised, I want to put these ideas to the test by offering a reading of prosopopoeia at work. I want to examine an act of reading taking place as it envisages the drama unfolding. I take Hardy's *Tess of the d'Urbervilles* in this instance as an example of reading as prosopopoeia (a reading-prosopopoeia), but my choice is somewhat arbitrary in the sense that I could literally take any piece of literature as my example. I choose Hardy here, simply because I have been teaching him lately and still find this work, after so many years of reading and rereading, to be one of the most extraordinary novels I have ever read. The experience of reading this work is consistently eventful, in the full resonance of that word. I find also, fortuitously or not, and on closer inspection, how oddly apt this text is to the topic at hand.

For present purposes, *Tess* is chock-full of references to seeing and sight. The more you look, the more you see: from Angel's first encounter with Tess ('As he fell out of the dance his eyes lighted on Tess Durbeyfield, whose own large orbs wore, to tell the truth, the faintest aspect of reproach that he had not chosen her') to Tess's doomed encounter with Alec Stoke-d'Urberville's 'bold rollling eye' ('She had an attribute which amounted to a disadvantage just now; and it was this that caused Alec d'Urberville's eyes to rivet themselves upon her'), to Mrs d'Urberville's literal and figurative blindness to her own son's character ('compelled to love her offspring resentfully'), to the tragically ironic unseen rape of Tess, to Tess's broken view of the world as a maiden no more, as she ('gazed over the familiar green world beyond, now half-veiled in mist'). Indeed Hardy describes Tess early in the novel as a woman 'doomed to be seen' by the wrong man – a prophetic imagining that will control every aspect of her life until, as Hardy famously puts it, 'the President of the immortals had ended his sport with Tess'.[13]

Perhaps, as Hardy himself, after seeing, at sixteen, Martha Brown being hanged outside Dorchester prison for murdering her husband, understood this visual trauma as also a trauma of reading. His question must have been how to apostrophise the memory in order to retell the story of a desperate woman driven to a desperate act, responsibly – at least responsibly to the memory of having seen it. In order to tell the story, Hardy has had to recreate a fictional representation of a significant real-world happening. He's had to raise a ghost. This event in August 1856, the catalyst for the book, is not only a profound visual stimulus for the story, it is also a crisis in representation which Hardy famously reflected on in his letters much later in his life, claiming he was ashamed at having ever witnessed it. Seen in this light, *Tess* operates as a work of voyeuristic penance. As in Ian McEwan's *Atonement*, Hardy responds to the tragic by immortalising it in text, by writing through it and commiting it to history. Only when Tess is read, does she appear to us as a living soul. Only when we pick it up and see her again does the tragedy unfold again in a haunted parallel universe. Only when we raise her ghost and Hardy's with it does she begin to live for us. Thus *Tess* is undoubtedly an extraordinary literary example of the collision of carnality and conceptuality, of vision and insight, the real and the surreal, in an ever increasing series of extraordinarily scopophilic renderings.

No one who reads *Tess of the d'Urbervilles* can fail to be struck by Hardy's peculiar oral fixation either. That Tess is primarily drawn in the reader's mind erotically isn't exactly understated in the text. Her 'mobile peony mouth and large innocent eyes', her 'bouncing handsome womanliness' and her 'luxuriance of aspect' and 'fullness of growth' are entrancing, as are all those references to her mouth. Examples of this are superabundant and far too many to recount here. Suffice it to mention the moment Alec feeds Tess those fateful strawberries through parted lips at Trantridge; that oddly tantilising moment when Alec tutors Tess in the art of whistling – only to surreptitiously watch her mouthing sounds from behind closed curtains; all those stolen cursory kisses from Alec on the road back and forth from Marlott; Angel's remembrance of Tess's kisses as the taste of 'butter and eggs and milk and honey'; even Angel's very own 'kiss of charity', which is really a kiss of death to Marion at Talbothays, and so on and so forth.

Perhaps the most obvious example, however, is Angel's aberrant orgasmic lunge at Tess in Chapter 24:

> How very lovable her face was to him. Yet there was nothing ethereal about it; all was real vitality, real warmth, real incarnation. And it was in her mouth that this culminated. Eyes almost as deep and speaking he had seen before, and cheeks perhaps as fair; brows as arched, a chin and throat almost as shapely; her mouth he had seen nothing to equal on the face of the earth. To a young man with the least fire in him that little upward lift in the middle of her red top lip was distracting, infatuating, maddening. He had never before seen a woman's lips and teeth which forced upon his mind with such persistent iteration the old Elizabethan simile of roses filled with snow. Perfect, he, as a lover, might have called them off-hand. But no – they were not perfect. And it was the touch of the imperfect upon the would-be perfect that gave the sweetness, because it was that which gave the humanity.
>
> Clare had studied the curves of those lips so many times that he could reproduce them mentally with ease: and now, as they again confronted him, clothed with colour and life, they sent an *aura* over his flesh, a breeze through his nerves, which wellnigh produced a qualm; and actually produced, by some mysterious physiological process, a prosaic sneeze.[14]

One of the marvels of Hardy's narrative art is his ability to manipulate point of view, and this citation is an excellent example. Point of view shifts through the third person vicariously from Clare to Hardy and back to Clare in this section, so that the reader is hitch-hiking in the consciousness of the narrator, then Angel, then the narrator. The piece, ironically, shifts point of view again, a little further on, culminating in Old Pretty, a 'puzzled' cow, kicking her hind leg anxiously while the lovers embrace beneath her.

Here Tess is sexualised and doomed yet again by the gaze of others. She is helpless, in this moment, just as she is helpless in the eyes of her readers throughout the novel. Perhaps that's her real tragedy. We see her almost entirely through the gaze of Alec and Angel, and, of course, Hardy's disembodied voice, and a host of peripheral characters. She is essentially a protagonist controlled and manipulated by the gaze of her peers and her readers, a protagonist as Peter Widdowson convincingly argues, that we simply don't get to know: 'we know almost nothing substantive about Tess's "character", for the novel never attempts to penetrate her secret being'.[15] Tess herself is therefore a ghost haunting Hardy's imagination and the imaginations of Angel and Alec, not a substantive being. Again, like Pygmalion, the 'pure woman, faithfully presented' (as Hardy ironically called her in his controversial subtitle) is anything but in the eyes of Victorian moralists. She is not pure and she is not faithful to anything but the germ of Hardy's story.

What we get with *Tess* therefore is a novel that prioritises the act of seeing so much so that the titular character is a focal point that fails to dislodge its secret. We see so much and yet know so little of her. Just as the three major moments in the novel are not narrated, so we come to realise that Hardy's strategy is to leave us guessing and not to present at all. Hardy's 'faithful representation' is doubly ironic at such moments because it simply does not depict. We are not privy to the rape of Tess; we only get a question: 'Why it was that upon this beautiful feminine tissue, sensitive as gossamer, and practically blank as snow as yet, there should have been traced such a coarse pattern as it was doomed to receive.'[16] Neither do we see Tess's act of murder. What we get is Mrs Brooks (the prying landlady) peering through the keyhole at Tess's tragedy followed by an oblong blood stain on the ceiling.[17] Lastly, we see only Liza-Lu and Angel gazing at a black flag symbolising Tess's doom in the final moments of the book.[18]

As a moral, *Tess* narrates the 'cruelty of lust and the fragility of love'.[19] Among its lessons is that seeing and believing are enmeshed in impressionistic desires; that, however else we may look at it, our gaze is motivated by a need: to understand, to obtain, to touch, to own, to embrace, to bring to life. Looks can be destructive both ways, from the beholder to the beheld. In this sense, *Tess* narrates an innate failure to see through seeing, to understand it for what it is. We may think we understand our desires. We may think we know why we see things the way we do. But we are perpetually undone by our blindness to understand why we see the way we do both in literature and in life. Moments of exposure to ideological or sensuous bias do not preclude us from making the same mistakes. We may read to see clearly but we are apt to stumble again because the initial act of reading, the first prosopopoeia, sets us off in a direction we have no way of understanding from a vantage point or from some prospect above that act itself. When it comes to this *im*possible trope we are always already within and without, looking beyond the future and back to an illusory past – simultaneously facing and defacing ourselves and others as we try to read.

I See Dead People

My claim here has been that *Tess* is a novel that in many ways foregrounds the trope of prosopopoeia. I have used it as an example to qualify Miller's assertion that the primary trope of literature (indeed,

I would say, of all reading) is prosopopoeia and therefore it is as such undeconstructible. My example, I can now say after my brief analysis, is strangely befitting, since Hardy is consistently drawing the reader's attention to ways of seeing in that novel. If you were inclined to follow this topic analytically and count them all up, you would find that there are 158 references to eyes in *Tess*, 176 in *A Pair of Blue Eyes*, 190 in *The Mayor of Casterbridge* and 246 in *Jude the Obscure*.[20] But this really tells us nothing more than Hardy uses the word quite a bit. What we ought to see is that beyond the simple data there is a propensity to disguise what is fundamentally apparent. In other words, there is a propensity in these novels to claim, however paradoxically, that the more we see the less we are aware of what we are seeing and how we are seeing it.

Take for instance the following description of Tess harvesting in the fields by the local townsfolk – Tess is considered a pitiful creature at this stage by her peers for being left alone to raise Alec's child:

> It was a thousand pities, indeed; it was impossible for even an enemy to feel otherwise on looking at Tess as she sat there, with her flower-like mouth and large tender eyes, neither black nor blue nor grey nor violet; rather all those shades together, and a hundred others, which could be seen if one looked into their irises – shade behind shade – tint beyond tint – around pupils that had no bottom; an almost standard woman, but for the slight incautiousness of character inherited from her race.[21]

Notice how Tess's eyes are described here. They are neither one colour nor another, shaded and tinted beyond definition, bottomless and unreadable. The more we look, the less we see. Hardy's description of them later in the novel is likewise unsettled:

> At first she would not look straight up at him, but her eyes soon lifted, and his plumbed the deepness of the ever-varying pupils, with their radiating fibrils of blue, and black, and gray, and violet, while she regarded him as Eve at her second waking might have regarded Adam.[22]

Tess's ever-varying pupils are indicative of a difficulty not only of chromatic equivalence but with a deeper existential awareness. The more intently Angel traces the lineaments of Tess's features, the more Hardy muddies the waters, as it were.

Reading passages like this cannot but make the reader infer that Hardy himself has fallen in love with his own creation. So finely wrought are those details that one can almost believe that this is the case, though of course we can never know for sure. Hardy has created a ghost of angelic proportions. By this I do not mean to suggest that Tess overshadows a phantom essence, an essence that conspicuously controls our reading of the text. My claim is merely that Hardy's art is to show us that our desires and projections create and control our readings in ways that we can never fully understand. We are directed by what we see but have no sure means of knowing that we are reading rightly.

This, finally, is the possibility and impossibility of good reading. If Miller's law is correct, and our theories are complicated and exceeded by our closest readings, then we can only return to *Tess* each time with an open mind, if we are to read it well. We ought to expect its excesses. Literature, as Miller says of it, 'speaks the unspeakable and finds resemblances for what resembles nothing else'; it affords us a privileged access to an otherness that is in no other way approachable.[23] When we read a character like Tess, we fill in the blanks and are guided along by a sense that we are correct in seeing things the way we see them. Perhaps, ultimately, nobody can make us see it differently once we have committed to our own readings. This is both clear to us and unclear simultaneously. We are directed by the text and our personalities, by what comes with us as much as what comes to us. Knowing that we project our desires and wishes into these resemblances is no guard against reading awry. Seeing things this way is seeing that reading is part of what Miller (after Henry James and Ralph Waldo Emerson) calls the conduct of life. It is our responsibility to the living and to the dead. It is also a way of doing things with words, a speech act for which we are ultimately responsible, though to what exactly, only our own eyes can tell us. Open Sesame!

Notes

1. By way of quick acknowledgement, I want to express a profound gratitude to my students for helping me think through some of the issues that follow here, especially as they relate to Hardy's *Tess*. Thank you kindly to my English literature students in Bangkok, Thailand, for making Hardy come alive for me once again in the most unexpected ways imaginable. To Zora, Tiger, Primi, Nash, Tejas, Rohan, Mindy, Fourth, Pun, Arnesh, Maek and Faye, thank you. Finally, to J. Hillis Miller, who, like Barkis, has always been willin' to help us all read better, a very happy 90th birthday.
2. Plath, 'Child'.
3. Miller, *Versions of Pygmalion*, p. 13.
4. Ibid. p. 20.
5. Joyce, *Ulysses*, p. 144.
6. Dickens, *Great Expectations*, ed. Charlotte Mitchell, p. 3.
7. Miller, *On Literaure*, pp. 24–45. Here Miller comments on the irruptive and 'violent' event of virtual immersion. That 'violence', Miller claims, is also pleasurable in that it covertly enacts the violences of death, of sexuality and of the irrationalities and absurdities of language. Virtual realities are portals for raising ghosts in our minds, ghosts that refuse to be exercised.

The characters in the stories we read remain in an alternative psychic universe and haunt us continuously. This violence, as I see it, is another way of thinking about the lack of control we readers actually have over this phenomenon in our lives. Do we really have any say over what virtual landscapes inhabit our imaginations?
8. De Man, 'Shelley Disfigured', in *Deconstruction and Criticism*, p. 68. De Man continues: 'No degree of knowledge can ever stop this madness, for it is the madness of words. What *would* be naïve is to believe that this strategy, which is not *our* strategy as subjects, since we are its product rather than its agent, can be a source of value and has to be celebrated and denounced accordingly.' A magnificent paradox this! Language gives and it takes away at the same time, just as de Man's language produces performatively a hypothesis about reading that is undermined in the language he uses to describe it. He says, 'to read is . . .' which is then followed by a series of contradictions. The argument is, I take it, that the contradiction is necessary to see that we have no control over what happens in the event of reading. Another way to formulate this in de Manian terms would be to say that language promises, but what it promises can never be known for sure. Its promises are always excessive. There would, of course, be much more to say of this essay and what de Man is calling Shelley's 'coercive forgetting' in terms of Miller's views of prosopopoeia in Plato. What I am arguing is a necessary form of unlearning in Miller strikes me here as yet another form of this forgetting.
9. See Miller's discussion of 'the aporia of reading' in *On Literature*, pp. 122–6.
10. See 'Face to Face: Faces, Places, and Ethics in Plato', in Miller, *Topographies*, pp. 57–79.
11. Plato, *Protagoras and Meno*, pp. 61–2 (329b–e).
12. Miller, *Topographies*, p. 70.
13. Hardy, *Tess of the d'Urbervilles*, int. Robert B. Heilman, p. 360.
14. Ibid. pp. 147–8.
15. Widdowson, 'Introduction: Tess of the d'Urbervilles Faithfully Represented By', p. 19.
16. Hardy, *Tess of the d'Urbervilles*, p. 71.
17. Ibid. p. 373.
18. Ibid. p. 390.
19. Ibid. p. 276.
20. Marshall, 'Thomas Hardy's Eye Imagery'.
21. Hardy, *Tess of the d'Urbervilles*, p. 89.
22. Ibid. pp. 166–7.
23. Miller, 'A Critical Story So Far', p. 251.

II
Self and World

Chapter 5

J. Hillis Miller's Hopkins: Poet of the Anthropocene

Claire Colebrook

As we settle into the Anthropocene we might feel increasingly justified that we have left deconstruction behind. Even before the awareness of irrevocable planetary damage to the point of altering the earth as a living system and requiring a new geological marker, many had pointed out that deconstruction's emphasis on textuality and inscription was irresponsibly blind to environmental forces (Clark 2008; Cohen 2010). Writing about justice to come, democracy to come, forgiveness and an open future were profoundly human ethical issues. This is especially so if we think of deconstruction in its ethical (Levinas-inflected) phase as paying heed to the singularity of the other, where the other was either another human blessed with their singular world (Critchley 2014), or even an animal whose gaze towards us provoked an even more intense awareness of our personal singularity (Derrida 2008). When Jacques Derrida wrote about the end of the world, the world was – as it was for phenomenology – the lived world of sense, and not the planet, and when he wrote about nuclear catastrophe the erasure was one of the archive in its production of sense and lived fictions, and not of inscription at a pre-human level (Toadvine 2018). It is no surprise that even before the Anthropocene there were a series of 'turns', – the ethical turn, the inhuman turn, the affective turn, the realist turn, the theological turn, new materialisms and new aestheticisms, all geared towards insisting that there is something outside the text. And if one is, in a manner of planetary responsibility, stepping outside deconstruction and the ethics of reading, then no figure would seem to be more necessary to surpass than J. Hillis Miller. When Miller claimed that deconstruction was not nihilism he turned towards the need to negotiate texts, formalism and reading (Miller 1987: 9). At least, we might concede, Derrida took on the criticisms of deconstructive nihilism and thought about every other person's death as the end of the world, and recognised that there was no such thing as animality or the animal. By contrast, Miller's *The Ethics of Reading* is, like the Kantian text it takes as an object, an isolated affair. One (Derridean) side of deconstruction not only turns towards otherness; it insisted that we cannot avoid somehow incorporating or reducing the radical otherness of the other (Derrida 1978). Derrida increasingly turned his attention to the worlds of others, the singularity of a world that we are struck by but can never grasp. Here, Derrida was perhaps akin to the Romantic poets so often read through deconstruction; the world offers us a sense or promise that we are impelled to acknowledge, and yet that remains forever deferred.

Another side of deconstruction – and the one I'll pursue through J. Hillis Miller – is far less oriented to the infinite, the intimation of a presence forever deferred, and is instead cut off, defaced, or more like a severed hand (Cohen 2009) than a face that, in its alterity, is justice. Here, one might think not so much of the deferral and promise of sense, but of the stubborn insistence of a text that is materially sublime, nothing more than itself (de Man 1996). This is perhaps why Miller was first drawn to Victorian poetics, especially the Hopkins whose sprung rhyme and incredibly visceral poetics captured the force of language's resistance. Perhaps what enabled Miller to transition from being someone interested in Victorian poetics, to become central to literary deconstruction, and then finally to turn to the predicament of the Anthropocene was a Victorian or post-Romantic sense of the end of the world. This was not Derrida's end of the world or end of man, where the end always has a promise of a beyond (1969). It is more like the end that Shelley (despite being a Romantic) purveys and surveys in 'The Triumph of Life': to look at the end of the world is to be stunned or paralysed by a disarray that seems to demand that there must be more, even if all one reads and sees keeps pulling us back to disconnected matters. The gaze in 'The Triumph of Life' is quite different from Derridean futurity, where the drive of anticipation opens the present to the infinite. Here, the force of life is, necessarily, destructive: life is drive, a propulsion that might be opposed to what Miller refers to as reading. The point of view of the poem is not taken up by the movement and drive of life, but is instead stunned and silenced by the bodies that are fragmented because they have no sense other than that towards an ever-open future:

> This was the tenour of my waking dream.
> Methought I sate beside a public way
> Thick strewn with summer dust, & a great stream
> Of people there was hurrying to & fro
> Numerous as gnats upon the evening gleam,

> All hastening onward, yet none seemed to know
> Whither he went, or whence he came, or why
> He made one of the multitude, yet so
> Was borne amid the crowd as through the sky
> One of the million leaves of summer's bier. –
> Old age & youth, manhood & infancy,
> Mixed in one mighty torrent did appear,
> Some flying from the thing they feared & some
> Seeking the object of another's fear,
> And others as with steps towards the tomb
> Pored on the trodden worms that crawled beneath,
> And others mournfully within the gloom
> Of their own shadow walked, and called it death . . .
> And some fled from it as it were a ghost,
> Half fainting in the affliction of vain breath.
> But more with motions which each other crost
> Pursued or shunned the shadows the clouds threw

The 'vain breath' noted here is at once the breath that is futile, being merely life, but also vain in the sense of self-regarding, so caught up in the motion of driving forward that there is no sense of what might be other than life. This moment in Shelley captures a counter-vital deconstruction that always marked Miller's work, especially in his early reading of Hopkins. Hopkins's sense of God, despite being given in every particular, is anarchically counter-vital. It is because things are never reducible to some single force of life, and because God is not a unifying so much as a singularising force, that the eye of the poet sees things in a manner that is materially sublime. If things are signs of divinity this is not because they offer some narrative or sense, but because – like the pageant viewed by Shelley – they cut into the driven connectedness of what appears all too coherently as life. In 'The Wreck of the Deutschland', the God that appears as a unifying mastery, almost giving things a boundedness, is nevertheless a ground that is likened to granite, and that stills motion. This type of sovereignty is given not in some promise of future abundance, but hides behind death, past all grasp:

> I admire thee, master of the tides,
> Of the Yore-flood, of the year's fall;
> The recurb and the recovery of the gulf's sides,
> The girth of it and the wharf of it and the wall;
> Staunching, quenching ocean of a motionable mind;
> Ground of being, and granite of it: past all
> Grasp God, throned behind
> Death with a sovereignty that heeds but hides, bodes but abides

It is not only that God is distant, difficult, disappearing, but that the sense of that granite that holds life together is what tears life apart.

We might fast forward to the two other motifs in Miller's work, where reading and the ethics of reading are also destructive but not nihilistic, or are at least a form of active nihilism: to be able to tear apart the seeming coherence and self-evidence of things, to be struck, assaulted by the very particulars that had once seemed to compose something as apparent as life. This, in turn, yields a counter-vital Anthropocene that takes its cue from late Romanticism or early Victorian poetics, rather than the Wordsworthian sense of the world as dwelling and bounded home for an intimated humanity. 'The Wreck of the Deutschland' witnesses catastrophe as an assault, as a mark of the divinity that strikes us not as a unifying futurity, but as a break in the present that strikes down our sense of the prima facie value of this life.

> Five! the finding and sake
> And cipher of suffering Christ.
> Mark, the mark is of man's make
> And the word of it Sacrificed.
> But he scores it in scarlet himself on his own bespoken,
> Before-time-taken, dearest prizèd and priced –
> Stigma, signal, cinquefoil token
> For lettering of the lamb's fleece, ruddying of the rose-flake.

The five nuns aboard the doomed Deutschland are already cast out from life, expelled from Germany, but their apartness is intensified and rendered divine when they are viewed through a poetics of inscription. As 'ciphers' of the suffering Christ, they signal or mark what it is in human life ('the mark is of man's make') that is merely an aspect of a broader scarring, lettering, marking, signalling, from which life must be cut. The truth is given in a cutting off, an apocalyptic shortening of the time of life. Here, Hopkins presents a counter-vital apocalypticism that is worth heeding in the era of the Anthropocene. Far from life's wreckage of the earth being an occasion for a new humanity that must and will save itself, the single catastrophe cuts into the sense and trajectory of life, the wreck of the Deutschland's thwarted journey opening a whole series of inscriptive layers that range from stigma to ruddying of the rose-flake:

> Nature, then, for Hopkins as for the Middle Ages, is the 'book of nature' in which we may read 'news of God'. But there is one crucial difference: the medieval doctrine of analogy has almost disappeared from Hopkins. For the Christian of the middle ages each object in the natural world repeated some particular aspect of the supernatural world. It was thus a means of knowing that supernatural world in detail. For Hopkins all the world is 'charged with the grandeur of God', and we know through the things of this world simply the power and presence of God, not details of the supernatural world. (Miller 1955: 302)

The world is like a book of nature, but the book reads like *Finnegans Wake*. Once we are distracted from life by the marks of the world, by the catastrophic temporalities that violate everyday trajectories, we are exposed to multiple and divergent inscriptive systems. What Miller finds in Hopkins is a unifying principle of rhyme where it is the materiality of inscription that creates relations that are not those of everyday coherence, not those of the simply given world, an intimation of an inhuman or radically material inscription.

If we link these three strands of Miller's work – Victorian poetics, deconstruction, climate change – it is possible to look back and read poets like Hopkins as poets of the Anthropocene. This is not to say that their work registers climate change, but that the Anthropocene exposes new modalities of reading that Miller insisted upon throughout his career. Inscription was not, as I have already suggested, a radicalisation of sense that would open meanings to a futurity that was infinite, but a more malevolent force of diremption. Rather than the promise of presence springing forth from a text, forever deferred, forever outstanding (in the manner of the Romantic sublime), the unreadability of texts, their stubborn materiality that is not ours, generates a quite different responsibility. As Miller argued in 'The Critic as Host', 'the impossibility of reading should not be taken too lightly. It has consequences, for life and death, since it is incorporated in the bodies of individual human beings and in the body politic of our cultural life and death together' (218). To say that the impossibility of reading is incorporated in the bodies of individual beings is at once to signal that being able to say 'I' and to have a world is to be bound up with complex systems of inscription one neither authored nor can comprehend, but also that our very modalities of touching, feeling, being affected and simply being embodied are also inscriptive systems.

Here, one might turn to 'The Wreck of the Deutschland', where what appears to be the immediacy of perception, with the body being struck by the force of experience in its disjunctive intensity, occurs as a form of assault, both witnessed and experienced:

I am soft sift
In an hourglass – at the wall
Fast, but mined with a motion, a drift,
And it crowds and it combs to the fall;
I steady as a water in a well, to a poise, to a pane,
But roped with, always, all the way down from the tall
Fells or flanks of the voel, a vein
Of the gospel proffer, a pressure, a principle, Christ's gift.

The self as bounded and fastened soft sift that is 'mined with a motion' is typical of a whole series of images in this poem, where the touch of God appears to be not so much graceful as pressured or mined. As Miller says in his early work on Hopkins, there is a general principle of life where the singular differences of every aspect of existence nevertheless generate a form of rhyme, if one can only view the world with the poet's eye; at the same time, that condition of poetic vision cuts one off, to the point where the ipseity of the self is like being imprisoned within the very self-sameness that constitutes one's life. The art of poetry becomes one in which one marks out one's self, along with the differences of nature, such that one's very being becomes one of the ways in which the world signs the joy of itself. At the same time this marking also risks cutting the self off, such that saving the self may cost the earth:

> In non-human nature the law is transformation, flux, but the law for man is absolute destruction, since his identity, though incarnated, is too subtle, too spiritual, to retain its distinctness through even so many changes as a tree or flower will endure. The final lesson man learns from nature is that he, too, is part of nature and that this means but one thing for him: death . . .
> Even if a man could achieve through the poetising of his perception of nature an unwavering and permanent identity, it would be all dismembered and unbound in a moment at his death. But even within the limits of earthly life the project is bound to fail. As we have seen, the ability to 'instress' nature is intermittent and can be replaced in a moment by the most agonising spiritual impotence. If the self is unable to selve, as it often is, it will be cut off entirely from the world which can give it such delight. In times of spiritual dryness, of spiritual paralysis, the self is locked entirely within its self-torment and cut off entirely from the outside world[.] (Miller 1955: 314–15)

The balance of poetry is a balance of life and non-life, of at once marking, inscribing, rhyming and catching the differences of the world such that the world is brought to expression; and yet that all too human marking that saves the world also risks becoming so bound up in itself that only a castastrophic assault to the self allows life to be more than mere life, to become expressive. In 'The Wreck of the Deutschland' the eye/I that views the catastrophe continually expresses what it sees as a traumatic rupture. The poem narrates a series of visual, spiritual and existential assaults on the boundedness of the self, beginning with the self as nothing more than this joyous sense of ruptured interiority:

> Thou hast bound bones & veins in me, fastened me flesh,
> And after it almost unmade, what with dread,
> Thy doing: and dost thou touch me afresh?
> Over again I feel thy finger and find thee.

Throughout the poem there are two modes of perception, two ways in which events are registered; one is by a marking that demands reading (in Miller's sense of cutting into and halting the flow of perception and sense), as though the world were itself inscription, composed in a pattern rather than a semantic or communicative sign: 'Stroke and a stress that stars and storms deliver.' The other mode of perception is of being physically touched, hurled, trodden, motioned, lashed or wrung: 'Father and fondler of heart thou hast wrung.' What Miller notes in Hopkins, a vital and counter-vital dialectic whereby the marking of the world renders the world expressive, while nevertheless generating a blindness or imprisonment from the world – a prison that is joyously undone by catastrophe – is worth recalling as we enter the Trumpocene. (Here I use the term 'Trumpocene', following Bernard Stiegler and Tom Cohen, as a post-Anthropocene reaction formation. In the face of destruction one adopts a mode of reading whereby all one encounters becomes nothing more than fake news: 'it threatens my being, and therefore must be a hoax' [Cohen 2017; Stiegler 2018]). Miller, after Hopkins, notes that nature is at once inscription, with the singularity of each aspect of existing marking itself out, as an ongoing variation on the same rhyming power of difference; at the same time as that very instress or inscape is never reducible to life itself. Like Deleuze and Guattari's concept of 'the refrain', every seemingly distinct thing comes into being through rhythm, expressive of a life that gives itself in variation (and not as an essence that is elevated above instances) (Deleuze and Guattari 1987: 310). And, also like Deleuze and Guattari's concept of the refrain, the very rhythm that marks out the earth is the same rhythm that can become deterritorialised, either as a seemingly rigid and imprisoning system of marks (the despotism of the signifier) or through a higher and inhuman poeisis that opens out to the cosmos. The resonances between Miller's early work on Hopkins, and Deleuze and Guattari's aesthetic, are timely: both are inflected by Duns Scotus's problem of immanence, and a world that sings the glory of a God that is nothing other than expressiveness, and both are directed against the flattening of inscription to a single human-all-too-human level of language.

The Anthropocene has levelled out just this problem of inscription: for many in Anthropocene studies the geological strata that indicated the history of man allowed all other forms of textuality to be subsumed as marks of a single human history. Clive Hamilton insists that climate change inaugurates a new hardcore realism (Hamilton 2017). Dipesh Chakrabarty (2009) insists that the realisation of the Anthropocene should generate a negative universal history: at the end of time we realise what we have been all along. Accordingly, the witnessing of possible catastrophe has become a way of generating a single imperative: the geological scale signals one story, one in which the very 'man' who destroyed the earth must become its saviour and survivor. 'The Wreck of the Deutschland' offers another modality of witnessing that is poised impossibly between reading – witnessing marks that cut into the flow of sense – and annihilative rupture, or being lashed by what one sees.

One of the ways the Anthropocene has been domesticated and has allowed for a rejuvenation of literalisms has been by one strata of inscription acting as the ground for all the others: suddenly there is a single Anthropos whose unified history has marked the planet at a geological level. As Miller points out, the predicament of the Anthropocene is made up of multiple and divergent registers of inscription. Rather than phenomenalisation, or a simple acceptance that the world is readable to produce a single sense, Miller insists on unreadability, where inscription cuts into the too easy belief that one can sort the world into hardcore facts versus fake news: 'Ideology is a confusion of linguistic with natural reality as the latter appears to our eyes, ears, taste, and touch. In my terms here, ideology means taking a lie, a citational construction, as true in reality so-defined' (Miller 2016: 142). Unreadability is not only the system of signification within which we speak and think, but includes the cuts, marks and breaks of the body and its milieu. 'The Wreck of the Deutschland' is a poem about unreadability in a general and also quite singular manner. The event of the wreck is itself a cut in the world, an unreadable catastrophe, despite the Job-like addresses of the narrator. It cuts into the ship's journey, the sense of the world's justice, and the narrator's very self as he witnesses – by way of the poem as testimony – the nun's standing apart, seeming to demand some type of interpretation, and yet majestic precisely because of her resistance to the general sense of wreckage. Even she, though, is majestic because her very skeleton becomes the site of divine intrusion:

> Ah, touched in your bower of bone
> Are you! turned for an exquisite smart,
> Have you! make words break from me here all alone,
> Do you! – mother of being in me, heart.
> O unteachably after evil, but uttering truth,
> Why, tears! is it? tears; such a melting, a madrigal start!
> Never-eldering revel and river of youth,
> What can it be, this glee? the good you have there of your own?

At once touched and turned, the nun seems to make words break, as though the poetry of this type of perception destroys recognition; it is precisely in being touched from elsewhere that the nun is also there on her own. Throughout the poem we encounter what Miller noticed in the early Hopkins: a sense of the integrity of every perception, as though each aspect of the world unfolded to its own infinite, and as if each perception were itself marking the world, causing words to break: 'Hopkins' experience of nature as inscaped leads to a vision of the universe as a great multiude of strongly patterned things. There are throngs of each kind, and all of each kind are alike, and rhyme, but each throng is apparently unrelated to any of the others. Nature is organized but only partially' (Miller 1963: 294). This is accompanied also by a contrary sense of difference, where precisely because of that distinction – or the highly singular nature of every aspect of existence – it can appear as indistinct. In the lines above, utterance and unteachabiity, melting and madrigals combine. We do not have the concepts or words to mark the complexity of existence; this is at once the challenge of poetics, where cutting into language tears it away from the everyday sense of things.

This is what makes Hopkins a poet of the unreadability of the Anthropocene. As 'The Wreck of the Deutschland' testifies to a single catastrophe, the nature that is witnessed intimates a force beyond any human reckoning, as if the destruction of the present were always apocalyptic, about to tear nature apart to reveal its justice that is also injustice. All the fragments of a world that is being dismembered offer themselves as sacrificial signs of a promised unity that never arrives. The spirit of the nuns is not of this world; their death is a sign of another world, while also marking out the way in which heaven – in this event – is 'astrew' in the world:

> Loathed for a love men knew in them,
> Banned by the land of their birth,
> Rhine refused them, Thames would ruin them;
> Surf, snow, river and earth
> Gnashed: but thou art above, thou Orion of light;
> Thy unchancelling poising palms were weighing the worth,
> Thou martyr-master: in thy sight
> Storm flakes were scroll-leaved flowers, lily showers – sweet heaven was
>   astrew in them.

In this respect 'The Wreck of the Deutschland' continues the post-apocalyptic tradition that runs (at least) from Mary Shelley's *The Last Man* to the present. Witnessing an end sharpens the urgency of living on. In contemporary post-apocalyptic culture, it is because the species is threatened with destruction that one heroic narrative after another replays the human capacity to step back from the brink of annihilation. This occurs both in Shelley's *The Last Man*, where Lionel's witnessing of the end, with all the failures of grand heroism, leaves him as the last man who can then perceive the world anew. In 'The Wreck of the

Deutschland' the poet/narrator's witnessing of the nobility of the end – the nun's capacity to embrace annihilation as a form of elevation – is at once a form of salvation, but also, and more importantly, a severing of redemption. Unlike the dominant tone in Anthropocene studies, where realisation of the destruction of the planet generates a single narrative, a unified 'we' and an imperative to live on, 'The Wreck of the Deutschland' cannot include the series of positive destructions it narrates in its own reckoning of sense. The poet/narrator views both the souls who simply struggle and fall to death, and the defiantly death-embracing nuns, recognising the distance, difficulty and dread of the divinity that marks out the world, and yet fails to appear. What makes 'The Wreck of the Deutschland' radically post-apocalyptic is what Miller identifies as unreadability pushed to its limits. The very form of the poem cuts into its own sense, not offering the triumph of witnessing, where viewing the end allows one to be somehow elevated. 'The Wreck of the Deutschland' destroys the logic of the Anthropocene whereby destruction generates a coherent point of view of survival; instead, what it witnesses are multiple losses and violences, all of them given as assaults that seem at once to promise grace and yet deny its arrival. This is not a scene of destruction that generates a humanity to come; this is an event that isolates every witness, ending any sense of coherence.

The Anthropocene – as a geological record that will finally restore and save humanity – is pre-empted and severed in 'The Wreck of the Deutschland': to witness an end, to see a force of destruction that opens up the complacency of life, is to unleash an inhuman and untimely force. Hopkins's God is not simply hard to grasp. He takes hold of the human, binds it back to its visceral materiality, destroying any easy recuperation. What occurs in 'The Weck of the Deutschland' is reading: the poet witnesses an event that at once marks him, but that also appears as a series of violent marks. The ethics of this reading is one of diremption, of not passing from the witnessing of catastrophe to its recuperation. Instead one is left with rereading, with traces that remain of marks.

It is the encounter with the text, the burden of being placed in a predicament of reading, that captures the structure of ethics: in the absence of a foundation or ground for the sense we make of a text, when all we have is the text in its isolation, every event of reading is a decision. And yet, what one refers to when one speaks about texts and reading is, in the tradition that runs from Romanticism to Miller himself, not the human-produced book but non-human systems and rhythms; if enlightenment transcendental idealism insists on the systems through which we order and represent the world, post-enlightenment difference is something we encounter. In this sense Miller continues a tradition that he identifies in Wordsworth, Keats and Hopkins: 'the self is formed not through inter-personal relations but through experiences of non-human nature, experiences which simply ignore the existence of other human beings' (Miller 1955: 306). That description of Hopkins's relation to nature, and the possibility of intuiting the datum itself, to then capture and memorialise that singularity in text might be fairly applied to Miller's deconstruction, despite everything that has been said about deconstruction not acknowledging anything outside the text. It is perhaps not surprising that literary deconstruction found a home in Romanticism: the sense of our lost origin being the effect of inscription, along with poetry itself as abundant recompense, was in line with Derrida's notion of necessary impossibility. Our finite experience of the world intimates an infinity we cannot erase, and yet any sense of the infinite is given from this world and its sublime intimation of something far more deeply interfused. This would be why Derrida recognised that concepts (in their repeatability) operate by creating a force that exceeds any present while Derrida also deformed that power of concepts by creating inscriptive disruptions that would foreground the materiality of the letter. But Derridean materiality was always inscriptive materiality, words like '*differance*' or other Joycean variations were ways of thinking conceptuality's (and thought's) dependence on systems of difference, on spacing, deferral and delay. Such a materiality is not matter; it is the differential movement, or radically passive synthesis, by which something like matter comes into being. In this respect deconstruction extends a Kantian tradition of liberal formalism; we cannot know things in themselves, and it would be irresponsible to speak in a godly manner, as if we had a direct grasp of the world. We know, and speak, and judge always with others and in the absence of any directly given foundation. What we live through are relations, relations that will always defer any imagined pure justice, democracy or law, which would always remain 'to come'.

This materiality without matter, a condition of being situated within relations that intimate a ground that one must assume but never grasp, is profoundly akin to the ways in which Miller describes writers like Gerard Manley Hopkins in *The Disappearance of God*. There is at one and the same time a sense of the urgency and powerful presence of nature in itself, along with an ongoing loss, distance and immediacy due to our creaturely finitude. Yet I would argue that for all that similarity between Derrida and Miller there is a subtle and important difference between a deconstruction of differential inscription that emerges from phenomenology and the conditions of knowing the world, and Hillis Miller's deconstruction that is generated from an encounter with

Victorian poetics. In *The Ethics of Reading* Miller gives an account of matter, not as that which is produced through inscription (as something we must presuppose, after the event, as a prior ground) but as a far more positive materiality. That is, one might contrast a highly critical post-Kantian deconstruction – where we only know what is through relations – to a Leibnizian mode where relations proliferate from a materiality that is always given positively in all its expressions. Here, we might note that even though many consign high deconstruction to the 1980s (particularly the Yale school with which Miller is associated) it is Kantian critique that has survived in the twenty-first century. For all the reaction against Judith Butler, her insistence on performativity – that we become who we are, with the bodies that matter, through repetition of norms – dominates how we think of sexual identity. Against that critical tradition, one might think of all the appeals to the work of Gilles Deleuze, for whom differences are positive; differences emerge from a matter that endlessly generates traces and tracks that are never matter itself. Miller, writing after James, draws attention to matter as that which appears as the field of snow across which one walks, such that one's footsteps do not create the space but are nevertheless made possible – necessary – by the matter one is required to traverse: 'It is rather a blank field of "matter" to be traversed' (Miller 1987: 111). If one is narrating a story, one needs to somehow get across a space of matter (both get across in terms of traversing space, but also get across in terms of communication). Narration is like tracking through snow; it doesn't create the snow, but it does mark it out. And to say that the snow or field is undifferentiated is not to say that one can narrate the story in any manner one likes, but that every track is a decision as just how to take each step:

> The vision is of what James calls 'the clear matter' of the story, that is it is a vision of the wall itself, in one image, or of shining snow, in the other. It is a vision of that against which both the shadow and the silhouette are projected. Or, in the other image, it is a vision of that undifferentiated field across which he walks either in the first written version or in the 're-vision', which is James' name for the act of re-reading his earlier writings. The story itself is a patterned or differentiated representation of the unpatterned and undifferentiated, the clear matter in the sense of a field without marks or discriminations. . . .
>
> If the matter, that field of shining unmarked snow, is at the same time the 'matter' of the story in the sense that one speaks of underlying intrigue or archetypal fable, the footprints in the snow, as opposed to the synchronic image of the shadow cast on the wall, suggest a temporal progress from here to there, like the 'march' of a story. Each footprint might be thought of as corresponding to a word, a phrase or an episode, as the writer traces

out a trajectory across the untrodden 'matter', or to use another of James' words for it, the 'thing' of which the story is the narrative, relation or written account. If the best writing is a species of 'vision' of this 'shining expanse of snow', or in James' admirable phrase for it later, 'fields of light', the later re-reading is a 'revision', but not in the sense of re-writing. (Miller 1987: 113)

One might think of deconstruction then as having two tendencies or inflections, different ways of thinking about difference. The first, which would definitely have resonance in Victorian poetics, would be a critical deconstruction that might come close to a negative theology. Here, one must always be oriented towards some presence or revelation that is presupposed by the very structure of appearances (because appearances are always appearances of . . .), but such presence is always deferred, given through the differences that intimate its insistence and persistence. By contrast, there would be another deconstruction, one that would be neither located within differences (forever distanced from presence) nor like all the new realisms abandoning the differential, material or inscriptive condition. This deconstruction would, like Miller's description of reading and rereading, be oriented to the matters, fields, shadows, tracks and steps that proliferate, and that we both decide to take in order to make our way, while also being drawn to that very matter as that which must be crossed. Rereading is not some passive repetition of that tracking but an ongoing decision and predicament of negotiating the matters we have crossed. We might say that reading and rereading give us a cartography as much as an ethics (and the hint of Deleuzianism is deliberate). Matter is there to be traversed, and the traversal is (as Deleuze and Guattari also argued) a map and not a tracing (Deleuze and Guattari 1987: 11): we make, mark, step and inscribe our way, for matter itself is there to be traversed, and yet the path we take (the steps we take in narration) is not determined in advance. Once we make those steps they are at once ours, but also not ours, for neither the matter of the field nor the patterns that we deploy emerge ex nihilo. This is not a modernist ethic or aesthetic of artist as creator ex nihilo, nor of the subject as self-made work of art. If we read, walk, trace, step or mark (and one should think of marking in the sense of making an inscription, but also of taking note, and of marking time), one has both decided one's path, drawn across the field that is before us, while also casting shadows that we may not see but that nevertheless compose matter's visual field.

This takes us to a different Victorian poetics, one that I first noticed in the path that Miller traces across his reading of Gerard Manley Hopkins. We are at once caught by what we see; we do not (as some cartoon versions of deconstruction would have it) structure the world according to our language. On the contrary, what we encounter prompts a mark. And there is not a self who composes the field of differences before them; one simply is whatever emerges from being caught by the matters that elicit the distinct perceptions we have of them. Poetry, for Hopkins, becomes the burden of capturing visual matters in verbal matters. This is a Victorianism, not of negative theology, forever distanced from presence, but of an earth that is teeming with life and difference, an earth that is being fruitful and multiplying. In the first stage of Miller's reading of Hopkins there is this highly non-Kantian, joyous multiplicity of differences that generates and demands an equally rich creation of verbal matters. Language does not organise or even mirror the world; rather, the world gives itself to be felt, sensed and marked, with words being bound up with the world's self-marking. The world sings the glory of itself. Again, we seem closer to Deleuze than to Derrida: differences giving themselves to be marked, perceptions opening out singular worlds. There is a simple reason for that resonance. When Miller writes on Hopkins he picks up on the Victorian poet's debt to Duns Scotus, the thinker to whom Deleuze attributed the philosophy of immanence. In the tradition of the philosophy of immanence every aspect of the world intimates a sense of the whole. It is not that there is some order that grants the world its sense and value – some transcendent God that we can think, imagine, pray to, but never know – but rather that everything sings the glory of God, and God gives himself forth in each and every one of his varied expressions. Language would not then be, as it is in the Kantian critical tradition, a condition of difference that enables the synthesis of the world but that itself forever recedes from being sensed. Words, as much as things, have their own singular being. And, as Miller makes clear in his reading of Hopkins, it's the task of poetry to have the singularity (rather than generality) of words shine forth.

I would argue, then, that there are two potentialities of deconstruction that cannot be neatly set apart or attributed to distinct authors but that nevertheless mark important tendencies. First, there is the deconstruction that has – with the advent of new materialisms and affect studies – been consigned to a limited and primarily critical mode of reading, where all we can know are texts and differences, and where the only politics is one of a promissory 'to come'. Second, though, is a deconstruction of positive materiality. Rather than *differance* as an operation that intimates but also precludes presence, materiality is at once so singular as to be deadening and yet in that very separation or refusal of the coherence of relationality it bears a more sublime form of expression: not a standard Kantian sublime of what must be thought but not known, but a sublimity of inhuman refusal:

> If every specter, as we have amply seen, is distinguished from spirit by an incorporation, by the phenomenal form of a quasi-incarnation, then Christ is the most spectral of specters. . . . I suspect de Man and Derrida would read Marx in almost the same way. I say 'almost' because Derrida was tempted much more than was de Man by the lure of some 'wholly other' and by what he called 'a messianic without messianism' . . . This formulation attempts to avoid any belief in an actual Messiah to come, any belief in the Incarnation. It is still, nevertheless, tempted by the messianic. De Man would not, I imagine, have altogether agreed with Derrida's formulations. Nevertheless, a reading of Marx by de Man, I suspect, if he had done one, would have stressed, as Derrida does explicitly in *Specters of Marx*, that for Marx the source of all ideological delusions is the spectral and baseless mystification of religious belief. More specifically, all ideological aberrations are modeled on belief in the Incarnation, that is, belief that in Christ the Word spirit and matter were conjoined (Miller 2014: 143)

It is this second mode of deconstruction, materiality and sublimity that allows us to draw a connection between Miller's early work on Hopkins, his ethics of reading and the later writings on the Anthropocene. Briefly, what runs through all these strands in Miller's writing is a quite distinct notion of reading. A straightforward Kantian/liberal/deconstructive mode would insist that any event of reading, no matter how much context, biography, archival detail and attention we have, would ultimately be undecidable, precisely because reading is always a decision. (I quite deliberately tie one mode of deconstruction to liberalism on this aspect alone: anti-foundationalism. In the absence of anything other than the text itself and any surrounding particulars we choose to take into consideration, all we have is the decision of reading.) What Miller's reading of Hopkins (and Miller's work on reading more generally) brings into play is a force of materiality that troubles the heightened responsibility of readerly decision. Yes, we are compelled to read and reread, and yes each event of reading is singular and emerges from a range of potentialities. The Derridean emphasis on futurity, promise and radical alterity is replaced or displaced in Miller's work by the disappearance of futurity. In Hopkins, for example, every perception, every affect, every word and every inflection does seem to open out to the infinite, but at exactly the same time, that passage to infinity and the burdensome divinity of everything is utterly unmanageable. It catches us but cannot be grasped, and the sheer multiplicity and fecundity of the universe can be so rich and godly as to paralyse us, to preclude speaking, to cut off anything other than the exquisite singularity of the present.

In a heavy-handed and somewhat violent manner I would like to draw two rough contrasts: first, between a reading focused on decision in the face of undecidability (Derrida) and a reading that is always rereading, always mired or bogged down in the tracks it makes through the matter of the text (Miller). Second: there would be a contrast between writing as that which exists as some quasi-transcendental inscriptive force, such that we would never know presence itself but only its promise and deferral, as opposed to writing as something menacing, enclosing, destructive and radically counter-historical. Writing would not simply be that within which we think, experience and act, but would operate in an uncanny, menacing and dissolute manner. One way of summarising deconstruction in general would be to think of it as a refusal of relationality. The notion that experience is present to itself, and might be proximate to itself in speech or introspection, is displaced by the problem of difference. In order for anything at all to be it must bear some relation to itself, whether we think of that as a relation through time, continuing to be the same or relatively same thing, or space, continuing to occupy this field or region. Relations require distance, and so sameness relies upon at least some minimal non-identity. But there is a slight inflection to the different ways in which non-relationality panned out. Derrida increasingly thought of iterability as generating ever more open, promissory and (ideally) just futures. Miller, especially in his focus on reading and the reading of Hopkins, draws attention to poetry's capacity to do quite the opposite of opening to futurity. This might seem to be a counter-ethics, if we think of ethics as some type of ethos; what emerges – to take the example from Hopkins and the way Miller picks up on instress – is the force of singularities, bits of matter, that are possibly like tracks across snow, but not connecting to a path or exit so much as forcing us to a halt. Yes, a word can open out to the world, but the more we try to get poetry to be singular and catch this moment of world, the more poetry will be a trail of wreckage, a monument to what has been lost or cannot ever have been captured. In *Twilight of the Anthropocene Idols* Miller reminds us of the inscription of reality: the financial crisis, carbon emissions, ocean acidification and extinction rates are issued with the same inscriptive force as climate change denial, supposed weapons of mass destruction and the refusal to believe that Barack Obama was born in America. No leap out of textuality is possible, or desirable. Rather than fight alternative facts with facts outside inscription, which is not possible, all that is left for us to do is attend to reading matters and intensify, rather than diminish, the rigours of textuality, inscription and reading. If we follow Miller following de Man and think of ideology as the refusal of the distance and difference between inscription and appearance, if we insist on what simply is in the clear light of day, then we erase the composition of the real. What happens, as Miller presciently suggested quite recently (but before the advent of the

Trumpocene) is a new literalism where facts, fake news and alternative facts get hurled across lines without negotiation, without reading. But one needs to be careful here with what one means by reading. One mode would be liberal (and would explain why Derrida and Habermas could ultimately achieve a rapprochement): with competing discourses and no foundation all we can do is enter into discussion with an ideal of consensus even if such unity would never arrive. By contrast, what Miller produces as reading is far more destructive: whatever unproblematic, self-evident and unquestionable facts and verities we think might give us common ground, including those idealities that might provide some futural or messianic hope, are bound up with inscription. Even though one cannot conflate the writers who catch Miller's attention with Miller himself (and even though the notion of 'Miller himself' or any writer speaking for themselves is impossible) it is worth noting this point about Hopkins: what holds the world all together is rhyme. There is neither a foundational principle that one might posit prior to difference, nor some ideal or regulatory unity 'to come'. Rhyme is an intimation of likeness with difference and, according to Miller, is related to Hopkins's peculiar theory of life and/as aesthetics. If evolution were simply the random mutation and then selection of differences, what emerges would be statistical regularities. If, however, there are forms towards which difference and movement tend, then it would follow that the proliferation of language would bear the same similarity within difference of all of life's forms. This might seem to be at odds with everything we have come to think of as poststructuralism, but that is only so if we have a very linguistic conception of difference and inscription. Deleuze, for example, followed Raymond Ruyer and Henri Bergson in thinking of evolution not as the selection of random variations but as the outcome of ever more subtle tendencies towards difference (Deleuze 1994). Difference was positive – productive of variation – rather than negative (the differences between terms that emerge only through negation). Rather than think of selfish genes, or basic units that will triumph regardless of larger forms, evolution is a tending towards forms, precisely because of the eternal possibilities or potentialities those forms possess. There is nothing necessary about any living form, but if there were to be a form that possessed language, vision, archives, history and life as it has come to be, it would probably have an eye that sees, hands that grasp and write and touch. Miller, reading through Hopkins, notes that the conception of rhyme as expressive of the order of the world is in line with a certain Platonism, the endurance of forms towards which life tends. As I have already suggested, this is Miller reading Hopkins, but as Miller notes in his work on the ethics of reading, the paths we make through texts are not determined in advance. What was it about Hopkins's poetry, and a certain mode of Victorian aesthetics, that allowed Miller to discern a new mode of difference and life that would eventually carry through into very specific questions about the materiality of inscription, climate change and the Anthropocene?

One of the reasons why deconstruction might seem to have failed the twenty-first century is the intensely open sense of futurity and ideality. If we can think of justice, forgiveness, democracy or friendship 'to come', this is because once a word is inscribed it has the possibility to open new contexts; one could never close down the possibilities of any of these terms, nor cite any one instance as justice as such, forgiveness as such, and so on. This is why Derrida writes so often of necessary impossibility: one cannot close down the thought of justice, and yet the fulfilment of the term will never arrive. In some ways such an ethics is sublime, and akin to a certain modality of late Romanticism: everywhere we are given intimations of a plenitude, spirit or force that is irreducible to this world, and yet all such positings are bound up with the finitude of the world, always deferred. Another mode of deconstruction would attend less to the idealities made possible by inscription, and focus instead on the non-human materiality of inscription. In *Twilight of the Anthropocene Idols* Miller looks to all the ways in which inscription exceeds comprehension. Rather than tracing the passage from word to spirit, from text to abundant futurity, the matters from inscription would be destructive of our temporalities and the notion of the only future being that of the human imagination. The very chastening mode of Hopkins poetry is at once tied to a God whose force expresses itself supremely in the visceral force of language, while also cutting off any human-all-too-human demands for a futurity of ownness.

Today, when there is so much passion for the post-Apocalyptic, and when the Anthropocene has yielded a proliferation of narratives that see the threat to the earth as an imperative for human triumph – where we will survive, we must survive – it is worth looking back at Miller's Hopkins. Here, the formal power of poetry destroys any possibility of the post-apocalyptic: the stress and pressure of inscription take us away from the parochial, towards the catastrophic.

Chapter 6

Walter Pater in the Wilderness
Megan Becker-Leckrone

> Walter Pater is the grandfather of whom his grandchildren are not always entirely proud.
> J. Hillis Miller, *The Johns Hopkins Guide to Literary Criticism and Theory*[1]

> The wager, ultimately, is that we can expand our repertoire of critical moods while embracing a richer array of critical methods. Why – even as we extol multiplicity, difference, hybridity – is the affective range of criticism so limited? Why are we so hyperarticulate about our adversaries and so excruciatingly tongue-tied about our loves?
> Rita Felski, *The Limits of Critique* (2015)[2]

> A book is a machine to think with.
> I. A. Richards, *Principles of Literary Criticism* (1924)[3]

It's easy to track the re-emergence of Walter Pater as a figure of study for literary critics of differing persuasions, but harder to trace his role among literary critics, as himself part of the history of literary critical theory. I am intrigued by Pater's role in the formalist, objectivist, largely Anglo-American New Critical theory that dominated criticism for the first half of the twentieth century – even if that role is a ghostly one, more easily identified by the contours of its absence than in invocations serving serious discursive engagements or theoretical critique.[4] I am interested in Walter Pater's strange exile-in-place within the English literary critical canon in the first half of the twentieth century and his reemergence from it in the second. My hypothesis is that Pater suffered less for being aesthetically out of step with literary high modernism than for being philosophically out of step with the criticism's hard positivist turn – toward avowedly practical, quantitative, even 'scientific' methods for approaching literary or aesthetic study – in the first half of the twentieth century. When J. Hillis Miller asserts that 'Nietzsche is the Pater of the German-speaking world' or Geoffrey Hartman observes that T. S. Eliot's real problem with Pater was not that he was insufficiently modernist, but insufficiently English, they gloss a similar point: Pater is not entirely at home with his fellows.[5] The dominant discourse of twentieth-century criticism had no place for Pater, at times manifestly expressed with dismissiveness or disdain, but more often only latently detectable in uncanny absences and odd rhetorical negotiations that tell a significant story about critical history, highly readable, though lately, rarely read. Returning to that story, really reading it, tells us something about not just a critical encounter, but a *missed encounter* nearly a century ago, as literary critics were endeavouring to found a discipline. It offers suggestive insights about some of the critical encounters in our own moment, as literary critics ponder how and whether the discipline can be saved.

To be sure, Pater's prescription for finding specific instances of beauty in the data of one's own consciousness may have had little to offer new critical efforts to legitimise literary study as a discipline in its own right and to establish iterable principles for its practice and pedagogy. The actually heterogeneous projects of critics we generally regard as New Critical – those of T. S. Eliot, I. A. Richards, William Wimsatt, Cleanth Brooks, Monroe Beardsley, John Crowe Ransom, Yvor Winters, René Wellek and others – have at least this judgement in common. But there are other discontinuities at play as well, and because Pater's work has never been easy to categorise, this encounter offers a particularly rich site for understanding a number of clashes, indeed deep schisms, between the fairly open and heterogeneous 'schools' of criticism and theory within literature departments and the supposedly originary departments from which they had emerged. We have understood for a long time that it is no accident that, in so many Anglophone universities today, psychologists don't read Sigmund Freud and philosophers don't read Jacques Derrida. Because Pater is British, Victorian, and literary, famous and influential in his own century, his reemergence in the English departments of the twentieth and twenty-first centuries is less conspicuously analogous to those dislocations. But in fact, the same intellectual rift, the continental drift, that created such exiles had, decades earlier, made one of Pater as well. Each has, in past decades, not simply found havens in literature departments, but become a dynamic force driving literary criticism in his own right. What, then, are we to make of Walter Pater's long exile from and robust return to the scholarly discipline that, for him, and to borrow his phrasing, would seem 'most home-like'?

A familiar, persuasive answer to that question is that a critical revaluation 'after the New Criticism' newly embraced Pater's subjectivist thick description as a way of reacting against the objectivist experiment and the limits of formalism.[6] Pater's criticism fell out of step with the formalising New Criticism that would supplant it, then once again found sympathy with the poststructuralist, phenomenological or deconstructive turns of a subsequent generation of literary critics. Myriad transformations of method, scope, canonicity and self-definition within nineteenth-century studies, too, offered his work a newly hospitable disciplinary environment and more receptive readership. Pater was brought back into the fold, along with so many other neglected figures, because the tyranny of T. S. Eliot's taste-making, for example, had run its course and a recalibration was in order: less Coleridge, more Wordsworth. The commonsense understanding of intellectual history as a longstanding dialectic, loosely speaking, thesis and antithesis, repetition with a difference, offers a serviceable rubric for all of the above explanations. For other reasons too, this critical metanarrative feels familiar – philosophically, poetically and, not least, similar to Pater's signature mingling of the two. It calls to mind both Socrates' banishment of poetry from his *Republic*, for failing to make a logical defense, outside its gates, for 'her' readmission, and Aristotle's 'reversal and recognition', the constitutive elements of a complex plot. And as always seems the case, Pater's analysis, in *Plato and Platonism* and elsewhere, of both the creation and legacy of Plato's 'philosophical literature' maps out an exemplary model for understanding his own: 'the seemingly new is old also', has 'already lived and died many times over', its 'life-giving principle' readable in 'the expressiveness which familiar thoughts attain by novel expression' (2–3, *Plato and Platonism*). But while all of these explanations hold some truth, they are not complete.

The story of an intellectual's misreading by his inheritors is one of our culture's oldest, and it would be unremarkable if Pater's wilderness years among the New Critics were only that, only a stint of exile while what he had to offer went out of fashion. Pater did not simply return to critical discourse as part of some eternal cycle, some familiar dialectic, however, but by another and less likely path. Examining Pater's place among those most dogmatically invested in the 'newness' of the discipline's critical principles and practice in the twentieth century reminds us that what sets their positions apart cannot be reduced to relative coordinates on the subjectivist/objectivist spectrum of aesthetic debate. Neither his exile nor his return should be explained away as merely reactionary.

Attending to this distinction guards against the widespread error of assuming that because certain premises (and, in notable cases, the politics) of these critics were 'conservative', they were not also radical, even extreme, that they did not represent a profound interruption to the long history of criticism, not just an especially influential dialogic instance within it. Indeed, the most influential of these critics often self-consciously represented their ideas in this way: as utterly and transformatively new, their break from the past not just deliberate but inevitable. Theirs was not merely a principled rejection of the past, but a disavowal of its existence, a rejection of its validity not just *in theory*, but *as theory*.

In *The Theory Mess*, Herman Rapaport hypothesises that 'the New Criticism was aberrant in its presuppositions that its mode of criticism could be more systematic and rigorous that the critical trends of the nineteenth century' (17).[7] As Rapaport's retrospective distance suggests, there is an enormous difference between the radicality I wish to identify and that which certain New Critics claim for themselves. Reading the ghostly inscription of Pater in their discourse of radicalism – of rupture with the past, genealogical divorce from the aesthetic tradition, rewriting the terms of the debate, delegitimising the questions that preoccupied their forebears, ventriloquising his texts in service of arguments he would never support – lends clarity to both the ambitions of their critical project and the significant implications of its attempt. In identifying the Paterian adumbrations in the work of I. A. Richards, for example, and even more, by isolating his most starkly anti-Paterian assertions, we can see precisely why it is accurate to call these presuppositions 'aberrant', and why we should bother to notice that they are. Ironically, though, we have long since homogenised the voluminous discourse that emerged around and in the wake of I. A. Richards' earliest claims for a 'science' of criticism and a 'psychology' of literature in *Science and Poetry* (1923) and *The Principles of Literary Criticism* (1924). In fact, we have all but levelled out the complex response to these works, including the many who critiqued his premises and methods or otherwise distinguish their positions from his, and now tend to treat New Criticism, to the extent that we consider it at all, as one collective effort to elaborate and refine his *Principles*, to perform the practice of his *Practical Criticism* (1929), the famous book Richards describes in the 'Preface' to *Principles of Literary Criticism* as its 'companion volume' (x). Thus, in the strong sense that Rita Felski describes, and as the vitiating standardisation of his practice has ironically come to reflect, Richards founded 'a repertoire of critical moods' that supposed itself devoid of mood, that literally made limiting the 'affective range of criticism' the inevitable choice and self-regulating ideal of a grand, unifying epistemology, a would-be scientific revolution. It is important to note that Richards did not see his critical endeavour as merely different from Pater's in taste, method or outlook. He saw it as part of a fortuitous and unprecedented moment in human history that rendered Pater – and not only Pater, but almost everyone and everything along with him – obsolete. Richards did not set out, in other words, to *distinguish* himself from Pater; he sought to *extinguish* him.

That Pater has vitally emerged from the diminished status to which the New Critics relegated him is precisely what lends force to a new comparative analysis. In our current moment, contemporary readers are more familiar with Pater's writing than with anything but the most anthologised specimens of New Criticism. Most often, their rejection of Pater and everything he stood for is offered in genial announcements that, while the aesthetic tradition has for centuries been the province of amateurs, serious people are finally ready to intervene. But if we are attuned to the rhythms and force, the openness and eclecticism of Pater's writing, with his accreted, capacious sense of history, in which unlike things can coexist without anything being lost, with his unusually nuanced figures for the vicissitudes of consciousness, we can read just how jarringly unlike him his inheritors are in every way. We can return to the New Critics their bracing strangeness, including a relationship to the past that, dressed up as positivism, at times comes close to nihilism.

In an intellectual climate invested in defining literary studies as an autonomous discipline by clearly articulating what it was not, the obscure aims of Pater's 'appreciations', 'imaginary portraits', and 'studies in art and poetry' appear out of step and fashion in every way. The dense, poetic prose of Pater's 'aesthetic criticism', where '[n]ot the fruit of experience but experience itself, is the end', was utterly at odds with a project, however diversely realised, suspicious of such ecstasies and convinced of their incompatibility with the newly prized aims of 'practical' and 'pragmatic' reading practices, grounded in principles that could be put widely into use and motivated by specific, positivist understandings of what a very narrowly defined 'aesthetics', 'linguistics' and 'psychology' had to offer this endeavour.[8] Every facet of his heirs' critical project runs counter to the moods and methods of Pater's 'critical spirit', to use his phrase. His epistemic understanding of what 'the aesthetic' is, to what tradition it belongs, what he is doing when he reads, writes, expresses, feels: these are, in remarkable and underappreciated ways, torn asunder by the generation of critics after Pater who sought to systematise this business of, as Ransom famously put it, 'Criticism, Inc.'[9] It was not simply that Pater's influences, interests, style and sensibility seemed old-fashioned; nor that maintaining the ecstasy of the 'hard, gem-like flame' no longer felt like a critic's highest priority. (Although all of those things are also true.) According to the New Critics, what Pater was doing was not criticism at all.

*

I borrow my essay's title from Geoffrey Hartman's 1980 book, *Criticism in the Wilderness: The Study of Literature Today*, which he borrows from the rueful conclusion to Matthew Arnold's 'Function of Criticism at the Present Time'. It also serves as Hartman's epigraph.[10] In his account, what Pater called 'aesthetic criticism' or the 'critical spirit' belongs to the intellectual tradition that brought us Nietzsche and Freud, but also Lukács, Benjamin, Adorno and Derrida. 'It makes a difference whether philosophical texts are also considered literary texts,' writes Hartman, and he sides with considerations that attend to that 'also', for all of the names listed above. Identifying a troubling continental divide, he wonders 'how these critical traditions grew apart . . . to identify the forces driving their increasing alienation from each other' and 'whether mediation is possible'. Hartman asks, at his own present time:

> Why so little exegetical daring? Why were historical and critical studies further apart than ever? Why the gulf between *philosophic* criticism and *practical* criticism, the former flourishing in Continental Europe, the later insulating the writings of English and American teachers? When we set Arnold beside Nietzsche, or set Eliot, Richards, and Leavis beside Lukács, Benjamin, and Valéry, the differences cannot be overlooked.[11]

He finds his answer in what he calls the 'colorful past' of critics like Pater. They are practitioners of a 'creative criticism', of 'intense and focused philosophy' that nevertheless dares to be 'brilliant' – witty, stylised, self-conscious, enthusiastic; in a word, creative – in all of the ways Eliot finds excessive, even dangerous (190–1). Eliot handles Pater's brilliance first-hand by snuffing it out, creating a straw man he can summarily dismiss.

Hartman cites Georg Lukács' 1910 text, 'The Nature and Form of the Essay', for understanding just what possibilities the 'new philosophic criticism' might hold, with a 'scope that . . . seems to stand in a complex and even crossover relation to both art and philosophy'.[12] Set against Eliot's assertion in 'The Function of Criticism' (1923) that criticism can never be truly creative because it must always be *about* another thing, along with the larger push by I. A. Richards and others for 'a stricter, more principled, even "scientific"' ground for examining art, Lukács' early essay poses a 'diverted question' about the link between 'the status of the essay' and 'the inner tendency of all reflective, self-critical discourse' (189, 191–2). That 'tendency' has the weight of all philosophy on its side, if one recognises there is an essentially 'literary form to philosophy' and that its first great practitioner was Plato. This idiosyncratic reading of Plato as a 'philosophic essayist' draws directly from Pater's *Plato and Platonism* (1893), a book that demonstrates the breadth of philosophical knowledge, both classical and modern. Asking whether criticism could ever be a science or if it qualifies as art, Lukács' startlingly Paterian essay – rife with references to Pater himself, the Renaissance and 'Winckelmann's dreams of Greece' – answers with dynamic ambivalence, acknowledging the necessity of a 'science of the arts' but claiming it is something all the 'greatest essayists ... transcend' (13). Lukács writes: 'I speak, of course, of Plato, the greatest essayist who ever lived or wrote, the one who wrested everything from life as it unfolded before his eyes and who therefore needed no mediated medium; the one who was able to connect his questions, the most profound questions ever asked, with life as lived' (13).[13] Hartman emphasises the 'peculiar twist of intellectual history' by which, as a consequence of Lukács' encounter with *Plato and Platonism*, this Hungarian Marxist theorist came 'to view the German Romantics, and especially Hegel, through Pater's conception of the Socratic conversation' (191).[14] This first essay in Lukács' first book, written in German, exemplifies the complex genealogies Pater's work posits, claims membership within, and influences in posthumous readers in cross-cultural contexts. It also testifies to the reach of Pater's influence, across the borders of language, nation and century, and serves as a useful contrast to the subsequent encounters I will explore where, much closer to home, the reception was very different.

I agree with Hartman that Pater, after his death and into the twentieth century, falls victim to bad historical timing and gets caught on the wrong side of a decisive 'continental drift', subject to a peculiar mixture of exile and domestication to which Pater's compatriots relegated his work. But it is important to stress that the so-called *philosophic* and *practical* 'gulf' was deliberate and, at the hands of some on Hartman's list, aspired to be absolute. The divisive, suppressive effort calls to mind the memorable etymology lesson that serves as the introduction to Freud's essay 'The Uncanny' (1919). Pater's heirs render him 'home-like' (*heimlich*), but in the double, incompatible sense Freud outlines in the definition that begins his 'aesthetic' exploration:

> *Heimlich*, adj., subst. *Heimlichkeit* (pl. *Helimlichkeiten*): I. Also *heimelich*, *heimelig*, belonging to the house, not strange, familiar, tame, intimate, friendly, etc. ... (*a*) (Obsolete belonging to the house or the family, or regarded as so belonging (cf. Latin *familiaris*, familiar) ...) II. Concealed, kept from sight, so that others do not get to know of or about it, withheld from others.[15]

When J. Hillis Miller casts the problem of Pater's critical legacy as a generational drama, as in my epigraph, he recognises that Pater's 'relation to his precursors and successors is complex', his 'significance for the theory of criticism and for its practice' underappreciated and his reputation chronically susceptible to narratives of 'suppressed influence' (1994: 556). Miller combats such genealogical forces by consistently emphasising the uncanniness of Pater's oeuvre, not just thematically, but structurally. In the language of psychoanalysis, Freud says 'the uncanny [*unheimlich*] is something which is secretly familiar [*heimlich-heimisch*], which has undergone repression and returned from it' (245). Four years before Hartman's book, Miller's essay, 'Walter Pater: A Partial Portrait' (*Daedalus*, 1976), similarly endeavours to remind readers of the richness of Pater's oeuvre, the continental scope of his thought and the genealogical distortions the New Critical *Heimlichkeit* had effected. As I have indicated above, when he calls Nietzsche 'the Pater of the German speaking world', the description is both evaluative and, in a sense, recuperative. To reckon fully with his legacy as not only 'one of the four greatest English literary critics of the nineteenth century', but even more, 'of the four, the most influential in the twentieth century and the most alive today', Miller stresses, is to grapple with discontinuity and displacement. Understanding how Pater's critical 'influence can be found on writers who deny or are ignorant of what they owe to him' while he is at the same time 'a precursor of what is most vital in contemporary criticism' – that is to say, understanding his dual, if not bifurcated, legacy – requires attunement to the strange, familiar unfamiliarity Miller describes.

Tracing Pater's genealogy beyond the borders of his homeland, Miller reminds his readers of the 'filiations' that have always been proper to Pater, but subject to 'suppressed influence' by his critical inheritors. Miller's analysis repatriates Pater among his philosophical, aesthetic and critical fellows; an effort, of course, that is not just geographical but temporal, historical. This effort too summons the logic of the uncanny, which 'leads back to what is known of old and long familiar', but has been forgotten (220).[16] For the most pernicious feature of Pater's decades in the wilderness of Anglo-American criticism, throughout the long dominance they enjoyed, is that it lacked the generosity of imagination to set him free, as it were, to let him 'live' where he had always been most intellectually at home, to reconnect his discourse with both ancient and contemporaneous continental conversations with which he had already been in step from the most fertile years of his career.

When Miller reads Pater as part of the spirit of an age that also produced Emerson and Nietzsche, and of an ancient, still vital philosophical discourse that stretches back to the pre-Socratics, he does so to make a case, fundamentally, for again reading his work carefully and comprehensively, for sticking with him. His 1976 essay, in other words, was as much an act of will as a specimen of criticism. In finding common cause with the mode of criticism Pater engaged, yoking Pater's lifelong interest in the literature of consciousness, Miller highlights the rich discontinuities and aporias that seem to mark the best efforts to figure the self, 'not so much the hidden center of a personality as an enigma exceeding personality' (101). Miller repairs the frayed, if not severed, thread that connects his own critical project with the criticism of the nineteenth century, which nearly half a century of Anglo-American literary critical discourse had actively sought to disrupt. This recuperative act does involve identifying the ways in which Pater's work is not unlike Miller's own, in mood and approach, asserting from the beginning that 'Pater is effective today as a precursor of what is most vital in contemporary criticism,' and even, in the end, suggesting that his work 'can be defined as an exploration and deconstruction of the problematic trope of personification' (97, 112). His more basic imperative, however, is simply to restore Pater's 'major author' status in the English canon and, even more modestly, make a case for reading closely and sticking with his 'great' works:

> Pater's writings, like those of other major authors in the Occidental tradition, are at once open to interpretation and ultimately indecipherable, unreadable. His texts lead the critic deeper and deeper into a labyrinth until he confronts a final aporia. This does not mean, however, that the reader must give up from the beginning the attempt to understand Pater. Only by going all the way into the labyrinth, following the thread of a given clue, can the critic read the blind alley, vacant of any Minotaur, that impasse which is the end point of interpretation. (112)

Miller's final call for a readerly patience when it comes to Pater's texts adumbrates most starkly what his immediate critical inheritors, in their 'missed encounter' with Pater, refused him. In *Theory Mess*, Rapaport consolidates his definition of this concept by deferring to African American critic Ann duCille's analysis of the specific kind of bad faith involved in the 'disavowal, avoidance, disrespect, [and] taking for granted' that drives critical theory's most conspicuous missed encounters, when critics fail to treat a rich, established field 'like a discipline with a history and a body of rigorous scholarship and distinguished scholars underpinning it' (3, 2). In rejecting Pater as a nineteenth-century relic – quaint, outmoded and unserious; the 'grandfather' of whom they are 'not . . . entirely proud' – his 'grandchildren' wilfully miss what a generation of more distant heirs both recognised and revived.

*

'The Child in the House' (1878) begins as the fictional Florian Delal overtakes an older man on a walk 'one hot afternoon' and, sensing that the man is weary, 'helped him on with the burden which he carried, a certain distance'.[17] On their walk, the story the man tells Florian happens to include the name of a place 'where Florian had passed his earliest years, but which he had never since seen'. Having told his story, Walter Pater tells his reader, the man 'went forward on his journey comforted'. Florian's 'reward for his pity', for the kindness of stopping and listening, the coincidental mention of his childhood home, unfolds later that night in a 'dream of that place ... which did for him the office of the finer sort of memory, bringing its object to mind with a great clearness, yet, as sometimes happens in dreams raised a little above itself, and above ordinary retrospect' (172). This brief narrative provides the entire fictional frame for Pater's story-essay, the first of a new subgenre of lyrical, meditative nonfiction Pater would call the 'imaginary portrait'. It serves as occasion for Pater to contemplate the largely internal, unexpressed process he calls 'brain building'. When Pater editor William E. Buckler modestly defines the 'imaginary portraits' as 'non-fictional fictions and critical non-criticism', he gives a sense of their hybridity, but lays greater stress on the formal, critical and epistemological urgency that brought the genre into being. 'The Child in the House' demonstrates, he argues, that Pater

> had creative intuitions that were inadequately satisfied by even the most imaginative reaches of conventional criticism, but also that prose literature itself lacked a precisely appropriate form for the expression of certain kinds of awarenesses that were being pressed upon the imaginative consciousness by mutually reinforcing developments in modern thought and in modern man's need to announce his spiritual whereabouts.[18]

The notion that Pater's *modernity* was such that it demanded new modes of expression, that he found new forms for new 'awarenesses' impressed upon the 'imaginative consciousness' – a legacy to which artists like Virginia Woolf and James Joyce pay homage – gets effaced entirely by the critical scholarship contemporaneous with modernism.

When it comes to Rita Felski's concern about the 'affective range of criticism', such 'awarenesses' demonstrate that Walter Pater is excruciatingly eloquent about his loves. Perhaps no modern critic has been so famously, or infamously, so. Pater is the eloquent proponent of 'unmethodical ... method', the 'lover of words for their own sake', who saw the essay as part of an ancient tradition, perfected by Plato, of 'continuous discourse with one's self, being ... co-extensive with life itself – a part of the continuous company we keep with ourselves through life'.[19]

As many critics have observed, Pater was like the very figures he chose to study, his descriptions of their lives and intellectual dispositions apt characterisations of his own. What he praises in Pico della Mirandola aptly describes Pater's own rootedness in the knowledge 'system[s]' of the past, and an eclectic method grounded in synthesis, rather than analysis. Pater collects and absorbs; he does not break down or exclude. Of Pico, he writes:

> He had sought knowledge, and had passed from system to system, and hazarded much; but less for the sake of positive knowledge than because he believed there was a spirit of order and beauty in knowledge, which would come down and unite what men's ignorance had divided, and renew what time had made dim. . . . And so, while his actual work has passed away, yet his own qualities are still active, and himself remains, as one alive in the grave, . . . and he has a true place in that group of great Italians who fill the end of the fifteenth century with their names, he is a true *humanist*. For the essence of humanism is that belief of which he seems never to have doubted, that nothing which has ever interested living men and women can wholly lose its vitality – no language they have spoken, nor oracle beside which they have hushed their voices, no dream which has once been entertained by actual human minds, nothing about which they have ever been passionate, or expended time and zeal.[20]

Pater's final volume was published posthumously in 1895. It was followed by an age that prized defining criticism down to determinations of 'fact' and 'value', in the name of propriety and rigour, with a hubris disguised as humility.[21] The critical enterprise taken up in England a generation after Pater, especially that of T. S. Eliot and I. A. Richards, establishes its own legitimacy and judges the value of specific critical projects – their own, but even more so, all the many others they deemed wanting – by criteria antithetical to 'the essence of humanism' as Pater defines it here. 'Positive knowledge' becomes the goal of criticism; the measure of its value, the degree to which criticism 'purifies' itself of Pater's sentimental fictions. For them, plenty that has 'interested living men and women' should be consigned to an ignorant past. Thus T. S. Eliot declares, contemplating Matthew Arnold's famous distinction between the 'creative' and 'critical' enterprises, that 'a critic must have a highly developed *sense of fact*', a quality that is 'by no means trifling or frequent'.[22] Eliot echoes Oscar Wilde's 'The Critic as Artist', but even more closely repeats Pater's essay on 'Style', from which Wilde draws liberally. Pater's finely wrought examination of the moment in the 'literature of prose', scientific and historical and critical prose alike, when 'the composer gives us not fact, but his peculiar *sense of fact* whether past or present, or prospective' is especially relevant (4). Eliot cites neither Pater nor Wilde, and *his* 'sense of fact' has none of Pater's, but rather subserves an exhortation to 'decide what is useful and what is not' to the critical enterprise (pessimistic that we are even 'competent to decide') and to forgo the assumption 'that we are the masters and not servants of facts' (20–1). For Eliot, defining 'fact' down in this way is the only way to save it from pretension or corruption (21).

When Pater pays Pico his highest compliment by observing how deeply his writing impresses upon the critic 'reading him' that 'his thoughts, *however little their positive value may be*, are connected with springs beneath them of deep and positive emotion', we see precisely the formula Pater's inheritors are at pains to overturn (102, emphasis mine). Like Eliot, I. A. Richards reorients the critical project around presumably objective matters of fact, specifically, the question of literary 'value.' Selectively eliding several decades of aesthetic criticism, Richards reaches back even further than Eliot's Arnold to Jeremy Bentham for his grounding of key concepts. 'Value' for Richards is a 'psychological' concept, which can be identified in organised 'units' of experience ('impulses') of varied 'importance'. By Richards' logic, what is important is what's 'good'; what's good is what's 'pleasing' or 'positive', a 'view [that] plainly has close connections with Utilitarianism' (43).[23] Citing Bentham's effort to isolate those 'moment[s] of action' in each individual that constitute 'his real greatest happiness', Richards aims to isolate '[w]hat gives the experience of reading a certain poem its value' (49, 2). Proper criticism begins by asking '[w]hat is a picture, a poem, a piece of music? How can experiences be compared? What is value?' (2). In the first of Richards' questions, readers of Pater would recognise the latter's famous effort '[t]o define beauty, not in the abstract, but in the most concrete terms possible' in the 'Preface' to *The Renaissance*. To do so, Pater says we must begin by asking, subjectively:

> What is this song or picture, this engaging personality presented in life or in a book, *to me*? What effect does it really produce on me? Does it give me pleasure? And if so, what sort or degree of pleasure? How is my nature modified by its presence, and under its influence?[24]

The answers to these questions, for Pater, are the 'original facts . . . which the aesthetic critic' must discover 'for oneself, or not at all' (viii). But remarkably, Richards is either unaware or uninterested in Pater's precedent, and the relatively abstract questions of 'experience' and 'value' that follow are a clue. As William Wimsatt and Cleanth Brooks observe in *Literary Criticism: A Short History*, Richards draws heavily from George Santayana's *The Sense of Beauty* (1896), an unacknowledged late nineteenth-century source, that saw the 'sense of beauty' as an 'animistic' vestige of our tendency to attribute to objects qualities that are, in fact, 'the objectification of our own emotions'.[25] From Santayana comes the humble hubris that '[t]heory helps us to bear our ignorance of fact', but also the peremptory jettisoning of the entire aesthetic tradition in favour of a 'psychology' of beauty.[26] More than Bentham or Pater, acknowledged or otherwise, it is from Santayana that we can see most clearly that the 'positive value' Pater alludes to in 'Pico della Mirandola' bears no resemblance to Richards' understanding of either term. Santayana offers a lucid summation of these terms for the Anglo-American positivist criticism Richards is most often credited with establishing:

> We have now reached our definition of beauty, which, in terms of our successive analysis and narrowing of the conception, is value positive, intrinsic, and objectified. Or, in less technical language, Beauty is pleasure regarded as the quality of a thing. . . . Beauty is a value, that is, it is not a perception of a matter of fact or of a relation: it is an emotion, an affection of our volitional and appreciative nature. . . . In the second place, this value is positive, it is the sense of the presence of something good . . . it is never a negative value. . . . No form in itself gives pain. . . . Beauty is therefore a positive value that is intrinsic; it is a pleasure . . . aesthetics [has only to do] with pleasure. (51–2)

*

In *Science and Poetry*, Richards considers the 'positive value' of poetry in the starkest of terms, and presents himself, in his specific historical moment, as uniquely qualified to consider '[w]hat reasons there are for thinking it valuable' (9). Though he uses Wordsworth's sonnet, 'Westminster Bridge', as his first specimen of 'experience' (in 'the right sort of reader', at least), an occasion for understanding 'in general how the mind works in an experience, and what sort of stream of events the experience is', the choice seems indifferent (10). He has little to say about the poem itself, but rather treats it as a manageable unit, 'ten minutes of a person's life' he can begin to 'describe in broad outline'. Science, specifically psychology, has made it 'at last possible' to understand what happens when we read a poem, from its initial moment ('the impression of the printed words on the retina') to the mental 'agitation' excited by that event, the various 'streams' of thought it elicits, the 'impulses', 'attitudes' and 'interests' they generate in the 'system' that is the mind, thinking (*Science and Poetry*, 10–14). That Wordsworth wrote this specific poem, on this subject and in this way, is immaterial to Richards. He might have chosen any poem and left the 'analysis' that follows unchanged. It is not an analysis of what this 'poem *says* that matters, but what it *is*'; namely, a communicative tool for reproducing in a reader an activity of 'consciousness *as a means of ordering, controlling and consolidating* ... experience' (25–7, emphasis Richards).

This explanation unfolds in a chapter entitled 'The Poetic Experience', but as Murray Krieger has pointed out,

> [t]he poetic process is described with almost no reference to the medium; ... and [it is] his theoretical neglect of his medium [that] allow[s] Richards to make such broad analogies among the various arts. Thus there is no explanation ... for the fact that the artist chooses the particular art that he does or, to narrow the field to literature, the particular genre that he does. In fact, we can see no reason for him to bother to communicate his experience at all, except out of a sheerly altruistic regard for the less highly organised people about him.[27]

Richards' citation of poems serves as the barest of props for a theory of experience that exists, for the poet, wholly 'prior to the act of expression', Krieger charges. For Richards, to read a poem as specifically communicating 'any set of perceptions or reflections ... about other things' is to '[m]isunderstand' it, to read it 'wrongly'; these things are 'irrelevant' to the 'scientific' critic, who rightly sees his task as the effort to see how the poem expresses and, in turn, elicits a mechanistic 'system' of balancing, orienting and organising stimuli and impulses. Like the needle of a compass in the field of powerful magnets, the mind in the force field of a poem 'waggles as we move and comes to rest pointing in a new direction whenever we stand still in a new position' (15). Richards extends the magnet metaphor across several paragraphs of elaboration, as 'Westminster Bridge' recedes from view, but so does the experience of reading or writing a poem, much less poetry or literature as such. In fact, he mentions the poem once more only to suggest substituting 'a simpler case' to explain the mental activity he theorises. Suppressing laughter that 'it is absolutely necessary to conceal, in Church or during a solemn interview' involves the same 'activity of the impulses'; the 'impulses a poem excites are not different in principle' (19–20). This explanation culminates in the assertion that, 'primarily ... Man is a system of interests,' of 'impulses stirred' into disequilibrium, then by means of that very system, organised again into equilibrium (21, 23). The 'sound and feel' of poetic language stirs the impulses in a way that is both pleasing and unique, different in kind from the effect of 'scientific' language, which only serves to convey information, not excite feeling. In *Science and Poetry*, Richards states without justifying this distinction, except to invoke fleetingly the content/form dichotomy with which the New Criticism is typically associated.

Given the wholly 'psychological' focus of Richards' argument, his aim of explaining what happens 'in the mind' *when a poem happens to it*, there is no hyperbole when Krieger trenchantly calls Richards a 'would-be neurologist' whose theory 'leads not merely to a distinction between, but to a separation of, content and form that is as primitive as any in the recent history of literary theory' (59). Ironically, 'the experience of' really reading Richards, reading the content of books whose 'formalist' reputation rests, these days, almost entirely on the critical activity promised by their titles (*The Meaning of Meaning, The Foundation of Aesthetics, The Principles of Criticism, Practical Criticism, Science and Poetry*) is wildly disorienting. It makes one incredulous that Richards is unwaveringly considered, as the back of the Routledge Classics edition of *Principles* calls him, 'one of the founders of modern literary criticism'. It is a check on one's sanity to see Krieger marvel at the distance between the eccentricity of Richards' 'science of mind' and its influence in Anglo-American criticism: 'Indeed it seems to be an amazing feat on the part of those of the new critics who spring from Richards that, with a theory so inadequate on the level of technique, they ... have been able to produce so much excellent criticism' (118).

Indeed, everywhere, Richards works to slough off influence, cut ties with his literary past, and at most, condescend to those who came before him. In *The Principles of Literary Criticism*, he dispenses with the entire history of aesthetics in three paragraphs, with Kant's three *Critiques* in one (9–12), dismisses one of its sublime progenitors as 'the wiseacre Longinus' (32) and adds to a disapproving rejection of Wordsworth's Aristotelian appeal in the 'Preface' to *Lyrical Ballads* as 'mystical' a speculation without evidence that 'Wordsworth probably heard about Aristotle ... from Coleridge' (241). What he gleans from all philosophy and criticism concerned with the nature of aesthetic experience is 'that there is no such mode' (12). His proof, against what he reads in Wordsworth's elevating reminder that 'Aristotle ... has said that poetry is the most philosophic of all writing,' involves positing that '[w]hen we look at a picture, or read a poem, or listen to music, we are not doing something quite unlike what we were doing on our way to the Gallery or when we dressed in the morning' (240, 12). But what Richards misses when he rejects peremptorily the great 'unremarkable Wordsworth', whom Geoffrey Hartman argues is most extraordinary when his verse seems most plain and his subject most humble, is the extent to which Wordsworth proves that very point far better, in fact, than Richards himself ever does. The potential for aesthetic experience exists everywhere for Wordsworth, 'on our way to' any place, at any time, 'morning' or otherwise.[28] Pater, who enlists Wordsworth's

'Preface' to sanction his claim that, in both poetry and prose, the possibility of '"fine" as opposed to merely serviceable art, exists', operates everywhere according to this principle. For Wordsworth, as for Pater, the elevation of poetry and prose to 'philosophic . . . writing' occurs not in the exclusionary logic of the 'quite unlike', but rather by extending aesthetic possibility out to any experience, 'to the real language of men, however, not on the dead level of their ordinary intercourse, but in select moments of vivid sensation, when this language is winnowed and ennobled by excitement'.[29]

The third chapter of *Science and Poetry* is entitled 'What is Valuable' – a statement, not a question – and here Richards turns from his 'reading' of Wordsworth's 'Westminster Bridge' to 'the general structure of . . . experiences' as such. How do we determine their 'value'? First, by recognising 'that poetic experiences are valuable (when they are) in the same ways as any other experiences. They are to be judged by the same standards' (28). Offering readers a putative 'unit' of human experience, Richards asks us to imagine a 'hypothetical' man in artificial isolation, purely 'experiencing', with no one and nothing and doing nothing of consequence, for an hour. 'He is going to cease to exist when the clock strikes – but for our purposes he must be imagined not to know this – and no one is to be a whit the better or worse whatever he thinks, feels or does during the hour' (30–1). The most 'valuable' way he can spend this hour? By 'engag[ing] as many of his impulses as possible', to feel as little pain as possible; 'the more he lives and the less he thwarts himself the better' (33). An hour spent thusly, 'abstractly', 'feels like and is the experience of poetry'; this is 'our answer as psychologists', Richards concludes tautologically. In a short chapter on 'Memory', Richards reports that the 'old theory of a kind of Somerset House of past impressions has given place to an account in terms of facilitations of neural paths, lowered resistances in synapses, and so forth'. But for once, he expresses bipartisan dissatisfaction: 'Neither view is adequate' (95). 'Somerset House' serves as a clever metaphor for the 'old associationists'' concept of the brain as an enormous archive of past events, but having already dismissed him as an outmoded aesthete leaves Richards apparently ignorant of Pater's own more nuanced architectural metaphor for the associative nature of memory.

How impoverished and provisional Richards' imaginary and hermetically isolated man-of-an-hour appears, as if it were only possible to hypothesise human experience discretely by stipulating that he will 'cease to exist when the clock strikes' but not know of his imminent artificial mortality. Compare this thought experiment with the richly gorgeous and perceptive, and in fact far less fictional, 'imaginary portrait' of Florian Delal in 'The Child in the House', where we are asked to consider one individual, where almost nothing happens with almost no one else around, as an entire world gets made. In its most figuratively layered moments, we see that the titular 'house' is not just a half-remembered 'place' to which Florian owes 'tones of sentiment afterwards customary with him', but also a powerful figure for the imbricated, indissociable structure of memory as such (176). For Pater, memory is the raw material of 'brain-building', the continuous process by which human consciousness is formed:

> How insignificant, at the moment, seem the influences of sensible things which are tossed and fall and lie about us, so, or so, in the environment of early childhood. How indelibly, as we afterwards discover, they affect us; with what capricious attractions and associations they figure themselves on the white paper, the smooth wax, of our ingenuous souls, . . . giving form and feature, and as it were assigned house-room in our memory, to early experiences of feeling and thought, which abide with us ever afterwards, thus, and not otherwise. The realities and passions, the rumours of the greater world without, steal in upon us, each by its own special little passage-way, through the walls of custom about us: and never afterwards quite detach themselves from this or that accident, or trick, in the mode of their first entrance to us. (177)

It is in the irrevocable distance between these two 'houses' that the missed encounter between Pater and the New Criticism can be felt most acutely.

*

Richards' declaration that the aesthetic is a 'phantom state', and the discourse upon it proves useless for determining what is valuable does not preclude his own ability to decide, in other words, 'what is useful and what is not', what is 'good' versus 'bad' in 'the experience of poetry'. But in what Krieger rightly calls Richards' 'theoretical neglect', reference to the specific 'medium' of poetry, or literature as such, drops out of his consideration, if not his estimation, altogether. Given his self-fashioning 'as a psychologist', it is hard to see why Richards bothers to write about poetry, or purports to do so, at all.

Set next to the twentieth-century advances of 'science', Richards asserts, aesthetic and ethical philosophies of the 'value' of art stand as mere relics. Philosophy is merely the 'special passion for knowledge for its own sake', one 'invent[ion]' among many toiling in the pre-dawn of what is 'not yet Science' (248). 'Science' alone is 'autonomous' and crucially, Richards has no doubt that he holds the key to a literary criticism wholly within its sphere (249). The history of these other disciplines' attempts, which he surveys and summarily finds 'defect[ive]' in the first three paragraphs of his first chapter (entitled 'The Chaos of Critical Theories'), leads him to conclude that an 'exact psychological analysis [is] needed in order to explain value' (34). Reoriented around a utilitarian understanding of value (and, by extension, what is 'good') as that which 'satisfies' positive psychophysiological 'impulses' ('appentencies', not 'aversions'), Richards clears the ground and names the stakes for a newly defined literary criticism to emerge (42–3). While Richards does not suppose his *Principles of Literary Criticism* represents 'a contribution to neurology', he does assume without misgivings that, as 'Science has opened out field after field,' a new literary criticism dwells in this new opening. His inquiry into the mental 'impulses' and modes of cognitive 'reference' by which poetry is produced is among those 'fields' (248–9). 'To declare Science is autonomous is very different from subordinating all our activities to it,' Richards allows, and poetry and imaginative fiction are among such 'human activities' (249). That allowance, however, serves mainly to distinguish poetry from the project of theorising it, and to separate, as the title of this penultimate chapter announces, 'The Two Uses of Language', one proper to each.

In a discussion that recalls ancient and modern delineations of literal and figurative language but acknowledges none of them, Richards links language to 'mental processes' of association, of 'impulses' with 'stimuli'; the 'ways in which we use . . . the stimuli we receive' constitute various forms of 'reference', which are either 'distorted' or 'undistorted' (244–7). Science, unsurprisingly, engages 'undistorted reference' and 'has advanced' most swiftly in pursuits where it has transcended 'a position of subjection to some instinct or emotion or desire' (249). According to Richards, criticism engages the '*scientific* use of language', poetry the '*emotive* use of language' (250).[30] This distinction serves as the foundation of Richards' theory of linguistic reference, but it also certifies the truth-value of his critical enterprise. Segregating critical discourse from its object on the basis of how each 'uses' language establishes 'The Analysis of a Poem' as the metalanguage of literature.

The depth of Richards' investment in this *cordon sanitaire* manifests itself throughout his work, largely without the context of what contemporary readers would recognise as language philosophy or a nascent speech act theory. In such instances, it is easy to read the insistent separation of 'emotive language' from the 'science' of criticism as a straightforward, reactionary distaste for the work of an earlier age. When he dismisses 'art for art's sake' with an alliterative slur ('a doctrine definitely and detrimentally dated'), he clearly sets his project apart from Paterian aestheticism (ix, 64). When he disdains 'aesthetic emotion' as a 'calamitous' attempt to 'fit Beauty into a neat pigeon-hole with Feeling', we might also think of Pater's interest in defining aesthetic criticism against 'abstract' definitions of 'beauty, excellence, art, poetry' in his 'Preface' to *The Renaissance* (1877: vii). But Richards' references here are to Vernon Lee's *The Beautiful* (1913) and Bernard Bosanquet's *Three Lectures on Aesthetics* (1915), not the *fin de siècle* figure with whom we most readily associate aestheticism. Richards in fact rarely sets his theoretical gaze to the past; his endeavours to be a criticism of the future.

His faith that the 'distinction' between scientific and emotive language 'once grasped is simple' justifies his principled rejection of any 'emotive' discourse that is not poetry. It also dictates the anti-style he conspicuously adopts. While distinguishing the scientific from emotive use of language segregates critical discourse from its object of study, so too does it make clear what Richards must do, in the service of such 'purity':

> My book, I fear, will seem to many sadly lacking in the condiments which have come to be expected in writings upon literature. Critics and even theorists in criticism currently assume that their first duty is to be moving, to excite in the mind emotions appropriate to their august subject-matter. This endeavour I have declined. (ix)

Established in the first pages of his 'Preface', added to the book's third edition in 1928, this principled refusal to be 'moving' or exciting stands in contrast to the critical conventions he hopes to supplant.

Aesthetics is the history of discourse describing the experience specific to encountering art, but Richards closes himself off from this history, rejects any anxiety of influence. Indeed, early in his treatise, he makes the influential argument, within these other claims, that 'the aesthetic' is no privileged domain, but rather a type of experience different from other sorts of experience perhaps in degree but not in kind. While the ideological implications of the aesthetic make that proposition politically suggestive and overdetermined, here I would simply like to point out that, in subordinating aesthetics and ethics to a supposedly utilitarian psychological literary criticism, the 'literary' drops out, at various points in his analysis, almost entirely. As the above explication illustrates, Richards spends far more time purging the poetic from criticism than he does writing anything genuinely critical about poetry. For a work everywhere hailed as a foundational text of modern literary criticism, *The Principles of Literary Criticism* is an astonishingly un- or even anti-literary book.

Richards is a critic in a lab coat, who cheerfully imagines that the 'knowledge the men of AD 3000 will possess, if all goes well' will make our current state of understanding seem 'pitiful', and 'would wish this book to be regarded as a contribution towards [this] future' (x). Although he calls for 'purer science and purer poetry', with the same deprecating arrogance as Eliot, Richards outlines his own critical endeavour as necessarily hybrid, his method dictated by necessity (ix). Though he elsewhere establishes that proper criticism engages the '*scientific* use of language', he often cedes that disciplinary ground to other fields. 'No other choice seemed open if I did not wish ... to be understood, than to include as a preliminary what amounts to a concise treatise on psychology' (viii). But just a few sentences later, what Richards calls a 'preliminary' helpmeet to a more fundamental job gets implicitly promoted to the job itself: here, he describes a project that links relatively incidental 'commonplaces of criticism' to 'a systematic exposition of psychology', and one feels the latter getting the upper hand (ix). In his first chapter, 'The Chaos of Critical Theories', Richards names the questions criticism 'is required to answer' and finds the answers 'yielded by the best minds' wanting. After three paragraphs dismissively surveying the history of not only literary criticism, but also that of 'Philosophers, Moralists and Aestheticians', he again puts himself favourably in league with the psychologists, 'the collection and analysis of concrete, particular facts and to empirical research', and nods knowingly about 'laboratory methods' (4). He alludes to experimental work he does not cite or describe, psychologists he does not name, and mocks the vocabulary of aesthetics. He decries the 'defects of almost all ... work on aesthetics' in favour of experimental psychology. His knowing asides claim rightful place in the worlds of the critic and the scientist, as self-evident authority, which 'anyone who has *both* looked at a picture or read a poem *and* been inside a psychological laboratory or conversed with a representative psychologist will understand' (4, emphasis Richards'). Most urgently, however, he worries about the health of human thought writ large, because things are in a sorry state, and in this sense, *The Principles of Literary Criticism* is, above all, a corrective exercise in epistemological purity. His work rights the long history of error aesthetic discourse has trafficked in, and rescues criticism from its 'debilitated ... taste for speculation'. He warns that '[m]ixed modes of writing which enlist the reader's feeling as well as his thinking are becoming dangerous to the modern consciousness with its increasing awareness of the distinction' (ix). This apocalyptic, messianic sensibility pervades all of his work, and is its most radical element. It is what makes Richards' texts deeply, profusely strange, the sense of which we lose when we reduce him to summary or remember him by the benign, seemingly pragmatic titles of his books.

*

At the same time Richards was fashioning a literary criticism as an anti-stylistic 'treatise on psychology', T. S. Eliot was, in the name of a similar rigour and discernment, artfully eviscerating his critical adversaries. In 1923's 'The Function of Criticism', Eliot leaves contemporary readers wondering whether it is more or less insulting that he spilled more ink in opposition to the critical musings of John Middleton Murry than he did for Walter Pater. In the sneering 'Arnold and Pater' (1930), he levels at Pater's oeuvre such a sweeping, wholesale rejection it scarcely qualifies as critique. Eliot dismisses Pater as a sentimental moralist with vague ideals, simultaneously denying his work as a coherent theory or practice of 'art for art's sake', or anything else. When aiming at theory, Pater's work manages only to be inadvertently practical: 'The theory (if it can be called a theory) of "art for art's sake" is still valid in so far as it can be taken as an exhortation to the artist to stick to his job; it never was, and never can be valid for the spectator, reader or auditor' (392). As practice, it either suffers by comparison to the greats ('The right practice of "art for art's sake" was the devotion of Flaubert or Henry James; Pater is not with these men') or embarrasses itself with a 'profession' for the beautiful that 'is most vocal', but not 'professional'. 'If we wish to understand painting', Eliot argues, '[w]e have specialists, such as Mr Berenson, or Mr Roger Fry' (393, 389). Again, what might seem merely petty strikes significant notes. The emphasis on expertise and the 'professional', the distinction and rejection of the 'moralist' from those engaged in the real work of criticism, the partisan siding with 'greats' who can understand the principles of their aesthetic because they engage the 'practice' of it: Eliot's sortings express the critic's new sense of himself in the twentieth century. In none of these categories does Pater make the cut.

T. S. Eliot presents 'The Function of Criticism' first as an extension of the principles put forth in his 1919 essay, 'Tradition and the Individual Talent', namely the notions that national literatures do not exist in isolation but as 'organic wholes' and that a 'common inheritance and a common cause unite artists consciously or unconsciously' and 'mostly unconscious'.[31] This 'inheritance' is both spatial and temporal: 'Between the true artist of any time there is, I believe, an unconscious community' (13). Eliot's 1919 essay was concerned largely with the discourse of 'the artist', the latter with that of the critic. As its title suggests, 'The Function of Criticism' interpolates Matthew Arnold's famous formulation of the respective roles of artist and critic in 'The Function of Criticism at the Present Time'. Eliot suggests that he will opt 'for the general use of the word "criticism"' to refer to discourse *about* literature, distinct from literature itself. And though he purports to use the word criticism 'as Matthew Arnold uses it in his essay', Eliot also declares he 'shall presently make several qualifications' to Arnold's formula (13). He gives almost no indication that, in the fifty-eight years since Arnold's publication, any significant 'qualifications' on that subject have intervened. ('To us ... Arnold is rather a friend than a leader. He was a champion of "ideas" most of whose ideas we no longer take seriously,' declares Eliot in 'Arnold and Pater').[32] Having set his sights in this essay on doing battle with contemporary John Middleton Murry, Eliot can only harken back, in a move that proves characteristic of the New Critics, to Matthew Arnold, as if the half-century of critical discourse that engaged directly with it simply never took place. Yet in earlier sections of the essay, Eliot mercilessly rails against the pious ahistoricism and cultural hubris in Murry he finds absurd, and reserves for special contempt Murry's suggestion that 'the English ... inherit no rules from their forbears; they inherit only this sense that in the last resort they must depend upon the inner voice' (16). In the name of the 'inner voice' comes every sin against rigour and accuracy, Eliot complains, any obligation to say not 'what comes *easy* to us, but what is right' (17, emphasis Eliot's). 'Inner Voice' is the enemy of 'Outside Authority', and therein threatens a critical free-for-all that casts aside every 'value' true criticism upholds – of 'discipline', 'law', 'discrimination', 'labour.' He writes:

> For they will not be interested in the attempt to find any common principles for the pursuit of criticism. Why have principles, when one has the inner voice? If I like a thing, that is all I want; and if enough of us, shouting all together, like it, that should be all that *you* (who don't like it) ought to want. (17, emphasis Eliot's)

Pulling back from this near-anarchy, which he hyperbolically compares to 'worship[ping] Baal' before settling on a more characteristic insult ('the name I suggest is Whiggery'), Eliot admits he may have digressed. In the final section of the essay, he places himself back among more worthy company, and recalling his essay's namesake, again invokes Matthew Arnold, though even here he cannot refrain from condescending. Returning to Arnold's 'use of the terms "critical" and "creative" by one whose place, on the whole, is with the weaker brethren', Eliot offers a final, resigned observation: 'it is fairly certain that "interpretation" ... is only legitimate when it is not interpretation at all, but merely putting the reader in possession of facts he would otherwise have missed' (20). The value of criticism, if it has any, lies not in any 'truth and beauty' it may reveal, but in '[c]omparison and analysis'; any inquiry that 'produces a fact even of the lowest order about a work of art is a better piece of work than nine-tenths' of existing criticism (21).

Richards, in the same way, asserts that the 'research into aesthetics' is worthy of mention only as a servant to psychology; psychology, it seems, is even the master of literary study itself. And *that* is what is strange above all in Richards' *Principles of Literary Criticism*: that it has so little interest in and performs so little literary criticism. Of his method, Richards starts by saying he cannot articulate the titular 'principles' without 'some understanding of the nature of experience' or 'theories of valuation and communication'; these are 'more fundamental studies' (viii). Paraphrasing with a telling difference Pater's 'Preface' to *The Renaissance*, Richards says such a treatise is preliminary to 'the fundamental questions ... criticism is required to answer ... What *is* a picture, a poem, a piece of music?' (2) Aesthetics cannot answer these questions, Richard asserts, without ever acknowledging that Pater's aesthetic criticism asked almost identical questions to very different ends. For Richards, 'emotion' dooms aesthetics to error, and besides, 'psychology has no place for such an entity' (2). Circularity notwithstanding, Richards goes on to reject Vernon Lee's suggestion that, aside from 'aesthetic emotion', we might consider 'empathy' a mode of experience in which literature might find a privileged home. We might, but Richards will not. It's too 'ambiguous' (11). Despite its incipient state, 'experimental psychology' is where the answers are and shall be. Even though 'only the simplest activities are at present amenable to laboratory experiments', the way of the future is here, 'inside [the] psychological laboratory' and in conversation with 'a representative psychologist' (4).

Richards never names this, or really any, psychologist in the service of the criticism whose principles this book purports to explain. Readers looking to this text for practical models for interpreting literature will be disappointed, if not baffled. Nowhere is that clearer than in the chapter entitled 'The Analysis of a Poem', perhaps the book's most curious specimen. It does not analyze a poem, though it cites a few, but rather explains the mental 'events which take place when we read a poem' (106). There are six events, and Richards spends much of the chapter cataloguing them. Perhaps because he theorises these events in wholly visual terms, from the act of laying eyes on the poem, 'the printed words', to the cognitive translation of those words into mental 'images', Richards resorts to a diagram. A string of words, uncited – it is, in

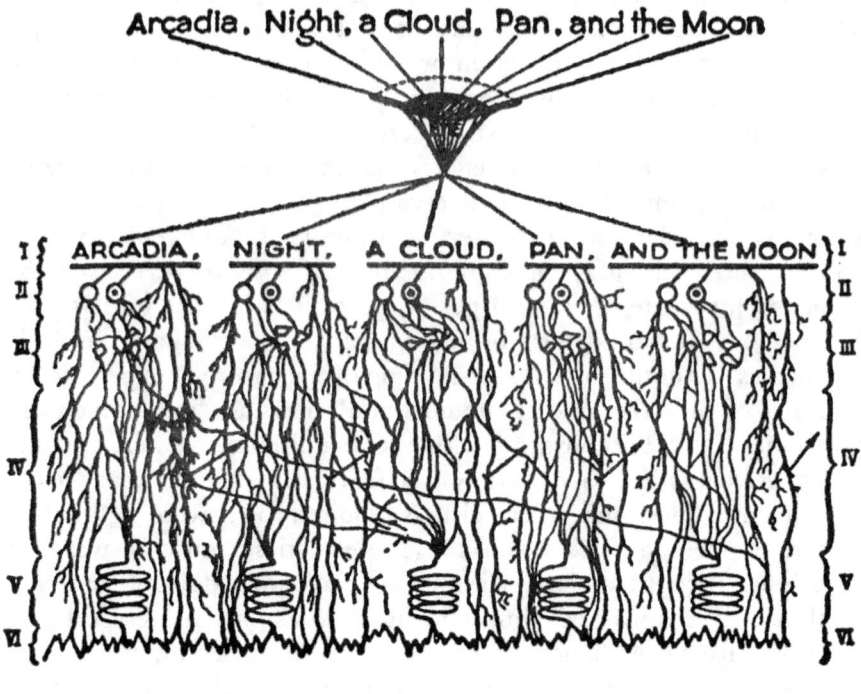

Figure 6.1 From Richards' 'The Analysis of a Poem', *Principles of Literary Criticism*, p.107.

fact, the final line of Robert Browning's 'Pan and Luna' – stands above a decidedly unscientific illustration (Fig. 6.1). Richards concludes this chapter by reminding us that '[t]here are plenty of ecstatic instants that are valueless' and that the intensity with which such instants impress themselves upon consciousness 'is no certain sign of [their] excellence' (120). With no hint of doubt or irony, Richards sets his picture of the mind against that of Pater's 'Conclusion' to *The Renaissance*, the '*locus classicus*' of the ecstatic instant; he, by contrast, privileges the vicissitudes of its 'after-effects', which his 'Analysis' has just outlined. Against the most famous few pages in all of Pater's oeuvre, which he mistakenly calls 'The Epilogue', Richards suggests his theory of the 'modifications in the structure of the mind' at work in an artistic encounter. 'No one is ever quite the same after any experience,' he concludes, with no trace of sense that Pater has said that much and more (121).

These claims to a 'purer science', and his pervasive insistence on a profoundly idiosyncratic, largely *sui generis* 'psychology' of what happens in an act of encountering a poem, likely make little sense to a contemporary reader curious to see what the so-called father of New Criticism put forth as its principles, without recognising that Richards' claim to theoretical legitimacy derives entirely from his faith in the stable truths of logical positivism, ordinary language philosophy and a very specific definition of 'psychology' these projects, at this time, all share. 'Psychology' for Richards and his colleagues is understood narrowly to mean 'cognition', and 'cognition' even more narrowly refers to the mechanisms by which mind processes experience, as Richards explains in a footnote in Chapter Six of *Principles*: 'Throughout this discussion "experience" will be used in a wide sense to stand for any occurrence of the mind. It is equivalent to mental state, or process' (33). While he allows that experience 'ha[s] parts which are not conscious and not accessible to introspection', they are also 'not as important as those which are' (33). Richards' occasional and marginalised acknowledgement of 'unconscious' thoughts should be understood as almost wholly divorced from Freudian psychoanalysis, which he disdainfully rejects in *The Meaning of Meaning*; that work serves as the occasion for dispatching, also, Henri Bergson, Ferdinand de Saussure and many other contemporaneous theorists Richards reads but misses.

Such divisions, importantly, extended as well to Anglo-American analytic philosophy and experimental psychology, disciplines to which I. A. Richards explicitly yoked his own critical project, psychology especially, for what he considered its historically sound logical grounding and cutting-edge scientific rigour. In shorthand, his is a psychology of thinking without feeling, and of mind without an unconscious. Even today, it might be difficult to explain to scholars in many disciplines outside of literary criticism and theory why this divide over what we mean when we say 'psychology' would baffle or matter so much. But it's rather astonishing to readers of Pater, not to mention of Marx, Nietzsche, Bergson and Freud, that *this* sense of the word 'psychology' would, for Richards or his local audience, be considered a given.

Pater's own pre-Freudian account of consciousness, in works from *The Renaissance* to 'The Child in the House', 'Style', and *Plato and Platonism*, is hardly less alien to Richards' definition of conscious experience than the more than quarter century of work Freud himself had published by 1924, from *The Interpretation of Dreams* to *Beyond the Pleasure Principle*. In English departments, journals and presses, Anglo-American New Criticism dominated the discourse and dictated the pedagogy of literary study for more than half of the twentieth century, which left Pater's work in a strange exile for just as long, and one from which Freud, in the discipline he arguably invented, has never returned. Yet the very same elements of Pater's aesthetic criticism which, for Anglo-American positivists, doom his work to the dustbin of critical history, also place him rather centrally and dynamically within a larger discourse on the phenomenon of consciousness, the mechanisms by which consciousness perceives and makes sense of external reality more generally. Edmund Husserl spent all of the 1890s writing *Logical Investigations*; the dense two-volume reckoning with logical positivism, in which this work is firmly grounded, also conceives of 'psychology' as the study of cognition. He published it in 1900, the same year Freud, himself active in the 1890s, published *The Interpretation of Dreams*. Within *this* conversation, Pater's work is continuous with an intellectual genealogy that includes Marx and Nietzsche on the one hand and Bergson, Freud, Husserl and Merleau-Ponty on the other.

In offering this list, I don't simply mean Pater was a psychoanalyst or phenomenologist *avant la lettre*, nor a Marxist without knowing it. Still, that much of this work has its roots in Pater's own most fertile period, the 1870s to 1890s, is a point worth emphasising. Aside from the obvious chronological overlapping of Nietzsche and Pater, there is Henri Bergson's *Essai sur les données immédiates de la conscience* (1889), published just as the *fin de siècle* purportedly gave aesthetes and decadents their final act, and his still-radical *Matière et mémoire* (1996), published two years after Pater died.[33] To me, Pater's incidentally gorgeous exploration of the moments and sensations, the susceptibilities and passions that participate in the process of what he calls 'brain-building', present as thrillingly prescient language 'experiments' in Bergsonian phenomenology. Bergson's emphatic rejection, in the 1893 *Essai*, of the positivist tendency to collapse qualitative into quantitative intensities, his attention there to time and duration as inseparable from any more abstracted sense of self and his insistence on the actual materiality of the body in the manifestation of consciousness in *Matière et mémoire* are all of a piece with Pater's 'Child in the House', where Pater offers a particular – if imaginary – account of the aesthetic intensities by which an individual consciousness emerges. Here a series of aesthetic intensities, in which bodily sensation and affective responses to external experiences are not clearly differentiated from what might come from 'within', so to speak, as part of the tendencies that draw him to the morbid, make him quick to read, grant him his 'susceptibilities'. In this sense, we might see Florian Delal as a characterological prop for a philosophical proposition, for the 'story of his spirit' that more generally offers 'a certain design', namely, 'that process of brain-building by which we are, each one of us, what we are'.

Pater stresses everywhere the singularity of the aesthetic subject's formation, '[o]ut of so many possible conditions, just this for you and that for me', that to me could be put into useful dialogue with Emmanuel Levinas and Derrida, who both formulate an ethics with a certain absolute alterity ('the other is wholly other') as its starting point, but importantly, *just* a start. From there comes responsibility to the other, in every sense of the word 'response'. In 'The Child in the House', Pater also presents a scene in which young Florian encounters a reproduction of David's portrait of Marie Antoinette on her way to execution. Here is an aesthetically constituted consciousness out of which ethics emerges. As Pater offers it in this moment, but also in the fictional frame that begins the story, 'pity' describes one specific reaction to the world around Florian, one of the 'cells' that contribute to the brain-building of consciousness. Its classification belongs with other experiences that involve another human being – not to say *living* being, for so much of the data of Florian's world, real and imagined, is alive – and together, they constitute the stirrings of a 'care for the other', so to speak, that the child does not think to call ethical or moral. Even the adult Florian experiences the world affectively, not through conscious expression of what is Good in any dogmatic sense, but rather in his 'recognition of the element of pain in things' (182). In this exquisite episode, Pater seems to offer an implementable ethics of care for the other, particularly in its corrective iterability, for as Florian closes the book for the first time, he also takes note of it 'as a thing to look at again, if he should at any time find himself tempted to be cruel' (183). Pater situates this impressive moment, and the possibility of renewing that impression as a way of refining consciousness, as a constant work in progress.

*

Where, finally, does Pater fit in our own critical moment? What do these critical afterlives, these previous reappearances of his peculiar 'critical spirit', have to say about an eclectic disciplinary era that seems to have room for the neuroscientist and the phenomenologist alike, and where Pater's criticism of self-conscious aesthetic intensity might, from a fresh perspective, hold common cause with critical movements with which we have not typically associated it – might even have the potential to forge bonds with modes of criticism that are as yet only nascent? Like his favourite figure, *La Gioconda*, Walter Pater's work has 'lived many lives'. In the spirit of the 'wager' Rita Felski offers in my essay's epigraph, I believe now may be an especially good moment to bet on Pater yet again.

Felski's subject in *The Limits of Critique* – the enormous field of criticism, that which broadly belongs to the enterprise motivated by the darker, more rigid, self-limiting moods and stances of the 'hermeneutics of critique' – is *not* the one I have been examining in this essay. In many ways, the critical theory that fits within this rubric grew up in ideologically principled opposition to the arid formalisms of Richards and those who issued from him.[34] But just as Felski insists throughout her book, my effort is to identify a tendency, an 'affective stance' most often characterised by its refusal to admit to having one, and like Felski, I am looking to identify, in contrast to this affective mode, an alternative. In her conclusion, she expresses the desire 'to move on: to try out different vocabularies and experiment with alternative ways of writing, to think in a more sustained and concentrated fashion about what other moods and methods might look like' (192–3). A return to Pater's criticism, with this imperative in mind, has always had many capacious 'moods and methods' to offer.

The kind of 'critique' Felksi finds limited and limiting for its 'affective inhibition' which creates the conditions for a reading practice that too often 'blocks receptivity and inhibits generosity', and in which we 'are shielded from the risks, but also the rewards, of aesthetic experience', poignantly captures the sadness of what was lost amidst the heady messianic zeal Richards everywhere expresses in imagining just how much old, bad intellectual production shall be cast into the heap of discarded ideas (188). The apotheosis of this zeal appears towards the end of his *Science and Poetry*:

> For science, which is simply our most elaborate way of *pointing* to things systematically, tells us and can tell us nothing about the nature of things in any *ultimate* sense. It can never answer any question of the form: *What* is so and so? It can only tell us *how* so and so behaves. And it does not attempt to do more than this. Nor, indeed, can more than this be done. Those ancient, deeply troubling, formulations that begin with 'What' and 'Why' prove, when we examine them, to be not questions at all; but requests – for emotional satisfaction. They indicate our desire not for knowledge but for assurance, a point which appears clearly when we look into the 'How' questions and requests, of knowledge and desire. Science can tell us about man's place in the universe and his chances; that the place is precarious and the chances problematical. It can enormously increase our chances if we can make wise use of

it. But it cannot tell us what we are or what this world is; not because these are in any sense insoluble questions, but because they are not questions at all. And if science cannot answer these pseudo-questions no more can philosophy or religion. So that all the varied answers which have for ages been regarded as the keys of wisdom are dissolving together. (52–4)

As one finds with the more self-conscious Santayana, Richards' extremism in this moment offers a useful, if unwitting, candour. Still more, it serves as a cautionary example of what is lost when one's critical vision has on its horizon the question of whether *any* discourse dare wonder at the meaning or purpose of existence, most of all one's own. When he holds up 'science' as the privileged realm of discovery and knowledge, able to answer 'how' but not 'what' or 'why', and when he furthermore relegates to pseudo-statements the ancient musings that begin with those words and asserts that they are 'not questions at all', Richards says more about his own pursuit than he realises. The entire history of intellectual speculation he is willing to discard in *Science and Poetry* has been driven not by true knowledge, but 'desire'. With unearned dualist logic, these pursuits are 'not questions' because they are instead 'requests – for assurance ... for emotional satisfaction'. But what Richards demonstrates most clearly is his *own* 'desire' for an explanation of aesthetic experience that holds the iron-clad 'assurance' he believes only 'science' provides.

In *The Expressiveness of the Body*, Shigehisa Kuriyama reads eighteenth- and nineteenth-century accounts from Western doctors who traveled to Asia to observe the art of reading pulses, not for how those accounts evaluate Eastern methods for a Western audience, but for what they tell him about their own preconceptions. Kuriyama's brilliant book retraces the remarkable similarities between the ancient West's obsession with 'pulsation' (Galen alone devoted a thousand pages to this delicate art) and that of the ancient East. In Western medicine, a once capacious language of the body's pulses was defined down to what modern medicine deemed its only variable traits – frequency, and the pressure of the systole and the diastole; in other words, only what could be quantified. Galen's quest, for example, to *feel* the difference between the systole and the diastole by palpation, by touch alone, has been so thoroughly abandoned in Western medicine, while remaining vital in Chinese medicine and acupuncture, that Kuriyama's meticulous study on 'the divergence of ancient Greek and Chinese medicine' often has the force of revelation. Kuriyama's reading of eyewitness observation, by 'modern' Western medical practioners, of the 'ancient' Eastern tradition offers a compelling picture of just how much they presumed they gained by defining down even their own, once-voluminous language of 'pulsation' to mere 'pulse', by abandoning what it considered outmoded and mystified. Of course, they found the haptic, highly metaphorical techniques of Chinese diagnosticians and practitioners – in this case, the felt reading of pulses – to engage 'styles of knowing' that 'fundamentally *used words differently*', even if they did not express the differences with such rhetorical awareness.[35] John Floyer, in 1707, described the difference as follows: 'Europeans excel in reasoning and judgment, and clearness of expression, [whereas] Asiatics have a gay luxurious imagination' (62). Despite the glaring Euro-logocentrism of Floyer's characterisation, he did acknowledge that Chinese medicine *worked*, and was a rich, ancient and valid form of knowledge; in this sense, he is far more open-minded than I. A. Richards is on shakier ground. What Kuriyama reads in encounters like Floyer's is not Europe's well-developed methods of scientific 'reason and judgment', yielding clarity, but rather, 'above all the fierce *yearning* for clarity' (64, emphasis Kuriyama's). When Richards embraces 'Science' (and the supposedly 'scientific psychology' he takes for granted he's practising, in all his work) at the expense of so much else, he does not model a lucid, definitive literary criticism, but rather exposes the ferocity of his '*yearning* for clarity'. He demonstrates, in other words, the very need for 'assurances', for the 'emotional satisfaction' of a criticism on the side of the only possible form of knowledge not on the verge of 'dissolving together' in the first decades of the twentieth century.

That he remains inured to so much speculative thought that had, and was in his own time, engaged with scientific and medical observations (Freud's practice of the talking cure, Bergson's interest in aphasia, Merleau-Ponty's serious engagement with early research on phantom limb pain), lays bare how very unscientific Richards' 'psychology' is, and how little it has to offer us today. It helps explain why Pater had so little to offer his brand of criticism, and why only a paraphrase of New Criticism remains in contemporary accounts of its place and moment. A few remaining anthologised essays are read these days, and usually in the context of surveys that, as I describe above, tend to read New Criticism as a dialectical reaction to aestheticism, thereafter itself surpassed by structuralism. And it explains why so very much of Richards' supposedly cutting-edge work is rarely among them. In fact, the greatest irony of English New Criticism's missed encounter with Pater is that, had they paid closer or more humble attention, Eliot and Richards might have recognised that, in a sense, Pater proleptically understood them – could imagine them – far better than they were capable of imagining him. Though he enlists a paragraph from Pater's essay on 'Style' in *Principles*,

Richards misunderstands a similar respect for precision articulated there in Pater's vision of what constitutes the highest aesthetic criticism: at once stripped of 'surplusage' (what Richards oddly calls the 'condiments' of style) and 'attendant to the metaphor that is mixed in all our speech, though a rapid use may involve no cognition of it' (17). For Pater, 'style' is indissociable from method, and while 'restraint' and 'omission' distinguish the true aesthetic scholar or artist, so does an awareness that, '[i]n this late day, no critical process can be conducted reasonably without eclecticism' ('Style': 14, 15, 13). Pater's aesthete will thus be 'well aware of physical science', but also that 'the scholar is nothing without the historic sense' (12).

Eliot, having dismissed Pater as a 'moralist' and minor figure, similarly lacks the grace or generosity to be eloquent not just about what he disdains or abhors, but what he might 'love'. In 'The Function of Criticism' and 'Arnold and Pater', Eliot esteems the high-minded Ruskin and Arnold, but is blind to the rigour and import of Pater's singular transmutation of them. More pointedly, Eliot forgets what Felski, nearly a century later, feels she must reassert:

> Talking about the force and lure of art works need not commit us to breathless effusions or antipolitical sentiments. It can open the way to a renewed engagement with art and its entanglement with social life . . . And here literary theory would do well to reflect on – rather than condescend to – the uses of literature in everyday life: uses that we have hardly begun to understand. Such a reorientation, with any luck, might inspire more capacious, and more publicly persuasive, rationales for why literature, and the study of literature, matter. (191)

Felski goes on to explain why she endeavours 'to show why reading critically – or what I have preferred to call reading suspiciously – should not be taken as the ultimate horizon of thought. It has no a priori claims to philosophical rigor, political radicalism, or literary sophistication. It is one way of reading and thinking among others: finite, limited, and fallible' (192). Richards' mistake, in *Science and Poetry* most egregiously, but in *The Principles of Literary Criticism* too, is to take the view from where he stood as the 'ultimate horizon of thought', which justified a stunning rejection of what came before him, but more importantly, a myopic ignorance about what was going on all around him – evidenced by the alacrity with which he summarily rejects Bergsonian phenomenology, Freudian psychoanalysis and Saussurian structural linguistics in *The Meaning of Meaning*. His even greater error was not to see how his radical rejection of whatever is not or not-yet fully 'scientific' blinded him to the possibility of imagining the potential dead end of such a stringent and restrictive criticism, much less to the subsequent generation's critique, and ultimate rejection, of his own most dearly held critical assumptions.

A contemporary community of literary scholars sees Pater for the multiform polymath he always was and recognises his place as no mere minor figure within theory, but a writer in the tradition of Nietzsche, Freud, Bergson, Bachelard, Merleau-Ponty, Levinas, Deleuze and so many others. If, as Hillis Miller attests, Pater's multilinear genealogy has been restored to him across such a diversity of thought, it should be possible to make the case for the force of Pater's work more generally, as a 'theorist', in the discourses of the human and social sciences. We should not underestimate the power of Pater's 'renaissance', understood broadly as an ethos he praises in the work of Pico della Mirandola: the concept that nothing that has ever passionately occupied man's thought could truly lose its vitality. It is the antithesis of T. S. Eliot's quest for a criticism of mere fact and I. A. Richards' zealous rejection of everything that does not yield 'a purer science' or 'purer poetry'. We should not discount the power of discovery and return, the key tropes Jacques Lacan used to re-introduce Freud, in bringing Pater to new readers and insisting on his rightful participation in unlikely discourses. In his next renaissance, which the publication of the newly published *Collected Works* will no doubt engender, I see Pater's work, in its entirety, as having the potential to be a truly animating force in the critical theory *à venir*, in our own, still young century.

Notes

1. Miller, 'Walter Pater', p. 556.
2. Felski, *The Limits of Critique*, p. 13.
3. Richards, *Principles of Literary Criticism*, p. vii.
4. Treating 'the New Criticism' as a proper noun draws most directly from American critic John Crowe Ransom's monograph *The New Criticism* (1941). I will maintain this convention, mindful of the anachronism and geographical displacement of applying that name to the work of the two critics, writing in England, I examine most closely, T. S. Eliot and I. A. Richards. The critical texts on which I will focus predate the book that gave the 'movement' its name. For this reason and others, the name is an imperfect one. Nevertheless, 'New Criticism' and 'New Critics' are sufficiently common terms, I believe, to justify their use – hereafter without quotation marks – in my essay. I also recognise the heterogeneity of the authors typically considered New Critical, who are diverse in method, style, training and ideology. The name New Critic does not imply unanimity of opinion; many of these critics took issue with one another. In 'A Psychologist Looks at Poetry' (*The World's Body*, 1938, 143–65; *I. A. Richards and His Critics*,

2001, 440–56), for example, Ransom himself takes issue with Richards' reductive, 'jaunty faith in what "modern psychology" says' about poetry, and his concomitant dismissal of the aesthetic insights of other knowledge traditions as mere 'pseudo-statements' (p. 442). He may have read 'the stock philosophers', from 'the Greek aestheticians' to the 'Neo-Hegelians', Ransom observes, but 'he ought to read them more humbly' (p. 450).
5. Miller, 'Walter Pater: A Partial Portrait', p. 97.
6. The phase refers to Frank Lentricchia's *After the New Criticism* (1980). I borrow this phrase and concept of the 'missed enounter', or the *'faux bond'*, from Herman Rapaport's discussion of it in *The Theory Mess*.
7. Rapaport's passing observation is part of a larger meditation on the 'eclipse' of theory in the late twentieth-century academy, which he argues requires first addressing 'a much more significant issue, namely, the decline of philosophy as the ground for the human and natural sciences'. By way of theorist Rosi Braidotti, he proposes that 'theory' may be a name or stand-in for intellectual work that occurs in this decline, or 'is itself the afterlife of philosophy' (p. 16). Though it is beyond the scope of this essay to synthesise the projects of all the theorists I cite here, I do see a unified effort across the many names (philosophy, criticism, philosophical criticism, theory) Miller, Hartman, Felski, Rapaport, Braidotti and others give to moods or modes of discourse that challenge the misplaced 'scientific' or anti-speculative drive.
8. Pater, 'Conclusion', *The Renaissance*, p. 236.
9. Ransom, 'Criticism, Inc.' This essay was first published in the *Virginia Quarterly* and subsequently in *The World's Body* (1938).
10. It comes from the last lines of Matthew Arnold's essay: 'The epochs of Aeschylus and Shakespeare make us feel their pre-eminence. In an epoch like those is, no doubt, the true life of literature; there is in the promised land, toward which criticism can only beckon. That promised land it will not be ours to enter, and we shall die in the wilderness: but to have saluted it from afar, is already, perhaps, the best distinction among contemporaries; it will certainly be the best title to esteem with posterity' (pp. 40–1).
11. Hartman, *Criticism in the Wilderness*, pp. 4–5.
12. Lukács, *Soul and Form*, p. 191.
13. The thesis here might echo *Plato and Platonism*, and the exuberant style might follow familiar rhythms, but Lukács is not, here, equal to Pater's precision and rigour. Though Pater suggests Plato's dialogue 'is essentially an essay', he does not conflate the forms entirely; nor does he assume the Socratic dialogues tell us anything about the 'life' of the man who wrote them down (Pater, quoted in Hartman, p. 191).
14. See also Lukács' 'Platonism, Poetry, and Form: Rudolf Kassner' (1908) for further indications of his indebtedness to 'the Platonist Pater' (26), also in *Soul and Form*.
15. Freud, 'The Uncanny' (p. 220).
16. The element of fear and strangeness that accompanies the uncanny, which the New Critics also sought to purge from a theory of poetic 'value' made up of only 'positive' terms, I will address in relation to Richards below. That Edmund Burke's *Philosophical Enquiry* treats fear as the foundational emotion of the sublime and also insists it is a 'positive', so defined within his proof that pain is never simply the absence of pain, is just one of countless

ways in which the discourse on poetic 'value' forecloses an astonishingly vast tradition of discourse, in the name of 'progress'.
17. 'The Child in the House', in Pater, *Miscellaneous Studies*, p. 172.
18. William E. Buckler, 'Introduction', in *Walter Pater: Three Major Works* (1986, p. 39).
19. In Pater's 'Style' (p. 17) and *Plato and Platonism* (pp. 168–9) respectively.
20. Pater, *The Renaissance* (p. 49).
21. *Miscellaneous Studies* was published in August, 1895. *Greek Studies* was published earlier that same year. Pater died on 30 July 1894.
22. T. S. Eliot, 'The Function of Criticism', in *Selected Essays*, pp. 18–20.
23. See Chapter 7, 'A Psychological Theory of Value', in Richards' *Principles of Literary Criticism* for this elaboration. At moments, his division of 'impulses' into positive ('appentencies') and negative ('aversions') resembles the theory of 'drives' elaborated by Sigmund Freud's contemporaneous texts (especially *Beyond the Pleasure Principle*, 1920), but Richards acknowledges Freud only once in this text, and only to observe that 'psycho-analysts tend to be peculiarly inept as critics' (24).
24. Pater, 'Preface', in *The Renaissance*, p. vii.
25. Though they are similarly dismissive of Freud, Wimsatt and Brooks do spend the time with his forbears Richards does not (including substantial readings of Pater, A. C. Bradley, Henri Bergson), and direct contemporary readers to texts lately relegated to relative obscurity. That Richards, by contrast, cites Freud offhandedly and only once in *Principles of Literary Criticism* simply adds another layer of mystery to this strange text. In the first of two chapters devoted to Richards in their 'short history', they use side-by-side passage citations to show how pervasively he borrows from Santayana, largely without attribution (Wimsatt and Brooks, *Literary Criticism*, pp. 613–20).
26. Santayana, *The Sense of Beauty*, p. 125. Notably, it is Santayana who first demotes aesthetics as the privileged domain for considering beauty, and emboldens the scientism present everywhere in Richards' work. In his 'Conclusion', for instance, Santayana reminds readers that 'our sense of beauty, an appreciation of sensible material, . . . and another of associated values, we have been merely following the established method of psychology, the only one by which it is possible to analyze the mind' (p. 260).
27. Krieger, *The New Apologists for Poetry*, p. 259.
28. Hartman, *The Unremarkable Wordsworth*.
29. 'Wordsworth', in Pater, *Appreciations*, p. 50.
30. In the '*scientific* use of language', statements convey information about what is or is not, and the relationship of 'references to one another must be . . . logical' (251). It uses words 'for the sake of the reference they promote'. The '*emotive* use of language' proper to poetry engages language 'for the sake of the attitudes and emotions which ensue' (250).
31. T. S. Eliot, 'The Function of Criticism' (1923), in *Selected Essays*, pp. 12–13.
32. T. S. Eliot, 'Arnold and Pater' (1930), in *Selected Essays*, pp. 384.
33. Bergson's doctoral dissertation, this text was first published in English in 1910 as *Time and Free Will: An Essay on the Immediate Data of Consciousness*, trans. F. L. Pogson, London: Allen and Unwin. Bergson,

who died in 1922, was posthumously awarded the Nobel Prize in Literature in 1927.
34. One could make a compelling case, however, that a certain strain of British Marxist critique *does* in fact have roots in the aesthetic demystifications and psychophysiological levellings of I. A. Richards, despite the temptation merely to equate his position with the famously 'elitist' F. R. Leavis, one of the first recipients of Cambridge's PhD in English and Richards' student, and to imagine, in turn, what an odd bedfellow he made with with longtime colleague Raymond Williams. Michael Sprinker, who subscribes to such a narrative ('Raymond Williams never felt entirely at home in Cambridge'), traces such a lineage in his review of books by two of Williams's students (Sprinker, 'Review').
35. Kuriyama, *The Expressiveness of the Body*, p. 64.

Chapter 7

'This world is now thy pilgrimage': William Michael Rossetti's Cognitive Maps of France and Italy

Eleonora Sasso

In *Some Reminiscences* (1906), Rossetti admits, '[F]or the French, along with the Italians, I have always felt a strong national predilection' (2: 356), mainly due to his strong sense of democracy and revolutionary spirit. But it was, first and foremost, the frightful memory of the invasion of 'gli austriaci' or 'i tedeschi', announced by his father, that indulged this predilection when Italy was under the heel of the Austrians. Born in a cosmopolitan milieu, Rossetti, the third son of a political Neapolitan refugee in England, soon developed ultra-liberal and revolutionary views. These are expressed in his most acclaimed collection of poems, *Democratic Sonnets* (1907), a political manifesto against tyranny and oppression, promoting the struggle for liberalism and democracy as embodied by historical figures such as Napoleon, Mazzini, Cavour and Garibaldi. This manifesto also attests to Rossetti's real and imagined journeys throughout Europe in the late nineteenth century. Taking these references into account, I reread *Democratic Sonnets* as a cognitive map of Rossetti's mental framework determined by French and Italian landmarks (Paris, the island of St Helena, the Alps, the Venice Lagoon, Mount Vesuvius and so forth), which function as orientation points that are tied to the historical events of the Italian Risorgimento.[1]

To Rossetti, employee of the Excise Office between 1845 and 1894, 'the idea of extensive and adventurous travel was always highly attractive' (Rossetti, *Some Reminiscences* 343). It is not by chance that after seeing the sea for the first time at Herne in 1846 his role as a secretary and editor working for the Pre-Raphaelite Brotherhood was characterised by a series of repeated journeys to Europe (Belgium, France, Germany, Italy, Holland, Scotland, Spain and Switzerland), including one unfortunate voyage to Australia on the ship Nineveh, which was infested with the smallpox. If it is true, as Frédéric Gros suggests, that 'boredom is immobility of the body confronted with emptiness of mind' (157), then Rossetti's repeated journeys to Europe constitute a remedy for the boredom of a sedentary and uneventful existence, slowing time and thereby freeing him from routine.

It is highly significant that Rossetti always travelled eastward to the Old World – the history, art and literature of the past. But apart from the more conventional aspect of the Grand Tour, that is preaching the unity of morality and taste, his motives for touring Europe were on the one hand to discover his Italian roots, a return to an ancient, ancestral home, and on the other hand to figure out the crimes and atrocities of war and study the works of art and literature, retracing the steps of his own Italian race. Metaphorically speaking, Rossetti's life is a journey, a journey to the East leading to the origins of the world. As a pilgrim of hope looking for personal and historical truths, he nourishes his soul with walks and visions, confirming Thoreau's philosophy of walking according to which our real treasure is the quantity of the representations that we have taken in and conserved, the sum of all the individuals' spaces experienced in a lifetime.[2] Rossetti's tourist activities included visiting the Louvre during the year of the Universal Exhibition of Paris in 1855, buying blue china and Japanese books at the shop of Madame Dessoye in the Rue de Rivoli, and going to the opera house in Aix-la-Chapelle to see Donizetti's *Lucrezia Borgia*, as well as dining at Pedrocchi's in Padua, paying homage to the Tomb of Dante, and visiting the Palazzo Galletti in Pisa where the Shelleys lived from January 1820 to April 1822.[3] These activities, then, are to be seen as Rossetti's urban explorations which, in Gros's words, 'giv[e] access, via the diversity of humanity and of the behaviour of our fellows, to detailed small discoveries, enchanting to the mind' (165).

According to Gros's taxonomy of walking, Rossetti's solitary strolls around the cities of Europe recall Nerval's wanderings.[4] They have a melancholy, dreamlike quality, the melancholy of names and memories, as in the case of the Bientina, a small town not far from Pisa, the birthplace of his grandfather Gaetano Polidori, whose lake had been drained in 1860. In the following excerpt, Rossetti recalls his first visit to Italy, as well as to the 'Lago of Bientina', which here appears to be an epiphanic place of sorrowful memories:

> My first visit to Italy was made, as already shown, in 1860, in company with Mr Vernon Lushington. Our chief goal was Florence; but we saw besides various other cities Como, Milan, Parma, Piacenza, Bologna, Pisa, Siena, Leghorn, Genoa. I visited also the birth-place of my grandfather Polidori, a small town named Bientina, not far from Pisa. I had often heard him speak of a 'Lago di Bientina'; but this sheet of water, whatever might have been its

dimensions towards 1788 when he bade a final adieu to Tuscany, was not to be discovered in 1860 – it had been drained away. The whole experience was, and could not but be, one of the leading landmarks in my life. (*Some Reminiscences* 347)

However, first and foremost Rossetti exemplifies the subversion enacted by the urban *flâneur*, the ghost of the metropolis, who sees without being seen. Like the urban *flâneur*, Rossetti moves slowly across the streets, and his mind is gripped by a thousand things at once: by the newly written street inscriptions in Verona after the departure of the Austrians, by the Prussian soldiers at Dijon, and by the ruins of the Tuileries, the Arc de Triomphe and the Jardin des Plantes, whose beasts died of hunger in 1871. By resisting the speed of violence, war and business, Rossetti's slowness becomes the condition for a higher agility: that of the mind. To put it in Gros's words, 'The urban stroller moves slowly, but his eyes dart about and his mind is gripped by a thousand things at once. . . . He has better things to do: remythologize the city, invent new divinities, explore the poetic surface of the urban spectacle' (179–80). Reminiscent of Gandhi's mystic and political choice between two energies, between calm force and perpetual agitation, between a civilisation of transmission, prayer and manual labour and one of speed, machinery and accumulation, Rossetti's journeys to France and Italy attest to the centrality of walking and in more general terms of travel in the creation of literary and artistic meaning. Walking, according to Gros, is among the most creative activities – the cure for all modernity's indignities.

Paris as a Blended Space of Life and Death: W. M. Rossetti's Cognitive Map of French History

As early as 1853, Rossetti crossed the Channel, as he had been haunted by an eager desire to visit Paris, the city of Victor Hugo, home of 'fine churches and splendid inns' (*D. G. Rossetti: His Family Letters* 73), a city whose most glorious view from the very top of Notre Dame made Dante Gabriel and William Holman Hunt 'shout in the spirit' (61).[5] Like Dante Gabriel and his Pre-Raphaelite brothers, who enjoyed Paris immensely, Rossetti felt such a fascination with the city, which according to him was 'an instinct of the civilized man' (*Some Reminiscences* 344), and he was amply conscious of it. After this first visit to Paris, during which he witnessed the vast changes (such as the extension of the Rue de Rivoli and the new portion of the Louvre) that Napoleon III had begun to make after his coup d'état, Rossetti visited Paris a great number of times (at least forty). These repeated visits to Paris appear to engender 'a state of well-being', fostered by 'the pleasure of repetition'; the beautiful city he finds so fulfilling offers a renewed pleasure that increases with each visit (Gros 142).

It is worth mentioning Rossetti's trip to Paris in 1855, the year of the first French Universal Exhibition, which was 'in many respects more extensive and complete than the London Great Exhibition of 1851' (*Some Reminiscences* 344). Compared to Dante Gabriel's disappointing artistic experience in 1849 – when he found he preferred the Can-Can at Valentino's (an infamous Paris dance hall) to the paintings exhibited at the Louvre that he defined as 'maps/of sloshy colours' in 'Last Sonnet At Paris' (*Rossetti: His Family Letters* ll. 9–10, p. 73) – Rossetti's visit to the French museum was an absolute discovery. As Rossetti recalls, he felt 'the keenest interest in looking at this collection, in which the great French painters of Louis Philippe's time were amply represented' (*Some Reminiscences* 345). In addition to the works by Ingres, Delaroche, Delacroix, Decamps and some others, Rossetti was particularly attracted by a separate gallery exhibiting Gustave Courbet's collection of paintings, whose naturalism may be associated, according to nineteenth-century critics, with the Pre-Raphaelite obsession with detail. He firmly believed that his Pre-Raphaelite brothers should have imported into their works some of Courbet's 'directness of view and powerful handling' (345). In *Some Reminiscences*, Rossetti clearly expresses his admiration for Courbet's painting, whose naturalism he thought was different from the Pre-Raphaelite attention to detail:

> I had recently heard Courbet spoken of as if he were doing in France much the same sort of work that the Pre-Raphaelites had set going in England. I amply admired much of what I here saw of Courbet's art: but I perceived that, both in spirit and in method, he was on a distinctly different tack from the Pre-Raphaelites, aiming at naturalism through breadth, whereas they strove to embody inventive thought through exactitude of detail. (*Some Reminiscences* 2: 345)

Great was Rossetti's shock, then, when the Louvre, chronotope of meeting (where he encountered Legros and Gerome), was set on fire by the Parisian revolutionists in 1871. That year he recorded in his diary that it was 'a most hellish deed and a miserable stigma on the advanced democracy . . . The Louvre is burning . . . one awaits the end in fear and trembling' (*The Diary of William Michael Rossetti* 64).

Cognitively speaking, Rossetti is a figure whose cultural and ideological path is determined by Parisian reference points or landmarks for orientation and is tied to what he regards as the present state of the world. If we reconstruct Rossetti's cognitive map – his mental representation of the environments that he experienced – then we will be able to trace Paris's spatial characteristics: the distance and direction between places and the inclusion of one place within another, as well as the range of motion events, that is, events where some entity changes its position in space, activated by the moon, the stars and the lights of Paris. Analysing Rossetti's motion events in relation to the Louvre, the Tuileries, the Arc de Triomphe, the Jardin de Plantes, Montmartre and so forth, we can determine the scope of his mapping, whose goal-oriented movement is metonymically related to a purposeful or intended action. To put it simply, the motion event that involves the motion towards the landmarks of Paris is related to the sole purpose of personal and historical remembrance and 'truth at all costs' (*Some Reminiscences* 370). In the following diary entry, Rossetti describes the ruins of a Paris whose grandeur is still perceptible in its damaged landmarks: 'Before reaching the inside of the city, I saw no traces worth mentioning of the damages of war . . . Went about chiefly to look at ruins – Tuileries, Finances (the worst), Cour d'Escomptes, Luxembourg and Arc de Triomphe slight . . . Jardin des Plantes' (*Diary* 112). He still considers France to be a great country whose republican government gives ideological strength and stability to its patriots. In his letter to Mrs Gilchrist (4 December 1870), he clearly expresses his deep admiration for this country, projecting the conceptual metaphor FRANCE IS A GREAT FIGHTER:[6]

> France is indeed in a horrible condition – but I think one may and must now say not in a disgraced condition, which is a great consolation to myself & others who love a Republic. La République has applied herself patriotically & energetically & daringly to retrieving if possible, the disasters & shame inherited from the Empire . . . She has made a great fight – an astonishing fight under the circumstances, it seems to me . . . will be entitled to show her horrid wounds & rents with lofty self-respect. . . . Great men were living before Agamemnon & great conquerors have had to turn tail prior to King William of Prussia. (Rossetti, *Selected Letters* 69–70)

For Rossetti, Paris is a blended space, a space of life and death, of liberty and slavery, an allegorical city in which he maps stories onto other stories, stories of historical figures: Robespierre, Danton, Napoleon, Lamartine, Emile Ollivier, Louis Philippe and Napoleon III. In a famous letter sent to Walt Whitman (31 March 1872), Rossetti reveals the list of the most important and influential people of the last 100 years in Europe, in which Napoleon I is defined as 'the greatest genius as a conqueror and ruler': 'I suppose anyone is to be allowed to admire him enormously, whether one approves him or not' (*Selected Letters* 286). It is not by chance that to Napoleon I he dedicates an elegiac sonnet entitled 'Napoleon Re-Buried, 1841', whose antonymic structure recalls

Alessandro Manzoni's dual rendering of Napoleon as both a man-tyrant and a suffering man in the poem 'The Fifth of May' ('Il cinque Maggio' [1821]).

First buried on St Helena, Napoleon's remains were exhumed and brought to Paris in 1840 on the orders of King Louis-Philippe for burial at the military hospital, the Invalides. Rossetti's sonnet invokes the need for this second burial by cognitively mapping the geographic space in order to have a sense of historical agency in the world. Cognitive mapping in this context would be an essential part of a political culture, which seeks to endow the individual subject with some new heightened sense of his place in the global system. Rossetti writes:

> Bear, bear him home with honour. From the rock
> Where England's vampire sucked the captive's blood,
> Along the South and North Atlantic flood
> To his remotest Paris bear him. Lock
> With clamps of steel into the porphyry block
> The bones of the unparagoned lord of men,
> And self-incredulous let History's pen
> Write – 'Here for aye lies he whose deeds made mock
> Of all the ages spread o'er all the world,
> Napoleon.' Read it, France, and, Europe, read.
> Think of a continent of slaughtered sons,
> Thought chained, a discipline of pomps and guns.
> Think also – This was Freedom's heir who hurled
> Her down, yet reigned by Freedom's grace indeed. (*Democratic Sonnets* xxv)

Rossetti invites the reader to start a journey eastward across four spatial and mental dimensions: 1) the island of St Helena, 2) the South and North Atlantic Ocean, 3) Paris (Invalides, 7th arrondissment) and 4) Europe. His wayfinding behaviour includes the task of orienting the reader towards nonvisible locations and planning the route to bear the bones of Napoleon, 'the unparagoned lord of men' (l. 6), from 'the rock where England's vampires sucked the captive's blood' (ll. 1–2) to the remotest area of Paris (Invalides). If the first part of the sonnet draws a cognitive map which suggests a humanised representation of Napoleon as a victim, a captive of 'England's vampire' (l. 7), deserving a warrior's burial 'with clamps of steel into the porphyry block' (l. 5), then the following sestet focuses on the military man who followed 'a discipline of pomps and guns' (l. 7) and slaughtered the sons of Europe in the name of Freedom ('Think of a continent of slaughtered sons', l. 11). From the remotest island in the Atlantic Ocean to the central arrondissment of Paris, the echo of Napoleon's deeds reaches its climax in the epitaph penned by a self-incredulous History, reminiscent of

Manzoni's Earth standing 'amazed, smitten and dazed' at the announcement of Napoleon's death ('So the Earth, smitten and dazed/At the announcement, stands amazed', Manzoni, 'The Fifth of May', ll. 5–6), as if to attest the apparent immortality of a myth. Rossetti's blending of such metonymic binaries as rock/blood, flood/block and sons/guns well reproduces the picture of Napoleon as the arbiter and controller of two historical worlds: the secular and the religious. In its negotiation of the gap between local subjective experience and a vision of an overall environment, Rossetti's cognitive map is an apt figure to make sense of and move through history.

Orientated towards the Light: Rossetti's Cognitive Maps and Wayfinding in Italy

Even more than through France, Rossetti travelled almost every year through some part of Italy that he considered his 'native country almost in equal degree with England' (Peattie 699), as clearly expressed in a letter to Walt Whitman (31 March 1972). As Angela Thirlwell argues, Italy was 'a central inner resource which nourished his English intellectual life' (34). The first trip to Italy in 1860 is considered by Rossetti as one of the leading landmarks in his life. In company with Mr Vernon Lushington, a Pre-Raphaelite sympathiser and friend to William Holman Hunt, Rossetti visited Florence, Como, Milan, Parma, Piacenza, Boulogne, Pisa, Siena and Genoa. Needless to say, his chief goal was Florence with its Uffizi, Pitti Palace and Santo Spirito, where he deeply admired Leonardo, Lippo Lippi and Giorgione. Surprisingly, his tourist promenades and urban *flâneurie* in such a *civitas peregrina* were soon interrupted by the invitations of Robert Browning to visit him at the villa at Marciano some miles from Siena, and of Mr Seymour Kirkup, an English painter of some celebrity in Florence, admirer of Gabriele Rossetti's theories of Dantesque interpretation, who was made a Barone of the Italian Kingdom, an honour due, in part, to his conspicuous achievements. At the pleasant villa at Marciano, Rossetti witnessed the Brownings' involvement with the Risorgimento and the Italian search for political identity, for those were the days following the Franco-Sardinian war against Austria in 1859. Equally astonishing was the discovery that the Brownings had a keen interest in spiritualism; they introduced Rossetti to Kirkup, a spiritualist who believed in guardian angels and above all in his ability to communicate with the spirit of Dante Alighieri. Memorable is the séance held in Kirkup's apartments on the Ponte Vecchio by his housekeeper, a medium claiming that the spirit of Dante protected Giuseppe Garibaldi as an 'angelo custode' but only appearing when Garibaldi was in Florence.[7] In a letter to Rossetti (6 March 1867), Kirkup explains how Garibaldi was haunted by Dante's ghost and how his medium Olimpia, a young uneducated girl, used to give proof of the presence of spirits through physical demonstrations:

> My somnambula, Olimpia, tells me that Dante is Garibaldi's angelo custode. He never comes but when Garibaldi is in Florence, which I always know by that. I met G[aribaldi] in the street the other day. I said nothing to her; and sure enough Dante came, and she did not know it, though D[ante] told us where he, G[aribaldi], was lodging. He was always with him during the war. ... You ask why the window of the small room is left open. It always is, by their desire, that they may take the object. They cannot get it through stone walls, though they can pass themselves. There is no window beyond it, as it is a corner-house, and there is none over it; and the chair is in the middle of the room, not close to the window. My studio is the next room to it, where I mostly sit, and where you once sat. (*Rossetti Papers* 254–5)

Rossetti's originally sceptical involvement in such paranormal activities (table turning and rapping, as well as the use of the ouija) soon became a real obsession throughout his life. He was repeatedly involved in séances in 1866 at the home of the historian Thomas Keightley, then at the Scotts' home, at the Marshalls' (on 12 May 1866), in the back sitting room of Charles Howell's house and in the studio at Cheyne Walk in 1867, trying to communicate with the spirit of Elizabeth Siddal. From this perspective, Rossetti's trips to Italy appear to be unmissable adventures of discovery, discoveries of history, literature, culture and above all of what Gros calls eternities, 'the eternity of things, endlessly renewed' (101) as well as the eternity 'of all that is resistant, unchanging' (82) exemplified by the rocks, the plains and the skylines.

The following trips to Italy were equally unforgettable, characterised by a series of misadventures, as when in 1873 Edward John Trewlany asked Rossetti to fulfil a small commission as a literary spy in Florence. Rossetti was supposed to accomplish the mission of buying a number of documents concerning Shelley and Byron in possession of Claire Clairmont, the stepsister of Mary Shelley and lover of Lord Byron. But when he arrived in her residence in the Via Valfonda (Florence), Rossetti found Clairmont 'lying outside her bed, unable to move about the room so as to bring out and explain her papers' (*Some Reminiscences* 352). Among the numerous misadventures reported in *Some Reminiscences*, Rossetti also recalls being robbed of about 800 francs in his own railway carriage during the journey through Verona to Venice in 1868, as well as his lost baggage while travelling by rail towards Verona in 1871, and other small incidents such as his broken watch stopping suddenly at intervals, the mosquito demons haunting his hotel room in Padua and his attacks of gout on reaching Naples in 1896, which obliged him to rush back to London. Another memorable event was the terrible earthquake that occurred in San Remo on Ash Wednesday (23 February 1887) before sunrise when he was staying at the 'Hotel Pension Anglo-American' with his wife Lucy Madox Brown, who would never forget that shocking experience. As reported by Rossetti, a certain tremor continued lurking in his wife's nerves, and for this reason the fourth day after the cataclysm they left San Remo. Christina Rossetti's letters, sent to his brother (28 February 1887) and Lucy (21 March 1887), also attest to Lucy's incapacity to overcome this trauma. The following empathic words written by Christina and addressed to Lucy well exemplify her troubled condition: 'I fully agree with you that it is impossible to pass through so awful an experience without deep impressions: the suspense I was in on all your accounts made its impression on me and sent me to prayer' (Rossetti, *Family Letters of Christina Rossetti* 163).

For Rossetti, travelling to Italy also meant a quest for love and romance: on 26 May 1873, he arranged a trip to Rome, Florence and Venice in a party of five (Mr and Mrs Bell Scott, Miss Boyce, Lucy Brown and himself) to continue his courtship of Ford Madox Brown's elder daughter, and he eventually proposed to her in Switzerland when the journey was almost over. They became engaged on 1 July 1873, and the following year they spent their honeymoon in Naples, Rome and Florence. Both trips were conducted for pleasure, which according to Gros is 'a matter of encountering. It is a possibility of feeling that finds completion in an encounter with a body, element or substance' (140). This is what happened to William and Lucy, who enjoyed the moonlight view of the Colosseum and the Roman and Ligurian sunlight, finding moments of pure pleasure, of agreeable sensations, sweet and unprecedented, as a result of encounters with the Italian landscape and works of art. Walking across the streets of Rome, Naples and Florence allowed them the opportunity to marvel at the beauty of the day and night, the brightness of the sun and the moon in a 'firework-like explosion of successive flashes' (Gros 181). Their shared interests led them also to visit botanic, zoological and public gardens in general, a real obsession for Rossetti, whose favourite Italian gardens were the Ravenna Pine Forest, the famous Pineta celebrated by Dante in Canto XXVIII of *Purgatorio* and by Byron in *Don Juan*; this was also where Byron and Shelley used to ride. In addition, he visited the Botanic Garden in Padua, the oldest Botanic Garden in Europe with 'splendid magnolias and a superb *araucaria excelsa*' (*Diary* 92). Far from being what Gros calls 'concerts of intrigues', as in the case of Tuileries whose variety of showcases made it 'a play in which all were actors and spectators' (172), Italian gardens are to Rossetti visual reminders of his childhood, of the time spent in the Zoological Gardens in London with Christina and Dante Gabriel looking at bears, wombats and owls, since 'behind all differences, gardens are all alike' (Gros 173).

Another peculiar trait of Rossetti's trips to Italy was the constant recording of the achievements and anecdotes of Giuseppe Garibaldi, whom he regarded as the 'greatest and most flawless personal hero' (Peattie 286). Fondly interested in the private lives of his heroes, Rossetti not only investigated the cause of Garibaldi's separation from Anita while visiting Ravenna on 10 August in 1871, but also appeared obsessed with staying in the hotels and pensions which had once accommodated Garibaldi. These included the Albergo d'Italia (Brescia), in which Garibaldi occupied room no. 6, shortly before Aspromonte and 'La Croce di Malta' Hotel, in Lecco, which Garibaldi visited twice in 1859 during his anti-Austrian campaigns. Indeed, there are countless anecdotes of Rossetti's detective-like search for traces of the presence of Garibaldi in Italy, but the most significant is the boat trip he took on Lake Como with his sister Christina in order to locate the hill where Garibaldi fought and triumphed over Austrian soldiers in an attempt to free Como from Austrian dominance. At that very moment, Rossetti and Christina heard a nightingale, a pure Romantic moment celebrating Garibaldi's immortality, eternalised by the bird's 'geno-song', a melancholy song dealing with death and the unknown (Barthes 182):

> After dinner C[hristina] and I went out in a boat on the lake for an hour: the boatman a good-looking characteristic Italian, who spoke with great enthusiasm about Garibaldi's achievements hereabouts in 1859. Almost opposite our starting-place is a not lofty hill where 11,000 Austrians were posted; upon whom Garibaldi fell suddenly with 3,000, and routed them very rapidly, and made them all clear out of Como: this succeeding other the like achievements at San Fermo and Varese. The Comaschi looked on in boats applauding (!). The boatman speaks very highly of Maximilian, and even enthusiastically of Radetsky, under whom he himself served in, or perhaps before, 1848. It seems Radetsky was very partial to his Italian and Hungarian soldiers, preferring them much for hill-service to Germans, and very indulgent in granting furloughs etc. Heard a nightingale on the wooded hills overlooking the lake, and saw the house which Queen Caroline used to occupy also the historic tower of Baradello, '*del tempo*' as the boatman said, '*dei Romani e di Federigo Barbarossa*'. I asked the boatman whether the people of Como would like to be under the Austrians again: he replied no, but with less decisiveness of phrase than similar questions generally elicit. (*Rossetti Papers* 111–12)

In this diary entry dated 2 June 1865, Rossetti provides a cognitive map of Como as a locus of historical memory. According to the Spatial Framework Hypothesis, an illuminating behavioural approach investigating a character surrounded by objects, Rossetti and Christina are participants in a scenario whose main character, the boatman, is described as facing a particular landscape and whose response times to access information about the surrounding objects (the lofty hill, the house of Queen Caroline and so forth) are assessed.[8] It is highly significant that the boatman's response time to Rossetti's last question is slower and less determined than the response time to landscape objects. The presence of a conversational partner (Rossetti) and his historical questions influence spatial frame selections. The boatman initiates utterances faster and more enthusiastically when speaking from a viewer-centred perspective (the boatman speaks enthusiastically about Garibaldi's achievements in the areas surrounding Como), next fastest from an object-centred view (the boatman's attention is attracted by a nightingale singing from the hills surrounding the lake, by the house in which Queen Caroline used to lodge and by the historic tower of Baradello) and surprisingly slowest from an addressee-centred frame (the boatman seems to react with less decisiveness to Rossetti's questions). In this sense, aspects of the broader conversational setting can affect spatial frame processing, since the boatman – who probably suffered for being under the Austrians – hesitates to answer Rossetti's hypothetical question.

Such a humanised vision of history may be explained by Rossetti's memorialist vein, which prompted him to write *Lives of Famous Poets* (1878) and *Some Reminiscences*, a 'formidable and inutile' book (Huneker 23), according to the mottoes 'Know thy self' and 'Memento Mori', which are the foundations of a western philosophical and humanist tradition. In Rossetti's view, historical events and poetic production are inseparable parts of the same process, a process according to which art takes reality in its stride, accepts it and absorbs it, since 'the greater the artist, the more numerous and significant the points of contact between artistic creation and historical circumstances' (Hauser 71).

Reconstructing Rossetti's cognitive maps of his repeated journeys to Italy suggests that Garibaldi's campaigns and motion events played a significant role in Rossetti's selection of itineraries leading to historical sites. This is clearly exemplified by his Petrarchan sonnet paying tribute to Garibaldi, eponymously entitled 'Garibaldi, 1871', in which a list of enumerated toponomies (America, Rome, Como, Sicily, Naples, Mentana, France and Nice) appears throughout the lyric as if to create Garibaldi's map of battlefields.[9] From America to Nice, the poet recalls the adventurous life of a hero who started to fight for the rebel movement in South America (Brazil and Uruguay). Rossetti writes,

> The hero of the word. America
> Has seen him charging in the battle's stress;
> And Rome has seen him in her bitterness,
> That brief eternal glory of her sway
> Triumviral; and Como's mountain-way
> Acclaims his swoop ere Austria yet may guess
> His talon's fury; Sicily no less
> And Naples see and worship. When his day
> Is almost done, and while Mentana's scar
> Sill rankles deep, he fights for prostrate France –
> In Rome his Judas double-dyed, in Nice
> His very birthright's prey-bird. Utterance
> Here falters: Men, who hail his light afar,
> Name 'Garibaldi', and then hold their peace. (*Democratic Sonnets* xviii)

In this circular poem, in which the hero's name is evoked both in the third and the last line, the reader can perceive what Thirlwell calls Rossetti's 'stark contrasts and social sarcasm' (258). An alternation of victories (Rome, Como, Sicily and Naples) and failures (Rome, the Battle of Mentana and France) is enacted through the use of an oxymoronic expression – 'at brief eternal glory of her sway/Triumviral' (l. 4).[10] Many are the implied references to Garibaldi's Hunters of the Alps ('and Como's mountain-way/Acclaims his swoop . . .' [ll. 5–6])[11] and the Expedition of the Thousands ('And Naples see and worship . . .' [l. 8]),[12] but what emerges from this celebratory poem is the strength and glory of a hero who against the odds can never surrender.

If a cognitive map is characterised by a fixed orientation, then Rossetti's poem, which exalts Garibaldi's vehemence ('His talon's fury' [l. 7]) and resoluteness ('and while Mentana's scar/Still rankles deep' [ll. 9–10]) against Austrian and French enemies and above all against Italy's traitors ('In Rome his Judas double-dyed' [l. 11]), is orientated towards the light of Garibaldi, always represented by his luminous aura.[13] The poem is inspired mainly by the meaning of the word *Risorgimento*, indicating the period of or the movement for the liberation and political unification of Italy, as conveyed by the verbal root *risorgere*, that is, reawaken, here from the land of the dead in the darkest hour. Rossetti's concluding lines 'Men, who hail his light afar,/Name 'Garibaldi', and then hold their peace' (ll. 13–14) are aimed at creating 'a moment's monument', a monument to the memory of Garibaldi's historical moment, or, in Dante Gabriel's words, a 'memorial from the Soul's eternity/to one dead deathless hour' ('The Sonnet', ll. 2–3, *Collected Writings* 275). Rossetti's *Democratic Sonnets* appears to be a most valuable document attesting to the relationship between historical events and poetic production, confirming Arnold Hauser's assertion that it is possible 'to learn more about history from the works of [authors] than from all the history books' (6). In Rossetti's view, history is a succession of key figures and key places of freedom and independence that humanise history and make it a part of the existential world of the living, and it is this view that grounds his own pilgrimage.

Notes

1. The term Risorgimento was first used in the context of national identity by Saverio Bettinelli in his cultural history of Italy, *Del Risorgimento d'Italia dopo il mille* (1775).
2. See Thoreau, *Walking*.
3. 'Caffè Pedrocchi' was a well-known café during the troubled years of the Risorgimento.
4. Chapter 17 of Gros's *A Philosophy of Walking* is devoted to Gérard de Nerval, whose walks through the streets of Paris are characterised by a feeling of melancholy. According to Gros, through gentle and easy walks, Nerval recalls sorrows and dreams, thereby rediscovering 'the solitary stroller' (149).
5. D. G. Rossetti, letter to William Michael Rossetti, 4 October 1849.
6. The use of small capitals to indicate conceptual metaphors has become conventional in Cognitive Stylistics and other fields, so I use them here for clarity. See Kitchin and Freundschuh, *Cognitive Mapping*.
7. Rossetti writes, 'I will add here (though with only partial relevancy to my context) that I have myself seen something of table turning and rapping, the use of the ouija, and the like, both with professional mediums and in private company. I have seen it, and I don't know what to infer about the phenomena, still less whether "spirits" have anything to do with them. I must however in candour say this much that I think movements and rappings do really take place without any intended or conscious action of the bystanders to produce them' (*Some Reminiscences*, p. 241).
8. According to the spatial framework hypothesis, spatial location serves as an event *framework*, and *spatial* directions serve as relational information within that *framework*. On this topic see Franklin and Tversky, 'Searching Imagined Environments', as well as Schober, 'Speakers, Addresses'.
9. Rossetti composed various sonnets on the figure of Garibaldi as clearly expressed in *Some Reminiscences*: 'I wrote the first, on Garibaldi, when I was absent from London, in January 1881 to deliver some lectures. I then for a while proceeded rapidly, scarcely a day passing when I did not draft a sonnet – occasionally more than one. I found that my facility in this first drafting work was fully adequate, or even ample – reviving the memory of olden times when bouts rimés sonnets were rattled off by Dante Gabriel and myself. . . . I had written a fair number of these sonnets when my brother, in the month of April, thought I was expressing strong

and subversive opinions with dangerous freedom' (*Some Reminiscences*, p. 474).
10. The Battle of Mentana (1867), named after a village in Rome, was fought between the allied French and Papal Armies and the Volunteer Forces of Garibaldi.
11. As early as 1859 Garibaldi offered his services to the King of Sardinia, and, having formed a detached corps, called 'Hunters of the Alps', he gained several victories over the Austrians at Varese, San Fermo and Como.
12. On 5 May 1860, about a thousand poorly equipped, badly armed men, wearing red shirts and slouch hats, set sail from Genoa in order to support the Sicilians. Among Rossetti's poems, 'The Red Shirt, 1860–1867' stands out for its visual quality pivoting on a potent republican symbol of independence, freedom and courage: Garibaldi's red shirts. Garibaldi's army selected red shirts as part of their uniform purely by chance; initially meant for Argentinean butchers, the shirts were available at low cost. Garibaldi took advantage of the colour, recalling the French legacy of red as colour of revolution in 1789 and 1848 and transforming the red shirts into a historical symbol of rebellion.
13. Like Rossetti, Walter Savage Landor and Mary Braddon envisioned Garibaldi as a luminous figure in their poems. In Landor's 'Ad Garibaldum' (1859), Garibaldi is 'the star of Columbia' ('I qua stella Comubiae refulgent'), guiding South American popular revolts, while in Mary Braddon's 'Garibaldi' (1861), Garibaldi is defined as a 'living light', shining ever and whose fullest majesty is revealed at night.

Chapter 8

Personal and Political Fainéance in George Gissing's *Veranilda*

Tom Ue

> I am hateful to myself. For though born to do something worthy of a man, I am now not only incapable of action, but even of thought.
> George Gissing, *Veranilda* (149)

J. Hillis Miller's seminal study *Fiction and Repetition: Seven English Novels* recovers the importance of repetition as a device that 'generate[s] meaning or . . . inhibit[s] the too easy determination of a meaning based on the linear sequence of the story' (2). 'Any novel', he argues, 'is a complex tissue of repetitions and of repetitions within repetitions, or of repetitions linked in chain fashion to other repetitions. In each case there are repetitions making up the structure of the work within itself, as well as repetitions determining its multiple relations to what is outside it . . .' (2–3). Invoking Gilles Deleuze's *Logique du sens*, Miller identifies two kinds of repetition that routinely intertwine: 'one asks us to think of difference on the basis of preestablished similitude or identity' and 'the other invites us on the contrary to think of similitude and even identity as the product of a fundamental disparity' (qtd in 5). *Fiction and Repetition* aims, ultimately, 'to devise a way to remain aware of the strangeness of the language of literature and to try to account for it' (21). This chapter answers Miller's call for replication studies by taking as a test case George Gissing's unfinished novel *Veranilda* (1904) and by showing how its meaning is realised in part by its repetitions. Gissing had long entertained the idea of writing a historical novel. As early as 1881 he thought of writing a story about Greek history during the end of the Peloponnesian War, but it was not until early July 1903, in Ispoure, that he settled on his story for good, the novel-in-progress being different from what he had composed in late 1900 and early 1901 (Coustillas, *Veranilda* xii–xv). Gissing's death in 1903, at the age of 46,

Fainéance in George Gissing's Veranilda 185

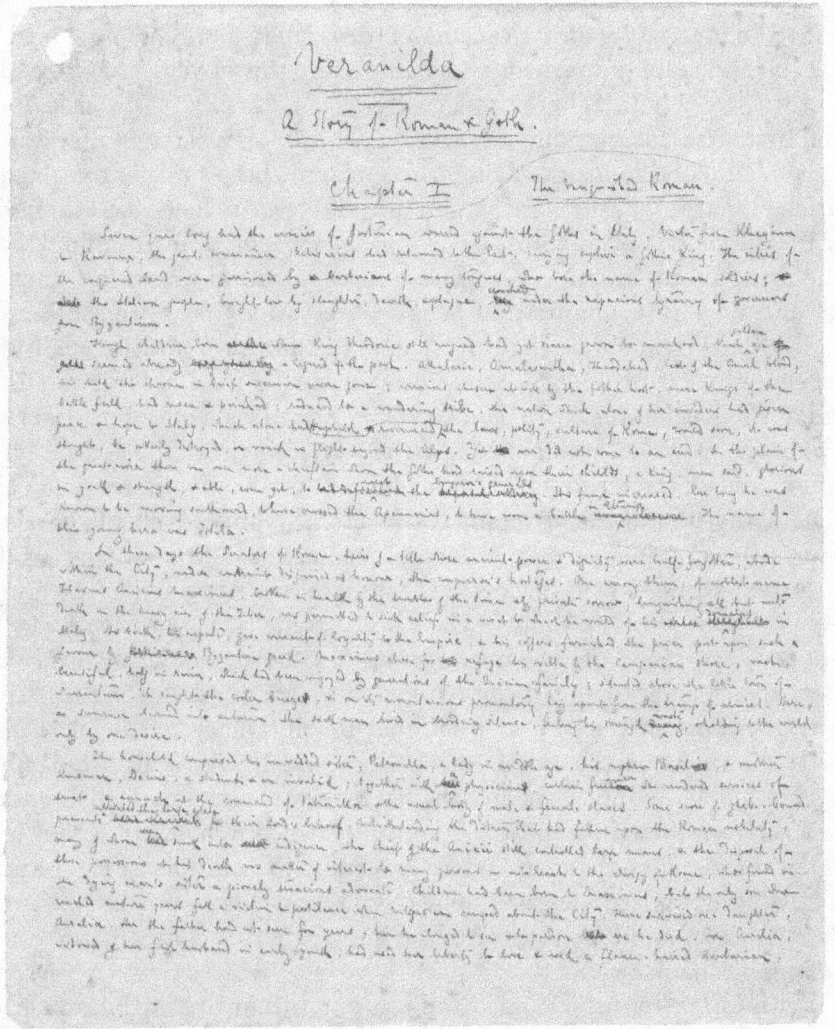

Figure 8.1 Manuscript page of *Veranilda: A Story of Roman & Goth* (1903; 49; MS; Gissing MSS. MS Department, Lilly Library, Bloomington).

left *Veranilda* with five remaining chapters unwritten; and the most part of the novel's manuscript is now held in the Lilly Library at Indiana University (Fig. 8.1).

Scholarship has regularly called attention to its treatment of action. Samuel Vogt Gapp, for instance, praises the novel's characters and descriptions of topography, notwithstanding its somewhat shaky chronology, yet he disparages its (lack of) action: 'The plot is well conceived, the action eminently true to the period, and the idea is a good one; but it does not move. It reminds one too much of the medieval representations of battles in tapestry form. It seems a little strange that [Gissing] failed to put life and color, movement and passion into this novel' (153–5). More recently, Robert L. Selig has suggested that it 'smells of the sickroom' and that it is a 'death-haunted project': 'This book written in illness is in turn filled with illness: the dying Maximus, the hero's uncle; the plague-stricken Petronilla, the hero's aunt; and the fever-ravaged hero himself' (93). The central protagonist Basil 'concentrates on doing nothing' (94), and an endnote directs us to scenes of his protracted illness in Chapters 21 and 24 (133). Gapp's and Selig's observations are insightful, and, as this essay will show, the novel's chain of inaction and, relatedly, its recurring motif of illness operate as synecdoche for the larger state of paralysis that haunts it. In *The Crisis of Action in Nineteenth-Century English Literature*, Stefanie Markovits has argued for the centrality of action and character to our thinking about post-Romantic writing: 'The generic division of the novel into novels of plot and novels of character shows the dominance of the debate over action and character in the Victorian age; it was in this period that these two Aristotelian categories became indispensable tools of the critical trade' (2). Markovits identifies the recurrence of two major storylines that emanate in texts that treat the struggle with action: frustrated marriage plots (or those that entrap people in them) and frustrated revolutionary or social reform plots (4–5). My essay builds on Miller's and Markovits's scholarship by attending to the ways in which Gissing characteristically repeats and offers commentary on the conflicts between individual agency and deterministic circumstances, and between action and inaction.[1] I argue that Gissing undermines a simplistic reading of his character Basil as a passive victim, and demonstrates the importance of contemplation as a coping mechanism.

Set in sixth-century Rome, and against the historical backdrop of warfare between the Roman emperor Justinian and the Gothic king Totila, this novel relates the love story of the Roman Basil and the Goth Veranilda. When the titular heroine is kidnapped, her lover attempts, unsuccessfully, to find her, as do both the Roman emperor and Totila for their independent political motives. Basil's friend Marcian, who serves both courts, becomes jealous of him and, when he is eventually entrusted with Veranilda, begins to fall in love with her. Feverish after a raid during his journey to join Totila, Basil learns from Marcian's deceptive servant Sagaris of his friend's betrayal, and suspects that Veranilda has become unfaithful. Basil arrives at Marcian's villa, kills his friend and then falls ill himself. He is sent to Benedict's monastery, where he regains his health and learns of his wrongs, after which he eventually joins forces with Totila and becomes promised to Veranilda. Gissing's writing stops with the imminent raid of Rome. My focus, in the first half of this essay, is on the conclusions proffered by Gissing's contemporaries and the ending that is foreshadowed by the parts that he completed. In so doing, I reveal how Gissing seems to insist upon the futility of an individual's actions notwithstanding his or her best intentions. As David Grylls has argued, Gissing's writing evinces an interplay between pessimism and willpower, a pattern introduced in his first published novel *Workers in the Dawn* (1880): 'a weakness of will in one of the protagonists that makes him or her excessively reliant on other people or on circumstances; a compensatory determination to resist the ensuing disadvantages; and a state of mind in which this resistance, taking the form of strenuous activity, is fuelled by both a conscious acceptance of suffering and the persistence of an almost unconscious hope' (14). My argument in the second half of this essay expands upon Grylls's by homing in on Basil's social position as an aristocrat, arguing that its attendant qualities in class and bearing, if privileged, could not have prepared him for the challenges of dealing with the novel's conflicts. I suggest that there is something positive in Basil's hesitations and his mental activities by analysing his development from being a victim of circumstance to having independence and free will – terms that are prevalent for our thinking about Gissing's larger oeuvre.[2]

Veranilda and the Problem of Endings

By Chapter 30, the end of the completed portion, Heliodora, the highly influential courtesan whose lovers once included Basil and who loves him still, is captured by the Roman leader and her lover Bessas, and it is likely that she can influence him to exercise her revenge upon Basil and her rival. Here, the novel's possible endings diverge. Gissing's friend H. G. Wells, in a rejected preface to *Veranilda* which he nonetheless published in the *Monthly Review* in August 1904 and in the *Eclectic Magazine* in November 1904, finds that 'the end for [Gissing's] two principal characters, the Princess and Basil is practically told':

> But the main threads run clear to their end; in a moment the tumult of the assailing Goths, terrible by reason of their massacre at Tibur, would have become audible, and the wave of panic that left Rome to the dogs and vermin have swept us to the end. And the end was morning, a sunlit silence upon the empty Forum, upon the as yet unruined Palatine Hill, upon the yet unshattered Basilica of Constantine. For just that one tremendous moment in her history Rome lay still. (586)[3]

W. L. Courtney's review in the *Daily Telegraph*, on 28 September 1904, completes the image evoked here: 'We want to hear of the sack of Rome by the Goths; we miss the final scene, as Mr Wells suggests it would have been, a sunlit silence upon the empty Forum in Rome, shattered but unruined, and the hero, Basil, and the heroine, Veranilda, at last joined in happy union' (441). Writing in 1937, Gissing's son Alfred makes 'conjectures as to the likely tendency of the five unwritten chapters':

> [W]e believe that, contrary to the habit of the earlier Gissing, he intended, as far at any rate as the affairs of Basil and Veranilda are concerned, to make the story end happily. His own experience of life had taught him much as to the perversity of human affairs; but now he was not dealing with the life around him; he was depicting an age widely remote from his own, an age which in the long vista of the past was covered with the bloom of distance and veiled in a golden haze – the glamour and romance of Roman history – an age in which it was possible for ideal things to take place. And we know that the last chapter of all was to contain a picture of Rome in all the fearful desolation of her forty days of utter abandonment – streets and great buildings empty and forsaken, and a ghostly stillness reigning within the mighty heart which had then ceased to throb. (90–1)

By contrast, Gissing's third wife Gabrielle Fleury suggests, in a letter to Clara Collet, that it might have remained 'in Gissing's mind to have Basil be killed and Veranilda enter a convent' (Coustillas, *Veranilda* xviii).[4] In her recollections about Gissing, she too describes an empty and silent Forum, but in dystopian terms that are reminiscent of Mary Shelley's in *The Last Man* (1826):

> The last [chapter] was to be at Rome, & to describe this city *absolutely deserted*, without a living creature, human or animal, as it was during 40 days after Totila had entered it, everybody having been driven out of the town, every animal having been devoured during the long siege. That unique spectacle of the still magnificent town without a soul, with that absolute silence over it, had taken a strong hold on G.'s imagination. He often spoke of that, & pictured so vividly in his mind the impression it ought to have made. And he often said: 'I feel I can make a strong chapter with it; it will be very striking'. – He was very glad to have found such [an] end for his beloved romance. (277; original emphasis)

Gissing had planned the book meticulously, and Fleury's report is worth quoting more fully for the light that it sheds on his method:

> Before beginning actual writing of his works, G. thought a great deal & for a long, long time. In fact he had the work long *ready* in his mind, before beginning writing, & only began it when he felt it so ready. And often made one, or even two, beginnings, & then gave it up, feeling the work was not ripe

enough in his head. So was it for 'Veranilda', his romance of the 6th Century, which he first began at Paris, in winter 1901, under the title: 'The Vanquished Roman', & he often afterwards, at Ispoure, expressed his delight of having abandoned it then, saying it wld have been so immature, so less strong. (And he thought the new title 'Veranilda', which he had found in the spring 1903, when once reading Cassiodorus' letters on the balcony of Villa Lannes, at Ciboure), was so charming, so much better than the previous one 'which might suggest a depressing subject'.) So, feeling the work quite ready in his mind, he began actual writing, but of course altered many things – episodes, details – whilst writing, new ideas came, improvements, changes suggested themselves, etc. – But he never *wrote* a plan of the book. It was all in his head. He then wrote with more or less rapidity, sometimes only a few lines in a sitting of 2 or 3 hours, sometimes much more. Corrected his pages, very often rewriting them. Made many corrections on the typescript [sic], & some again on the proofs, was most careful & fastidious about style & beauty & perfection of language. – G. often said that a book had its growth just like a plant. One felt it grow, slowly grow, develop in the mind – & sometimes it is growing quite unconsciously, – after you have been working at it very hard in your head, & let it rest for a time – then if you try to hurry its natural growth, instead of waiting the right moment, instantly you begin to try & write, you feel it is immature. (284)

Fleury reveals that it was not Gissing's practice to discuss a novel-in-progress in substantial detail, though he dwells again on the strength of the ending that he had in mind: 'You will see, you will see, . . . I can tell you I have got a strong last Chapt. I may be mistaken, but I think it will be very striking' (290).

Gissing's preparatory notes for *Veranilda*, also held in the Lilly Library, reveal some of his intentions. He writes regarding Basil:

> In taking part of Totila, remembers the principles of Cassiod.
> Totila sends him (after Casinum) as bearer of letter to Senate. Says to him: 'Get me Rome without a conflict – & Veranilda is yours.'
>
> B. goes into besieged Rome, to try to plot for its surrender. (Scenes with brother about this). He is arrested as traitor, imprisoned, & lives on nettles. At capt of Rome, Heliod. manages that he alone shall remain in prison, when Rome deserted. Veran., in despair at husband's disappearance, goes with Felix to seek him.
> Heliod. has told Totila (meaning thus to make marriage with V. impossible) that Basil has turned traitor and gone with Bessas. The traitorous servant of Marcian, become lover of Heliod. (who is mistress of Bessas) at length kills Heliod before Mithras, whom they both had worshipped secretly. He knows she is going to betray treasure & give herself to Totila. He it is, also, who tells Basil's servant that B. remains in prison – in the same house where Heliod. dead.[5]

Tantalisingly reticent regarding the fates of Basil and Veranilda, this ending is nonetheless foreshadowed through a comparison that Gissing

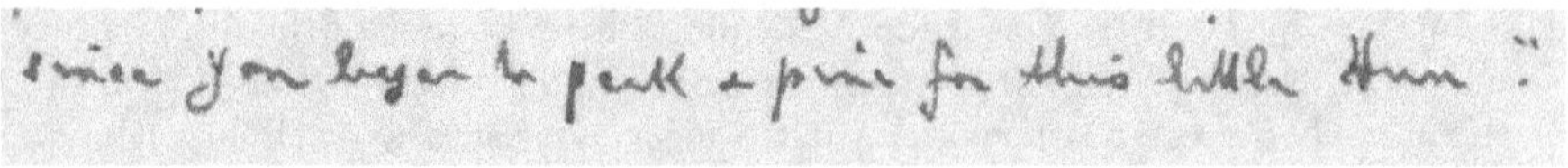

Figure 8.2 Gissing alludes to Macbeth (1903; 49; MS; Gissing MSS. MS Department, Lilly Library, Bloomington).

unobtrusively draws between Heliodora and one of the witches from Shakespeare's *Macbeth* in an earlier scene.[6] P. F. Kropholler identifies, as a reference to Act 1 Scene 3, Heliodora's chiding of Basil for devoting all of his energy in search for Veranilda (16). Heliodora is quoted as saying: 'And in truth, lord, your courtesy has suffered since you began to peck and pine for this little Hun' (141). Kropholler, informed by Pierre Coustillas, has noted the misprint of 'peak' as 'peck' (Fig. 8.2). Readers of Shakespeare will recognise the scene when the First Witch describes having been denied chestnuts by a sailor's wife, and the witches' plan to cause a storm and make the sailor 'dwindle, peak, and pine' (1.3.22) at sea, an incident that alerts us that they are not only agents that prophesy but also forces with agency. Based on the portion that Gissing finished writing, this allusion, an instance of repetition, has not led us to a direct analogy as yet. While the witch condemns the sailor and his wife by punishing the sailor, Heliodora seems to have little power over Veranilda's absence – and indeed, the novel's larger marriage and social plots. Yet evidence of Heliodora's danger is ample. Near the start of *Veranilda*, Basil learns that her husband, a little-respected senator, had suddenly died – an event for which she may have been responsible. She sent Basil a lock of hair, tied with gold thread, and a message saying, 'I am free' (15). Much later, Heliodora's friend Galla will scream accusingly at her: 'Wanton! witch! poisoner!' (177) Gissing may leave it unclear whether or not Galla is merely repeating gossip, but he privileges us to more concrete evidence of Heliodora's violence through her seduction and manipulation of Sagaris to bring about her rival Muscula's execution. More to the point, Heliodora threatens Basil 'in a deep note which was half friendliness, half menace': 'I am not wont to have my requests refused. Leave me thus, and you have one more enemy – an enemy more to be dreaded than all the rest' (142). And again in their final meeting, when Basil asks that they 'part and think of each other no more': 'Leave me thus, and your life shall pay for it' (180).[7]

The network of significance here seems to resist our classification of the novel into the forms of comedy and tragedy. The different endings – Basil's and Veranilda's reconciliation (according to Wells, Courtney and Alfred Gissing), Basil's death and Veranilda entering a convent (Fleury) and Basil's arrest as a traitor (Gissing's notes) – leave unanswered the social questions over which the novel meditates, questions that are apparent, for instance, in Basil's interactions with Totila. The Roman noble holds romanticised views of the Gothic king following a short interview, one that left him 'bewildered, aware of nothing, his eyes turned vacantly upon some one who addressed him': 'He had ever worshipped the man of heroic virtues; once upon a time it was Belisarius who fired his zeal; now his eyes dazzled with the glory of Totila; he burned to devote a loyal service to this brave and noble king' (313). Basil's unconditional and uncritical devotion to a set of heroes that now includes Totila is shown to be misplaced and unreciprocated. When Totila questions Basil about his killing Marcian, an event about which Totila clearly expresses concern, the Roman noble confesses the truth and views his friend at his best: 'Gracious lord, that I accused him falsely, I no longer doubt, having had time to reflect upon many things, and to repent of my evil haste. But I am still ignorant of the cause which led him to think ill of me, and so to speak and act in a way which could not but make my heart burn against him' (310–11). Totila tests even as he studies Basil, and if at first he looks upon the Roman with 'a gaze of meditative intentness' (310), then this quickly intensifies to one of 'thoughtful interest' (311). As they speak, 'his eyes still searching Basil's face' (311), '[a]ll but a smile of satisfaction lurked within his eyes' (311), and finally, 'His eyes were again fixed upon Basil with a look of pleasant interest' (312). Gissing's language here is conspicuously similar to his description of Bessas's interest in Basil in an earlier scene. When the characters first meet, Bessas speaks 'much as he might have spoken of viewing a horse that interested him', and he demonstrates 'that affectation of bluff good-nature which always veiled his designs' (120–1). Gissing is visibly linking the two leaders, as he puns on, and blurs, the double sense of interest as '[t]he relation of being objectively concerned in something, by having a right or title to, a claim upon, or a share in' ('Interest, n.', I. 1. a.) and '[t]he relation of being concerned or affected in respect of advantage or detriment; esp. an advantageous relation of this kind' ('Interest, n.', I. 2. a.).

The glitter in Totila's eyes implies valuation, and Gissing hints, through a reference to Basil turning to a 'monk' (312), at the Gothic king's thought-process. Basil's feelings are not reciprocated by the king, who makes plans for him, and who preys on Basil's conscience by referring to his need for 'penance' (312). The king views Basil as a vehicle that is potentially useful in furthering his own military and political aspirations, as the narrator, from Totila's perspective, will make clear: 'Meanwhile, having spoken with the young Roman whom Veranilda loved, he saw in Basil a useful instrument, and resolved, if his loyalty to the Goths bore every test, to reward him with Veranilda's hand. The marriage would be of good example, and might, if the Gothic arms remained triumphant, lead to other such' (338). The marriage plot is regularly used as a laboratory for exploring social problems in the Victorian novel; as Talia Schaffer writes, 'marriage is a symbolic resolution to a cultural problem' (3). Joseph Allen Boone has persuasively argued that the proverbial 'happy ending' in a courtship, where 'converging lovers are rewarded with the bliss of matrimony and countless progeny', and 'the tragically closed outcome', for those who abuse the ideal, 'equally conspired to uphold a belief in romantic marriage as the most desirable end of existence and, hence, as a virtually unassailable, closed truth' (65).[8] More germane to the argument that I am making, marriage incorporates the language of action (Markovits 5). Totila may be pressing for action, but his identification of Basil as an 'instrument', which comes with the suggestion that he is replaceable, his use of Veranilda as bait for procuring and retaining Basil's loyalty, and finally, his translation of Basil's sacred trust into an 'example' all taint what might have been a moral union and call attention to the difference between Basil's worshipful stance towards Totila and the king's actual feelings.

Totila's indifference and his fundamentally selfish goals in retaining control and expanding his realm encourage us to read the novel's conclusion as being deeply troubling. His actions are occasioned by his political motivations, as Marcian suggests to Basil: 'This Totila . . . seems to be not only a brave and capable commander, but a shrewd politician. Everywhere he spares the people; he takes nothing by force; his soldiers buy at market; he protects the farmer against the taxing Greek. As a result his army grows; where he passes he leaves a good report, and before him goes a welcome' (16–17). Accounts of Totila's charity pepper the novel: in a chapter titled 'Whispers', officers relate how, in his attempt to help the Neapolitans who are famine-stricken, Totila 'ministered to their needs even as a friendly physician would have done, giving them at first little food, and more as their strength revived' (183). Yet the king's benevolence is contested by report of his massacre of the people of Tibur, relayed in the penultimate chapter that Gissing wrote. This event deprives the Goths of the Romans' support and spurs them to turn to their extremely corrupt governor rather than to accept this invasion. The informed narrative voice imparts one possible reason for Totila's condoning this violence, through free indirect discourse:

> Wearied by marchings and counter-marchings, the Gothic warriors were more disposed to rest awhile after their easy conquests than to make a vigorous effort for the capture of Rome. Totila himself, heroic redeemer of his nation, turned anxious glances towards Ravenna, hoping, rather than resolving, to hold his state upon the Palatine before Belisarius could advance

against him. He felt the fatigue of those about him, and it was doubtless under the stress of such a situation, bearing himself the whole burden of the war, that he had ordered, or permitted, barbarous revenge upon the city of Tibur. (336–7)

Totila's soldiers are increasingly bored from doing nothing (in contrast, to use Markovits's terms, to 'inner doings' [6]) and the king desires an easy victory. Totila's imminent triumph becomes even more terrifying for the Romans, and in fact, for anyone who does not openly support him, as Gissing suggests to Fleury: '[Gissing] expressed the opinion that the explanation of it might be in the fact of the place being perhaps a Gothic settlement. In which case this Gothic unfaithfulness & treachery could very well have appeared to him as requiring an exceptional vengeance, in order to make an example' (278). Gissing incorporates this possibility into his novel. In the vernacular of gossip, the narrator speculates: 'Some offered as explanation the fact that many Goths lived in Tibur, whose indifference or hostility had angered the king; others surmised that this was Totila's warning after the failure of his proclamation to the Romans' (334). The 'example' motif would lend support to my reading of Totila's attempted conversion of the Roman Basil for his Gothic ends. Even if the king achieves greater prosperity and power, he will not become a more humane ruler. The outcome of Basil's and Veranilda's romance can neither obviate nor mitigate the political and military problems that Gissing's novel evinces.

Indecision, Inaction and Individualism

In this climate, and positioned so that one 'can only choose between [the] evils' (155) of a corrupt governor, 'who first of all fed his soldiers, and then sold [grain] at a great price' (335), and the merciless Totila who intends 'by patient blockade to starve the Romans into surrender' (336), it follows that many characters, including Basil and Marcian, suffer from indecision. Their aspirations are incongruent with their current times, as the narrator implies: 'Hence the sympathy between [Marcian] and Basil, both being capable of patriotism, and feeling a desire in the depths of their hearts to live as they would have lived had they been born in an earlier time' (134). While his city slowly perishes from starvation, Bessas continues to live in almost unchanged luxury, perhaps, as Gissing suggested to Fleury, because he was 'getting fishes from the Tiber, fishes that had escaped the nets put of course by the Goths in the river' (278). His corruption is the stuff of public knowledge, as we might infer from Heliodora's reflection, that 'she had objects of value, such as were daily accepted by Bessas in exchange for corn and pork' (342). Yet she had no opportunity to make an exchange: she was captured and her house pillaged. More pressingly, though, even the fishes (should they be responsible for their survival) will become scarce with time, especially with so many soldiers to feed. Ultimately, it is the Romans who suffer, making untenable the positions to which Romans like Basil and Marcian aspire. Following his unsuccessful search for Veranilda over a six-month period, Basil becomes increasingly lax, as his costume and behaviour register: 'He was carelessly clad, walked with head bent, and had the look of one who spends his life in wearisome idleness. Without speaking, however, he threw himself upon a couch and lay staring with vacant eye at the bronze panels of the vaulted ceiling' (149). Basil's indecision is repeated and matched by Marcian's. After he secures Veranilda, he is 'torn between spiritual fervour and passions of the flesh' (226), between the homosocial affection that he bears towards Basil and jealousy over his love for Veranilda. Marcian oscillates, furthermore, between loyalty to Basil and duty to Totila, and he finally betrays both parties by becoming 'traitor now for his own ends':

> To defeat Basil's love was his prime end, jealousy being more instant with him than fleshly impulse. Yet so strongly had this second motive now become, that he all but regretted his message to the king: to hold Veranilda in his power, to gratify his passion sooner or later, by this means or by that, he would perhaps have risked all the danger to which such audacity exposed him. But Marcian was not lust-bitten quite to madness . . . By skillful use of his advantages, he might bring it to pass that Totila would grant him a supreme reward – the hand of Veranilda. (255–6)

In Basil's education and training, Gissing provides a possible explanation for his wasted potential and his difficulty with coping with his circumstances: 'Sound of body, he needed to put forth his physical energies, yet had never found more scope for them than in the exercise of the gymnasium, or the fatigue of travel; mentally well-balanced, he would have made an excellent administrator, such as his line had furnished in profusion, but that career was no longer open' (149). Basil can no longer repeat. The profession of so many from his family is not a viable option, and he does not channel his training toward a more outward-facing goal. Similarly, his mental wellbeing is constrained and never challenged sufficiently, as he confesses to his kinsman Decius: 'When I was young – how old I feel! – I looked forward to a life full of achievements. I felt capable of great things. But in our time, what can we do, we who are born Romans, yet have never learnt to lead an army or to govern a state?' (149) As an aristocrat, Basil is educated for things other than being a soldier or a politician. His schooldays are spent:

in the practice of sophistic argument, and the delivery of harangues on traditional subjects . . . Other youths had shown greater aptitude for this kind of eloquence; he did not often carry off a prize; but among his proud recollections was a success he had achieved in the form of a rebuke to an impious voluptuary who set up a statue of Diana in the room which beheld his debauches. Here was the nemesis of a system of education which had aimed solely at the practical, the useful; having always laboured to produce the man perfectly equipped for public affairs, and nothing else whatever. (150)

Basil's indifference to scholarly endeavours speaks to his uncompetitive nature: the school prizes that he earns are few and far between. He has long forgotten his grammatical learning and he had written 'no lyric or elegy in Veranilda's honour' – the fact that it is unclear whether love or grief is more prevailing registers his indecision – or, in fact, any poetry since he was sixteen (150–1). In short, his circumstances entitle him to a comfortable lifestyle wherein, under non-war conditions, he would simply rely on his substantial inheritance and a familiar narrative. Yet Basil is not Marcian, and as Miller would suggest, we do well to attend to their differences in spite of their similarities. Basil's vitality and his retention of imaginative stories, which prevail over the seemingly contagious gloom that envelops his friend, are central in this diegesis, which is bereft of these very things.

Viewed in this context, illness assumes greater meaning. As a synecdoche, it offers a partial reflection of the emotional and psychological states of paralysis experienced by many characters, and this is discernible in Basil's illness and recovery. Basil and his followers are attacked by marauders in his trip to the Gothic camps:

Advancing with fierce threats, the robbers commanded him and his men to alight, their chief desire being no doubt to seize the horses and arms. Though outnumbered, Basil shouted defiance; a conflict began, and so stout was the resistance they met that, after several had fallen on either side, the brigands drew off. Not, however, in final retreat; galloping on in hope of succour, Basil found himself pursued, again lost two or three men, and only with the utmost difficulty got clear away.

It was the young Roman's first experience of combat. For this he had been preparing himself during the past months, exercising his body and striving to invigorate his mind, little apt for warlike enterprise. When the trial came, his courage did not fail, but the violent emotions of that day left him so exhausted, so shaken in nerve, that he could scarce continue his journey. He had come out of the fight unwounded, but at nightfall fever fell upon him, and he found no rest. The loss of some half dozen men grieved him to the heart; had the brave fellows fallen in battle with the Greeks, he would have thought less of it; to see them slain, or captured, by mere brigands was more than he could bear. When at length he reached Aesernia, and there unexpectedly met with Venantius, he fell from his horse like a dying man. (245–6)

The narrator's juxtaposition of the battle scene with a clearer manifestation of Basil's illness – 'He was aching from head to foot, and a parched mouth, a hot hand, told of fever in his blood' (245) – link the violence to illness, and, more importantly, this analogy, combined with his demonstrated grief over fallen comrades, humanises Basil, showing his sensitivity towards not only Veranilda but also his fellow man. Indeed, after he kills Marcian, Basil falls ill again, though he assured Venantius that he is 'quite restored' and that his 'fever has passed' (243). 'Basil lost consciousness of present things; and many days went by before he again spoke as a sane man' (279), yet this illness and his experiences in Benedict's monastery provide him with the opportunity to learn in more profound ways than had his earlier education or the raid.

Within the monastery's walls, Basil has the time and space to learn about his wrongs. Gissing describes Basil's feelings following his confession to Benedict:

> The telling of his story was to Basil like waking from a state of imperfect consciousness in which dream and reality had indistinguishably mingled. Since the fight with the brigands he had never been himself; the fever in his blood made him *incapable of wonted thought or action*; restored to health, he looked back upon those days with such an alien sense that he could scarce believe he had done the things he related. Only now did there move in him a natural horror when he thought of the death of Marcian, a natural distress when he remembered his bearing to Veranilda. Only now could he see in the light of reason all that had happened between his talk with Sagaris at Aesernia and his riding away with Venantius from the villa on the island. As he unfolded the story, he marvelled at himself, and was overcome with woe. (298; emphasis added)

The narrator may be echoing Marcus Tullius's letter, which appears in this essay's epigraph (that is, 'I am hateful to myself. For though born to do something worthy of a man, I am now not only *incapable of action, but even of thought*.'). As Miller would suggest, these characters' resemblance is ironically heightened by their difference. The insistence on the present – with the anaphora 'Only now' – situates Basil's misdeeds in the past and suggests a change in him. The distance between the time of his actual experience and the time of narration contributes to Basil's awakening and catharsis, and the intrusion of 'reason' empowers him with a bifocal perspective with which he can view his friend and beloved more critically and objectively. Even if Marcian and Veranilda had betrayed him, Basil realises that he had acted rashly and unreasonably. Here Gissing seems to be suggesting that inaction – as Markovits writes, 'both frustrated external action and heightened internal action' (4) – is still preferable to rash action and that proper action remains, however distant, a possibility. Gissing repeatedly reminds us that this learning process is gradual. Basil joins the monastery's other members for his evening meal that day because he wishes to accept part of his penance, 'for, though the brothers knew not of his sin, he could not meet their eyes for shame, and such humiliation must needs be salutary' (299).

Such references to his 'shame' and 'humiliation' suggest his selfishly inclined feelings over his actual remorse over the tragedy he had caused and for which he can offer no reparation. If, in his first combat, Basil's grief owes in large part to how his men were lost – 'had the brave fellows fallen in battle with the Greeks, he would have thought less of it' (246) – then his experience will move him to regard, as an equal, Deodatus, the son of a serf on his land who was reluctantly summoned to follow him into battle: they kneel side by side in prayer and Basil finally releases him from service and allows him to take the vows of Benedict's community. Basil achieves another level of self-knowledge through his regular reading of appointed psalms, a practice that we can hold in contrast with his empty repetition of the self-deprecating remarks that he had learned as a child:

> One day, as he closed the book, his heart was so full of a strange, half-hopeful, half-fearful longing, that it over-flowed in tears; and amid his weeping came a memory of Marcian, a tender memory of the days of their friendship: for the first time he bewailed the dead man as one whom he had dearly loved. (306)[9]

While Gissing does not dismiss Christian teachings as irrelevant, the wholesale import of this learning is shown to be less useful than more nuanced reflection over fewer and more meaningful passages. This kind of reading has the capacity to make Basil more perceptive and to enable him to face his love and his political choices with greater clarity. What is striking about Basil's acceptance of his wrongs is not only his remembrance of Marcian at his best, and his active display of remorse over his actions, but Gissing's use of the past tense to describe Basil's affection, which comes with the awareness that feelings can and do change. Basil's learning makes him a markedly different Roman from the one who had entered the monastery and a more humane leader than the merciless Totila, who knows only to value people in accordance to what they can bring him.

Basil sees monks who 'busied themselves in reproducing not only religious works but also the writings of authors who had lived in pagan times' (305). This image of quiet industry fundamentally changes Basil's views about the monastery, while arguing for the importance of the distribution of literature as a vehicle for instigating larger social changes:

> All at once the life of this cloister appeared before him in a wider and nobler aspect. In the silent monks bent over their desks he saw much more than piety and learning. They rose to a dignity surpassing that of consul or praefect. With their pens they warred against the powers of darkness, a grander conflict than any in which men drew sword. (306)

Gissing's military metaphor foregrounds the importance of the monks' work in actively preserving and promoting knowledge and culture, and it suggests, furthermore, the urgency of keeping art alive at a time when literature so often becomes lost.[10] Nevertheless, as Adrian Poole has remarked, Basil necessarily returns to his own world: '[T]he refuge of the main character Basil at the Benedictine monastery at Monte Cassino produces a response that seems close to Gissing's own. Basil, and Gissing, admire this enclave of calm unworldliness, but cannot suppress their own instinctual need for continued engagement with "the world"' (205). So too does Grylls: 'But Basil discovers that he lacks the constitution to commit himself to ascetic life. He leaves the monastery, re-enters the world and is reconciled with Veranilda – the perfect heroine, the feminine ideal' (151). Basil must employ what he learns in an attempt to make a difference in a world where his privileges in class can no longer promise him a place. While it strikes me that Basil's faith in Totila is troubling, it nevertheless operates as an important antithesis to the novel's diegesis, where friendship, love and trust are constantly sacrificed – the alliteration in the title of Chapter 21, 'The Betrayer Betrayed' suggests circularity and invites us, in Miller's terms, to observe the similarities of, in spite of the differences between, these parties – and we cannot divest it from Basil's attempt to make his society, if only temporarily, a better place. When Basil aligns himself with Totila's and the Goths' cause, he does so by attaching greater value to the good of the many and also by carving out a space for himself to grow: 'I honour the Goth, even as I love my country' (312). *Veranilda* argues for the value of contemplation – even if this is mediated through inaction and indecision – as a way of reacting and coping with public politics. Basil's learning enables him to (re)negotiate the conflict between individual will and circumstance. Early in the novel, Basil asks Veranilda, 'Had I been the enemy of Totila ... could you still have loved me as a wife should love?' (76) By the end, we are not so different from his beloved and we, too, are moved by Veranilda's determination to see Basil as Basil: 'I had not asked myself ... for it was needless. When I look on you, I think neither of Roman nor of Goth' (77).

Acknowledgements

I thank Christine Bolus-Reichert, Hélène Coustillas, John James, Katherine R. Larson, Joan Marshman, J. Hillis Miller, Monique R. Morgan, Diane Piccitto, Patricia Pulham, Monika Szuba, Julian Wolfreys and the reviewers for their incisive feedback; Coustillas, Adam Guy, Philip Horne, Morgan, and Greg Zacharias for their insights; audience members at the *Apocalypse and Its Discontent* conference at the University of Westminster for their kind attention; and Penny Ramon, Frank Tong and the staff of the Lily Library at Indiana University, McGill University Library and the University of Toronto Libraries for their research help. I am enormously grateful to Jane Gissing and the Lily Library for permission to publish archival material relating to *Veranilda*, and to the Social Sciences and Humanities Research Council of Canada, Dalhousie University, Indiana University, McGill University, University College London and the University of Toronto Scarborough.

Notes

1. Stefanie Markovits employs the term 'action' as opposed to 'agency' 'to invoke explicitly the connections between actions of characters and the structures of plot used by authors' (*The Crisis of Action*, pp. 5–6) and 'inaction' 'to stress the link between not doing and inner doings, between inaction and character' (ibid. p. 6). As Markovits writes, 'My claim is that on some level, in literature at least, if not in life, we are who we are, not by virtue of what we do, but by what we have failed to do. Frustrated action – inaction – is character building' (ibid.). Markovits's argument is prevalent in looking at my epigraph, which comes from a letter by Marcus Tullius that Decius gives Basil to read. The letter similarly distinguishes, even as it suggests a synergy, between action and thought. This episode is resonant, furthermore, because it follows a six-month period of obstruction that is registered, at the level of narrative, by a break between Chapters 12 and 13.
2. Gissing (re)turns regularly to a character type that he identifies in his short story 'A Victim of Circumstances' (1893): in it, the painter Horace takes credit for his more talented wife's work, and she stops painting to make him feel better. The story ends twenty-one years later, significantly, on a New Year's Eve – a time that traditionally brings together family members – with Horace, now a widower, telling his story and complaining in a bar to anyone who would listen: 'I'm a victim of circumstances . . . if ever man was. It puzzles you, no doubt, that I should once have done great things, and yet at my age, only fifty, be nothing but an obscure drawing master. You don't understand the artist's nature. You can't imagine how completely an artist is at the mercy of circumstances' (p. 24). Continuing to claim

credit for his wife's surviving work, Horace blames his marriage, 'a rash, indeed a fatal, step' (p. 25), which circumscribed his ability to realise his full potential. Through the ironic disparity between how the implied author and the reader see the painter and how he views, or at least represents, himself, Gissing emphasises the greater importance of individual agency over deterministic circumstance. This debate, in David Grylls's terms, between 'determinism and determination' (*The Paradox of Gissing*, p. 18) is apparent in many of Gissing's works, including *Workers in the Dawn* (1880), *New Grub Street* (1891), *Born in Exile* (1892) and *The Private Papers of Henry Ryecroft* (1903).

3. For an insightful discussion of the quarrel behind this preface, see Coustillas, 'The Stormy Publication of Gissing's *Veranilda*'.
4. Gissing's brother Algernon corroborates a part of this account, in a letter held at the Lily Library, to Gissing's literary agent J. B. Pinker on 25 January 1904: 'My brother had no notes at all as to its conclusion. The orig points that he had spoken of, & which I shall be quite willing to put into the form of a brief note, were these. That Veranilda goes into a convent & that the author had in his mind what he called "a strong last chapter – Rome deserted." This is all.'
5. I am grateful to Hélène Coustillas for her assistance with this transcription and to Philip Horne for his advice. The word 'make' was inserted between 'to' and 'marriage', and the cancelled words 'that' appear after 'Heliod. has told Totila' and 'wa' after 'become' in the manuscript. Pierre Coustillas has shown the rewards of examining Gissing's preparatory materials in his edition of *Veranilda* for Harvester Press.
6. As Horne convincingly argues in 'Poetic Allusion in the Victorian Novel', 'serious allusions nearly always convey some tension or ambivalence beyond their easily explicable textual or narrative function' (p. 610). In my forthcoming monograph *Gissing, Shakespeare, and the Life of Writing*, I examine the nature of Gissing's intense lifelong engagement with Shakespeare and inspect Shakespeare's canonicity in the late nineteenth century in the context of Gissing's and some of his contemporaries' imaginative literature.
7. Heliodora's danger is taken seriously – even by Basil. In response to his plans to marry Veranilda and to return to Rome, Marcian wondered, 'could he suppose . . . that Heliodora would meekly endure his disdain, and that the life of Veranilda would be safe in such a rival's proximity?' (p. 46). This threat, combined with the dangers of war, is sufficient to drive Basil away from Rome: 'Basil gnashed his teeth and handled his dagger. Why return to Rome at all? he cried impatiently. He had no mind to go through the torments of a long siege such as again threatened. Why should he not live on in Campania –' (p. 46).
8. Joseph Allen Boone describes how the late Victorians' concern about 'the unease of unhappy wedlock' found expression in the forms of their writing: 'developing structural techniques that involved dislocation, duplication, juxtaposition and, ultimately, unresolved endings, such writers began to counter the formulaic patterns of traditional love-plots and give expression to formally as well as thematically innovative fictions' ('Wedlock as Deadlock', p. 72). Recent work by Talia Schaffer has distinguished between

what she calls 'familiar marriage' and 'romantic marriage': the former 'stresses trust, comradeship, practical needs, and larger social organization' and it addresses a void that romantic marriage has failed to fill (*Romance's Rival*, p. 3). David Grylls classifies the doomed romantic relationships in Gissing's fiction into two kinds: 'either the lovers fail to unite, the result being loneliness and misery; or the lovers succeed in uniting, the result being company and misery' (5).

9. We might compare Basil's reading here with his early education in Christianity, which did not help him become more selfless:

> Owning himself, in the phrases he had repeated from childhood, a miserable sinner, a vile clot of animated dust, at heart he felt himself one with all the beautiful and joyous things that the sun illumined. With pleasure and sympathy he looked upon an ancient statue of god or hero; only a sense of duty turned his eyes upon the images of Christian art. (p. 150)

The words that Basil is made to learn are both empty and at odds with his pre-Christian spirit, which is contrasted with, and fundamentally challenges, what he is pressured to memorise.

10. The threat of literature becoming lost is both suggested and demonstrated. Early in the novel, the narrator explains the invalid Decius's impatience to go to Rome: '[Basil's] kinsman, under the will of Maximus, enjoyed a share in the annual revenue of this Surrentine estate; moreover, he became the possessor of many books, which lay in the Anician mansion of Rome, and it was his impatience, thought Aurelia, to lay hands upon so precious a legacy, which might at any time be put in danger by the events of war, that prompted him to set forth' (p. 64). In a much later scene, Marcus, the poet monk, tells Basil that he would have met Benedict when he had first arrived, but for the loss of a book: 'You would have seen him on the day of your arrival, ere yet you became distraught, but that a heaviness lay upon him because of the loss of a precious manuscript on its way hither from Rome – a manuscript which had been procured for him after much searching, only to be lost by the folly of one to whom it was intrusted . . .' (p. 281).

Chapter 9

Great Expectations: Narration, Cognition, Possibility

Dianne F. Sadoff

Any reader of this volume will already know the critic to whom it pays homage, since J. Hillis Miller has been perhaps our most productive and innovative critic of nineteenth-century literature since the 1950s. Miller began his remarkable career with *Charles Dickens: The World of his Novels* (1958). There, Miller scans the 'gaudy and ghastly sight' in 'rapid panorama' of European cities as 'totalit[ies]'; the 'swarming multiplicity' of characters jumbled into these cities, he says, constitute an imaginative 'entire society' (viii, xv, 44). Two later books focus on fictional form: *Thomas Hardy: Distance and Desire* (1970) and *The Form of Victorian Fiction* (1968). In Hardy's novels, Miller argues, 'all forms of engagement lead ultimately to disaster', yet his 'watchers at a distance' – including the narrators – desperately hope that love will prove an 'escape from the poverty of detachment' (73). In *Form*, Miller anticipates our current focus on a work's 'inner structuring principles', which for him emanates from the 'interaction of the imaginary minds of the narrator and his characters' (xi). Focusing on temporality, ontology and consciousness, the chapters observe isolated figures who enter a 'collective mind' (93).

My readers will have already recognised Miller's early dedication to Georges Poulet's 'criticism of consciousness' (*Repetition* 18). Yet in the 1970s, as member of the Yale 'Gang of Four', Miller entered Jacques Derrida's and Paul de Man's orbit, helping to innovate and popularise for American theory what he then called post-structuralism or deconstruction. Arguing against 'univocal' readings in *Repetition and Fiction* (1982) and adding to Derrida and de Man both Sigmund Freud and Jacques Lacan, Miller's book traces the ways 'counterparts' and 'subversive ghost[s]' vex yet exist alongside binary oppositions (234, 9). In the new millennium, Miller has explored speech-act, media and technology, and transnational theories. Investigating the 'permeable frontier' between J. L. Austin's *How to Do Things with Words* and the novels of Henry James, *Literature as Conduct* (2005) examines the concept of performativity in six James tales and tomes; in *The Medium is the Maker* (2009), Miller ranges over the nexus between the literary text and contemporary communication technologies; in *Thinking Literature Across Continents* (2016), Miller and Ranjan Ghosh discuss their styles of 'contrastive reading', undertaking a purposive 'rhythm' of dialogue 'across continents' (231). Whereas Ghosh grounds his readings in Sanskrit poetics, Miller calls his redefined deconstruction 'rhetorical reading', which displays the 'tropological dimension of any discourse [as] interfere[ing] with its statement of a clear, logical meaning' (96). Needless to say, no other living critic has so brilliantly borrowed *and* invented theoretical concepts, so fruitfully and energetically provided the rest of us with constructive ways to read literature. In my essay for this volume, I experiment with cognitive theory as a new way to read Charles Dickens's *Great Expectations*.

I

I argue, then, that nineteenth-century narratives trigger readers' enactment of cognitive modes that blend conceptual scenes, display and evoke intuitive predictions and notions of possibility, and so foster experiences of immersive or emotive reading. I deploy cognitive-scientific literary theories, which provide critics new and sophisticated tools for thinking about the ways narratives cue readers to use fictions. For narratologists, cognition has become a crucial tool, whether in theories of mind, or in hermeneutically informed neuroscientific accounts of the brain's functioning during reading, or in histories of cognition as emerging from Victorian physiological psychology.[1] I also argue that intuitive thinking, which generates impressions, feelings and inclinations, which enjoys cognitive ease and seeks narrative coherence and consistency, counters cognitive rationality, for readers employ conceptual blending's unconscious cognitive moves *and* intuitive thinking even as they logically articulate judgements, project prospects and make choices about fictive probabilities. In *Great Expectations*, the author's and narrator-character's conceptual blends seek to articulate rational cognitive and intuitive thinking, even as disjunctions in figural perspective trouble and often disrupt that link.

Blending becomes visible in Pip's metaphors, fabricated stories and visualised scenarios as well as in his linguistic constructions. He deploys, in particular, the coordinating conjunction 'as if', which creates the possibility that disnarration or unnarration may leak into or out of coherent narration. Pip's pervasive use of 'as if' allows me to revise or complicate conceptual blending, so that the experiencing figure's 'seeing' is not necessarily or not always the remembering narrator's 'understanding'. Reading blended scenarios against plot possibilities, the reader must also formulate new understandings about the nature and function of Dickens's understanding, of the character's and narrator's knowledge and of the novel's multiple endings. In this essay, I argue for a more expansive and flexible view of blending's effects, especially when used in character narration, a complex discourse of desire and miswanting – a pun on lacking and yearning – that may stimulate narratorial and readerly errors of affective forecasting.

Gilles Fauconnier and Mark Turner's theory of conceptual blending anchors my argument that blending demands complication or revision so as better to inform critical interpretation. Daniel Kahneman's challenge to the rational model of judgement and decision-making provides the tools for my complication. First, an explanation of conceptual blending's usefulness. Blending enables critics to think creatively about 'emergent structure', which 'conveys meaning . . . not present in either of the input spaces' (Hilpert 107). Composition and completion generate emergent structure in the blend, and, along with elaboration, aid compression in running the blend. The reader or thinker links two items that are selectively projected from mental input spaces into the blend; on completion, he or she understands familiar patterns by recruiting widely ranging unconscious background knowledge to finalise the blend's work (*Think* 47–9). Ralf Schneider explains: composition 'establishes links' between 'comparable elements' from the inputs; completion enables background knowledge to '"seep[]" into the blend' and thereby shortcut 'conscious thinking' (6). Compression creates conceptual blends from mental spaces that are 'connected to long-term schematic knowledge called "frames"' and to 'long-term specific knowledge' belonging to the thinker's past experience (*Think* 40). According to Fauconnier and Turner, moreover, the 'creative possibilities of blending stem from the open-ended nature of completion and elaboration', which 'recruit and develop new structure' that is 'principled but effectively unlimited' (*Think* 49).

The reader's capability to compose, complete and elaborate blends also depends on his or her intuitive predictions about narrative form and plot. Narrative predictions facilitate cognition by constructing frameworks: associating like representations, deriving 'analogies between input and memory' and so generating story possibilities ('Top-down'

161). For Martin Hilpert, 'the ability to reason about cause and effect crucially draws on conceptual integration' yet also involves 'mental simulation of an alternative counterfactual scenario' whose outcomes may be different from a probable consequence: the reader hypothesises, predicts, invents possible patterns that might be confirmed or disavowed in later reading moments (107–08). In *Great Expectations*, Dickens's grammatical counterfactual conditionals also propose scenarios of cause and effect that alert the reader to simulated scenarios, that also instruct him or her to apprise the narrative's counterpart linkages even as they 'change dynamically' across networks (*Think* 45). Ultimately, conceptual blending, itself a fusion of cognitive modes to analyze and interpret storied or lived events, scenes and memories, must coordinate with intuitively perceived inferences, hypotheticals and projections by both narrators and readers ('Top-down' 149). When conceptual processing and intuitive predicting correspond, a narrative's conclusion stages their successful correlation – or, if discordant, it may orchestrate their disjunction. From this perspective, intuitive thinking may facilitate cognition or contradict it, creating either prospect confirmation or a cognitive illusion (Kahneman 27–8).

Intuitive narrative predictions, in addition, may be either confirmed or disconfirmed by a tale's discourse. In narrative, disanalogy deletes details from a source story if they don't fit the target story (Turner, *Mind* 64–7) and unnarration masks the narrative fissure. Robyn Warhol defines unnarration as discourse in which 'the narrator can't ... or won't tell what happened' and disnarration as a story moment in which 'the narrator tells something that did not happen [rather than] what did' (231). Deploying cognitive linguistics to theorise Dickens's narrators' refusals to tell, she traces patterns of 'disnarration through negation' and 'disnarration through the use of subjective constructions', arguing that in Dickens's late style, 'disnarration', 'narrative refusals' and 'counterfictionals' become 'dominant mode[s] of narrative discourse, maybe even *the* dominant mode' (230, 231, 232). In counterfictionals or counterfactuals, 'false antecedents are always phrased subjunctively', although 'auxiliary verbs' carry 'different degrees of force' (227) – the auxiliary verb 'would' exercises more authority than do other available auxiliaries in English, such as 'might' or 'may' or 'could'. The subjunctive mood and the coordinating conjunction 'as if' may thus serve to support or disconfirm narrative prediction and readerly inference patterns, or may violate expectations of fictional possibilities.

Disnarration and counterfictionals, however, do not necessarily eradicate narrative meaning. Warhol aptly links counterfictionality to Richard Saint-Gelais's sense that disnarration 'suggests what it denies', makes 'erasure visible' and 'create[s] possible worlds *in* a fictional world' (242; emphasis in text). Disnarrations also articulate unrealised possibilities and counterfactual emotions, such as Gerald Prince's mixed list of 'unfulfilled expectations, unwarranted beliefs, ... crushed hopes, suppositions and false calculations, errors and lies' (3).[2] Warhol also notes that a text's unnarrated and disnarrated events produce a 'vividly *present absence*', what Prince calls 'events that *do not* happen' but are 'referred to' in a 'hypothetical mode' (Warhol 231, Prince 2; emphasis in text). The narrative's present absence points toward the discourse's displacements, gaps and elisions, as well as toward the unconscious knowledge of correlations and locations that must be recalled for conceptual blending to evoke and 'transfer ... emotions' across narrative networks (*Think* 44, 49). Dickens's and Pip's 'as if' conjunctions often recount present absences as hypotheticals, alerting the reader to narrative disjunctions and failures of understanding but also seeking to enforce interpretive knowledge. For Patrick Colm Hogan, imaginative triggers, which recruit 'concrete imagery' and 'emotional memories', create for readers 'sensory vivacity' (245, 247). Pip's conceptual blends combine the experiencing self's concrete images and sensory vivacity with the remembering narrator's emotional memories to solicit the reader's immersive reading experience.

II

Dickens's use of cognitive triggers and intuitive projections, then, may produce analogies or disanalogies and create disnarrations or unnarrations. In the 'as if' locution, characters may also see what is not seen but represent it as visible, even if the reader understands its nature as metaphorical or nonexistent. Opening a space for disjunction between the experiencing character and remembering narrator, Dickens's 'as if' instructs the reader to assess links between comparable elements in the character's and narrator's knowledges, to seek analogy and coherence along with completion. The coordinating conjunction transfers figural properties and roles, and transfers emotions from one character to another and, via the narrator or implied author, to the reader. Yet the doubled figure of Pip and Dickens's 'as if' also forces the reader to seek to align intuitive prediction with conceptual blending and rational cognitive processing. Because, as Pip's tale demonstrates, cognitive threats outweigh certainties and put opportunities at risk, the reader must make intuitive projections, must judge, even as he or she experiences transferred emotions of dread, terror and anxiety. Resisting the 'lure of hindsight and the illusion of certainty', the reader spies the implied author lurking in the 'as if' (Kahneman 14).

As Pip meets the convict on the marshes, his retrospective narrative blends his look at the scene with unnarrated scenarios. Indeed, the convict's seeming to rise from his father's grave unsettles the young Pip's 'impression of the identity of things', as, turned upside down, he watches the 'church jump[] over its own weather-cock' (26). As Pip later looks back at the criminal, the marshes' and river's 'long black horizontal line[s]' and the sky's 'row of long angry red lines ... intermixed'. The word 'intermixed' signals a conceptual blend, and Pip proceeds to run the blend, faintly visualising the 'only two black things in all the prospect that seemed to be standing upright': a sailors' 'beacon' and a 'gibbet' with hanging chains that had 'once held a pirate'. The convict limps toward the gibbet, he imagines, 'as if he were the pirate come to life, and come down, and going back to hook himself up again' (25). Here, Pip selects frames of knowledge that constrain even as they produce meaning, yet this blend creates cross-space mappings between input spaces with clashing frames (sailors lost or pirates marauding at sea; Pip on the marshes). Pip's sight of gibbet and beacon on a horizontal landscape blends two, even three, inputs, and associates thievery with both upright figures, which signify hanging and looking out. Pip compresses his own look at the marshes with the guilt of convicts and the predation of pirates, whose predicted transportation or hanging may or will confirm their role as criminals.

Pip's conceptual blends often compress two spaces – one seen, another not seen – with the two temporalities of experiencing and remembering (113). The remembering Pip recounts his adventures at Satis House to Joe and Mrs Joe:

> If they had asked me any more questions I should undoubtedly have betrayed myself, for I was even then on the point of mentioning that there was a balloon in the yard, ... my invention being divided between that phenomenon and a bear in the brewery. ... Now, when I saw Joe open his blue eyes and roll them all round the kitchen in helpless amazement, I was overtaken by penitence. (81)

Pip's word 'now' refers to a past the narrator remembers, and his 'then' refers to the boy's immediately past experience at Satis House. This temporal doubling makes us sympathetic with the guilt-ridden boy even as the adult narrator distances the reader from his imaginative grandiosity. Pip's remembered visualisation also blends seemingly past scenes of exotic, fantastic, unreal beings and objects – balloons and bears, coaches and gold goblets – with present scenes of disuse and decay he sees at

Miss Havisham's grotesque mansion: the balloon, which cues the reader to recall Cruikshank's *Sketches by Boz* frontispiece, and the bear, which blends a hypothetical scenario with the house's unnarrated past in commodities and trade, a vocation into which Pip will move at the book's end. Yet the tale of balloons and bear is disnarrated: these scenarios did not happen, and Pip has created counterfictionals to shield himself from the 'hurt' he felt when Estella humiliated him. Pip's retrospective emotion, contrition, for lying to Joe about Satis House, unnarrates his shame at having called the knaves 'jacks', of having 'coarse hands' and wearing 'thick boots': things that stand for his labouring-class status at the forge and arouse in the reader counterfactual speculations of, 'if only Pip had known . . .' (73; Kahneman 354).

The two Pips – one figural and experiencing, the other remembering and narrating – use different language and have different perspectives, interests and values. When Pip claims he 'often served [Mrs Joe] as a connubial missile', the metaphor and vocabulary, which identify Pip's body as pawn in a marital struggle, belong to the remembering narrator, the adult Pip, although his subjective affective experience – his terror about the Tickler – is located in his childhood past (29). The two Pips also appear in 'two input spaces . . . separated in time', yet 'cross-space mapping connects child to adult' (*Think* 65, 66). The reader is projected into the blend as the listener, he or she who must judge the remembering Pip's appraisals of the experiencing boy. Pip's narratorial role forces him to 'maintain simultaneously what look like contradictory representations' and the reader to understand that young and adult Pips are linked not only by 'nonsimultaneity' but also by a vital relation, by 'memory, change, continuity, [and] simultaneity' (*Think* 84, 96). Pip's narrative depends upon the doubled logic of retrospection, on the remembering narrator's mediation between character and reader, which immerses the reader in the boy's youthful fears and wishes even as it cues him or her to recognise the adult narrator's more mature assessments.

Pip's scenarios also establish the boy and the convict as counterparts in the blend, as the act of seeing transfers properties and roles from convict to terrified boy, roles the narrator, too, fails to understand. Pip's conceptual blend creates a '[m]etonymy of associations' between Pip and Magwitch, in which Pip will now view himself as possessing the convict's guilt and taking on his role; because he steals victuals for, and thus is identified as analogous to, the chained man, his blend unconsciously enacts a 'property transfer' (Turner, *Death*: 26, 29). Via the '[p]ersonification of properties', then, Pip will bear the convict's criminality, as the 'composition of projections from the input' creates spectacular emergent emotions of culpability as well as dramatic psychological changes for the experiencing Pip; our narrator, the remembering Pip, may have perceived but nevertheless fails fully to understand this property-and-role transfer's significance (*Death* 21–2; *Think* 48; Kahneman 381).³ Scenarios produced by conceptual blending thus project aspects of vital relations, such as identity, and associate things that may conventionally stand for other, unlike things, such as kinship, role or property (*Think* 93). As Fauconnier and Turner note, identity is perhaps the most crucial of vital relations, one easily compressed with kinship, time, space, role or properties, and one crucially linked to the projection of spectacular emotions such as fear and terror (*Think* 24).

As he compresses his identity with the convict's, the remembering Pip also transfers to himself emotions appropriate to accused men and criminals. When first in Jaggers' office, he spies a skylight 'eccentrically patched like a broken head, and the distorted adjoining houses looking as if they had twisted themselves to peep down at me through it' (162). This new, fuzzy scenario transplants the figurative head's property of human vision to London's down-and-out buildings, as though windows were eyes and skylight glass a distorting lens capable of knowing the boy's secret guilt and generating a transfer of emotions from the other occupants of Jaggers' den to Pip: he then becomes the vulnerable boy who feels that misshapen things in the world will accuse him of rightfully being in the wicked lawyer's office, as are the criminals whose heads leave greasy marks on Jaggers' walls. When he runs across the moors with Mrs Joe's pork pie, he transfers human properties to animals even as he criminalises his small self. He fancies that the 'gates and dykes and banks came bursting at me through the mist, as if they cried as plainly as could be, 'A boy with Somebody-else's pork pie! Stop him!' The cattle came upon me with suddenness, staring out of their eyes and steaming out of their nostrils, 'Holloa, young thief!"' (35–6). As the narrator of these scenes, Pip mobilises imagination by calling on the energy of elaboration: treating scenes or scenarios as 'simulations and running them imaginatively' (*Think* 48–9). These conceptual blends transfer to himself an intention to commit crimes: they compress Pip's apprentice past at the forge with his dubious guilt, overweighting improbable outcomes by falsely and figuratively predicting a future on trial (Kahneman 314).

The conjunction 'as if' intensifies the strong emotions about class that Pip transfers across networks. His unknowing panic about being defiled by lower-class men means Pip fears possible but improbable violence against his young self: the man with the file at the Jolly Bargeman, 'still cocking his eye, as if he were expressly taking aim at me with his invisible gun' acts, Pip imagines, 'as if he were determined to have a shot at me at last' (87, 88).⁴ Here, blending makes a dumbstruck Pip target of a possible murderer who understands the boy's denied past links to criminals. Later, Orlick, jealous of Pip's promotion at the forge, lunges 'as if he were going to run a [red hot poker] through my body', but instead, he 'whisked it round my head, laid it on the anvil, hammered it out – as if it were I, I thought, and the sparks were my spirting blood' (119). Here, Pip imagines a shady journeyman seeming to attack his body, likening the anvil's strike and spark to his physiological sense of his heartbeat pounding, his blood gushing. Although his self-identifying phrase, 'I thought', seeks to separate body and emotion, it expresses physiological fears appropriate to scenes of physical endangerment and loss of control. Pip's blends, then, compress and so heighten intentionality: the quality of his emotional states.

The conjunction 'as if' also expresses Pip's disavowed boyish desires to harm upper-class males who demean and declass him. The past subjunctive, moreover, expresses his inability to act in the face of the possible violence he imagines they may wield against him. During his second visit to Satis House, for example, Pip follows the pale young gentleman, 'as if [he] had been under a spell'; the boy, Pip recalls, 'eyeing my anatomy as if he were minutely choosing his bone', commands, in the simple present imperative, 'Come and fight'; Pip expresses 'surprise' when, after the first blow, he 'saw [the boy] lying on his back, looking up at me with a bloody nose and his face exceedingly foreshortened' (99–101). Here, the past subjunctive and 'as if' protect Pip from the necessity to claim his own violent acts as volitional, even when associated with the spatial dislocations of perception created by his fuzzy perspectival vision. As he ponders the gentleman's 'puffy and incrimsoned countenance', he sees that 'village boys could not go stalking about the country, ravaging the houses of gentlefolks and pitching into the studious youth of England, without laying themselves open to severe punishment' (102). The reader spies the implied author here, for Pip has not pillaged Satis House, where this scene takes place, and he has misattributed erudition and diligence to a boy he doesn't know. This scenario blends scenes of violence against those who humiliate and declass the experiencing Pip, even as the remembering Pip protects himself from understanding them, and the implied author predicts retributive justice.

The remembering Pip's conjunction also transfers retaliatory emotions along networks, especially against women who humiliate him. Pip banishes Estella from the scenes in which she disgraced him, as he fancies he sees her 'pass among the extinguished fires, and ascend some iron stairs, and go out by a gallery high overhead, as if she were going out into the sky' – as though she were returning to the firmament her name suggests. This kind of conceptual blend functions most fully, however, with the figural Miss Havisham, who possesses the prized girl for whom Pip longs. 'I saw a figure hanging ... by the neck' on a great wooden beam, a form in 'yellow white [and] faded trimmings', beckoning 'as if she were trying to call to me'. Terrified, Pip runs from and then toward the paradoxically accusatory and helpless effigy of Miss Havisham, yet finds 'no figure there' (75–7). These wild cognitions, dynamic yet fantastic blends, substitute phantoms for visualised figures, establishing seeing as *not* seeing and *not* knowing. These phantoms also create 'spectacular emergent emotions' that force the reader to begin to cognise the experiencing and remembering Pip's unknowing and disavowed desires.

Other phantoms, ghosts and hauntings transfer strong emotions across networks via another vital relation, 'representation', for the narrating Pip's conceptual blends also compress his boyish identity with theatricalised criminal figures (*Think* 97–8). Pip was 'stung' by the bumbling play-actor Wopsle's 'identification' of George Lillo's murderous apprentice in *The London Merchant* with himself; when George Barnwell 'began to go wrong, ... I felt positively apologetic, ... [as] I was made to murder my uncle with no extenuating circumstances whatever' (123). Pip's coordinating conjunction voices the boy's unknowing hostility toward that uncle, the hypocrite who takes credit for Pip's expectations; '"Take warning, boy, take warning!"' Pumblechook growls, 'as if ... I contemplated murdering a near relation [or] benefactor' (123). The verb 'contemplated', which links seeing with understanding and predicting, forces the reader to realise that the boy does unknowingly ponder a figurative murder. With his 'head full of George Barnwell', Pip returns home, believing himself guilty of 'the attack upon [his] sister', since he seems a 'more legitimate object of suspicion than anyone else' (125). When Wopsle, bungling on stage as Hamlet, sees a man behind Pip in the audience, a man 'like a ghost', his report makes Pip feel a 'special and peculiar terror' at Compeyson's haunting of him (353–4). As ghost, Compeyson parodies and prophesies Pip's failure yet also predicts criminal violence against his person, undertaken by Orlick, Pip's felonious ancestral counterpart at the forge. Orlick slouchingly haunts Pip, turning up after *The London Merchant* (123); after attempting Pip's murder at the limekiln, Orlick accuses the boy of killing Mrs Joe: '[I]t was your doing – I tell you it was done through you. ... You was favoured, and he was bullied and beat. ... You done it; now you pays for it' (389). Efficient and creative, these representations produce spectacular emotion, recruiting emotional memories through ghostly images, as the experiencing Pip, the narrating Pip and the reader experience sensory vivacity: the immense fear and terror transferred across representational spaces.

Pip's persistent use of 'as if' and the conditional mood not only transfers role and properties and creates disnarrations, but also inflects his narrative's grammar strongly toward what the reader must view as 'unreal or impossible' conditions (Vaihinger 258). In the subjunctive mood – an *irrealis* verb form that voices wishes or fears, possibilities or improbabilities – the 'as if' locution also expresses counterfactual emotions of disappointment, regret, guilt and shame, emotions understood only in retrospect (Zeelenbert and van Dijk 147). When apprenticed by the Justices, the boyish Pip imagines that Pumblechook pushes him, 'as if I had at the moment picked a pocket or fired a rick', holds him 'as if we had looked in [at the court] on our way to the scaffold' (112). But Pip did not fire a rick, nor was he en-route to his own hanging but to the forge, despite the criminal guilt spun out here through metaphor. In a series of hypotheses about Dickens's disnarrations and unreal conditions, Warhol muses about the comparative function of Dickens's counterfactuals, about what 'if the story were different'; she invokes phrases such as 'if only' as she considers *'what might have been and yet is not'* (230; emphasis in text). Pip's 'as if' also signposts his transfer of counterfactual emotions from one frame or source story to another. After the scenes I cited above, Pip crawls into bed feeling 'truly wretched', with a 'strong conviction' that Joe's trade will not suit the boy condemned to practise it: the reader asks counterfactually, what if he must not? (113). For the reader, then, the counterfactual conjunction creates a 'series of hypotheses' and predictions about Pip's future class status, his family situation and his possible happiness – or misery (Herman, *Logic* 321).[5] Pip's counterfactual scenarios, even if false, portend potentialities, possibilities and hypotheticalities that aid readers to run blends and forecast outcomes.

Critics have not failed to notice Pip's 'as if', and have suggested its use for character narration. J. Hillis Miller elegantly notes that, among other functions, the 'as if' locution 'testifies to the copresence of Dickens' childish view and his mature, disillusioned view, and points to the persistence of the former as the source . . . of Dickensian imagination' (*World* 152). G. L. Brook, invoking Miller, mistakenly calls the 'as if' locution 'fanciful', the 'invention of some improbable but amusing explanation' for figural appearance or behaviour (33). Roger Fowler rightly notes that the conjunction 'emphasize[s] interpretation rather than factual report'; using *'words of estrangement'* such as 'seems' alongside the conjunction, the narrator describes 'some internal state' about which 'he cannot be sure' (92, qtng Uspensky; emphasis in text). Applying to the novel computational analysis of textual corpora, Michaela Mahlberg identifies 266 uses of 'as if' in *Great Expectations*, demonstrating both this novel's 'highest normalized frequency' for the phrase when compared with Dickens's other texts, and its more frequent occurrence when compared with nineteenth-century texts by other authors (23, 26). Believing what he calls 'conditional analogy' provides the 'fundamental syntax of Dickensian character', Jonathan Farina implicitly contradicts Mahlberg, counting 411 iterations of 'as if' in *Dombey and Son* (1846–7), 393 in *David Copperfield* (1840–50) and 392 in *Our Mutual Friend* (1865). Yet these are all significantly longer novels than is *Expectations* (427; see also *Everyday Words*). Of the critics I cite, Miller and Fowler most clearly suggest that Dickens's implied author produces Pip's temporally disjunct doubled discourses as constituting his failure to understand.

Nevertheless, the conjunction 'as if', if we read with Mahlberg, must complicate or revise Turner's rule that 'UNDERSTANDING IS SEEING' (*Death* 17–18). Mahlberg notes that the implied author's and the remembering narrator's 'as if', which seems to enable the reader to 'see the world of the novel through Pip's eyes' (27), nevertheless demonstrates that 'seeing is *not* knowing' (31, 28, 29). For Mahlberg, the reader sees from the experiencing Pip's perspective even as he or she understands the remembering Pip's own failure to have known, his persistent unnarrations and disnarrations (256). Turner's rather insistent, capitalised slogan points to his maxim's blind spot: the typeface asserts the identity of seeing and understanding even as the analysis admits that vision and cognition exist in 'different, though related, domains of experience'. Turner seeks to nuance his capitalised rule, for what 'we see depends upon where we stand and where we direct our gaze': images seen may be 'sharp or fuzzy'; we may see 'clearly or hazily or through a glass darkly'; we may close our eyes and so not see (*Death* 17). Intuition and partial perception may thus obscure rather than facilitate knowledge. Yet Turner nevertheless insists that seeing is 'related to understanding in a systematic way', because '*metaphor is so deeply entrenched in our conceptual systems*'; for 'where we intuitively understand properties as being shared, they are shared by virtue of some metaphorical understanding' (*Death* 18; emphasis in text). The typeface of Turner's second maxim, italics, again displays his theory's blind spot, as he works out his nevertheless critically useful notions of blending. Yet as Mahlberg suggests without quite saying so, Pip's 'as if' conjunctions alert the reader to the boy's youthful lack of understanding, to the adult narrator's disnarrations and unnarrations and to the reader's own necessary projections and predictions of narrative outcomes.

As I've suggested above, the remembering Pip's 'as if' also opens a space for the implied author, who manipulates his tale's teller to affect the reader's experience. As James Phelan notes, 'meaning' arises from 'the feedback loop among authorial agency, textual phenomena, and reader response'; authorial agency, moreover, is located in the 'implied rather than the actual author' (*Living* 45, *Telling* 204). Phelan's feedback loop corresponds to my notion of the ways conceptual blending links the textual character and narrator with the implied author; despite the reader's – and the two Pips' – lack of full understanding, the reader performs an activity like the implied author's, as he unriddles the character's failures to understand, his counterfactual emotions and experiences of terror; he understands, too, the narrator's disnarrations, unnarrations and hypotheticals as present absences. After the boy stays at the Blue Boar rather than the forge, as he intended, the narrator notes: 'All other swindlers upon earth are nothing to the self-swindlers, and with such pretences did I cheat myself' (216). The reader can only assign such high-level generalisations to the implied author, since they so forcefully judge the experiencing character. Yet the implied author's omnipresent representations of Pip's failures to understand, say, Biddy's right readings of the boy's refusals to know makes the reader suspect Pip's ability to see: 'Are you quite sure, then, that you WILL come to see [Joe] often?' she asks Pip. The remembering Pip accuses himself of a youthful 'virtuously self-asserting manner'; the implied author rightly suggests that Pip's anger at Orlick's 'dancing at' Biddy signifies jealousy, which subtends the whole scenario (267). Indeed, the implied author preaches to the reader about his character's failures to know and his narrator's as-yet impartial understanding: if the marshes' mists 'disclosed to me, as I suspect they did, that I should not come back, and that Biddy was quite right, all I can say is – they were quite right too' (268). Whereas the remembering Pip feels counterfactual regret – the outcome might, he realises, have been different – and the implied author inscribes his clear understanding, the reader feels coerced to know, too, as the implied author's preachments become a kind of bullying (*Think* 52, 145).

The remembering narrator's conditional conjunctions also warn the reader that Pip's prospect theory might well be flawed. Thinking that Miss Havisham has chosen him for Estella and surreptitiously provided his fortune, Pip's expectations prevent him from 'anticipat[ing]' the possibility of 'disappointment', a powerful counterfactual emotion known only in retrospect (Khaneman 287). Magwitch's return to the narrative contravenes Pip's intuitive projection into the future of his hopes, wants and desires, and confirms the reader's emerging conjecture that Pip's great expectations will prove to be in vain. When, amid signs and portents, Magwitch reenters Pip's life, he claims his function as metonymic parent: 'Look'ee here, Pip. I'm your second father. You're my son – more to me nor any son' (298–9). Here, Magwitch compresses his identity with a vital relation of kinship; he claims his role as figurative cross-class progenitor: 'And then, dear boy, it was a recompense to me, look'ee here, to know in secret that I was making a gentleman' (299). Yet as a returned transport, Magwitch's unlawful reappearance signifies his doubled criminality and, projected onto Pip's desired trajectory into the gentry, means the boy will not become a gentleman, will not inherit a fortune, will not marry Estella. The experiencing Pip responds, feeling the 'sharpest and deepest pain of all', since for the convict he 'had deserted Joe' (301). As the remembering Pip realises he had 'disguised from [his] recognition' his 'uneasiness' about his treatment of Joe and his condescension toward Biddy, he also understands imagined or recalled 'mysterious warnings' of Magwitch's return (236, 301). Fearing the knockings and whisperings outside his door – the reader wrongly but wittingly predicts Orlick's lurking or Compeyson's crouching – Pip has unknowingly cued the reader to reinterpret the 'messengers' Magwitch's 'wicked spirit' has visited upon him: Orlick, Compeyson and Magwitch seem ghostly reminders of Pip's self-attributed criminality (301).

As the novel ends, Pip's blended scenes and intuitive predictions produce wild cognitions that the reader can only view as *irrealis*, as hypotheticals that identify present absences. When Pip infers that Estella is Molly's rather than Miss Havisham's child, he blends his look at the housekeeper's scarred hands with his sight of Estella's fingers, knitting, identifying the two women as kin. Tellingly, as he looks at Estella, Pip twice sees in the girl the 'ghost' of a likeness, although she's different from her supposed mother, Miss Havisham; seeing his face, Estella presciently asks, 'Are you scared again?' (227). He is; yet due to its improbability, the reader is loath to accept his hint that a phantom stimulates this wild cognition. When Herbert tells Pip his story of Miss Havisham, Pip likewise infers that Magwitch fathered Estella, an even more improbable prediction. When he confronts Jaggers, Pip makes the lawyer 'start'; he confirms Pip's conjecture only by positing another hypothetical tale: 'Put the case . . .' (375, 377). On his preceding visit to Satis House, Pip paused to look back: 'A childish association revived with wonderful force . . . and I fancied that I saw Miss Havisham hanging to the beam. So strong was the impression, that I stood under the beam shuddering from head to foot before I knew it was a fancy' (367). Again, the reader's inference predicts Pip's unknowingness, for his seeing is not seeing, even as his seeing is not understanding.

This wild cognition, projected from the fantasied scene on his first visit to Satis House, displays Pip's fancying a repeated counterfactual scene, for his *irrealis* verbs point explicitly to the 'web of connections across spaces in an integration network involving a counterfactual scenario of harm' (*Think* 64). He sees a 'great flaming light spring up' around Miss Havisham, a 'whirl of fire blazing all about her'; dragging the cloth from the table and destroying the decayed wedding feast, Pip 'closed with her [and] threw her down' as he and Miss Havisham struggle 'like desperate enemies' (368). The 'extinguished fires' of Pip's early brewery scenario leap into being here, in this blended scene of reviled 'mother by adoption' both hanging and burning (333). The conjunction 'as if' also signals Pip's transfer of criminal role from himself (and his second father) to Miss Havisham: 'I still held her forcibly down with all my strength, like a prisoner who might escape ... as if I unreasonably fancied (I think I did) that if I let her go, the fire would break out again and consume her' (368). As she lies in the place she predicted for her death, Pip sees 'the phantom' of her guilt, as he begins to align seeing and understanding, sensing the effigy a fancy (369). Despite Pip's emergent understanding, the reader conjectures or deduces this fantasied scene's forecast of eventual narratorial knowledge.

Pip's intuitive predictions undone and burned, his counterfactual scenarios confirm the reader's doubts about the boy's great expectations. The narrative tension between expectation – the experiencing Pip's supposition that he will gain gentlemanly wealth, happiness and leisure in the future – and fatalism – the reader's strong belief that Pip cannot control future events – creates the novel's dense heterogeneity of multiple contrary prospects. Pip's faulty cause-effect reasoning mentally simulates alternative counterfactual scenarios with outcomes the story suggests but the narrator fails to foresee: the narrative's affordance to connect events over time and prophesy others. The reader has hypothesised, predicted and inferred possible patterns that might later be encountered, confirmed or denied. Some potential outcomes appear figurally in Pip's tale and provide ghostly reminders of the tension between his expectations and his possible failed futures. When he goes home, Pip knows that he 'must stay at Joe's', although the reader predicts he'll lodge at the Blue Boar, a hypothesis that is almost immediately narratively confirmed. On the coach, two criminals ride behind him: the man Pip recognises from the Three Jolly Bargemen tells the other convict about two one-pound notes, in Pip's own words. Pip feels 'certain' the man 'had no suspicion of [his] identity', but the reader predicts a contrary outcome: the upwardly mobile 'Handel' will somehow be found out and again become the guilty young man at the forge (220). This conceptual blend of past story event and present occurrence once again produces sensationally vivid emotions, for Pip felt 'a dread' with 'no distinctness of shape' that seemed a 'revival' of childhood 'terror' (220).

Pip's failure to perform as parallel the cognitive acts of conceptual blending and intuitive predicting produces the novel's problematic multiple endings. The original, unpublished version portrayed the triumph of probability over possibility: the remembering narrator surmises that Estella's 'suffering... had given her a heart to understand what my heart used to be' (Carlisle 440). Yet the three revised versions of 1861 and 1862 predict, prophesy or estimate possible vistas of marital partnership. The manuscript and proof revision read, 'I saw the shadow of no parting from her, but one,' as the ghost of mortality steps in to disrupt or complicate the narrator's desire (Carlisle 440). Later, Dickens struck the final phrase, 'but one', from *All the Year Round*'s and the triple decker's texts, unnarrating even while hinting at a hypothetical wedding, and suggesting eternal love. As Pip's great expectations unravel, the reader's hypotheses efficiently and creatively project different possible outcomes, futuresand prospects, all of them undone by Dickens's unnarrations.

Strikingly, all four endings represent a spectacular form of narratorial unnarration. The original ending, as transcribed and footnoted by John Forster, temporally compresses Estella's married life into one paragraph, all its details prefaced by the narrator's absence and incapacity: 'I had heard...' he intones three times, before sketching brief details of marital abuse, separation, death, remarriage and fall in fortune (Forster 737–8, Rosenberg 100–2). Yet the revisionary unnarrations produce a vividly present absence, a lack that points toward the story's displacements and elisions, as well as toward the discourse's unknowing understanding of its figural counterparts, identities and class positions. Yet the one-volume edition's 'no shadow of another parting from her' unnarrates the tale's vital relations of time and change, for the necessary 'outcome of the chain of causes and effects that constitutes plot' predicts separation rather than worldly and spiritual unity for Pip and Estella (Carlisle 440–1, Sadrin 168).

Nevertheless, Dickens's friend Bulwer-Lytton convinced him to alter the ending he had 'originally conceived' (Johnson 968). Having apparently read the proofs while Dickens visited him at Knebworth, Bulwer-Lytton was 'very anxious' about the first ending, Dickens told Wilkie Collins; to Bulwer-Lytton, he wrote 'the alteration... is entirely due to you' (*Letters* 428, 429, 433). As Dickens disclosed to John Forster, Bulwer-Lytton 'supported his views with such good reasons' that Dickens rewrote it, not once but thrice (*Letters* 433). Dickens's biographer, E. D. H. Johnson, speculates that the 'changed ending' expressed Dickens's 'desperate hope' that he and Ellen Ternan would never part – although his statement unnarrates a marital implication (969). Nevertheless, Johnson argues that Bulwer-Lytton's 'poor counsel' caused Dickens to 'undo', or to disnarrate, Estella's upbringing, which he believes predicts Pip's disappointment (992–3). Fred Kaplan notes that Ellen no doubt read the proofs, too, or that Dickens read them to her; Kaplan supposes that she probably agreed with Bulwer-Lytton (437). Strikingly, both biographical accounts deploy Dickens's narrator's refusals to tell: Johnson disnarrates and unnarrates; Kaplan supposes and projects. Although Dickens had 'no doubt' that the changed ending would make the novel 'more acceptable' to his readers, that belief, too, supposes and predicts what his contemporaries would feel (*Letters* 433). Yet one contemporary reviewer understood Pip's delusive expectations, knew the 'ghastly recluse' did not confer wealth on the boy and felt 'held in thrall by the knowledge' that Magwitch would return.[6] Others praised the plot's 'unity' or 'genius', the 'felicity' of prolonging expectation and the 'series of surprises' that support the 'logic of passion and character'.[7] Although Dickens hypothesised what his contemporary flesh-and-blood readers might have preferred, his predictions about his readers seem flawed. Nonetheless, his alterations' discourse unnarrated the plot's seemingly necessary trajectory, with Pip and Estella unwed.

Twentieth-century critics generally prefer the original ending, as do I.[8] Pip's desire – to see 'the shadow of no parting from her' – represents what Kahneman calls '*miswanting*', a term that describes the 'bad choices' that result from 'errors of affective forecasting' (406; emphasis in text). A counterfactual emotion, miswanting makes Pip – and the implied author – overweight improbable outcomes. As Kahneman notes, a story recounts 'significant events and memorable moments, ... and the ending often defines its character' (387). Due to what Kahneman calls the 'peak-end effect', the author, implied author and remembering narrator compose stories with peaks and ends that define the tale's meaning; the reader, too, recalls narrative peaks and ends, and these significant events determine or affect the reader's emotive response to the story's significance (407). As such, the conclusion provides the remembering and reading selves an intuitive takeaway from its privileged position as both peak and end. As Estella prepares to part from Pip once again in the tale's final chapter, she speaks the line that Dickens transposes from the manuscript's remembering narrator: 'suffering has ... taught me to understand what your heart used to be' (439). Strikingly, however, at least one of Dickens's contemporary reviewers thought the ending flawed. 'The plot ends before it ought to. ... The heroine is married, reclaimed from harshness to gentleness, widowed, made love to, and remarried, in a page or two. This is too stiff a pace for the emotions of readers.'[9] Pip's refusal to accept Estella's version of their story's peak and end creates for modern readers counterfactual emotions of disappointment and regret at the end's improbability.

Martin Meisel rightly calls another scene the novel's 'true ending' (327). Indeed, Meisel's choice appropriately serves as the tale's peak and end. Prior to the novel's conclusion, its final counterfactual scene represents Joe's son, 'little Pip', as Pip himself, reborn and given a second chance of life at the forge. On his final visit to the forge, Pip marvels, 'there, fenced into the corner with Joe's leg, and sitting on my own little stool looking at the fire, was – I again!' (436). Fittingly, Pip takes his 'little likeness' to his own father's grave and 'set[s] him on a certain tombstone there', as through temporal compression and cross-space mapping, little Pip becomes counterpart of the boy, Pip, and the now-adult Pip becomes his second father, or becomes father to himself: in the web of connections across spaces, this integration network activates and circulates the reader's intuitive inferences about Pip's and little Pip's identities and kinship (*Letters* 432, *Expectations* 436). The centrality of tombstone and grave also create pattern recognition, as the remembering narrator recalls and repeats the graveyard-meeting peak as end. The scene compresses the narrative's most emotionally laden peak moments and repeats its pattern of criminal counterparts, here cleansed and purified; it overweights a less improbable, because metaphorical, outcome than does the supposed wedding, an unnarrated present absence. As Dickens's discourse ends with yet another version of Pip's characteristic seeing is *not* understanding, the novel's existing peak and end – the hint of Pip and Estella's marriage – screams counterfactuality to a modern reader. 'Conceptualization always has counterfactuality available,' Fauconnier and Turner say, and Dickens wildly indulges it as his novel concludes (87).

III

As coda, I'd like to thank J. Hillis Miller for having introduced me, when an undergraduate, to Dickens's world, in *World*. And for having taught me, as a young assistant professor, about post-structural and French Freudian theory. May we all thank him for his incredible critical generosity, on his ninetieth birthday.

Notes

1. See, respectively, Zunshine, Armstrong and Dames.
2. I follow Jameson in distinguishing 'emotion' from 'affect'; Jameson argues that affect, conceptualised at mid-century, refocused realistic fiction on

physiological sensation. I also draw on Hogan, whose 'neurobiological sensitivity model' argues that emotion is a 'crucial part of the function of imagination' and that 'literary feeling' – although without 'actional outcomes' – emerges from triggered 'emotional' and 'implicit memories' the reader experiences while reading (*The Antinomies of Realism*, pp. 243–5).
3. Grossman attributes Pip's association of himself with Magwitch's guilt – and his story's shift from first-person toward omniscient narration – not through conceptual blending but via the exponential growth of transport networks ('Living the Global Transport Network', pp. 238–40).
4. The classic essay about Pip's psychology is, of course, by Moynahan ('The Hero's Guilt'). See also Herman, on the 'perspectival indices that cluster around' what he calls hypothetical focalisation and often serve as 'the formal markers of skepticism, detachment, even paranoia' (*Story Logic*, p. 328).
5. Interestingly enough, when Herman theorises the counterfactual conditional, he deploys the locution 'as if' – an instance of the ways fictional discourse is taken up by its critics (*Story Logic*, p. 321).
6. See Chorley, 'Review', p. 44.
7. See Forster, '*Great Expectations*', p. 453; Whipple, 'Review', p. 428.
8. See especially Rosenberg, Sadrin, and Meisel.
9. Anonymous, '*Great Expectations*: Reviews', p. 69.

III

Histories, Historicities

Chapter 10

How Not to Historicise a Poem: On McGann's 'Light Brigade'

Henry Staten

Literary critics have rarely been very rigorous historians, but that didn't much matter in an older tradition of criticism that treated history broadly, as background. In the early 1980s, by contrast, new techniques of historical interpretation were developed that claimed to penetrate the very quick of lived historical experience reflected in literary works, and thus to supersede mere close reading. The common factors in the various new styles of historicism were (1) their approach to history as the realm of representation, a conveniently vague notion that managed simultaneously to appeal to the Real of history while opening history to the imaginative activity of the critic as never before; and (2) their adoption of moral and political high ground that was sometimes explicitly Marxist but more often remained evasively leftist or progressive.

The reading on which I focus, Jerome McGann's pages on Tennyson's 'Charge of the Light Brigade' in his 1985 book *The Beauty of Inflections*, is exemplary of these new styles of historicism, which remain influential today. No one, not even the Marxists, laid claim to the ethico-political probity of these new styles more aggressively than McGann in this reading. Using the New Critics as his foil, as was common at the time, McGann claimed (in a startling, revisionist echo of Matthew Arnold) that his approach to historical reconstruction had recreated the 'human drama' of Tennyson's poem 'as in itself it really is' (193). His argument sounds familiar today even if we haven't read it: Tennyson's apparently simple, and rather naïve, poem is actually a complexly coded ideological intervention, motivated by the interests of the ruling class. The English cavalry, McGann argued, was perceived by the British public as a peculiarly aristocratic institution; but this same public had come to perceive the aristocracy as 'effete' (196), 'dandified' and 'enervated' (201). Because the units sent to the Crimea, and especially the Light

Brigade, were among the *most* 'socially élite' units in the British army, the charge at Balaclava was seen by Tennyson's public as an aristocratic drama (194). *The Times*, in its editorial comments, pushed the view that this drama redounded to the glory of the aristocracy, and so, according to McGann, did Tennyson's 'patently aristocratic' poem (197).

McGann's reading subsequently became a standard reference. In an essay published in 1990, Marjorie Perloff lionised it as a model of historicising criticism, contrasting its rigour with what she saw as the empty gestures toward history by John Brenkman and Frederic Jameson in their contributions to the noted *Poetry after Formalism* anthology.[1] And recent work on the context of the 'Charge' by Trudi Tate and Stefanie Markovits has accepted the interpretive agenda set by McGann. Tate and Markovits propose new interpretations of Tennyson's motive, but they accept McGann's central claims that 1) the cavalry represented the aristocracy in Tennyson's mind and in the perception of his audience, and 2) this being so, the poem can be interpreted as intervening in the political debate of the period over the fitness of the aristocracy to rule.[2]

McGann's reading is now decades old, yet it is worth revisiting because our graduate students continue to learn the style of historicism that it helped to establish, and of which it can easily still serve as a model. In the 1980s and after, this kind of reading came to be felt by many as the only truly responsible form of criticism. Yet its combination of ethico-political uprightness and imaginative gymnastics seems to have exercised an anaesthetising effect on the critical faculty of many readers, who accepted the most dubious historical claims as long as they were packaged in the approved kind of argumentation. McGann's reading of the 'Charge' is exemplary in this regard, so masterfully achieved a display of the critical rhetoric of representation historicism that it lulled even so astute a critic as Perloff into accepting its flimsy recourse to history.

Perhaps an analysis of McGann's problematic claims can serve a useful pedagogical function at present. My entire essay will circulate around the question of just what the Light Brigade was in reality, what it would have represented, and how it is represented in the poem, considered in relation to the reality and perception of class at the time.

I

In his reading of the 'Charge of the Light Brigade', McGann paraphrases the opinion of *The Times*, which he takes to be also Tennyson's, as follows: 'The six-hundred dead cavaliers are "noble" still, not merely by virtue of their actual class position, but by reason of their deeds, and the spiritual "nobility" which their deaths have shown' (196). This single assertion, which makes two patently false claims, ought already to awaken the reader's historical scepticism. In the first place, as any reader of the poem knows, not all of the six hundred were killed, since it refers clearly to those who rode 'Back from the mouth of Hell'; and Tennyson's audience would have known from the report in *The Times* that more than two thirds of the brigade had survived.[3] More significant than the number of dead, however, is the fact that McGann refers to the six hundred as though they were all aristocrats. His reference to the dead as 'cavaliers' is ambiguous, a cavalier being literally a horseman but historically an aristocratic horseman; the sentence and essay as a whole show that McGann does indeed mean it in the latter sense. The purportedly dead six hundred supposed 'cavaliers', McGann's paraphrase asserts, are noble 'still', meaning that they must have been noble before; but this nobility which they 'still' possess is now 'not merely' a matter of class, meaning that that's all it was before the charge. McGann thus implies not only that the brigade as a whole was aristocratic, but also that each man in it was an aristocrat.

If McGann were observing any distinction between aristocrat and non-aristocrat within the Light Brigade, he would mention the vast majority of the Light Brigade's members who were commoners; and he never does. McGann's entire argument, thus, rests on a simple fallacy of composition, one which Tennyson's original audience would never have committed. This audience would have been intensely aware that the vast majority of those reported dead or missing were enlisted men, members of what McGann in reference to the infantry calls 'the lower orders' (196); and that even among the dead officers, most were not aristocrats. In the entire British cavalry in 1847, in fact, there were barely one hundred aristocrats, and the numbers reported by *The Times* for the dead confirm this scarcity.[4] According to the *Times* leader for 13 November, of the 169 killed or missing, thirteen were officers ('London, Monday, November 13, 1854' 6), and according to the dispatch from William Howard Russell on the 14th ('The War in the Crimea: The Cavalry Action at Balaklava' 7), who names ten of them, only one bears a title.[5]

The notion of six hundred dead 'cavaliers' begins to look radically different in the light of these numbers; but perhaps the main thrust of McGann's argument could still be preserved. Not all the brigade died, and of those who died only a few were aristocrats; nevertheless it's undeniable that, as the words quoted by McGann from *The Times* assert, in England the infantry and cavalry were historically distinguished 'along class lines', the cavalry being 'the favourite resort of the aristocracy' (195). To make matters worse, the specific units sent to the Crimea were 'notoriously affected groups', the 'most socially élite' in the British army (194–5); and their incompetence had been shown up shortly before Balaclava by the victory of the infantry at the battle of the Alma, where the cavalry had for various reasons remained out of the fighting. Are not a few aristocrats at the top enough to make the Light Brigade as a whole 'aristocratic', at the level of representation, so that Tennyson's readership would, indeed, have seen the 'Charge' as a 'patently aristocratic poem' (197)? And in that case, it would be valid to inquire into what Tennyson intended to say about the aristocracy by means of his poem.

As I show, the apparent plausibility of this line of defence crumbles under historical scrutiny. But first I want to follow the next turn in McGann's argument, because it is only after he thinks he has established the nature of Tennyson's ideological intention that McGann starts making imaginative historical juxtapositions of the kind that characterise the new historicisms, and which beguiled Perloff. He begins now, with a bravura air of mastery, to jump across historical periods, cultures and representational modalities, arguing that Tennyson's little poem is actually a bold act of historical revisionism that, in its attempt to glorify the English aristocracy, appropriates an iconographic tradition developed by French painters following the French Revolution. I will pay very close attention to the way McGann introduces painting, and, glancingly, sculpture, into the dossier, because his juxtaposition of literature with visual media, which has no doubt helped to inspire numerous dissertations, opens to the critical imagination a realm in which the most fanciful of claims and the loosest of analogies can gain a respectful hearing, as long as they make the appropriate nods to the Left.

II

McGann claims that 'one of the principal technical means' by which Tennyson's poem was enabled to 'cross class lines and speak to the nation at large' – despite the fact that it glorifies the bravery of the aristocracy in the face of their ineptitude – is that it draws the 'form' of its images from an iconography of heroism that Tennyson appropriates (197), an iconography that 'is almost entirely French and emerges out of the Romantic styles that were associated with Napoleon' (199):

> The poem's images present the cavaliers as if they were cast in a tableau, or in a heroic painting – and in one case at least, as if they were statues. The Light Brigade comes before us in Tennyson's poem as an aesthetic object, as

we see very clearly in the fourth stanza, where the riders are made to assume the classic pose of the equestrian hero in action. Such a figure lived in the nineteenth century's eye in a whole array of paintings and statues, some great (e.g., in the work of David, Gros, Gericault, and Delacroix), some merely ordinary (e.g., in the statuary familiar throughout the cities of Europe).

Flashed all their sabers bare
Flashed as they turned in air.

The fact that the military gestures in 'The Charge of the Light Brigade' are modeled upon a certain tradition of heroic military art is extremely important to see. [...]

In a moment I will look more closely at this set of claims; but first let us pause over the evidence that McGann provides to support the notion that French painting is even relevant to Tennyson's poem. His evidence for this claim is precisely two lines from the poem: 'Flashed all their sabers bare/Flashed as they turned in air.' That's it. The entire argument about the relation of Tennyson's poem to France, French painting and the ideological struggle after Waterloo depends on our accepting this single image as evidence that the representation of the Light Brigade is modelled on French Romantic painting, and thus tied to a certain unspecified French ideology that is presented as antithetical to that of the aristocratic English cavalry.

What other images, a naïve reader might wonder, would one find in a poem about a cavalry charge with sabres, other than charging and sabres? As for the 'flashing' – whenever cavaliers draw their swords in poetry, be it in the romances of Chretien de Troyes or the Shah Nameh of Ferdosi (Atkinson's translation had appeared in 1831), their blades are unfailingly described as bright, glittering, shining; why, then, does Tennyson's image call for such a specialised derivation? So much for common sense; add a bit of research and we find that the specific figure of flashing blades, like so much else in Tennyson's poem, is taken directly from Russell's prose in *The Times*. Like Tennyson, Russell even repeats his figure twice: 'they never halt or check their speed an instant ... with a halo of flashing steel above their heads ... they flew into the smoke of the batteries'; 'Through the clouds of smoke we could see their sabers flashing' ('The Cavalry Action at Balaklava' 7). McGann's claim for the provenance of the figure thus fetches far to seek a source that lies very near to hand.

This fact alone is enough to render McGann's theory about French painting superfluous; but let us stay with his argument. There are three reasons to keep alive the tenuous hypothesis that the flashing of sabres all by itself could link this poem to an entire tradition of French painting: 1. Perloff buys it. 2. It exemplifies the loose way in which visual imagery can be marshalled as evidence, and often is. 3. It is McGann's main evidence for his claim that he is elucidating the 'form' of the poem.

Here is how McGann continues:

> One has merely to compare, say, David's famous portrait of Napoleon with any of the portraits of Wellington, or even of Nelson, in order to perceive the gulf which separates their ideological points of view. Like Gros's portrait of Murat at the Battle of Aboukir, or Géricault's famous picture of the chasseur of the Imperial Guard, David's picture is charged through with various signs of Romantic motion, force, and energy. English painting of the same period never triumphed in this style. Consequently, in the immediately subsequent history the French chasseurs of the Napoleonic wars became heroic models throughout European art and culture, whereas the English cavaliers are either models of equestrian decorum, or objects of broad ridicule – in the last instance, mere aristocratic dandies. Besides, the fact that the heroic French chasseur did not come from the well-born and elite classes of society was an important element in his ideological significance. In this respect he came to stand for the human meaning of the historical events which tore Europe apart at the end of the eighteenth century. Napoleon's world-historical import was epitomised in the figure of the French chasseur, whose exploits in battle overshadowed and surpassed in glory the military acts of Europe's congregated and élite forces.

McGann here tantalisingly suggests that in 1854 Napoleon's chasseurs represent the 'human meaning' of a broad set of 'historical events which tore Europe apart' and which encompassed both Napoleon and the preceding revolution, with its pursuit by the 'lower orders' of liberty, equality and fraternity. This vaguely conceived 'human meaning' is, of course, one that must command the sympathies of any Left-leaning literary critic; it is the historical beginning of that very revolt against oppression and subjugation in which such a critic participates today. Tennyson's intention, by contrast, McGann indicts of supporting the counter-revolutionary tendency, and of doing so by perverting the symbols of that revolution to his reactionary purpose. His poem is an '"Englishing", as it were ... of certain French possessions' in 'an act of revisionist historical criticism' (200).

Karl Marx, for his part, in 1852 wrote in the 18th *Brumaire* of Louis Bonaparte that the historical meaning of 1789 and its aftermath was 'the unchaining and setting up of modern bourgeois society' (16). Marx, of course, had been expelled from France in 1845 for his radicalism, and lived from 1848 and worked the rest of his life in England, where he had the liberty to do his work. But conceive the revolution of 1789 as ideally as you like: how can Napoleon, who sought to establish his own family as a new hereditary royalty, be treated as an emblem for the ideals of popular democracy, except by the loosest possible conception of the 'human meaning' of unspecified 'historical events'? Napoleon did of course carry forward the impetus of the revolution in certain ways; yet he is also the very model of the modern dictator, the man who developed what Marx called the 'appalling parasitic body' of an 'executive power with its enormous bureaucratic and military organization, with its ingenious state machinery' (18th *Brumaire* 121), who militarised France and professionalised its army in the interest of conquest – a man to whom 'manpower ... was a commodity like any other' and who once wrote that a million dead human beings did not matter to a man like him (Forrest 19). By what strange alchemy does McGann make the Napoleonic mounted chasseur a pure and simple expression of the purported fact that England – the birthplace of the ideas of liberty that inspired the French revolution – had 'lost to France the ideological struggle' in the decades following the battle of Waterloo (200)? The non-aristocratic mounted chasseurs, McGann claims, 'became heroic models throughout European art and culture' as embodiments of the 'human meaning' of the paroxysm of the late eighteenth century, thus giving France the 'brilliant aesthetic triumph' that constitutes its ideological victory over England (200).

Viewed in terms of the actual, concrete historical 1854 context of Tennyson's poem, at the time of the Crimean War the entity called France signifies to the English not the ideal heritage of 1789 but a despotism – that of Louis Napoleon – that has yet again discredited the French revolutionary tradition and now is felt by many in England to threaten English liberties. Not the least of the ironies of this moment is that the universal suffrage which continued to elude English reformers had been reinstituted in France at a stroke by Louis Napoleon, 'chief of the Paris lumpenproletariat', as Marx calls him in the 18th Brumaire (83), not in token of the triumph of French revolutionary ideology, but as the necessary base for absolute imperial power. And whatever the French cavalry might have meant fifty years earlier, Marx notes sardonically that it had in 1850 publicly raised the shout 'Vive Napoléon! Vive les saucissons!', having been bought to the despot Louis Napoleon's side with champagne and garlic sausages (78). At this point in history, the specifically English model of freedom, founded on the preservation of traditional forms of association and the mediation of state power through these forms, appeared, to the English themselves, and to many observers on the Continent, to have been vindicated against the periodic spasms of at least partly proletarian revolution that afflicted France, and which had been regularly, and immediately, betrayed by other forces. As Marx notes, Bonapartism achieves absolute, centralised state power by a process that 'annihilates the aristocratic intermediate grades between the mass of the people and the state power' (129); but Bonaparte continued to 'represent' the power of the big bourgeoisie even as he abolished the parliament that still 'represented' it in the other sense of the term that Marx distinguishes.[6] In England, however, which had the most powerful and richest aristocracy in Europe, this class was still able to play the role of bulwark against absolutism and military despotism.[7] The system of purchase of commissions in the army, which seems so irrational to us, was historically justified in terms of this role; it was thought that officers who have a stake in the established order of society cannot be bought by a despot, as was possible with a purely professional army like that of the French. The purchase of commissions, of course, infected the British army as a whole – not just the cavalry – with 'the weakness of caste' to which *The Times* refers, but as Marx better than anyone knew, every historical force is transected by multiple lines of cause and effect that push in contrary directions.[8]

However, let us set aside the question of the intelligibility of the notion of France's ideological triumph over England. Assume that it makes sense, and even that it happened. What about the most imaginatively stimulating part of McGann's thesis, the notion that the vehicle of this triumph was a tradition of French painting exemplified by Gros, Gericault and David, a tradition that turned the Napoleonic mounted chasseur into a Europe-wide symbol of a certain 'human meaning' having something to do with the aspirations of the lower orders?

Such a victory, if it existed, could only be ideological in the worst sense of the term – a merely imaginary glorification that altered nothing in the class structure of Europe, the aristocracies of which were at mid-century as busy trying to hold on to their power as always, and the big bourgeoisie of which was busy, as always, cooperating with the aristocracy to hold down the classes that the chasseur supposedly represents, so that it could manoeuvre for power against that same aristocracy.

But set that aside too. What, exactly, is the 'aesthetic triumph' that McGann evokes? He says early on that the 'inexorable rhythm of Tennyson's poem ... perfectly mirrors the cavalry's implacable movement' (197), but when he makes the turn to the French painters he says the poem presents the 600 English 'cavaliers' (as he insists on calling them) as if they were 'cast in a tableau ... and in one case ... as if they were statues' (199). Which is it to be, implacable Romantic movement or static tableau/statue? McGann says first that Tennyson's riders 'are made to assume the classic pose of the equestrian hero in action' as this hero 'lived in the nineteenth-century's eye' in French paintings and in 'the statuary familiar throughout the cities of Europe' (199); and then invokes the notion of 'Romantic motion' as the overarching quality that will now, in the loosest way imaginable, hold together the static-dynamic qualities of poem, paintings and statues.

In support of his claim, McGann names three French paintings, of which only one, by Gericault, is actually of a mounted chasseur. The other two are Gros's portrait of Murat at Aboukir, and David's portrait of Napoleon – presumably the one of Napoleon crossing the Alps. Napoleon famously crossed the Alps on a mule, but David's portrait depicts him on a magnificent charger who is pointlessly rearing; Napoleon gestures rhetorically, attired in imperial magnificence, and there is neither enemy nor sabre in sight. Was the imagination of all mid-nineteenth-century Europe fired with thoughts of the lower-class origins of Napoleon's chasseurs when they saw this blatant glorification of the French emperor, originally commissioned by Charles IV of Spain? Napoleon himself, of course, was not exactly from the 'lower orders', and even if he had been, the example he set of upward mobility would have been equivocal (think of the Napoleon-inspired career of Julien Sorel in *The Red and the Black*). The portrait of Murat is more to McGann's point; here there is an actual battle, and Murat displays his unsheathed sabre. But this sabre is the only point at which Gros's painting could be compared to Tennyson's poem. Murat's charger is not charging but, it appears, drawing back as if beginning the picturesque motion of rearing, and Murat's sabre is not 'flashing' in the painting, either in the sense of reflecting light or of rapid motion; he is holding it out ceremonially at arm's length, in a pose that corresponds to the latently neoclassical composition of the work rather than to anything that might occur in a battle. The whole composition is, like that of David's portrait of Napoleon, reminiscent of statuary, but precisely for that reason neither of these paintings has anything to do with the 'implacable movement' of either the actual charge of the Light Brigade or its representations in *The Times* or Tennyson's poem – and certainly nothing to do with the 'Romantic motion' emphasised by McGann. McGann incoherently throws the tradition of statuary into his discussion in response to the static quality of these paintings, without attempting to bridge the gap between them and the Romantic dynamism that is his primary concern. And Murat himself, who was in 1808 created King of Naples by his brother-in-law, the emperor, and who was known as the 'Dandy King' for his love of finery, is another puzzling symbol for the non-aristocratic 'human meaning' that the French chasseur is supposed to represent. Gericault's painting comes closest to the mark; it is actually of an anonymous chasseur (who is, however, as gorgeously attired as any aristocrat), and there is both a scene of battle and something approaching a gesture of combat (Fig. 10.1). While the composition of this painting is significantly more

Figure 10.1 Théodore Géricault, *The Charging Chasseur*, c.1812. Found on Wikimedia Commons, reproduced under a Creative Commons License.

dynamic than that of the other two, it remains primarily rhetorical and static. The horse is not charging but in the de rigueur pose of rearing, and the chasseur is twisting on his horse in a way that would be very awkward in life, yet is here represented as though he were in repose, his torso perfectly erect, his face reflecting no intense physical effort of the sort that would be required if he were twisting completely around in the

Figure 10.2 Lady Elizabeth Butler, *Scotland Forever!*, 1881. Found on Wikimedia Commons, reproduced under a Creative Commons License.

saddle of a rearing horse to slash down at an attack from behind. There is, moreover, no sign of an attacker; the whole thing looks posed for the painter. There is a sort of Romantic motion here, but it is of a formalised sort, completely lacking in the forward rush of attacking cavalry – by contrast, for example, with the depiction in Lady Elizabeth Butler's famous 1881 painting of the charge of the Scots Greys at Waterloo, *Scotland Forever!* (Fig. 10.2). All three of McGann's examples glorify an individual figure on a rearing or almost rearing horse, whereas the image presented by Tennyson's poem is of anonymous hundreds engaged in what is, after all, essentially and irreducibly, a charge, and, according to the poem, a wild charge.

In no sense, then, can Tennyson be said to have derived the 'form' of his poem from the French, and McGann's entire argument about Tennyson's 'appropriation' of French iconography for ideological purposes falls to the ground.

III

Now let us return to the question I left hanging at the end of Section I. Is McGann's treatment of the 'The Charge of the Light Brigade' as representation of an essentially aristocratic spectacle based on bad logic, a simple fallacy of composition, or is there an alternate logic of representation by means of which the effete aristocratic nature of a few leaders smears itself over the six hundred who charged, determining the character of the action as historical representation? The quotations McGann provides from *The Times* and from historians Michael C. C. Adams and Cecil Woodham-Smith appear to strongly support his claims. The *Times* leader for 14 November said the cavalry and infantry were distinguished 'along class lines', claiming that, as 'the favourite resort of aristocracy', the cavalry was affected by 'the weakness of caste' ('London, Tuesday, November 14, 1854' 6). Adams refers to the 'wasp-waisted officers' who were 'objects of caricature' (419); and Woodham-Smith chronicles the extraordinarily dandified character of the field commanders of the Light Brigade, Lords Lucan and Cardigan.

In fact, however, the picture of the aristocratic officers that McGann's sources draw is quite different from what these scattered references suggest. Adams places the poem in the mid-century context of the pervasive transatlantic anxiety about the old heroic ethos of the nation-state that was being eroded by the economic self-interest championed by the middle class. Tennyson, like many others in Britain and the US at the time, looked to war as a rejuvenating force for the 'ancient virtue' that was in decline (Adams 421). Adams mentions the aristocracy only in passing, as the class whose virtues were under assault by those of the 'entrepreneur' (413). In an isolated remark that McGann cites, Adams mentions that the Britons had doubts about the 'mettle' of the 'wasp-waisted, dandified army officers' who were sent to lead the army in the Crimea (419), but Adams's point concerns not the state of the aristocracy per se but the possibility that even the aristocracy had been infected by the decay emanating from the commercial bourgeoisie. When Adams discusses 'The Charge of the Light Brigade', he makes no further mention of the aristocracy; he reads the poem as Thoreau did at the time, and as the unsuspicious reader naturally would, given that there is not a single mention of aristocratic standing in the poem, as a celebration of the actions of ordinary soldiers – many of whom, as Adams notes, 'came from the lowest levels [of society]' (420) – who showed 'that the English had something of the ancient virtue about them yet' (421).

The fact that Tennyson's poem never mentions the officers, only 'the 600' over and over, forms a sharp contrast with the *Times* leader of the 13th, which explicitly draws the distinction between the enlisted men and their aristocratic leaders, in order to assign the major part of the glory only to the leaders. McGann quotes these remarks in part, but elides the crucial words, which I here place in italics:

> Whatever the case of the common soldier, and however little he might know the full horrors of his position . . . *the officers who led him on* . . . *knew well what they were about. Nor were those officers mere soldiers of fortune, with nothing to lose but themselves, and no inducements out of their profession. They were men who risked that day all the enjoyments that rank, wealth,*

[and] good social position . . . can offer . . . Splendid as was the event on the Alma, yet that rugged ascent . . . was scarcely so glorious as the progress of the cavalry through and through that valley of death . . . ('London, Monday, November 13, 1854' 6)

McGann replaces 'officers who led him on . . . risked' with 'the Light Brigade risked' (194). It's hard not to see this as tailoring the facts to fit the interpretation. In McGann's sentence, all 600 are risking what *The Times* explicitly denied to all but the leaders. Tennyson's poem, by contrast with *The Times*, omits any mention of the leaders, making the entire six hundred the subjects of glory.

If this is a covert way of affirming the aristocracy, it was not evident to the common British soldiers of the time, among whom it became wildly popular, as a superb article by Christopher Ricks and Edgar Shannon has documented; and Tennyson was so moved by their response that he went to great lengths to make sure copies of the poem would be distributed to any soldier who wanted it.[9]

In fact, the entire to-do about dandification of the aristocracy at the time of the Battle of Balaclava primarily circulated around exactly two aristocrats, Lords Lucan and Cardigan. Most of Woodham-Smith's book on the charge of the Light Brigade is about these two, as he chronicles in what appears to be disbelieving wonder the bizarre characters and careers of these two members of the highest British aristocracy. But he never hints at any sign of 'enervation' in them, or any lack of martial valour, only uncontrolled tempers, aristocratic arrogance and a lack of experience and wisdom – especially not with regard to Lucan. Similarly, *The Times* speculates that the two orgulous princes, their high blood roused, rushed into the valley of death not for any rational military motive but in order to prove their aristocratic manhood – an action that is said to be unsurprising for the aristocratic leaders of the cavalry. The weakness of caste with which *The Times* says aristocracy has been infected is not that of effeteness and enervation, but of aristocratic pride and incompetence, and even an excess of warrior mettle.

Nor are the class lines mentioned by *The Times* what they seem. While aristocrats in the cavalry were more numerous, and generally wealthier, than those in the infantry, there were, as the numbers I cited earlier show, aristocrats in both. In addition, the class lines along which cavalry and infantry were distinguished involved the common soldiers as well as their leaders. Both cavalry and infantry drew their recruits 'from the least skilled sections of the working-class', and drew particularly heavily on casual labourers, the unemployed, the indebted, and impoverished Irishmen (Spiers 44–52); but 'the educational and social backgrounds of cavalry recruits were superior to those of the infantry' (Strachan 54), which, by contrast, allowed 'much of the scum of urban Britain' into its ranks (Anglesey 1: 116). Thus, not just the officers, but the rank and file of the cavalry were of a higher, but decidedly not aristocratic, class, than those of the infantry. And even within the officer corps of the cavalry, the difference, not between aristocrat and non-aristocrat, but between wealthy and poor officers, substantially complicates the homogenised picture of the dandified cavalry officer. The mere mention of the name 'Cardigan' would have reminded Tennyson's audience of these complications, for James Brudenell, Lord Cardigan had been the central figure of two major, widely publicised scandals in the 30s and 40s – scandals that led him to be booed and hissed in public – and the first of these scandals had centred, precisely, on the question of the dandified uniforms that he required his officers and men to wear.

According to Woodham-Smith, regimental officers detested colonels who dandified their men out of their own pockets almost as much as they detested colonels who pocketed the army allotments for their normal clothing, because, while the colonels paid for the men, the officers had to pay for their 'splendour' themselves – a hardship for the poorer officers (38).[10] The order to buy new clothing was particularly galling when there was still wear in the old. The scandal to which I am calling attention erupted when one Captain Wathen protested to Brudenell that new jackets were unnecessary and that the men had grumbled at getting them, and Brudenell had Wathen arrested, and eventually court-martialled. These doings were widely reported in the press, and there was widespread outrage against Brudenell, to the degree that crowds at the opera and in the street assailed him when he appeared in public. Brudenell had become, says Woodham-Smith, 'a figure of national detestation' (72). Amid the outcry against Brudenell, Wathen was acquitted and Brudenell was removed from his command. This anecdote allows us a glimpse of the layered, and conflicted, economic and social reality within the cavalry officer corps itself, which Tate calls a 'group of aristocrats in short jackets and tight red trousers' (161) – a reality that was well known to the public for which Tennyson wrote.

If what Tennyson had wanted to show was the glory of the aristocratic cavalry, why did he not forthwith write a poem about the impressive victory of the Heavy Brigade, under the leadership of Lord Lucan and Sir James Scarlett, that took place just hours before that of the Light Brigade, and which was praised in *The Times*? This charge was, intriguingly, carried out by those very same Scots Greys who had been primary actors in the famous charge against the French infantry squares at a turning point at Waterloo – a charge that belatedly became the painted icon of British cavalry glory that McGann notes was still missing in

1854, the 1881 painting I mentioned earlier by Lady Elizabeth Butler, *Scotland Forever!* Here, in the charge of the Heavy Brigade at Balaclava, and especially in the actions of the Scots Greys, was the stuff out of which British cavalry legend could have been woven – if that had been Tennyson's aim.[11] In fact, Tennyson was eventually persuaded to write a poem about the charge of the Heavy Brigade ('The Charge of the Heavy Brigade at Balaclava') – one in which the brigade's leader, Sir James (second son of a baron), was duly glorified – and a resoundingly dull poem it was. Tennyson's heart clearly wasn't in it.

Notes

1. See Perloff's 'Can(n)on to the Right of Us, Can(non) to the Left of Us: A Plea for Difference', in *Poetic License*, pp. 7–29.
2. See Tate's 'On Not Knowing Why: Memorializing the Light Brigade' and Markovits's 'Giving Voice to the Crimean War: Tennyson's "Charge" and Maud's Battle-Song'. Tate and Markovits both disagree with McGann about the nature of that intervention; they think the poem is ambivalent in its attitude toward the charge. As Tate correctly notes, it was not the martial heroism of the aristocracy that was being questioned at the time, but its administrative competence, and the questioning came not on behalf of the lower orders but on behalf of the commercial and financial middle class that was competing with the aristocracy for control of England. But she accepts McGann's fundamental contention that in this poem Tennyson is struggling with the meaning of the charge as an aristocratic spectacle – 'a spectacular martyrdom which only the aristocracy could provide' (p. 174) – as does Markovits, who reminds us that 'these are after all cavaliers that [Tennyson] is writing about' (p. 484). A measured and not entirely clear dissent from this consensus is offered by Kathryn Ledbetter, who provides an expansive account of the media context that spawned Tennyson's poem. Ledbetter provides a middle-class perspective on the poem, but makes room for McGann's reading of the poem as 'patently aristocratic' as an alternative 'ideological focus' (*Tennyson and Victorian Periodicals*, p. 122). Ledbetter does not give her own reading sufficient credit; it is not just differently focused from McGann's, but far more rigorous in its historical method.
3. The reader of poetry will also know from Kipling's 1890 poem 'The Last of the Light Brigade' not only that thirty-six years later there were still at least twenty survivors of the charge, but that these 'cavaliers' were starving and in tatters.
4. 'In 1830, 21 per cent of British officers were aristocrats, 32 per cent landed gentry and an overwhelming 47 per cent middle-class. A check of the Army List in 1847 revealed that of 5,000 infantry officers, only seventy-three were titled (including younger sons of peers), and even the allegedly exclusive cavalry and Foot Guards could muster only a further 103 aristocrats between them' (Strachan, *Wellington's Legacy*, p. 110).

5. Some of the dead officers might have been untitled scions of nobility, but at most the number of dead aristocrats would still have been very small.
6. See the very lucid explanation of these matters in Göran Therborn's *What Does the Ruling Class Do When it Rules?*, pp. 198–9.
7. See Woodham-Smith's *The Reason Why*, pp. 22–3. Woodham-Smith is cited – very selectively – by McGann as one of his main historical sources.
8. By another historical irony, Louis Napoleon was the ally of the British in the Crimea, and it was French cavalry that helped to secure the retreat of the Light Brigade from the valley of death.
9. Shannon and Ricks judge that in the poem Tennyson's 'strong silent emphasis was to be on the commonality of courage, not upon rank' ('"The Charge of the Light Brigade"', p. 14).
10. Once alerted to the economic issues surrounding officers' clothing, one is moved to wonder how the splendid uniform of Gericault's chasseur – who looks as much a dandy as any English officer – would have been paid for.
11. Recent military history has questioned the actual effectiveness of the charge on Napoleon's infantry squares at Waterloo, but at the time it was considered devastating.

Chapter 11

Hellenising the Roman Past: Walter Pater's *Marius the Epicurean* and Anthony Trollope's *Life of Cicero*

Frederik Van Dam and Melanie Hacke

In his 1865 biography of Julius Caesar, the French Emperor Napoléon III maintained that the French Empire was the spiritual successor to imperial Rome. Among the many reactions that this claim provoked, that of the English critic Walter Bagehot stands out. According to Bagehot, it was the English who kept the Roman legacy alive, albeit in an unexpected way: the English rivalled the Romans of old in 'real sound stupidity' (2: 398). Like the Romans, Bagehot writes, the English 'beat the ideas of the few into the minds of the many' (2: 444), thus forestalling revolution and creating the stability needed for a prosperous nation. Even though Bagehot's views are not to be taken as representative of his day and age, it is significant that he and many of his contemporaries fell back on the image of Rome as a mirror for the present. In the following two case studies, we aim to explore some of the details of this practice in the work of two Victorian writers whose interest in the Roman past led them to write in genres that differed from those they were accustomed to. We will examine how the novelist Anthony Trollope engaged with the idea of Rome in his biography of Cicero, and how the critic Walter Pater represented second-century Rome in his novel *Marius the Epicurean*. What separates these two writers from mainstream writing about Rome, we argue, is that they attempted to infuse writing about Rome with the values of Hellenism.[1]

Mainstream Victorian writing about the Roman past was dominated by two contexts, politics and religion. In both of these, a positivist perspective vied with various forms of traditionalism. On the one hand, many Victorian writers turned to ancient Rome as a prefiguration of their own proto-imperialist moment. In Victorian public discourse, as Jonathan Sachs remarks, 'Rome [came] to stand for the spread of ideas and institutions through empire' (Sachs 323). Within this political context, one can make a distinction between two competing perspectives, positivism and heroism. British positivists such as Richard Congreve, Frederic Harrison and Edward Spencer Beesly believed that the despotism of Caesar was the outcome of a long process and, as such, the herald of an age of progress. The disciples of Thomas Carlyle, in contrast, emphasised Caesar's individual genius and heroic qualities. It was in Caesar's ability to hold sway over his contemporaries, they argued, that an alternative for the woolliness of British modernity was to be found. James Anthony Froude, one such disciple of the so-called Great Men theory, out-Carlyled Carlyle by suggesting that Caesar prepared the way for the coming of Christ. The example of Froude also fits in a second context that structured Victorian writing about the Roman past. Many writers used the Roman past as a backdrop for the presentation of their religious views. In an age where God was disappearing, as J. Hillis Miller famously puts it, certain writers returned to the history of the early church to buttress their beliefs. For Cardinal Newman, Catholicism derived its authority from the martyrs of the early church, who were persecuted by the Romans, while for Charles Kingsley, Christianity was saved through the infusion of Northern blood and Protestant values. Positivist writers, in contrast, criticised such narratives about the early church. Writers such as David Friedrich Strauss, Ernest Renan and John Seeley exposed the Gospels and the life of Christ as the stuff of legend. It is within, or rather against, this texture that we must situate Trollope's and Pater's pictures of ancient Rome.

An Active Citizen of a Free State: Trollope's *Life of Cicero* (1880)

In *The Life of Cicero*, Trollope's engagement with politics and religion is marked by ideas that are more commonly associated with Victorian Hellenism. As depicted by Trollope, Cicero's politics are a veiled version of civic republicanism, a tradition of political thinking which emphasises the necessity of participation in public life. This theory posits that the cultivation of individual liberty must be complemented with a concern for the common good. While his allusions to civic republicanism align Trollope with liberal thinkers such as John Stuart Mill, they separate him from British positivists such as Edward Spencer Beesly as well as from representatives of the heroic school such as James Anthony Froude. At the same time, Trollope suggests that Cicero was a Christian before the First Coming, an idea which does not tally with positivist scepticism, nor with muscular Christianity or Catholicism, while it does show points of overlap with the liberal Christianity of Frederic William Farrar.

Even though he considered it the 'opus magnum for [his] old age' (*Letters* 842), critics have neglected Trollope's *Life of Cicero*. Begun in 1878 and published in 1880, Trollope's biography is ostensibly polemical: it opens with an attack on Mommsen, Merivale and Froude, who in various ways represent the Great Men theory. Froude bears the brunt of Trollope's ire. Trollope is particularly troubled by the fact that Froude twists and turns Cicero's words to make them suit his purpose: 'it is not too much to demand that when a man's character is at stake his own words shall be thoroughly sifted before they are used against him' (1: 6). The seeds of Trollope's discontent can be found in the margins of his own copy of Froude's *Sketch*, which radiate with criticism on factual errors and erroneous translations (see Booth). His criticism of the positivists is less manifest. Indeed, we know that Trollope's feelings on first reading Beesly's articles were generous: in his letters, for instance, we read that Trollope is 'so given to rebellion in politics that [he is] delighted to see and hear any Catiline defended, and any Cicero attacked' (*Letters* 306). In one of the footnotes of the *Life*, however, it appears that this delight has evaporated. Although Beesly is not cited, Trollope bristles when he considers how Cicero has been attacked for embellishing his writings with 'mendaciuncula', little white lies. This concept was a key element in Beesly's attack, which Trollope puts down to an Evangelical distaste of humour: 'Such "mendaciuncula" are in the mouth of every diner-out in London, and we may pity the dinner-parties at which they are not used' (1:195–6).

It is in Trollope's in-depth engagement with Cicero's moral essays that we find his alternative to Caesarism. According to Trollope, Cicero's essays encourage one to live a 'full active human life, in which [the citizen] might achieve for himself all the charms of high rank, gilded by intelligence, erudition, and refined luxury, in which also he might serve his country, his order, and his friends' (1: 112). *The Life of Cicero* portrays the ancient Roman as an antidote to atomised individualism, and valorises a holistic and civic vision of the nation and an ethically vital tendency towards equality. This may be read as Trollope's version of civic republicanism. Many such versions were at his disposal: extending back to Plato, Aristotle and the 'Machiavellian moment' of Renaissance Florence, civic republicanism had experienced a revival in the works of Victorian poets such as Robert Browning, Elizabeth Barrett Browning, Arthur Hugh Clough and A. C. Swinburne. It is to John Stuart Mill's promotion of 'active and disinterested participation in public affairs' (Miller 89), however, that we should trace the kind of republicanism that shimmers through in Trollope's representation of Cicero.

Central to Trollope's argument, as it is to Mill's, is the imbrication of individual freedom with civic virtue. For Trollope's Cicero, liberty and civic participation are mutually constitutive: liberty was 'very dear to [Cicero] – dear to him not only as enjoying it himself, but as a privilege for the enjoyment of others' (1: 81–2). Cicero therefore exerted himself on behalf of his fellow citizens to ensure that their rights were maintained: 'this liberty, though it was but of a few, was so dear to him that he spent his life in an endeavour to preserve it' (1: 82). Mill, too, considered the distinction between civic virtue and individual freedom to be moot: 'To Mill the fundamental character that a democracy must possess in order to safeguard liberty, was a high degree of popular participation in public life' (Biagini 62). According to Trollope, Cicero put this task above his own personal welfare, as when Caesar offered him a high position to secure his support:

> It was open to Cicero, without disloyalty, to accept the offer made to him; but with an insight into what was coming, of which he himself was hardly conscious, he could not bring himself to accept offers which in themselves were alluring, but which would seem in future times to have implied on his part an assent to the breaking up of the Republic. Αἰδέομαι Τρῶας καὶ Τρῳάδας ἑλκεσιπέπλους. What will be said of me in history by my citizens if I now do simply that which may best suit my own happiness? (*Life* 1: 354)

Such disinterested behaviour is an important spring of action in Mill's motivational psychology. Trollope seems to qualify it, however, by elsewhere suggesting that to accomplish this goal the pursuit of power is justified: 'How shall a patriot do the work of his country unless he be in high place; and how shall he achieve that place except by cooperation with those whom he trusts?' (*Life* 1: 213). The political representative, then, must embody a paradox. He has power but must see this power as a trust. This, too, reflects a typical conundrum in Mill's philosophy:

> In whatever way we define or understand the idea of a right, no person can have a right (except in the purely legal sense) to power over others: every such power, which he is allowed to possess is morally, in the fullest force of the term, a trust. But the exercise of any political function, either as an elector or as a representative, is power over others. (Mill, *Considerations* 353–4)

Finally, Trollope's characterisation of Cicero dovetails with Mill's own admiration for the Roman orator. If we are to judge by Mill's enthusiastic review of Macaulay's *Lays of Ancient Rome*, Cicero is the 'greatest orator, save one, of antiquity' (*On Liberty* 42). For Mill, Cicero is surpassed only by Demosthenes: 'As for prose, we give up Cicero as compared with Demosthenes, but with no one else' ('Macaulay's *Lays*' 532). The comparison is illuminating. Paradoxically, Demosthenes made his appearance when Athenian democracy was about to be overrun by the Macedonians, led by Philip the Great. As Mill writes, his 'life was an incessant struggle against the fatality of the time, and the weaknesses of his countrymen' ('Grote's Greece' 312). This is mirrored in Trollope's depiction of republican Rome: 'Ciceronic compromises were, and must have been, equally ineffective. The patient was past cure' (*Life* 1: 376; see also 2: 58).

Mill's pairing of Cicero with Demosthenes suggests that Trollope's civic republicanism should be understood as an expression of Hellenism. Civic republicanism is, indeed, an important if not widely recognised substratum in Victorian Hellenism. For Mill, the institutional configuration of Athens served as a reminder that individual liberty, the freedom from external restraints, could not function without the responsibility that comes with participatory citizenship. As he writes in the *Principles of Representative Government*,

> What is still more important than even this matter of feeling is the practical discipline which the character obtains from the occasional demand made upon the citizens to exercise, for a time and in their turn, some social function.... Notwithstanding the defects of the social system and moral ideas of antiquity, the practice of the dicastery and the ecclesia raised the intellectual standard of an average Athenian citizen far beyond anything of which there is yet an example in any other mass of men, ancient or modern. The proofs of this are apparent in every page of our great historian of Greece. (254)

The 'great historian of Greece' that Mill refers to is George Grote, whose best-selling *History of Greece* (1846–56) Mill reviewed enthusiastically, and who can be said to be the founder of Hellenic civic republicanism. Grote's Hellenism was well received in radical university circles. Edward Augustus Freeman, later Regius Professor of History at Oxford, for instance, enthusiastically endorsed Grote's work; both writers thought that the present-day Swiss cantons were closest to the Greek 'co-existence of freedom and self-imposed restraint, of obedience to authority with unmeasured censure of the persons exercising it' (Grote 154). Trollope seems to have had affinities with this circle. In his obituary on Trollope, Freeman mentions that he was genuinely impressed by Trollope's knowledge of Cicero when they first met, in Rome, and hints at the fact that Trollope was writing in the Hellenic tradition of civic republicanism initiated by Grote:

> it was because Mr Trollope had seen a good deal of men and things in England and Ireland and other parts of the world that he was able to understand men and things at Rome also. I know not how it may sound either at Balliol or at Berlin; but nothing is more certain than that Arnold and Grote, simply

because they were active citizens of a free state, understood ten thousand things in Greek and Roman history which Mommsen and Curtius, with all their fresh lights in other ways, fail to understand. (238)

Freeman's suggestion that Trollope was also treading in the footsteps of Dr Arnold hints at a second way in which Trollope challenged the assumptions of contemporary writing on the history of ancient Rome. According to Arnold, the institutions of the Roman Empire ultimately helped further the spread of Christianity. Trollope takes up an even more radical stance by suggesting that a pagan, Cicero, did so as well:

But there was a humanity in Cicero, a something almost of Christianity, a stepping forward out of the dead intellectualities of Roman life into moral perceptions, into natural affections, into domesticity, philanthropy, and conscious discharge of duty. (*Life* 1: 2–3)

As the final cadence of this quotation suggests, civic republicanism and Christianity are not mutually exclusive. Throughout his biography, indeed, Trollope posits that Cicero's concern for the welfare and liberty of others at the expense of his own interests was guided by an innate understanding of Christian principles. The Christian subtext of Trollope's argument is a challenge to mainstream Caesarism as well.

On the one hand, Trollope's emphasis on the relevance of Christianity defies positivists such as Harrison and Morley, who thought that the liberal Christianity of their time was 'a phase of soft, autumnal decay' (Willey 263). Trollope's belief in the truthfulness of Cicero's account of his own life, moreover, counters the sceptical methodology of Strauss, Renan and Seeley in their respective biographies of Christ, in which they exposed the Gospels as the stuff of legend. Trollope does not seek to reveal the man behind the myth.

On the other hand, his presentation of Cicero as scrupulous and conscientious is a stab at the 'muscular' form of Christianity which Froude found in Caesar. For Trollope, Caesar is not a rewarding subject because 'the character of the man is unpleasant to contemplate, unimpressionable, very far from divine. There is none of the human softness necessary for love; none of the human weakness needed for sympathy' (*Life* 2: 212–13). Cicero, in contrast, is aware of his own limitations, being one of those 'whose intellects are set on so fine a pivot that a variation in the breeze of the moment, which coarser minds shall not feel, will carry them round with a rapidity which baffles the common eye' (*Life* 1: 19). Like heroes in Trollope's novels such as Phineas Finn or Plantagenet Palliser, Cicero is prone to vacillation. In exile, for instance, Cicero contemplated suicide but decided against it. Trollope remarks that, ironically, this token of Christianity has been held against Cicero because he thus did not conform to practices of his time:

> It is because he dared to live on that we are taught to think so little of him – because he had antedated Christianity so far as to feel when the moment came that such an escape was, in truth, unmanly. He doubted, and when the deed had not been done he expressed regret that he had allowed himself to live. (*Life* 1: 367)

This weakness is a token of 'that superiority of inward being which makes Cicero the most fit to be loved of all the Romans' (*Life* 1: 16).

Trollope's rejection of positivist scepticism and of muscular Christianity does not mean that he embraces the views of Froude's main opponent, Cardinal Newman, whose *The Arians of the Fourth Century* (1833) and *The Church of the Fathers* (1840) had 'helped make the early church a fiercely contested arena for Christians' (Goldhill, *Victorian Culture*, 203). Believing in the promise of eternal life, Newman's protagonists are willing to sacrifice themselves for what they believe to be the greater good. Newman and Trollope may have been friends, but Newman would have found much to disagree with in Trollope's biography of Cicero. Cicero is certainly not given to sacrifice: had he 'adhered to truth at the cost of being a martyr, his conduct would have been high though we might have known less of it; but, looking at all the circumstances of the period, have we a right to think that he could have done so?' (*Life* 2: 134). A more fundamental point is that Cicero was a pagan and thus, for Christians, beyond redemption. Trollope's biography, however, rests on the assumption that one can be a virtuous Christian even without having read the Gospel – that, as Freeman puts it, 'there may be some place in the economy of things where Tully may welcome the Anthony who has been his zealous champion' (240).

As such, Trollope's *Life* seems to defer to a Hellenist kind of Christianity. Trollope's biography is an expression of Hellenism insofar as it is fascinated by the tension between Cicero's pagan beliefs and his quasi-Christian identity. Trollope never fully accounts for his feeling that there 'is such a touch of humanity in [Cicero's words], such a feeling of latter-day civilisation and almost of Christianity, that we are apt to condemn what remains in them of paganism' (*Life* 1: 178–9). By focusing on a figure who predated the coming of Christ, Trollope effectively challenges his contemporaries' views about the development of Christianity, a recurring concern in writing about ancient Rome. He was not alone in thus being caught between two worlds: 'Many serious Christians – Frederick William Farrar would be a paradigm – combined Anglican sermons, liberal educational reform, and a love of things

Greek' (Goldhill, rev. of *British Aestheticism*, 476). Trollope's thesis that Cicero's pagan beliefs foreshadow Christ's teaching dovetails with Farrar's *Eternal Hope*, a series of sermons delivered in 1877 and published in 1878, in which Farrar attacks the idea of eternal torment and dismisses the doctrine of purgatory. Furthermore, the *Life of Cicero* is similar in its conception to Farrar's *The Life of Christ* (1874), a romantic and conservative biography which 'encouraged belief, comfort, and joy in Christian tradition' (Goldhill, *Victorian Culture*, 155). Perhaps the example of Farrar explains why Trollope chose to tell Cicero's life through a biography rather than through his form of choice, the novel; and that he should do so as a believer, not a sceptic.

The way in which Trollope makes the study of the Roman past an integral part of his religious beliefs presents a parallel to his investment in civic republicanism insofar as both arguments are part of his attempt to Hellenise the history of Rome. The theological dimension of Trollope's biography reinforces the political: like the Messiah whom he prefigures, Trollope's Cicero is hopeless advocate, whose call for a return to the republican forms of the past interrupts the present – the Roman as well as the Victorian present – and points the way to a radically different future.

Walter Pater's *Marius the Epicurean* (1885)

Whereas Trollope's claim to fame rests on his novels, Walter Pater is best known for his work as a critic. The essays collected in *Studies in the History of the Renaissance* (1873) established him as the founding father of British aestheticism. Pater's one novel, *Marius the Epicurean* (1885), at first sight seems a mere elaboration of the aesthetic theories propounded in *The Renaissance*. But *Marius the Epicurean* is more than a simple exercise in translating aesthetic theories into the form of the novel. As in Trollope's biography, in this novel the Roman past has a particularly complex function. As a *Bildungsroman* that traces the mental development of the protagonist Marius from paganism through Epicureanism to early Christianity, *Marius the Epicurean* is a plea for a critical and eclectic consciousness. An anecdote in Thomas Wright's 1907 biography of Pater suggests that the religious dimension of this plea should not be played down: when a friend asked Pater why he had written *Marius*, Pater replied: 'To show ... the necessity of religion' (Wright 1: 87).

Pater was not the first Victorian novelist interested in the possibilities that the history of ancient Rome presented for a discussion of religious concerns in the present: one thinks of Edward Bulwer-Lytton's *The Last Days of Pompeii* (1834), Charles Kingsley's *Hypatia* (1853), Cardinal Wiseman's *Fabiola* (1854) or Cardinal Newman's *Callista* (1855). Through their depiction of the Greco-Roman world, authors could comment on contemporary religious issues. The majority of these novels portrayed the early church in a romanticised way, thereby advocating a return to a purer faith. Pater also promotes a return to religion, but his call for a Hellenic eclecticism challenges traditionalist narratives. *Marius* stands out from these religiously conservative novels through its Hellenised representation of the Roman world and its lenient portrayal of paganism. By analysing how *Marius* incorporates and subverts some of the topoi frequently used in fiction about Rome, we will demonstrate that Pater's exploration of religion is more subtle and complex than that of the average nineteenth-century historical novel. Indeed, Pater also criticises positivist scepticism by showing that a materialist worldview cannot lead to spiritual fulfilment. This religious message is enforced by the novel's references to the Roman poet Lucretius, a contentious figure in Victorian thought.

Like many other novels set in Rome, *Marius the Epicurean* ostensibly creates a parallel between Victorian Britain and second-century Rome. Pater seems to encourage such a contextual reading by rehearsing the popular argument that '[t]hat age and our own have much in common – many difficulties and hopes. Let the reader pardon me if here and there I seem to be passing from Marius to his modern representatives – from Rome, to Paris or London' (*Marius* 210). The novel's first chapter, 'The Religion of Numa', is a case in point: it all too clearly criticises the way in which rapid urbanisation in the late nineteenth century was making society lose touch with the simple pieties of English village life. From its opening lines onwards, *Marius the Epicurean* thus pleads for a revival of religion, as offering purpose and comfort for the individual and as providing the stuff that communities are made of.

The first chapter introduces Marius as a sensitive and thoughtful boy priest, piously participating in a pagan feast, and losing himself in 'ponderings on the divine nature' (*Marius* 5–6). Marius feels isolated from the other worshippers, for whom the pagan ceremonies are no more than a marker of their aristocratic identity. Marius's piety and the strong connection between his religion and his home echo Pater's childhood fascination with Anglicanism (Hext 66). At the same time, Marius's love of religious ceremonies (which is maintained throughout the whole novel) displays affinities with Catholic ritual. While the autobiographical elements in 'The Religion of Numa' thus establish the introverted Marius as Pater's alter ego, whose individual pilgrimage the reader is invited to follow, they also suggest that the novel can be read as a coded commentary on nineteenth-century socio-religious concerns. As such, the novel's opening addresses the perception that post-Darwinian Britain attached too much weight to rationalism and materialism, while neglecting traditional religious and communal values.

However, as Marius grows up and travels to Rome, where he enters the service of Marcus Aurelius, it becomes clear that Pater approaches the Roman setting in a way that distinguishes *Marius the Epicurean* from other Victorian fiction set in antiquity. Importantly, Victorian narratives about post-Augustan Rome tend to focus on the empire's corruption and decline. The topos of degeneration was used mainly to measure the purity of the first Christians against pagan immorality. It also provided authors with an opportunity to stage violence, sin, horror and other elements that had affinities with the conventions of the Gothic novel. Pater, in contrast, associates the ripeness of the Roman Empire with aesthetic perfection rather than with degeneracy: when the young Marius first enters Rome and is struck by the magnificence of its buildings, Pater suggests that his protagonist is fortunate to live in so late an age, because 'at no period of history had the material Rome itself been better worth seeing' (*Marius* 142). Because Greco-Roman culture is so old, it has amassed a wealth of cultural capital, most of which is still extant in the second century. In addition, the age of Marcus Aurelius possesses a vast 'accumulation of intellectual treasure' (*Marius* 120). Because of its abundant variety of philosophies and beliefs, the second century is a perfect age for young men like Marius, who are seeking to develop their subjectivity. The constant flux of sense impressions and the religious uneasiness attendant on the coexistence of a wide range of creeds enables Pater to draw another parallel between Marius's coming of age process and that of the late Victorian individual, who could benefit from this wealth of stimuli, but also risked being smothered by it.

Nevertheless, Pater does not entirely dismiss the omens of Rome's decline. The city's 'perfection . . . indicated only too surely the eve of decline' (*Marius* 142). The novel registers how war is raging at the empire's borders, how the Antonine Plague continues to claim lives and, most importantly, how the great multitude of religions causes tension in Rome's 'fervid and corrupt life' (*Marius* 191). Pater's most negative description of the Roman Empire can be found in the chapter 'Manly Amusements', in which Marius is invited to attend the gladiatorial games. This chapter furnishes another example of the way in which Pater's novel differs from its predecessors. Popular historical novels focusing on Rome's corruption generally included a violent scene in the amphitheatre, in which, for instance, a Christian martyr dies for his or her faith. 'Manly Amusements' explicitly criticises the use of this motif:

> For the long shows of the amphitheater were, so to speak, the novel-reading of that age – a current help provided for sluggish imaginations, in regard, for instance, to grisly accidents, such as might happen to one's self: but with every facility for comfortable inspection. (197)

Here Pater suggests that the violent scenes in popular fiction about Rome were intended for people who were intrigued by 'grisly accidents', as long as they could observe them from a safe distance. These novels, while claiming to spread a Christian message, offered detailed descriptions of bloodshed to get their readers' 'sluggish imaginations' going.

As the novel progresses, Rome's degeneration is increasingly emphasised and its positive aspects gradually disappear. This development in the novel's setting has an effect on the development of its protagonist. In the first half of the novel, Marius's life is determined by the aesthetic quest for splendour, just as the cultural heritage of the late empire is associated with the quest for perfection. From the second half of the novel onwards, however, Marius is confronted with the question of community and religion, and gradually comes to the conclusion that 'these Romans were a coarse, a vulgar people; and their vulgarities of soul [were] in full evidence here' (*Marius* 362). Instead, Marius is attracted by Aurelius's altruism, and later by the values of the Christian community, to which he is introduced by his friend Cornelius.

The tipping point in Marius's coming-of-age process is the chapter 'Second Thoughts', in which Marius realises that his aesthetic Epicureanism is too egocentric. He resolves to correct this imbalance by incorporating religious and communal values, and to so transcend the gap between the individual and community, beauty and sympathy, or thought and feeling. Marius gradually learns to do this through his encounters with a group of Christians. Like Newman, Pater depicts the early Christian brotherhood in a surprisingly conservative and positive manner. Cornelius, for instance, seems to carry 'such a breeze of hopefulness – freshness and hopefulness, as of a new morning, about him' (*Marius* 192). Like a typical conversion novel, *Marius the Epicurean* thus connects early Christianity with the commencement of a new and innocent era, which will replace the decline and corruption of the pagan world. However, Pater not only praises the Christian community for its puritan values of chastity, homeliness and hard work, but also associates its focus on ritual with his own Hellenic commitment to beauty.

Because of the novel's favourable depiction of early Christianity, Marius's death has often been read as that of a recently converted martyr, a common ingredient in conversion novels. However, we should refrain from reading *Marius the Epicurean* as a conversion novel. As Simon Goldhill has pointed out, the peasants who care for Marius during his final illness 'hold ... his death, according to their *generous* view in this matter, to have been *of the nature* of a martyrdom' (*Marius* 383–4, emphasis ours). The narrator's qualifications suggest that the goodly country people may be wrong; Marius's death may resemble a Christian martyrdom, but this is merely their interpretation (Goldhill, *Victorian Culture* 218–19). The same logic can be applied to the first allusion to Marius's end. In the second chapter, he looks forward to 'some great occasion of self-devotion, ... *as* the early Christian looked forward to martyrdom' (*Marius* 14, emphasis ours). In another flash-forward, the same passage states that by the end of the novel Marius will have 'learned to think of all religions as indifferent' (*Marius* 14). The fact that the novel's description of early Christianity is preceded by a chapter in which Marius speaks with Apuleius, and followed by a conversation with Lucian, further proves that Pater does not want to present Christianity as the ideal faith, since both Apuleius and Lucian are agnostics who argue that no philosopher can ever be certain that his principles are the only path to truth. As such, Pater's novel differs from Newman's Catholic novels as well as from Kingsley's more 'manly' Protestant genre by making Marius an eclectic: he does not commit himself to one creed, but selects the most suitable principles from different religions and philosophies.

Pater's references to the Roman poet Lucretius (*c.*99–55 BC) add an additional layer of meaning to the novel's Hellenism, thus further reinforcing its difference from contemporary sceptical engagements with the Roman past. The novel's engagement with Lucretius – a contentious figure in nineteenth-century thought – highlights the dangers of radical materialism, and thus enforces Pater's call for a religious consciousness founded on the contemplation of beauty. Lucretius left only one work, the Epicurean didactic poem *De Rerum Natura*, or *On the Nature of Things*, one of the first works to introduce atomic theory. By uncovering that everything in nature arose from a material cause, and that the gods lived in *intermundia* (spaces between the worlds) where they did not control the fate of man, Lucretius wanted to rid people of their fear of the gods. During the Middle Ages the Church branded Lucretius an atheist, even though today his religious position would be termed agnostic, and *De Rerum Natura* sank into oblivion. During the nineteenth century, however, the poem gained in popularity, partly due to its revolutionary treatment of religion. Many writers were drawn towards Lucretius's agnosticism, which symbolised the freedom of the human mind. Even so, most Victorians (such as Elizabeth Barrett Browning, Alfred Tennyson, Matthew Arnold) were ambivalent about *De Rerum Natura*'s philosophy: they were attracted by its rejection of the gods, but did not think that mankind could live without the idea of a personal deity.

Marius the Epicurean first alludes to Lucretius when Marius's childhood friend Flavian dies. Marius senses that Flavian's soul has perished together with his body, and looks for confirmation of this belief in the Epicurean philosophers. Marius is inspired by his reading, and adopts the Epicurean tenet of living in the present as a basis for his aesthetic mode of existence. Pater's description of Marius's Epicureanism adopts and thereby popularises a large number of Lucretian concepts and images. In *Marius* as well as in the 'Conclusion' to *The Renaissance*, aesthetic impressions are described as particle currents streaming towards the senses, an image for which Lucretius is famous. Lucretius, like Marius, pleads in favour of trusting man's perception. One particular Lucretian phrase illustrates that Marius has no other choice than to trust his senses, even though his perception might be unreliable: 'Aristippus of Cyrene too had left off in suspense of judgment to what might really lie behind – *flammantia moenia mundi:* the flaming ramparts of the world' (*Marius* 110). Aristippus thought up a practical philosophy, but did not work out a metaphysical system that explained what lay behind the belt of fire of which the Epicureans believed that it encircled the world (Lucretius 9, footnote). In other words, the philosopher ought not to look beyond the boundaries of the world, or beyond the material *moenia* of his senses. Throughout the rest of *Marius*, Pater repeatedly returns to the English phrase, and the broader concept of the limitation of the senses.[2]

However, Marius's encounters with Christianity soon make him feel that there is more than just the visible world. Pater suggests that Lucretius experienced a similar spiritual process, wherein he gradually came to question the absolute indifference of the gods. The first books of *De Rerum Natura* might thus have been the work of a young and sentimental Lucretius, still excited about the world, while the later books' invective against paganism resulted from embittered age: 'Was the magnificent *exordium* of Lucretius, addressed to the goddess Venus, the work of his earlier manhood, and designed originally to open an argument less persistently somber [sic] than that protest against the whole pagan heaven which actually follows it?' (*Marius* 85–6). A remark about Lucretius in the chapter 'Manly Amusements' confirms that Pater generally considered Lucretius's evaluation of paganism too severe. Pater expresses his disapproval of the games by stating that '[j]ust at this point, certainly, the judgment of Lucretius on pagan religion is without reproach – *Tantum religio potuit suadere malorum*' (198).[3] As a rule, Pater's comment implies, Lucretius's assessment of paganism does deserve reproach.

Another set of references to *De Rerum Natura* demonstrates Pater's ambivalent attitude to Lucretius's agnosticism and radical materialism. *Marius* contains an obscure allusion to Saint Jerome's famous account of Lucretius's death, which recounts how the poet committed suicide in an outburst of madness. Although this story is questionable, it remained influential in Lucretius's nineteenth-century reception, and was treated by, among others, Arnold and Tennyson. Pater provides his own spin on it by implying that Lucretius's suicide was caused by his dissatisfaction with *De Rerum Natura*. Though he had sought to prove that metaphysical speculation was useless, he could not wholly believe his own theory, and still wondered what lay beyond 'the flaming ramparts of the world':

> Men's minds, even young men's minds, at that late day, might well seem oppressed by the weariness of systems which had so far outrun positive knowledge; and in the mind of Marius, as in that old school of Cyrene, this sense of *ennui*, combined with appetites so youthfully vigorous, brought about reaction, a sort of suicide (instances of the like have been seen since) by which a great metaphysical *acumen* was devoted to the function of proving metaphysical speculation impossible, or useless. (115–16)

Interestingly, Pater considers Lucretius's fervent quest for an all-encompassing theory of the visible and invisible worlds a typical symptom 'at that late day' (*Marius* 115), a modern condition occurring in the Roman as well as the Victorian empire. A few pages onwards, Pater connects the impossibility of metaphysics with his favourite Lucretian phrase: 'that age of Marcus Aurelius [was] so completely disabused of the metaphysical ambition to pass beyond "the flaming ramparts of the world"' (*Marius* 120). This coupling may suggest that the passage above alludes to the death of Lucretius.

Although Pater admired Lucretius's philosophy and although he used *De Rerum Natura*'s theory of the mortal soul and of the senses, he objected to Lucretius's agnosticism. Pater did not believe in a providential God, but he could not accept the idea of life without religious ritual, either pagan or Christian: religious ceremony, in his view, could connect people and guide them towards their own individual philosophy of life. His criticism of Lucretius corresponds to Marius's ambiguous stance towards the material world. Though the Epicurean Marius maintains that 'he must still hold by what his eyes really saw' (*Marius* 272), the various religions around him, with their different conceptions of the divine, rouse his curiosity as to what lies beyond 'the flaming ramparts of the world' (*Marius* 120).

Conclusion

Both Trollope and Pater made use of the perceived similarity between the Roman Empire and Victorian Britain to interpret contemporary political and religious issues. While Christianity is gaining ground amid the steady degeneration of Roman society, Pater's Marius opts for an Epicurean and thus essentially Hellenist philosophy of life. By exploring this aesthetic Hellenism from within a Roman setting, Pater challenges mainstream Victorian modes of writing about Ancient Rome. So does Trollope, albeit in a different way: Trollope infuses Cicero's republicanism with Demosthenian values of individual liberty and civic virtue, and even with a Hellenist kind of Christianity. As such, both Trollope's *Life of Cicero* and Pater's *Marius the Epicurean* can be set apart from traditionalist as well as from sceptical perspectives on the Roman past.

Notes

1. Parts of this essay have appeared previously: an earlier and more detailed version of the case study on Trollope can be found in Chapter 5 of Frederik Van Dam's *Anthony Trollope's Late Style: Victorian Liberalism and Literary Form* (Edinburgh University Press, 2016), while parts of the case study on Pater have been published in Melanie Hacke, '"The Flaming Ramparts of the World": The Function of Lucretius in Walter Pater's *Marius the Epicurean*', *English Text Construction* 9.2 (2016), pp. 222–43. We thank Edinburgh University Press and John Benjamins for permission to reproduce parts of these writings.
2. In *De Rerum Natura* the phrase is used in praise of Epicurus, who 'extra/ processit longe flammantia moenia mundi' (1.72–3); 'marched far beyond the flaming walls of the world' (Lucretius 9). In contrast to Aristippus, Epicurus's philosophy does encompass the entire universe. In addition, Lucretius intended the phrase to evoke the image of an army general storming the city walls and setting fire to them (Lucretius 9, footnote).
3. Pater here alludes to the offering of Iphigenia; the citation can be translated as 'so potent was Superstition in persuading to evil deeds' (Lucretius 11).

Chapter 12

The Ghost in the Machinal: De-/Re-contextualising *Daniel Deronda*

Sundeep Bisla

> We wanted the touch of the real in the way that in an earlier period people wanted the touch of the transcendent.
> Catherine Gallagher and Stephen Greenblatt,
> *Practicing New Historicism*

G v. D

G says to D that a certain process of recontextualisation has been of absolutely no significance.

D replies that, actually, it has made from his perspective a great, even critical, 'difference'.

Now, what might be the implications of one's not being able to tell the difference between G's here signifying either George Eliot's character Gwendolen or the new historicist critic Catherine Gallagher and D's signifying Deronda or the deconstructionist philosopher Jacques Derrida? For one thing, such undecidabilities would suggest that the notoriously anti-programmatic[1] new historicists had all along had more of a 'theoretics'[2] at play in their practice than has usually been understood to be the case, and that the notoriously 'boring' and 'sterile' deconstructionists had actually been writing in their analyses what amounted to authentic ghost stories. But, viewing our set-up here from a meta-critical perspective, could we not be said to be immured in the realm of paradox: stuck actively employing the thinking of G (by disregarding obvious differences in context) while all the time agreeing, as we will see, with the perspective of D? So be it. This is actually a happy discrepancy, as it will turn out to be a motor for textual production.

Late in George Eliot's novel *Daniel Deronda* (1876), the title character comes to make the long-awaited revelation of his discovery of his ancestry to his friend Gwendolen Harleth. This is the moment when the main characters are forced to deal with – that is, as it turns out, to disclose to each other their contrasting attitudes with respect to – the main plot twist in the narrative, Daniel's second recontextualisation (his first having come off-stage, so to speak, when at the age of two he had been made the ward of an English gentleman). In Chapter 69, when Deronda breaks the news of his true heritage to Gwendolen, she is quite taken aback, in a manner that verges on the offensive:

> '[My mother] parted with me after my father's death, when I was a little creature. But she is now very ill, and she felt that the secrecy ought not to be any longer maintained. Her chief reason had been that she did not wish me to know I was a Jew.'
> '*A Jew*!' Gwendolen exclaimed, in a low tone of amazement, with an utterly frustrated look, as if some confusing potion were creeping through her system. Deronda colored, and did not speak, while Gwendolen, with her eyes fixed on the floor, was struggling to find her way in the dark by the aid of various reminiscences. She seemed at last to have arrived at some judgment, for she looked up at Deronda again and said, as if remonstrating against the mother's conduct –
> 'What difference need that have made?'
> '*It has made a great difference to me* [italics added] that I have known it,' said Deronda, emphatically; but he could not go on easily – the distance between her ideas and his acted like a difference of native language, making him uncertain what force his words would carry.
> Gwendolen meditated again, and then said feelingly, 'I hope there is nothing to make you mind. *You* are just the same as if you were not a Jew.'
> (Eliot 1991: 687)

Rather than feeling complimented by this reassurance, Deronda makes it clear that he has already 'converted', so to speak, to the new perspective: 'The discovery was far from being painful to me ... I had been gradually prepared for it, and I was glad of it. I had been prepared for it by becoming intimate with a very remarkable Jew, whose ideas have attracted me so much that I think of devoting the best part of my life to some effort at giving them effect' (687). Indeed, Deronda had been so ready to accept the revelation of his Jewishness that he could well at the crucial moment have said the same thing, *mutatis mutandis* of course, that Gwendolen says with regard to her witnessing of Grandcourt's drowning: 'I only know that I saw my wish outside me' (596).

The reference to Deronda's 'devoting' himself to completing his friend Mordecai's project recalls that moment when he had effused to Gwendolen during a party at Diplow about the effect on him of the impressive singing abilities of Mordecai's sister, Mirah. 'For my part', says Deronda,

> 'people who do anything finely always inspirit me to try. I don't mean that they make me believe I can do it as well. But they make the thing, whatever it may be, seem worthy to be done. I can bear to think my own music not good for much, but the world would be more dismal if I thought music itself not good for much. Excellence encourages one about life generally; it shows the spiritual wealth of the world.'
>
> 'But then if we can't imitate it? – it only makes our own life seem the tamer', said Gwendolen, in a mood to resent encouragement founded on her own insignificance.
>
> 'That depends on the point of view, I think', said Deronda. 'We should have a poor life of it if we were reduced for all our pleasure to our own performances. A little private imitation of what is good is a sort of private devotion to it.' (374)

Daniel is inspired (Mordecai would of course insist on the actual term 'inspirited') by excellence in the arts 'to try'. This is a potentially unclear statement: does he mean to try to do it 'to the same standard' or to have an unserious 'try' at the thing, to do it 'in addition to'? Because Gwendolen could think him to be expressing an impossibly egotistical belief in his abilities in all areas of artistic endeavour, he is quick to clarify that he does not intend to suggest that he thinks he can do *anything* to a masterly level of competence: 'I don't mean that they make me believe I can do it as *well*.' He simply feels called upon to do also, or '*as well*', the thing, to whatever (undoubtedly inferior) standard he is capable. And the inferiority of this copying is nothing to be ashamed of. It is itself a sort of prayer or religious homage, 'a sort of private devotion' to the original endeavour.[3]

Interpreting the statement in precisely the way that Deronda has explicitly disavowed intending it, and still stinging from the composer Klesmer's harsh evaluation of her vocal abilities, Gwendolen is in no mood to accept 'encouragement founded on her own insignificance': 'But then if we can't imitate it? – it only makes our own life seem the tamer.' Thus, Gwendolen – consistent with her character – insists on interpreting Deronda's 'try' (the etymologically related 'essay' might do just as well here) as if it were still situated in its initial setting (never mind that that initial setting had been based on a mistaken interpretation), that is, in this case, on reading it from the perspective of parity. Here we have yet one more example of Gwendolen's closed-mindedness. She refuses to allow Deronda's attempted recontextualisation of her original (mis)reading to take effect, and this discrepancy between the two perspectives results in the creation of text. That is, simply on a basic word-count level, we, readers and characters alike, find text being produced by recontextualisation as the clearing up and non-clearing up of a potential pun is here creating words and new page after new page that Eliot can then sell on the literary market. For our author, narrative momentum, paradoxically, is generated by rereading, by recontextualisation. Here – not for the last time in this novel – we are forcibly being broken free from, due to the possibility of language's being rhetorically *de trop*, the barren circle of non-production/exact reproduction.

It should be noted that also at the simple level of content what we encounter in this passage is the main characters speaking about productive and unproductive repetitions. Artistic mastery is a machine for productivity, for those, that is, of Deronda's persuasion. On the other hand, people like Gwendolen are inclined to shy away from the attempt or to view a 'feeble' one as somehow unreal, as making 'no difference' in the world. For her, if a repetition is not going to come close to equalling the original, if it is going to remain in some crucial respect inadequate, it cannot and does not signify; it is not actually what she might call 'a production'. This difference between the attitudes of these two characters – one allowing recontextualisation to be potentially 'productive', the other refusing this standpoint – remains consistent throughout the story.

A difference between productive and non-productive repetitions (the latter akin to a type of wealth generation without actual 'production' labelled by recent economists 'rent seeking')[4] is also evidenced in the stark contrast between the attitudes of our two twentieth-century thinkers, Gallagher and Derrida. The latter, outlining in his book *Limited Inc* a certain distinction that characterises his concept of linguistic iterability, or the repeatability of linguistic signs, breaks down the products of linguistic repetition, iterability's actualisations, into two categories, citations and iterations. In describing why he will be liberally quoting from the misreading of his work offered by the philosopher John Searle, Derrida remarks: 'iteration ... which ... was never confused with citation ... is at work, constantly *altering*, at once and without delay ... whatever it seems to reproduce ... Iteration alters, *something new* takes place' (Derrida 1988: 40; last italics added). J. Hillis Miller comments about this line, '[T]he difference between citation and iteration is clear enough. Citation is supposed to drag its original context implicitly along with it, while iteration may use the same words in a radically new context' (Miller 2001: 71). That is, while in the case of 'citation' the effect of the initial context overrides that of – or, better yet, pre-occupies the space of – the subsequent one, in that of 'iteration' the situation is just the reverse. Implicitly founded upon some form of the belief that '[previous] history repeats itself', all manifestations of 'historicism' are born privileging the citational over the iterational world-view.[5] Emphasising instead the iterational perspective, Derrida remarks that 'To write is to produce a mark that will constitute a sort of machine which is *productive* in turn, and which [the author's] future disappearance will not, in principle, hinder [in] its functioning, offering things and itself to be read and rewritten' (Derrida 1988: 8; italics added). Thus, by way of a slight shift in emphasis, a space opens up through which the self-sustaining 'machine' of recontextualisation-as-iteration is found to be allowing newness to enter the world.

On the other hand, in her classic new historical analysis of *Daniel Deronda*, 'George Eliot and *Daniel Deronda*: The Prostitute and the Jewish Question',[6] Gallagher, in setting out her approach, lays out a particular distinction that will be of great significance for her argument to come: that between the 'natural production of new things in the world' and its corollary antithesis the '"unnatural" reproduction of mere signs'. She derives this dichotomy purportedly from Aristotle and describes it as manifesting itself in the English Victorians' distinction between the metaphors of literary paternity and literary usury. Gallagher writes,

> It has been noted that Aristotle was uncertain about whether writing most resembled the natural generativity of plants and animals or the unnatural generation of money, which, in usury, proliferates through mere circulation but *brings nothing qualitatively new into being*. At times, Aristotle speaks of poetic making as a method of natural reproduction; at other times, he speaks of the written word as an arbitrary and conventional sign multiplying unnaturally in the mere presence of exchange. The former idea of language promotes the metaphor of literary paternity; the latter the metaphor of literary usury and, ultimately, literary prostitution. (Gallagher 1985: 40; italics added)

The immediate cause for which Gallagher is putting in service this 'counterhistory' of the usury/prostitution metaphor is so as to be in a position to complicate the too-simplistic case that had been made earlier by Sandra Gilbert and Susan Gubar in their seminal feminist work *Madwoman in the Attic* (1979): that in the nineteenth century the literary 'paternity' metaphor had been standing as an impediment to the full-scale and free expression of women's literary creativity. The manifestly less-than-complimentary metaphor of female author as prostitute, Gallagher contends, had as well.[7] In other words, the Victorian opprobrium against an economy of usurious exchanges was causing women writers to feel like unproductive copies (of male writers) who did not (deserve to) signify, to feel, that is, to use Gwendolen's terminology, like 'tame' triers. But there was another possible standpoint: that one that I am calling the 'iterational' or repetitionally productive one. My main argument in this chapter will be that Gallagher unfairly downplays the 'spiritual charge' of Eliot's *Daniel Deronda*, that is, that she slights, or, more properly, is led to slight,[8] the possibility in general of the attitude expressed by Deronda in the passage cited earlier (the 'iterational' perspective) as a result of her excessive focus upon and allegiance to the attitude expressed by Gwendolen (the 'citational' one).

Textualonomics

Thus it comes as no surprise that in a key passage in her essay Gallagher should find the strong temptation toward textual re-citation, or as her subject George Eliot in one of her essays puts it, the writer's temptation 'to do over again what has already been done, either by himself or others' (qtd in Gallagher 1985: 45), to be an example of an essentially unproductive usury as opposed to either a productive, devotional repetition or, on the other hand, an expression of, as Gilbert and Gubar would have it, the female's discomfort with the inherently masculine writing instrument. That is, one significant stroke of originality in Gallagher's historical approach itself would seem to be, ironically, the contention that derivative, unoriginal works – here we are to envision the prostitute's repetitive and unoriginal (i.e., unprocreative, unproductive) lifestyle – are not the result of 'a fear of writing or any anxiety about handling pens' (Gallagher 1985: 59) experienced by female writers in the mid-century, but instead are slottings in to (that is, are historical repetitions of) a usurer/whore metaphorical economy in common currency in the Victorian era:

> Many nineteenth-century statements about the false, imitative, and merely conventional nature of women's writing, statements that have been used to prove that the woman writer was considered a eunuch, *should be reread with these* [usurer and whore] *metaphors of exchange in mind*. . . . [George Eliot] argues that '"In all labour there is profit"; but ladies' silly novels, we imagine, are less the result of labour than of busy idleness.' . . . Such women rake off profits without production, without labor. (44; italics added)

Immediately after this passage, Gallagher succinctly summarises her critique: 'Eliot's dominant metaphor for authorship, both in her novels and essays, is not genealogy but commerce' (45). What Gallagher means by that latter term is clear enough: the interchange between production and exchange seen in classical times in the centralised Greek marketplace, as well as today in our own more dispersed ones. In this, she is following a common path in economic thinking. Indeed, there is a strong line of reasonableness running through Gallagher's article, and despite the foregoing criticism, it has to be admitted that in a general sense she is unquestionably onto something: there is a definite interest expressed in the narrative of *Daniel Deronda* with regard to the circulation between production and exchange. The roulette wheel with which the story begins conclusively establishes that theme, at the same time that the soul transfer with which the book ends rounds it off.

But I am suggesting that our critic is being here a bit too succinct. I believe the term 'commerce' requires more elaboration than Gallagher is prepared to give to it. While I applaud her having shifted the analytical paradigm away from the material body (particularly that entity's implicit recourse to spatiality) and toward the marketplace, I do not believe she has gone quite far enough. In Eliot's writing we are faced with, at least in the case of her novels, exchanges (whether strictly commercial or not) that are more immaterial (and yet nevertheless natural) than simply unnatural, and in that sense, ones that would be more accurately (or adequately) described as 'textual' rather than usurious or rent-seeking. Quite simply, as I might term it, the 'textual economy', as a direct result of the paradoxical mechanism of iterability undergirding it, is not operating like the material one, and it is a mistake to be treating the two similarly, indeed, in Gallagher's case to not even be distinguishing between the two.

In order to make clear the distinction I am attempting to draw, we might look at a moment from Gallagher's later major analysis of *Deronda*, the chapter '*Daniel Deronda* and the Too Much of Literature'.[9] There Gallagher is intent on clarifying that the excessiveness signalled by her chapter's title meant for Eliot not what today for us it 'tends to imply[,] the supplemental nature of the signifier, the doubling of mimesis, the simulacra, imaginary annexes or multiple worlds of fiction – all the ways in which, we've convinced ourselves, literature is not only constitutionally but also proudly de trop' (Gallagher 2006: 118). Instead, she argues, it meant for Eliot the assaults of 'feebl[e] imitations' and of authors' repetitions of themselves – this contention being supported with the quotation of a journal entry that has Eliot admitting to the worry of possibly 'sinking into an insistent echo of myself' – upon that concept that Gallagher has convinced herself is clearly enough understood simply through its naming, 'genuine originality': 'Eliot proceeded from the . . . bias [that] there should be *just enough* literature, which should be just sufficiently contained in books just adequate to express only the important thoughts of just those authors capable of genuine originality' (118). Here we once again find Eliot being held up as a champion of honest, real-world evident effort.[10]

In Gallagher's earlier consideration of *Deronda* we also find the distinction between 'honest' production and 'dishonest' or 'unnatural' *re*production being used to connect claims on behalf of 'originality' enunciated in several didactic passages from Eliot's letters and essays with a literary-critical conceptual schema that would have the world be neatly dividing itself according to a natural production/unnatural exchange binary.[11] This all seems reasonable enough. The neophyte entrant to any arena is often going to be prone to being harried by feelings of illegitimacy and the Victorian author long since deceased before 1966's *The Languages of Criticism and the Sciences of Man* conference at Johns Hopkins would come along to break open literary-critical discourse is quite likely not going to be thinking in deconstructive terms. But it has to be admitted that there has always been more to the world of textual repetition (a quite multifaceted one) than simply the effects of plagiarism, by others or by oneself of oneself. For one, there has constantly also been (constantly always also will be) the effects of *rhetoric*, a manifestly less 'immoral' consequence of the repetition of language. I am arguing here that Eliot as a fiction writer – and at that a very well-established one by this late stage in her illustrious career – could not have helped realising certain other 'excessive' aspects of the workings of language, mainly those having to do with the *productive* power of recontextualisation. Indeed, have we not already seen at least one of Eliot's characters being allowed – I am thinking of Deronda's having realised a multiplicity of significations to be inhabiting the phrase 'to try . . . as well' – to infer, contrary to Gallagher's contention in the 'Too Much' chapter, something 'de trop' to be arising from the various rhetorical possibilities made available by iterability-as-iteration?

Rhetorical Hope

Obviously, expecting simple linguistic 'repetition' to rise to the level of 'genuine originality', expecting it to, so to speak, make a 'difference', would seem to be too much to ask of certain fields, as for example is the case with the law.[12] But when such a repetition is rendered in the much more open-minded field of literature, as well as its offshoot literary criticism, a Derridean 'iteration', it clearly reaches (by definition) the level of a production through/as recontextualisation and thereby crosses over into the territory of, to use Gallagher's terms, *circulation* and *exchange*. In other words, no easy distinction between production and exchange can be allowed to stand when we view repetitions as possibly bringing 'something new' into the world (technically this would be, allowing something new to happen). If it is granted that a repetition can create newness – that repetition can 'create', period – one finds production, in the form of *re*production, to be bleeding over into the realm of exchange. This is not possible from the perspective of a solely materialist world view because materials are finite and limited and involved in a zero-sum game. Conservation of matter and all that. Also, with materials both the Law of Identity (where A=A applies both forward and backward) and the Law of Noncontradiction (where A cannot also equal not-A) are in play; with iterable elements they are not. Immaterial entities, such as textual repetitions, do not operate according to a zero-sum logic or according to the laws of Identity and Noncontradiction.[13] To offer one example of a clear violation of certainly the latter principle, and perhaps also the former, I would point to William Blackstone's contention in his well-known *Commentaries on the Laws of England* (1765–9) that 'the identity of a literary composition consists entirely in the *sentiment* and the *language*; the same conceptions, clothed in the same words, must necessarily be the same composition'.[14]

The distinction between the non-encroachment/encroachment of repetition of text upon the realm of productivity strikes me as the central point of contention between our two most significant recent developments in literary theory. And this difference manifests itself most forcefully with regard to the concept of 'spirit'. In the 'try' episode, Gwendolen's actual problem is, I believe, one of impatience. Too much is asked for too quickly. 'Genuine originality' puts up such a formidable barrier that it must appear conclusively impassable to those of Gwendolen's (and Gallagher's) persuasion. Thus, the strong temptation is just not to try. But in actuality, as any good teacher can tell you, the barrier between rote repetition – a key theme in *Daniel Deronda* – and actual learning (the actual 'production' of selves simultaneously located in the same space) is *not* impassable. Mere repetition, if carried on long enough and with enough enthusiasm, can eventually turn into access to the realm of the spirit. But this progress can only begin for those who first possess a modicum of the hope that it can, and thus the Gwendolens of this world have absolutely no chance of reaching this magical realm. That is, since allowing for the possibility for recontextualisations to be valid productions is the first necessary step in this mystical transformation, the historicists' world will always be one conclusively bereft of spirit.

In short, I am arguing here that there exist other ways of demarcating the category of 'commerce', and, specifically, its 'production' and 'exchange' domains, and that this recalibration is rendered obligatory when the goods under consideration are textual ones. This critique stemming from a desire to accord proper respect to the productive potential inherent in iteration – a wish to take proper account of the near-labourless, near 'magical' efficiency of the reproduction of the iterable commodity – allows for the articulation of two diverse aspects of culture: economics and literary criticism. If one views 'rhetoric' – for a good number of critics a favourite 'subversion' access point – as simply a term for taxonomising the many effects of the more or less productive recontextualisation of text, then the discourse of John Maynard Keynes at least momentarily meets up with that of Paul de Man. The latter, in his well-known essay 'Semiology and Rhetoric', contends that the 'rhetoric' of an utterance is often going to be out of sync with that utterance's 'grammar', that element focused on by what I am considering a new historical naïve referentialism. For de Man, rhetoric and grammar – in his senses of them 'the literary dimensions of language' and 'syntactical relations' (1979: 5 and 6) – work at cross purposes. In other words, multiplicity and reference[15] are in conflict and from de Man's perspective 'these days' (1979, but the same being true all the way up to 2010 or so) the victory seems to have been going more often than not to the latter:

> [Today] [w]e may no longer be hearing too much about relevance but we keep hearing a great deal about reference, about the nonverbal 'outside' to which language refers, by which it is conditioned and upon which it acts. The stress falls ... on the interplay between ... fictions and categories that are said to partake of reality, such as the self, man, society, 'the artist, his culture and the human community'(3)

However, de Man also sees a counter-discourse to be at work. While 'the perception of the literary dimensions of language is largely obscured if one submits uncritically to the authority of reference' (5), working against this submission stands the 'inordinate amount of attention' that the conspicuous and complex 'code' would be attracting to itself, a circumstance that results in the situation of 'literature necessarily breed[ing] its own formalism' (4).[16] This tension leads to a constant need for rereading: an initial reading taking place from the perspective of grammar, say, and then from that of rhetoric (or vice versa). This rereading will never result in a single interpretation in which the two simply unproblematically mesh. Left over will always be some sort of excess, some remainder.[17] Thus, this conflict between grammar and rhetoric results for de Man in repetitions that are productive, even if simply of disagreement. Whether one calls it grammar or aesthetic values, the 'turn to reference' by the new historicism is continually going to face the possibility of being undone by a turn to rhetoric, dissemination or the underlying linguistic structures (like iterational iterability) that allow the disruptions of ghostly reading to come about.

Gallagher's inquiry, relying heavily as it does on Eliot's 'historical', didactic documents (essay comments and diary entries) as opposed to the more figurative aspects of her fictional ones, seems always already to have foreclosed on the possibility of a mismatch between grammar and rhetoric or, to put it in other terms, between naïve referentiality and the 'too much' of literature. For example, the already-cited quotation offered by Gallagher of Eliot's judgement of many contemporary 'ladies' silly novels' being the result not of honest labour but of 'busy idleness' comes from an essay entitled, appropriately, 'Silly Novels by Lady Novelists'. Gallagher describes this essay as one of several contemporary Victorian 'outburst[s] against female authors emphasiz[ing] these authors' unearned ascendancy in the marketplace' (Gallagher 1985: 44). The feeling that Victorian women authors lacked a clear right to the earnings won by their writings was apparently creating for them a certain sense of illegitimacy. This illegitimacy was not simply being remarked on by Eliot but was, according to Gallagher, going on to affect as well her later-life fictional productions.

But was Eliot as naïve a referentialist as Gallagher makes out? Admittedly, it is an incontestable fact that Eliot's fetishisation of originality, evident in the application of the pejorative term 'silly novels' to especially formulaic productions of her time, moves against the rhetorics enabled by iteration. However, the complexities of the 'code' were (and are) always there. It is just that one needed to choose to look for them. Even in Eliot's more didactic writings, I believe, we can find evidence of both a rhetorics of iteration and a rhetorics from iteration. For example, in a letter of 3 January 1875 (the time of the composition of Book 1, and perhaps Book 2, of *Daniel Deronda*) Eliot describes, in what has become one of her more well-known sayings, her dislike of the disillusioning process of prooftext typesetting to which an author's manuscript brilliance must necessarily at some point in the publishing process be subjected:

> All writing seems to me worse in the state of proof than in any other form. In manuscript one's own wisdom is rather remarkable to one, but in proof it has the effect of one's private furniture repeated in the shop windows. (Eliot 1954–78: 6, 108)

The anomalous term *repeated* here (*displayed* would have been more expected) can be interpreted either in a restricted economy sense (Gwendolen's perspective) or a general economy sense (Deronda's perspective). The former perspective finds *repeated* to be simply meaning *displayed*: George Eliot's actual furniture is being placed in the shop windows. The latter finds *repeated* to be multiple, both in literal meaning and in 'force': these are new chairs and coffee and side tables – modelled upon Eliot's originals – being put in the windows, not the actual items from the drawing room in the Regent's Park Priory. But there is also a rhetorics *from* iteration here. The passage itself concerns the process of printing. It encapsulates (albeit perhaps more in the general spirit than the precise sense) the process at the basis of the title of that well-known work by Elizabeth L. Eisenstein, *The Printing Press as an Agent of Change*. The proof pages are either one's old furniture with all its faults now exposed by the glare of the marketplace or 'new' furniture modelled on and mimicking the old (to undo the metaphor – standardised and 'typed' simulacra of the crabbed manuscript text). The latter situation potentially allows newness to enter the world and, despite Eliot's apparent negative attitude toward this process, this possibility will actually be turning out to be, I will argue in the next section, opening up the mystical hope underlying the religious aspects of her last major novel.

Reading Hebrew

Much of what I have so far noted about the new historical 'programme' has been previously remarked. For example, the critic Joseph Litvak was in my experience the first to notice the importance of the production/exchange dichotomy for the otherwise fiercely-anti-programmatic new historicists when he questioned whether 'the production/exchange opposition' might not have been 'the new historicism's answer . . . to the Derridean speech/writing dyad' (Litvak 1988: 144). He also implicitly ascribed a certain guilt to their 'supplanting' of the deconstructionists (121). Litvak would go on in 1992 to remark of Gallagher's 1985 interpretation of *Deronda* that it had 'derive[d] much of its interest from its displacement of classic deconstructive motifs like textuality and dissemination into a more worldly register of economic and sexual exchange, presided over by those seductive emblematic figures, the "almost always Jewish" moneylender and prostitute'.[18] He was drawing out here the implications of points he had made in his earlier essay. There he commented that

> [N]ew historicists as a whole tend to swerve from the general and the theoretical to the local and the historical. . . . [They] resist the repetition-compulsion to which [Paul de Man's] totalizing and potentially totalitarian unreliability [inevitably to be disclosed by the 'technically correct rhetorical readings' he was calling for] would consign them, but they do so only by breaking that universal irony down into a series of local narratives or (hi)stories ('episodes', as Greenblatt calls them) designed to disguise the fundamental contradiction

lurking within every text, whether narrowly 'literary' (e.g., *Felix Holt*) or broadly social (e.g., the industrial revolution).[19] Thus, in keeping with the well-known ambiguity of the term, 'history' is constituted as the already-textualised repertoire of specific manipulations and concealments whereby the discovery of an essentially transhistorical or antihistorical undecidability may be postponed. (Litvak 1988: 125–6)

Litvak had also rehearsed D. A. Miller's contention that the critical appeal of deconstructive undecidability was not enough in itself and that in general 'Undecidability . . . must always be the undecidability of *something in particular*' (qtd in Litvak 1988: 128).

This obsession with always localising, with invariably-reductively 'specifying', had been recharacterised by Litvak as a desire on the part of the new historicists 'to recount the more engagingly particularized episodes . . . leading up to that discovery [of a deconstructive undecidability]', a desire that manifested itself in 'a concern for the specific interests of specific narratives [through which] narrative interest as such displace[d] epistemological severity as the order of the day' (Litvak 1988: 128). A better example of this process would, I imagine, have been difficult to find than Gallagher's contention in her analysis of *Deronda* that she would *not* be attempting with respect to the metaphors of author as whore and author as father 'to choose between [them] or to develop an abstract truth about authorship' (Gallagher 1985: 41). Instead, Gallagher's essay would be 'describ[ing] specific historical associations confronting professional women writers in the nineteenth century, when the metaphor of the author as whore was commonplace' (41). She had then gone on to point out that her 'purpose' was to 'register the peculiar Victorian resonances' of this metaphor (as well as of its alternate manifestation, the author-as-usurer) and to utilise it 'as a way of understanding' *Deronda* (41). Here we see the first half of Litvak's contention quite forcefully borne out, as patently evident in this piece interested in simply 'recount[ing] . . . episodes' ('describe', 'register', in Gallagher's terms) was the new historical 'swerve' away from deconstruction's general theoretical 'epistemological severity' (no 'abstract truth about authorship' here) and toward an obsession with the particular ('specific', 'peculiar'). Litvak characterised a section of Gallagher's book on the Industrial Revolution in similar terms, commenting, 'Thus, for example, if *Hard Times*, in familiar deconstructive fashion, is "about" the failure of metaphor, at stake here is not just a *general* principle of rhetoric but the ideology based upon the *specific*, paternalist metaphor of [Victorian] society as family' (Litvak 1988: 129; emphases added). Here the particular eclipses (or is made to eclipse, by a repetition-as-mere-reproduction-of-previous-context *Weltanschauung*) the universal.

The attitude espoused by D. A. Miller in the quotation above was not unique. Or if it was when he wrote it, it did not long remain so. The new historicism from its earliest manifestations has invariably been considered to have been the signalling of a degree of 'progress' in the practice of literary criticism. These critics often choose to characterise the deconstructionists as being merely interested in 'frozen' or 'sterile' aporias at the same time that they describe their own practice as opening up access to decided movement.[20] For instance, in his article 'Towards a Poetics of Culture',[21] Greenblatt at one point catalogues three different but related recent trends in conceptualisation in the humanities that all according to him could be seen to 'pul[l] away from a stable, mimetic theory of art [in the] attemp[t] to construct in its stead an interpretative model that will more adequately account for the unsettling circulation of materials and discourses that is, I have argued, the heart of modern aesthetic practice'. He holds that 'It is in response to this practice that contemporary theory must situate itself: not outside interpretation, but in the hidden places of negotiation and exchange' (Greenblatt 1987: 13–14). Here Greenblatt's 'more adequately' is meant to contrast the representation of reality offered by his three theorists of 'circulation' and 'exchange' – the thinkers Wolfgang Iser, Robert Weimann and Anthony Giddens – with that system of representation that had been offered previously by the presumably one-way textualist discourse of the deconstructionists. The primary desire of the new historicists having always been to get things (the blood cells?) 'circulating', not leave them locked up in deconstruction's (seemingly) progressless paradoxes, this instance of implicit substitution in Greenblatt's essay is simply one among many to be encountered in the new historical canon.[22] There has always been a quite distinct difference in world views setting apart the two literary critical approaches I am considering here: one a discourse governed by the metaphor of a circulatory system and the other a style of inquiry launched toward the continual disclosure of an apparently 'frozen' aporia or impasse. However, I contend that things stand actually the other way around. The citational world-view on which the new historicism is based (on which, as I have already noted, any and all other forms of 'historicism' must be based) – the fundamental assumption that 'history repeats its[old]self', that the old context continues to predominate when a story, anecdote or historeme is transplanted to a new one – is a freezing of 'progress', while it is actually the iterational perspective, that world view preferencing the non-identity of the repeated, that would be allowing new (and often mystical) things to enter the world.

The passage I would wish to highlight in the context of the new historicism's uneasy supplanting of deconstruction is that one from

Gallagher's essay dealing with Mordecai's 'printing' in Chapter 38 of his words upon young Jacob Cohen's intelligence. At this point in her argument, Gallagher quite forcefully attempts – to my mind decidedly unpersuasively – to deny the mystical realm to the deconstructionists:

> It is true that this union [between Deronda, Mirah and Mordecai] seems to have textuality at its heart, but that textuality rigorously excludes all that Eliot has previously meant by 'art'. For art, like money in this novel is international, widely disseminated through modern printing, and bent on the creation of fungible, cosmopolitan selves. The Cabbala, on the other hand, is a set of exclusive, closely guarded and hand-copied esoteric texts, bent on the creation of a cumulative but nevertheless unique Jewish self. Indeed, Mordecai's way of disseminating his culture evinces a desire to dispense even with these texts. His teaching of little Jacob, for example, proceeds by 'a sort of outpouring in the ear of the boy' of 'a Hebrew poem of his own'. Jacob cannot even understand the words, but Mordecai assures himself that 'The boy will get them engraved within him ... it is a way of printing' ... Mordecai may believe that this kind of 'printing' will one day influence Jacob, but as Eliot would be the first to point out, this activity has nothing to do with authorship. No one is culpable for it. (Gallagher 1985: 58)

Here Gallagher – as a means of establishing, apparently, the radical individuality of one's Jewishness through the envisioning of a Jewish self that while it may be 'cumulative' is still 'nevertheless unique' – explicitly denies there to be a concern with textuality in this episode. Authorship for Eliot, Gallagher argues, necessarily is characterised by the seemingly-very-material discourses of culpability, labour and originality. In other words, nothing 'new' is created without authorial labour, and specifically potentially 'culpable' authorial labour of an original kind.

It is, however, necessary to point out that this type of 'printing' of Jewishness can, at least from Mordecai's perspective, result in no less than the founding of the state of Israel. The narrator describes Jacob's pleasure in 'this fascinating game of imitating unintelligible words'. This fascination becomes for Mordecai the potential means of establishing a Jewish nation: 'My words may rule him some day. Their meaning may flash out on him. It is so with a nation – after many days' (Eliot 1991: 409). This establishment of missionary zeal, as he repeatedly explicitly makes clear, is also the agenda underlying his instruction of Daniel in Hebrew. The 'printing' here in this famous passage – despite Gallagher's attempt at a radically transformative recontextualisation of it – is George Eliot's undeniable acknowledgement of the force of the iterability of language.[23]

The iterational perspective also casts in a new light a particularly striking scene from later in the narrative. In Chapter 48 we are presented with a tableau that re-presents the whole of the story writ small, that one in which Gwendolen, on a 'pretext' (504) (quite literally this is a pre-text as in 'before text' situation),[24] visits Mirah at the lodgings she shares with her brother. She claims she is there to invite Mirah to perform at an evening party to be held at her house. She is actually visiting, of course, to convince herself of the baselessness of the supposition her husband has just offered regarding the nature of Mirah and Deronda's relationship: 'Men can see what is his relation to her' (502). Gwendolen is brought into 'a room where there [are] folding-doors, and she hear[s] Deronda's voice behind it':

> 'Mr Deronda is in the next room.'
> 'Yes,' said Mirah, in her former tone. 'He is reading Hebrew with my brother.'
> 'You have a brother?' said Gwendolen, who had heard this from Lady Mallinger, but had not minded it then. (505)

Here we have the two love triangles in the story (Gwendolen-Deronda-Mirah, Grandcourt-Gwendolen-Deronda) intersecting in the foreground while the tale of Deronda's slow, laboured conversion to Judaism is taking place in the background, 'in the next room'. One recalls here F. R. Leavis's and Henry James's suggested separation of the novel into two – good and bad – parts. But this scene is not just the whole of the narrative writ small in that sense; it is also an allegory for the theoretics of linguistics, that is, for the structural workings of iterability. Here we have, in what resembles nothing so much as a figurative print shop, 'real life' going on in the front room while all the while the 'machine' of dissemination is (re)enunciating away behind the folding doors in the back room.[25] I might add that this situation of folding doors through which Deronda's voice can still be heard is an excellent example of that phrase 'separateness with communication' (620) that Deronda uses to describe to Joseph Kalonymos what type of Jew he will be attempting to be.

The process of Deronda's 'reading Hebrew' is undoubtedly akin to the tutoring in Hebrew that Eliot and George Henry Lewes undertook under the tutelage of their friend Emanuel Deutsch (considered by some critics a possible model for Mordecai).[26] In the scene of Gwendolen's visit, we find the strangeness of Deronda's reading Hebrew left out of play, its having been eclipsed by the issue of generational reproduction, until, that is, two pages later when the issue is once again brought up by the narrative: '[T]he phrase "reading Hebrew" had fleeted unimpressively across her sense of hearing, as a stray stork might have made its peculiar flight across her landscape without rousing any surprised reflection on its natural history' (507). With this reminder – one that calls us back to a passage that might have fleeted past us on our own first or second reading of the text, until on our third it perhaps 'flash[ed] out on' us – the text almost seems to *require* us to notice this activity going on behind the folding doors, to explore the 'natural history' of that distinction standing behind the process of rote learning: the unproductive reproduction/productive reproduction one. The idea behind that type of learning seems to be that 'mindless' repetition eventually magically *can* turn at some point into actual learning, real internalisation. There is an explosive efficacy inherent in this potential 'flash[ing] out' that calls up that explosive efficacy characteristic of the essentially-labourless labour inherent in the end-case-efficient iterability of text.

It is not just a revolutionary vs. reactionary attitude toward recontextualisation that I am considering here. The contrast can also be described as that distinguishing additive from subtractive copying. Recall Mordecai's description of the Cabbalistic transmigration of souls: 'a soul liberated from a worn-out body may join the fellow-soul that needs it, that they may be perfected together' (461). This is in line with the narrative's earlier reference to his having pictured another person who would come to help him in his endeavours: 'his imagination had constructed another man who would ... be a blooming human life, ready to incorporate all that was worthiest in an existence whose visible, palpable part was burning itself fast away' (406). These two entities would create an 'expanded, prolonged self' (406). This line of inquiry is summarily dismissed by Gallagher when she writes, 'Eliot is drawn to the Cabbala for its principle of exchange, but she never confuses this with the exchanges of authorship' (Gallagher 1985: 57). In contrast, my contention is that however essential it may be for the new historicist critic, given her discipline's allegiance to materialised exchanges, to view Eliot's attitude to the Cabbala, among other things, in this way, this necessity does not dispel the evident 'mysticism' surrounding these exchanges. The sound of the, so to speak, 'machine' of reproduction in operation in 'the other room' will necessarily be penetrating into the one in which Mirah interacts with her guest, the room in which the 'exchanges' of society take place, whether the literary critic or her mode of criticism would have it or no. The effect of this encroachment should not be ignored, for this 'machine' is itself part of the real world. What had caused us to have difficulty 'hearing' its workings was the whirring and clicking of a 'machine' of a different sort, the machine of new historicism's enforced material-making, that is, its theoretically-enforced materialism.

Reclaiming Marx

A significant problem, I believe, for the New Economic Criticism – a late-90s potential offshoot of the new historicism – stems from its conceptual basis in an inveterate reification of dissemination.[27] My own *new* new economic criticism, on the other hand, would be founded upon a different proposition: that literary (iterable) property is fundamentally different from other, non-iterable forms of property. It is my contention that the iterable economy fundamentally differs, to no small extent, from the domestic and international materialist political economies (at least from the wholly material aspects of those economies). I would be tempted to label it a 'shadow economy', were it not for the fact that all of us have been made conscious recently of the staggering effects of the Internet upon the world economy. Back in 1992, the copyright historian Mark Rose already was commenting on the significant impact of this intangible economy: 'Approximately twenty-five percent of current US exports, I have heard, are in one way or another dependent upon intellectual property laws' (Rose 1991–2: 146). More recently, another copyright historian, Peter Baldwin, writes, 'In 2010 industries heavily based on intellectual property provided 27 percent of US jobs' (Baldwin 2014: 18). I contend that the difference between the iterable and non-iterable economies must be brought, in the economic realm no less than the literary critical one, to the level of conscious acknowledgement, specifically into one's calculations and theoretical formulations, or else there will result an undue weighting in favour of materiality, particularly in favour of that markedly inadequate model (the Siren Song apparently of new historicist criticism), a fully materialised textuality.

I will be contesting Gallagher's characterisation of the thinking of Marx shortly, but first I would like preliminarily to contest her characterisation of the thinking of Aristotle. Gallagher's foundational distinction between usury and natural production comes from that philosopher's *The Politics*. Marc Shell, Gallagher's source for her understanding of this text (Gallagher 1985: 60 n. 3), makes a telling choice in the passage with which he chooses to define *chrematistics* (Aristotle's term for unnatural wealth-generation). Shell cites the definition provided in Aristotle's concluding remarks on the concept, the philosopher's definition emphasising the unnaturalness of the concept of interest: '[M]oney was brought into existence for the purpose of exchange, but interest increases the amount of the money itself . . . . [C]onsequently this form of the business of getting wealth is of all forms the most contrary to nature' (*Politics* 1258b; qtd in Shell 1978: 94). In this context, Aristotle will mention a certain opprobrium attaching to the 'chrematistical' (immaterially productive) realm: 'Usury is most reasonably hated, because its gain comes from money itself and not from that for the sake of which money was invented' (*Politics* 1258b; qtd in Shell 1978: 94). This somewhat nefarious economy matches up for Gallagher, as we have seen, with the Victorian opprobrium against the Jewish usurer and actress/prostitute, as well as with the profits made through the circulation of unoriginal compositions.

Shell's work is ritually invoked at the beginnings of studies like Gallagher's. Besides the prominent acknowledgements by Gallagher in her books *The Body Economic* ('Some of the earliest examples of what came to be called the "new economic criticism" include Marc Shell's *The Economy of Literature* and *Money, Language, and Thought* . . .' [Gallagher 2006: 2 n. 1]) and *Nobody's Story: The Vanishing Acts of Women in the Marketplace 1670–1820* ('Examples of this new economic criticism include Marc Shell, *The Economy of Literature* . . . and *Money, Language, and Thought*' [Gallagher 1995: xiv n. 4]), we also have Mary Poovey's acknowledgement in *Genres of the Credit Economy* of the models offered her by 'Jean-Joseph Goux's discovery of a "structural parallel" between money and language [and] Marc Shell's claim (following A. R. J. Turgot) that speech and money are both languages'.[28] Shell himself, committed to putting forward an argument biased in favour of materialism (a bias that is particularly surprising given that his book begins with the following sentence: 'Those discourses are ideological that argue or assume that matter is ontologically prior to thought' [Shell 1978: 1]) and less perspicacious than his classical subject, begins his chapter on Aristotle with a common, unfortunate collapse, that of iterable products with material ones. He comments, '"Economy" refers etymologically to the conventions (*nomoi*) of and distribution (*nemesis*) within the household (*oikos*). Domestic economy concerns production and distribution in the household. . . . Political economy concerns production and distribution in the polis. . . . Literary economy concerns *similar* problems of production, distribution, and relations' (89–90; last italics added). Earlier, Shell will have commented, along the same lines, that one goal of literary criticism 'is to understand the connection between the smallest verbal metaphor and the largest trope'. Thus, his book will be an attempt 'to understand the relation between . . . literary exchanges and the exchanges that constitute the political economy. It looks from the *formal similarity* between linguistic and economic symbolism and production to the political economy as a whole' (7; italics added). Compare this with Poovey's remark in *Genres* that she will be exploring the ways in which three forms of writing, imaginative, monetary (which means among other things 'forms of credit'), and econometric (for example, writings about economic theory), 'sometimes *shared formal features*' (Poovey 2008: 2; italics added).

It is surprising that Shell does not offer the definition of *chrematistics* given by Aristotle at the beginning of Chapter 9: 'the other [means of wealth generation] is not natural, but carried on rather by means of a certain acquired skill [*empeiria*] or art [*technē*]'.[29] (Indeed, had he done so, he would have rendered his discourse a good deal less helpful to Gallagher, since art – still even at this moment – would seem to be quite a bit less obviously 'sterile' a practice than is usury.) This 'art' has often been characterised as being both good and evil at the same time. It is akin to the art of writing, that skill that is described by Plato using the ambiguous term *pharmakon* (cure/poison). It is no accident that one of Derrida's preferred ways of describing iterability is as a type of *technē*. When referring to Socrates' criticism of writing as a tool that because it repeats is rendered fundamentally 'unproductive', he writes,

> Socrates ties up into a system all the counts of indictment against the *pharmakon* of writing ... Socrates' first argument [is] writing is not a good *tekhnē*, by which we should understand an art capable of engendering, pro-ducing, bringing forth. ... [The thinker using writing] would not know that he already knows what he thinks he is learning through writing, and which he is only recalling to mind through the types. ... Writing ... only intervenes at a time when a subject of knowledge already possesses the signifieds, which are then only given to writing on consignment. (Derrida 1981: 134–5)

Of course, Derrida will go on to criticise this perspective on writing, remarking that 'the technique of imitation ... has always been in Plato's eyes manifestly magical, thaumaturgical' (139). Derrida points out that imitation necessarily involves a certain type of productivity, the productivity of difference so that the imitation can actually constitute itself (its-*self*) – albeit as an 'imitation' – in opposition to the imitated thing itself:

> A perfect imitation is no longer an imitation. ... Imitation does not correspond to its essence, it is not what it is – imitation – unless it is in some way at fault or rather in default. It is bad by nature. It is only good insofar as it is bad. (139)

It is this 'magical' aspect of the imitation that is in some way essentially 'off' that funds textualonomics with its ever-increasing reservoirs of newness.

The thinking of Karl Marx, that famous 'materialist', is, not surprisingly, instrumental for the new historicists. But even in his work we can find signs of the existence of that shadow world of iterability. This seems to have been what J. Hillis Miller was suggesting, in his well-known 1986 Modern Language Association Presidential Address, subtitled 'The Triumph of Theory, the Resistance to Reading, and the Question of the Material Base', when he called for a critique of that base through a deconstructive 'rereading' of Marx's work. Miller made this point while arguing that those on the 'so-called left' who might oppose theory (I take it from the larger context that he was specifically referring to the new historicists) needed to make their peace with their deconstructive foes since the former critics' resistance to theory that was also a resistance to reading was bound eventually to be co-opted by conservative forces:

> [Y]ou should make common cause with those who practice a rhetorical study of literature, that is, with the multiform movement called 'deconstruction'. ... Your commitment to history, to society, to an exploration of the material base of literature ... will inevitably fall into the hands of those with antithetical positions to yours as long as you hold to an unexamined ideology of the material base, that is, to a notion that is metaphysical through and through, as much a part of Western metaphysics as the idealism you would contest. 'Deconstruction' is the current name for the multiple and heterogeneous strategies of overturning and displacement that will liberate your own enterprise from what disables it. Among its tasks is that rereading of Marx in which ... many ... younger scholars are currently involved. (Miller 1991: 326)

It is in that spirit that I have in a general sense been considering the contrast between deconstruction and the new historicism as one between textualonomics and materialist economics, and it is in that spirit that I would like now in particular to offer my own rereading of Marx, a rereading that challenges Gallagher's implicit subsumption – a direct consequence of her (standard) understanding of a singular conception of Marxian labour – of the textual and mystical economy. Gallagher describes a type of 'Marxist thought' that has Marx sounding like nothing so much as a late-twentieth-century new historicist himself:

> [P]rostitution in the nineteenth century is linked to writing through their joint inhabitation of the realm of exchange. ... [T]he processes of exchange, of circulation, are distinguished from those of production by all political economists. The sphere of production, rather than that of circulation, is then identified as the source of value, the source of real wealth. The Marxist critique of political economy, with its distinction between the production and realization of surplus-value, only refines the qualitative difference between these economic realms. These realms, of course, interpenetrate, for the essence of capitalism ... is production that depends on the exchange of two underlying commodities: labor (or labor-power) and money. The stated source of value (and of surplus-value), however, remains the productive labor of the worker, that which brings some new things into the world. (Gallagher 1985: 41–2)

Here, Gallagher's principal principle is clear enough: no labour, no value. 'The source', she writes, 'of value ... remains the productive labor of the worker.' Despite their 'interpenetration', the two 'economic realms' of production and exchange maintain for her their fundamental distinctness, with the former playing the role of the sole source of value creation because it is the one that serves as the region of 'creation' per se: only 'productive labor ... brings ... new things into the world'.

However, at one point in his writings Marx writes the following: there is 'a vast difference which affects the formation of wealth, between labour which is engaged on reproductive articles and labour concerned purely with luxuries'.[30] Clearly, Gallagher's monolithic view of Marxian labour is irreconcilable with a Marx who finds the 'labour concerned ... with luxuries' to be distinct (indeed, 'vastly' distinct) from the 'labour which is engaged on reproductive articles'. In making this remark Marx was introducing into his work a type of thinking profoundly disruptive of the natural production/unnatural exchange binary. Here the thinker so dear to the exclusively materialist new historicists had the conception – a quite correct and fundamental one, in my opinion, and one forming the basis of a particularly significant strain of deconstructive critique – that there is a serious distinction needing to be drawn between the wealth accruable to a producer by the creation of luxury goods and the wealth accruable by the creation of iterable, or at least proto-iterable, ones (*reproduktiven Artikeln*).[31] Thus, at least at one point in his writings, Marx recognised the fact that in the case of iterable products there is involved no 'labour' per se (or to be technically precise, a very different sort of labour than that which Gallagher is envisioning when she refers to the 'productive labor of the worker'). *Pace* the common understanding of Marx's concept of labour, 'new' things can indeed be brought into this world, this passage from the *Resultaten* seems to be implying, by mere reproduction. Marx here opened up, in the case of easily reproducible property (such as, for example, pirated books), a path toward the acknowledgement in his conceptualising of the essentially free creation of surplus-value, of value in general, without the need for the expenditure of 'labour' as we commonly understand that term. Admittedly, this is not our usual understanding of Marx's thinking. But that is a function of our closed-mindedness, not Marx's.

Escaping Reproducing the Old

Given my emphasis on the rhetorical dimensions of Eliot's novel, it should come as no surprise that I find her text to be uncommonly productive of 'new' readings. To offer in closing just one, I might turn to that moment when we find our author expressing, so to speak, 'behind' the overt meaning of her narrative, her allegiance to productive reproductions. Midway through the novel, Sir Hugo Mallinger, while showing Grandcourt and Gwendolen around the Abbey at Monk's Topping amidst a walking party that includes Deronda, remarks on his preference for 'not attempting to remedy the mixture of the undisguised modern with the antique' which apparently has caused this one of his estates to resemble a grouping of 'architectural fragments'. When the party pauses before 'a beautiful pointed doorway' that is 'the only old remnant in the east front', Sir Hugo is prompted to comment,

> Well, now, to my mind ... that is more interesting standing as it is in the middle of what is frankly four centuries later, than if the whole front had been dressed up in a pretense of the thirteenth century. Additions ought to smack of the time when they are made and carry the stamp of their period. I wouldn't destroy any old bits, but that notion of reproducing the old is a mistake, I think. (Eliot 1991: 356)

The practice of 'reproducing the old' is a sterile one, not to mention severely lacking in the mysticism that makes the world a realm of spirit as well as of matter. Here Daniel's father figure's last sentence – as they so tellingly say – 'takes on new meaning', given the context in which I am choosing to place it. I believe we can actually figuratively 'hear' Eliot differing from Gallagher's standpoint with regard to repetitions – 'that notion of reproducing the old [context] is a mistake, I think' – and siding with the world view of iterations over that of citations. Sir Hugo, or perhaps his author herself, would seem to be suggesting, to repurpose an old phrase myself, that there are more things in Heaven and Earth than are dreamt of in the new historicism's philosophy.

Notes

1. Gallagher and Stephen Greenblatt in the aptly named *Practicing New Historicism* repeatedly contend that new historical practice is backed by no general theoretical programme: 'One of the recurrent criticisms of new historicism is that it is insufficiently theorized. ... We speculated about first principles and respected the firmer theoretical commitments of other members of our discussion group, but both of us were and remain deeply skeptical of the notion that we should formulate an abstract system and then apply it to literary works. ... The effect on the two of us was to underscore the difficulty of constructing an overarching theory, prior to or independent of individual cases. ... [N]ew historicism is not a repeatable methodology or a literary critical program. ... So we sincerely hope you

will not be able to say what it all adds up to; if you could, we would have failed' (Gallagher and Greenblatt, *Practicing New Historicism*, pp. 2, 3, 19). I will be arguing here that the new historicists do indeed have a programme, one that might be described as a 'historicism'-inflected 'thick materiality' undergirding a would-be impermeable natural production/unnatural exchange binary.

2. I am following along in a tradition of theorists who have suggested certain programmatic structures to be underlying the new historicists' practice. See, for one example, J. Hillis Miller writing that the proponents of this school, as well as theory resisters on the right, 'need to point the finger of blame against theory to avoid thinking through the challenge theory poses to their own ideologies' (*Theory Now and Then*, p. 315).

3. The 'pay-off' to this set-up regarding trying and inspiration will come near the end of the novel when Deronda says to an ailing Mordecai, 'It is quite true that you and Mirah have been my teachers. . . . If this revelation [of my Jewishness] had been made to me before I knew you both, I think my mind would have rebelled against it. . . . But it has been the gradual accord between your mind and mine which has brought about . . . full consent. . . . It is through your inspiration that I have discerned what may be my life's task . . . to bind our race together in spite of heresy. . . . I mean to work in your spirit. Failure will not be ignoble, but it would be ignoble for me not to try' (Eliot, *Daniel Deronda*, p. 642).

4. See Krueger originating the term in her 1974 article. See also Thomas Piketty remarking that individuals and families under Capitalism 'evolve' toward rent seeking: 'Capital is never quiet: it is always risk-oriented and entrepreneurial, at least at its inception, yet it always tends to transform itself into rents as it accumulates in large enough amounts – that is its vocation, its logical destination' (*Capital in the Twenty-First Century*, p. 144), and Joseph Stiglitz pointing out that taxation is one means of derailing rent seeking systems: 'Rent seeking is, on average, destructive, because the rent-seekers gain for themselves less than they take away from others. . . . The more those gains are taxed, the fewer the resources that get devoted to rent seeking, and the more the efforts that get devoted to activities that may not pay as well, but that increase the size of the nation's income and are satisfying in their own right' (*The Price of Inequality*, p. xxxiii).

5. The *OED* offers as one definition of *historicism* the following: 'Belief in the importance or value of historicity or of the past . . . [R]egard for or preoccupation with the styles or values of the past'. Less 'pre-occupied' with/by the past, the Derridean perspective will be making room for the productive aspects of a certain '*différance*', or 'this *sameness* which is not *identical*' (Derrida, 'Differance', p. 129; italics in original).

6. Gallagher, 'George Eliot and *Daniel Deronda*'. This essay must have been considered by Gallagher one of her more representative efforts as years later she chose to have it serve as her contribution to Veeser's *The New Historicism Reader* (pp. 124–40).

7. The question of how truly 'productive', per se, Gallagher's own inquiry could be said to be, being derived as it is to some extent from the terms originally deployed by Gilbert and Gubar, is left unasked by Gallagher. In other words, is she not – by profiting from the perspective of *D* here while

nevertheless purportedly solely espousing the philosophy of G – just as conflicted as we, only in the opposite direction?

8. Lest I should appear to be too severe against Gallagher, I must point out that it is my contention that this allegiance is to be ascribed more to the thinking of her critical school than to Gallagher herself. And already my opening gambit is falling apart.
9. In Gallagher, *The Body Economic*, pp. 118–55. Gallagher conducts this study from the perspective of William Stanley Jevons' 1871 discussion of surplus value theory. I will be leaving this analysis largely out of play here, not because I believe it to be innocent of the charge of foreclosure upon the iterable but because I find the previous *Deronda* essay to be more pertinent and instructive a model for implicitly commenting on a myriad of new historical inquiries, especially those composed between 1985 and 2006.
10. We have evidence that in her life Eliot approved of at least one type of 'imitative' writing, the reprinted saying. Rosemarie Bodenheimer, in discussing Eliot's sanctioning of Alexander Main's quotations from her works in his *Wise, Witty, and Tender Sayings*, facetiously comments, 'The literal repetition and republication of what she had already said does not, it seems, qualify as [part of the] "too much" [of literature]' (*The Real Life of Mary Ann Evans*, p. 175). While it could have been a function of mere vanity, there is also another possible explanation for this willingness on Eliot's part to repeat herself: disseminating 'good' literature – no matter how often that practice is repeated – is the point of writing and the epigram by George Eliot, decontextualised though it might be, seems invariably to reach the level of genuine originality.
11. It is the new historical default to the materialist perspective when faced with the potentially anomalous character of textuality that keeps this binary safely in place. For example, in critiquing the deconstructive obsession with textuality, Gallagher and Greenblatt comment that this obsession, while 'licens[ing] a certain kind of attention', also necessarily draws notice to – in a negative manner – all the issues that that type of inquiry would be foreclosing upon. Foremost among the ignored aspects is the especially 'solid' nature of the material things referred to by the various texts' immaterial words. In contrast, the new historicists, wishing for a return to 'real' matters, are 'call[ing] for a sharp attention to genre and rhetorical mode, to the text's implicit or explicit reality claims, to the implied link (or distance) between the word and whatever it is – *the real, the material,* the realm of practice, pain, bodily pleasure, silence, or death – to which the text gestures as that which lies beyond the written word, outside its textual mode of being' (Gallagher and Greenblatt, *Practicing New Historicism*, p. 23; emphasis added).
12. This possibility has been explicitly denied by the US Supreme Court's 1991 decision in *Feist v. Rural Telephone*, a decision denying copyright protection to reprinted compiled telephone numbers and addresses. Sandra Day O'Connor delivered the Court's judgement: 'The white pages do nothing more than list Rural's subscribers in alphabetical order. . . . This time-honoured tradition does not possess the minimal creative spark required by the Copyright Act and the Constitution. We conclude that the names, towns, and telephone numbers copied by Feist were not original to Rural,

and therefore were not protected by the copyright in Rural's combined white and yellow pages directory. As a constitutional matter, copyright protects only those constituent elements of a work that possess more than a *de minimis* quantum of creativity. Rural's white pages, limited to basic subscriber information and arranged alphabetically, fall short of the mark' (*Feist Pubs., Inc. v. Rural Tel. Svc. Co., Inc.*, p. 363).
13. Barbara Johnson writes, 'Instead of a simple "either/or" structure, deconstruction attempts to elaborate a discourse that says *neither* "either/or", *nor* "both/and" nor even "neither/nor", while at the same time not totally abandoning these logics either' (*A World of Difference*, p. 12).
14. Blackstone, vol. 1, bk. 2, p. 405. This attitude has never afterwards been seriously contested in the subsequent Anglo-American copyright regime, although, admittedly, Learned Hand did hold that someone who had independently created a poem that happened to be the same as Keats's 'Ode on a Grecian Urn' would not be guilty of the violation of copyright: 'if by some magic a man who had never known it were to compose anew Keats's "Ode on a Grecian Urn" he would be an "author", and, if he copyrighted it, others may not copy that poem, though they might of course copy Keats's' (*Sheldon v. MGM Pictures Corp.*, p. 54).
15. Derrida in an early essay points to this tension in Georges Bataille's thinking (particularly in the books *L'Expérience intérieure* and *La Part maudite*) and labels the two, respectively, 'general economy' and 'restricted economy'. See 'From Restricted to General Economy: A Hegelianism without Reserve' in Derrida 1978: 251–77. In that essay he comments about the difference between the thinking of Bataille and Hegel: 'To be indifferent to the comedy of the *Aufhebung*, as was Hegel, is to blind oneself to the experience of the sacred, the heedless sacrifice of presence and meaning' (p. 257).
16. In his later essay 'The Return to Philology', de Man uses an alternate set of terms with which to cast the tension he so often was exploring: 'Literary theory raises the question whether aesthetic values can be compatible with the linguistic structures that make up the entities from which these values are derived'. He continues, 'What is established is . . . that the manner in which the teaching of literature, since its beginning in the later nineteenth century, has foreclosed the question is unsound, even if motivated by the best of intentions' ('The Return to Philology', p. 25).
17. Derrida labels this process 'dissemination': 'Dissemination . . . can be led back neither to a present of simple origin . . . nor to an eschatological presence. It marks an irreducible and *generative* multiplicity. The supplement and the turbulence of a certain lack fracture the limit of the text, forbidding an exhaustive and closed formalization of it, or at least a saturating taxonomy of its themes, its signified, its meaning' (*Positions*, p. 45; emphasis in original).
18. Litvak, *Caught in the Act*, p. 153. Leaving aside the issue of the specific 'seductions' commonly deployed by the new historicists, I would recast that process characterised by Litvak as one of the transformation of textuality and dissemination into particular economic and sexual exchanges instead as a process of the materialisation (through reifying commodification or embodiment in a 'more worldly register') of the immateriality of textuality.

19. This line seems a pointed reference to Gallagher's book *The Industrial Reformation of English Fiction 1832–1867*, Chapter 9 of which is an extended revision of her essay on *Felix Holt*: 'The Politics of Culture and the Debate over Representation'.
20. J. Hillis Miller notes the tendency of deconstruction's many critics to label it a 'sterile' practice: 'The word *sterile*, used in the attacks from both [right and left] sides as an epithet defining theory, carries a large sexual freight. The implication is that theory is narcissistic, even self-abusive. Theorists are impotent while the opponents of theory on both the left and the right are men and women of power. They make things happen in the real world in a way whose model is procreation – either male or female reproduction' (*Theory Now and Then*, p. 314).
21. This essay would seem to stand as a manifesto of sorts for the new historicism, having not only been written by one of the two main proponents of the movement but also reprinted multiple times (see Greenblatt, 'Towards a Poetics of Culture', pp. 3–15, Greenblatt, *Learning to Curse*, pp. 146–60, and Greenblatt, *The Greenblatt Reader*, pp. 18–29; it also serves as the *opening* piece in the collection *The New Historicism* [Veeser, pp. 1–14]).
22. Explicitly contrasting their practice with that of the deconstructionists, Gallagher and Greenblatt in their introduction to *Practicing New Historicism* make clear, through an obsessive (and over-compensatory?) concern with movement, their desire that their practice be viewed as a type of progress: 'We are intensely interested in tracking the social energies that circulate very broadly through a culture, flowing back and forth between margins and center, passing from zones designated as art to zones apparently indifferent or hostile to art, pressing up from below to transform exalted spheres and down from on high to colonize the low. ... This ambition to specify the intriguing enigmas of particular times and places distinguishes our analyses from the contemporary pan-textualism of the deconstructionists, who have their own version of the proposition that a culture is a text. Stressing the slippages, aporias, and communicative failures at the heart of signifying systems, linguistic or otherwise, their cultural textualism has no historicist ancestry' (pp. 13–14). I have already noted how the 'historicist ancestry' of the new historicists manifests itself in a preference for citational over iterational iterability, for the previous over the subsequent context. This preference must be tied, I suspect, at some deep psychological level to the New Historicists' need to begin their essays with a seemingly-fortuitously-encountered minor anecdote (one that is actually a 'plant') that then seemingly-adventitiously would be opening up to a wonder-filled reading of a particular canonical or otherwise-culturally-significant text by an old master, or, as they describe their practice at one point, 'to pick up a tangential fact and watch its circulation' (p. 4). This tendency toward auto-wonderisation, so to speak, seems to have been at the basis of Joel Fineman's critique of new historical practice in his superb essay 'The History of the Anecdote', the argument of which Gallagher and Greenblatt themselves could be understood to be succinctly summarising in their book when they admit to the 'problem' with this pre-'planting' of the opening anecdote. Gallagher and Greenblatt write, 'There is an obvious problem with this procedure: one chose an anecdote

... because it "sounded like" a passage in Marlowe or Shakespeare, and then achieved a spurious effect of surprise and confirmation when it turned out to sound like Marlowe or Shakespeare' (p. 47). Focusing on a particular example from an essay by Greenblatt, Fineman describes the process in this way: '[W]hen Greenblatt explicates the gynecological commentaries on the anatomy of the sexual apparatus[,] he introduces, on the basis of what seems to be his own volition, the metaphor of the inside-outside rubber glove, a metaphor that then subsequently appears to be historically significant when it reappears in the quotation from *Twelfth Night*. . . . But because the metaphor comes to Greenblatt from Shakespeare, and not from the gynecologists . . . it seems very clear that it is Shakespeare's literary text that controls Greenblatt's reading of the history of medicine, and that, correlatively, it is not the case that the history of medicine opens up, on this reading, a novel way to read Shakespeare. . . . [T]he medical texts are, for Greenblatt, nothing but Shakespearean' (Fineman in Veeser, *The New Historicism*, p. 75). Gallagher and Greenblatt's apparent response to this temporality problem of their amnesia-like auto-wonderisations does not, to my mind, actually address the substance of the critique: 'The histories one wanted to pursue through the anecdote might, therefore be called "counterhistories", which it would be all the more exhilarating to launch if their destinations were as yet undetermined and their trajectories lay athwart the best traveled routes' (p. 52). That 'launch if', Fineman was suggesting, was actually a 'launch *as* if'. Thus the 'newness' – another word for the sense of 'wonder' aimed at by the new historicists – contained in new historical productions turns out to actually require the critics' *manufacturing* it, since the new historicism, like the old historicism from which it was desperately trying to distinguish itself through this wonder-creating trick, is in the end based on a citational paradigm that fundamentally interdicts the entry of 'newness' in the course of the rest of the analysis. Starved for newness, the new historicists are required to conjure it themselves, with their citational perspective serving as the unacknowledged negative-impetus for the 'spurious' temporality of their productions.

23. It seems appropriate to point out that Cicero in *De Natura Deorum* (bk. 2, ch. 28) ascribes the etymology of *religion* to *re-legere* (those who are *religious* being those who 'reread' script/scripture): 'They who prayed whole days and sacrificed, that their children might survive them (*ut superstites essent*), were called superstitious, which word became afterward more general; but they who diligently perused, and, as we may say, read or practised over again, all the duties relating to the worship of the Gods, were called *religiosi* – religious from *relegendo* – "reading over again, or practising"; as *elegantes*, elegant, *ex eligendo*, "from choosing, making a good choice"; *diligentes*, diligent, *ex diligendo*, "from attending on what we love"; *intelligentes*, intelligent, from understanding – for the signification is derived in the same manner. Thus are the words *superstitious* and *religious* understood; the one being a term of reproach, the other of commendation' (*Tusculan Disputations*, p. 282). Clearly this etymology has at its basis the implicit suggestion that a rote repetition could possibly someday turn into something mystical. In this context we have to ask if it is simply a coincidence that Deronda should first encounter Mordecai in

'a second-hand book-shop' which the latter is minding (*Daniel Deronda*, p. 325). There could hardly be a more apt setting for the initial meeting of these two eventually very 'religious' individuals.

24. While I recognise that the etymology of *pretext* would be rendering it a pulling of the wool over the eyes of (or an appearing in disguise, a veiling of oneself, in front of) someone, a putting of the fabric (text) before (pre) the eyes of another party or of the self, I nevertheless would contend that it is also working here in the temporal sense of 'before text[uality]' (even in the rather technical and modern sense in which I am understanding that latter term) somewhere in the consciousness of George Eliot.

25. This print shop scene is for me also implicitly suggesting a Daniel Deronda/ *Daniel Deronda* connection. The fact that both these entities owe the specific structures of their existence to a female artist whose profession is based on her productive recontextualisation of the gestures and mannerisms – in the one case through acting (surely the practice Gwendolen is involved in here), in the other through literary re-presentation and printing – of people from real life implies a sort of covert conjunction between the Alcharisi and Eliot to be occurring in this scene.

26. See Rosemary Ashton writing, 'Deutsch was an enthusiast for a Jewish homeland; when he visited Palestine in 1869 he wrote that all his "wild yearnings" had been fulfilled. ... Deutsch and his experience, including his painful decline and death from cancer in 1873, were etched in George Eliot's mind as she wrote about Daniel Deronda and his Jewish mentor Mordecai in her last novel' (*George Eliot: A Life*, p. 304; see also p. 335).

27. Besides this reification, another common strategy adopted by inquiries in this field is to conclude the book, article or chapter at the precise moment when iterability comes unavoidably into play. This might be described as the 'taking one's ball and going home' strategy. See, to offer two examples, Chartier, *Inscription and Erasure*, pp. 142–3, and Pettitt, *Patent Inventions*, p. 299. In a sense Marx could also be accused of this as his *Capital* acknowledges the special nature of iterability only in an unpublished passage, one cited below in this section.

28. Poovey, *Genres of the Credit Economy*, p. 25. I will have to leave the thread leading to Turgot's and Goux's understandings (or misunderstandings) of coining's iterable inscription/material metal distinction for others to follow.

29. Aristotle, *Politics* 1257a. Shell's focus on the usury passage is understandable given that he is attempting to set up an analysis of Oedipus's family's complex genealogy and to establish an equation between incest and usury, specifically, by way of their conjoint practice of creating despite uncomfortably close similarity, or as Shell puts it, their conjoint appeal to the process of 'like generated from like' (see Shell, *Economy of Literature*, pp. 99–100).

30. Marx, 'Appendix', p. 1046; trans. modified. The German is this: '*ein grosser Unterschied mit Bezug auf die Bildung etc. des Reichtums, zwischen der Arbeit, die sich in reproduktiven Artikeln und andrer, die sich in blossen luxuries darstellt*' (Marx, 'Resultate des unmittelbaren Produktionsprozesses'). The English rendering of the *Resultaten*, as it is generally known, is preceded by the following headnote: '"The Results of the Direct Production Process" is part of a third draft of *Capital* which Marx wrote between the summer of 1863 and the summer of 1864, based

on a plan Marx made for the work in December 1862. This manuscript has been lost. . . . The pagination and content of this sixth chapter indicate that it followed on from five previous chapters. By the time *Capital* was completed however, this chapter had not been included' (Marx, 'Economic Works of Karl Marx'). Is it an accident, I am prompted to ask, that Marx stops thinking, and suppresses his conclusions, just at the moment when his inquiries butt up against the necessary conceptualisation of iterability? It seems clear that complicating his heretofore monolithic view of labour in this way would have involved him necessarily in a wholesale deconstruction of his philosophy all the way back to the concepts of the alienation of the worker from his or her commodity as well as from his or her labour. After all, how much of the muscle-memorised seasoned swing of the hammer of the 'old hand' at carpentry – as distinct from the apprentice's thumb-threatening frenzied flailings – can be said to be *truly* his or her own?

31. There are degrees of being repeatable, as well as repetitive. Textuality seems to represent the zero-degree definition-condition of iterability. The phrase 'mind-numbingly repetitive' when used to describe some process or other is an indication that some degree of iterability is in play: the repeated movements of certain human-performed jobs (as well as, of course, of certain robotics applications) make use to some extent or other of iterability's seemingly out-of-this-world efficiency (a transformational coming-together very much akin to the 'flashing-out' hoped for from rote learning). Design stealing, miniaturisation, copying plant adaptations – all rely to some degree on this efficiency, as do also coining (legitimate or illegitimate) and cloning, as well as procreation in its various forms. Some aspects of the last (particularly the RNA transcription process, carried on for example by the entities that Miller chooses to have exemplify what even he seems to mischaracterise as the '[implicitly wholly-material] Material Base', that is, the plants of the 'old bean field still stick[ing] out here and there in odd corners' in 1986 at the Orange County Performing Arts Center site [Miller, *Theory Now and Then*, p. 320]) are undeniably the result of the efficiency of iterability. Thus the fecund men and women Miller refers to are necessarily always already going to be vulnerable to having the revelation brought home to them that they are in part beholden for that fecundity (both literal and metaphorical) to a process they had so often previously denigrated as 'sterile'. (I thank Monica F. Cohen, Eamon P. Martin and John Maynard for reading and commenting on earlier versions of this chapter. Its writing was supported by a US Department of Education Grant provided to York College/CUNY.)

Chapter 13

J. Hillis Miller's All Souls' Day: Formalism and Historicism in Victorian and Modern Fiction Studies

Perry Meisel

Introduction

'*Bleak House*', writes J. Hillis Miller in his introduction to the Penguin edition of Dickens's novel, 'is a document about the interpretation of documents' (1971: 11). It was the moment for which we had all been waiting. We had been struggling to understand what the new criticism from France meant and how to use it in our own reading of fiction. Suddenly, everything fell into place. In one sweeping gesture, Miller's easy, avuncular remark showed us the way. No single insight could have made it clearer.

What did Miller reveal? Text and world were no longer copy and original. Narration and story, *récit* and *histoire* were now one and the same. Why? For a simple reason that changed the rules – the world itself was made up of languages. And language, by definition, was part of the world rather than its dim and fugitive reflection. It took years, however, for the consequences of this thunderclap to play out. The welcome rain came slowly, and without the aid of Bakhtin. It changed the way one read Victorian fiction, and, in a second wave of influence, it changed the way one read modern fiction.

The swell of textuality that makes the unlikely reflexiveness of Dickens's novels a template for Victorian fiction is not limited to Dickens alone. Casaubon's fruitless search for the 'key to all mythologies' in George Eliot's *Middlemarch* (1872) is, as Miller points out (1987), another *locus classicus* for the foregrounding of textuality in Victorian writing. The metaphor of reading makes the personal and the hermeneutical equivalent by virtue of the common activity of interpretation that they share. Casaubon's brutality as a husband and as a scholar who falls short of nuance in both spheres of life is Victorian fiction's most persuasive instance of what makes rudeness in one aspect of behaviour an index of cruelty in the other. Dorothea is victim in love to what makes Casaubon's intellectual project victim to a kin indecency. Casaubon's failure as an interpreter lies in his lack of fluency as a reader. Despite the theological subject of *The Key to All Mythologies*, the work of the Higher Criticism is unavailable to him because he cannot read German. It leads to his fatal universalism as an interpreter. It also leads to his failure as a husband. He cannot read Dorothea either, whose attraction to him is based on an interest in his work whose details he will not share with her. It is no surprise that her interest in architectural renovation strikes no answering chord in him. Renovation, whether intellectual or personal, is the interpretative impulse whose absence on his part dooms his work and their marriage even before the failure of his heart dooms them both.

Miller's signature insight also allows one to see that Henry James's indebtedness to Eliot proceeds from this starting point (2005). Dr Sloper's inability to understand his daughter's desires in *Washington Square* (1880) is, like Casaubon's inability to understand Dorothea, an inability to interpret as she does. James's concern with the clash of the social codes of Americans and Europeans in *Daisy Miller* (1879) or 'An International Episode' (1879) is also one that focuses on their lack of a common code of reading that underwrites their inability to understand one another. This is also what links the early, social James with the later, psychological James. Miller's reading of James as a whole regards both personal and social interaction as a series of speech acts that move and persuade one's thoughts and emotions. Its precondition is the notion that the psyche is a text. Here Miller's unexpected appreciation of Steven Marcus's edition of Freud's letters to Fliess (1977) comes into focus as entirely logical. The unconscious, too, is, to borrow Jacques Lacan's phrase, structured like a language.

Dickens and the Archive

It is customary to assign the source of Miller's reading of *Bleak House* to his shift from the early influence of Georges Poulet to the later influence of Jacques Derrida and Paul de Man. The deconstructive Miller, however, is already implicit in the phenomenological Miller of *Charles Dickens: The World of his Novels* (1958). Not only that; to read Miller's early book on Dickens in the light of his later reading of *Bleak House* is to be doubly surprised. The familiar tradition of complaint that Miller is not a historical critic of Dickens is misconceived. Not only is his phenomenological approach already structural; his presumable formalism is also historical. How does the identity of *récit* and *histoire* lead to a historical approach to fiction? One customarily regards seeing narration and story as doubles as an an infinite regress or *mise en abyme* –as two likenesses reduplicating one another forever, forsaking any referential function they may have and becoming endless, reflexive copies of themselves. Like Warhol's lithographs of historical figures such as Mao or Marilyn Monroe, historicity is presumably emptied out at the moment of its evocation. Far from being a retreat into the formal, however, the *mise en abyme* or infinite regress is actually an opening onto history. No falling away into a mysticism of textuality, it is an entrance into textuality as the archive. Foucault (1966, 1969) before the fact rather than Blanchot after the fact (1955), Miller's archive is the field of history in all its fugitive concreteness, the vortex of all the signs and their tokens left behind in the wake of time in its flight. Both specific and endlessly ungraspable, it is a reconceived resource for the critic and historian rather than a dead end.

While Dickens's fiction may seem to be a 'self-contained entity' (1958: viii), says Miller, 'it is' actually 'a better clue than any biographical data to the writer's intimate relation to the material world' (1958: ix). 'A thousand paths radiate from the same center' (1958: 14). *Pickwick Papers*, the entrance to Dickens's world chronologically, is 'a swarming' and 'simultaneous plurality' of 'centers' (1958: 13). *Bleak House*, later in Dickens's career, is the ripe fruit of this early plant, a novel that adduces plural 'perspectives from different viewpoints of a condition of reality too complex to be seen from any one perspective' (1958: 163). The doubling of *récit* and *histoire* in the novel is manifest, but it is in the service of discovering an archive, not a series of empty forms: 'Characters', chief among them the detective Mr Bucket, 'try to discover in the world an intelligible order' (1958: 167). Each character, Esther Summerson included, tries 'to put together the fragments of the world into a coherent whole' (1958: 170). 'The real detective' is 'the narrator himself, attempting . . . to discover the laws of the world he sees' (1958: 176). Jarndyce and Jarndyce is no formal model; it is a profoundly concrete one. Although it will 'never end' – indeed, 'it is the permanent condition of life in *Bleak House*' – the 'endless case . . . becomes a symbol in the novel of what it is to be in the world at all' (1958: 196). It is the very picture of the archive because it accounts for its complexity in terms of overdetermination, not closure: 'The world of *Bleak House*', says Miller, 'is a vast interlocking system in which any change or action in one place will have a corresponding and reciprocal effect on any other place' (1958: 206). Hardly a phenomenological or formalist reduction, Miller's reading employs the resources of both methods to produce something beyond them both: a model of fiction as a metatext that presents its own world as a model for discovering its plural relationships to the very real historical archives that prompt its production. The truth of this claim is played out in the subsequent history of Victorian criticism as it both accepts Miller's influence and wrestles with the anxiety it provokes.

Influence and Anxiety in Victorian Studies

Influence, as Harold Bloom reminds us, has a rocky history. It is marked not only by gratitude, but by quarrels that are not quarrels at all. They are the symptoms of indebtedness that provoke anxiety rather than gratitude. The movement of Victorian studies in fiction in the decades subsequent to Miller's reading of Dickens reveals both. It shows how prescient Miller's earliest work on Dickens is, not only in relation to his later, deconstructive handling of Dickens in the infamous introduction to *Bleak House*. It also shows how much both kinds of readings enable the historicism that presumably comes to displace deconstruction.

George Eliot is not the only major Victorian novelist who is part of the holistic paradigm for reading that Miller finds in Dickens. Walter Kendrick's definitive study of Anthony Trollope, *The Novel-Machine* (1980), reveals an equivalent identity of textuality and manners in a writer presumably immune from such reflexivity. For Kendrick, a formalist approach leads to a formalist conclusion, or so it seems. Trollope's conception of himself as a writer in his autobiography is that of a machine. He conceives of himself as an engine of production not unlike the world of industrial capitalism whose wealth and manners he represents, a world with which his writing is in point of fact identical as a project and an activity. Realism, according to Kendrick, has a surprising and unexpected precondition: 'Writing', he says, is 'prior to the representation of reality', not the other way around (1980: 3). Writing is primary, reality is secondary. Writing does not represent; it 'transmits' (1980: 4). Kendrick appears to verify the notion that Miller's formalism begets more formalism. But, as with Miller himself, Kendrick's formalism contains a surprise. It is really an implicitly historical assessment of Trollope based on a theory of writing whose referential function derives from the psychological forms that reader and writer alike share at the level of their unconscious assumptions about Victorian life. Kendrick's use of Trollope's autobiography to find these principles is not in itself psychological or historical, but the assumptions that Trollope shares with his readers are both physiological and historical in the broadest sense because they are social.

Trollope's novels do not therefore copy life. Their referentiality comes from elsewhere. They come from what Kendrick calls 'conceptions' (1980: 8) – from an archive of ideas in Trollope's mind. They are located in the novelist's imagination and in the minds of Trollope's readers. They meet in a field common to them both – an archive of assumption based on a knowledge of Victorian habit. The Archdeacon Grantly in *The Warden* (1855), for example, is not a copy of anything real, but the result of Trollope's own 'consciousness' (1980: 19). The imitation is simultaneously reflexive and realistic. The imagination copies, as it were, itself. 'Two things become identical' – the image and its representation – 'without losing their difference' (1980: 20). 'The result is duplication without imitation' (1980: 23). Trollope neither recollects nor imitates. Rather, he 'brings his two halves' – half Trollope the writer, half Trollope his own reader – 'by letting one sympathize with the other' (1980: 23). The novel exists in its prior conception and in its later reading. What is represented exists nowhere but in this relation. Writer and reader co-mingle in the archive that they both share. Novels convey reality precisely because they do not. Because life for Trollope is the life almost exclusively of the drawing-room, its set of conceptions is extraordinarily strict and delimited. No wonder Lizzy Eustace in *The Eustace Diamonds* (1873) measures her own being in a misguided relation to Shelley and to Byron (1980: 66). 'The world is structured just as the mind is' (1980: 86), not as a merely psychological principle but as a representational one. 'The world and the minds in it speak the same language' (1980: 87). 'The Trollopian mind is a sort of internal debating society', concludes Kendrick, 'containing an audience and two speakers who compete for the reader's attention' (1980: 87). Like Miller's conception of the world of Dickens, 'the structure of any particular novel is unimportant by comparison with the total structure to which each novel contributes a part' (1980: 87). Kendrick privileges *He Knew He Was Right* (1869) because it is a departure for Trollope. Its singularity exposes the methodical regularity of his other books because Louis Trevelyan's madness exposes the single real danger to the novel-machine: 'the boundless proliferation of signs that the novel is designed to contain and subjugate' (1980: 131). Here the threat of textuality to express itself and overwhelm the realist illusion reveals its endemic presence in the repression to which it is characteristically subject in Trollope's other novels. Because madness is a proliferation of signs or 'conceptions', the result is the potential exposure of the endless textuality that Trollope ordinarily makes disappear.

In this way, Trollope's realism is always based on the textuality whose control is its repressed and preponderant condition.

Even more explicit in showing the identity of world and texts is D. A. Miller's study of Victorian fiction, *The Novel and the Police* (1988). While employing Foucault's vocabulary from *Discipline and Punish* (1975) as a smokescreen, Miller the Younger is actually using Miller the Elder's approach to Victorian writing. It is not surprising that he takes Miller the Elder's reading of *Bleak House* as his polemical target. Miller the Elder's view of the novel as 'an interminable proliferation of signs' is 'decisive' (1988: 67), but this 'identification of form and content' (1988: 84) is insufficient to account for the novel's wider activity. 'The practices of the world' exceed 'the practices of representing it' (1988: 84), particularly the *mise en abyme* of textuality into which novel and world alike are thrown by the insistence upon their isomorphism or shared technical structure. 'Differentiating' the two spheres is required (1988: 84). Among the first of the New Historicist critics to employ Foucault's use of Bentham's Panopticon to explain narration in fiction, Miller the Younger exploits it to great effect. The Panopticon – the central tower in a prison occupied by a guard whose surveillance of the prisoners cannot be seen by them – is a screen onto which characters and reader like Bentham's prisoners, project their own fears and anxieties. This exposes the Victorian novel's famed morality for what it is: a system of social tyranny and fiction. Text and world are not the same. The world may employ textual practices – the control of society through duplicitous fictions – but they are not identical with narrative textuality. Narrative textuality is presumably unbiased. Mimetic rather than tendentious, transparent rather than persuasive. Textuality and the social uses of representation may be similar, but they are also distinct.

Miller the Younger gives us Wilkie Collins rather than Dickens to make his point. Far from identifying *récit* and *histoire*, Collins's *The Moonstone* (1868) separates 'the relevant signifiers from the much larger number of irrelevant ones' (1988: 33). Not everything counts, even if it requires measuring the difference between one signifier and another to do so. Sergeant Cuff, the official detective, knows this: '"I have never met with such a thing as a trifle yet"' (1988: 35). Cuff fails because the novel's strategies reach beyond the goals of detection – to the pursuit of a plot distinct from narration. There is no isomorphism between them. Textuality has as its project the discovery of an end to interpretation even though its real effect is to produce the proliferation of interpretation. Miller the Younger's distinction is no distinction at all. Instead, it leads, ironically, to an identity between the Panopticon and the novel's own narrative method – the very identity it presumably rejects.

The exclusion of the official police in *The Moonstone* introduces policing of a different order in the margins of the text. The official police become the unofficial police to be found in the psyche of the characters and in the novel's own narrative method, one which introduces unofficial policing in the reader. '*The Moonstone* dismisses the police altogether,' says Miller, 'and the mysterious crime is worked to a solution by a power that no one has charge of': the power of 'gossip and domestic familiarity', which themselves produce the effect of surveillance (1988: 49). Surveillance now occurs in 'closed clubs and houses ... The intention to detect is visible only at a microscopic level', not at a manifestly institutional one (1988: 49). The result is the creation of a new kind of institutional authority, one which, like the Panopticon, is everywhere and nowhere: a social authority produced by the effects of Collins's writing. Here narration and story are redoubled in a way that may exceed isomorphism, but which requires it in order for it to be overcome. This is how *The Moonstone* satisfies 'a double exigency: how to keep the everyday world entirely outside a network of police power and yet at the same time to preserve the effects of such power within it' (1988: 50).

The same can be said of the novel itself. Its textual strategies both identify and distinguish between the two because, like the world it represents, it is also a Panopticon. Nor is the novel, as Miller the Younger claims, a 'monological' text in Bahktin's sense (1988: 54). On the contrary, because of 'discontinuities and incoherencies' (1988: 56) – emblems of the blind alleys down which signifying chains of different authority or dialects may lead – the novel is, by definition, resolutely dialogical. Otherwise, the novel's buckshot proliferation of anxieties and the fears that prompt them would be impossible to create in either the novel's characters or in its reader. It creates them in order to control them both. Panoptical authority, by definition, exists everywhere and nowhere. Its effectiveness derives from the presence of its absence. Foucault's Benthamite device is not an empirical one but a psychological one. Its power comes not from the guard's actual surveillance of those incarcerated – whether or not there is even a guard on duty in the central tower is always an open question – but from belief that he is. Surveillance is an effect of the Panopticon's structure, not its cause. The same may be said of the role of the omniscient Victorian narrator, everywhere and nowhere at once. The narrator is an effect in which the reader believes, calculated by the text rather than by its speaker. Text and speaker are analogous to Panopticon and guard. The former creates the illusion of the latter. Their relationship may be distinct but, when all is said and done, it is also equivalent.

This is not simply the structure of Victorian narration. It is also the story Victorian fiction tells, again and again. While presumably differing from Miller the Elder's notion of narration and story, Miller the Younger reconstitutes it by means of its rejection. Miller the Younger's anxiety of influence redoubles the structure of authority that he finds at work in Collins. Miller the Elder's authority returns in a repressed form. Miller the Elder's authority functions the way authority functions in *The Moonstone*. The strategic departure of the official police has as its ironic result the return of authority in a secret way that expands rather than inhibits its effects.

D. A. Miller's early New Historicism prefigures the far more thoroughgoing materialism of later studies of the Victorian novel such as Elaine Freedgood's *The Ideas in Things* (2006). It is a fine example of the difference from Miller the Elder's pioneering work as well as its repressed continuity with it. Like D. A. Miller's, Freedgood's enabling rejection of Miller the Elder returns her to its theoretical assumptions. Like Miller the Younger, she, too, begins by claiming to move beyond the formalism of Miller the Elder, casting aside his reading of Dickens in order to do so (2006: 16–17). This allows her to return, consciously or not, to a heightened recapitulation of his enabling premise that texts are about the interpretation of texts. For Freedgood, a material approach leads to a formal one. Absorbing the influence of the New Historicism along with the influence of a reflexive reading of fiction, Freedgood's focus on 'things' shows how effective a materialist supplement to Miller the Elder's approach can be. The most microscopic details of novelistic representation are mirrors, not of an object-world, but of an object-world that is itself a world of texts and representations. They disclose their historicity because they are parts of a discursive chain that reveals the endless signatures of their productive mechanisms, particularly the production of material goods. 'Victorian novels' penchant for the representation of the emblematic hodgepodge of objects' (2006: 6), she writes, reveals an 'overdetermined material' history (2006: 5) that links the political, social, and mercantile in 'a grammar of meaning' available to the attentive reader (2006: 6). This reader becomes a historical reader, because this reader has already learned to become a formal reader trained in the belief that 'documents' are 'documents about the interpretation of documents'. A heightened formalism, as Roland Barthes once proposed, returns us to history in a fresh and vivid way.

Like D. A. Miller's, Freedgood's argument is a clearer and more extraordinary one than her polemical assertions might lead one to believe. 'Cultural knowledge is stored in a variety of institutional forms', including 'the word' (2006: 23). 'The commodity is both a material object and a trope' (2006: 27). It is symbolic because it is real and real because it is symbolic. This kind of formalism produces 'an interpretative open end of dizzying potential' (2006: 14) that allows the winds of real history to fill the novel with fresh life and lead to a new encounter with the real.

The real, of course, is implicitly redefined in the process. It is the archive to which Miller the Elder is led in his early study of Dickens. Objects in Dickens's *Great Expectations* (1861) are archives of their real histories of production, storehouses of meaning available precisely because they are texts to be interpreted. Freedgood's particular focus is the 'Negro-head tobacco' that Magwich smokes in *Great Expectations*, an object that is 'a very particular kind of memorial' because it contains the history of both aboriginal genocide in Australia and imperial consumerism as a whole (2006: 83). The London press featured mass coverage of the atrocities in Australia alongside advertisements for products whose manufacture depended on the resources of colonialism and whose protection depended on the violence of British military practice.

Negro-head tobacco is, writes Freedgood, 'a kind of unsupervised metonymic archive: a nearly infinite catalogue of compressed references to social facts' (2006: 84). The well-known and well-documented awareness in contemporary Victorian England of this history is one that the text of the novel assumes on the part of its reader. 'It was part of', says Freedgood, 'the "hubbub" of social discourse to which Dickens listened' (2006: 86). Freedgood's New Historicism is the direct result of her close formalist reading not a reaction to close reading, but its best effect. Once again, Miller the Elder's text within a text becomes the occasion for New Historicist specificity – precisely that which it presumably forecloses. What we today call 'brands' are the sign and signature of a world of texts whose literal specificity is what realist fiction represents. In a hyperbolic realist like Dickens, these accents of the real have a feverish aura and an unexpected exactitude. They complete the vision of Dickens that Miller the Elder enables.

Indeed, Freedgood's title and the method it employs constitute a broadside deconstruction of the notion of immanence and of the thing-in-itself as a category. Despite the logocentrism of Bill Brown's 'thing theory' in *A Sense of Things* (2002), Freedgood's critical practice is not only materialist, but also deconstructive. 'No ideas', says William Carlos Williams, 'but in things' (1963: 6), even as sensory entities. Things exist as ideas, but not because they are the phenomena that express the *noumena* of Platonic forms or inherent ideas. It is the other way around: Things exist as ideas because they are the tokens of the types conceived of by the production of material goods and the categories of pertinent perception, even in a pre-capitalist setting. The type/token ratio, as Umberto Eco calls it (1976), measures the way something concrete is the function of its satisfaction of the demands of a semantic inventory. A table is a table because it corresponds to the notion of what a table is. Virginia Woolf gives a familiar exemplification in *To the Lighthouse* (1927). When Lily asks what Mr Ramsay's work is about, his son Andrew advises her 'to think of a kitchen table . . . when you're not there' (1927: 38). This is not an idealist presentation of a thing-in-itself, but a presentation of the 'thing' as it is presented by Freedgood. Victorian objects, like all objects, are 'things' because they are parts of a protocol of sensory production, whether mechanical or biological. The result is a formidable critical synthesis that is both formal and concrete, synchronic and diachronic, deconstructive and historical.

In Memoriam Virginia Woolf

What lies beyond the archive? No metaphysical question, this, too, is a strictly material one. What lies beyond the archive is also what lies beyond its vortex: the ungraspable end to interpretation known as death. Here the continuity between Victorian and modern is, as it were, palpable. Without Miller to guide us, however, this palpability is evanescent and inexact. Like Jarndyce and Jarndyce, death, too, is not an end but a constant new beginning. Not the moment when there is no page left to turn, death is, like Borges's 'Book of Sand' (1975), a volume with no beginning and no end. It has new pages every time one consults it. This book of death is the archive, which, for those left behind, becomes a book of new life. Those who are left behind to mourn are the readers. Virginia Woolf is the most eloquent exemplar of this new kind of life within death.

Miller's shocking essay on *Mrs Dalloway* (1982), originally written a year before his introduction to *Bleak House* (1970), cleared away the customary assumption that the modern novel is characterised by the inner speech of its characters in favour of a radical assertion – that a novel like *Mrs Dalloway* (1925) has, like a Victorian novel, an omniscient narrator. It also gave the notion of the omniscient narrator a new weight. The omniscient narrator is not simply an observer or even an interpreter. The narrator also has an additional role – that of the mortician. *Contra* Pater, art no longer aspires to the condition of music. It aspires to the condition of film. 'It embalms time', to use André Bazin's words, 'rescuing it from its proper corruption' (1945: 14). The narrator of Woolf's novel gathers up all the novel's characters, living and dead, in a loving embrace. This is true not only of Septimus, who has committed suicide, but also of the old lady whom Clarissa observes in the window across from hers as she imagines her imminent decline as the novel concludes. This Miller calls the modern novel's funereal function as 'the raising of the dead', as he puts it in *Distance and Desire* (1970), his book on Hardy. Here the continuity between Victorian and modern fiction is made explicit in a way that not only throws special light on the modern novel, but also spells out the way the modern novel elaborates what is already at work in the nineteenth-century novel.

What Clarissa sees in the window is the continuity between herself and everything around her, living, dead and about to die. Her act of sympathy is an epistemological one. So expansive is the field of determinations within which Woolf's omniscient narrator situates Clarissa's character that character as such – discrete, individualised, specific – ceases to exist. In the very act of exalting subjectivity to its presumably most decisive moment in the history of literature, subjectivity is in point of fact disassembled. No wonder Clarissa appears to die at the novel's close. The machinery of both consciousness and its representation unpacks the coherence of both because it apprehends them both at their real moment of emergence in a social and a historical field – in an archive. This deconstructive turn in the procedure of the modern novel does not separate its achievement from the fiction of the past. It actually recapitulates the structure of the nineteenth-century novel in overdrive. The characteristic structure of the *Bildungsroman* is a double one, focusing on both the development of an individual and on the grand sweep of historical events that underwrites birth, life and death. Woolf's narrator does precisely what its precursors in Dickens or Flaubert do, revealing a continuity with them that vitiates our customary assumption that a radical break has occurred in the movement from one century to the next. This double focus is a dialectic, one that shows how the individual is a function of cultural forces and how cultural forces are processed through and by the agency of individual subjects. When Woolf expands character to the point of showing how it dissolves into the public force fields that constitute and determine it, she is simply drawing out the implicit dialectic of the *Bildungsronman* in an explicit way.

Poised between specificity and oblivion, character inhabits the archive. Once again the infinite regress of textuality is not a hollow formalism, but its very opposite. The fall into the archive is not a fall into a vacuum but into a plentitude. This for Miller is Woolf's 'All Souls' Day' (1970) – the condition of literary immortality. This literary immortality is located in the reader because the reader also is the archive. 'The reader', says Barthes, 'holds together in a single field all the traces by which the written text is constituted' (1968: 148). Generation to generation, the reader as archive is where the threads of literary memory are held together.

It is in *To the Lighthouse* that Miller's insight is played out to greatest effect. Here Virginia Woolf's own immortality is vouchsafed in an unparalleled instance of this funereal mechanism. *To the Lighthouse* registers the death of Julia Stephen in the death of Mrs Ramsay. This is the classic understanding of the novel from an autobiographical point of view. It is Woolf's way of mourning her mother, and of terminating her melancholia. The novel is an act of Kleinian reparation – a forgiving of the mother because of her imagined cruelty to the child. Because the Duckworth brothers' abuse of the young Virginia is the direct result of Julia's death – the mother is no longer there to protect the child – Woolf retrospectively blames her mother for the abuse. She is not there to protect her because she is dead. Woolf unconsciously revenges herself upon her by disrupting her wholeness in her memory. Lily's completion of her painting, as generations of critics have noted, is the sign and seal of the lifting of this revenge and the salutary closure of the daughter's depression. Mourning replaces melancholia.

After 1941, however, mourning takes on an entirely new and different status in the novel. In the light of Woolf's own death, the novel's object of mourning is no longer Julia Stephen, nor is the mourner Virginia Woolf. The mourner is now Virginia Woolf's reader and the object of mourning is Virginia Woolf herself. *To the Lighthouse* becomes a mausoleum. The plural reality to which it is subject as a book of mourning requires us to conceive of it as an archive of souls. The distance with which the reader beholds the novel as Woolf's mourning for her mother has a second kind of life when it becomes the longing the reader feels for the departed author. It gains speed as history speeds up, and it is infinitely personal because it is not personal at all. We create the woman whose death we mourn. It leads to a new kind of archive – the myth of Virginia Woolf.

Coda: *Apophrades*

Woolf's prophetic account of her own futurity returns us to Miller's prophetic role in the later history of the study of Victorian and modern fiction as a whole. His enabling recognition that texts are about texts not only opens our awareness of the novel as a form to the reflexivity of its realism, whether the social realism of Victorian fiction or the psychological realism of modern fiction. It also enables the methodology of its presumable opposite, that of the New Historicist reading of fiction. Far from a formalist criticism, Miller's criticism alerts us to the production of discourse as the key activity in both fiction's representationalism and in its represented worlds. Even more, it provides an enabling role for the reader that unlocks this daunting and endlessly provocative style of critical will. It is, moreover, a reflexive instance of what it describes. It enacts its principles in its own behaviour as criticism. All influences gather in an empyrium not unlike the return of the dead in *Mrs Dalloway* or *To the Lighthouse*. Poulet, Derrida, Iser, Barthes, Austin, Foucault, even Freud and Lacan – all come to rest in his work.

IV

Strange Pleasures

Chapter 14

The Comedian as the Letter C: Wit in *Martin Chuzzlewit*

Robert Douglas-Fairhurst

'Dickens often emphasised the comic aspect of his work,' J. Hillis Miller notes in his pioneering 1970 article, 'The Sources of Dickens's Comic Art: From *American Notes* to *Martin Chuzzlewit*', and 'To investigate the genesis of Dickens's comedy may help to identify its special qualities.'[1] In this essay I attempt to reopen some of the questions Hillis Miller first broached nearly fifty years ago. Investigating the genesis of Dickens's comedy, I will argue, involves returning to several other cultural sources, and in particular to a central mid-Victorian debate over the difference between 'wit' and 'humour', together with their collaboration – whether this is viewed as a narrative double act or as an unresolved squabble – in *Martin Chuzzlewit* (1842–4),[2] a novel that reveals some of the special qualities of Dickens's writing while threatening those very qualities at their origins.

In Edward Albee's play *Who's Afraid of Virginia Woolf* (1962), Martha tells a story about how her father once accidentally knocked her husband George into a huckleberry bush: 'It was awful, really,' she remembers. 'It was funny, but it was awful.'[3] The idea that some events might be funny *and* awful, or even funny *because* they are awful, is one that intrigued Dickens from the start of his career. The *Pickwick Papers* includes the story of an alcoholic clown who begs for money, his glassy eyes staring out from thick white greasepaint, before staggering away, only for a 'roar of laughter' to greet his next tumble onto the stage.[4] There is also the example of Joseph Grimaldi, the clown whose memoirs Dickens edited for publication in 1838, and whose life seems to have been one long comedy of errors, whether he was falling down a trap-door and continuing to perform despite being in agony, or accidentally shooting himself in the foot so that his boot 'puffed out to a great size, presenting a very laughter-moving appearance to everybody but the person in it'.⁵ Dickens's sketch 'The Pantomime of Life' (1837) goes even further in muddling together theatrical comedy and the contingencies of real life, describing a man who falls in the street and is cuffed around by a crowd of bystanders, as if the situation were merely another piece of slapstick with additional audience participation.⁶ Dickens's own attitude is rather different, because as the sketch develops there is a widening gap between the seriousness of the scene and the facetiousness with which it is described. Like that notoriously unflinching line from *The Tale of a Tub* (1704) when Swift's narrator coolly recounts how 'Last Week I saw a Woman *flay'd*, and you will hardly believe, how much it altered her Person for the worse,'⁷ Dickens affects a callous disregard for his subject in order to provoke a very different response from his readers; he tempts us into a comic unconcern and then reminds us how often we observe actual suffering with similar equanimity. As Coleridge observed in one of his notebooks: 'Poetry – excites us to artificial feelings – makes us callous to real ones.'⁸

This is also a common worry in Dickens's early fiction, where the characters who laugh loudest and longest are often those who treat the misery of other people merely as a comic interlude in their own lives. In *The Old Curiosity Shop* (1840–1), Dick Swiveller winds up some mournful reflections on being jilted with 'Ha, ha, ha!' and the narrator points out that he is following the standard model found in melodramas known as 'laughing like a fiend' – 'for it seems that your fiends always laugh in syllables', he notes, 'and always in three syllables, never more nor less'.⁹ Much the same is true of Dickens's wickedest characters, who rarely make jokes but regularly punctuate their speech with mirthless bursts of 'Ha, ha, ha!' For example, in *Oliver Twist* (1837–9) Oliver himself almost never laughs, probably because he realises that he has little to laugh about, whereas characters like Fagin and Noah Claypole prove themselves to be pure Hobbesians at heart, with each chuckle or guffaw announcing their latest triumph over human weaknesses like trust or love:

> 'Stop!' said the Jew, laying his hand on Noah's knee. 'The kinchin lay.'
> 'What's that?' demanded Mr Claypole.
> 'The kinchins, my dear,' said the Jew, 'is the young children that's sent on errands by their mothers, with sixpences and shillings; and the lay is just to take their money away – they've always got it ready in their hands, – then knock 'em into the kennel, and walk off very slow, as if there were nothing else the matter but a child fallen down and hurt itself. Ha! ha! ha!'
> 'Ha! ha!' roared Mr Claypole, kicking up his legs in an ecstasy. 'Lord, that's the very thing!'
> 'To be sure it is,' replied Fagin; 'and you can have a few good beats chalked out in Camden-town, and Battle-bridge, and neighbourhoods like that, where

they're always going errands; and you can upset as many kinchins as you want, any hour in the day. Ha! ha! ha!'

With this, Fagin poked Mr Claypole in the side, and they joined in a burst of laughter both long and loud.[10]

Their unrelentingly cheerful response to human misery reveals not just 'a momentary anaesthesia of the heart',[11] as Henri Bergson summarised the moral condition of someone who laughs at a joke, but something more like a permanent narcosis of feeling. Yet while Dickens appears to register their attitudes with careful neutrality, once again he builds little moments of resistance into his own style. For example, Fagin is frequently described as 'the merry old gentleman', and that is how he really appears to Oliver's innocent eyes, but as 'merry old gentleman' was a euphemism for the devil the phrase also allows us to see him from a more knowing angle. The result is not just irony but an expression of wit: the creation of a complex form of ethical perspective that emerges from what T. S. Eliot once described as the 'recognition, implicit in the expression of every experience, of other kinds of experience which are possible'.[12]

Of course that's not the only possible definition of wit, a word that touches on fine distinctions between many different kinds of understanding, intellect, reasoning, mental agility, capacity to entertain and more. The *OED*'s definitions work their way down several columns, subdividing at various points like a river's tributaries and obscure backwaters, before settling on popular variants such as a 'talent for saying brilliant or sparkling things, esp. in an amusing way', or 'the apt association of thought and expression, calculated to surprise and delight by its unexpectedness'.[13] Yet in practice things are rarely so straightforward. So delicately edged with ambiguity is the word that it is unusually good at creating surprises as well as describing them. Even in a single piece of writing, trying to pin down a definition of 'wit' is like putting your finger on a blob of mercury. That is why William Empson could devote an entire chapter of *The Structure of Complex Words* (1951) to Pope's 'incessant play' with this 'smart flat little word' in 'An Essay on Criticism' (1711);[14] thinking about wit means having to keep your wits about you. We might expect this to be especially true of the period when 'wit' was a topic of stringent philosophical and literary debate – roughly speaking, between the mid-sixteenth and mid-eighteenth centuries – but the aftershocks from this debate continued to ripple through the Victorian period. New linguistic compounds included 'wit-contest', 'wit-shaft' and 'wit-pointed', while as late as 1902 an anthology of extracts was published as *Wit and Wisdom from Dickens* – the sort of 'wit-gathering' (another nineteenth-century coinage) that had long been popular with readers who wanted to recall their favourite author's best moments, or were happy to let an editor do their forgetting for them. At the same time, 'wit' itself was often puzzled over by Victorian critics, usually in relation to 'humour'. Sometimes these terms were treated as synonyms or supplements of each other, whether in anthologies like Percy Fitzgerald's *Pickwickian Wit and Humour* (1903), or in the hands of reviewers who repeatedly found themselves reaching first for one word and then the other, like someone spinning a coin. In 1837, the *London and Westminster Review* suggested that 'The qualities for which every body reads and admires [Dickens] are his humour and wit'; in 1858, Walter Bagehot in the *National Review* was still praising him in the same terms: 'Writers have attained the greatest reputation for wit and humour whose whole works do not contain so much of either as are to be found in a very few pages of his.'[15] As Malcolm Andrews has pointed out,[16] other critics were keen to establish some distance between these terms. Wit signalled artfulness, archness, turning other people into the butt of our jokes: it was a quality that manifested itself chiefly in laughing at. Humour, by contrast, signalled generosity, sympathy, recognising that we are all potentially ridiculous in each other's eyes: it was a quality that manifested itself chiefly in laughing with. Some writers prioritised one, some the other; but across Dickens's lifetime there was a steady cultural drift away from wit and towards humour.

Another coinage at the start of Dickens's career – 'wit-starved' – foreshadows how many later critics would come to view his writing in particular as a triumph of heart over head, the helpless belly laugh over the controlled curl of the lip. In 1852, for example, when Thackeray lectured on 'Charity and Humour', he naturally found himself gravitating towards Dickens to support his idea that 'the best humour is that which contains most humanity, that which is flavoured throughout with tenderness and kindness'.[17] It is as if humour was really just another expression of charitable feelings, or what Carlyle had earlier and ambitiously characterised as a 'warm, tender fellow-feeling with all forms of existence'.[18] By 1872, when Forster published the first volume of his life of Dickens, describing his friend as a humorist was almost as natural a move as introducing him by name: 'Charles Dickens, the most popular novelist of the century,' he began Chapter 1, was also 'one of the greatest humorists that England has produced.'[19]

The same movement from wit to humour is also reproduced in miniature in some of Dickens's most popular works. Michael Slater has pointed out that in *A Christmas Carol* (1843) Scrooge begins by sharpening his wit against other people, as he makes sour wisecracks about gravy and the grave, or grimly tells his nephew that 'every idiot who goes about with "Merry Christmas" on his lips, should be boiled with his own pudding, and buried with a stake of holly through his heart'.[20] Only after Scrooge is reformed is he capable of producing the sort of infectious laughter that spills over and unites him with other people: 'a splendid laugh, a most illustrious laugh ... The father of a long, long line of brilliant laughs.' Put another way, Scrooge is gradually overwhelmed by the style of his own story, with its overflowing syntax and toppling lists that describe Christmas as a time of 'great, round, pot-bellied baskets of chestnuts, shaped like the waistcoats of jolly old gentlemen, lolling at the doors, and tumbling out into the street in their apoplectic opulence'; a time when people throw snowballs as if they are exchanging presents or swapping jokes, 'laughing heartily if [each one] went right and not less heartily if it went wrong.' Even the carol of the title offers a clue about the kind of story Scrooge finds himself in, because when the carol singers offer a version of 'God rest ye merry, gentlemen, Let nothing ye dismay', they could also be offering a good working definition of their own narrative, in which there are many risks to human happiness but ultimately no real cause for dismay.[21]

A similar pattern is worked into some of Dickens's longer early works, albeit in strange and subdued forms. For example, *The Old Curiosity Shop* is dominated by Quilp, a Punch-like figure who has apparently escaped from the world of knockabout comedy and is determined to make real life play by the same rules. Yet although he too is quick to laugh at the misfortunes of other people, frequently spicing up his repertoire of villainous grimaces and scowls with 'Ha, ha!' or the full melodramatic 'Ha, ha, ha!' even he cannot prevent the spirit of humour from welling up and finally winning out. Although Kit's children weep to hear about Nell's death, they soon cheer up when he tells them how her grandfather 'had been used to say "she always laughs at Kit"; at which they would brush away their tears, and laugh themselves to think that she had done so, and be again quite merry'. The moral seems plain: a world that has been split apart by malice can be healed by sociable laughter; a sense of humour is more or less equivalent to a sense of proportion.

Of course Kit's children are British, and one popular Victorian assumption was that humour was also a characteristically, if not peculiarly, British quality. It is as if the word still contained lingering traces of the 'humours' or fluids of the body, ancient associations which, as they had weakened, had spread themselves more thinly to include national as well as personal characteristics. Humour was as British as hearts of oak and joints of roast beef; it was democratic; it was at once a social lubricant and a form of social glue. When Hippolyte Taine published his

History of English Literature in 1874, he argued that the word itself was 'untranslatable in French, because in France they have not the idea', and concluded with Gallic disdain that 'Humour is a species of talent which amuses Germans, Northmen; it suits their mind, as beer and brandy suit their palate.'[22] Many British writers would have happily agreed with him. It's noticeable that Thackeray's lecture on 'Charity and Humour' was originally delivered in New York, as if he saw himself as an emissary charged with bringing the good news about good humour, and also that on Dickens's first trip to America in 1842 he singled out humour as a quality that this new country appeared to have abandoned, or perhaps not yet properly developed. 'I should think there is not, on the face of the earth, a people so entirely destitute of humour,' he told Forster. 'It is most remarkable. I am quite serious when I say that I have not heard a hearty laugh these six weeks, except my own.'[23] Indeed one way of viewing Dickens's trip would be as a quasi-anthropological encounter between wit and humour, or what he viewed as cleverness and aggression coming up against his own desire for the sort of comedy that was heartfelt, large-hearted and in every other way 'hearty'.

The standard critical view of this trip is that Dickens was disillusioned by America because, as he travelled through the country, it failed to measure up to the version he had previously mapped out in his head. As he told William Macready, 'This is not the Republic I came to see. This is not the Republic of my imagination.'[24] Often it is the little words that do the heaviest lifting in Dickens's writing, and in *American Notes* (1842) it is 'expect' and its variants that take on much of the force of his disappointment. From the fact that on the passage out there was 'less whist-playing than might have been expected', to the sad stories of emigrants who arrived in New York 'expecting to find its streets paved with gold', the word's contours of meaning gradually thicken on the page as Dickens's own hopes crumble away.[25] But of course disorientation and disappointment can also be powerful generators of comedy, from the slapstick of a clown tripping over his own shoes, to the more sophisticated surprises of a novel like *Great Expectations* (1861). Even the expectations we have about comedy can be the subject of further comedy if they are stymied or knocked off course; a good deal of laughter is provoked by what Kant memorably described as 'the sudden transformation of a strained expectation being suddenly reduced to nothing'.[26]

Dickens told one correspondent that 'I never laughed in my life as I did on this journey,'[27] and he worked hard to make America funny on his own terms. Much of this activity involved him retrieving an unexpected comic accent from within ordinary expressions such as 'Yes,

Sir', which initially he found disconcertingly strange, but with a bit of effort could be naturalised within a genre of writing where such ambiguity was more obviously at home. Towards the end of his journey, Dickens confessed that, like Sampson Brass in *The Old Curiosity Shop*, 'the still small voice is a singing comic songs within us',[28] but this comic undersong was one that accompanied him throughout his travels. As I have already suggested, comedy often involves the creation of a counterfactual world – an elsewhere; a version of the world in which things happen otherwise – where characters who run off the edge of cliffs turn to face the camera before giving a plaintive final wave, or where the seaside attracts mismatched pairings of scrawny husbands and impossibly voluptuous wives. And one of the ways Dickens responded to America was to create a parallel comic world that he liked to pretend had been lurking in the cracks of his surroundings all along.

Someone who met him in Boston recalled that after bounding into his hotel, Dickens greeted curious bystanders with Joseph Grimaldi's catchphrase: 'Here we are!'[29] It was an early clue that he had decided to view the city as a place that was as shiny and superficial as a stage set, where everything was 'so slight and unsubstantial in appearance', he later explained in *American Notes*, 'that every thoroughfare in the city looked exactly like a scene in a pantomime.' But of course Victorian pantomimes involved far more than glitzy scenery. They were also famous for their transformation scenes, where rapid costume changes and complicated sets with hidden flaps and pivots allowed a pumpkin to turn into a coach, or children to reveal themselves as fairies. As Dickens wrote in 'A Christmas Tree' (1850), pantomime was a world where 'Everything is capable, with the greatest ease, of being changed into Anything; and "Nothing is, but thinking makes it so."'[30] Having decided to view the rest of America in a similar way, Dickens set about turning his perceptions into a style.

Repeatedly, in *American Notes*, he tries to match physical movement with linguistic travel, as he invents metaphors – literally a 'carrying across' – that imagine one thing as something else. A wardrobe is so small he treats it as a shower cubicle; a wooden church is so new it looks like a packing case left in the street; the sparks from a railway engine create 'a storm of fiery snow'. Categories are conflated; boundaries are crossed and blurred. Individual words, too, sometimes take an unexpected turn. Dickens hates spitting, for example, but is fond of words like 'expectorating' or 'expectorator', which add an edge of Kantian comedy to social encounters that kept being punctuated by a shower of phlegm: strained expectations that ended in expectoration. (Given how strongly Dickens responded to spitting – it's a good example of what Forster called the 'profound attraction of repulsion' in his work – his later hymn of praise to Niagara Falls starts to look suspiciously like an attempt to wash away his earlier memories, as if trying to reassure himself that there was only one step from the ridiculous to the sublime.)[31] Other words came close to squirming free from his control entirely. 'Fix', for example, turns out to be a little model of the national character, which Dickens characterised as 'impatience of restraint' because it too is irrepressible, uncontainable. You can 'fix' yourself by dressing up, or 'fix' your enemy by giving him a dressing down; a tailor can 'fix' you some trousers, or a doctor can 'fix' you with some medicine. In fact just about the only thing that can't be fixed in America, it seems, is the meaning of 'fix'. But here too Dickens tackles his anxiety with a comic undersong, because if he pretends to be exasperated by the word's shifty qualities, he also gleefully exploits them. Take his description of a cramped coach ride:

> 'Any room, sir?' cries the new passenger to the coachman.
> 'Well, there's room enough,' replies the coachman, without getting down, or even looking at him.
> 'There an't no room at all, sir,' bawls a gentleman inside. Which another gentleman (also inside) confirms, by predicting that the attempt to introduce any more passengers 'won't fit nohow.'
> The new passenger, without any expression of anxiety, looks into the coach, and then looks up at the coachman: 'Now, how do you mean to fix it?' says he, after a pause: 'for I *must* go.'
> The coachman employs himself in twisting the lash of his whip into a knot, and takes no more notice of the question: clearly signifying that it is anybody's business but his, and that the passengers would do well to fix it, among themselves. In this state of things, matters seem to be approximating to a fix of another kind, when another inside passenger in a corner, who is nearly suffocated, cries faintly, 'I'll get out.'[32]

What such writing recognises is that a good joke is intimate with its target. Only a writer who has a sneaking admiration for such linguistic resourcefulness would be so attracted to a word that, unlike the coach, manages to accommodate the needs of so many different people without any sense of strain.

Add these examples together, and gradually the tone of *American Notes* reveals itself as an accomplished double-act, as Dickens's excited early hopes encounter the voiceover of his older, wiser self. As he explained to Thomas Mitton a few days after his arrival, 'I keep my eyes open, pretty wide,'[33] and this nicely captures the twin perspective he would later employ in his written accounts: wide-eyed with wonder, but also taking care that nothing escaped him. Later in his career, of course, he would develop a similar double-voiced discourse for narrators like Pip or David Copperfield, and in America too it allowed him to turn disillusionment into a kind of rueful comedy: smiling at American pretensions, but also smiling at himself for having once taken them at face value. It is this ability not only to make or take a joke, but to turn oneself into one, that Baudelaire would later single out as the comedian's greatest skill: 'the capacity of being himself and someone else at the same time.'[34] Or, to borrow a model Dickens knew and admired, it is the same quality Falstaff had earlier characterised as wit: 'Men of all sorts take a pride to gird at me,' he points out in *Henry IV Part 2*, but 'The brain of this foolish-compounded clay, man, is not able to invent anything that intends to laughter, more than I invent or is invented on me. I am not only witty in myself, but the cause that wit is other men.'[35]

Dickens's comic response to America shouldn't come as any great surprise. Expecting X but getting Y is a standard recipe for comedy, as several of Dickens's contemporaries pointed out, including Schopenhauer, who argued in *The World as Will and Representation* (1819) that often what makes us laugh is the difference between our subjective assumptions about the world and the objective realities against which they chafe or collapse. There's also the fact that pointing out disguises while ruthlessly stripping them away is central to Dickens's imagination. As many readers have noticed, he often constructs elaborate fictions that revolve around characters who fail to see through their own illusions, whether this is Pip telling himself one story while actually living out another, or David becoming a novelist who is blind to the romantic heroine patiently waiting under his nose. And this isn't solely a matter of plot; it's also a matter of style. In his preface to *Bleak House* (1852–3) Dickens pointed out that he had 'purposely dwelt upon the romantic side of familiar things',[36] but in much of his fiction he proves to be equally good at exposing the familiar side of romantic things, as he punctures illusions and brings high-flown rhetoric crashing back down to earth. Sometimes these attitudes are pinned onto a character as a scapegoat, but more often they involve Dickens mocking his own most cherished ideals, as if he was unable to catch sight of himself looking serious without wanting to pull a funny face. The result is a style of narrative in which each page behaves like a warped carnival mirror, reflecting not only the world outside the novel, but other pages of the same text.

How does this work in practice? One way of thinking about the surprise that accompanies a joke is that it can encourage us to think more carefully about the values it is poking fun at. Take jokes about selfishness; for example: 'I'm really worried about my parrot. He keeps saying, "I can't go on, I hate my life." My husband's far too selfish to notice. He just sits in a corner crying'; or: 'My wife just called me selfish, which completely ruined my 10th wedding anniversary.' Most people feel that selfishness is wrong, and jokes like these explore a wide range of possible responses towards such feelings, from covert celebrations to appalled parodies. Such flexibility is typical of a comic response to complex situations. Paolo Virno has argued that 'Every joke puts into focus ... the variety of alternatives that come forth in applying a norm,'[37] and this applies even to jokes about people who seem unable to imagine how the world looks from someone else's point of view. Put crudely, jokes about selfishness ask us to adopt a distinctly unselfish attitude if we are to find them funny. But of course the notion of a 'variety of alternatives that come forth in applying a norm' can also be central in much longer narrative forms.

It has become traditional to praise *Martin Chuzzlewit* as one of the funniest of Dickens's novels. Some critics have gone even further: for R. C. Churchill, it is 'the greatest work of comic genius in the whole of English literature';[38] for A. E. Dyson, it is 'the funniest book in the language'.[39] Dickens's intentions were clear from the outset. Much attention has focused on the list of names he drew up as he sought the right grammatical texture for his title, trying out Martin Chuzzlwig, Martin Chubblewig, Chuzzletoe and Chuzzlebog, and then Martin Chuzzlewig, Martin Sweezleden, Martin Chuzzletoe, Martin Sweezleback and Martin Sweezlewag, before finally settling on Martin Chuzzlewit (724). A 'sweezle' or 'swizzle' is a swindle, as in the old schoolboy expression 'what a swizz', and several critics have pointed out that 'chuzzle' is another slang term meaning to cheat or defraud, pushing the name of the main character closer to the sort of thing one might expect to find in a Restoration comedy. As for why the hero is named Martin Chuzzle*wit*, that is probably because there are in fact two characters with this name in the novel. The title therefore singles out an individual and doubles him up, and so sets the tone for a novel that, as John Bowen has pointed out, is full of uncanny doubles and secret selves.[40]

These figures include Montague Tigg, who reverses his name and reinvents himself as Tigg Montague, like someone looking in a mirror; Mrs Gamp, who has a 'twofold profession' (363), carries her imaginary friend Mrs Harris around inside her like an invisible twin, and in her second-hand coat looks as if she's being embraced from behind by its original owner; General Scadder, who is literally two-faced, with an immoveable and sightless eye that seems to be coldly observing what the other side of his face is up to; and Jonas Chuzzlewit, who is 'not only fearful *for* himself but *of* himself' (619) after his crime, and half expects when he returns home to find himself asleep in bed. There are also many smaller examples of the same narrative tendency. From the 'double eye-glass' (11) owned by Pecksniff, to the fact that Mrs Prig has a deep voice and a beard, almost nothing in *Martin Chuzzlewit* is straightforwardly singular. Language too frequently doubles up, whether it is investigating the punning potential of terms such as 'capital' and 'credit', being mashed together in portmanteaux words, or creating gleeful parodies as literary equivalents of the novel's many human parasites. There is also a tendency for the narrative to multiply itself through repetition, reminding us that if 'Nothing propagates so fast' (255) as change then language rarely lags far behind. Unsurprisingly, the worst offender is Pecksniff, who treats words rather as he treats other people, by pretending to linger seductively over them while really trying to bully them into compliance. '*Have* I influence with our venerable friend, do you think,' he asks Mary, 'Well, perhaps I have. Perhaps I have,' before his mask slips to reveal the creepy erotic charge that lies behind his refusal to leave words alone: 'You will consent, my love; you will consent, I know. Whatever you may think; you will' (416–17).

Yet for a supposedly comic novel, it's remarkable how many jokes fall flat or appear to emerge by accident, as when Mrs Gamp confides that Mr Mould the undertaker 'has undertook the highest families in this land' (272), or how often characters express amusement in a way that is singularly free from comedy. Repeatedly, figures like Montague Tigg or Pecksniff break out with a 'Ha! Ha! Ha!' that is about as funny as a rash. As young Martin points out, 'There is a sort of jesting which is very much in earnest, and includes some pretty serious disgust' (205). In fact, for much of the novel it appears that, in order for the plot to go right, comedy has to go wrong. Sometimes the basic ingredients are present but misapplied, like someone who takes a pizza base, mozzarella cheese and tomato sauce and tries to assemble them into a type of novelty breakfast cereal. For example, a surprising amount of attention is given to red noses – one sentence contains no fewer than five references (52) – but usually in the context of petty quarrels rather than clowning. There is some lively confusion of the animate and inanimate, or what Bergson refers to as the comic principle of 'something mechanical encrusted on the living',[41] as when Jonas hears a strange noise and remarks 'Something wrong in the clock, I suppose' (262), but this humorous potential too is quickly squashed when the noise turns out to be his father suffering a stroke. At other times, jokes are drawn out so long they become the cover for private obsessions:

> 'Hollow *elm* tree, eh?' said Mr Mould, making a slight motion with his legs in his enjoyment of the joke. 'It's beech in the song. Elm, eh? Yes, to be sure. Ha, ha, ha! Upon my soul, that's one of the best things I know!' He was so excessively tickled by the jest that he couldn't forget it, but repeated twenty times, 'Elm, eh? Yes, to be sure. Elm, of course. Ha, ha, ha! Upon my life, you

know, that ought to be sent to somebody who could make use of it. It's one of the smartest things that ever was said. Hollow *elm* tree, eh? Of course. Very hollow. Ha, ha, ha!' (346)

The more often characters burst out with 'Ha, ha, ha!' the more hollow their laughter sounds: a hollow that is good at creating echoes but is increasingly excavated of meaning. In particular, Jonas Chuzzlewit is a great laugher, and like his precursors in the earlier novels, what he laughs at is primarily his ability to triumph over other people. Presumably that is why his first action on marrying a character called Merry is systematically to destroy her sense of humour. From laughing at everything she ends by laughing at nothing, a sad demonstration of the truth contained in her father's warning: 'Let us take heed how we laugh without reason, lest we cry with it' (14).

As for why comedy too takes such a beating in the novel, one clue is provided by a repeated slippage in Mrs Gamp's speech from 'just' to 'jest', as when she explains that her patient Mr Chuffey is 'jest as usual' (349), or recalls how Mrs Harris 'jestly says to me, but t'other day' (398). It is like a keyhole into a world where almost nothing is quite what it seems, and where some people have apparently mistaken comic attitudes for acceptable kinds of moral behaviour. If this sounds reminiscent of *A Christmas Carol*, it is worth recalling that Dickens wrote the two works side by side; and just as Martin goes off to America, so Dickens seems to have enjoyed creating another kind of double plot, by echoing many of the situations of his novel in his Christmas story. For example, the instalment of *Martin Chuzzlewit* that he published in October 1843 contains the episode when Mrs Gamp pinions the arms of her patient to his sides to see what he would look like if he were dead. The same month Dickens described Scrooge lying in bed and being shown what it would be like if he were to die. Put the scenes side by side, and it seems that Dickens too enjoyed the challenges of a 'twofold profession'.

The clearest example of comedy going wrong is the character of Pecksniff. We are introduced to him with a piece of slapstick, although because he takes himself so seriously he is unable to see the joke:

> The scared leaves ... got into unfrequented places, where there was no outlet, and where their pursuer kept them eddying round and round at his pleasure; and they crept under the eaves of houses, and clung tightly to the sides of hay-ricks, like bats; and tore in at empty chamber windows, and cowered close to hedges; and, in short, went anywhere for safety. But the oddest feat they achieved was, to take advantage of the sudden opening of Mr Pecksniff's front-door, to dash wildly into his passage; whither the wind following close upon them, and finding the back-door open, incontinently blew out the lighted candle held by Miss Pecksniff, and slammed the front-door against

Mr Pecksniff who was at that moment entering, with such violence, that in the twinkling of an eye he lay on his back at the bottom of the steps. Being by this time weary of such trifling performances, the boisterous rover hurried away rejoicing, roaring over moor and meadow, hill and flat, until it got out to sea, where it met with other winds similarly disposed, and made a night of it. (8)

It is like a miniature version of the novel as a whole, in which selfishness is defeated by generosity, and high spirits overwhelm high seriousness. By the end even the public fountain gets in on the act: 'Brilliantly the Temple Fountain sparkled in the sun, and laughingly its liquid music played, and merrily the idle drops of water danced and danced' (698). Interestingly, a fountain was also Thackeray's metaphor for humour in his lecture on 'Charity and Humour', where he suggested that it is humour that 'bids the fountain gush and sparkle',[42] and both writers consider humour to be primarily a sociable quality; both realise that sharing a joke is one of the most revealing kinds of social interaction you can have that doesn't involve taking your clothes off.

In some ways, *Martin Chuzzlewit* might therefore be viewed as another example of humour putting wit in its place. Yet when Dickens tried to explain how he wrote, he suggested that he could 'fancy or perceive relations in things which are not apparent generally', and although Forster interpreted this as one of the 'exquisite properties of humour',[43] it sounds far more like a definition of wit. Compare Leigh Hunt: 'Wit is the clash and reconcilement of incongruities,' he writes in 'An Illustrative Essay on Wit and Humour' (1846), 'the meeting of extremes round a corner; the flashing of an artificial light from one object to another, disclosing some unexpected resemblance or connection.'[44] *Martin Chuzzlewit* is full of narrative meetings where the light from one passage flashes unexpectedly across another. Thus Mary Graham is described as 'composed' (424) a few chapters after Mr Mould 'compose[s] his features' to look professionally sorrowful (276), and both episodes reflect strangely on the flimflam of American newspapers, which boast of drawing from 'the well of Truth, whose waters are black from being composed of printers' ink' (226). At one end of the novel, Merry Pecksniff is dismissed as 'a gushing thing' (10); at the other, Ruth Pinch meets John's confession of love with 'gushing tears of joy, and hope, and pride, and innocent affection' (700), which is so sympathetic a description it risks sounding equally gushing. Strangest of all, Pecksniff and the narrator appear to have read the same rhetorical handbooks:

'Old Tom Pinch!' said Mr Pecksniff, looking on him with affectionate sadness. 'Ah! It seems but yesterday that Thomas was a boy fresh from a scholastic course. Yet years have passed, I think, since Thomas Pinch and I first walked the world together!' (72)

> And that mild figure seated at an organ, who is he? Ah Tom, dear Tom, old friend!
> Thy head is prematurely grey, though Time has passed thee and our old association, Tom. But, in those sounds with which it is thy wont to bear the twilight company, the music of thy heart speaks out; the story of thy life relates itself. (715)

How are we supposed to interpret these 'unexpected resemblances or connections'? In *Knowing Dickens* (2007), Rosemarie Bodenheimer helpfully lists some possible strategies; helpful not just in themselves, but also because she offers them in the form of questions, which remind us that this is also what each part of a novel like *Martin Chuzzlewit* represents: a silent question to which the other parts offer various forms of reply, retort or reproof. When we read a passage like 'Ah Tom, dear Tom, old friend,' with its awkward echo of Pecksniff, Bodenheimer asks,

> Is it unintentional self-parody? Conscious ambiguity? Self-knowledge, or self-critique? Is it a defensive flight from emotional investment, or a self-protective ironic shield against critical attack? Is it Dickens's comedic instinct revenging itself on his Victorian piety? Is it simply that Dickens believed in whatever he wrote at the moment?[45]

Other critics have tended to narrow down this range of options. For John Carey, Dickens's comic episodes were a kind of vandalism he enacted on the serious parts of his plots; for G. K. Chesterton, while Dickens believed in whatever was at the end of his pen from one moment to the next, laughter was the only way he could approach whatever he took seriously.[46] However, there is a slightly different way of thinking about Dickens's narrative shifts and swerves in *Martin Chuzzlewit*, and we can approach it through another imaginary voyage to America: Wallace Stevens's 'The Comedian as the Letter C'.[47]

'Can one man think one thing and think it long?' Stevens asks towards the end of his poem; 'Can one man be one thing and be it long?' The joke is that his own language is everything by turns and nothing long, as 'think' gives way to 'thing', then reverts to 'think', and finally settles on 'thing' again, like a weathercock revolving in a gale. But the idea itself is straightforward enough. To engage in such self-revision is not only to be a comedian, in Stevens's sense of the word; it is primarily an exercise in wit. To borrow another line from the poem, it is the writer's acknowledgement of 'the unavoidable shadow of himself' that is cast across the page in the act of composition and is then permanently fixed in print. For Dickens this manifests itself in various ways. It can be seen in the double plots and other structural devices that show how one life finds echoes in many others. It can be seen in characters like John Westlock, who does not have 'the least objection to laugh at himself' after gravely telling the waiter that the wine he has ordered is 'a pretty tidy vintage' (172), or Ruth Pinch, who asks Tom whether he minds if the pudding she is planning to make should turn out to be 'a stew, or a soup, or something of that sort', and then breaks into 'a merry laugh at her own expense' (514). Finally, it can be seen in Dickens's willingness to put the underlying genre of his own writing at risk. The final illustration nicely captures the vulnerability of a scene that draws on the conventions of melodrama, yet also shows how easily melodrama can topple over into farce (Fig. 14.1).

Figure 14.1 Warm reception of Mr Pecksniff by his venerable friend.

Perhaps that is why Martin appears to be holding a real stick that is also a slapstick, and why some of the witnesses to this moment seem unable to keep a smile off their faces. It is as if they have worked out how easily one kind of story can become something rather different. 'Turn and turn about' (665), as Mrs Gamp says; 'Turn and turn about.'

Notes

1. Miller, 'The Sources of Dickens's Comic Art', p. 467.
2. All subsequent page references are to the Oxford World's Classics edition (1984, repr. 1998), which reprints the text of the definitive Clarendon Press edition ed. Margaret Cardwell (Oxford: Clarendon Press, 1982).
3. Edward Albee, *Who's Afraid of Virginia Woolf?* (1962, repr. New York: Scribner Classics, 2003), p. 57.
4. Dickens, *The Pickwick Papers*, ed. James Kinsley, p. 34.
5. Dickens, *Memoirs of Joseph Grimaldi*, p. 135.
6. Repr. in Dickens, *Dickens's Journalism*, vol. 1: 500–7.
7. Swift, *A Tale of a Tub and Other Satires*, p. 109.
8. Coleridge, *Coleridge's Notebooks: A Selection*, p. 3.
9. Dickens, *The Old Curiosity Shop*, p. 432.
10. Dickens, *Oliver Twist*, pp. 291–2.
11. Bergson, *Laughter*, p. 5.
12. T. S. Eliot, 'Andrew Marvell', p. 170.
13. *OED*, 'wit', 7 and 8a.
14. Empson, *The Structure of Complex Words*, p. 84.
15. Repr. in Collins, *Charles Dickens: The Critical Heritage*, pp. 55, 407.
16. Andrews, *Dickensian Laughter*, pp. 19–23; see also Martin, *The Triumph of Wit*.
17. Thackeray, 'Charity and Humour', p. 196.
18. Carlyle, 'Jean Paul Friedrich Richter', p. 16.
19. Forster, *The Life of Charles Dickens*, vol. 1: 3.
20. Slater, 'The Triumph of Humour'.
21. Dickens, *A Christmas Carol, and other Christmas Books*, pp. 11, 78, 46, 15.
22. Taine, *History of English Literature*, vol. 3: 299.
23. To John Forster, 24 and 26 April 1842, *The Pilgrim Edition of the Letters of Charles Dickens*, vol. 3: 208.
24. To W. C. Macready, 2 March 1842, *Letters*, vol. 3: 156.
25. Dickens, *American Notes*, pp. 18, 245.
26. Kant, *The Critique of Judgement*, p. 199.
27. To C. C. Felton, 31 December 1842, *Letters*, vol. 3: 415.
28. To David C. Colden, 29 April 1842, *Letters*, vol. 3: 218.
29. Collins, *Dickens: Interviews and Recollections*, vol. 2: 305.
30. Dickens, *Household Words* 39 (21 December 1850), p. 292.
31. Forster, *The Life of Charles Dickens*, vol. 1: 11.
32. Dickens, *American Notes*, p. 124.
33. To Thomas Mitton, 31 January 1842, *Letters*, vol. 3: 43.

34. Baudelaire, *Selected Writings on Art and Literature*, p. 160.
35. *Henry IV Part 2*, I.ii.
36. Dickens, *Bleak House*, p. 6.
37. Quoted in Bevis, *Comedy: A Very Short Introduction*, p. 4.
38. 'Charles Dickens', in Ford, *A Guide to English Literature*, p. 120.
39. A. E. Dyson, '*Martin Chuzzlewit*: Howls the Sublime', *Critical Quarterly* 9:3 (September 1967), p. 234.
40. Bowen, *Other Dickens: Pickwick to Chuzzlewit*, ch. 7: 'The Genealogy of Monsters: *Martin Chuzzlewit*'.
41. Bergson, *Laughter*, p. 37.
42. Thackeray, 'Charity and Humour', p. 202.
43. Forster, *The Life of Charles Dickens*, vol. 2: 273.
44. Hunt, *Wit and Humour*, p. 9.
45. Bodenheimer, *Knowing Dickens*, p. 35.
46. See Carey, *The Violent Effigy* and Chesterton, *Charles Dickens: A Critical Study*.
47. Quotations are taken from the text published in Wallace Stevens, *Collected Poems* (2006), pp. 23–41.

Chapter 15

Dickens's Theatre of Shame
James Eli Adams

'Lord, Lord – to think of it – it's as good as a play! As good as a play!' So an elderly woman in Chapter 5 of *Oliver Twist* responds to, of all things, the body of her daughter, who has just died of starvation (48). The hysteria informing this 'hideous merriment', as the narrator calls it, brings home the brutalising effects of poverty in the world of Dickens's novel. But it also foregrounds the pervasiveness of theatre and theatricality in Dickens's writing. Of course that preoccupation has hardly been overlooked; indeed, it has been so widely recognised that it might organise an entire history of Dickens's critical reception. One particularly suggestive episode in such a history would be J. Hillis Miller's 1971 essay, 'The Fiction of Realism', a telling moment in his move away from the phenomenology of his early work towards an engagement with deconstruction. In Miller's account, the pervasiveness of theatrical reference in *Sketches by Boz* and *Oliver Twist* drives home the figurality of Dickens's realism, and – more generally – exemplifies 'literature as a use of language which exposes its own rhetorical devices and assumptions' (147).[1] Curiously, however, even as Miller insists that 'All language is beside itself. There is no "true" sign for the thing', his ostensibly deconstructive account repeatedly invokes an idea of *authenticity*, a realm of experience somehow outside the subversive play of language, and a fundamental ground for gauging its effects. The characters of *Sketches* are 'hopelessly imprisoned within the cells of a fraudulent culture' (139), their theatricality a mode of 'inauthentic repetition' in which 'Character after character ... is shown pretending to be what he is not'. A 'fundamental theme of the *Sketches*' is '[t]he imprisonment of the human spirit in its conferring of meaning' (139). It is not obvious how the appeal to an authentic culture or true identity or spiritual freedom can be reconciled with the strenuous skepticism informing the conclusion, 'all language is beside itself'.

The persistence of this familiar humanistic vocabulary in Hillis Miller's criticism, as in much of American deconstruction, would be a rich topic in its own right. But I want to make the narrower case that this tension in Miller's argument reproduces a tension in Dickens's own preoccupation with theatricality. Theatricality in Dickens in fact has a powerfully mimetic function, inasmuch as it foregrounds an inescapable dimension of everyday social exchange. Far from constituting 'a deformation in Boz's mirroring of the "real" London' (134) Boz's attention to theatre amplifies the theatricality of the quotidian. Social life is structured by a host of conventions that function like scripts for various situations, defining roles which for the most part we perform mechanically, unreflectively. But on occasion, the scripts of social life can become objects of acute self-consciousness: when we are in unfamiliar settings, when the appropriate public role seems unusually at odds with private feeling, or when we see an opening to exploit conventions to advance our own interests in new ways. Sometimes we may even feel that our speech and actions shade into the projection of an idealised self, or an effort to impersonate another being. It is in this light that theatricality in Dickens is so often associated with figures of social mobility.

This dramaturgic understanding of social exchange has been most influentially developed in the work of the sociologist Erving Goffman, notably in *The Presentation of Self in Everyday Life*. As Goffman puts it,

> ordinary social intercourse is put together as a scene is put together, by the exchange of dramatically inflected actions, counteractions, and terminating replies. Scripts even in the hands of unpracticed players can come to life because life itself is a dramatically enacted thing. All the world is not, of course, a stage, but the crucial ways in which it isn't aren't easy to specify. (72)

It's not hard to see the powerful resonance of such theatrical dynamics in Dickens's fiction. But the paradigm carries an unsettling implication, akin to the deconstructive conclusions of Miller's argument. The dramaturgic exchange as Goffman understands it gives us no access to an essential self in the social agents involved:

> A correctly staged and performed scene leads the audience to impute a self to a performed character, but this imputation – this self – is a product of the scene that comes off, and is not a cause of it. The self, then, as a performed character, is not an organic thing that has a specific location, whose fundamental fate is to be born, to mature, and to die; it is a dramatic effect arising diffusely from a scene that is presented, and the characteristic issue, the crucial concern, is whether it will be credited or discredited. (253)[2]

Human character is thus reduced to sheer externalised convention – a 'peg on which something of collective manufacture will be hung for a time'. This reduction appears as a recurrent background effect in Dickens's fiction, notably in images of human beings as mere mechanisms, such as the lawyers in *Bleak House* leaping up and down like piano keys. Such figures clearly serve as foils to constructions of more substantive, autonomous selfhood in Dickens's major characters. But how might Dickens's writing convey that sense of selfhood as an effect in itself enacted and dramatic, something more than narrative assertion?

Dickens's discomfort with the theatricality he so insistently represents is brought home, I will suggest, in repeated representations of disrupted or failed theatricality, which are bound up with the experience of shame. Throughout his fiction, a character's shame is manifested in the rupture of performance, whether as conscious repudiation of a role or as an abrupt loss of composure, the faltering of self-possession before an audience, which undercuts the authority of a performed identity by suggesting the presence of a contending identity or perspective. In such moments, shame is manifested as a public spectacle that enables an audience to recognise social performance as such; it enforces a reassuring distinction between a performing self and a separate, more authentic self behind the role.

Moments of failed or thwarted performance are particularly notable in Dickens's representations of fallen women, where they have the further appeal of suggesting an ongoing moral awareness that seems effaced by their outward degradation. Dickens's prostitute is recognisable first and foremost as a spectacle, whose debasement tends to be registered by her comfort in, or at least disregard for, a sense of being observed. A faltering of composure, by contrast, expresses a sense of shame, which insinuates the persistence of an essentially 'feminine' conscience, and with it the prospect of moral redemption. Dickens rehearses this contrast from the outset of his career, in *Sketches by Boz*, where the repeated juxtaposition of 'hardened' and 'anguished' women clearly derives from the conventions of stage melodrama. In *Sketches*, however, the prospective moral reform signalled by shame is repeatedly disabled by a seemingly irresistible arc of downward mobility. That narrative clearly works to contain the threatening sense of sexual 'contagion' embodied in such compromised figures, even as it evokes a pathos so essential to the appeal of melodrama. In *Oliver Twist*, however, novelistic structure allows Dickens to develop this juxtaposition into a more sustained exploration of the theatre of shame, in which moments of arrested or failed performance convey something more than an ideal of feminine purity redeemed through suffering. Such moments also become vehicles of uneasiness about the sheer pervasiveness of performance in everyday life: anxieties not only about the challenge of recognising such performance, but also about the power of social convention to constrain human agency and the capacity for self-determination.

I

The sense of theatricality that pervades Dickens's work is especially vivid, and potentially most disconcerting, in the arena of social mobility, which embraces both the ambition to ascend and the fear of falling. Of course there is nothing new about – as Boz puts it in 'London Recreations' – 'the wish of persons in the humbler classes of life, to ape the manners and customs' of those above them (*Sketches* 115): witness Malvolio, among countless other aspiring spirits from early modern drama onwards. But Dickens registers with special force the newly dynamic social order of nineteenth-century Britain, where a pervasive sense of potential mobility gave new urgency to social life as an arena of performance, and to the social utility of adept self-presentation and 'impression management', in Goffman's phrase – along with the corresponding challenge of distinguishing true from feigned identity. That challenge assumes comic form in 'Horatio Sparkins', one of the earliest of the *Sketches by Boz*, from February 1834. Young Sparkins impresses the newly affluent Malderton family as 'the most gentleman-like man' they have ever met, but his 'theatrical air' turns out to be just that (409, 415). Horatio Sparkins, they discover, is a fictional identity, a role written and performed by one Samuel Smith, the assistant at a 'cheap shop'. Of course the sketch deflates the pretensions of the credulous Maldertons, whose snobbery expresses their deep insecurity in their new but brittle social distinction. At the same time, the sketch flatters readers who have sensed the imposture from the beginning and can thereby feel reassured of their own social understanding, which is that of a spectator well-versed in the conventions of both the theatre and the drawing-room.

In both regards, however, the sketch contains a more unsettling possibility: that social performance might be difficult to recognise, that the distinction between person and role, true and feigned identity, might even be fundamentally insecure. Might it be that every self is a performing self, and that the forms of recognition that we solicit and extend in organising social life are grounded less in morality than in theatricality? The world at large might in this sense be suspected of what Fagin so fears in Nancy: 'deep play', understood not merely as treachery, but as sustained performance so dexterous that it unsettles one's confidence in distinguishing between true and false. This unsettling prospect will of course engage Dickens on a larger scale later in his career, as it will a host of Victorian novelists fascinated by financial fraud and assumed identities. In his early writing, Dickens attends to the disappointment of more limited ambitions, of a kind affiliated with the world of Samuel Smith. Tellingly, we learn nothing more of Smith's actual identity than his bare name and occupation – in keeping with Boz's focus on satirical observation. But one can imagine the sketch recast in a very different perspective, perhaps under the title 'Samuel Smith', as a story in which Smith's aim to impress is constantly shadowed by fear of exposure, which brings with it the possibility of shame. Once again exposure would reinforce the social order, would indeed only weld the aspiring performer more tightly to the social niche he dreamed of escaping. But this alternative perspective, as it brings home the pathos of frustrated ambition, would also reinforce the moral distinctions that the virtuoso performer puts into question. The failed performance, that is, as it arouses a sense of shame, registers awareness of a distinction between moral and social identity, between a performing self and a true self.

Sketches rarely foregrounds the challenges of recognising a deceptive theatricality. But theatrical self-presentation is a central burden of Boz's well-nigh mesmerised fascination with the prostitute as a public spectacle. That theatricality is brought home in a persistent doubling of such figures, in which a 'hardened' comfort with, or oblivion to, one's audience is set against an anguished loss of composure. Occasionally the contrast is captured backstage, as it were, in figures unaware they are being observed. In 'A Visit to Newgate', for example, the narrator catches sight of an old, impoverished woman – 'it is impossible to imagine a more poverty-stricken subject' – in conversation with a younger woman, presumably her daughter, 'a good-looking robust female, with a profusion of hair streaming about in the wind – for she had not a bonnet on'. That wind-blown hair is a sure emblem of moral abandon, which is confirmed when the younger woman is 'perfectly unmoved' at her mother's expression of 'mental anguish'. 'Hardened beyond all hope of redemption', the daughter 'took no more apparent interest in the conversation than the most unconcerned spectators' (237). The contrast between the hardened and the anguished is more overtly theatrical in another sketch, 'The Prisoner's Van', where the first prisoners to emerge from the van are two teenage prostitutes, apparently sisters, 'though two additional years of depravity had fixed their brand upon the elder girl's features as legibly as if a red-hot iron had scarred them' – again Dickens's vehement sense of moral degradation is something legible in the very countenance. More telling, though, 'It is impossible to conceive a greater contrast than the demeanour of the two presented. The younger girl was weeping bitterly – not for display or in the hope of producing effect, but for very shame; her face was buried in her handkerchief' – whereas her sister banters with the crowd 'with a flaunting laugh' (316). The experience of shame, expressed in a recoil from performance or 'producing effect', is underscored by contrast with a 'flaunting' appeal to an audience.

We might expect that 'weeping bitterly ... for very shame' would signal a prospect of moral redemption. But the narrator foretells no escape: 'What the younger girl was then, the elder had been once; and what the elder then was, she must soon become. A melancholy prospect, but how surely to be realised: a tragic drama, but how often acted!' Shame encourages the possibility that the 'hardened' demeanour of the prostitute is itself merely a performance, and thus leaves an opening for some authentic self to crowd it aside into a life of repentance and even reform.[3] But here the spasm of moral awareness seems to have no effect beyond the moment, at least to the fallen themselves. Nothing, it seems, can arrest their descent; indeed, the contrast seems to accelerate that trajectory, as Miller and many other readers have pointed out. That sense of irresistible decline would become central to an emergent social discourse of prostitution, as in William Tait's *Magdalenism* (1840): 'The general law in regard to them appears to be, like that of gravitation, always pressing downwards ... till they sink into the lowest state of degradation into which it is possible for a human being to fall' (Nead 145–6). As an account of social and moral 'gravitation', it might seem that narrative itself subdues the dangers bound up with the prostitute.

The experience of shame thus might seem to mollify fears of the prostitute as a social threat, locus of a manifold 'contagion', both by framing her existence as narrowly self-destructive, and perhaps, as Lynda Nead points out, thereby absorbing the figure into a victimhood that might elicit readerly compassion and philanthropy (138–9). Yet Dickens's early writing rarely aligns the prostitute with a larger sense of social danger (that association becomes prominent in cultural discourse only in the 1840s, when it clearly informs *David Copperfield*). In framing Tait's 'gravitation' as a 'tragic drama', Dickens instead focuses attention on individual stigma and suffering, within which shame might offer consoling evidence of the resilience of human conscience, as well as our own capacity as readers to sympathise with the woman's moral struggle, or even a colder, more narrowly aesthetic pleasure in suffering as a spectacle of exquisite pathos. (These representations of moral awareness as a form of public spectacle tend to elide the distinction between shame and guilt; both are forms of moral distress understood in relation to an audience.) But all of these appeals seem bound up with the fascination of an imagined surrender to external forces – 'fascination' as the experience of a profound ambivalence, as in 'the fascination of repulsion' that Dickens attributes to Rosa Bud in *The Mystery of Edmund Drood*.

That fascination seems aroused by a radically abridged sense of agency, a sense of imprisonment by, or surrender to, external forces. In *Tainted Souls and Painted Faces*, Amanda Anderson has argued that the figure of the prostitute has a special appeal to the novelist in this regard: the figure is an epitome of social determination, against which other characters might seem to accrue by contrast a fuller agency and freedom. And yet, Anderson notes, the fallen character also 'reminds the author that he can never fully own himself, and that his *own* history, as well as the story that he tells about that history, is determined by a number of forces beyond his control' (11). That susceptibility to external forces pervades *Sketches* in versions of a falling away from earlier prosperity or contentment – often brought about, ironically, through the forces of 'improvement.'[4] The life of the prostitute captures a vividly foreshortened, melodramatic version of this decline, which is condensed in the moment of shame.

This function is most fully elaborated in 'The Pawnbroker's Shop', which presents a sequence of women at various stages on the road to ruin; as several critics have remarked, the sketch might be dubbed, with a nod to Hogarth, 'The Harlot's Progress'. The stages on that descent are registered, tellingly, in relation to an audience, real or imagined. Customers of 'habitual acquaintance' are 'indifferent to the observation of their companions in poverty', whereas 'the more timid or respectable [. . .] shroud themselves from the notice of the remainder' (224) – a distinction brought home in Cruickshank's illustration for the sketch. Among that latter group, concealed from wider view in a 'box' in 'the darkest and most obscure corner of the shop', are a mother and daughter, 'struggling to avoid the observation even of the shopman'. Despite their outward respectability, their descent is well under way: they are pawning sentimental trinkets, 'parted with now without a struggle, for want has hardened the mother, and her example has hardened the girl . . . And the prospect of receiving money coupled with a recollection of the misery they have both endured from the want of it . . . appears to have obliterated the consciousness of self-humiliation which the bare idea of their present situation would once have aroused' (228). Here is Dickens's characteristic rhetoric of fallen women as 'hardened', disfigured by a moral coarsening that can be read in their appearance, which expresses a state of mind in which 'consciousness of self-humiliation' has been 'obliterated'.

But how is pawning a possession something akin to prostitution? Why not read their conduct as a brave, stoic effort to cope with unhappy circumstance? The answer, I think, is that the women have already been pulled into an irresistible social descent, which leads inexorably to prostitution, and their lives bear the mark of that looming stigma. They have not always been poor: the 'misery' they have endured involves 'the coldness of old friends – the stern refusal of some and the still more galling compassion of others'. Thus they presumably have grounds for humiliation that the habitually poor have not, and Dickens interprets their lack of shame not as discipline but as emotional numbness – particularly given the nature of the objects they are selling: a small gold chain and a ring, 'given her in better times, prized perhaps once for the giver's sake, but parted with now without a struggle . . .' They are selling without regret a token of affection – which suggests a shamelessness pointing the way to the young woman selling herself. ('What is a prostitute?' asks William Acton. 'She is a woman who gives for money that which she ought to give only for love' [Nead 101].) Indeed, their transaction is witnessed by yet another young woman whose 'miserably poor, but extremely gaudy' attire 'too plainly bespeaks her station in life . . . where the practiced smile is a wretched mockery of the misery of her heart'. Here is another actress striving to conceal her degradation with a 'practiced smile', but the sight of the mother and daughter 'seems to have awakened in the woman's mind some long-slumbering recollection, and to have changed, for an instant, her whole demeanor'; when she looks more closely at the two, and they 'involuntarily shrink from her', she 'cover[s] her face with her hands, and burst[s] into an agony of tears'. Here, for a passing moment, the prostitute has recovered her own 'consciousness of self-humiliation', once again registered in the faltering of studied demeanour, apparently prompted by having glimpsed an earlier episode in her own life.

> There are strange chords in the human heart . . . which will vibrate at last to some slight circumstance apparently trivial in itself, but connected by some undefined and indistinct association, with past days which can never be recalled, and with bitter recollections from which the most degraded creature in existence cannot escape. (228)

This dense, epiphanic moment evokes an extraordinary self-division that pits memory against helplessness. The young prostitute has recalled past days 'that can never be recalled': she remembers them but cannot undo them, they cannot be recalled because they are irrevocable. And so too, it seems, are their after-effects. Hence the recollections that outwardly soften and humanise her, that work against her 'degraded condition', also imprison her; they are 'bitter', because they ultimately mock her inability to escape her degradation. As so often in Dickens, memory chastens and redeems with images of better, more innocent times – much as the sight of Oliver delivered into evil, in Nancy's words, 'turns me against myself'. But once again the experience only confirms a form of helplessness. That fate is brought home by yet another female spectator, 'the lowest of the low; dirty, unbonneted, flaunting, and slovenly'. Even for this degraded being the spectacle of the pawnbroking prompts 'an expression of something like interest' to break in on 'her half intoxicated leer', 'and a feeling similar to that we have described, appeared for a moment, and only a moment . . .' Only a moment, because her end is near and clear. 'Who shall say how soon these women may change places? . . . How many females situated as her companions are, and as she may have been once, have terminated the same wretched course, in the same wretched manner. One is already retracing her footsteps with frightful rapidity' (229).

The interest that these women take in one another, 'the feeling similar to that we have described', seems an 'interest' less in another person than in an earlier version of themselves; they are witnessing an image from their own lives, experiencing a pang of memory from a time before their social degradation was so palpable. In such moments, they recover what had been otherwise obliterated, 'the consciousness of self-humiliation'. That experience will become pivotal to *Oliver Twist*, notably in the character of Nancy, where far more explicit and expansive arcs of moral reform and irresistible descent converge in a conflict that structures much of the novel. That conflict is played out, moreover, in a sustained preoccupation with performance, which underscores not only its pervasiveness in everyday life, but the peculiar interpretive demands it poses for both character and reader.

II

The challenges of recognising and interpreting social theatre are brought home in *Oliver Twist* even in what might seem the broadest mode of performance, the comedy of hypocrisy, where the disjunction between character and role seems especially glaring. '"Gracious goodness! Is that you, Mr. Bumble, sir?" said Mrs. Mann, thrusting her head out of the window in well-affected ecstasies of joy' (21). Mrs Mann's performance of course says much about her character: it is 'well-affected' because she has spent many years rehearsing how to conceal her disdain both for the orphans in her care and for the parochial authorities. We have no hint that Bumble recognises the imposture, presumably because Mrs Mann's solicitous 'joy' gratifies his considerable vanity. But we as readers could not recognise that tone, or the imposture it conveys, without the narrator's assistance; the bare substance of Mrs Mann's words does not in itself convey their theatricality. We require the knowledge condensed in the narrator's prompt, 'well-affected', and, more subtly, in the hyperbole of 'ecstasies of joy'.

Oliver himself of course possesses no such guidance, and this leaves him at the mercy of performers of all kinds, because he cannot grasp disjunctions between surface and substance. But his innocence also leaves him at the mercy of observers of all kinds. Because the social typology of the parish boy conflicts with the refinement expressed in Oliver's manners and countenance – 'His mug is a fortun' to him', as Toby Crackit enviously remarks (177) – nearly everyone he meets suspects him of imposture. Throughout the novel, casual observers take up a vantage akin to that of both a jury and a theatre audience, who must judge which of those characteristics, the social standing or the demeanour, expresses (or disguises) the 'real' boy. In this light, Oliver's very birth underscores the power of appearances in organising social life, as Oliver is costumed in a manner that blazons his social standing. He is 'badged and ticketed' within the social order when he is enveloped in the old calico robes of the parish child: 'What an excellent example of the power of dress, young Oliver Twist was!' (5). Of course this rhetoric takes its force from the assumption of an inherent disjunction between an individual and a social role. Some of us are born theatrical, but we all have theatre thrust upon us. The theatricality of everyday life is clearest in worlds where social types are most sharply delineated – witness 'Horatio Sparkins' – but the enduring alignment of human identity and clothing suggests that theatre is an inescapable feature of social life.

The novel thus summons up a theatricality more elemental than that of the stage proper, or of the various social rituals that Dickens holds up for ridicule as solemn hypocrisies. Recognising the pervasiveness of social theatre underscores just how singular and vulnerable Oliver is in his 'artlessness'. It also brings home how much readers in turn require the supplementary presence of the narrator to illuminate Oliver's experience, which in turn amplifies our consciousness of the theatre of everyday life. Consider, for example, the scene in Chapter 9, where Oliver in a trance-like state observes Fagin as he sifts through his treasures and then, on becoming aware of Oliver, 'furiously' seizes a bread knife. When Oliver's earnestness, with its characteristic power, disarms Fagin's suspicion, Fagin carefully modulates his anger:

'Tush, tush, my dear!' said the Jew, abruptly resuming his old manner, and playing with the knife a little, before he laid it down: as if to induce the belief that he had caught it up in mere sport. 'Of course I know that, my dear. I only tried to frighten you. You're a brave boy. Ha! Ha! You're a brave boy, Oliver!' (69)

Unlike the passage involving Mrs Mann, here the commentary might seem superfluous to the reader's recognition that Fagin is acting. Presumably we could infer as much without the phrase, 'as if to induce the belief that he had caught it up in mere sport'. Indeed, to a reader accustomed to modernist strategies of narration, this might seem a distracting example of Dickensian over-emphasis: why not just show us rather than tell us? But Dickens's narration at this juncture aims less to underscore Fagin's performance than to point up the limits of Oliver's understanding as a spectator: the phrase captures an inference, a recognition, not available to Oliver. Thus the comedy of Oliver's innocence – 'Oliver thought that the old gentleman must be a decided miser to live in such a dirty place, with so many watches' (69) – is shadowed by a sense of the vulnerability bound up with it. And that innocence in turn allows the narrator to underscore the intricacies of an acting Oliver cannot fathom.

Indeed, Oliver will never fully fathom the acting of Nancy, who first appears in this same scene. Her introduction, focalised through Oliver, underscores his innocence:

They were not exactly pretty, perhaps; but they had a great deal of colour in their faces; and looked quite stout and hearty. Being remarkably free and agreeable in their manners, Oliver thought them very nice girls indeed, as there is no doubt they were. (71)

Again the emphasis suggests Oliver's naivete: who else could fail to grasp the social type blazoned in Nancy's appearance? But Dickens aims to complicate the typology, and that process begins with Nancy's gifts as an actress. The brio with which she rehearses and then performs her role as Oliver's sister (101–2) suggests her resourcefulness in this line. But as it captures her acting talents, it also individuates her. This complication emerges in Chapter 16, when Nancy returns Oliver to Fagin's lair, but then discards her assumed role, growing furious over the treatment of the boy when he tries to escape. When she threatens to inform on the gang if the boy is mistreated, Fagin tries to disarm the tension with his own posturing. 'Why, Nancy,' he remarks, 'You – you're more clever than ever tonight. Ha! Ha! my dear, you are acting beautifully!' (131). (The 'Ha! Ha!' is one of the signatures of Fagin's theatricality.) But of course at this juncture Nancy is not acting, and her unfeigned passion undermines Fagin's pretense:

The Jew saw that it would be hopeless to affect any further mistake regarding the reality of Miss Nancy's rage; and, shrinking involuntarily back a few paces, cast a glance, half imploring and half cowardly, at Sikes ...' (131–2)

Nancy's sincerity, underscored by the ostentatious surrender of her earlier role, undercuts Fagin's own performance. Moreover, her unforced anger, the narrator claims, instantiates a broader truth: 'There is something about a roused woman, especially if she is to add to all her other strong passions the fierce impulses of recklessness and despair, which few men like to provoke' (133). The roused, reckless, and despairing woman might seem worlds removed from Rose Maylie, but Nancy's passionate fury is invested with a moral force closely akin to Rose's gentleness (and indeed to Oliver's earnestness, which can move even Bumble and Fagin). That moral force checks the aggression of the most callous men. Fagin, perhaps the most subtle and adept performer in the novel, is for once at a loss, while Sikes can do little more than splutter, unleashing a barrage of curses, 'the rapid production of which reflected great credit on the fertility of his invention' – which is to say, his own ineptitude as a performer (132).

Sikes is canny enough, however, to grasp another means of controlling Nancy: 'Do you know who you are, and what you are?' he asks her (132). It's not really a question, of course – it's a reminder, like the sorts of bullying that Oliver frequently endures, of how thoroughly her identity and her freedom are circumscribed by her place in the social order. Nancy, unlike Oliver, does not dispute the world's suspicions; instead, she tries to deflect Sikes's insult: 'Oh, yes, I know all about it,' she replies. 'I know all about it' suggests that 'who you are, and what you are' circulates as a mere social report, a form of news or gossip or innuendo. But Nancy cannot deny it; she can only *act* as if it doesn't matter to her. Yet she's unable to carry off that performance. Instead, she replies 'laughing hysterically, and shaking her head from side to side, with a poor assumption of indifference' (132). Note that 'poor assumption of indifference' is a prompt much like Mrs Mann's earlier 'well-affected' joy, but here it works to underscore a *failure* of theatricality. Without the phrase, we might not appreciate that 'laughing hysterically' is not a performance, but instead a sign of performance breaking down. And this is crucial to recognise, because that collapse is a marker of shame, which is registered in Nancy's inability at this moment to assume or display 'indifference' to her own degradation.

Indifference belongs to the woman who is truly 'hardened'; as throughout *Sketches*, it defines a woman who is untroubled by an audience, or utterly oblivious to it. Shame, by contrast, registers for Dickens in the disruption or faltering of a pose, or as an experience that altogether inhibits performance; the consciousness of an audience becomes unnerving, degrading. Nancy's sense of shame in turn reflects a moral sense not yet extinguished. At this moment she loathes herself not merely, or even primarily, because she is a whore, but because she believes she has led Oliver into ruin: 'He's a thief, a liar, a devil: all that's bad, from this night forth.' Of course she does not appreciate the strange resilience of Oliver's innocence. (Who could?) But as she thus excoriates herself, she is affirming a moral awareness that heralds her subsequent efforts to rescue Oliver. As she puts it later, 'The sight of him turns me against myself and all of you' (209).

The ready capacity for shame and remorse heralds the possibility of redemption: it suggests that 'the woman' in Nancy is not quite dead. This is the logic played out in Chapter 40, when Nancy has her fateful conversation with Rose Maylie. 'There was something of the woman's original nature left in her still,' the narrator remarks; 'she felt burdened with the sense of her own deep shame . . .' (332). Shame is the expression of an enduring spark of womanly virtue, which has been fanned into a blaze in her efforts to save Oliver. It is that shame 'which alone connected her with that humanity, of which her wasting life had obliterated so many, many traces when a very child' (333). The term 'obliterated' again suggests that 'humanity' itself is something visible: Dickens is thinking of Nancy as a spectacle, and at this juncture this is precisely how she envisions herself. The whole world, Nancy tells Rose, instinctively recoils from the very sight of her: 'Do not mind shrinking openly from me, lady . . . I am well used to it. The poorest women fall back, as I make my way along the crowded pavement' (333–4). This is a familiar convention of 'fallenness', but it is striking here simply because it is not consistent with the earlier depiction of Nancy the virtuoso actress. When she performs the role of Oliver's sister, the crowd does not shrink from her; it does not sense a disguise. In Chapter 40, however, Nancy in effect claims that nothing could disguise her character, that she has no capacity whatsoever to shield herself from the world's contempt. It is as if we have two different Nancys – or rather, as if the experience of shame has split her very existence in two, and she is revising her own past in light of her new self-consciousness. She remains a spectacle, to be sure, but she is no longer an actress (at least with regard to Rose). And in this respect she is aligned with Oliver, not only through her moral support for the boy, but as she at this moment embodies a kind of artlessness that bespeaks unextinguished virtue, 'something of the woman's original nature in her still'.

Of course Nancy's fate ultimately reenacts the seemingly inexorable decline that shadows the prostitute throughout *Sketches by Boz*. But there is a profound irony informing her sordid death: it is the by-product less of her illicit sexuality than of a selfless fidelity to her lover, and as such it is an outgrowth of what the novel would have us believe is 'woman's essential nature'. In Nancy's fate, an ideal of domestic femininity culminates in a form of self-immolation. Oliver's resilience, by contrast, enacts not only the conventions of the moral progress but the gendered asymmetry in Dickens's narratives of social vulnerability. That distinction is brought home in 'A Visit to Newgate', for example, where the first group of inmates the narrator encounters is a group of young male pickpockets, who clearly rehearse the dynamics of Fagin's gang:

> As to anything like shame or contrition, that was entirely out of the question. They were evidently quite grateful at being thought worth the trouble of looking at; their idea seemed to be that we had come to Newgate as a grand affair, and that they were an indispensable part of the show. (241)

Naturally they are a part of the show; the narrator's disavowal is curiously disingenuous, since why else has he come to Newgate, if not for a bit of theatre? 'We never looked upon a more disagreeable sight,' the narrator continues, 'because we never saw fourteen such hopeless and irreclaimable creatures before.' But 'irreclaimable' hardly mutes the vitality of their performance – any more than it will that of the Artful Dodger in *Oliver Twist*. (Indeed, in the 1850 edition of *Sketches*, Dickens dropped the term, to make the phrase 'hopeless creatures of neglect'.) While the spectacle of the shameless young pickpockets, like that of the Artful Dodger, retains a comic fascination, the young women on their downward path enact 'a tragic drama', within which no amount of suffering can grant them any sort of real agency, any power to resist their fate.

The peculiar burdens attached to compromised femininity are brought home in *Sketches* by contrast with another social type which, like the prostitute, bodies forth social decline in theatrical form: the shabby-genteel man. In 'Shabby-Genteel People', the narrator declares, 'A very poor man, "who has seen better days," as the phrase goes, is a strange compound of dirty-slovenliness and wretched attempts at a kind of faded smartness' (304). Once again the effort to conceal one's degradation, in a performance of 'faded smartness', inadvertently underscores it – which suggests a fairly exact parallel to the prostitute's trajectory. But, the narrator continues, 'only men are shabby-genteel'. This is perplexing, but consider the earlier sentence with 'woman' instead as the subject: 'A very poor woman, "who has seen better days," as the phrase goes, is a strange compound of dirty-slovenliness, and wretched attempts at a kind of faded smartness' (304). A woman's degradation almost irresistibly summons up that of the prostitute, the model and nadir of such a descent, an extreme the shabby-genteel man never reaches. Hence the shabby-genteel man calls out in Boz more unqualified pathos than the fallen woman. 'A glance at that depressed face, and timorous air of conscious poverty, will make your heart ache – always assuming that you are neither a philosopher, nor a political economist' (305). Here once again is the familiar inculcation of redemptive sympathy, which is contrasted, as so often in Dickens, with the heartless discourse of systematic reason, epitomised by political economy. But as that sympathy is extended to the spectacle of the shabby-genteel man, Dickens makes a very large allowance for moral weakness: 'The miserably poor man (*no matter whether he owes his distresses to his own conduct, or that of others*) who feels his poverty and vainly tries to conceal it, is one of the most pitiable objects in human nature' (emphasis added). This generosity again is alien to political economy, but also to Dickens's own account of fallen women. When it comes to shabby-genteel men, the matter of agency is bracketed altogether: the inculcation of pity not only mitigates our judgement, it entirely suspends any issue of responsibility.[5]

'The consciousness of self-humiliation', finally, suggests a further energy informing Dickens's fascination with the prostitute's theatre of shame. That 'consciousness' pointedly recalls Dickens's narrative of childhood trauma in the blacking factory. Steven Marcus has offered a particularly suggestive account of the bearings of this episode on *Oliver Twist* ('Who is Fagin?') but the performative dimensions of shame are not confined to Oliver's ordeal; they are amplified in being displaced onto the figure of the prostitute. (Lurking behind this association is a long-standing association of writing for hire with social degradation, which surfaces in a wry self-identification in the sketch 'Seven Dials': a mysterious shabby-genteel man is 'very naturally suppose[d] to be an author; and rumours are current in the Dials, that he writes poems for Mr. Warren' (95) – Warren of course being the owner of the blacking factory where the young Dickens worked.) Dickens's narratives of the prostitute's irrevocable decline certainly capture an anxiety about the power of social determination generally, but they also serve as implicit foils to the trajectory of Dickens's own career: while he retained the memory of that humiliation, it was animated and shaped (and re-shaped) by the triumph of having overcome it, of having defied what might have seemed *his* fate. In this context, Oliver's own resilient endurance of humiliation, as he imagines Mr Brownlow's bad opinion of him, is a mark of resistance as well as submissive virtue. It defies what Nancy imagines to be his own implacable, irresistible doom: 'he's a thief, a liar, a devil, all that's bad, from this night forth' (132).

Hillis Miller's provocative reading of *Sketches* finds in these patterns of 'apparently inescapable' degradation 'excellent demonstrations of the metonymic basis of realistic narrative' (132–3). They are that, to be sure, but that need not imply that realism lacks any purchase on a world outside the play of language. I think Miller's formulation is of its time in aligning 'realism' with a naive faith in transparency of reference, which could be subverted by the mere existence of figurative language. The limits of that assumption are brought home by his own appeal to an 'inauthenticity' in Dickensian theatricality; the writing that shows us language as deformation must evidently also capture the reality it deforms. It is this referential dimension in Dickensian mimesis that makes his metonymic and theatrical strategies such powerful components not only of narrative structure but of social anxiety and reflection, as Anderson and other critics have brought home. His theatre of shame is as good as a play – but it's never just play.

Notes

1. Compare his 1962 Introduction to *Oliver Twist*: 'The London of *Oliver Twist* . . . is a literal representation of the city as it was in the early nineteenth century' (Hillis Miller 1962, 33). Miller's collection of his early essays, *Victorian Subjects*, commendably makes no effort to efface such shifts, which are central to the interest of his rich career.
2. Goffman's work has been notably neglected within literary study. As Leila May points out, Goffman's analysis might well seem to 'swallow up' Judith Butler's influential formulation (thirty years later) that gender is 'performatively constituted': 'If all identity is performed, then the news that gender is performative is perhaps not as dramatic as Butler hoped it would be' (31).
3. This prospect presumably informed Dickens's lengthy, energetic commitment to Angela Burdett-Coutts's 'Urania Cottage' project for reclaiming 'fallen' women (Hartley, *Charles Dickens and the House of Fallen Women*). How that commitment might be related to his fictional representations of the prostitute is a fascinating question, but beyond the scope of this chapter.
4. Jaffe (34) is especially astute on this social dynamic. Hillis Miller, *Subjects* 131–3, offers a very different understanding of the pattern as an index of the power of metonymy in Dickens's writing.
5. But this discrepancy does not entail, as Deborah Nord suggests, that in *Sketches* women are 'the sole casualties of a usually buoyant urban world' (68) – only that they embody different forms of social and psychic damage.

Chapter 16

Critical Listening and Rhetorical Reading: Performative Utterance in George Eliot's *Felix Holt*
Helen Groth

In his prelude to *Reading for Our Time* Miller begins with a question: 'Can reading *Adam Bede* and *Middlemarch* today be at all justified, in this time of irreversible global climate change, worldwide financial meltdown, with a new financial bubble already building, and the bamboozling of the American electorate (and other electorates around the world) by the media, advertising, the politicians, and hidden right-wing contributors into voting in ways exactly contrary to their interests?'[1] Miller's work invites us to consider both the nuanced pleasures and precarious responsibilities of rhetorical reading at this particular moment in time; a time in which, as the historian Kathryn Hughes argued in a compelling opinion piece published in the *Guardian* in the wake of Brexit, returning to Eliot's work is not only justified, but enlightening.[2] A rhetorical reading of Eliot takes time, as Miller's work exemplifies, it requires paying attention to linguistic details, to the strange texture of prose style, to the subtle insistent demystification of unexamined words that expose the inherent fragility of speech acts more generally.

Reading Eliot in our time in this fashion recalls Nietzsche's salutary reminder of the 'vanishing existence of the aesthetic listener' in *Birth of Tragedy*.[3] Nietzsche's aesthetic listener, like Miller's rhetorical reader, reveals the potential loss or risk of failing to hear or recognise 'the incomprehensibly different' amidst the noise and chatter of contemporary social and media systems. Eliot's writing turns on such risky moments. The incomprehensible wonder of a scene is momentarily captured, a voice or seemingly trivial, yet revelatory, word uttered, the silent interiority of a character 'telepathically known' by an imaginary narrator, as Miller elegantly notes. The inherent complexity and contingency that this mode of reading and writing privileges requires a persistent unsettling of assumed understandings of self, of meaning, of the real; a critical approach that is both uniquely suited to Eliot's exacting form of aesthetic listening and to the purpose of this chapter, which is to extend Miller's version of rhetorical reading into a reconsideration of the enduring force of Eliot's literary interrogation of political speech acts in *Felix Holt*. Before turning to *Felix Holt*, it is important to clarify how this essay will mobilise Miller's understanding of rhetorical reading as a sustainable form of critical listening in an increasingly digitised, data-driven global environment: a world where what it means to read at all is being fundamentally reconfigured and reimagined. The following section explores this alignment of rhetorical reading and critical listening first in the context of Miller's work and then by tracing parallels with Eliot's critical interest in voice and the noise and confusion generated by misinterpretation.

Rhetorical Reading as Critical Listening

Miller, responding to Jonathan Loesberg's somewhat premature 1993 summation of his critical oeuvre as an exercise in contradictory close reading, clarified the key characteristics of his work in the wake of his transformative encounter with Paul de Man and Jacques Derrida.[4] Avowing his debt to speech act theory, as mediated by de Man and Derrida, Miller elaborated on the implications of the shift from his earlier work's stress on consciousness to his later focus on the 'constitutive powers of language'.[5] For Miller, rhetoric is inherently catachrestic. It is also 'performative language as opposed to cognitive language' (125). Miller describes this formative transition more specifically in a slightly earlier essay on 'Speech Acts in Hopkins's Poems', where he recounts the critical innocence that led him to believe that reading literature involved 'transparent and affective access to the mind of another'.[6] What replaces this misguided faith in a 'successful *introspection d'autrui*', to adapt Miller's description of his method, is a rigorous examination of literary writing's 'performative making' of what it 'seemed merely to report' (174). Miller accordingly examines the definitional conundrum Hopkins's poetry presents to Austin, de Man and Derrida's understanding of an efficacious performative speech act as an inherently nonpoetic, contingent, intersubjective, social and material phenomenon that 'depends on the presence of a whole set of conventions, agreements, contracts, laws, constitutions' (180).

What Hopkins called 'vowelling on and vowelling off',[7] and Miller characterises as 'strongly marked and echoing sprung rhythm' (184), requires enlisting performative locutions such as imperatives, pleadings, interjections, prosopoetic apostrophes, as well as poetic devices such as alliteration, assonance and rhyme to 'make words into things and things that have power to do other things in their turn by a performative transformation that makes them embodied or materialised breathings, sighs, cries, saying yeses' (184). With typical acuity Miller highlights Hopkins's ingenious capacity to 'keep words at the level of sound' (188), to heighten the stress on the 'pure sounds of speech as opposed to their meaning'. As Hopkins put it: 'Poetry is speech framed for contemplation of the mind by the way of hearing or speech framed to be heard for its own sake and interest even over and above its interest in meaning.'[8] Listening is, in this sense, inherently privileged by both Miller and Hopkins as intrinsic to reading poetry. Hopkins materialises speech, sounding out an inscape that is insistently specific and distinct, a sounding out that Miller's critical reading further amplifies and in so doing makes relevant to other literary forms.

Many years later in *Reading for Our Time*, Miller returned to the synonymous representational duties of 'articulated sounds' and 'black marks inscribed on white' (13). Through a reading of George Eliot's *Adam Bede* he argues for an understanding of her prose as inherently performative in the sense he had elaborated in his analysis of Hopkins as 'speech framed for contemplation'. He also argues for the novel's prescient convergent analysis of performative speech and the false interpretations it generates, which is reflected in the enduring 'human propensity' as Miller puts it, 'to invent fictions on the basis of strong feeling and to live by them as if they were true' (21). Belief in a universally known truth is predicated on the linguistic error of taking the figurative literally and the novel explores the risks of doing so. The sympathy that belief elicits, as Eliot typically characterises it, is both constitutive of and dangerous to community, given it is necessarily contingent and precariously maintained by fictions, such as those simultaneously generated and omnisciently destabilised by the novel's narrator. Likewise, the figures of speech on which the experience of community and the fiction of transparent communication are predicated – metaphor, metonymy, synecdoche, prosopopoeia, catachresis – are constitutive elements of everyday language use in the novel, and yet also performative in their contingently rhetorical manifestation of shared beliefs or assumed truths.

Miller's acute reading of Eliot is enhanced by their mutual interest in listening out for what Michel Serres characterises as the static or interference of what is excluded or suppressed in the process of creating fleeting illusory moments of consensus; there is always some static or background noise that intermittently disrupts the signal. As Serres reminds us in *Genesis*: 'In order to succeed, the dialogue needs an excluded third.'⁹ Usefully, for the purposes of this essay's ultimate interest in Eliot's examination of the distortive effects of political rhetoric in *Felix Holt*, Serres invokes the metaphor of the crowd in *Genesis* to dramatise the multiple ways in which noise is channelled, potentially working as an agent of change, but not always or uniformly so:

> Like the noise of the crowd that thunders and rumbles, at times breaks up, and at times gets bigger. At each crossroads, it breaks up or grows further. Noise is parasitical, like interference, it follows the logic of the parasite, a very tiny thing, an insufficient reason, a cause without consequence at times, which may vanish to the left of the dovetail, which may increase and magnify to the right of the instauration. This soft sound which has just begun, who is now impinging on our ears, we have forgotten that it might well have died. It never stops being unstable, left or right, immense or non-existent, new music or silence. (57)

Eliot consciously experimented with the way listeners are variously sensitised to the excluded noise that reverberates just beneath the threshold of consciousness, as her memorable observations on 'the roar on the other side of silence' in *Middlemarch* palpably exemplify. Noise functions differently, however, in Eliot's characterisation of Dinah Morris's impassioned Methodist preaching in *Adam Bede*: 'The effect of her speech was produced entirely by the inflections of her voice.'[10] Vocal timbre and accent both operate here in the manner of Serres's account of parasitic yet constitutive noise, intensifying the affective force of the medium rather than the message. United by the performative event, Dinah's audience hears but fails to listen; distracted by the medium, they are diverted onto their own interpretative trajectories. They enjoy the 'mellow treble' and musicality of her voice but remain unconverted to the precepts of Methodism, despite Dinah's 'pleading' reproaches and 'severe appeals' (81–8).

Eliot's publisher John Blackwood described her ear for voices as a negative characteristic in 1861: 'her great difficulty seems to be that she, as she describes it, hears characters talking'.[11] From Eliot's perspective, however, this was a strength, not a failing. Eliot returned repeatedly to the risks of not listening carefully to the voices of others, and the consequent misinterpretations generated. In her essay 'The Antigone and Its Moral' (1856), for example, Eliot questioned superficial interpretations of Sophocles' drama which idealised the heroic suffering of Antigone at the hands of a tyrannical Creon; a reading that ultimately links this earlier essay with the moral argument that shapes her analysis of the risks of political speech in *Felix Holt*.[12] Encoded in Eliot's rejection of a reductive binary reading of Sophocles' tragedy is an implicit challenge to Hegel's prior interpretation of Antigone's burial of her brother as an act of civil disobedience driven by sisterly fealty, and Creon's punitive response as an act of paternalistic civic responsibility that exceeds the bounds of the familial; an interpretation that aligns Antigone with the feminine sphere, shaped by individual and domestic concerns, and Creon with the masculine sphere of political collective action and legal imperatives.[13] Eliot argues instead that Sophocles' tragedy turns on the 'dramatic collision' of conflicting principles of equal value, and that any reconciliation that involves the submission of one to the other is therefore inevitably in 'opposition to a good' (264). The good in this context is the sacrifice of moderation and reverence in the interests of the resolution of a violent conflict, as Eliot concludes: 'Perhaps the best moral we can draw is that to which the Chorus points – that our protest for the right should be seasoned with moderation and reverence' (266). Vital here, as Kathryn Kruger has noted, is Eliot's shift of focus away from Creon and Antigone as the source of 'the moral of the tragedy' and towards the Chorus, 'a multiplicity of voices directed in a shared delivery' (70). This emphasis on a middle term suggests an alternative solution to the emblematic conflict between Antigone and Creon; a non-violent resolution that requires moderation and an ethics of mutual recognition.

If the moral is moderation, the following passage from the same essay, which is often read as exemplifying Eliot's conservative approach to reform, can be read as a pacific plea for non-violent forms of political representation or protest:

> Reformers, martyrs, revolutionists, are never fighting against evil only; they are also placing themselves in opposition to a good – to a valid principle which cannot be infringed without harm. Resist the payment of ship-money, you bring on civil war; preach against false doctrines, you disturb feeble minds and set them adrift on a sea of doubt; make a new road, and you annihilate vested interests; cultivate a new region of the earth, and you exterminate a race of men. (Pinney 264)

The 'lofty words' of universalism are 'not becoming to mortals' (Pinney 264), Eliot concludes. The so-called heroic gains achieved by violent acts, by riot, sacrifice and colonisation, are predicated on harm and loss. Eliot's reading thus exposes the dangers of both passionate beliefs predicated on self-serving misinterpretation and grand gestures that discount the potential human and ethical costs of fermenting violence or dissent.

There are clear continuities between Eliot's critical insistence on community and responsibility and Miller's sustained parallel theorisation of the ethics of reading and 'communities in fiction', culminating in his recent work on the muted yet essential performative efficacy of modern literary speech acts in post-Holocaust 'communities in conflagration'.[14] For Miller the critical intervention of the novels of Eliot, Trollope, Hardy and others lies not in their mimetic capacities but in their performative modelling of behavioural and communal ideals. Miller argues, for example, that the narrator's invitation to the community of Barset to 'Follow me!' at the opening of Trollope's *The Last Chronicle of Barset* transforms the novel into an 'extended speech act' that exceeds the local, drawing readers from across time and space into Trollope's fictional world.[15] While Eliot associates such folksy forms of direct address in *Middlemarch* with the bygone days of Fielding and the eighteenth-century *Bildungsroman*, her descriptive preludes to novels such as *Middlemarch*, *Adam Bede* and *Felix Holt* share Trollope's desire for a complicit audience who can knowingly enter into a carefully constructed fictional community. In these novels, Eliot invites the reader to follow the narrator as she takes them deeper into the respective communities she describes.

Eliot's introduction to *Felix Holt* is striking in this regard, simulating the experience of a stagecoach ride: the narrator assumes the role of both travel guide and local historian, taking the reader back thirty-five years to the events leading up to the first reform bill of 1832, whilst moving the traveller/reader through a series of industrial and pastoral Midland scenes towards the fictional Loamshire town of Treby Magna where the main events of the narrative take place:

> In these midland districts the traveller passed rapidly from one phase of English life to another: after looking down on a village dingy with coal-dust, noisy with the shaking of looms, he might skirt a parish all of fields, high hedges, and deep-rutted lanes; after the coach had rattled over the pavement of a manufacturing town, the scene of riots and trade-union meetings, it would take him in another ten minutes into a rural region, where the neighbourhood of the town was only felt in the advantages of a near market for corn, cheese, and hay, and where men with a considerable banking account were accustomed to say that 'they never meddled with politics themselves'.[16]

Miller's resistance to the concept of omniscient narration in his reading of Trollope's novel can also be applied to the narrating voice in the above passage. Eliot's narrative voice is communal in tenor, conveying local knowledge, rather than a mystified all-seeing access to an objective truth. The narrator only knows what they know and speaks for and to that knowledge. Eliot's use of the past tense signals the transmutation of the present tense and individual knowledge of the speaking voice into a communally experienced past. As Miller puts it in the context of Trollope: 'Writing it down relocates what was once a present happening into an indefinitely close or remote past, into a kind of essential pastness' (40).

What is equally striking about the above passage, to return to my opening allusion to Nietzsche's account of the aesthetic listener in *Birth of Tragedy*, is the evident pleasure Eliot takes in the slow immersion of her readers in the nuance and complexity of ordinary life, whilst insisting on the 'unintelligible effects' that are intrinsic to the experience of reading narrative art.[17] The environs of Treby Magna are simultaneously rendered familiar and 'incomprehensibly different' to those who choose to attend closely to a dense descriptive prose that models a multi-faceted interpretive approach to the rhetorical constitution of community by both its insiders and outsiders. Further drawing on the alignment of Miller's sustained engagement with J. L. Austin's *How to Do Things with Words* in his reading of nineteenth-century fiction and Eliot's sustained attention to the errors caused by the literal interpretation of seemingly transparent statements of fact, the following section maintains the focus on rhetoric and rhetorical reading by turning to the novel's mediation of the political speeches of Felix Holt, Eliot's contentiously received radical artisan.

Eliot is forensically interested in the interaction between convention and utterance, and the consequent effects on the words chosen and the actions those words materialise. Performative utterance is inherently contingent on both the participants and circumstances, as well as the procedures they invoke, in Eliot's novel. This is palpably enacted in Felix's 'unhappy' participation in the political process of electioneering as a self-selected counter voice. Drawn into circumstances beyond his control, he participates with characteristic passion in the performance of opposing political beliefs in the local pubs of Treby Magna as part of the election of the community's next political representative to Westminster. But Felix's refusal to recognise the rules of the political game, inherent in his failure to be heard or understood by the working people he claims to represent and culminating in his being inadvertently swept up by the riots that break out on election day, reinforces Eliot's critical treatment of both the limits of political speech and the systematic inequities that riddled the political process in both 1832, when the novel is set, and 1866, when it was written. Far from embracing the universalising rhetoric of Arnold's *Culture and Anarchy*, catalysed by the riots in Hyde Park and elsewhere in response to the Reform Bill of 1867, Eliot's novel provides a prescient reminder, as the historian Kathryn Hughes argued in *The Guardian* in the immediate wake of Brexit, of the destructive consequences of Westminster-centric demagoguery.[18]

The Limits of Radical Speech

The historical reception of *Felix Holt* is riddled with biographical fallacy and misinterpretation. E. S. Dallas, the influential literary critic for *The Times*, wrote with unabashed contempt for Eliot's romantic over-identification with her hero:

> Womanlike, George Eliot has more affection for him than men are ever likely to feel. Men may admire various points in his character – as his honesty, his nobleness of aim, and his strength of purpose; but it is only women who are willing to put up with the arrogance and self-conceit of conscious rectitude. Felix means well and does well, but in his youthful zeal he has such a tendency to be didactic and indignant that we fear if we ever came to know him in the flesh we should vote him a confounded bore.[19]

Readers attempting to glean some sense of the novel from Dallas's patronising appraisal would have been seriously misled. The didactic paternalism that shapes Felix Holt's expression of his desire for Esther, whilst a significant character flaw, is one strand of a complex multidimensional plot that is far more concerned with the politics of enfranchisement and disinterested critical citizenship than romance. The central questions that drive the novel, and which continue to haunt contemporary British politics, are: what justification is there for concentrating the power to determine a nation's fate in the hands of a privileged, self-interested minority? Can democratic process triumph over the corrupting effects of power? If democracy fails, what are the risks for the majority that it disenfranchises? Does the solution lie in a form of practical politics or localised civic action motivated by free-thinking individuals with the critical capacity to generate legitimate political consensus? Eliot, informed by her close reading of Mill's *On Liberty*, and to a lesser extent Arnold and Schiller, enacts these dilemmas through her elaboration of the competing impulses that shape Felix's character.[20]

Urged by Esther's adoptive father, the radical preacher Rufus Lyon, to attend the nomination of the candidates for North Loamshire and act on his hitherto abstract principles, Felix describes himself thus:

> 'I shall get into a rage at something or other,' Felix had said. 'I've told you one of my weak points. Where I have any particular business, I must incur the risks my nature brings. But I've no particular business at Duffield. However, I'll make a holiday and go. By dint of seeing folly, I shall get lessons in patience.' (184)

The narrator's subsequent analysis of the implications of this speech makes it clear that Felix is an object of analysis, not an object of desire.

Felix's violent surges of emotion risk the advances made by his 'long-trained consciousness' towards the self-regulated autonomy of the liberal citizen with the potential to participate and transform collective life (285). As Mill notes in *On Liberty* (1859): 'A person whose desires and impulses are his own – are the expression of his own nature, as it has been developed and modified by his own culture – is said to have a character. One whose desire and impulses are not his own, has no character, no more than a steam-engine has a character.'[21] At this stage of the plot, the narrator sounds a note of concern that later builds to a crescendo when Felix's passions ultimately overwhelm him as he risks and fails to resolve the election day riots resulting in his false arrest and trial for being in violation of the Riot Act: 'Felix had a terrible arm: he knew that he was dangerous; and he avoided conditions that might cause him exasperation' (285).

As the narrator makes clear, such conditions include nomination day, which Eliot describes as 'a great epoch of successful trickery, or to speak in a more parliamentary manner, of war-stratagem, on the part of skilful agents' (285). The disarticulation of speech from political values by 'skilful agents' who corrupt democratic process for financial gain contrasts starkly with the liberal ethos that drives Felix's struggle to maintain the balance between passionate utterance and rational deliberative exchange. As the narrator observes:

> To have the pleasure and the praise of electioneering ingenuity, and also to get paid for it, without too much anxiety whether the ingenuity will achieve its ultimate end, perhaps gives to some select persons a sort of satisfaction in their superiority to their more agitated fellow-men that is worthy to be classed with those generous enjoyments of having the truth chiefly to yourself, and of seeing others in danger of drowning while you are high and dry. (285)

Eliot unmasks the coercive rhetoric and 'vulgar cant' of the worst of these political agents, Johnson (an apt name for readers returning to Eliot in the context of Brexit), by focusing on the listening crowd's reactive 'cheering', 'hustling', 'roaring' and 'hissing' (287). Felix listens to Johnson on the reader's behalf, critically filtering and effectively muting his corruptions of Mill's ideals of representative government: 'It was a little too exasperating to look at this pink-faced rotund specimen of prosperity, to witness the power for evil that lay in his vulgar cant, backed by another man's money, and to know that such stupid iniquity flourished the flags of Reform, and Liberalism, and justice to the needy' (287).

Notably, there are only two speakers who are given air time in this critical scene in the novel. The first is an unnamed trade unionist who takes his place on the 'projecting stone' outside the 'Fox and Hounds' in the 'ultra-liberal quarter of the High Street' (288), and Felix Holt, who steps onto the stone in his wake. Both men speak at length, the first making the case for extending the franchise to all, and the latter, Felix, presenting a case for the need to reform the system and extending access to education to all before doing so. Eliot distinguishes the two men and the resonant force of their message on the basis of their voices. The distinction is striking in a scene where so much emphasis is placed on forms of speaking and the ethics of passionate utterance. Eliot characterises the Trade Unionist thus: 'He lifted up one forefinger, and marked his emphasis with it as he spoke. His voice was high and not strong, but Felix recognised the fluency and the method of a habitual preacher or lecturer' (288). By contrast, the description of Felix's first utterance, in response to the trade unionist's calls for an equal share 'in what goes on in life', stresses the force of his voice and instant charismatic hold on his audience:

> 'Hear, hear!' said Felix, in his sonorous voice, which seemed to give a new impressiveness to what the speaker had said. Every one looked at him: the well-washed face and its educated expression along with a dress more careless than that of most well-to-do workmen on a holiday, made his appearance strangely arresting. (289)

Then when Felix steps onto the projection stone, the narrator drives the contrast home in heroic terms suggestive of both Arnold and Carlyle:

> Felix Holt's face had the look of habitual meditative abstraction from objects of mere personal vanity or desire, which is the peculiar stamp of culture, and makes a very roughly-cut face worthy to be called 'the human face divine'. Even lions and dogs know a distinction between men's glances, and doubtless those Duffield men, in the expectation with which they looked up at Felix, were unconsciously influenced by the grandeur of his full yet firm mouth, and the calm clearness of his grey eyes, which were somehow unlike what they were accustomed to see along with an old brown velveteen coat, and an absence of chin-propping. When he began to speak, the contrast of voice was still stronger than that of appearance. The man in the flannel shirt had not been heard – had probably not cared to be heard – beyond the immediate group of listeners. But Felix at once drew the attention of persons comparatively at a distance. (291)

What he offers instead of the largely unheard sermonising rhetoric of the 'man in the flannel shirt' is the secular 'opinion' of an educated liberal subject, an action that aligns with Mill's ideal of democratic citizenship. As Colene Bentley has argued, at this pivotal moment Felix enacts one of the unresolved tensions in the novel, between 'contemplation and participation'.[22] Expanding on this point, Bentley takes Eliot to task for her failure to recount the history of Felix's 'citizenship training' that has impressed 'the stamp of culture' on his 'roughly cut' physiognomy; to write a more coherent *Bildungsroman*, in other words, although Bentley does not invoke this term:

> Felix espouses the values of rational autonomy and self-reflection, which mark his liberal personhood; but as a character he often lacks narrative realisation because at key moments in the novel Eliot does not provide an account of how her protagonist came to hold the opinions he in fact does. Furthermore, during the Duffield riot and ensuing trial, Eliot accords Felix an authority before others that depends not on his association with cultivated reason but on his public display of personal charisma. Taken together, these episodes pose the perplexities of democratic citizenship as a formal matter: in the absence of narrative (or, for Mill, public) justification, do the dynamics of citizenship in the public sphere risk becoming merely aestheticised? (276)

Eliot's fictional realisation of Felix, as Bentley rightly notes, lacks a coherent developmental arc or literal alignment to the tenets of nineteenth-century liberalism. The form of the novel is equally episodic and uneven in its realisation, which may suggest that Eliot was more interested in narrative as an event than as a relation of an event, to quote Blanchot, from whom this distinction is drawn: 'Narrative is not the relating of an event but this event itself, the approach of this event, the place where it is called upon to unfold, an event still to come by the magnetic power of which the narrative itself can hope to come true.'[23] Pertinently, Miller cites this passage from Blanchot in the context of his argument in *Thinking Literature Across Continents* as a theoretical justification for why imaginative narrative matters as an unique opening up of an endlessly receding vanishing point of unknown possibility; a movement that is infinitely dynamic and participatory in its generation of multiple interpretations and points of entry.[24]

Read through this lens, the two speeches that form the centrepiece of the event that unfolds at Duffield on nomination day offer an alternative point of entry into Eliot's interest in the irresolution and ambiguity that this narrative episode generates – that is, that both the Trade Unionist's sermonic speech and Felix's resonantly asserted opinion fail to educate their intended listeners to think otherwise about the limits of representative government in its current incarnation. This failure points to Eliot's abiding interest in the fallibility of human communication and the infinite potential of both interpretation and misinterpretation, rather than an uncomplicated or romanticised advocacy of either man's political ethos. In the case of the trade unionist, the reader, like Felix, tunes in midstream to an emphatic rhetorical accumulation of wrongs done by the governing classes:

'Not a pig's share,' the speaker went on, 'not a horse's share, not the share of a machine fed with oil only to make it work and nothing else. It isn't a man's share just to mind your pin-making, or your glass-blowing, and higgle about your own wages, and bring up your family to be ignorant sons of ignorant fathers, and no better prospect; that's a slave's share; we want a freeman's share, and that is to think and speak and act about what concerns us all, and see whether these fine gentlemen who undertake to govern us are doing the best they can for us. (289)

These are the words, the narrator informs us, that no one hears, with the exception of Felix and the reader. What this brief excerpt demonstrates is Eliot's interest in the narrative enactment of ethical propositions that are designed to stimulate action in the reader – in this case, the active thinking through of the foundational concepts of liberty and representative government. Fundamental to this critical process for the reader is weighing up the significance of the fact that the above damning anaphoric enumeration of the wrongs of the current political system fails to elicit the passionate identification that it demands from the crowd. An angry response, a riot even, inspired by the audience's legitimate demands for an equitable share in the profits of their labour would have been less surprising at this point in the novel than when it actually occurs on election day, whipped up by the deceptive cant of Spratt, the 'hated manager of Sproxton colliery' (285). Instead an expectant, passive silence ensues, prompting calls for further oratorical diversion, which Felix obligingly provides.

In contrast to the passionate utterance of the previous speaker, Felix speaks with a 'vibrating voice', eschewing the collective and emotive listing of wrongs in favour of apparently reasoned opinion delivered in the first person:

'In my opinion,' he said, almost the moment after he was addressed, 'that was a true word spoken by your friend when he said the great question was how to give every man a man's share in life. But I think he expects voting to do more towards it than I do. I want the working men to have power. I'm a working man myself, and I don't want to be anything else. But there are two sorts of power. There's a power to do mischief – to undo what has been done with great expense and labour, to waste and destroy, to be cruel to the weak, to lie and quarrel, and to talk poisonous nonsense. That's the sort of power that ignorant numbers have. It never made a joint stool or planted a potato. Do you think it's likely to do much towards governing a great country, and making wise laws, and giving shelter, food, and clothes to millions of men? Ignorant power comes in the end to the same thing as wicked power; it makes misery. It's another sort of power that I want us working men to have, and I can see plainly enough that our all having votes will do little towards it at present. I hope we, or the children that come after us, will get plenty of political power some time . . .' (292)

Whilst the content of their respective speeches may differ, both speakers enlist the same rousing and rhythmic effects of anaphora to amplify the impact of their arguments. Where they diverge is in Felix's first-person interrogative style, which performatively insists on being taken seriously in circumstances that Eliot has created to ensure that the reverse eventuates. While the trade unionist recognises the limits of performative utterance amidst the chaos of nomination day, Felix fails to recognise the conventions of the event, lets his passions override his reason, and his call to action consequently results in mockery and inertia. Eliot, as her earlier Mill-inspired observations on the dangers of Felix's unruly passions foreshadowed, makes clear that the blame for this failure is shared by both speaker and listeners alike: 'Felix had seen every face around him, and had particularly noticed a recent addition to his audience; but now he looked before him without appearing to fix his glance on any one. In spite of his cooling meditations an hour ago, his pulse was getting quickened by indignation, and the desire to crush what he hated was likely to vent itself in articulation' (294). Overcome by a desire for revenge against Johnson, Felix disconnects from his audience and the opportunity to affect change eludes him. All that remains is Eliot's summative narration, which ensures the reader remains attentive to the plot twist that concludes this chapter and reinforces the novel's ultimate critical interest in exposing systemic inequities silently maintained and tenuously upheld by ruling elites – in this instance the unwittingly false inheritance of property and thus the right to stand for election by Harry Transome, one of the nominated candidates for the contested seat of North Loamshire.

As Kathryn Hughes argues in her wonderful *Guardian* opinion piece, 'What is the role of the left in times of political crisis? Reading George Eliot after Brexit', returning to *Felix Holt* amidst the chaos and violence of contemporary British politics in 2016, or indeed 2018, reveals unexpected resonances and forgotten parallels. *Felix Holt* is a thought experiment in many ways, as Hughes succinctly puts it, that attempts 'to write a new kind of politics into being' (4). Idealistic, yes, but not naïve or romantic in the novel's insistence that the corrupted political system that drove the Reform Acts of 1832 and 1867, both of which led to more rather than less wealthy upper-class men represented in Westminster, needed more reform before broadening the franchise could lead to meaningful change. Politics in the wake of the passage of the 1867 act was still a game only the wealthy could afford to play, even more so, with some middle-class members forced to resign under the new system, and efforts to manipulate the working-class vote causing further political instability under Conservative rule. Eliot was intimately aware of the local costs of the struggle for political representation. As a young girl she had watched from the window of the school house at Nuneaton during the election of 1832 as Radical and Tory candidates came to blows in the streets outside – events which resulted in the reading of the Riot Act, the scrambling of the militia and the death of a local man. These events find their way into *Felix Holt* but, as Hughes notes, they create an anachronistic 'fuzziness', given that the labouring classes were of little interest to those spruiking the Great Reform Act of 1832 to the predominantly urban property owners who stood to benefit. Yet the question of historical veracity is ultimately irrelevant to the critical process or form of rhetorical reading that Eliot's novel invites. *Felix Holt* exemplifies both Eliot's acuity and the enduring relevance of her careful observation of human interaction and the intricacies of communal life. Her argument in *Felix Holt*, which is that meaningful change is slow, attentive and sensitized to historical precedent and the limits of human communication, seems more relevant now than it has ever been.

Notes

1. Miller, *Reading for Our Time*, p. xi.
2. Hughes, 'What is the role of the Left in times of political crisis?'.
3. Nietzsche, *Birth of Tragedy*, p.61.
4. Loesberg, 'From Victorian Consciousness to an Ethics of Reading'.
5. Miller, 'Response to Jonathan Loesberg', p. 125.
6. Miller, 'Naming and Doing: Speech Acts in Hopkins's Poems', p. 174.
7. Hopkins, cited in Miller, 'Naming and Doing', p. 184.
8. Hopkins, *Journals and Papers*, p. 289.
9. Serres, *Genesis*, p. 57.
10. Eliot, *Adam Bede*, p. 81.
11. Haight, *The George Eliot Letters*, vol. 3, p. 427.
12. Eliot, 'The Antigone and Its Moral', p. 264.
13. Kruger, 'The Antigone and Its Moral': George Eliot's Antigonean Considerations'.
14. Miller, *The Conflagration of Community*, p. xiii.
15. Miller, *Communities in Fiction*, p. 35.
16. Eliot, *Felix Holt. The Radical*, p. 6.
17. Nietzsche, *Birth of Tragedy*, p. 67.
18. Hughes, 'What is the role of the Left in times of political crisis?', online version.
19. Dallas, 'Review of *Felix Holt*'.
20. Harris and Johnston, *The Journals of George Eliot*, pp. 126–7.
21. Mill, *On Liberty and Other Essays*, p. 67.
22. Bentley, 'Democratic Citizenship in Felix Holt', p. 276.
23. Blanchot, 'The Song of the Sirens', p. 6.
24. Miller, *Thinking Literature Across Continents*, p. 66.

Chapter 17

Repetition and/of/in Victorian Pleasures

John Maynard

With no apology I offer this paper on the issues raised by John Stuart Mill's pig satisfied (happiness as wallowing in pleasure) rather than his Socrates unsatisfied. But wallowing is not without conceptual challenges and practical problems in continuation.

Two views of repetition: One we find repeated again and again in postmodern orthodoxy, where the construction of difference over repetition always dominates. Difference is the universal that inhabits all repetition, inserting itself in the closest similarity, calling every redo a new beginning, every retake a new shot, every reprint a new issue, above all in literary study, every reread a new meaning. Difference inhabits repetition like a spirit that cannot be exorcised, try as we might to restore similarity to identity. The biggest game of course is identity itself; nothing is as it is; we are not as we were or will (be).

Three especially familiar touchpoints, of many, to a central movement in late twentieth-century philosophy, just to ground these assertions about the priority of difference in their habitual repetition in recent thinking; many other examples of the same sort about difference could be given. First, of course, Gilles Deleuze, whose dazzling and perhaps dazing *Difference and Repetition* (French, 1968) opened the way to the broader speculations on rhizomatic, non-repeating organisations in his and Felix Guattari's *A Thousand Plateaus* (1980). With Deleuze, repetition itself has been invaded and eaten up by difference. It is, in his reading of proto-moderns Søren Kierkegaard and Friedrich Nietzsche, a unique, willed event, carefully set off from what most of us think of repetition as being. All the usual suspects for repetition – events, things, dates and celebrations, and certainly representations–are simply defined away as not repetitions at all but mere resemblances or generalities. The Platonic form or idea has been swept away by the new appearance, the simulacrum – likeness without any unifying ground at all.[1]

Second usual suspect, Jacques Derrida, the philosopher of *différance*, not only seconds Deleuze's attack on traditional idealist philosophy's creation of ideal forms that allow repetition of the same despite irrelevant accidents; he also beautifully asserts the uniqueness in textuality: as 'Signature Event Context', 'Limited Inc' and an Afterword in *Limited Inc* affirm, every new reading is a resituation, recontextualisation (136–7), therefore necessarily invaded by difference. To read a pleasure, in any sense of read – textual or experiential – would be to find not a repetition but a new pleasure.

Add, finally, in this brief tour of the well-known postmodern context, Hillis Miller's own now classic literary study, *Fiction and Repetition*. After reviewing the systems of Deleuze and Deleuze's Nietzsche, he puts them in more dynamic, dyadic literary action: nineteenth-century novelists tend to 'intertwine' grounded (idealist, form-al) and ungrounded repetition, creating characters or texts that invest hopes in the possibility of actions, ways of life, personal connections, things, repeating; but Miller reads them as proto-modern/postmodern persons or texts that reveal their failure to find/achieve repetition.[2] Literature is invested with ambivalence on this central issue.

To descend from this brief and sketchy look at philosophical heights to cultural practice, certainly 'make it new', make it different, would be the mantra of both the modern and postmodern periods. When we turn to an economy of pleasures, the particular topic of this intervention, a regime of new pleasures would seem to be just what the doctor of the modern ordered for the satiated late Victorian world. The Oscar Wilde figure, Ménalque, in Gide's *L'immoraliste* lectures the protagonist Michel on the need to come to each pleasure as a widower from the last: 'I don't like looking back,' he lectures the protagonist, 'and I leave my past behind me the way a bird leaves its shady tree in order to fly away. I tell you, Michel, each joy still awaits us, but must find the bed empty, must be the *only one*' (112). Wilde's own mentor, Pater, in the conclusion to *The Renaissance* had of course already dictated, following Fichte, 'our failure is to form habits' (189). Each pleasure of sensation should be a new one. The generation before the Victorians, following the broad turn to the individual that Foucault in *The Order of Things* maps out as occurring from the Renaissance on, often agreed. Romanticism had moved away from the centre, like modernism as C. F. G. Masterman famously and platitudinously captured it, taking the two voyages of new internal, psychological investigation and new external exploration. Perhaps not always happily. World-weary late Byron portrays a Juan who might have preferred a rut of pleasure – coming 'always [again and again] back to coffee and Haidee'. But being Don Juan, life and his drives will lead him to a jading satirical world of ever-changing pleasures.

Always making it new or always making a new woman offers endless difference. But of course from another view, it falls into another repetition. Freud also, of course, also on the cusp of modernism, would find all Don Juans, even distanced, satirical ones, victims of repetition compulsion, forced to re-experience earlier pain even in the repeated act of pleasure. Lacan would find all pleasure-seeking activity, even as it moves along a line of difference from symbol to symbol, repeatedly attempting to recuperate a lost Real of initial pleasure and plenitude. Both would seem to be finding roots of desire for repeated pleasure even as they participated in modernism's critique of the need they explained. The poor hero Nathaniel, immortalised theoretically in Freud's reading of Hoffmann's 'The Sand-Man' ('The Uncanny') is of course tragically doomed in his search; but he is certainly on the way to forming habits about girls and dolls – as Oscar Wilde was about young men in his repetitive dining with panthers at the Café Royal (alas and incidentally closed in December 2008 and remade into a glitzy commercial hotel with swimming pool after so many years of visitors seeking to repeat Wilde's dining experiences).

Freud's repeating obsession with obsessions of repetition tells us something universal but it also may profitably be located in his age.[3] It was not hard for him to find such repeaters in his society when the broader story, I will assert, is that the Victorian age as a whole, sick or sound, quested not for the unique and new in pleasure but for the same old – the second view of repetition that I promised in my opening. In their outlook, it was difference, not repetition, that was to be overcome and made subordinate. Repetition was essential. It is easy for us postmoderns to get into the skin of pleasure-seeking moderns – always looking for the new new thing and new frisson. Much harder to understand from within the many Victorians. I say 'the many' because obviously one size never fits all; there was many a proto-modern or late Romantic among Victorian pleasure-seekers, indeed a preponderance among culturally creative people by the late 1880s on. And it was certainly not that the Victorian age did not produce difference. Everywhere change was environing their habitats. Industrialisation, urbanism, merchandising, practical technology, empire-building, expansions of print culture all were producing difference at an alarming rate. It was just this pressure that made the Victorians different from 2,400 years of essentialists who looked for the continuity that created identity and repetition out of the changes of life. Traditional ideas of reassuring unity and identity were being challenged by upcoming modernity as they had never been before. Political thinkers such as John Stuart Mill or Walter Bagehot could even define the uniqueness of their age as that of change against the racist stereotype they created of Chinese or 'Oriental' stasis.[4] Victorians expected political evolution; they believed in history as one progression or another; they celebrated their innovations; they eventually even bought into the long reaches of change in Darwinian evolution. But they fought back against flux and deracination in their hearts and in their pleasures. A radically conservative thinker like Gerard Manley Hopkins could cut to the chase and spell out ultimate Heraclitean alternatives, resolving in his deep discouragement that nature was a self-consuming fire of flux only to be given repetition and identity in the unchanging immortal diamond of religious belief: 'That Nature is a Heraclitean Fire and of the Comfort of the Resurrection' (65–6). For the broad centre there was a finer balancing act: living with change but recuperating it for larger unity and identity by insisting on the possibility of repetition. We are used to looking for difference in every apparent repetition. Victorians more often looked for repetition in every apparent difference.

It was not done (my next main point) without stress and strain. As indeed Hillis Miller himself does in his general approach to repetition in Victorian fiction, I find some of the most interesting moments in Victorian culture of pleasure at points of tension or confusion between unique and repeating pleasure. To start, Victorians regularly like to insist, not without significant justification, that pleasure cannot be apprehended as something new: it exists by virtue of the recognition of its repetition – a point Freud and Lacan would agree with while colouring the pleasure compulsive.[5] A philosophical point too, as the copy of pleasure especially identifies and establishes the pleasure in the second place, creates recognition by re-cognition. The second taste of something renders the first delicious. In Robert Browning's 'Up at a Villa – Down in the City' it is the speaker 'person of quality's' absence from the raucous pleasures of the city that allows him to represent for himself his desire: his urbanist picture of drums tootling and the rest. If the modern seeks *toujours la première fois*, the Victorian only begins to live in the second rolling in the clover (a World War II song, I should say, however Victorian its approach). 'There's no such pleasure in life!' (538) says Browning's speaker, having recognised it in his own re-representation of it.

Freud and Lacan are not to be too easily dismissed. To stay with Robert Browning, who has stayed with me for a good number of years of Victorian study, for another set of examples, Robert's odd love poems (once read I think more than now for their purported philosophy of the good moment becoming the infinite moment) regularly celebrate repetition of pleasure as the one thing holding life fully together – just at the moment of its rupture. If the lover of 'Love Among the Ruins' can affirm his love relation in the teeth of massive archeological evidence of change since violent classical times, the more interesting speaker of 'Two in the Campagna' portrays himself always about to re-seize the day. Then that 'good minute goes' (729) rather than comes. Pleasure is real by its repeated pursuit, not in its achieved repetition. The truly strange speaker of 'The Last Ride Together' manages almost to hypnotise himself into assurance that his final ride with his rejecting mistress – certainly the great riding pleasure and possibly great love of his life – will somehow last forever: 'What if we still ride on, we two/ With life for ever old yet new,/Changed not in kind but in degree,/The instant made eternity,–/And heaven just prove that I and she/Ride, ride together, for ever ride?' What would be breakup and hurt in Hardy late in the century ('Neutral Tones' offering identity as death-in-life, the repetition only of the lover's deadly face at the moment of disuniting, or the later 'The Voice' representing and re-presenting love as dissipated and lost in the repetition) is somehow turned into endless pleasure by a will of return. I will not dignify this as a Nietzschean return and make it palatable to Deleuzian exceptional repetition.[6] The Browning poems portray not the somewhat material reality of the repetition of pleasure but the cultural investment in the idea of repeated pleasure. The speaker of 'The Last Ride Together' ends with a question mark and with heaven as a place of recovery, to which I will return in other writers seeking renewing pleasure.

We are well aware that Victorians did take repeated pleasure in material matters, in their beer, in their pipes, in their dogs, in their tea rituals, in their formal repetitions in etiquette (ladies remove themselves, men drink and talk, then the twain remeet in the drawing room – always!) and these were perhaps for years untroubled repetitions. The cultural insistence on shared rituals of pleasure (like watching sport on TV today) served to enculturate and dominate those called by their class assignments to participate. So we could add less innocent repeated pleasures such as hunting to hounds, dining at the club, cricket matches, vacationing abroad and above all, Christian rituals, which grew and grew during the Victorian period.[7] These compare drastically with a modern revision of pleasure in a writer like Georges Bataille, where pleasure is a unique event that spends rather than accrues social capital. Forgive however another case of sexual pleasure, here more material, which demonstrates, again, a conflicted drive toward both difference and repetition. Steven Marcus long ago christened Walter, of

My Secret Life, as not just a repeat fornicator, which he so colossally was, but tried to place him in his *The Other Victorians* in relation to a special world of repetition, what he called pornotopia. 'A typical piece of pornographic fiction', he remarked, 'will usually have some kind of crude excuse for a beginning, but, having once begun, it goes on and on and ends nowhere. This impulse or compulsion to repeat, to repeat endlessly, is one of pornography's most striking qualities' (279). Marcus places this compulsion to repeated representation of repeated pleasure in a transhistorical, psychological frame (for which Foucault or Fredric Jameson or their many followers would slap his wrists) but he is fascinated by Walter's account, which is what he gives most of his attention to in this study of Victorian pornography. And what is fascinating at first glance in Walter is his abundant novelistic detail within his plot dynamo of repeating desire. But for all his detail from a real world invested/infested by change (which makes his work much more interesting than the seamless money-shot repetition of usual Victorian pornography), for all his quest for varied sexual experience, Walter cannot help but fall into patterns. As Marcus concludes, despite its other qualities enhancing one-handed reading, it is 'deeply and typically of his time. Indeed, *My Secret Life* is nothing if it is not a representative Victorian work' (190). Tarrying with apparent experimentation and difference becomes habituation – even to as outlier and black swan an activity as repeatedly ejaculating in another man's seed. 'It is singular,' wrote Walter, insisting on a fine distinction between his fantasy about other sexual clients and those actually seen, 'but I write what occurred, that I rarely seemed to have the same excitement, pleasure, or even desire in trailing the women whom I had seen fucked, as I did those who came into me from other rooms . . . I *always desired those who'd been stroked in other parts of the house* [italics his] – I always fancied the sperm was that of handsome young men' (quoted Marcus 175). Yes, it is easy to read this intense interest in different repetitions as about not-very-repressed bisexuality or homosexuality in Walter, and he does in fact have full homosexual relations as well as incredibly numerous heterosexual ones.[8] But it is the repetition that interests me. This is not one adventure but one that he delights in contemplating as repetitive, 'always'. The sexual adventurer of the age becomes slave to his own need for repetition. 'What often astonishes me is my desire to do again everything sexual and erotic which I have already done. . . . I want to do everything over again. All former gratifications which were a little out of the common seem to have faded from my recollection somewhat. – I don't clearly enough recollect my sensations or the quality of the pleasure they gave me. I wish to refresh my memory by repeating the amorous exercises' (quoted Marcus 180). As we indeed find when our delight at his specificity yields to repetitive boredom in reading his formulaic sexual repetitions. Is this just the nature of pornography as a universal itch? Partly, but I would argue that Walter, who made a life's profession of using his money for much sex, needed to assure himself with his kind of infinite moment as non-other-Victorians did as well.

In this brief chapter I want to look at one other area where repeated pleasure creates a permanence that forestalls – though it does not halt – difference. This is the pleasure of repetitive artistic creation, which of course Walter, writer of eleven volumes and 4,200 pages, knew as much of as any Victorian, along with everything else they didn't necessarily know. Repetition by representation seems to have been at the foundation of Victorian stabilising attempts. So it is not surprising to find Victorians taking and giving pleasure by writing about pleasures using technical devices of repetition to enhance repetitive representations: rhymings, refrains, repeating metrical patterns and the like.[9] Clough's song from *Dipsychus* is a good example just because he was, overall, looking to shock by difference and extreme honesty: 'How pleasant it is to have money, heigh ho!/How pleasant it is to have money' (II ii 'In a Gondola') – a scandalously honest refrain which today we may be tempted to ascribe to CEOs at Goldman Sachs or Merrill Lynch or indeed to Bernie Madoff himself. In a mid-Victorian context it marks, from out of the belly of the drifting gondola, Clough's difference from Victorian closed-mouthedness on spending. But pleasure is still rendered as repetition: 'So pleasant', 'How pleasant', etcetera, stanza after stanza, ending 'How pleasant . . .' The formal repetition takes away the sense of difference that would normally infest this attempt to represent life as easygoing consumption.

Lewis Carroll's 'The Walrus and the Carpenter' (from *Through the Looking-Glass*) is another hard case, as it is no namby-pamby poem of happy repetition (like, for instance, 'The Owl and the Pussy-Cat' by lovable Edward Lear – 'What a beautiful Pussy you are,/You are,/You are!/What a beautiful Pussy you are'). Carroll's thugs take their repeated pleasures at other critters' expense. The happy stanzaic and rhyming repetitions (the six-line stanzas rhyme ab, cb, db, giving a hard regular return of the rhyme, especially as the lines, in ballad measure, are easily read out as three long lines, each rhyming, rather than six lines so can be taken as fourteeners: 'Four other Oysters followed them, and yet another four;/And thick and fast they came at last, and more, and more, and more–/All hopping through the frothy waves, and scrambling to the shore') suck us into their obscene, gluttonous pleasure even as we experience as severe moral difference as we may in a play by Pinter or Mamet.[10] Form here, a simple, almost bodily pleasure of repetitive aural effects, overwhelms our sense of diversity in reality.

The same dissonance of form and content is true in the happy ending structure of many Victorian novels, which end not with marriage but often with marriages. For instance, *Bleak House* insists on placing multiple couples – the Woodcourts, the young Turveydrops, and Charley and her miller husband – in endless marital bliss even in the teeth of its demonstration of destruction (difference) in society and even after its manifold attacks on stagnation. (And notwithstanding Caddy's deaf and dumb child!) When focus is on a single couple, as in *Jane Eyre*, repetition takes the form of a kind of marriageotopia, with a sense of ongoing unchanging bliss. The (to us) objectionable Ferndean is so claustrophobic (buried deep in the wood) because it is to be the scene of repetitive cuddling and coddling. That St John intrudes, provoking so many different interpretations, suggests at least a resistance to Jane's conclusion: Change and martyrdom and death versus endless pleasure. The latter is a fairy-tale ending, but the other is no less unreal – apocalyptic. We post-Victorians are put on the horns of a dilemma: repeating dank and green pleasure or senseless mountain striving, change and death.

Death: the very word is like a knell bringing me to my final topic. Were Victorians able somehow to equate repetition in the form of the eternal changelessness of death with their much favoured repetition of pleasure, thus bridging prospectively the gap Freud would find between pleasure principle and death instinct? The answer is yes they did, yes, yes, yes. When we come to the end, as this brief paper is about to, among many Victorians pleasure does not stop, and it does not stop repeating itself. If sexual pleasure, repeated, approaches pornotopia, pleasure in death tends toward a thanatosotopia, endless death as endless life of repeated pleasure. In this, most believing and writing Victorians seem to agree, if on nothing much else. Cathy (II) in *Wuthering Heights* reports Linton's heaven was

> lying from morning till evening on a bank of heath in the middle of the moors, with the bees humming dreamily about among the bloom, and the larks singing high up over head, and the blue sky and bright sun shining steadily and cloudlessly. That was his most perfect idea of heaven's happiness – mine was rocking in a rustling green tree, with a west wind blowing, and bright, white clouds flitting rapidly above; and not only larks, but throstles, and blackbirds, and linnets and cuckoos pouring out music on every side, and the moors seen at a distance, broken into cool dusky dells . . . and the whole world awake and wild with joy. He wanted all to lie in an ecstasy of peace; I wanted all to sparkle and dance in a glorious jubilee.

I said his heaven would be only half alive, and he said mine would be drunk; I said I should fall asleep in his, and he said he could not breathe in mine, and began to grow very snappish. (248)

Obviously Cathy's vision is more in keeping with the amazing natural vitality celebrated in the entire novel. What should be salient, however, is that both expect the same thing in expectation: a heaven of repetition of their kind of pleasure. Grownups of all kinds, thinking forward to their heavens, imagined a place of repeating and termless communion with their beloveds or loved ones. Even Christina Rossetti's bitter sounding nun-in-training in 'The Convent Threshold' looks forward to a stasis of familiar pleasure with her beloved – if only he will heed her warnings and accept change now: 'Look up, rise up: for far above/Our palms are grown, our place is set;/There we shall meet as once we met/ And love with old familiar love' (59). Coventry Patmore, who worried a good deal about meeting all three of his wives in heaven,[11] found a happy house for angels all circulating forever about the holy Lamb in his 'Deliciae Sapientiae de Amore'. This ode from the series *The Unknown Eros* (which re-establishes the traditional move from earthly to heavenly love) asks us to look through the heavenly 'Palace portals, and behold/ The dainty and unsating Marriage-Feast.' 'Gaze' in that heaven 'and be not afraid,/Young Lover true and love-foreboding Maid./The full moon of deific vision bright/Abashes nor abates/No spark minute of Nature's keen delight./'Tis there your Hymen waits!' In perpetuity of bliss, with desire begetting only more desire! Robert Browning in 'Prospice' heroically imagines the great difference of enduring death – ending in eternity with (we trust) Elizabeth: 'Then a light, then thy breast,/O thou soul of my soul! I shall clasp thee again,/And with God be the rest!' (815). Thus also Tennyson dreams (*In Memoriam* 103) of death as a ship on which he will clasp the monumental figure of Arthur Hallam around the neck. Cultures project into their eternal futures the types of their deepest psychology. The Victorians found in their afterlives the endless return of pleasure that they worked so hard to snatch out of the change and difference that surrounded, overshadowed and limited their living quests for unchanging, renewing pleasures. Repetition without difference: play it again, Sam. Play it forever. Roll me over in the clover, roll me over, lay me down, and do it again and again and again.

In case these begin to be too pleasurable thoughts for a serious paper on repetition, let me end with a Foucauldian serious thought: repeating pleasure under stress versus quest (compulsive or not) for ever new pleasures seems to mark an epistemic fault line, beginning perhaps with early modernity, alighting briefly in the Romantic period, but falling decisively somewhere around late Victorian and *fin de siècle*, one as significant as other more conceptual changes (punishment, sexuality). If late Victorian literature offers to Miller a fair field for study of broken attempts at repetition, the earlier Victorian literature and broader culture offer numerous cases of a general struggle to recruit pleasure out of change and destruction for the final comfort of seemingly seamless repetition. Clearly Victorians were fighting against a tide of epistemic change. But of course repetition is dead; long live repetition: what does the thoroughly modern student desire: *Foucault dosim repetatur*. Repeated pleasure in subordinating history's differences and mixed stuff to desire's pleasure in system. Our compulsion is perhaps that we can't live with repetition but can't live without it.

Notes

1. See also Deleuze, 'Plato and the Simulacrum'. Unlike Baudrillard, Deleuze is not concerned to detach all signs from predecessors, but he does wish to unsettle their relations by insisting on the resituating or reframing that exists in all successor signs.
2. I am not quite sure if Miller saw these at this time as two philosophical points of view that also had successive historical life, as in effect a display of a change in attitude toward repetition. In my brief discussion of the theory of repetition I am indebted to the sophisticated reconsideration of repetition as a concept in current work by Deep Bisla, which the author kindly shared with me.

    Perhaps this is the place to thank the editors of this volume for inviting my little contribution in honour of Miller: a person whose work I obviously admire greatly as the finest in theoretical and practical criticism but who has also demonstrated on many occasions his generosity to members of our profession – repeatedly responding to requests for evaluations of colleagues' work despite his so substantial commitments to criticism.
3. In his Foucauldian study *Obsession*, Lennard J. Davis broadly surveys the development of what are called manias in the nineteenth century, obsessional neuroses by Freud, and eventually get renamed and resited in the twentieth century as clinical obsessive-compulsive disorders. He notes the obsession with obsession in patients, doctors, writers and society generally, especially in the nineteenth century and since. His useful interrogation of any clear partition between clinical obsession-compulsion and 'normal' desire for repetition usefully suggests that Victorian repetitions and repetition compulsions were only separated by degree, not kind. Contemporary clinical definitions of obsessive-compulsive disorders define them as based on thoughts that are 'distressful, persistent and recurrent' (p. 11). The distress would seem even in the nineteenth century to offer in theory a way of distinguishing obsessive-compulsive behaviour from pleasurable repetitions, but the distinction can be in practice difficult: Lennard cites the nineteenth-century reception of Casanova, who would become in the

twentieth century the eponym of obsessive-compulsive sexual behaviour, as devoid of any sense of compulsion or pain: he is merely sensual and/or tasteless (pp. 171–2). On nineteenth-century versions of sexual monomanias see also Helen Small's study of *Love's Madness*.

4. 'A large part, a very large part, of the world seems to be ready to advance to something good – to have prepared all the means to advance to something good – and then to have stopped, and not advanced. India, Japan, China, almost every sort of Oriental civilisation, though differing in nearly all other things, are in this alike. They look as if they had paused when there was no reason for pausing – when a mere observer from without would say they were likely not to pause.

   The reason is that only those nations can progress which preserve and use the fundamental peculiarity which was given by nature to man's organism as to all other organisms. By a law of which we know no reason, but which is among the first by which Providence guides and governs the world, there is a tendency in descendants to be like their progenitors, and yet a tendency also in descendants to *differ* from their progenitors. The work of nature in making generations is a patchwork – part resemblance, part contrast. In certain respects each born generation is not like the last born; and in certain other respects it is like the last. But the peculiarity of arrested civilisation is to kill out varieties at birth almost; that is, in early childhood, and before they can develop. The fixed custom which public opinion alone tolerates is imposed on all minds, whether it suits them or not': Bagehot, *Physics and Politics*, p. 40. Cf. Mill on the sway of 'custom' over the East: *On Liberty*, pp. 41–2.

5. Freud's concept of *Nachträglichkeit* as shock experienced only in repetition – as in the Wolf Man's experience of parental sex – would be an unpleasing version of this mechanism. A parallel but pleasing one would be the recognition of sex as pleasure in the second lovemaking in the film of Marguerite Duras's *The Lover*. But the belated version can exist on a purely cognitive plane that also allows pleasure: the second hearing of a repeated motif in a musical piece – indeed second hearing or reading or seeing of any work of art.

6. Though it is somewhat like Kierkegaard's choice of the past revisited over the necessary failure of future attempts to repeat a past happiness. It is also oddly similar to Homi Bhabha's use of *Entstellung* as the repositioning of a received discourse (here of romantic love) in a restatement (refiguration) that serves a postromantic's needs – as the needs of the postcolonial subject are served by repetition with a difference but a difference that is denied: see the essay 'Signs Taken for Wonders'.

7. These are in effect social performances in repetition. They could be considered broadly, though I do not go there here, in relation to Victor Turner's ideas of repeat performance to create social action or Judith Butler's ideas of gendering as repeated performances, or Althusser's grounding of ideology in (repeated) material practices.

8. The form of his pleasure of course also suggests René Girard's concept of triangulated desire and its development in Eve Sedgwick's *Between Men*.

9. Gertrude Stein offers one well-known version of the modern alternative in 'Portraits and Repetition', where she says, 'No matter how often what

happened had happened any time anyone told anything there was no repetition.'
10. Worth also noting here Victorian fascination with highly structured verse forms presented in extensive series – Lear again with his limericks, the many sonnet sequences, *In Memoriam*, *The Rubaiyat* (so many quatrains). Victorians liked repeated readings and treasuries of well-known verse (e.g. Palgrave's *Golden Treasury*) and resisted the postmodern view that rereadings are necessarily re-sitings and reinterpretations.
11. Specifically in the late poem 'Amelia'.

Chapter 18

Philanthropic Rot in Print Run for Profit: The *Tu-Quoque*-Time-Bomb in Conrad's *Heart of Darkness*
Ortwin de Graef

> ... eventually the thing grew into a study of other sorts of savages at home and the civilized man's helpless plight among them.
>
> Evelyn Waugh[1]

> If this white-handed man with the perpendicular profile had been sent to govern a difficult colony, he might have won reputation among his contemporaries. He had certainly ability, would have understood that it was safer to exterminate than to cajole superseded proprietors, and would not have flinched from making things safe in that way.
>
> George Eliot[2]

'It had become so pitch-dark that we listeners could hardly see one another. For a long time already he, sitting apart, had been no more to us than a voice' (Conrad, *Heart* 70). In the darkness on board the *Nellie*, four men – the Director of Companies, the Lawyer, the Accountant and the featureless fourth who frames the tale – listen to Marlow, a man reduced to a voice recalling his quest in search of Kurtz, a man 'present[ing] himself as a voice' which he, Marlow, feared he might never hear.

> 'I made the strange discovery that I had never imagined him as doing, you know, but as discoursing. I didn't say to myself, "Now I'll never see him," or "Now I'll never shake him by the hand," but "Now I'll never hear him." The man presented himself as a voice.' [...]
> There was a pause of profound stillness, then a match flared and Marlow's lean face appeared, worn, hollow, with downward folds and dropped eyelids, with an aspect of concentrated attention. And as he took vigorous draws at his pipe it seemed to retreat and advance out of the night in the regular flicker of the tiny flame. The match went out. (92)

But of course Marlow did get to hear Kurtz:

'Oh yes! I heard more than enough. And I was right too. A voice. He was very little more than a voice. And I heard – him – it – this voice – other voices – all of them were so little more than voices – and the memory of this time itself lingers around me impalpable like a dying vibration of one immense jabber, silly, atrocious, sordid, savage or simply mean, without any kind of sense. Voices, voices – even the girl herself – now . . .'
He was silent for a long time. (93)

After that silence, Marlow at last begins to recount his encounter with Kurtz – hearing his voice, reading his handwritten report for the International Society for the Suppression of Savage Customs:

'Seventeen pages of close writing he had found time for! But this must have been before his – let us say – nerves, went wrong and caused him to preside at certain midnight dances ending with unspeakable rites, which – as far as I have reluctantly gathered from what I heard at various times – were offered up to him – do you understand – to Mr Kurtz himself. But it was a beautiful piece of writing. The opening paragraph, however, in the light of later information, strikes me now as ominous. He began with the argument that we "whites from the point of development we had arrived at must necessarily appear to them (savages) in the nature of supernatural beings – we approach them with the might as of deity," and so on, and so on. "By the simple exercise of our will we can exert a power for good practically unbounded," etc. etc. From that point he soared – and took me with him.' (95)

In his excellent Cambridge edition of *Heart of Darkness*, Owen Knowles provides the following textual note to this passage:

Conrad's barely perceptible inverted comma before 'whites' evidently left the typist or editor with the task of determining where the direct quotation from Kurtz's pamphlet begins. Conrad's own indicator, 'began with the argument', supports MS's punctuation. (423)

In the first published version of the text, in *Blackwood's Edinburgh Magazine* in 1899, the 'direct quotation' is marked as beginning with the word 'must'. I have not had access to the manuscript, and have no reason to doubt Knowles's perception of Conrad's barely perceptible inverted comma, but the tense use in Conrad's sentence does not, in fact, seem to support the manuscript punctuation and favours the *Blackwood's* version instead. The sentence's tenses enact the weird work of memory Marlow performs, stretched between the present tense of 'appear' and 'approach' in the past words of Kurtz and the past tense of Marlow's own 'began' and, arguably, 'had arrived' uttered in the 'now' of the narration, when Kurtz's words have turned 'ominous'.

Such philological niceties must seem obscene in the face of the 'unspeakable rites' that Marlow now, 'in the light of later information', reads into Kurtz's writing. Yet Conrad's barely perceptible inverted comma does alert us to the essential strangeness of his text as it imagines a disembodied voice recalling a tale by another disembodied voice told at some unspecified time on board a boat and which then suddenly, in total darkness, begins to quote directly from a document that isn't plausibly there – absurdly even inserting an editorial explanatory parenthesis: 'them (savages)'.[3] Had Marlow learnt the report off by heart before handing it over to Kurtz's cousin back in Brussels? Probably not all of it, the 'peroration' being 'magnificent; though difficult to remember, you know' (95). The postscript, on the other hand, 'scrawled evidently much later in an unsteady hand' is notoriously memorable: 'It was very simple and at the end of that moving appeal to every altruistic sentiment it blazed at you luminous and terrifying like a flash of lightning in a serene sky: "Exterminate all the brutes!"' (95).

The direct quotations from Kurtz's pamphlet offer authoritative evidence, piercing the fabric of Marlow's dodgy memorial work with real historical writing confirming the horror at its heart. A man of noble altruistic sentiment falls prey to 'brutal instincts' and 'monstrous passions' (113) leading him astray into some lightless region of subtle horrors (104). But will that really do? Is that how the riddle reads? The text's insistence on the sheer materiality of the document it both reproduces and redacts is an instance of what J. Hillis Miller has called 'the linguistic moment': 'a breaking of the illusion that language is a transparent medium of meaning', a moment of 'suspension' that can have 'such momentum that it tends to spread out and dominate the functioning of the whole' text (*Linguistic* xiv). That language is not a transparent medium of meaning is not quite the exciting discovery it may have once seemed, but that was never the point: what remains of interest is how these moments indeed acquire momentum, generating ripples riddling the text with barely perceptible resonances that can never quite be read to rest. To remain stuck in such matters of medium reading a text with stakes as high as those of *Heart of Darkness* may seem like a case of moral myopia, yet there is just too much of this stuff to cloak it with the mantle of meaning. Hence, arguably, the 'affect' Miller has elsewhere confessed Conrad's tale inspires in him: 'uneasiness' ('Prologue' 30).

In what follows I propose to pursue a number of moments of unease riddling Conrad's text – some of them well-worn cruxes in Conrad scholarship, others coming to the surface now with the aid of digital databases that allow us to scan much more efficiently the vast empire of print in which Conrad leaves his, and Kurtz's, mark, opening new opportunities for exercises in transtextual 'delayed decoding' that render this tale even more unreadable than it always already was.[4] I will first reiterate some of the distinctions set up and knocked down again in the movements of the text before Marlow's final passage to Kurtz's Inner Station – distinctions between 'force' and 'work', 'conquest' and 'colony', 'profit' and 'philanthropy', 'efficiency' and 'mere show', 'apostle' and 'impostor', 'virtue' and 'rivets'. The instability of these distinctions, often underscored by anagrammatic effects, gives discursive shape to the absence of clear and conclusive evidence as to what it is precisely that Kurtz was and is up to, an absence that memorable readings of *Heart of Darkness* by Sven Lindqvist and Philippe Lacoue-Labarthe which I shall briefly revisit are productively in denial about. Yet while such denial may be admirable and arguably even advisable, it glosses over some of the intriguing unclear and inconclusive evidence Conrad's text does recall, so I next turn to two scenes Marlow bears witness to towards the end of his tale: his discovery of the heads stuck on stakes outside Kurtz's station, and the stand-off with the native woman as the steamer is about to take Kurtz away. Both scenes harbour alternative perspectives Marlow leaves unread, ready as he remains to stick to the 'unspeakable rites' reading. Finally, in lieu of a conclusion, I re-examine the all-too-readable postscript.

'Brute force' and 'real work'

Marlow's first musings before he begins his tale proper involve a return to the time when Britain, too, was 'one of the dark places of the earth' (45). He imagines how a Roman commander ordered to go up the Thames might have felt, or a young Roman citizen travelling 'in the train of some prefect, or tax-gatherer, or trader even': 'the growing regrets, the longing to escape, the powerless disgust, the surrender – the hate' (46–7). But no sooner is the implied similarity between the Roman and the British Empire entertained than it has to be denied: 'What saves us is efficiency – the devotion to efficiency' (47). The Romans, by contrast, are no 'colonists', really, they are merely 'conquerors, and for that you only want brute force' (47). The distinction is too self-serving to stand up to scrutiny, and it would in all likelihood have puzzled many of Conrad's turn-of-the-century readers, accustomed as they were to diagnoses of the similarities between the Roman Empire and the British Empire as it increasingly expanded into regions peopled by cultures with which it shared very little history.[5] Not to mention the Roman roads still leading out of London two millennia after their construction – lasting testimony to the very Roman efficiency Marlow himself praised a little earlier when he commended the 'wonderful lot of handy men' who had built the boats that brought the Romans to Britain 'apparently by the hundred, in a month or two, if we may believe what we read' (46). As he continues his musing, Marlow concedes the point in a slippage of the pronoun. After having briefly described the actions of the conquerors, as distinct from the colonists, as 'robbery with violence, aggravated murder on a great scale', he concludes:

> 'The conquest of the earth, which mostly means the taking it away from those who have a different complexion or slightly flatter noses than ourselves, is not a pretty thing when you look into it too much.' (47)

The reflexive pronoun 'ourselves' now involves Marlow and company in the ugliness of conquest, so he recoils to something that 'saves us' by redeeming it – this time no longer named 'efficiency' but just 'the idea only'.

> 'What redeems it is the idea only. An idea at the back of it; not a sentimental pretence but an idea; and an unselfish belief in the idea – something you can set up, and bow down before, and offer a sacrifice to.' (47)

What that idea might be remains to be read. Or not.

Marlow embarks on his tale proper, which starts at a time in an unspecified past when he had 'just returned to London' after a six-year stint in 'the East': 'I was loafing about hindering you fellows in your work and invading your homes – just as though I had got a heavenly mission to civilize you' (48). Tired of loafing and hindering – never mind civilising – he then started looking for something else. He recounts how, ever since he was 'a little chap' (48), he had wanted to visit the blank spaces on the map, and that now he formed the plan to go to the Congo. Aided by an aunt with connections in Brussels, he landed a job with a Continental Trading Company who 'were going to run an oversea empire, and make no end of coin by trade' (50). Brussels, Belgium and the Congo remain unnamed throughout, as does Britain, yet Marlow's comments on the map of Africa he sees in the Company's waiting room are unmistakable:

> 'There was a vast amount of red – good to see at any time because one knows that some real work is done in there, a deuce of a lot of blue, a little green, smears of orange, and, on the East Coast, a purple patch to show where the jolly pioneers of progress drink the jolly lager-beer. However, I wasn't going into any of these. I was going into the yellow. Dead in the centre.' (50–1)

Only the unnamed British Empire delivers 'real work', it would appear – the Continental Company's projected activities of running 'an oversea empire' and making 'no end of coin by trade', by implication, seem 'unreal', as Marlow will indeed confirm when his tale turns to the Company's Central Station (65, 66). But first he has to say goodbye to his aunt.

While they are having tea, it becomes clear that not only did she successfully lobby for his position as captain of a river steamboat, she also entrusted him with a mission:

> 'It appears [. . .] I was also one of the Workers, with a capital – you know. Something like an emissary of light, something like a lower sort of apostle. There had been a lot of such rot let loose in print and talk just about that time, and the excellent woman living right in the rush of all that humbug got carried off her feet. She talked about "weaning those ignorant millions from their horrid ways", till, upon my word, she made me quite uncomfortable. I ventured to hint that the Company was run for profit.' (53)

'Rot in print' versus 'run for profit': that these phrases should be near-anagrams suggests that the difference between Marlow's 'hint' and what is let loose in 'print' may not be as straightforward as he might wish (see also Wollaeger 75). Rot in print is run for profit, too: the rot in print his aunt recycles is a close echo of phrases in Henry Morton Stanley's 1885 *The Congo and the Founding of its Free State: A Story of Work and Exploration*, and the Gospel of Work with a capital, preached earlier in the century by Carlyle, was also invoked later by Stanley in 1898 to justify Leopold II's exploits in the Congo.[6] Clearly the neat distinction between British 'real work' and Continental involvement in the business of Empire is as compromised as that between British colonists and Roman conquerors.

The aunt's reply to Marlow's 'hint' compounds the confusion: '"You forget, dear Charles, that the labourer is worthy of his hire," she said brightly' (53). This phrase, too, was used by Stanley in *The Congo and the Founding of its Free State*, but its original source is the King James Version of the Gospel of Luke (10:7), where it is rendered as a saying by Jesus to the disciples he sends out to spread the word. The jury is out on what the historical Jesus may have meant by the proverb, if indeed he did use it, but in Luke's account of the so-called 'mission charge' it ties in with then contemporary questions about the lawfulness of profiting from prophecy or preaching: working the word deserves a reward.[7] Conrad, as we know from a 1914 letter to Edward Garnett, was deeply suspicious of Christianity and its spread across the earth:

> I am not blind to its services but the absurd oriental fable from which it starts irritates me. Great, improving, softening, compassionate it may be but it has lent itself with amazing facility to cruel distortion and is the only religion

which, with its impossible standards, has brought an infinity of anguish to innumerable souls – on this earth. (*Letters* 5: 358)

Marlow's aunt has no such misgivings about the 'glorious idea' (49) and for her there need be no conflict between mission and money; for Marlow that just goes to show how queer women are:

> 'It's queer how out of touch with truth women are! They live in a world of their own, and there had never been anything like it, and never can be. It is too beautiful altogether; and if they were to set it up it would go to pieces before the first sunset. Some confounded fact, we men have been living contentedly with ever since the day of creation would start up and knock the whole thing over.
> After this I got embraced, told to wear flannel, be sure to write often and so on – and I left. In the street – I don't know why – a queer feeling came to me that I was an impostor.' (53)

Following close on the observation of women's 'queer' truth-deafness instantiated in his aunt's conception of his mission as that of some sort of 'apostle', Marlow's 'queer feeling' that he is an 'imposter' once again ties lines he tries to disentangle into letter-knots. For is not this 'queer feeling' an indication of a lingering awareness on the part of Marlow that there is something false in his venture, that it is he who is out of touch with truth? After all, he professes disdain both for the Company's commercial 'rapacity' (65) and for the 'philanthropic pretence' (66) that accompanies its operations – the question then being what on earth he thinks *he* is doing, other than opportunistically making use of the occasion to satisfy a boyhood dream. What is the unsentimental 'idea at the back of it' (47) redeeming *his* participation in the enterprise? As the story continues, Kurtz is the figure who will increasingly take over the blank space in Marlow's make-up where ordinarily purpose would be located: Kurtz becomes Marlow's motive, and the core of the conundrum is Kurtz's purpose.[8]

Virtue versus Rivets

Upon arrival at the Central Station, Marlow learns that the boat he is supposed to steer up to the Inner Station, which is where Kurtz holds court, has struck some stones in the river and has sunk with a hole in its bottom. It will take months to repair, giving Marlow plenty of time to get sick of the Central Station.

> 'It was as unreal as everything else – as the philanthropic pretence of the whole concern, as their talk, as their government, as their show of work. The only real feeling was a desire to get appointed to a trading-post where

ivory was to be had, so that they could earn percentages. They intrigued and slandered and hated each other only on that account – but as to effectually lifting a little finger – oh, no.' (66–7)

The Central Station represents the Company's lack of both efficiency and an 'idea at the back of it' – although something pretending to represent such an idea is clearly in the air, attached to the name of Kurtz and, to Marlow's surprise, to his own, as becomes clear in his conversation with the 'first-class agent' in charge of brickmaking who keeps 'pumping' Marlow about his Brussels connections. Marlow recalls: 'At first I was astonished, but very soon I became awfully curious to see what he would find out from me' (67). As are we, as we read this now, for the irony is at least double: Marlow mocks the first-class agent for thinking he, Marlow, has some secret something to share, something Marlow ironically pretends to be curious about, presumably knowing full well himself whatever there is to be found out from him; yet the further irony is that that is precisely what he does not know, and what we as readers are awfully curious to find out. Marlow turns the tables and questions the first-class agent:

'"Tell me, pray," said I, "who is this Mr Kurtz?" "The chief of the Inner Station," he answered in a short tone looking away. "Much obliged," I said, laughing. "And you are the brickmaker of the Central Station. Every one knows that." He was silent for a while. "He is a prodigy," he said at last. "He is an emissary of pity and science and progress, and devil knows what else. We want," he began to declaim suddenly, "for the guidance of the cause entrusted to us by Europe, so to speak, higher intelligence, wide sympathies, a singleness of purpose . . ." "Who says that?" I asked. "Lots of them," he replied. "Some even write that; and so *he* comes here, a special being – as you ought to know—" "Why ought I to know?" I interrupted, really surprised. He paid no attention. "Yes. Today he is chief of the best station, next year he will be Assistant Manager, two years more and . . . but I daresay you know what he will be in two years' time. You are of the new gang – the gang of virtue. The same people who sent him specially also recommended you. Oh, don't say no. I've my own eyes to trust." Light dawned upon me. My dear aunt's influential acquaintances were producing an unexpected effect upon that young man.' (67–8)

To his surprise, then, Marlow finds himself associated with Kurtz as one of the 'gang of virtue'. This is clearly not a cause held in high esteem by the first-class agent, but it is also not a cause taken seriously by Marlow: it is, after all, the deluded dream of his aunt, more of the lot of rot let loose in print and talk at the time. Yet Marlow finds himself uncomfortably unable to disabuse the first-class agent and allows his identification as one of the 'gang of virtue' to go unchallenged, thinking that somehow this performance of 'pretence' 'would be of help to that

Kurtz whom at the time I did not see' (69–70). He feels 'captured' (70) by Kurtz – a name for which he does not yet have an image, and that troubles him. The text underscores the importance of this moment by having Marlow's narrative break down at this point, in a famous confession of expressive impotence:

> '... No, it is impossible; it is impossible to convey the life-sensation of any given epoch of one's existence – that which makes its truth, its meaning – its subtle and penetrating essence. It is impossible. We live, as we dream – alone. ...' (70)

Increasingly haunted by the worrying idea of 'virtue', Marlow turns to issues of efficiency, or rather the lack of it:

> 'What more did I want? What I really wanted was rivets, by heaven! Rivets. To get on with the work – to stop the hole. Rivets I wanted. There were cases of them down at the coast – cases – piled up – burst – split! You kicked a loose rivet at every second step in that station-yard on the hillside. Rivets had rolled into the grove of death. You could fill your pockets with rivets for the trouble of stooping down – and there wasn't one rivet to be found where it was wanted.' (70–1)

The textual disposition of Conrad's composition once more produces the temptation of the anagrammatic, scrambling the word 'virtue' that haunts Marlow as the curse of Kurtz into 'rivets'. Rivets represent efficiency: they fasten things, repair holes, keep together the instruments of empire as an industrial-commercial undertaking performing 'real work': they have nothing to do with ideas like 'virtue' – except all but one of its letters. At the level of the letter, the anagrammatic relation of 'virtue' and 'rivet' itself functions as a rivet tempting us to stop the holes in Conrad's text by dint of pure pun. There is the real work of efficient enterprise and there is the delusion of the civilising mission: rivets versus virtue, and to confuse the one with the other spells disaster. Yet that is the confusion the text cannot dispel: it is what it, as text, as tool for thought, can only compound.

Intent as he is on getting his hands on rivets, Marlow remains riveted by virtue. Turning away from the first-class agent, he goes to his wrecked steamer, a negative icon of efficiency, an instrument of work rather than ideas, now useless for lack of rivets to repair it with, but still a comforting reminder of work. Not that Marlow likes work, as such:

> 'No. I don't like work. I had rather laze about and think of all the fine things that can be done. I don't like work – no man does – but I like what is in the work – the chance to find yourself – your own reality – for yourself, not for others – what no other man can ever know. They can only see the mere show – and can never tell what it really means.' (72)

Work, then, or what is 'in' it, allows you access to 'what it really means' – but only for yourself: it allows man to find himself for himself, as a man – which, not quite incidentally, translates into Latin as the root of virtue. Conversationally unremarkable, the pronominal positioning in the passage, slipping from 'I' to 'you' to 'they', once again testifies to the shifty set-up of the Marlow show: the belief is in some inner private truth unaffected by the rest of humanity, yet that belief can only be expressed through the marker of the ethical relation to the other – you – from which the other others – they – must be excluded (see also Sayeau 349). 'They can only see the mere show' of work, just as Marlow in the Central Station can only see 'their show of work' (*HoD*, 66), as opposed to, presumably, the 'real work' he can read in the red on the Map of Empire. But what about Kurtz's work?

Denial

Finally fed up with worrying about rivets ('One's capacity for that kind of folly is more limited than you would suppose' [74]), Marlow has 'plenty of time for meditation':

> '[. . .] now and then I would give some thought to Kurtz. I wasn't very interested in him. Still, I was curious to see whether this man, who had come out equipped with moral ideas of some sort, would climb to the top after all and how he would set about his work when there.' (74)

The lasting haunting impact of Conrad's narrative is doubtlessly partly due to the fact that we don't really know what Kurtz was up to, that we don't really know what he actually did do.[9] One response to that predicament is to deny it – and such denial is perfectly legitimate in the face of the 'luminous and terrifying' injunction scribbled on the last page of Kurtz's now 'ominous' Report: 'Exterminate all the brutes!' (95) A powerful case in point is Sven Lindqvist, who opens his book named after that injunction with the following thought:

> You already know enough. So do I. It is not knowledge we lack. What is missing is the courage to understand what we know and draw conclusions. (Lindqvist 2)[10]

At the end of the book, he spells out the point:

> In practice, the whole of Europe acted according to the maxim 'Exterminate all the brutes!'
> Officially, it was, of course, denied. But man to man, everyone knew. That is why Marlow can tell his story as he does in Conrad's novel. He has no need

> to count up the crimes Kurtz committed. He has no need to describe them. He has no need to produce evidence. For no one doubted it.
>
> Marlow-Conrad was able to assume quite calmly that both the listening gentlemen on the yacht, the *Nellie*, and the readers of *Blackwood's* silently knew quite enough to understand the story and in their own imaginations develop details the novel only implied. This knowledge is a fundamental prerequisite of the book. (171–2)

Yet even as the silent knowledge of that public secret must indeed be assumed (though the extent to which it really remains known is a cause for concern), Conrad's text also implies details whose imaginative development runs counter to what we know and must complicate the conclusions we draw – if any.

An alternative denial of our lack of knowledge of Kurtz's actual activities is to read *Heart of Darkness*, as Philippe Lacoue-Labarthe has done, as the myth of the West, the performance of its innermost truth: the horror.

> The myth of the West, which this narrative [*récit*] recapitulates (but only in order to signify that the West is a myth), *is*, literally, the thought of the West, is that which the West 'narrates' about what it must necessarily think of itself, namely – though you know this already, as you have read these pages – that the West is the *horror*. (Lacoue-Labarthe 112)[11]

What we who have read these pages know – *pour faire vite* – is that Kurtz represents 'the *figure* par excellence of the West': the artist or genius whom nature (*physis*) has endowed with *technē,* the gift to possess all gifts that supplement his own limitation, 'starting with the gift of gifts: language' (115). The horror – *our* horror – is the recognition of what this gift carves into being: the abyssal emptiness which gives rise in Western practice to '*technical* agitation' (117). As a reaction-formation to the denaturalising delimitation installed by *technē*, the West develops itself as a culture, or rather *the* culture, of power:

> The response to the vertigo of *techne* is *technical* agitation. And it is probably also in order to avert the horror (of art) that Kurtz tried to lose 'himself' in ivory trafficking and colonial royalty. Therein, precisely, is the *lure* par excellence, namely the Western lure itself – that is, as long as the West [. . .] is understood as that which will have always shrunk from the dread of knowledge (another word to translate, in its full meaning, the Greek *techne*) by taking refuge in know-how [*savoir-faire*], and as that which will have always confused ability [*capacité*] (the gift) with power. (117)

The whole of Western culture is predicated on its horror of itself, hence 'its work of death and destruction, the evil it generates and spreads to the confines of the earth [. . .] Such is its curse, and such is the gloom it imposes on the whole world: pain, sadness, an endless lament, a mourning that no work will ever diminish' (119). Such then is the curse of Kurtz as the embodiment of Western will to power, pre-eminently the power of ideology unleashed in language: the technique of death (119).

Like Lindqvist, Lacoue-Labarthe is aware of what we do not know, but he too counters this non-knowledge with another knowledge that encompasses all detail – in this case the knowledge of *technē* as destructive, disastrous creation. But he ends on a question: if *Heart of Darkness* spells the myth of the West as the myth of *technē*, and *technē* is also always art, what about *Heart of Darkness* as art, and more particularly *literature*, 'the *mythical* usage of the original *technē* that is language'? (120) Addressing this question requires a turn to what Conrad withholds but does not deny.

Voice, Invoice, Ivory

Marlow continues: one evening lying on the deck of his boat he 'heard voices approaching': the Manager of the Central Station and his uncle, the leader of the recently arrived Eldorado Exploring Expedition. The Manager complains to his uncle about Kurtz, who one year previously dismissed his assistant from the Inner Station, informing the Manager that he 'had rather be alone than have the kind of men you can dispose of with me.' (74)

> '"Anything since then?" asked the other hoarsely. "Ivory," jerked out the nephew. "Lots of it – prime sort – lots – most annoying, from him." "And with that?" questioned the heavy rumble. "Invoice," was the reply fired out, so to speak.' (74)

Unaware of Marlow's presence, the two continue their conversation. Marlow cannot pick everything up, but the gist is that Kurtz travelled down with the ivory only to then decide about halfway to return to the Inner Station and to have the ivory delivered by his 'English half-caste clerk'. (75)

> 'The two fellows there seemed astounded at anybody attempting such a thing. They were at a loss for an adequate motive. As to me, I seemed to see Kurtz for the first time. [. . .] I also did not know the motive. Perhaps he was just a fine fellow who stuck to his work for its own sake.' (75)

Perhaps. But again: what *is* Kurtz's work? The standard reading is that he works for the Company collecting ivory, for which he is presumably paid in percentages, and that, in addition, he is on some kind of civilising mission. The standard reading is further that in both lines of work he loses the plot: entering into conflict with the Company, which then cuts off his supply in trading goods and medical support so he begins to resort to unsound ways; and fashioning himself into a divine sovereign, subjecting the savages to violent rule on pretence of civilising them, culminating in the disastrous final resolve to 'exterminate all the brutes'.[12] Yet all the standard reading has to back any of this up is what the text allows the primary narrator to recall of Marlow's unreliable memory work, itself fed with information from various questionable characters – chief among them Kurtz's dubious devotee, the Russian 'harlequin' (98), 'bewildering' Marlow as 'an insoluble problem' (100).[13]

Can we entertain an alternative account? Disgusted with the rapacious cruelty and mendacity of the enterprise he is involved in, Kurtz has decided to change course. Building an alliance with the villages in the vicinity of the Inner Station, he sets out to put into real practice what the Company's PR machine merely preaches by making the natives proper stakeholders in the ivory trade – labourers worthy of their hire, so to speak. Kurtz appears throughout primarily as a 'voice' – but there is also the ivory 'invoice', and nothing in the text decisively forbids us to read this invoice as a demand for just reward. Marlow has no time for such a spin on Kurtz's 'immense plans' (113), primarily remembering Kurtz's 'broken phrases [. . .] in their ominous and terrifying simplicity [. . .] his abject pleading, his abject threats, the colossal scale of his vile desires, the meanness, the torment, the tempestuous anguish of his soul' (121). But he never really tells us what these 'broken phrases' were precisely – and when he does quote some phrases of Kurtz's spoken in 'his collected languid manner', he summarily dismisses them:

> '"This lot of ivory now is really mine. The Company did not pay for it. I collected it myself at a very great personal risk. I am afraid they will try to claim it as theirs though. H'm. It is a difficult case. What do you think I ought to do – resist? Eh? I want no more than justice." . . . He wanted no more than justice. No more than justice!' (121–2)

Given the fact that nothing of what happened gets past Marlow to us, and that Marlow's mind is made up, it is hard to resist his sarcastic verdict – yet precisely because Marlow's mind is quite literally made up by Conrad as a mind much does get past, his text does invite such resistance. Yes, the ivory is Kurtz's, and inasmuch as his 'immense plans' involve a fair share of the profit for the native stakeholders, what he wants is indeed justice.

'Rebels!'

Objection: there is no mention of anything like native stakeholders in Kurtz's operation – on the contrary, what we do get is heads of natives stuck on stakes outside Kurtz's house. The Russian, Kurtz's 'admirer' (104) and 'last disciple', explains that 'these heads were the heads of rebels', which leads Marlow to laugh: 'Rebels! What would be the next definition I was to hear? There had been enemies, criminals, workers – and these were – rebels.' (105) Yet still – and yes, this special pleading is revolting but if we want to get to the heart of the horror we must resist the comforting and ultimately aesthetic revulsion at this gruesome scene as a spectacle that doesn't involve us – yet still, as the Russian says: we have 'no idea of the conditions' (105). We don't know for certain that Kurtz himself was directly or indirectly responsible for this atrocity, and if he was, we don't know what brought this outrage on – were they natives opposing Kurtz's rule of their own accord, were they hired by Kurtz's adversaries in the Company, were they enemies of the villages Kurtz had formed an alliance with? We don't know. We know, as Conrad knew, that heads were put on stakes by the Belgian Captain Léon Rom 'as a decoration round a flower-bed in front of his house' after a punitive raid against Africans in 1895.[14] But we also know that Kurtz is not, or not just, Rom (Conrad, *Heart* xlii–xliii). And we know, as Conrad must have done, that rebel heads on stakes are nothing new – that that is what is likely to happen to rebels if they happen to get caught.

Conrad started writing 'The Heart of Darkness' (as it was then titled) late in 1898, the year of the centenary commemoration of the Irish Rebellion, which received considerable attention in British journals and newspapers, including *Blackwood's*, the magazine Marlow's tale first appeared in, which raised concern in its March 1898 issue about a 'festival of revenge' it feared would break loose ('The Looker-On' 438).[15] One of the casualties of the 1798 Rebellion was the rebel priest John Murphy, who was first tortured by the British and then 'stripped, flogged, hanged, decapitated, his corpse burnt in a barrel of tar and his head impaled on a spike' ('John Murphy'; see also Maxwell 185). Murphy was not alone: as *The Review of Reviews* recalled in its July 1898 piece on the centenary of the Rebellion: 'Hell was let loose on the unfortunate country. In towns, grisly heads of decapitated insurgents grinned from spikes upon the passers-by' ('The Topic of the Month' 75). And fast-forwarding to the early twentieth century, here is another Irish Rebel, involved in the Easter Rising seventeen years after 'The Heart of Darkness' was first published:

> Where all your rights become only an accumulated wrong; where men must beg with bated breath for leave to subsist in their own land, to think their own thoughts, to sing their own songs, to garner the fruit of their own labours – and even while they beg to see these things inexorably withdrawn from them – then surely it is a braver, a saner, and a truer thing to be a rebel in act and deed against such circumstances as this than tamely to accept it as the natural lot of men. (Casement 211)

These are the words of Roger Casement, hanged for high treason shortly after in August 1916. Conrad got to know Casement in the Congo around 1890, when they were roommates for a few weeks – as he wrote in a 1916 letter to John Quinn: 'the work he was busy about then was recruiting labour. He knew the coast languages well. I went with him several times on short expeditions to hold "palavers" with neighbouring village-chiefs' (*Letters* 5: 596–7).[16] Casement later joined the British Foreign Office as a diplomat, and it was his 1904 report on atrocities in the Congo which significantly contributed to reform. He then turned his attention to abuses of the Putumayo Indians in Peru, and to human rights in Ireland – the first got him a knighthood, the second got him hanged. Obviously, Conrad did not know about Casement's eventual execution as a rebel when he was writing 'The Heart of Darkness', but the fate of his old friend adds an uncanny retroactive ring to Marlow's laughter at the word 'rebels'. For even if the heads on stakes were Kurtz's work, the derisive dismissal of the very thought that they were indeed rebels is at least curious, coming as it does from a citizen of a country with routine expertise in the routing of those it unreservedly calls rebels.

Restored to its original context in *Blackwood's Edinburgh Magazine*, the High Tory organ of British Imperial self-congratulation, Marlow's ridiculing of the notion of rebellion sounds even more incongruous, though in the main the false note in all likelihood fell on deaf ears.[17] 'The Heart of Darkness' first appeared as a three-instalment serialisation in the February, March and April 1899 issues of the magazine. The January 1899 issue just preceding this serialisation featured an unsigned piece on the occasion of the publication of a *Life of Charles Stewart Parnell*. The Irish nationalist politician Parnell died in 1891, having led the Irish Parliamentary Party for just under a decade at the time, but as the title of the *Blackwood's* piece makes clear, they're not having it – to them Parnell is 'The Rebel King', and they're not planning to mince their words. I use the third person plural, because the unsigned article is written in the first person plural, impersonating the voice of the magazine whose readership's consent it assumes:

> [...] let there be no misunderstanding. We purpose to employ very plain language in dealing with our subject. We are not to mince matters; we are to

make no lavish use of periphrasis. We shall take the liberty of calling treason and murder by their proper names, and of applying the terms "traitor" and "murderer" to any instigator, as well as to any perpetrator, of those crimes. For the truth is that Mr Parnell was nothing if not the inveterate and implacable enemy of England. ([Millar] 138)[18]

That being the truth, it little matters what the 'rebel king' did or did not do or write, and like him, *Blackwood's* concludes, 'may they all perish who shall seek to compass the ruin and degradation of England!' (150)[19]

Two months later, in the issue that features the second instalment of 'The Heart of Darkness', *Blackwood's* has two further unsigned pieces focusing on rebellion. One deals with William Hodson, praising him for his 'daring capture' of the 'figurehead and the leaders of the great rebellion', the 1857 Indian Mutiny, though grudgingly admitting that it would have been better if Hodson had not then proceeded to shoot three of his captives with his own hand ([Cardew] 533, 535).[20] What the article does not mention is that Hodson subsequently ordered the bodies of the rebel leaders to be displayed in front of a police station 'there to be seen by all' ('William Stephen Raikes Hodson').[21] The second rebellion piece in the same issue is a scathing review of the first volume of the Whig politician and author Sir George (Otto) Trevelyan's *History of the American Revolution*, which *Blackwood's* cannot stomach. Trevelyan's 'theory of rebellion' seeks to explain the American Revolution as justifiable resistance to British misrule, but for *Blackwood's* this is to side with 'gentlemen who talked "patriotism" when they meant perfidy, and "liberty" when they meant rebellion' ([Griffin] 584).[22] And rebellion must be crushed, not spuriously justified – in Ireland, in India, as it should have been in America.

As in the piece on Parnell, *Blackwood's* prides itself on calling things by their proper name: they know a rebel when they see one. But when Marlow sees one in its pages, he cannot believe his ears: 'Rebels! What would be the next definition I was to hear? [. . .] Those rebellious heads looked very subdued to me on their sticks' (105). Well, yes, they would. Yet again, Marlow's incongruous, and in this instance curiously callous, irony backfires: there is such a thing as rebellion, not only but certainly also very emphatically in the *Blackwood's* sociolect, and no matter how justifiable or inexcusable, no number of subdued rebel heads on stakes can alter that.[23] Assuming that is what they are – which we only have on the deeply dubious authority of the Russian, who for all we know put them there himself while Kurtz was living among the natives in the villages on the lake, to get back at them for having told Kurtz he stole ivory from them which he claims he was given as a reward for shooting game, leading Kurtz to threaten to shoot him in turn (102).[24] I know, you know, we know, I'm making it up as we go along, and that is precisely what Conrad's tale maddeningly allows, and indeed demands, when you read it against the enough that you think you know.

Fury

But perhaps the suggestion is that the natives of the Congo have not got it in them to rebel against exploitation and injustice, that they, unlike the Irish, in the words of Casement, 'tamely [...] accept it as the natural lot of men'. This would resonate with Lacoue-Labarthe's reading of the opposition in the tale between the voice of Kurtz and the sounds of the savages in the forest – 'angry and warlike yells' giving way to 'a tremulous and prolonged wail of mournful fear and utter despair as may be imagined to follow the flight of the last hope from earth' (Conrad, *Heart* 91): 'the two voices that structure Marlow's narrative: the savage, undifferentiated clamour and the voice of Kurtz [...] are, purely and simply, the voice of nature (*physis*) and the voice of art (*techne*)' (Lacoue-Labarthe 116). Yet thus to identify the Africans with savage nature and to reserve articulacy for the West is to invite the charges of racism famously levelled at Conrad by Chinua Achebe when he decided it was 'clearly not part of Conrad's purpose to confer language on the "rudimentary souls" of Africa' (1787).[25]

Achebe notes that the speech of the savages in *Heart of Darkness* mainly consists of 'short grunting phrases' (Conrad, *Heart* 84), adding that the two occasions when they are given direct speech, 'even English speech', only serve to strengthen their representation as 'dumb brutes' (1788). There is, however, one rarely read passage in the text that critically qualifies this. Kurtz is watched over by Marlow and the Company men on board the boat that is to take him back, and then the natives appear on the shore, headed by 'a wild and gorgeous apparition of a woman' who appears to be in charge somehow (107). Achebe identifies her as 'obviously [...] some kind of mistress to Mr Kurtz', though no hard evidence for this can be found in the text, and he underscores her 'structural' role in the overall set-up of the tale as 'savage counterpart' to Kurtz's fiancée, the Intended, the 'most significant difference' being 'the author's bestowal of human expression to the one and the withholding of it from the other' (1787). The African woman indeed does not speak, instead suddenly raising her arms, in what seems like a signal for the other natives. 'A formidable silence hung over the scene,' Marlow adds (108), and in the manuscript version Conrad had further amplified this silence: 'Her sudden gesture was as startling as a cry but not a sound was heard' (361). The contrast with the Intended's 'exulting and terrible cry [. . .] of inconceivable triumph and of unspeakable pain' (125–6) in the final movement of the text seems clear: the subaltern cannot speak. But the text continues. The woman turns away, and the possible threat of an assault on the boat seems averted, to the relief of the Russian, who turns to Marlow:

> '"If she had offered to come aboard I really think I would have tried to shoot her," said the man of patches, nervously. "I had been risking my life every day for the last fortnight to keep her out of the house. She got in though one day and kicked up a row about those miserable rags I picked up in the store-room to mend my clothes with. I wasn't decent. At least it must have been that for *she talked like a fury to Kurtz for an hour*, pointing at me now and then. *I don't understand the dialect of this tribe*. Luckily for me, I fancy Kurtz felt too ill that day to care, or there would have been mischief. I don't understand. . . . No – it's too much for me. Ah, well, it's all over now."' (108, emphasis added)

Clearly, the African woman and the Russian harlequin are not on speaking terms – small wonder, given that the 'man of patches' may be read as the figure of Empire itself, as the text suggests when it describes his clothes as 'covered with patches all over, with bright patches, blue, red and yellow' (98), recalling the patches on the map of Africa in the Company's waiting-room. Patches, significantly, in all likelihood stolen from the African woman, who turns to Kurtz to demand justice – in her own language, which Kurtz, unlike the Russian, understands.[26] Kurtz is too ill to help, but the important point is surely that the Russian knows he would have if he could have. Like Casement, Kurtz knows the language of the natives and engages in 'palavers' with them – to him, they are not Achebe's 'dumb brutes'.[27] Yet he does write, 'Exterminate all the brutes!'

At least, that is what Marlow has us believe. But Conrad makes him admit that the note was 'scrawled evidently much later in an unsteady hand' and lets him add that '[t]he curious part was that [Kurtz] had apparently forgotten all about that valuable post-scriptum' (95–6). And for good measure, Conrad has Marlow destroy the evidence before he hands over the report back in Brussels. On the basis of what fictional evidence we do have, then, it is at least possible that Kurtz never wrote this death sentence in the first place but that it was added to the manuscript by someone else – for instance, the assistant he had dismissed back to the Central Station, to the Manager's chagrin; or even the Russian, angered by Kurtz's palavering with the African woman. Not quite straightforwardly a forgery, but Marlow's reading makes it so.[28] And even if it was Kurtz who scrawled the postscript, its very simplicity is deceptive: which brutes, precisely?[29] From what we can cobble together about his 'immense plans', it seems at least as likely that the 'brutes' he wished to see exterminated are the Belgians, the British and all the other European tribes working disaster in Africa by 'brute force'.

Postscript: 'Exterminate' and 'Brutes'

So who did order the brutes to be exterminated? Lindqvist is right: all of Europe acted according to this maxim, but let's be bloody literal-minded about it and check the actual words.[30] *British Periodicals* is an online database consisting of four separate collections, the first two of which comprise searchable facsimile page images for some 460 mainly nineteenth-century British journals, amounting to some six million pages. A search in the first two collections for 'exterminate' and 'brutes' in publications before 1900 yields 107 hits. Of these, there are only three where 'exterminate' is the verb and 'brutes' the object in the same sentence. One involves the culling of wolves in Russia and France.[31] The most recent occurs in the second instalment of Conrad's 'The Heart of Darkness' in the March 1899 issue of *Blackwood's*. The oldest comes at the end of an 1874 unsigned seven-page piece, also in *Blackwood's*, titled 'Ashantee: Extracts from the Journal of a Naval Officer Addressed to His Wife'.

The journal records part of the January 1874 expedition under the command of General Garnet Wolseley from the British Gold Coast to Kumasi, the seat of the Ashanti King, whom the British are out to force into submission. The author, identified in the *Wellesley Index* as Captain Percy Putt Luxmoore of the Naval Brigade, complains about the miserable conditions and especially about the unreliability of the bearers they have recruited among the native people: 'These brutal Fantees bolt if only they have the chance, and the night before last 400 of them deserted *en masse*. The General is now going to try what can be done in the way of gentle persuasion by powder and ball' ([Luxmoore] 522). And a week later, the journal notes: 'The so-called king of one of our so-called "friendly tribes" was going to be shot for allowing his people to bolt, but the General will not allow that, so he is only going to be hanged "pour encourager les autres"' (522–3). The 'friendly tribe' in question here are the Fante, a coastal people with a long history of enmity with the Ashanti, and part of the mission of the British expedition, in the words of its authorised chronicler, was to prevent 'the enslavement of the whole Fanti nation to [the] terrible, bloodthirsty, and despotic rule' of the Ashanti (Brackenbury *Ashanti* 26).[32] But the closing sentences of Luxmoore's journal reveal a different idea, luminous and terrifying, like a flash of lightning in a serene sky:

> I am sorry to tell you that my *valet* Krooboy has got so aristocratic that he won't answer to his name 'Jem Will', but comes directly I say 'James William', and that is such a mouthful to get out in this weather. I wish Sir Garnet would make one more stipulation with the Ashantees, and I am not alone in saying so, viz. – that they should immediately collect all their fighting men and come down after we leave and *exterminate* UTTERLY these brutes of Fantees. They are fifty times worse than any Ashantee. ([Luxmoore] 524)[33]

Kurtz may have written 'Exterminate all the brutes!', but even if he did – and if he did, he would have written it in French[34] – even if he did, he only did so as a figment of Conrad's imagination. Luxmoore (Fig. 18.1) wrote this sentence of death himself, and unlike Conrad's Kurtz's version, it is referentially precise: the 'brutes' to be exterminated are an African people, the commissioned executioners are another African people, the offence to be punished is disobedience – not to mention an annoying insistence on verbal civility in hot weather. And the voice delivering the extermination sentence is that of an Officer of the British Empire, published in the very magazine which would print pretty much the same sentence a quarter-century later for the instruction and entertainment of readers invited to shudder at such atrocity as a symptom of bad because un-British colonial rule.[35, 36]

Did Conrad read Luxmoore's journal in *Blackwood's*?[37] We know he read many issues of the journal sent to him by its editor before he started writing 'The Heart of Darkness', but these were probably relatively recent (Knowles and Moore 39). On the other hand, as Conrad would later write to his then agent J. B. Pinker, *Blackwood's* was available in every 'single club and messroom and man-of-war in the British Seas and Dominions' (*Letters* 4: 506). So it is not unlikely that browsing through back issues, he would have been intrigued by this piece from a naval officer on the 1874 Anglo-Ashanti War, especially given that the 1896 Ashanti expedition was still relatively fresh in the public memory, and a new Ashanti war was in the making (Wasserman).[38] But whether intentionally planted as such or not, the phrase 'exterminate the brutes' was always a *tu-quoque*-time-bomb ticking away in the libraries of the British Business Empire.[39]

Of course, Kurtz never wrote a thing, being wholly written up by Conrad, who could have made matters clear but decided not to – instead first giving us an excuse to condemn Kurtz that on closer reading turns out to be too comfortable for comfort, then leaving us with the uneasy sense that we(stern) humans, still digesting the cultural fall-out of Christianity

Figure 18.1 Rear Admiral Captain Percy Putt Luxmoore (b. 1835), CB, Royal Navy c.1873–4 (RCIN 2501002, Royal Collection Trust).

– that 'oriental fable' whose 'impossible standards' informed the civilising mission of the West – all work under the curse of the man-made-deity Kurtz, engaging in the interminable palaver of *Gattungswesen*, whistling in the dark. Call it Kurtzianity. We are all compromised.

Heart of Darkness is the text of that compromise, precisely to the extent that it withholds clarity and presents itself as a record of Marlow's 'inconclusive experience' of Kurtz's unreadable 'extremity' (47, 118). Conrad could be clear if he wanted to. In a letter to his friend R. B. Cunninghame Graham written shortly after finishing 'The Heart of Darkness' he states, in French:

> L'homme est un animal méchant. Sa méchanceté doit être organisée. Le crime est une condition nécéssaire de l'existence organisée. La société est essentielment criminelle – ou elle n'existerait pas. C'est l'égoisme qui sauve tout – absolument tout – tout ce que nous abhorrons tout ce que nous aimons. Et tout se tient. Voilà pourquoi je respecte les êxtremes anarchistes. – 'Je souhaite l'extermination generale' – Très bien. C'est juste et ce qui est en plus c'est clair. On fait des compromis avec des paroles. Ça n'en finit plus. C'est comme une forêt ou personne ne connait la route. On est perdu pendant que l'on crie – 'Je suis sauvé!' (*Letters* 2: 159)[40]

But instead of saying this in print, he publishes, for profit, a tale that cannot not keep up the philanthropic pretence it nonetheless denounces as rot – a compromise with words forever failing to come to terms with extermination in the name of humanity's 'impossible standards'. It would be good to be able to say this is good, that this is how Conrad's text interrupts the technique of death it is compromised by. But perhaps Conrad's own verdict should stand: 'Somme toute c'est une bête d'histoire qui aurait pu être quelque chose de très bien si j'avais su l'écrire' (*Letters* 2: 158).[41]

Notes

Keith Carabine, Nidesh Lawtoo, Pieter Vermeulen and Steven Vervaet have generously shared their thoughts about this piece with me. I hope I have done them justice in trying to clarify what can never be clear here.

1. Waugh's comment on the genesis of *A Handful of Dust*, qtd in the editor's introduction in Waugh, p. xiv.
2. Eliot, *Daniel Deronda*, p. 507.
3. For congenial thoughts on quotation marks in *Heart of Darkness* see Pecora, '*Heart of Darkness* and the Phenomenology of Voice', pp. 998–1000.
4. The phrase 'delayed decoding' (Watt, *Conrad in the Nineteenth Century*, pp. 175–9) was famously coined by Ian Watt to capture Conrad's curious reversals of cause and effect in descriptive passages, whereby readers, through Marlow, register strange sensations which only later begin to make sense.
5. See Kumar, 'Greece and Rome in the British Empire', and for an alternative account of Marlow's dubious reasoning here, singling out the same passages to different effect, Atkinson, 'Bound in *Blackwood's*', pp. 376–9.

6. See Knowles's textual notes in Conrad, *Heart*, pp. 444–5.
7. For a nuanced account of the case see Harvey, '"The Workman is Worthy of His Hire"'. An alternative reading of Conrad's use of the phrase is Steiner, 'Modern Pharisees and False Apostles'.
8. 'Marlow's structuring of his own *fabula* as *sjužet* has attached itself to Kurtz's *fabula*, and can find its significant outcome only in finding Kurtz's *sjužet*' (Brooks, 'An Unreadable Report', p. 247).
9. For a compelling, concise account of this lasting impact see Parry, 'The Moment and Afterlife of *Heart of Darkness*'.
10. The book's conclusion is identical to its opening, except for the change of 'enough' to 'that' (p. 172).
11. Lacoue-Labarthe's talk 'L'horreur occidentale' was presented at a seminar organised by *Parole sans frontière* in 1995–6 and is now available here: <http://www.parole-sans-frontiere.org/spip.php?article243> (accessed 12 February 2019). I leave aside here the implications of Lacoue-Labarthe's identification of 'the *horror*' with, specifically, 'the West', or more critically 'the myth of the West'. We are all compromised. See also Miller, 'Prologue', pp. 19–22; Dollimore; and Lawtoo, 'A frame', pp. 101–5.
12. There are many variations on what I all too conveniently assume as 'the standard reading' here, and there are numerous readings countering this 'standard reading', most famously perhaps Cedric Watts's 'covert plot' (*The Deceptive Text*, pp. 119–20). The alternative reading I sketch below goes further, foolishly perhaps, than any I have come across.
13. Conrad scholars, too, have been bewildered by the Russian harlequin, but generally give him a more favourable reading than I think he deserves. See Burgess, 'Conrad's Pesky Russian', and Galef, 'On the Margin'.
14. As reported by E. J. Glave in the *Century Illustrated Monthly Magazine* in 1897; see Knowles's explanatory note in Conrad, *Heart*, p. 453.
15. As detailed below, most of the data from nineteenth-century periodicals presented here were retrieved through ProQuest's *British Periodicals*.
16. In his 'Congo Diary', Conrad noted what 'a great pleasure' and 'a positive piece of luck' his making the acquaintance of Casement was: 'Thinks, speaks well, most intelligent and very sympathetic' (Conrad, *Last Essays*, p. 123). But in the letter to Quinn quoted above, he has changed his memory: 'He was a good companion; but already in Africa I judged that he was a man, properly speaking, of no mind at all. I don't mean stupid. I mean that he was all emotion. By emotional force (Congo report Putumayo – etc) he made his way, and sheer emotionalism has undone him. A creature of sheer temperament – a truly tragic personality: all but the greatness of which he had not a trace. Only vanity. But in the Congo it was not visible yet' (p. 598).
17. Highlighting the contrast between pro-Empire pieces in the magazine and Marlow's disgust with Continental incompetence in the Congo, Atkinson gives a plausible account of how *Blackwood's* readers might have digested 'The Heart of Darkness' as ultimately a confirmation of the superiority of British Imperialism. He touches on the question of rebellion ('Bound in *Blackwood's*', p. 376), but does not trace it back to Conrad's text or to other pieces in *Blackwood's* at that time, and so misses what I take to be a crucial further twist. For Conrad's position in the 'Blackwood circle' see Finkelstein, 'Decent Company'.

18. The article is unsigned, but the *Wellesley Index* identifies its author as John Hepburn Millar (1864–1929), a professor of constitutional law at Edinburgh University and a regular contributor to *Blackwood's*. In the 1000th issue of *Blackwood's*, which also featured the first instalment of 'The Heart of Darkness', Millar co-authored the unsigned opening piece ('Noctes Ambrosianae No LXXII') with G. S. Street; for perceptive comments on this piece, and on the overall voice of *Blackwood's*, see Atkinson, 'Bound in *Blackwood's*'.
19. The run-up to this conclusion gives a summary of Parnell's end eerily reminiscent of Kurtz's: 'The last year of Parnell's life was one of desperate and futile effort to retrieve his position. His health broke down; he was tortured by the pangs of disappointment; the cup of victory had been dashed from his lips at the very instant at which he was about to drain it. There was no rest or repose for him. From London to Ireland, from Ireland back again to London – thus the ceaseless, weary round went on. Racked by disease, blighted in his most cherished designs, he perished, solitary, unpitied and betrayed, like a wild beast in his den. Even so, and not otherwise, may they all perish who shall seek to compass the ruin and degradation of England!' (p. 150).
20. The *Wellesley Index* identifies the author of this unsigned piece as Francis Gordon Cardew (b. 1862), an officer in India. Atkinson ('Bound in *Blackwood's*', pp. 386–9) gives a fine account of the article's special pleading for Hodson and traces intriguing parallels with the case of Kurtz, though without mentioning the rebel heads on stakes, and assuming too easily that Kurtz is 'guilty'.
21. I have not been able to ascertain the extent to which Hodson's display of the dead rebels was common knowledge at the time.
22. The *Wellesley Index* identifies the author of this review as Martin Joseph Griffin (1847–1921), parliamentary librarian in Ottawa.
23. As the son of a Polish nationalist insurrectionist, Conrad arguably knew more than he wanted to about the reality of rebellion – more than he appears to have shared with Marlow, at any rate. For a concise account of Conrad's take on political rebellion see Bross, 'Eastern Europe'.
24. As Keith Carabine pointed out to me, given Conrad's father's involvement in anti-Russian agitation, the fact that it is a Russian who identifies the heads on stakes as rebels adds a further bang to the backfire.
25. For an excellent sustained revisitation of the Conrad–Achebe controversy see Lawtoo, *Conrad's Shadow*, pp. 129–207.
26. Like the Russian, the African woman has exercised Conrad scholars, but her quarrel with the Russian is rarely registered – an exception which reads that quarrel very differently from what I propose is Ketterer.
27. Robert Hampson also notes that the scene of the African woman talking to Kurtz reported by the Russian indicates 'an awareness of language and the ability to discriminate between different African dialects' at odds with the suggestion that Africans in *Heart of Darkness* are not credited with human language, but he does not develop the scene's intimation of Kurtz as a protector of the Africans ('"Heart of Darkness" and "The Speech that Cannot be Silenced"', p. 18).
28. Michael Greaney (*Conrad, Language, and Narrative*, pp. 70–1) has noted the resemblance between the pamphlet's 'postscript' and the Russian's

annotations in the seamanship manual, but does not entertain the possibility that they might actually be in the same hand. The fact that both the manual and the postscript are qualified as 'luminous' suggests that the postscript can also be un-read as cipher.
29. In his earlier Congo tale, 'An Outpost of Progress', Conrad has the trader Carlier talk more straightforwardly about 'the necessity of exterminating all the niggers' (Conrad, *Heart*, p. 452).
30. For an alternative exercise in literal-mindedness in reading *Heart of Darkness* see Schmitt, 'Tidal Conrad (Literally)'.
31. 'Even in France they cannot exterminate the ravenous brutes by killing them at the rate of 700 per annum' ('Statistics').
32. Published by Blackwood, Brackenbury's *Ashanti War* narrative unsurprisingly received a glowing review in *Blackwood's*. The review is unsigned, but the *Wellesley Index* identifies its author as the army officer William George Hamley, a frequent contributor to the magazine.
33. Underneath Luxmoore's 'Ashantee' piece, the *Blackwood's* editor writes: '[*We have been disappointed in receiving the rest of this Journal, but hope to give it in our next.*]' According to the *Wellesley Index*, only one piece by Luxmoore ever appeared in *Blackwood's*.
34. For a fine account of the silent translation at work between the lines of *Heart of Darkness* see Maisonnat, 'The Voice of Darkness', pp. 169–73.
35. Michael Greaney has convincingly described Marlow as 'a "Trojan Horse" figure, smuggling an outlandish literary voice into the conservative pages of *Blackwood's Magazine*' (*Conrad, Language, and Narrative*, p. 60); my suggestion here is that Kurtz's postscript figures as a second-order Trojan Horse tripping up Marlow in turn.
36. Rear Admiral Captain Percy Putt Luxmoore (b. 1835), CB, Royal Navy *c.*1873–4 (image, Royal Collection Trust) <https://www.royalcollection.org.uk/collection/2501002/rear-admiral-captain-percy-putt-luxmoore-b-1835-cb-royal-navy> (accessed 12 February 2019).
37. My thanks to Robert Hampson for his expert advice on this probably irresolvable issue.
38. Further speculation might involve imagining Conrad sufficiently intrigued to read Brackenbury's two-volume narrative of the Ashanti War published by Blackwood (referred to above), where he would have encountered the German missionary Kühne (also mentioned but not named by Luxmoore), who was held captive by the Ashanti for five years and served as an interpreter between Wolseley and the Ashanti King. That Ashanti business was still a live concern for *Blackwood's* in 1899 is illustrated by a review of William Butler's biography of George Pomeroy-Colley by the same Henry Brackenbury in its March 1899 issue, also featuring the second instalment of 'The Heart of Darkness', in which Brackenbury explicitly mentions having served together with Colley and Luxmoore in the Ashanti Expedition in January 1874 (Brackenbury, 'Pomeroy-Colley', p. 561). The uncanny result is that the real author of the extermination sentence, Luxmoore, is named in the same issue of *Blackwood's* that prints its fictional echo. In a further chilling twist, an early review of *Heart of Darkness* praised Conrad for his unparalleled treatment of what came to be called 'going native' but which the review names as 'the "going Fantee" of civilised man' (Clifford, 'The

Art of Mr Joseph Conrad', p. 389). See also Jasanoff, *The Dawn Watch*, p. 211.
39. As Edward Said has noted (*Culture and Imperialism*, p. 25), Conrad's choice of Marlow's narratees bespeaks his awareness that the business of empire has become the empire of business. Evidently, *British Periodicals* only covers a small amount of the print mass produced in nineteenth-century Britain, and more expansive searches also including newspapers may well yield additional precursors for Kurtz's extermination curse. For further indications that Kurtz is a medium of mass media see Lawtoo, 'Horror', pp. 255–6.
40. The translation supplied in the edition: 'Man is a vicious animal. His viciousness must be organised. Crime is a necessary condition of organised existence. Society is fundamentally criminal – or it would not exist. Selfishness preserves everything – absolutely everything – everything we hate and everything we love. And everything holds together. That is why I respect the extreme anarchists. – "I hope for general extermination." Very well. It's justifiable and, moreover, it is plain. One compromises with words. There's no end to it. It's like a forest where no one knows the way. One is lost even as one is calling out "I am saved!"' (*Collected Letters* 2, p. 160).
41. The translation supplied in the edition: 'In short, it's a stupid story that would have been very good, if I had known how to write it' (*Collected Letters* 2, p. 158).

V

Interviews

Chapter 19

The Pleasure of That Obstinacy: An Interview with J. Hillis Miller

Frederik Van Dam

> On the other hand, I should agree that 'the impossibility of reading should not be taken too lightly'. It has consequences, for life and death, since it is inscribed, incorporated, in the bodies of individual human beings and in the body politic of our cultural life and death together.
>
> J. Hillis Miller, 'The Critic as Host' (440)

In May 2015, I found myself travelling to Deer Isle, Maine, to interview J. Hillis Miller about the privileged place that the Victorian novelist Anthony Trollope occupies in his thinking. Like a Victorian novel, the story behind this interview begins with an unexpected legacy. A Flemish priest had contacted the University of Leuven in 2004 because he wanted to leave his worldly belongings to fund the study and promotion of the works of Anthony Trollope. As the resident Victorianists, Ortwin de Graef and I were given the task to find ways in which we could fulfil Father Paul Druwé's wishes. Among many other undertakings, we decided to organise a major academic conference to celebrate the bicentenary of Trollope's birth in 2015. Unfortunately, the advancing years of our keynote speaker prevented him from travelling. Undaunted, we hatched the plan of filming an interview at his home instead.

With the assistance and guidance of numerous colleagues, we turned our footage into an intellectual portrait, *The Pleasure of That Obstinacy*, in which J. Hillis Miller's reflections about Trollope lead him to consider the value of literature and the imagination in a world that is increasingly digitised and mediatised.[1] Since the notion of transparency is a recurring feature in Miller's ruminations, it has also been incorporated on the level of form: the film attempts to craft a narrative and visual language that performs the way in which Miller structures his own writing. The camera is positioned so that viewers are watching over the interviewer's shoulder: viewers know that J. Hillis Miller is talking to someone, but not to whom. The absence of a voiceover, the length of the shots, and a serene colour scheme all further serve to create the illusion of transparency; the stillness and tranquillity of the images complement the threatening implications of his words.

Like the deconstructive readings with which Miller transformed the academic landscape, *The Pleasure of That Obstinacy* refuses to sustain its own illusion. As the film progresses, the viewer becomes aware that its chronology is not linear. The film's different strands are interconnected, and, as in a Victorian multiplot novel, multiple narratives are made possible by their juxtaposition. In addition, the images that bridge and illustrate various moments create room for interpretation, as they shift between prolepsis and retrospection. The frequency of these images increases towards the end; this creates the sense of a crescendo, in which the illusion of transparency is eventually undone. Viewers, in short, have to adopt the posture of a critic if they are to unravel what is happening in front of their eyes.

In this contribution to the present book, I present an alternative version of this interview – a second remediation, one might say. Certain elements that have a performative function in the film have been excised; the linguistic register has been slightly adjusted to suit the standards of the written interview. In a similar vein, the order of the segments in the first half has been changed. Most importantly, each part of the interview is preceded by a question, but these questions merely echo the ones that I asked during the interview: they are a rhetorical construction that is supposed to guide the reader in the same way that images and sound guide the viewer of the film. I hope that this altered and remediated transcript can mimic the self-reflective quality of J. Hillis Miller's own prose.

FVD: Could you tell me a bit about the critics who influenced your views on Anthony Trollope?

JHM: One of my tasks at Johns Hopkins, in the fifties, was to teach the Victorian novel. Because I thought that I had to include Trollope in my list along with George Eliot and Charles Dickens, I chose, somewhat arbitrarily, *Barchester Towers*. During this time, Georges Poulet had become a very good friend and colleague. We used to have coffee every morning. And I complained to Poulet and said that I didn't have anything to say about *Barchester Towers* and that I was having difficulty filling up the several hours that I had allotted to this novel. It turned out that Poulet was a great reader of Trollope – that he had read all of Trollope's novels from one end to the other and essentially knew them by heart.

The main thing that I remember, and that is important still, was his notion that Trollope's novels express the 'collective consciousness of a community'. It is a metaphysical idea: it doesn't just mean that a lot of people think the same thing, but that there is a permeating consciousness which individuals share. For Poulet, that is what Trollope's novels represent. The narrator of Trollope's novels speaks for that collective consciousness, and all of the characters' minds are embedded in that collective consciousness. It is this that justifies or explains, according to Poulet, the transparency of characters to one another – the kind of intuitive understanding of what other characters are saying. This is a fascinating idea, but one that I would now be a little dubious about. I would qualify it by saying that in the late novels characters do not know what the other person is thinking. It is there to some degree; you get notations and various clues. But I think that Poulet's idea of transparency was exaggerated. Yet he made me realise that there really was something to do with teaching and understanding Trollope. This was a decisive moment in my understanding of Trollope's novels.

It's interesting to me that the greatest teacher that I've had was not a Trollope specialist, but a Trollope fanatic. Imagine that – somebody who read through all Trollope's novels and started again at the beginning. As Poulet said, 'I've read all of Trollope's novels; Trollope is very important for me. But I never had the idea of writing about him.' Ever since then, I've been trying to understand Trollope and reading more of his novels and writing about him.

FVD: Are there other, more general ways in which Poulet changed your critical practice?

JHM: You cannot imitate a great critic like Georges Poulet, but I did notice that his essays about Mme de Sévigné and Baudelaire were structured around citations. What he says is true because he makes citations. For me, that is a basic rule, which is often not obeyed these days.

You must remember that I began as a physicist. I even considered becoming a mathematics major when I was at Oberlin, so I have some scientific training. One thing that you learn from science is that you don't just say that black holes are made of green cheese. You get some data to prove that black holes are really made of green cheese. You don't make assertions without having collected some evidence. In the case of physics, evidence often takes the form of mathematical information.

So how would you catch *me* out? How would I defend myself? One way would be to show the passage that supports the general claim that I am making, and the other way would be to see whether my interpretation is reproducible. Do other people read the novel and come up with similar readings? That is where the analogy between science and literary interpretation breaks down. It breaks down because the data for black holes and from astrophysics – which is what I was especially interested in, but the same thing would go for nuclear physics – isn't the same thing as language. Language has got some special problems. Since literature is made of language, you cannot simply transfer scientific methodology from the study of black holes or supernovas to the study of literature. You have to recognise that the thing you are studying, in this case language, has got special rules and difficulties that make it very hard to get a consensus.

Why is it that people who are friendly would disagree in their ways of reading Trollope's *John Caldigate*? There are various answers to that, but I would give two. One is that the text of a novel like *John Caldigate* – not an enormous novel, but it is fairly long – gives a lot of data, if you compare it to the sort of data that people would get from black holes. And the data is not mathematical. The second thing, which is crucial for me, is that language and particularly the language of literature is full of figures of speech. That would be the simplest way to say this. Figurative language is an intrinsic part of literature, of language generally, and it creates problems.

A passage in Paul de Man's essay on Walter Benjamin's 'The Task of the Translator' sticks in my mind as a way to formulate that. He makes a distinction, based on Benjamin, between the hermeneutics and the poetics (de Man, 'Conclusions' 27). In Benjamin's essay, the distinction is between the meaning [*das Gemeinte*] and the way in which it is said [*Art des Meinens*]. In his typically challenging way, de Man says that you might wish that you could do hermeneutics (which is concerned with what the passage means) and poetics (which is concerned with how that meaning gets said) and reconcile them. It's not at all clear that this is the case. Figurative language – which is roughly what he means by poetics – interferes with hermeneutics.

FVD: Many critics allege that Trollope's style is colourless to the point of invisibility. How would you analyse, for instance, the way in which Lord Lufton courts Lucy Robarts in *Framley Parsonage*?

JHM: We get a figure which runs through the passage: '"So you have an unknown damsel shut up in your castle," [Lord Lufton] had once said to Mrs Robarts. "If she be kept a prisoner much longer, I shall find it my duty to come and release her by force of arms"' (99). This is a cliché from romances, or early nineteenth-century gothic novels. If she is an imprisoned damsel, he is the knight errant who is going to come and free her. It's a very powerful figure and it's not accidental; I think Trollope means us to understand what Lord Lufton is going to do. Behind this cliché is the image of the male who successfully courts the young maiden, who is a prisoner in her home. He frees her from that into adult life and adult sexuality. And this comes out in the last sentence: 'We may say she was fairly caught' (99). Now the figure is a little less innocent. She is not only liberated; she is caught. Lord Lufton, 'taking a pair of pheasants from the gamekeeper' – the picture shows him carrying them – 'and swinging them over his shoulder, walked off with his prey' (99). Is the prey the pheasants that he shot, or is the prey Lucy? An equivalence is made between the killed pheasants (because *he* shot them, not the gamekeeper) and Lucy: they are both his prey. So there is some slightly sinister aspect to this courtship.

Then you get the picture (Fig. 19.1). I must say that though Lucy looks like I imagine her to look – short and pretty – Lord Lufton does not correspond at all to the mental image I had. I didn't imagine those whiskers; I didn't imagine the clothes that he is wearing and the funny hat. I thought that he would have been slightly younger. In other words, it is one of those cases where I want to say to the illustrator that he has got it all wrong. And that is an interesting moment. Nevertheless, the image tells you how in the Victorian period an expert illustrator, John Everett Millais, imagined Lucy and Lord Lufton. So you have to take it seriously. The pheasants have got something to do with it. What is that birdhouse doing in the background? And the chickens on the ground, behind the doorway? What was in Millais's mind? You could say that this is just décor. There really would have been likely to be a dovecote. And doves were eaten. I know this because at my maternal grandfather's barn there was a dovecote at the top of the barn. My grandfather would go out with his shotgun and scare them out, shoot them, and we would have them for dinner. So, once again, the image of prey is there, as are the chickens. In short, we've got three different kinds of edible birds in Millais's picture. This goes beyond anything in the text, as good illustrations do. And you have to look at them to figure out what's going on in excess of the text. A good illustrator always puts something in.

Then they shake hands and they touch. There's a tactile relation, just before they separate, back at the farm; he is going in and help deal with Ponto, a hunting dog – not just a pet. I also would stress the following, strange phrase: 'I will carry a brace of pheasants with me and protect Miss Robarts from the evil spirits of the Framley roads' (99). This is another figure that adds into a general picture of the scene as being somehow like a gothic novel, with evil spirits, a damsel in a tower imprisoned, a knight who comes to protect her from the evil spirits, and so on. Anybody who says that Trollope's boring or that his style is totally transparent and uninteresting has not read very carefully.[2]

FVD: What actually happens in our minds when we read a novel – say, Trollope's *John Caldigate*?

JHM: I would like to read *John Caldigate* by way of a Husserlian epoché – which is to suspend everything, put all aside, and just try to

Figure 19.1 John Everett Millais's illustration of Lucy Robarts and Lord Lufton. Courtesy of Special Collections and Archives, Cardiff University.

make sense out of this novel. Trying to be as concrete as I can, I would say that reading *John Caldigate* creates an imaginary world in which my mind and feelings and body cooperate. It is a subliminal physical reaction. For example, when characters kiss, I do a little kissing of my own with my body. It's not quite the same as an emotion. In Trollope's fiction, we primarily imagine people and their thoughts and actions and interactions with one another. But we also see: I have a vivid idea in my mind of, for example, muddy roads and decrepit houses and Australian gold mines because Trollope's narrator tells me a good bit about these.

I would emphasise something that is very often forgotten by people who want to tie novels to the real world: you can meet John Caldigate, Hester Bolton and Timothy Crinkett and all the other people in this novel nowhere but in the pages of *John Caldigate*. They do not exist as real people. They exist only as this virtual imaginary world of the words on the page. No doubt there is some relation to the real world of that time. I wouldn't deny that. But in no sense is it a direct variant of people and their actions in the real world, even though real cities are mentioned.

What is the mode of existence of this virtual world? Where, how, what kind of thing is it? How can I put my finger on it? I think the answer to that is extremely strange, and often forgotten. It seems to be there all the time, waiting to be entered whenever I pick up the book, the printed book or an e-text. It seems to have a kind of permanent existence. Few people, certainly (except Poulet) could find time or have the ability to read *John Caldigate* at one sitting. I certainly couldn't – I have to stop it, I've got other things to do, I come back and pick it up. It is as if the story goes on happening somewhere, waiting for me to return and re-enter it at the temporal location where I had to stop reading. And I can get through it only through the word. The story exists in that strange place: it has a temporal sequence that has a quasi-musical rhythm, but it also consists of segments, marked out as chapters, with hiatuses between them that we feel the narrative voice could fill in, if it wished. The narrative just doesn't choose to tell you everything. In *John Caldigate*, you get a new chapter that says 'five months later' and the narrator never tells you what happens in those five months, but that doesn't mean you don't think that the narrator could.

My initial decision to shift from physics to English literature at Oberlin was motivated by a curiosity about that strangeness. I've written in a number of places about that. It was a very specific text, Tennyson's 'Tears, Idle Tears', which is a standard textbook text. It seemed to me, as a physicist and mathematician, really weird! What does Tennyson mean by saying that tears are idle? 'Tears of the depth of some divine despair' (266): what does that mean, exactly? My idea was that language ought to have some referential meaning. I ought to be able to paraphrase it. I couldn't. And I'm still fascinated by that.

FVD: Where does this fascination stem from?

JHM: The two books that I remember most are *Alice in Wonderland* and *The Swiss Family Robinson*. I don't know how I got the latter, but I thought it was great, and still do. When I first read it, I thought that it was about a real place. And my mother said that it wasn't real, that it was an imaginary place. I remember being very annoyed when she showed me the name of the author. I didn't think that it had an author; I thought it gave direct access through the words to a place that really did exist. I taught myself to read so I wouldn't be dependent on her. What I also really liked about the novel was the idea: it's like *Robinson Crusoe*, but with a whole family. They build a treehouse and live together. I learned from that novel to have a kind of confidence that if I were marooned in the woods I would just build myself a hut, I would find myself things to eat. I was trained by my father as a hiker; he was a great fisherman, and he taught me not to be afraid of the woods. I do have this illusion that, if I get stuck, I would be able to find berries and water. Henry David Thoreau's response was a more American one – more like my feeling about the deserts in California. He felt that rocks are completely inhuman and alien and have no sympathy whatsoever for human beings. I think that that is a more American reaction to the wilderness. What struck me when I first read *John Caldigate* and other of Trollope's colonial novels was the way in which he assumes that it will be quite easy to impose European or British customs, habits, ways of thinking, ways of behaving and so on, on alien places like Australia.

FVD: Should we still see nineteenth-century fiction as determined by a concern with social reality, or should we see it through more various lenses?

JHM: This brings us to the central issue in *John Caldigate*. In fact, the novel is not really about history or politics, or class or gender structures as such – even though you learn a lot about those, tacitly. The question, over and over in Trollope's novels, is: who will marry the unmarried maiden? Who will father the children that will inherit whatever the father possesses? The unmarried maiden, the young girl, is Trollope's big subject. Henry James was right when he said that he turned the English girl inside out (127). The members of the community are fascinated by her because she is a kind of wild card. Parents and uncles make a lot of effort to determine whom she marries; a lot is at stake. So Trollope's subject is courtship and marriage and the passing on from generation to generation of property, money, titles and standing in the world. Mary Wortle in *Doctor Wortle's School* will become a duchess and the mother of an earl because Carstairs happens to have fallen in love with her. John Caldigate will inherit his father's estate after all, and his first son will by primogeniture inherit after him. Hester Bolton, in her obstinacy, is the crucial link.

Trollope's young girls are amazingly stubborn, because they very often – and again, novel after novel – have to stick to a love commitment against total opposition from everybody. In the case of Hester Bolton, it is a horrible mistake because the man she marries happens to have been married already. But there are many versions of this, usually having to do with class. You might say that the unnamed centre of Trollope's novels – since it wasn't something that Victorian novels could really talk about, it could be spoken only indirectly – is the sexual intercourse between a lawfully married couple that will beget the next generation and their inheritance. It's the redistribution of property, wealth, status, titles.

What determines the choice of the good girls in Trollope's fiction is falling in love, as I have explained in an essay on *Ayala's Angel* ('The Grounds of Love'). You might say that falling in love is the 'God-term', in Kenneth Burke's sense (Burke 74), because it is indefinable. There is a moment when characters are not in love and there is a moment when they are. This applies to both men and women. All they can say is, 'I love her or him'. And the good girls stick to that choice, which, in a way, is not made by them, but by an inaccessible part of them. Hester Bolton doesn't say, 'I decide that I will love John Caldigate'; it just happens. And once it happens, for the good people, it is absolutely irrevocable. It is going to last for their lifetime. It is on that basis that they are so unknowingly stubborn, obstinate. One remembers all the efforts to get Hester back with her mother for the best reasons: she shouldn't live in proximity to somebody who is a sinner. But she says, 'no, I'm married to him, I don't care whether he's a bigamist. He is bone of my bone and flesh of my flesh'. Part of the pleasure of reading Trollope's novels is the pleasure of that obstinacy.

FVD: How would you respond to the charge that entering the imaginary community of *John Caldigate* is a waste of time in our dire present?

JHM: My answer to this would be partly in reference to the famous passage about ideology in Paul de Man's 'Resistance to Theory': 'What we call ideology is precisely the confusion of linguistic with natural reality, of reference with phenomenalism' (11). Ideology is a lie: it looks like referential language, but it doesn't refer to anything – like the verdict that says that John Caldigate was guilty of bigamy. It's a linguistic reference; it just doesn't happen to correspond to the outside real world. De Man makes this very counterintuitive claim: 'It follows that, more than any other mode of inquiry, including economics, the linguistics of literariness' – by which he means rhetorical reading, the study of figurative language – 'is a powerful and indispensable tool in the unmasking of ideological aberrations, as well as a determining factor in their recurrence' ('Resistance' 11). He not only identifies ideological mistakes but also explains how they come about, namely by the workings of the linguistics of literariness. 'Those who reproach literary theory', says de Man, 'for being oblivious to social and historical (that is to say, ideological) reality are merely stating their fear at having their own ideological mystifications exposed by the tool they are trying to discredit' ('Resistance' 11). In other words, they are afraid of theory because it might tell the truth about their own illusions. This reproach was often made in the old days. 'They are, in short, very poor readers of Marx's *German Ideology*' ('Resistance' 11). It's almost the only reference de Man makes to Marx. Why bring Marx in at this point? I think the answer is that Marx's *German Ideology*, which is an amazing book, demonstrates that ideology is based on linguistic mistakes.

I would argue that from reading *John Caldigate* in a very concentrated way you can learn how collective ideological mistakes are made – in this case, the whole community thinks that Caldigate is a bigamist – and how the performative power of lies may have big consequences. And the novel also teaches you that this happens especially when those lies are promulgated through the media and the metropolitan press: *The London Times* but also other less reputable journals for Trollope, Fox News and radio talk shows for us.

There are many people in the US and elsewhere, so-called 'Birthers', who believe that Barack Obama is a Muslim Kenyan, not born in the US, which is a requirement to be president of the United States. But he was born on Hawaii and is therefore an American citizen. There is a large percentage of American evangelical Republicans that think that he is the Antichrist come back to earth, just as Mrs Bolton believes that John Caldigate is an emissary straight from the devil. The analysis of religious fanaticism in Mrs Bolton is a big feature in *John Caldigate*. She is shown sympathetically, in the sense that she is doing what she thinks is right. And so are many such people in the US. Or take those people who still believe, against all the evidence, that humanly caused climate change is a hoax, concocted by scientists to fool people. Or those people who believe in the false analogy between household finances – in which you're taught, 'don't get over your head in debt' – and national finances. This is a very powerful argument for saying that the big national debt is disastrous. But they're not the same, because the government prints the money; you can't say that of any household. So I would say that teaching *John Caldigate* would be a big help in teaching students how to read the media.

Finally, it is important to remember that just 'unmasking' (de Man's word) ideological delusions by no means cures you or anyone else of those mistaken beliefs. Just to know that the manifold linguistic mistakes that have led to continuing the burning of fossil fuels has brought about irreversible climate change doesn't keep it from going on happening.

FVD: What is the role of education in addressing this challenge?

JHM: I don't think universities ought to be run by very highly paid non-academic people. How do they know what ought to be taught? And they're likely to go in for MOOCs [Massive Open Online Courses]. I think that these will put ordinary professors out of business. I mean, if I can take a course with the great Shakespeare professor at Harvard and pay very little for it, why should I take a course with the much less important gifted teacher in my own university? And the next step beyond that is, do we really need a local professor at all? But this is the law of technological development. MOOCs are like drones in the following way: once you learn that you can do it with new digital technology, it is irresistible. It will happen. It's all very well for me to say that I think that MOOCs are a terrible idea. That is not going to stop them from happening. Technological advances, particularly in the area of telecommunications, are unstoppable. It is all very well for me to say that I don't use Facebook, but I can't get along without e-mail at this point. I'm dependent on it. Computers have completely transformed my professional life, even though I was, to some degree at any rate, resistant of it. I think this means the end of the university as we have known it: the university depended on an earlier stage of technology, and when that state is transformed we are not going to need professors in quite the same way.

If I were a young person entering the profession, I'm not sure that I wouldn't become a specialist in computer games, because they have such a tremendous social power and importance. And they are analysable. They are a genre that has tremendous worldwide influence. Millions and millions of people play *Grand Theft Auto*. Even so, there is certainly still a lot of language around. You do need, in a broad sense, the ability to read in order to understand political speeches and news reports. Part of the point of my essay on multimedia is that there has always been multimedia. I don't deny that there is a difference between reading pictures and reading texts. As Paul de Man says, instead of paying attention to the visual dimension of texts, we need to 'learn to *read* pictures' (de Man, 'Resistance' 10; original emphasis). In their use of pictures, advertising and news commentary make use of what are in fact tropes. It is very valuable to recognise this – and there's nothing new about it. One of the basic tools of cinema is metonymy: you put two things side by side and the viewer assumes that there's some kind of relation between them. It is helpful to say that this is a trope called metonymy. In *Battleship Potemkin*, maggots are followed by the crowd, which is to say that the crowd is somehow like the maggots. And if I'm not mistaken, you plan to juxtapose things that I say with pictures of the lighthouse or drone pictures of the house. You will be using figurative expressions. There is nothing particularly sinister about the ability to do this, although sometimes it does involve things that are trying to be put over on you.

FVD: If technology has dramatically changed the way in which we experience the world by creating a state of near-constant surveillance, couldn't one argue that the Victorian novel paved the way for this state of affairs? Trollope's omniscient narrators naturalise a similar way of experiencing the world, don't they?

JHM: Characters are not shown as aware that any consciousness is introspecting them. This would be really weird – as if you and I and all the people here were being surveyed at this very moment by some kind of consciousness that might write it all down. And in traditional western thinking that would have to be God. Trollope never really quite says that. Telepathy would be better.

I want to take this opportunity to reflect a bit here about the circumstances of this interview, which are peculiar. So here I am – apparently just sitting here talking to somebody who's not visible – who can see me but who's not seen. And it's in the privacy of my home. I'm sitting in a chair in my living room. You might define it as a whole-scale invasion of privacy and a kind of surveillance. I'm being surveyed in ways that are hidden by, for example, not showing pictures of the cameras – you're supposed to forget that such a thing exists. So we're engaged in something that is very modern and just slightly spooky. And your team's use of drones makes that even more obvious.

In the latest *Harper's Magazine*, I just read a selection from a new book called *Unmanned: Drones, Data, and the Illusion of Perfect Warfare*. The author is reflecting mostly on the transformation of warfare by unmanned drones. Somebody in Idaho or Colorado pushes a button and somebody in Yemen is instantly killed, not unusually with some unintended civilian consequences. They now provide most soldiers with little drones, like the one you've got, but there are even smaller ones. It's part of giving them a rifle and binoculars.

> The civilian market for unmanned vehicles has expanded to serve scientific, industrial, consumer, educational and entertainment purposes. Drones

play an increasing role in industries as diverse as real estate and journalism, weather forecasting and agriculture. They identify forest fires and pipeline leaks, relay radio signals and assist in archaeological and environmental research. (Arkin n.p.)

All this is done by way of tremendous surveillance – a capacity which we saw in action yesterday. The owners of the lobster boats did not ask to have their picture taken. But the picture was taken. And our pictures were also taken by the drone. The drone came down – I could see the little eye pointed in my direction. Unmanned drones have participated in the total data collection these days at least in the US that more and more takes privacy away. What you are doing here looks innocent: 'we take a lot of pictures of Hillis Miller as he lives – who would not be interested in that?' It has no sinister purpose, but it is part of a larger operation.

FVD: Even though the film that we intend to make will not be able to sabotage this operation, we do hope that it will contribute, in a small and insignificant way, to your own project of arming people with the power to read.

Notes

1. The credits are as follows: interview and script by Frederik Van Dam, directed by Dany Deprez, cinematography by Jef Van den Langenbergh, sound recording by Tom Keymeulen, editing by Bob Mees, typography by Bram Bentein, colouring by Thomas Kumeling, soundscapes by James de Graef, sound engineering by Johan Vandermaelen, production by Frederik Van Dam and Ortwin de Graef. Première at the Trollope Bicentennial Conference (19 September 2015). This film was made possible through the generous support of the Paul Druwé Fund for Trollope Studies at the University of Leuven. The present essay has benefited greatly from the advice of Joanna Robinson.
2. For a different interpretation of this image, see Skilton, 'The Centrality of Literary Illustration in Victorian Visual Culture'.

Chapter 20

Toward an Appreciation of the Victorian *Umwelt*: An Interview with J. Hillis Miller

Monika Szuba and Julian Wolfreys

JW: I would like to continue the consideration of 'community' that you comment on in both *Communities in Fiction*, 'Rural Experience' and elsewhere, with a specific Victorian focus (something that is present in both those texts). In *Communities in Fiction*, you comment in your introduction on a number of theories of 'community'. Notably, you refer to Raymond Williams and Martin Heidegger, whose versions of community are markedly different, though both are implicitly ontologically 'whole', undifferentiated. Both men share too, a fundamental preference for the rural over the urban, whether that be through Williams's celebration of idealised classless rural communities or, in Heidegger's case, the implicit connection between a *Mitsein* (a being-together, a being-with) and the later notion of dwelling. Can you discuss Elizabeth Gaskell's vision of 'community' in *Cranford* and/or *Wives and Daughters* in the light of such theories of community and the rural? What role does gender play for Gaskell in the formation and/or disordering of 'community' and to what extent does Gaskell define or mediate, however ironically, 'community' through what you call in *Communities in Fiction* 'shared experience as *Gerede*, "idle talk"' (7), or to translate slightly differently, gossip or doxa?

JHM: I agree that theorists of community like Williams and Heidegger tend to idealise and falsely sentimentalise rural communities. A 'neighbourhood' in an American or European city is more or less as much a community as any rural groping, though they differ of course in various ways (fewer farmers in the cities (!) and less ethnic unity). In my experience of several rural communities both in the US north and in the US south actual rural communities are more the locus of class, race and gender divisions than of happy unanimity. Their *Gerede* is as much an expression of dissensus and bad ideological prejudices as of clear-seeing agreement. Many white Trump supporters in the US midlands today live in 'rural communities' and think Trump's truly awful racial, gender and anti-immigrant prejudices are just nifty.

I can write better about Gaskell's *Cranford* than about her *Wives and Daughters*. The community in *Cranford* is a little weird in that, as the narrator begins by saying, 'Cranford is in possession of the Amazons; all the holders of houses above a certain rent are women. If a married couple come to settle in the town, somehow the gentleman disappears.' The story *Cranford* tells, however, is of the gradual happy invasion of this community of old maids by men. The novel also gradually reveals that one of the two sister heroines, Miss Matty Jenkyns, has been the victim of truly horrible treatment by her elder sister, Miss Deborah Jenkyns. Deborah has taken over from their father the class prejudices that make her believe the prosperous farmer, Mr Holbrook, unsuitable as a husband for her. The small-town 'community' of Cranford ain't anything like Raymond Williams's fantasy image of happy rural Welsh communities. The community of Cranford is extremely complex and reticulated, like all real communities. A long essay would be necessary even to begin to do it justice.

MS: To refer again to *Communities in Fiction* (as well as your essay in *Twilight of the Anthropocene Idols*), you mention Derrida's law of 'auto-co-immunity', or 'com-mon auto-immunity', the desire for self-destruction which drives human cultures. Without a doubt (even if climate change deniers would disagree), we are witnessing an ongoing destruction of the planet, and we certainly cannot claim that it's 'Nobody's Fault', to employ Dickens's first title for *Little Dorrit*. If literary works may 'mirror the future', as you suggest, are there any Victorian novels which present a form of Freud's *Nachträglichkeit*, a proleptic foretelling of a present situation? Are there any which move beyond anthropocentric concerns, that do not focus on the self-centred world, human *Umwelt*?

JHM: A whole library of Victorian science fiction novels exists. [See <http://virtualvictorian.blogspot.com/2011/06/victorians-and-science-fiction.html> for one online entry about them.] Notable examples include the French novelist Jules Verne's *De la Terre à la Lune* (1865, English translation, *From the Earth to the Moon*, 1867). That novel imagined, 'with quite an uncanny accuracy, a three-manned aluminium spacecraft being launched from Florida by a cannon called Columbiad, which then returned to earth again by splashing down into the Pacific ocean'. Talk about 'proleptic'! H. G. Wells's *The Time Machine* (1895) is another example of a prophetic Victorian novel. Even so, I have the feeling that the changes in technology (airplanes, space ships, SUVs, computers, the

Internet and so on), global politics, new forms of media (TV, cinema [and what cinema!! *Black Panther!*], video games, virtual reality apparatuses, Facebook, Twitter, iPhones, the Internet, etc.), all appearing since the Victorian period, have been so radical that few novelists then had anything like a full 'proleptic foretelling of the present situation'. I add perhaps the most threatening new revelation: anthropogenic climate change. This is bringing melting arctic and antarctic ice, as well as melting of Greenland glaciers; more and stronger hurricanes; more inland storms with tornadoes; heat waves; forest fires; rising seawaters that will flood Manhattan and other cities around the globe, and so on, even including, paradoxically, an altered jet stream that exposes North America to the polar vortex and thereby brings huge snowstorms, nor'easters, three in 13 days this current January (2018). A recent authoritative (and truly terrifying) essay in *Scientific American* gives the latest prognosis. [See Jennifer A. Francis, 'The Arctic Climate Is Shattering Record After Record, Altering Weather Worldwide', *Scientific American* (April 2018), 48–53.] This essay repeats today's constant scientific refrain: 'Oh, this is happening much faster than we thought!' Scientists have tended to underestimate the acceleration of climate change caused by the feedback loop. Melting causes more and faster melting by exposing, for example, open sea, which absorbs heat, in place of ice, which reflects heat. Meanwhile, in the United States President Trump and Scott Pruitt, his head of the Environmental Protection Agency, are doing their best to remove regulations and hasten human-caused climate change. Their actions will destroy the United States as we have known it. It will become more and more uninhabitable, like the rest of the globe. This is an extraordinary example of what Derrida calls 'auto-immune self-destruction', unfolding before our eyes and in the new warmth of our bodies. In spite of the crucial advances of Victorian geology and the Victorian discovery of evolution, I suspect that if the Brontë sisters or Charles Dickens, George Eliot or either Trollope (Frances or Anthony), or even Jules Verne, were to return today they would be absolutely amazed and appalled at the way we live now, glued to our iPhones or computer screens, watching the sea levels rise out of the corners of our eyes. The best in the way of the proleptic Anthony Trollope can do in his late novel *The Fixed Period* (1882) is to imagine that in 1980 compulsory euthanasia would be imposed on those aged 67–68 and horseless carriages would be speeding around the countryside at 20 miles per hour.

MS: As you argue, Victorian novelists such as Charles Dickens, George Eliot, Elizabeth Gaskell, Anthony Trollope and others transmitted and often created ideologies, which included 'beliefs about gender, courtship and marriage, class divisions'. To what extent did they also 'unmask' certain 'ideological aberrations', to employ Paul de Man's term? Which Victorian authors may have freed their readers from their cosy cocoons by weaving counter-narratives?

JHM: Yes, such 'unmasking' happens pervasively and persuasively in the work of novelists such as those you mention. It happens most powerfully, however, not through direct preaching commentary, nor necessarily by 'weaving counter-narratives', but by straightforward narration of 'ideological aberrations' that is undercut by the irony indigenous to Victorian narrative technique. Elizabeth Gaskell more or less leaves it to the reader to figure out that Miss Matty, in *Cranford*, has been foully mistreated by her father and elder sister in the name of the ideological aberration that forbids a genteel girl to marry a farmer, even a prosperous one. A similar event happens in Anthony Trollope's *Framley Parsonage*. The latter novel centres on a 'counter-narrative' telling the story of an illegitimate girl's eventual happy marriage to an upper-class gentleman. Esther Summerson's happy ending marriage, in Dickens's *Bleak House*, to a physician, Allan Woodcourt, is another example of that theme. This story is pervasive enough in Victorian fiction as almost to be an ideological aberration rather than a counter-narrative. Society is happily ameliorated when illegitimate maidens marry well. The ideological presupposition is that class exogamy is good for middle- and upper-class society. This no doubt reflects actual changes taking place in the inherited rigidity of Victorian class structure, or it at least appeals to middle class novel-readers' wish that this rigidity might change to their benefit. All this, by the way, is exceedingly difficult to make plausible to American students in Victorian novel courses. They tend to say, 'If these two young people love one another, why don't they just marry and get on with it?' The issues your interview question poses are so important and so complex as to demand at least a whole book to deal with properly. Just untangling the treatment of class in Dickens's *Bleak House* would take many pages, perhaps a whole book in itself.

JW: There is now in the university and elsewhere a sustained interest in what, for want of a better term, is called 'Neo-Victorian fiction'. This is not that new, but has formed an ongoing commentary, a dialogue and a sanctioned discourse by the institutions of the university and criticism (seminars, journals, conferences etc.) for almost a generation. A perhaps not wholly unfair characterisation of this interest might be said to be in the critical interest in saying the apparently unsaid; to put this differently, a good deal of the critical attention devoted to the Neo-Victorian, so-called, is in its seeming ability and willingness to depict, represent, address and speak of, what the Victorians – many assume, *pace* Foucault – never said at all; or if they did, they did so in whispers, through apophasis. Taking whatever aspects of either Neo-Victorian writing or criticism of such that you wish, would you comment on your understanding of fictions such as A. S. Byatt's *Possession*, Sarah Waters's *Tipping the Velvet* and *Affinity*, Peter Carey's *Jack Maggs*, Michel Faber's *The Crimson Petal and the White* and the many other novels of the late twentieth and twenty-first centuries, and their purpose or, to take this from another angle, the *need or desire* for such fictions?

JHM: To my shame, I have not read a single one of the novels you mention. I am a true ignoramus in this field. I must therefore leave it to you, who seem to have read everything, to answer your own questions about 'Neo-Victorian fiction'. I suppose part, at least, of the reason people like reading such novels is nostalgia for an apparently happier and more stable time, before all those troubling new features I list in my answer to Monika's interview question above about prolepsis in Victorian novels. I say 'apparently'. Life was already pretty complicated for the Victorians, as Victorian novels attest if they are at all 'true to life'. Victorian novels themselves, by the way, say a good bit more about what you call the 'unsaid' than one might think, including even some details about sexual feeling and behaviour, warm kissing and embracing at least if not actual intercourse. I conclude my answer to this question by observing that these Neo-Victorian novels no doubt deserve all the attention they have received in the form of 'an ongoing commentary, a dialogue, and a sanctioned discourse by the institutions of the university and criticism (seminars, journals, conferences etc.) for almost a generation'. Nevertheless, I doubt if these new novels play today anything like the role played in the Victorian period by that period's novels. That role is now played, in my reluctant judgement, for better or worse, by cinema, TV, video games. Facebook, Twitter and all the new digital media. If you want to find out what our ideological aberrations are today, study video games, TV and films. Like Victorian novels in their period, these new media both reflect and create our present ideological presuppositions about race, class and gender, the sacred three 'chiens de faience' on the mantlepiece of cultural studies.

JW: A final, and possibly unfair question, impossible to answer, but prompted by Derrida's remark (in an interview with Derek Attridge, I believe) that he could never write on Samuel Beckett because he felt too close to the playwright and novelist: you've written on many of the canonical Victorian authors, novelists and poets. Is there one on whom you wish you'd written, or one to whom you feel 'too close' and have not?

JHM: I have always thought that Derrida in his remark to Attridge was somewhat disingenuously and ironically defending himself for an omission. I don't see that his writings are all that much like Beckett's. Tricky fellow, that Jacques. In my own case, I am not aware of any inhibitions in my choice of authors about whom to write. No doubt that is denegation, of whose cover-ups I am by definition unaware. I have been kept by my ignorance of their original languages from writing about some authors I immensely admire, such as Dostoevsky, though I have written about Kertesz, of whose native language I am profoundly ignorant. Some other important writers just don't interest me all that much for some reason, for example Wilkie Collins, Michel Foucault and Beckett himself, an unlikely threesome. I am particularly drawn to and challenged by authors like Dickens, Rimbaud, Henry James, William Carlos Williams, Yeats and Kafka, who are in one way or another strikingly idiosyncratic and difficult to 'read', that is, about whom it is difficult to write something sensible and halfway adequate. By 'sensible and halfway adequate' I would these days mean a 'rhetorical reading', that is, a reading that pays attention to figures of speech and nuances in words and syntax, as opposed to the conceptual paraphrases of 'hermeneutical readings'. I would no longer use the word 'deconstruction' at all, by the way, since a false understanding of it has won the day with the media and with many academics too. Better just to drop the word altogether in any context that involves literary study.

Afterword

Dickens in My Life
J. Hillis Miller

In Memory of Mrs Hamlin, who introduced me to Dickens
I am grateful to Malcolm Andrews for inviting me to tell the story of Dickens in my life. I am also grateful to him and his colleagues for giving me over twenty years ago the opportunity to write an essay for *The Dickensian* on *A Christmas Carol*.

My father was in the 1930s the president of a small (200-student) Baptist women's college: Keuka College, in upstate New York. This was while I attended a one-room school (the first six grades) in the fifty-family village of Keuka Park, on Lake Keuka, the little finger of the Finger Lakes. I then went on to go by school bus to Junior High School in Penn Yan, New York, about four miles north from Keuka Park. It was definitely the boondocks. Keuka College's president's house, where we lived, was quite grand, however, with a big ballroom on the third floor where my brother and I played table tennis. My parents were highly educated (father a PhD from Columbia; mother a small-town high school teacher in Virginia). My younger brother and I had and read a lot of books (the Pooh books, the Alice books, *The Wind in the Willows*, *The Swiss Family Robinson*), but I do not remember that we had books by Dickens, except possibly *A Christmas Carol*.

Unlike Henry James I did not read Dickens much, if at all, as a young child. James, in a wonderful passage in *A Small Boy and Others*, writes of his early reading of *Oliver Twist* that: 'It perhaps even seemed to me more Cruikshank's than Dickens's; it was a thing of such vividly terrible images, and all marked with that peculiarity of Cruikshank that the offered flowers or goodnesses, the scenes and figures intended to comfort and cheer, present themselves under his hand as but more subtly sinister, or more suggestively queer, than the frank badnesses and horrors. The nice people and the happy moments, in the plates, frightened me almost as much as the low and the awkward.' That passage strikes me as right on the mark. I encountered it, however, only much later in my life. It is cited in my essay of 1971 on Dickens and Cruikshank, mentioned below.

My early reading of Dickens, right up through my dissertation and then for my quite different published book on Dickens, was all in modern reprints that did not have the original illustrations. In those far-off days few people, including Dickens scholars, I among them, yet clearly realised that the Dickens books are multimedia creations, like Victorian novels generally.

To return to my first serious encounter with Dickens: My father was attempting with moderate success to raise money for Keuka College from a rich California lady whom I remember hearing about as just 'Mrs Hamlin'. She became interested in my family, as well as in supporting Keuka College. She paid for us (father, mother, my brother Bill and I) to drive to California from upstate New York (a big deal in those days). Mrs Hamlin put us up for some days in a grand Pasadena hotel, where my brother and I rejoiced in the fact that the hotel was 'American Plan'. That meant we could eat anything we liked, and as much as we liked, at breakfast, lunch and dinner. A bit later, if I remember the sequence correctly, Mrs Hamlin sent me as a present a wonderful set of little leather-bound Dickens works printed on 'Bible paper'. 4.25 by 6.25 inches. No illustrations except modern frontispieces. I still have the set on the shelf right here in the room where I am writing this: *The Works of Charles Dickens*, New Century Library (London, Edinburgh, Dublin and New York: Thomas Nelson and Sons, n.d.). Mrs Hamlin clearly thought, somewhat mistakenly, that I was up to Dickens and that I therefore ought to read him. She said that her favourite was *Bleak House*. So I started with that, but I don't remember that it made a great impression on me, as *Oliver Twist* with the Cruikshanks did on James. There's the difference between us, one among many others, to say the least! I could 'fly to the moon' more easily than I could write a James story or novel, much less a Dickens one. Some of those small volumes have marginal markings made much later, when I actually read Dickens seriously, perhaps in preparation for my PhD dissertation.

In the ensuing years I became good at physics and mathematics in high school and went off to Oberlin College, intending to become a physicist. In the middle of my sophomore year at Oberlin, I shifted from physics to English literature, with heroic (and wise) encouragement from Dorothy, my wife-to-be. (We thought of the shift as a vow of poverty for us both. That has not exactly happened.) I went off to Harvard two years later to take a PhD in English Language and Literature. Dorothy and I were married three months later, with no clear idea what we would live on, then or after. Getting my professional goals wrong at first as usual, I initially intended to specialise at the Harvard Graduate School in Renaissance literature. However, when it came time to choose a dissertation topic, I realised that what I really wanted to do was to write a dissertation on Dickens. This was in belated fulfilment of Mrs Hamlin's hopes for the role Dickens might play in my life.

Why Dickens? It was partly those little leather-bound volumes haunting me as an unfulfilled obligation and as a curiosity to see what I would make of Dickens. It was also partly the fact that I had not studied Dickens or Victorian literature generally in my Harvard graduate courses (or at Oberlin either), so his work had not been 'ruined' for me by courses good or bad. It was also partly just my slightly ornery and defiant propensities. (What's the use of doing just what everybody expects you to do? American individualism?) I chose Douglas Bush as my dissertation adviser, an odd choice, since he was not a Victorian specialist. I had briefly consulted Harry Levin, who advised me in preparation for writing a dissertation about Dickens to 'soak myself in Regency prose'. It was probably good advice, but I found it an appalling prospect of ten years of boring toil, and did not consult him again. Bush was a learned, tolerant and markedly shy Renaissance scholar. His only claim to knowledge about Dickens was his teaching, for some strange reason, an undergraduate lecture course at Harvard on the Victorian novel. I was a 'term-paper reader' for that course, but do not remember after this long time lapse one single thing he said in his lectures. That includes things he must have said about Dickens. Another case of a teacher who had not 'ruined' Dickens for me. I was already secretly reading 'theory' (Richards, the 'New Critics', Empson, Kenneth Burke, especially the latter two). I say 'secretly' because literary theory was anathema at Harvard in those days (1948–52). Reading theory was something you did, if at all, in private, behind closed and locked doors.

My dissertation was never published. It is called, somewhat pompously, 'The Symbolic Imagery of Charles Dickens'. It is an 800-page monster, two fat volumes in typescript. A copy is perhaps buried still somewhere in the Harvard Archives. I have another copy, a cast-off second copy sent back to me by Harvard. I think it may be now in the Critical Theory Archives at the University of California at Irvine. My dissertation was an attempt to use Kenneth Burke to show that Dickens's novels were what Burke called 'a strategy to encompass a situation'.

My thesis adviser, Douglas Bush, openly detested Burke, ostensibly because he used the editorial 'we', much disliked by Bush, but really because Burke was so manifestly an extravagant and irrepressible 'theorist'. I toiled away for about six months, happily with little supervision from Bush beyond five-minute progress reports each month during his office hours. (Me: 'Mr Bush, I think I can submit the dissertation in time for the June PhD granting.' Bush, smiling shyly at his shoes: 'Ah . . . you have great expectations!') Mr Bush 'read' the whole 800 pages in one weekend and accepted it, with a single comment: 'I think you might sometimes use "that" rather than "which".' I know the rule now, non-restrictive as against restrictive, but still do not know how to apply the rule in a given case. I guess Bush thought a dissertation so manifestly Burkean could not be either right or wrong, so he might as well pass it. Nevertheless, two years later he generously recommended me for a position at Johns Hopkins, getting 'which' was a turning point in my life. I suppose I could say, by starting a new sentence: 'Getting "that" was a turning point in my life,' or 'It was "that which" was the turning point of my life.' In any case, it *was* a turning point. I found Hopkins a wonderful university in those days, and my colleagues generously encouraged my work.

I got the appointment at Hopkins in part by way of a brief presentation about *Bleak House*, of all things, and spent my first few years at Hopkins trying to turn my dissertation into a book. Harvard University Press politely turned it down, not unreasonably, with a recommendation that I revise and shorten it, then resubmit. Three years later the new version that was submitted to Harvard and accepted for publication was radically different from the dissertation. It was not so much a revision as an entirely different way of looking at Dickens. I had now, by way of my Hopkins colleague Georges Poulet, come 'under the influence' (note that idiom) of the Geneva School 'criticism of consciousness'. *Charles Dickens: The World of His Novels* is an attempt to show that Dickens's work as a whole expresses a single distinctive 'imaginary world'. Nevertheless, I was still enough of a New Critic to organise the book as a chronological series of essays on individual Dickens works rather than as one big Pouletian essay with a-chronological citations from all over Dickens's writings.

Since I published that book in 1958 I have written a good many additional essays on Dickens. I have given many lectures or classes on Dickens. I have read many manuscripts on his work, directed or evaluated many Dickens dissertations, etc. All in an attempt to 'get Dickens right' at last.

Probably the most substantial of these subsequent essays is 'The Fiction of Realism: *Sketches by Boz, Oliver Twist* and Cruikshank's Illustrations'. This is my part of a little book of 1971 with David Borowitz called *Charles Dickens and George Cruikshank*, published by the William Andrews Clark Memorial Library. 'The Fiction of Realism' has been republished in various places.[1]

Part of my essay was given as a Clark Library Seminar under the Clark's auspices and those of the University of California at Los Angeles. It was the first lecture I had ever given that was illustrated by projected slides, in this case the preliminary drawings by Cruikshank for the *Sketches by Boz* plates. Those drawings are in the Houghton Collection of Harvard's Widener Library. Harvard permitted me to copy them and have slides made.

'The Fiction of Realism' is what I would now call 'rhetorical readings' of the *Sketches*, of *Oliver Twist* and of the great Cruikshanks that illustrated both those works. I was by then 'under the influence' of continental theory: Barthes, Genette, Deleuze, Jakobson, and especially my colleagues Paul de Man and Jacques Derrida. 'The Fiction of Realism' builds on a famous formulation by Roman Jakobson that (which?) associates metaphor with lyric poetry and metonymy with realist fiction. I showed that *Sketches by Boz* is comically constructed around metonymic assumptions (for example, that you can tell what a man is like by way of his doorknocker). 'As a man's surroundings are, so will his life be,' said I. 'This metonymic law functions implicitly everywhere' in the *Sketches*. The *Sketches*' relation to the Cruikshanks that illustrate it is also, I tried to show, metonymic. Finding metonymy everywhere in these verbal and graphic works gave me much pleasurable excitement, the excitement of discovery: 'Oh look! Here's another great example!' Much depends, of course, on what you do with all those discoveries.

In that same year, 1971, Penguin published a paperback edition of *Bleak House*, with a commissioned introduction by me. I still find that a good essay. It fulfils at last my obligation to Mrs Hamlin to take *Bleak House* seriously. The essay begins with the assertion that '*Bleak House* is a document about the interpretation of documents. Like many great works of literature it raises questions about its own status as a text. The novel doubles back on itself or turns itself inside out. The situation of the characters within the novel corresponds to the situation of its reader or author.'

I was thinking, as the essay goes on to show, of all the 'detectives' in the novel who piece bits of textual evidence together to uncover a secret: Tulkinghorn, Mr and Mrs Snagsby, Krook, Grandfather Smallweed, Guppy, Sir Leicester, Lady Dedlock, all the lawyers and judges, and so on. Among them is of course the well-named Inspector Bucket. Bucket is a professional detective who collects evidence. My central point in the essay is that all these 'interpreters' represent within the novel the situation of its readers. 'We' too must put signs together to make a plausible encompassing interpretation of them. Any reader who thinks that is an easy thing to do should remember the ominous epigraph from Nietzsche's *The Genealogy of Morals* that precedes my assertion that *Bleak House* is a document about the interpretation of documents: 'forcing, adjusting, abbreviating, omitting, padding, inventing, falsifying, and whatever else of the *essence* of interpreting'.

Though I do not disown any of the many books and essays I have written about Dickens, I do not feel that I have ever been entirely successful or 'encompassing' in what I have written about him. Dickens, in my view, is not only 'inimitable', but also not open to being mastered by any critical or theoretical 'approach'. What's the problem? The problem is that Dickens's greatness lies in a fantastic linguistic exuberance. That inexplicable gift is employed in the service of creating an amazing array of zany characters, each different from all the others. What I most admire in Dickens is the great comic characters and their loony dialogues. These are truly inimitable. The melodramatic main plots seem to me more or less vehicles for those dialogues, even the greatest of them, such as the Lady Dedlock story. Though such comic characters and such dialogues are everywhere in Dickens, for example Grandfather and Grandmother Smallweed in *Bleak House*, I perhaps prefer *Our Mutual Friend* to all Dickens's other work. I like it because it contains Silas Wegg, 'a literary man – *with* a wooden leg', and Mr Venus (pronounced 'Wenus'), the articulator of human bones. Wenus is usually found 'floating his powerful mind in tea'. I cannot, without laughing, think of Wegg reading to the Boffins *The Decline and Fall Off the Rooshan Empire*, or of Venus, who has the bone of Wegg's missing leg in his extensive collection, explaining to Wegg that his leg-bone has a twist to it and can't be got to fit into any of the skeletons Venus constructs and sells: 'No, I don't know how it is, but so it is. You have got a twist in that bone, to the best of my belief. I never saw the likes of you.' Or of Pleasant Riderhood rejecting Venus's offer of marriage by saying, '[I] do not wish to regard myself, nor yet to be regarded, in that boney [sic!] light.'

But I forbear. Such interchanges, complete with hyperbolic gestures and facial expressions, are truly inimitable. Each is different from all the others. I could go on citing them all day. Their timing and their crazy diction are perfect. I could do a 'rhetorical analysis' of them, for example of 'bony light', but I feel doing that would not get me very far. I have done many 'rhetorical readings' of Dickens nevertheless. Doing so is something like lamely explaining a joke. The best response is still probably delighted laughter. That laughter has been the main role of 'Dickens in my life'.

I conclude with a brief note about a recent promising way I have found to account for Venus, Wegg, the Boffins and all Dickens's other comic characters, dozens and dozens more if you include those in all the other novels along with those in *Our Mutual Friend*.

Quite recently I had the opportunity to read drafts of two chapters of a remarkable book in progress by Dr Jonathan Buckmaster, trained at Oxford and Royal Holloway. The book is on Dickens's *Memoirs of Joseph Grimaldi*. Grimaldi was a celebrated early nineteenth-century pantomime clown. This early work by Dickens (1838), or rather by 'Boz', was a rewriting of memoirs Grimaldi had written himself. They had, after Grimaldi's death, first been awkwardly rewritten and edited by a Grub Street writer, Thomas Egerton Wilks, and this work was then rewritten again by Dickens. The published work is brilliantly illustrated by Cruikshank. The title page says *Memoirs of Joseph Grimaldi, Edited by 'Boz', With Illustrations by George Cruikshank*. Here is the first of the Cruikshanks in the *Memoirs of Joseph Grimaldi*. It corresponds to the scene in Chapter One in which Grimaldi's father, also a pantomime clown, accidently throws the young Joe, dressed as a monkey and being twirled around his father's head by a rope, into the 'pit', that is, the front rows of the audience. The rope, as you can see, breaks. Cruikshank's 'composition', with Grimaldi, in this case as a child, at the centre, surrounded by amazed onlookers, recurs in his plates. It is a pantomime scene with a vengeance. It also gives the viewer an imaginary Cruikshankian vision of what early nineteenth-century pantomimes were like (Fig. Aft.1).

One chapter of his book that Buckmaster sent me argues plausibly that the *Memoirs* are a co-creation of 'Boz' and Cruikshank. Dickens's critics have paid little attention to this book over the years. It is usually considered hack-work, written in four months at age twenty-five to make three hundred pounds from the publisher Richard Bentley. Mrs Hamlin's gift set of Dickens to me does not contain it, nor is it anywhere else in my library. It has only recently been reprinted in expensive versions. Now, however, it exists in a number of free online versions, several with the Cruikshank illustrations included.[2]

To make a long story short, Dickens in his rewriting of the *Memoirs* put most of the dull factual material about performances, etc. in footnotes. He shifted the text from first person to third person, thus introducing 'Boz' as narrator. He starts with an 'Introductory Chapter' recounting Boz's (presumably Dickens's own) childhood fascination with clowns and with pantomime generally. Dickens's rewriting turns Grimaldi's *Memoirs* into a proto-Dickens novel, with rapid-fire episodes of hyperbolic violence or melodrama and with dialogue like that of the

Figure Aft.1 Joe's Debut into the Pit at Sadler's Wells.

plays in pantomimes. One example among many is the episode of 'The Pentonville Gang of Burglars' in Chapter Three. I am only now reading carefully the whole of the *Memoirs*, but my tentative hypothesis at this moment is that the 'origin' of Wegg, Venus, the Boffins and all Dickens's other great comic characters is his childhood fascination with English pantomime.

If I ever write this up it will be part of my current investigation of what really happens when we read a work of literature, criticism or philosophy. I claim that what happens is to a large degree an imaginary visual experience generated by the words and in this case also by Cruikshank's distinctive pictures. Expectations and associations, some arbitrary and accidental, help create that inner imaginary scene.

I saw a Christmas pantomime in London once. When I ('we'!) read *Our Mutual Friend* or any other work by Dickens, including the *Memoirs*, if I think of English pantomime, even in its present-day form, and of what Dickens says about his love of pantomime, that makes a lot of difference to what I see in my mind's eye. Doing that changes the role Dickens plays in my life.

Notes

1. For example, online at <https://books.google.com/books?id=VgMB9-tMS-MoC&pg=PA119&lpg=PA119&dq=Miller,+The+Fiction+of+Realism&source=bl&ots=s6BNJWCCpF&sig=1RZuK5AJWz5e47uJmYiuK1xg9f4&hl=en&sa=X&ved=0ahUKEwje-5-qiebLAhUPxmMKHZIPBPQQ6AEIKTAB#v=onepage&q=Miller%2C%20The%20Fiction%20of%20Realism&f=false> (accessed 12 February 2019).
2. See Wikipedia, 'Memoirs of Joseph Grimaldi'.

Bibliography

Works by J. Hillis Miller

'A Critical Story So Far: Interview with Christopher D. Morris', in David Jonathan Y. Bayot (ed.), *Reading Inside Out: Conversations with J. Hillis Miller* (Eastbourne: Sussex Academic Press, 2017).

'A Profession of Faith', in J. Hillis Miller, *For Derrida* (New York: Fordham University Press, 2009), pp. 1–9.

'Derrida and de Man: Two Rhetorics of Deconstruction', in Zeynep Direk and Leonard Lawlor (eds), *A Companion to Derrida* (Cambridge: Blackwell, 2014).

'Introduction', in Charles Dickens, *Bleak House* (Baltimore: Penguin, 1971).

'Naming and Doing: Speech Acts in Hopkins's Poems', *Religion and Literature* 22.2/3 (Summer–Autumn, 1990), pp. 173–91.

'Presidential Address 1986: The triumph of theory, the resistance to reading, and the question of the material base', in J. Hillis Miller, *Theory Now and Then* (Durham, NC: Duke University Press, 1991), pp. 309–27.

'Prologue: Revisiting "*Heart of Darkness* Revisited" (in the company of Philippe Lacoue-Labarthe)', in Nidesh Lawtoo (ed.), *Conrad's* Heart of Darkness *and Contemporary Thought: Revisiting the Horror with Lacoue-Labarthe* (London: Bloomsbury, 2012), 17–35.

'Reading Paul de Man While Falling into Cyberspace in the Twilight of the Anthropocene Idols', in Tom Cohen, Claire Colebrook and J. Hillis Miller, *Twilight of the Anthropocene Idols* (Ann Arbor: Open Humanities Press, 2016).

'Response to Jonathan Loesberg', *Victorian Studies* 37.1 (Autumn 1993), pp. 123–8.

'The Creation of the Self in Gerard Manley Hopkins', *ELH* 22:4 (December 1955), pp. 293–319.

'The Critic as Host', *Critical Inquiry* 3.3 (1977), pp. 439–47.

'The Fiction of Realism: *Sketches by Boz, Oliver Twist*, and Cruikshank's illustrations', in J. Hillis Miller, *Victorian Subjects* (Durham, NC: Duke University Press, 1991), pp. 119–78.

'The Grounds of Love: Anthony Trollope's *Ayala's Angel*', in J. Hillis Miller, *Black Holes*, with Manuel Asensi, *J. Hillis Miller; or, Boustrophedonic Reading* (Stanford: Stanford University Press, 1999), odd-numbered pp. 185–311.
'The Linguistic Moment in "The Wreck of the Deutschland"', in T. D. Young (ed.), *The New Criticism and After* (Charlottesville: University Press of Virginia, 1976), pp. 47–60.
'The Sources of Dickens's Comic Art: From *American Notes* to *Martin Chuzzlewit*', *Nineteenth-Century Fiction* 24:4 (1970).
'Virginia Woolf's All Saints' Day', in *The Shaken Realist: Essays in Modern Literature in Honor of Frederick J. Hoffman* (Baton Rouge: Louisiana State University Press, 1970).
'Walter Pater: A Partial Portrait', *Daedalus* 105: 1 (1976), pp. 97–113.
'Walter Pater', in Michael Groden and Martin Kreiswirth (eds), *The Johns Hopkins Guide to Literary Theory and Criticism* (Baltimore: The Johns Hopkins University Press, 1994), pp. 556–8.
Charles Dickens: The World of His Novels (Cambridge, MA: Harvard University Press, 1958).
Communities in Fiction (New York: Fordham University Press, 2015).
Fiction and Repetition: Seven English Novels (Cambridge, MA: Harvard University Press, 1982).
For Derrida (New York: Fordham University Press, 2009).
Illustration (Cambridge, MA: Harvard University Press, 1992).
Literature as Conduct: Speech Acts in Henry James (New York: Fordham University Press, 2005).
On Literature (New York: Routledge, 2002).
Reading for Our Time: Adam Bede and *Middlemarch Revisited* (Edinburgh: Edinburgh University Press, 2012).
Speech Acts in Literature (Stanford: Stanford University Press, 2001).
The Conflagration of Community: Fiction before and after Auschwitz (Chicago: The University of Chicago Press, 2011).
The Disappearance of God: Five Nineteenth-Century Writers (Urbana: University of Illinois Press, 1975).
The Ethics of Reading: Kant, de Man, Eliot, Trollope, James, and Benjamin (New York: Columbia University Press, 1987).
The Form of Victorian Fiction: Thackeray, Dickens, Trollope, George Eliot, Meredith, and Hardy (Notre Dame: University of Notre Dame Press, 1968).
The Linguistic Moment: from Wordsworth to Stevens (Princeton: Princeton University Press, 1985).
The Medium is the Maker: Browning, Freud, Derrida and the New Telepathic Ecotechnologies (Eastbourne: Sussex Academic Press, 2009).
Theory Now and Then (Durham: Duke University Press, 1991).
Thomas Hardy: Distance and Desire (Cambridge, MA: Harvard University Press, 1970).
Topographies (Stanford: Stanford University Press, 1995).
Versions of Pygmalion (Cambridge, MA: Harvard University Press, 1990).
'What the Lonely Child Saw: Charles Dickens's *Oliver Twist*', in J. Hillis Miller, *Victorian Subjects* (Durham, NC: Duke University Press, 1991), pp. 31–48.

Other Works

Achebe, Chinua, 'An Image of Africa: Racism in Conrad's *Heart of Darkness*', in Vincent B. Leitch (ed.), *The Norton Anthology of Theory and Criticism* (New York: Norton, 2001), pp. 1783–94.

Albee, Edward, *Who's Afraid of Virginia Woolf?* (New York: Scribner Classics, 2003).

Anderson, Amanda, *Tainted Souls and Painted Faces: The Rhetoric of Fallenness in Victorian Culture* (Ithaca: Cornell University Press, 1993).

Andrews, Malcolm, *Dickensian Laughter: Essays on Dickens and Humour* (Oxford: Oxford University Press, 2013).

Anglesey, Marquess of, *A History of the British Cavalry 1816–1919, Vol. 1, 1816–1850* (London: Cooper, 1973).

Anonymous, '*Great Expectations*: Reviews', *Saturday Review of Politics, Literature, Science and Art* vol. 12, no. 299, 20 July 1861, pp. 69–70.

Anonymous, 'The Looker-On', *Blackwood's Edinburgh Magazine* 163.989 (March 1898), pp. 422–38.

Anonymous, 'The Topic of the Month', *The Review of Reviews* 18 (1898), pp. 66–76.

Anonymous, *My Secret Life*, abridged (New York: Grove Press, 1962).

Aristotle, *Politics*, trans. H. Rackham (Cambridge, MA: Harvard University Press), <http://www.perseus.tufts.edu/hopper/text?doc=Perseus%3atext%3a1999.01.0058> (accessed 12 February 2019).

Arkin, William M., 'Loitering with Intent', *Harper's Magazine* (June 2015), <https://harpers.org/archive/2015/06/loitering-with-intent/> (accessed 12 February 2019).

Armstrong, Paul B., *How Literature Plays with the Brain: The Neuroscience of Reading and Art* (Baltimore: Johns Hopkins University Press, 2013).

Armstrong, Tim, *Haunted Hardy: Poetry, History, Memory* (London: Palgrave, 2000).

Arnold, Matthew, *Essays in Criticism* (London: Macmillan, 1986).

Ashton, Rosemary, *George Eliot: A Life* (London: Allen Lane, 1996).

Asquith, Mark, *Thomas Hardy, Metaphysics and Music* (Basingstoke: Palgrave Macmillan, 2005).

Atkinson, William, 'Bound in *Blackwood's*: The Imperialism of "The Heart of Darkness" in Its Immediate Context', *Twentieth-Century Literature* 50.4 (Winter 2004), pp. 368–93.

Bagehot, Walter, *Physics and Politics* (Boston: Beacon Press, 1956).

Bagehot, Walter, 'A Later Judgment: Caesarism after Thirteen Years', in Forrest Morgan (ed.), *The Works of Walter Bagehot*, 2 vols (London: Routledge and Thoemmes, 1995), pp. 440–7.

Baldwin, Peter, *The Copyright Wars: Three Centuries of Trans-Atlantic Battle* (Princeton: Princeton University Press, 2014).

Barthes, Roland, *Image/Music/Text*, trans. Stephen Heath (London: Fontana Press, 1977).

Bataille, Georges, *L'Erotisme* (Paris: Edition de Minuit, 1957).

Baudelaire, Charles, *Selected Writings on Art and Literature*, trans. P. E. Charvet (London: Penguin, 2006).

Bazin, André, 'The Ontology of the Photographic Image', in *What is Cinema?* vol. 1 (Berkeley: University of California Press, 2004), pp. 9–17.

Bentley, Colene, 'Democratic Citizenship in Felix Holt', *Nineteenth-Century Contexts* 24.3 (2002), pp. 271–89.

Bergson, Henri, *Laughter: An Essay on the Meaning of the Comic*, trans. Cloudesley Brereton and Fred Rothwell (London: Macmillan, 1911).

Bergson, Henri, *Matière et mémoire: essai sur la relation du corps à l'esprit* (Paris: Flammarion, 2012).

Bergson, Henri, *Essai sur les données immédiates de la conscience* (Paris: Flammarion, 2013).

Bettinelli, Saverio, *Del Risorgimento d'Italia dopo il mille* (Remondini: Bassano, 1775).

Bevis, Matthew, *Comedy: A Very Short Introduction* (Oxford: Oxford University Press, 2013).

Bhabha, Homi K., 'Signs Taken for Wonders', in Henry Louis Gates (ed.), *Race Writing and Difference* (Chicago: University of Chicago Press, 1985), pp. 163–84.

Biagini, Eugenio F., 'Neo-Roman Liberalism: "Republican" Values and British Liberalism, ca. 1860–1875', *History of European Ideas* 29 (January 2003), pp. 55–72.

Birke, Dorothee, Michael Butter and Tilmann Köppe, *Counterfactual Thinking – Counterfactual Writing* (Berlin: De Gruyter, 2011).

Bisla, Sundeep, 'The Elephant in the Room: Textual Repetition in the World of Real Things', unpublished study.

Blackstone, William, *Commentaries on the Laws of England*, 2 vols (Philadelphia: George Childs, 1868).

Blanchot, Maurice, *The Space of Literature*, trans Amy Smock (Lincoln: University of Nebraska Press, 1988).

Blanchot, Maurice, 'The Song of the Sirens', in *The Book to Come*, trans. Charlotte Mandell (Stanford: Stanford University Press, 2003), pp. 1–24.

Bodenheimer, Rosemarie, *The Real Life of Mary Ann Evans: George Eliot, Her Letters and Fiction* (Ithaca: Cornell University Press, 1994).

Bodenheimer, Rosemarie, *Knowing Dickens* (Ithaca: Cornell University Press, 2007).

Boone, Joseph Allen, 'Wedlock as Deadlock and Beyond: Closure and the Victorian Marriage Ideal', in *'For Better or Worse': Attitudes Toward Marriage in Literature (Part I)*. Special issue of *Mosaic: An Interdisciplinary Critical Journal* 17.1 (Winter 1984), pp. 65–81.

Booth, Bradford A., 'Trollope on Froude's *Caesar*', *Trollopian* 1.2 (March 1946), pp. 33–47.

Borges, Jorge Luis, 'The Book of Sand', in *The Book of Sand*, trans. Norman Thomas di Giovanni (New York: Dutton, 1977), pp. 117–22.

Bornand, Odette (ed.), *The Diary of William Michael Rossetti 1870–1873* (Oxford: Clarendon Press, 1977).

Bowen, John, *Other Dickens: Pickwick to Chuzzlewit* (Oxford: Oxford University Press, 2000).

Brackenbury, Henry, *The Ashanti War: A Narrative. Prepared from the official documents by permission of Major-General Sir Garnet Wolseley*, vol. II (Edinburgh: William Blackwood and Sons, 1874).

Brackenbury, Henry, 'Sir George Pomeroy-Colley', *Blackwood's Edinburgh Magazine* 165:1001 (March 1899), pp. 558–71.
Braddon, Mary, *Garibaldi and Other Poems* (London: Bosworth & Harrison, 1861).
Brontë, Emily, *Wuthering Heights*, ed. Ian Jack (Oxford: Oxford University Press, 1995).
Brook, G. L., *The Language of Dickens* (London: Andre Deutsch, 1970).
Brooks, Peter, 'An Unreadable Report: Conrad's *Heart of Darkness*', in *Reading for the Plot: Design and Intention in Narrative* (Cambridge, MA: Harvard University Press, 1984), pp. 238–63.
Bross, Addison, 'Eastern Europe', in Allan H. Simmons (ed.), *Joseph Conrad in Context* (Cambridge: Cambridge University Press, 2009), pp. 132–8.
Brown, Bill, *A Sense of Things: The Object Matter of American Literature* (Chicago: University of Chicago Press, 2003).
Browning, Robert, *The Poems*, Vol. 1, ed. John Pettigrew and Thomas J. Collins (New Haven: Yale University Press, 1981).
Burgess, C. F., 'Conrad's Pesky Russian', *Nineteenth-Century Fiction* 18.2 (September 1963), pp. 189–93.
Burke, Edmund, *A Philosophical Enquiry into the Origin of Our Ideas of the Sublime and the Beautiful* (Oxford: Oxford University Press, 2015).
Burke, Kenneth, *A Grammar of Motives* (Berkeley: University of California Press, 1969).
Cardew, Francis Gordon, 'Hodson', *Blackwood's Edinburgh Magazine* 165:1001 (March 1899), pp. 522–39.
Carey, John, *The Violent Effigy* (London: Faber & Faber, 1973).
Carlisle, Janice, 'The Endings of *Great Expectations*', in Charles Dickens, *Great Expectations*, ed. Janice Carlisle (Boston: Bedford, 1996), pp. 440–1.
Carlyle, Thomas, 'Jean Paul Friedrich Richter' [1827], repr. in Henry Duff Traill (ed.), *The Works of Thomas Carlyle, Vol. 26: Critical and Miscellaneous Essays I* (Cambridge: Cambridge University Press, 2010).
Carroll, Lewis, *Alice in Wonderland*, ed. Ronald J. Gray (New York: Norton, 1971).
Casement, Roger, 'Speech from the Dock (1916)', in Stephen Regan (ed.), *Irish Writing: An anthology of Irish Literature in English 1789–1939* (Oxford: Oxford University Press, 2004), pp. 203–12.
Cash, Peter, The Poems of Thomas Hardy: English Association Bookmarks No. 16 (Leicester: The English Association, [1994] 2011).
Chartier, Roger, *Inscription and Erasure: Literature and Written Culture from the Eleventh to the Eighteenth Century* (Philadelphia: University of Pennsylvania Press, 2007).
Chesterton, G. K., *Charles Dickens: A Critical Study* (New York: Dodd Mead and Company, 1906).
Chorley, W. H., '*Great Expectations*', review, *The Athenaeum* No. 1759 (13 July 1861), pp. 43–5.
Cicero, *Tusculan Disputations; also, Treatises on the Nature of the Gods, and on The Commonwealth*, trans. C. D. Yonge (New York: Harper & Brothers, 1899).
Clark, Timothy, 'Towards a Deconstructive Environmental Criticism', *Oxford Literary Review* 30:1 (2008), pp. 44–68.

Clifford, Hugh, 'The Art of Mr Joseph Conrad', *The Spectator*, 29 November 1902, repr. in Joseph Conrad, *Contemporary Reviews. Volume 1:* Almayer's Folly *to* Youth: A Narrative and Two Other Stories, eds Allan H. Simmons, John G. Peters and J. H. Stape (Cambridge: Cambridge University Press, 2012), pp. 386–90.
Clough, Arthur Hugh, *The Poems of Arthur Hugh Clough*, 2nd edn., ed. Frederick L. Mulhauser (London: Oxford University Press, 1974).
Cohen, Tom, 'Tactless – the Severed Hand of J.D.', *Derrida Today*, 2.1 (2009), pp. 1–22.
Cohen, Tom, 'The Geomorphic Fold: Anapocalyptics, Changing Climes and 'Late' Deconstruction', *Oxford Literary Review* (Summer 2010).
Cohen, Tom, 'Make Anthropos Great Again! Notes on the Trumpocene', *Azimuth* 9 (2017): *The Battlefield of the Anthropocene: Limits, Responsibilities and the Duty of Flight*, <http://www.azimuthjournal.com/2017/10/04/the-battlefield-of-the-anthropocene/> (accessed 12 February 2019).
Coleridge, Samuel Taylor, *Coleridge's Notebooks: A Selection*, ed. Seamus Perry (Oxford: Oxford University Press, 2002).
Collins, Philip (ed.), *Dickens: Interviews and Recollections*, 2 vols (London: Macmillan, 1981).
Collins, Philip (ed.), *Charles Dickens: The Critical Heritage* (London: Routledge, 1986).
Conrad, Joseph, *The Collected Letters of Joseph Conrad*, 9 vols, ed. Frederick R. Karl (Cambridge: Cambridge University Press, 1983–2008).
Conrad, Joseph, *Last Essays*, ed. Harold Ray Stevens and J. H. Stape, *The Cambridge Edition of the Works of Joseph Conrad* (Cambridge: Cambridge University Press, 2010).
Conrad, Joseph, *Youth, Heart of Darkness, The End of the Tether*, ed. Owen Knowles, *The Cambridge Edition of the Works of Joseph Conrad* (Cambridge: Cambridge University Press, 2010).
Courtney, W. L., 'Review of *Veranilda* by George Gissing', *Daily Telegraph* 28 September 1904, p. 6, repr. in Pierre Coustillas and Colin Partridge (eds), *Gissing: The Critical Heritage* (London: Routledge & Kegan Paul, 1972), pp. 440–4.
Coustillas, Pierre, 'The Stormy Publication of Gissing's *Veranilda*', *Bulletin of the New York Public Library* 72 (1968), pp. 588–610, <babel.hathitrust.org/cgi/pt?id=uc1.b3309922;view=1up;seq=7> (accessed 12 February 2019).
Coustillas, Pierre, 'Introduction', in George Gissing, *Veranilda* (Brighton: Harvester Press, 1987), pp. xi–xxx.
Coustillas, Pierre, *George Gissing: The Definitive Bibliography* (High Wycombe: Rivendale Press, 2005).
Critchley, Simon, *The Ethics of Deconstruction: Derrida and Levinas*, 3rd edn (Edinburgh: Edinburgh University Press, 2014).
Dallas, E. S., 'Review of *Felix Holt*', *The London Times*, 26 June 1866, p. 6, repr. in David Carroll (ed.), *George Eliot: The Critical Heritage* (London: Routledge and Kegan Paul, 1971), pp. 266–7.
Dalziel, Pamela, and Michael Millgate (eds), *Thomas Hardy's 'Poetical Matter' Notebook* (Oxford: Oxford University Press, 2009).
Dames, Nicholas, *The Physiology of the Novel: Reading, Neural Science, and the Form of Victorian Fiction* (Oxford: Oxford University Press, 2007).

Davis, Lennard, *Obsession: A History* (Chicago: University of Chicago Press, 2008).
De Man, Paul, 'Autobiography as De-facement', *Modern Language Notes* 94.5 (1979), pp. 919–30.
De Man, Paul, 'Promises (*Social Contract*)', *Allegories of Reading* (New Haven: Yale University Press, 1979), pp. 276–97.
De Man, Paul, 'Semiology and Rhetoric', *Allegories of Reading* (New Haven: Yale University Press, 1979), pp. 3–19.
De Man, Paul, 'Shelley Disfigured', in Harold Bloom et al., *Deconstruction and Criticism* (New York: Seabury Press, 1979).
De Man, Paul, 'The Resistance to Theory', *Yale French Studies* 63 (1982), pp. 3–20.
De Man, Paul, *The Resistance to Theory* (Minneapolis: University of Minnesota Press, 1986).
De Man, Paul, 'The Return to Philology', in *The Resistance to Theory* (Minneapolis: University of Minnesota Press, 1986), pp. 21–6.
De Man, Paul, 'Phenomenality and Materiality in Kant', in *Aesthetic Ideology* (Minneapolis: University of Minnesota Press, 1996), pp. 70–90.
De Man, Paul, '"Conclusions" on Walter Benjamin's "The Task of the Translator"', Messenger Lecture, Cornell University, 4 March 1983, *Yale French Studies* 97 (2000), pp. 10–35.
Deleuze, Gilles, 'Plato and the Simulacrum', in *The Logic of Sense* (New York: Columbia University Press, 1990), pp. 253–66.
Deleuze, Gilles, *Difference and Repetition*, trans. Paul Patton (New York: Columbia University Press, 1994).
Deleuze, Gilles, and Félix Guattari, *A Thousand Plateaus: Capitalism and Schizophrenia*, trans. Brian Massumi (Minneapolis: University of Minnesota Press, 1988).
Derrida, Jacques, 'The Ends of Man', *Philosophy and Phenomenological Research* 30:1 (September 1969), pp. 31–57.
Derrida, Jacques, 'Differance', in *'Speech and Phenomena' and Other Essays on Husserl's Theory of Signs*, trans. David B. Allison (Evanston: Northwestern University Press, 1973), pp. 129–60.
Derrida, Jacques, *Writing and Difference*, trans. Alan Bass (Chicago: University of Chicago Press, 1978).
Derrida, Jacques, *The Archeology of the Frivolous: Reading Condillac*, trans. John P. Leavey, Jr (Lincoln: University of Nebraska Press, 1980).
Derrida, Jacques, 'Plato's Pharmacy', in *Dissemination*, trans. Barbara Johnson (Chicago: University of Chicago Press, 1981), pp. 61–171.
Derrida, Jacques, *Positions*, trans. Alan Bass (Chicago: University of Chicago Press, 1982).
Derrida, Jacques, *Limited Inc.*, trans. Samuel Weber and Jeffrey Mehlman (Evanston: Northwestern University Press, 1988).
Derrida, Jacques, 'Signature Event Context', 'Limited Inc.', and an Afterword, *Limited Inc.* (Evanston: Northwestern University Press, 1988).
Derrida, Jacques, *Edmund Husserl's Origin of Geometry: An Introduction*, trans. John P. Leavey, Jr (Lincoln: University of Nebraska Press, 1989).
Derrida, Jacques, *The Problem of Genesis in Husserl's Philosophy*, trans. Marion Hobson (Chicago: University of Chicago Press, 2003).

Derrida, Jacques, 'Justices', in Barbara Cohen Dragan Kujundžić (ed.), *Provocations to Reading: J. Hillis Miller and the Democracy to Come* (New York: Fordham University Press, 2005), pp. 228–61.

Derrida, Jacques, 'What Remains by Force of Music', in *Psyché: Inventions of the Other, Volume I*, ed. Peggy Kamuf and Elizabeth Rottenberg (Stanford: Stanford University Press, 2007), pp. 81–90.

Derrida, Jacques, *The Animal That Therefore I Am*, ed. Marie-Louise Mallet, trans. David Wills (New York: Fordham University Press, 2008).

Derrida, Jacques, *Advances*, trans. and int. Philippe Lynes (Minneapolis: University of Minnesota Press, 2017).

Dickens, Charles, *Household Words* 39 (21 December 1850), pp. 292.

Dickens, Charles, *Oliver Twist*, ed. Kathleen Tillotson (Oxford: Clarendon Press, 1966).

Dickens, Charles, *Martin Chuzzlewit*, ed. Margaret Cardwell (Oxford: Oxford University Press, 1988).

Dickens, Charles, *Dickens's Journalism*, ed. Michael Slater, 3 vols (London: J. M. Dent, 1994).

Dickens, Charles, *Sketches by Boz*, ed. Dennis Walder (Harmondsworth: Penguin, 1995).

Dickens, Charles, *Oliver Twist, or The Parish Boy's Progress*, ed. Philip Horne (Harmondsworth: Penguin, 2003).

Dickens, Charles, *Bleak House*, ed. Stephen Gill (Oxford: Oxford University Press, 1996).

Dickens, Charles, *Great Expectations*, ed. Janice Carlisle (Boston: Bedford, 1996).

Dickens, Charles, *The Old Curiosity Shop*, ed. Elizabeth M. Brennan (Oxford: Clarendon Press, 1997).

Dickens, Charles, *The Pickwick Papers*, ed. James Kinsley (Oxford: Oxford University Press, 1998).

Dickens, Charles, *Great Expectations*, ed. Charlotte Mitchell (London: Penguin Classics, 2002).

Dickens, Charles, *American Notes*, ed. Patricia Ingham (Harmondsworth: Penguin, 2004).

Dickens, Charles, *A Christmas Carol, and other Christmas Books*, ed. Robert Douglas-Fairhurst (Oxford: Oxford University Press, 2006).

Dickens, Charles, *Memoirs of Joseph Grimaldi* (London: Pushkin Press, 2008).

Dillon, Jacqueline, *Thomas Hardy: Folklore and Resistance* (London: Palgrave Macmillan, 2016).

Dollimore, Jonathan, 'Civilization and Its Darkness', in Lawtoo (ed.), *Conrad's Heart of Darkness and Contemporary Thought: Revisiting the Horror with Lacoue-Labarthe* (London: Bloomsbury, 2012), pp. 67–86.

Eco, Umberto, *Theory of Semiotics* (Bloomington: Indiana University Press, 1976).

Eliot, George, *The George Eliot Letters*, ed. Gordon Haight, 9 vols (New Haven: Yale University Press, 1954–78).

Eliot, George, 'The Antigone and Its Moral', *Essays of George Eliot*, ed. Thomas Pinney (London: Routledge and Kegan Paul, 1963).

Eliot, George, *Felix Holt. The Radical* (London: Penguin, 1976).

Eliot, George, *Daniel Deronda*, ed., intro. and notes Graham Handley (Oxford: Oxford University Press, 1998).
Eliot, George, *Adam Bede* (Oxford: Oxford University Press, 2008).
Eliot, T. S., *Selected Essays* (London: Macmillan, 1960).
Eliot, T. S., 'Andrew Marvell' [1921], repr. in *Selected Prose of T. S. Eliot*, ed. Frank Kermode (London: Faber & Faber, 1975).
Empson, William, *The Structure of Complex Words* (Cambridge, MA: Harvard University Press, 1989).
Enstice, Andrew, *Thomas Hardy: Landscapes of the Mind* (Basingstoke: Macmillan Press, 1979).
Eyre, Banning, 'Éthiopiques 10: Tezeta: Ethopian Blues and Ballad', *Afropop Worldwide*, <https://afropop.org/articles> (accessed 15 March 2018).
Eyre, Banning, 'Kay Kaufman Shelemay: Ethiopia: Empire and Revolution (interview)', *Afropop Worldwide*, <https://afropop.org/articles> (accessed 15 March 2018).
Farina, Jonathan, '"Dickens's As If": Analogy and Victorian Virtual Reality', *Victorian Studies* 53.3 (2011), pp. 227–36.
Farina, Jonathan, *Everyday Words and the Character of Prose in Victorian Britain* (Cambridge: Cambridge University Press, 2017).
Fauconnier, Gilles, and Mark Turner, *The Way We Think: Conceptual Blending and the Mind's Hidden Complexities* (New York: Basic Books, 2002).
Feist Pubs., Inc. v. Rural Tel. Svc. Co., Inc. (1991), 499 US 340.
Felski, Rita, *The Limits of Critique* (Chicago: Chicago University Press, 2015).
Finkelstein, David, 'Decent Company: Conrad, *Blackwood's*, and the Literary Marketplace', *Conradiana* 41.1 (Spring 2009), pp. 29–47.
Fleury, Gabrielle, 'Appendix III: Gabrielle Fleury's Recollections of George Gissing', in Paul F. Mattheisen, Arthur C. Young, and Pierre Coustillas (eds), *The Collected Letters of George Gissing*, vol. 9 (Athens: Ohio University Press, 1997), pp. 275–321.
Ford, Boris, *A Guide to English Literature: From Dickens to Hardy* (London: Cassell, 1963).
Forrest, Alan, *Conscripts and Deserters: The Army and French Society During the Revolution and Empire* (New York: Oxford University Press, 1989).
Forster, John, '*Great Expectations*', review, *The Examiner* No. 2790 (20 July 1861), pp. 452–3.
Forster, John, *The Life of Charles Dickens*, ed. J. W. T. Ley (New York: Doubleday, Doran and Co., 1928).
Forster, John, *The Life of Charles Dickens*, ed. A J. Hoppé, 2 vols (London: J. M. Dent and Sons, 1966).
Foucault, Michel, *The Order of Things: An Archaeology of the Human Sciences*, trans. Alan Sheridan (New York: Random House, 1970).
Foucault, Michel, *The Archaeology of Knowledge*, trans. A. M. Sheridan Smith (New York: Harper & Row, 1972).
Fowler, Roger, *Linguistics and the Novel* (London: Methuen, 1977).
Franklin, Nancy, and Barbara Tversky, 'Searching Imagined Environments', *Journal of Experimental Psychology: General* 119 (1990), pp. 63–76.
Freedgood, Elaine, *The Ideas in Things: Fugitive Meaning in the Victorian Novel* (Chicago: University of Chicago Press, 2006).

Freeman, Edward Augustus, 'Anthony Trollope', *Macmillan's Magazine* 47.279 (January 1883), pp. 236–40.
Freud, Sigmund, 'The Uncanny', in *The Standard Edition of the Complete Psychological Works of Sigmund Freud, Volume XVII (1917–1919): An Infantile Neurosis and Other Works*, trans. James Strachey (London: Hogarth Press, 1955), pp. 217–56.
Freud, Sigmund, *Letters to Wilhelm Fliess*, trans. Eric Mosbacher and James Strachey (New York: Basic Books, 1977).
Freud, Sigmund, 'The Uncanny', *Pelican Freud Library: Volume 14: Art and Literature* (Harmondsworth: Penguin, 1985), pp. 335–76.
Frothingham, Nathaniel Langdon, 'Poetry of Manzoni', *North American Review* 112 (July 1841), pp. 169–74.
Furbank, P. N. (ed.), *Selected Poems of Thomas Hardy* (Basingstoke: Macmillan Press, 1967).
Galef, David, 'On the Margin: The Peripheral Characters in Conrad's "Heart of Darkness"', *Journal of Modern Literature* 17.1 (Summer 1990), pp. 117–38.
Gallagher, Catherine, 'The Politics of Culture and the Debate over Representation', *Representations* 5 (1984), pp. 115–47.
Gallagher, Catherine, 'George Eliot and *Daniel Deronda*: The Prostitute and the Jewish Question', in Ruth Bernard Yeazell (ed.), *Sex, Politics, and Science in the Nineteenth-Century Novel* (Baltimore: Johns Hopkins University Press, 1985), pp. 39–62.
Gallagher, Catherine, *Nobody's Story* (Berkeley: University of California Press, 1995).
Gallagher, Catherine, *The Body Economic: Life, Death, and Sensation in Political Economy and the Victorian Novel* (Princeton: Princeton University Press, 2006).
Gallagher, Catherine, and Stephen Greenblatt, *Practicing New Historicism* (Chicago: Chicago University Press, 2000).
Gapp, Samuel Vogt, *George Gissing, Classicist* (Philadelphia: University of Pennsylvania Press, 1936).
Ghosh, Ranjan, and J. Hillis Miller, *Thinking Literature across Continents* (Durham, NC: Duke University Press, 2016).
Gibson, James, 'Introduction', in *Thomas Hardy: The Making of Poetry* (Basingstoke: Palgrave Macmillan, 1971), n.p.
Gide, André, *The Immoralist*, trans. Richard Howard (New York: Vintage, 1970).
Girard, René, *Deceit, Desire and the Novel: Self and Other in Literary Structure* (Baltimore: Johns Hopkins University Press, 1966).
Gissing, Alfred, 'Gissing's Unfinished Romance', *National Review* 108 (January 1937), pp. 82–91.
Gissing, Algernon, letter to J. B. Pinker, 25 January 1904, 1904–1905, Gissing MSS: Correspondence. MS Gissing MSS, MS Department, Lilly Library, Bloomington, IN.
Gissing, George, *Born in Exile* (Edinburgh: Thomas Nelson and Sons, n.d.), n.p., <archive.org/details/borninexile00gissuoft> (accessed 12 February 2019).
Gissing, George, 'Basil', in *Veranilda – Notes*, 1903, MS Gissing MSS, MS Department, Lilly Library, Bloomington, IN.

Gissing, George, *Veranilda*, 1903, MS Gissing MSS, MS Department, Lilly Library, Bloomington, IN.

Gissing, George, *New Grub Street*, ed. Bernard Bergonzi (London: Penguin Group, 1985).

Gissing, George, *Workers in the Dawn*, ed. Pierre Coustillas (Brighton: Harvester Press, 1985).

Gissing, George, *Veranilda*, ed. Pierre Coustillas (Brighton: Harvester Press, 1987).

Gissing, George, 'A Victim of Circumstances', in *Collected Short Stories* vol. 2, ed. Pierre Coustillas, with the assistance of Barbara Rawlinson and Hélène Coustillas (Grayswood: Grayswood Press, 2012), pp. 3–26.

Gissing, George, *George Gissing, The Private Papers of Henry Ryecroft*, ed. Tom Ue (Edinburgh: Edinburgh University Press, forthcoming).

Goffman, Erving, *The Presentation of Self in Everyday Life* (Woodstock, NY: Overlooks Press, 1973).

Goldhill, Simon, review of Stefano Evangelista, *British Aestheticism and Ancient Greece: Hellenism, Reception, Gods in Exile, Victorian Studies* 52.3 (Spring 2010), pp. 474–6.

Goldhill, Simon, *Victorian Culture and Classical Antiquity: Art, Opera, Fiction, and the Proclamation of Modernity* (Princeton and Oxford: Princeton University Press, 2011).

Golledge, Reginald G., *Wayfinding Behavior: Cognitive Mapping and Other Spatial Processes* (Baltimore: Johns Hopkins University Press, 2010).

Greaney, Michael, *Conrad, Language, and Narrative* (Cambridge: Cambridge University Press, 2002).

Greenblatt, Stephen, 'Towards a Poetics of Culture', *Southern Review* 20:1 (1987), pp. 3–15.

Greenblatt, Stephen, *Learning to Curse* (London: Routledge, 1990).

Greenblatt, Stephen, *The Greenblatt Reader*, ed. Michael Payne (Oxford: Blackwell, 2005).

Griffin, Martin Joseph, 'Sir George Trevelyan as a Historian', *Blackwood's Edinburgh Magazine* 165.1001 (March 1899), pp. 581–90.

Gros, Frédéric, *A Philosophy of Walking*, trans. John Howe (London and New York: Verso, 2014).

Grossman, Jonathan H., 'Living the Global Transport Network', *Great Expectations. Victorian Studies* 57.2 (2015), pp. 225–50.

Grote, George, *History of Greece* (New York: Harper and Brothers, 1880).

Grylls, David, *The Paradox of Gissing* (London: Allen & Unwin, 1986).

Haight, Gordon S., *The George Eliot Letters* (New Haven: Yale University Press, 1954).

Hamley, William George, 'Brackenbury's Narrative of the Ashanti War', *Blackwood's Edinburgh Magazine* 116.705 (July 1874), pp. 96–126.

Hampson, Robert, '"Heart of Darkness" and "The Speech that Cannot be Silenced"', *English*. 39 (Spring 1990), pp. 15–32.

Hankins, John Erskine, *The Life and Works of George Turbervile* (Lawrence: University of Kansas Publications, 1940).

Hardy, Barbara, *Thomas Hardy: Imagining Imagination in Hardy's Poetry and Fiction* (London and New Brunswick, NJ: Athlone Press, 2000).

Hardy, Florence Emily, *The Life of Thomas Hardy: 1840–1928* (London: Macmillan; New York: St Martin's Press, 1965).
Hardy, Thomas, *Wessex Poems and Other Verses* (London: Macmillan & Co, 1898).
Hardy, Thomas, *Writings in Prose and Verse*, Anniversary Edition, 21 vols (New York and London: Harper & Brothers Publishers, 1920).
Hardy, Thomas, *Winter Words in Various Words and Metres* (New York: The Macmillan Company Publishers, 1928).
Hardy, Thomas, *Thomas Hardy: The Complete Poems*, ed. James Gibson (Basingstoke: Macmillan, 1976).
Hardy, Thomas, 'The Dead Quire', in *Thomas Hardy, The Variorum Edition of the Complete Poems*, ed. James Gibson (London: Macmillan, 1979), pp. 255–9.
Hardy, Thomas, *Tess of the d'Urbervilles*, int. Robert B. Heilman (New York: Bantam Books, 1992).
Hardy, Thomas, *A Laodicean*, ed. and int. John Schad (London: Penguin, 1997).
Hardy, Thomas, *The Mayor of Casterbridge*, ed. and int. Keith Wilson (London: Penguin, 1997).
Hardy, Thomas, *A Pair of Blue Eyes*, ed. and int. Pamela Dalziel (London: Penguin, 1998).
Hardy, Thomas, *Desperate Remedies*, ed. and int. Mary Rimmer (London: Penguin, 1998).
Hardy, Thomas, *Tess of the D'Urbervilles*, ed. Tim Dolin and int. Margaret R. Higgonet (London: Penguin, 1998).
Hardy, Thomas, *The Woodlanders*, ed. and int. Patricia Ingham (London: Penguin, 1998).
Hardy, Thomas, *Under the Greenwood Tree*, ed. and int. Tim Dolin (London: Penguin, 1998).
Hardy, Thomas, *The Return of the Native*, ed. Tony Slade, int. Pamela Boumelha (London: Penguin, 1999).
Hardy, Thomas, *Far from the Madding Crowd*, ed. and int. Rosemarie Morgan, with Shannon Russell (London: Penguin, 2000).
Hardy, Thomas, *Poems Selected by Tom Paulin* (London: Faber & Faber, 2005).
Harris, Margaret, and Judith Johnston (eds), *The Journals of George Eliot* (Cambridge: Cambridge University Press, 1988).
Hartley, Jenny, *Charles Dickens and the House of Fallen Women* (London: Methuen, 2008).
Hartman, Geoffrey, 'Literary Commentary as Literature', *Comparative Literature* 28.3 (1976), pp. 257–76.
Hartman, Geoffrey, *Criticism in the Wilderness: The Study of Literature Today* (New Haven: Yale University Press, 1980).
Hartman, Geoffrey, *The Unremarkable Wordsworth* (Minneapolis: University of Minnesota Press, 1987).
Harvey, A. E., '"The Workman is Worthy of His Hire": Fortunes of a Proverb in the Early Church', *Novum Testamentum* 24.3 (July 1982), pp. 209–21.
Hauser, Arnold, *The Sociology of Art*, trans. Kenneth J. Northcott (London: Routledge, 1982).
Heffernan, Julián Jiménez (ed.), *Into Separate Worlds* (Basingstoke: Palgrave Macmillan, 2013).

Heidegger, Martin, *Being and Time*, trans. John Macquarrie and Edward Robinson (New York: Harper and Row, 1962).
Heidegger, Martin, *Poetry, Language, Thought*, trans. Albert Hofstadter (New York, London: Harper Perennial, 2013).
Herman, David, *Story Logic: Problems and Possibilities of Narrative* (Lincoln: University of Nebraska Press, 2004).
Hext, Kate, *Walter Pater: Individualism and Aesthetic Philosophy* (Edinburgh: Edinburgh University Press, 2013).
Hogan, Patrick Colm, 'On Being Moved: Cognition and Emotion in Literature and Film', in Lisa Zunshine (ed.), *Introduction to Cognitive Cultural Studies* (Baltimore: The Johns Hopkins University Press, 2010), pp. 237–56.
Hopkins, Gerard Manley, *Poems and Prose*, ed. W. H. Gardner (New York: Penguin, 1953).
Hopkins, Gerard Manley, *Journals and Papers* (London: Oxford University Press, 1959).
Horne, Philip, 'Poetic Allusion in the Victorian Novel', in Lisa Rodensky (ed.), *The Oxford Handbook of the Victorian Novel* (Oxford: Oxford University Press, 2013), pp. 606–33, <www.oxfordhandbooks.com/view/10.1093/oxfordhb/9780199533145.001.0001/oxfordhb-9780199533145-e-001> (accessed 16 October 2018).
House, Madeline, Graham Storey and Kathleen Tillotson (eds), *The Pilgrim Edition of the Letters of Charles Dickens*, 12 vols (Oxford: Clarendon Press, 1965–2002).
House, Madeline, Graham Storey and Kathleen Tillotson (eds), *The Letters of Charles Dickens, 1859–61*, vol. IX (Oxford: Clarendon Press, 1997).
Hughes, Kathryn, 'What is the role of the Left in times of political crisis? Reading George Eliot after Brexit', *The Guardian*, 8 July 2016.
Huneker, J., 'Dull Confessions Brightly Reviewed: William Michael Rossetti's Prosy Reminiscences Suggest a Few Thoughts to James Huneker', *The New York Times*, 12 January 1907, p. 23.
Husserl, Edmund, *On the Phenomenology of the Consciousness of Internal Time (1893–1917)*, trans. John Barnett Brough (Dordrecht: Kluwer, 1991).
Husserl, Edmund, *The Essential Husserl: Basic Writings in Transcendental Phenomenology*, ed. Donn Welton (Bloomington: Indiana University Press, 1999).
Jaffe, Audrey, *Vanishing Points: Dickens, Narrative, and the Subject of Omniscience* (Berkeley: University of California Press, 1991).
James, Henry, 'Anthony Trollope', *Partial Portraits* (London and New York: Macmillan, 1984), pp. 97–136.
Jameson, Fredric, *The Antinomies of Realism* (London: Verso, 2013).
Jasanoff, Maya, *The Dawn Watch: Joseph Conrad in a Global World* (London: William Collins, 2017).
Johnson, Barbara, *The Critical Difference: Essays in the Contemporary Rhetoric of Reading* (Baltimore: The Johns Hopkins University Press, 1980).
Johnson, Barbara, *A World of Difference* (Baltimore: Johns Hopkins University Press, 1987).
Johnson, Edgar, *Charles Dickens: His Triumph and Tragedy*, 2 vols (New York: Viking, 1952).

Joyce, James, *Ulysses*, ed. Declan Kiberd (London: Penguin, 1992).
Kahneman, Daniel, *Thinking, Fast and Slow* (New York: Farrar, Strauss and Giroux, 2011).
Kant, Immanuel, *The Critique of Judgement*, trans. J. C. Meredith (Oxford: Oxford University Press, 1952).
Kaplan, Carola M., Peter Lancelot Mallios and Andrea White (eds), *Conrad in the Twenty-First Century: Contemporary Approaches and Perspectives* (New York: Routledge, 2005).
Kaplan, Fred, *Dickens: A Biography* (Baltimore: Johns Hopkins University Press, 1998).
Keats, John, 'Ode to a Nightingale', *Selected Poems and Letters*, ed. Douglas Bush (Boston: Houghton Mifflin Company, 1959), pp. 205–7.
Kendrick, Walter, *The Novel-Machine: The Theory and Fiction of Anthony Trollope* (Baltimore: The Johns Hopkins University Press, 1980).
Ketterer, David, '"Beyond the Threshold" in Conrad's *Heart of Darkness*', *Texas Studies in Literature and Language* 11.2 (Summer 1969), pp. 1013–22.
Kierkegaard, Søren, *Repetition* (Copenhagen: Bianco Luno Press, 1843).
Kitchin, Rob, and Scott Freundschuh, *Cognitive Mapping: Past, Present, and Future* (London: Routledge, 2000).
Knowles, Owen, and Gene Moore, *Oxford Reader's Companion to Conrad* (Oxford: Oxford University Press, 2000).
Krieger, Murray, *The New Apologists for Poetry* (Bloomington: Indiana University Press, 1963).
Kropholler, P. F., 'Archaisms in Veranilda', *The Gissing Newsletter* 21.4 (1985), pp. 10–17, <http://www.lang.nagoya-u.ac.jp/~matsuoka/gissing/newsletter-journal/newsletter-21-4.pdf> (accessed 12 February 2019).
Krueger, Anne O., 'The Political Economy of the Rent Seeking Society', *The American Economic Review* 64:3 (1974), pp. 291–303.
Kruger, Kathryn Brigger, 'The Antigone and Its Moral': George Eliot's Antigonean Considerations', *The George Eliot Review* 44 (2013), pp. 68–79.
Kumar, Krishan, 'Greece and Rome in the British Empire: Contrasting Role Models', *Journal of British Studies* 51.1 (2012), pp. 76–101.
Kuriyama, Shigehisa, *The Expressiveness of the Body and the Divergence of Greek and Chinese Medicine* (New York: Zone Books, 1999).
Kveraga, Kestutis, Avniel S. Ghuman and Moshe Bar, 'Top-down predictions in the cognitive brain', *Brain and Cognition* 65 (2007), pp. 145–68.
Lacoue-Labarthe, Philippe, 'The Horror of the West', trans. Nidesh Lawtoo and Hannes Opelz, in Lawtoo (ed.), *Conrad's* Heart of Darkness *and Contemporary Thought: Revisiting the Horror with Lacoue-Labarthe* (London: Bloomsbury, 2012), pp. 111–22.
Lakoff, George, and Mark Johnson, *Metaphors We Live By* (Chicago: Chicago University Press, 1980).
Landor, Walter Savage, *The Complete Latin Poetry of Walter Savage Landor*, ed. Dana Ferrin Sutton (Lewiston, NY: Edwin Mellen Press, 1999).
Langbaum, Robert, *Thomas Hardy in Our Time* (New York: St Martin's Press, 1995).
Lawtoo, Nidesh, 'A frame for "The Horror of the West"', in Lawtoo (ed.), *Conrad's* Heart of Darkness *and Contemporary Thought: Revisiting the Horror with Lacoue-Labarthe* (London: Bloomsbury, 2012), pp. 89–108.

Lawtoo, Nidesh (ed.), *Conrad's* Heart of Darkness *and Contemporary Thought: Revisiting the Horror with Lacoue-Labarthe* (London: Bloomsbury, 2012).

Lawtoo, Nidesh, 'The Horror of Mimesis: Echoing Lacoue-Labarthe', in Lawtoo (ed.), *Conrad's* Heart of Darkness *and Contemporary Thought: Revisiting the Horror with Lacoue-Labarthe* (London: Bloomsbury, 2012), pp. 239–59.

Lawtoo, Nidesh, *Conrad's Shadow: Catastrophe, Mimesis, Theory* (East Lansing: Michigan State University Press, 2016).

Ledbetter, Kathryn, *Tennyson and Victorian Periodicals* (Burlington: Ashgate, 2007).

Leigh Hunt, James Henry, *Wit and Humour, Selected from the English Poets* (London: Smith, Elder and Company, 1846).

Lindqvist, Sven, *'Exterminate All the Brutes'*, trans. Joan Tate (London: Granta Books, 2002).

Litvak, Joseph, 'Back to the Future: A Review-Article on the New Historicism, Deconstruction, and Nineteenth-Century Fiction', *Texas Studies in Language and Literature* 30:1 (1988), pp. 120–49.

Litvak, Joseph, *Caught in the Act: Theatricality in the Nineteenth-Century English Novel* (Berkeley: University of California Press, 1992).

Loesberg, Jonathan, 'From Victorian Consciousness to an Ethics of Reading: The Criticism of J. Hillis Miller', *Victorian Studies* 37.1 (Autumn 1993), pp. 99–121.

Lucretius, *De Rerum Natura*, trans. W. H. D. Rouse, ed. Martin Ferguson Smith (Cambridge, MA: Loeb-Harvard University Press, 1992).

Lukács, Georg, *Soul and Form*, trans. Anna Bostock (Cambridge, MA: MIT Press, 1974).

[Luxmoore, Percy Putt], 'Ashantee', *Blackwood's Edinburgh Magazine* 115:702 (April 1874), pp. 518–24.

Mahlberg, Michaela, 'A Corpus Stylistic Perspective on Dickens' *Great Expectations*', in Marina Lambrou and Peter Stockwell (eds), *Contemporary Stylistics* (London: Continuum, 2007), pp. 19–31.

Maisonnat, Claude, 'The Voice of Darkness', in Lawtoo (ed.), *Conrad's* Heart of Darkness *and Contemporary Thought: Revisiting the Horror with Lacoue-Labarthe* (London: Bloomsbury, 2012), pp. 164–80.

Manzoni, Alessandro, *The Sacred Hymns and The Napoleonic Ode*, trans. Joel Bingham (London: Henry Frowde, 1904).

Marcus, Steven, 'Who is Fagin?', in Steven Marcus, *Dickens from Pickwick to Dombey* (New York: Simon and Schuster, 1968), pp. 358–78.

Marcus, Steven, *The Other Victorians: A Study of Sexuality and Pornography in Mid-Nineteenth-Century England* (New York: Norton, 1974).

Markovits, Stefanie, *The Crisis of Action in Nineteenth-Century English Literature* (Columbus: Ohio State University Press, 2006).

Markovits, Stefanie, 'Giving Voice to the Crimean War: Tennyson's "Charge" and Maud's Battle-Song', *Victorian Poetry* 473 (2009), pp. 481–503.

Marshall, George O., 'Thomas Hardy's Eye Imagery', *Colby Quarterly* 7:6 (June 1966), pp. 264–8.

Martin, Robert Bernard, *The Triumph of Wit: A Study of Victorian Comic Theory* (Oxford: Oxford University Press, 1974).

Marx, Karl, *'Resultate des unmittelbaren Produktionsprozesses'* (1863),

<https://www.marxists.org/deutsch/archiv/marx-engels/1863/resultate/1-mehrwert.htm> (accessed 12 February 2019).

Marx, Karl, 'Economic Works of Karl Marx 1861–1864: The Process of Production of Capital, Draft Chapter 6 of Capital Results of the Direct Production Process: Introduction' (1864), <https://www.marxists.org/archive/marx/works/1864/economic/introduction.htm> (accessed 12 February 2019).

Marx, Karl, and Friedrich Engels, *The German Ideology. Critique of Modern German Philosophy According to Its Representatives Feuerbach, B. Bauer and Stirner, and of German Socialism According to Its Various Prophets. Collected Works*, vol. 5 (New York: International Publishers, 1976), pp. 19–539.

Marx, Karl, 'Appendix: Results of the Immediate Process of Production', in *Capital: Volume One*, trans. Ben Fowkes (New York: Knopf Doubleday, 1977), pp. 948–1084.

Marx, Karl, *18th Brumaire of Louis Bonaparte* (New York: International Publishers, 1987).

Maxwell, W. H., *History of the Irish Rebellion in 1798; with Memoirs of the Union, and Emmett's Insurrection in 1803* (London: H. G. Bohn, 1854).

May, Leila Silvana, *Secrecy and Disclosure in Victorian Fiction* (New York: Routledge, 2017).

McAlindon, Tom, 'Time and mutability in the poetry of Thomas Hardy', *English Studies* 97.1 (2016), pp. 22–41.

McGann, Jerome, *The Beauty of Inflections* (Oxford: Oxford University Press, 1985).

Meisel, Martin, 'The Ending of *Great Expectations*', *Essays in Criticism* 15 (1965), pp. 326–31.

Merleau-Ponty, Maurice, *Phenomenology of Perception*, trans. Donald A. Landes (London: Routledge & Kegan Paul, 1962).

Merleau-Ponty, Maurice, *The Primacy of Perception and Other Essays on Phenomenological Psychology, the Philosophy of Art, History and Politics*, trans. Carleton Dallery (Evanston: Northwestern University Press, 1964).

Merleau-Ponty, Maurice, *The Visible and the Invisible: Followed by Working Notes*, ed. Claude Lefort, trans. Alphonso Lingis (Evanston: Northwestern University Press, 1968).

Merleau-Ponty, Maurice, *The World of Perception*, trans. Oliver Davis (London and New York: Routledge, 2008).

Mill, John Stuart, *On Liberty* (London: Longmans Green, 1913).

Mill, John Stuart, 'Grote's History of Greece II' [1853], in J. M. Robson (ed.), *Collected Works of John Stuart Mill: Essays on Philosophy and the Classics*, vol. 11 (London: University of Toronto Press, Routledge and Kegan Paul, 1978), pp. 307–38.

Mill, John Stuart, 'Macaulay's *Lays of Ancient Rome*' [1843], in J. M. Robson and Jack Stillinger (eds), *Collected Works of John Stuart Mill: Autobiography and Literary Essays*, vol. 1 (London: University of Toronto Press, Routledge, and Kegan Paul, 1981), pp. 523–32.

Mill, John Stuart, *On Liberty and Other Essays*, ed. John Gray (Oxford: Oxford University Press, 1991).

Mill, John Stuart, *Considerations on Representative Government*, in *On Liberty and Other Essays*, ed. John Gray (Oxford: Oxford University Press, 2008), pp. 205–467.

Mill, John Stuart, *On Liberty*, in *On Liberty and Other Essays*, ed. John Gray (Oxford: Oxford University Press, 2008), pp. 5–128.

Millar, John Hepburn, 'The Rebel King', *Blackwood's Edinburgh Magazine* 165.999 (January 1899), pp. 138–50.

Miller, D. A., *The Novel and The Police* (Berkeley and Los Angeles: University of California Press, 1988).

Miller, Dale E., 'John Stuart Mill's Civic Liberalism', *History of Political Thought* 21.1 (January 2000), pp. 88–113.

Miller, J. Hillis, *Thomas Hardy: Distance and Desire* (Cambridge, MA: The Belknap Press of Harvard University Press, 1970).

Miller, J. Hillis, *Ariadne's Thread: Story Lines* (New Haven and London: Yale University Press, 1992).

Miller, J. Hillis, *Communities in Fiction* (New York: Fordham University Press, 2015).

Miller, J. Hillis. *The Linguistic Moment: From Wordsworth to Stevens* (Princeton: Princeton University Press, 1985).

Modiano, Patrick, 'Flowers of Ruin', in *Suspended Sentences*, trans. Mark Polizzotti (New Haven: Yale University Press, 2014), pp. 131–213.

Morris, William (ed.), *The American Heritage Dictionary of the English Language* (Boston: American Heritage Publishing Co. and Houghton Mifflin Company, 1969).

Moynahan, Julian, 'The Hero's Guilt: The Case of *Great Expectations*', *Essays in Criticism* 10 (1960), pp. 60–79.

Nancy, Jean-Luc, *La communauté désoeuvrée* (Paris: Christian Bourgois, 1986).

Nancy, Jean-Luc, *The Inoperative Community*, ed. Peter Connor, trans. Peter Connor, Lisa Garbus, Michael Holland and Simona Sawhney (Minneapolis: University of Minnesota Press, 1991).

Nancy, Jean-Luc, *The Ground of the Image*, trans. Jeff Fort (New York: Fordham University Press, 2005).

Nead, Lynda, *Myths of Sexuality: Representations of Women in Victorian Britain* (Oxford: Blackwell, 1988).

Nietzsche, Friedrich, *Birth of Tragedy*, trans. Walter Kaufmann (New York: Vintage, 1967).

Nord, Deborah Epstein, *Walking the Victorian Streets: Women, Representation, and the City* (Ithaca and London: Cornell University Press, 1995).

Ogden, C. K., and I. A. Richards, *The Meaning of Meaning: A Study of the Influence Upon Thought and the Science of Symbolism* (New York: Harcourt, Brace, 1956).

Parry, Benita, 'The Moment and Afterlife of *Heart of Darkness*', in Carola M. Kaplan, Peter Lancelot Mallios and Andrea White (eds), *Conrad in the Twenty-First Century: Contemporary Approaches and Perspectives* (New York: Routledge, 2005), pp. 39–53.

Pater, Walter, *The Renaissance: Studies in Art and Poetry* (London: Macmillan, 1877).

Pater, Walter, *Appreciations, with an Essay on Style* (London: Macmillan, 1889).

Pater, Walter, *Plato and Platonism* (London: Macmillan, 1893).

Pater, Walter, *Miscellaneous Studies: A Series of Essays*, ed. Charles Lancelot Shadwell (London: Macmillan, 1913).

Pater, Walter, *The Renaissance: Studies in Art and Poetry*, ed. Donald L. Hill (Berkeley: University of California Press, 1980).
Pater, Walter, *Marius the Epicurean: His Sensations and Ideas* (New York: Cosimo Classics, [1885] 2005).
Patmore, Coventry, *Poems by Coventry Patmore*, vol. 2 (London: George Bell and Sons, 1886).
Paulin, Tom, *Thomas Hardy: The Poetry of Perception* (London and Basingstoke: Macmillan Press, 1975).
Paulin, Tom, 'Introduction', in Thomas Hardy, *Poems Selected by Tom Paulin* (London: Faber & Faber, 2005).
Peattie, Roger W. (ed.), *Selected Letters of William Michael Rossetti* (London: Pennsylvania State University Press, 1986).
Peattie, Roger W., *Selected Letters of William Michael Rossetti and Christina Rossetti* (Philadelphia: Pennsylvania State University Press, 1990).
Pecora, Vincent, '*Heart of Darkness* and the Phenomenology of Voice', *ELH* 52.4 (Winter 1985), pp. 993–1015.
Perloff, Marjorie, *Poetic License: Essays on Modernist and Postmodernist Lyric* (Evanston: Northwestern University Press, 1990).
Pettitt, Clare, *Patent Inventions: Intellectual Property and the Victorian Novel* (Oxford: Oxford University Press, 2004).
Phelan, James, *Living to Tell about It: A Rhetoric and Ethics of Character Narration* (Ithaca: Cornell University Press, 2005).
Phelan, James, *Somebody Telling Somebody Else: A Rhetorical Poetics of Narrative* (Columbus: Ohio State University Press, 2017).
Piketty, Thomas, *Capital in the Twenty-First Century*, trans. Arthur Goldhammer (Cambridge, MA: Harvard University Press, 2014).
Pinion, F. B., A Commentary on the Poems of Thomas Hardy (London and Basingstoke: Macmillan Press, 1976).
Pite, Ralph, *Hardy's Geography: Wessex and the Regional Novel* (Basingstoke and New York: Palgrave Macmillan, 2002).
Plath, Sylvia, 'Child', *Sylvia Plath: The Collected Poems*, ed. Ted Hughes (New York: Harper Perennial Modern Classics, 2008), p. 265.
Plato, *Protagoras and Meno*, trans. W. K. C. Guthrie (London: Penguin, 1961).
Poole, Adrian, *Gissing in Context* (London: Macmillan Press, 1975).
Poovey, Mary, *Genres of the Credit Economy* (Chicago: University of Chicago Press, 2008).
Prince, Gerald, 'The Disnarrated', *Style* 22.1 (1988), pp. 1–8.
Ransom, John Crowe, 'Criticism, Inc', *Virginia Quarterly Review*, 13:4 (1937), pp. 586–602.
Ransom, John Crowe, *The New Criticism* (New York: New Directions, 1941).
Ransom, John Crowe, 'A Psychologist Looks at Poetry', in John Constable (ed.), *I. A. Richards and His Critics*, vol. 10, *I. A. Richards: Selected Works, 1919–1938*, 10 vols (London, Routledge, 2001), pp. 440–56.
Rapaport, Herman, *The Theory Mess: Deconstruction in Eclipse* (New York: Columbia University Press, 2001).
Richards, I. A., *Science and Poetry* (London: Kegan Paul, Trench, Trubner, 1926).
Richards, I. A., *Principles of Literary Criticism* (London: Routledge, 2001).

Rose, Mark, 'Review of *Contested Culture: The Image, the Voice, and the Law* by Jane M. Gaines', *Discourse* 14:1 (1991–2), pp. 146–9.

Rosenberg, Edgar, 'Last Words on *Great Expectations*: A Textual Brief on the Six Endings', *Dickens Studies Annual* 9 (1981), pp. 87–115.

Rossetti, Christina, *The Complete Poems*, ed. R. W. Crump and Betty S. Flowers (New York: Penguin, 2001).

Rossetti, D. G., *The Collected Writings of D. G. Rossetti*, ed. Jan Marsh (London: Dent, 1999).

Rossetti, William Michael (ed.), *D. G. Rossetti: His Family Letters with A Memoir* (London: Ellis, 1895).

Rossetti, William Michael (ed.), *Rossetti Papers 1862 to 1870* (London: Sands and Co., 1903).

Rossetti, William Michael, *Democratic Sonnets* (London: Alston Rivers, 1907).

Rossetti, William Michael (ed.), *The Family Letters of Christina Georgina Rossetti* (New York: Charles Scribner's Sons, 1908).

Rossetti, William Michael, *Some Reminiscences*, 2 vols (Cambridge: Cambridge University Press, [1906] 2013).

Royle, Nicholas, '"The Telepathy Effect": Notes toward a Reconsideration of Narrative Fiction', *The Uncanny* (Manchester: Manchester University Press, 2003), pp. 256–76.

Russell, William Howard, 'The War in the Crimea: The Cavalry Charge at Balaklava', *The Times*, 14 November 1854, Issue 2 (1898), p. 7.

Russo, John Paul, *I. A. Richards: His Life and Work* (Baltimore: The Johns Hopkins University Press, 1989).

Sachs, Jonathan, 'Greece or Rome?: The Uses of Antiquity in Late Eighteenth- and Early Nineteenth-Century British Literature', *Literature Compass* 6.2 (March 2009), pp. 314–31.

Sadrin, Anny, *Great Expectations* (London: Unwin Hyman, 1988).

Said, Edward, *Culture and Imperialism* (London: Vintage, 1993).

Said, Edward, *Beginnings: Intentions and Method* (London: Granta, 1998).

Saint-Gelais, Richard, 'How To Do Things With Worlds: From Counterfactuality to Counterfictionality', in Dorothee Birke, Michael Butter and Tilmann Köppe, *Counterfactual Thinking – Counterfactual Writing* (Berlin: De Gruyter, 2011), pp. 240–52.

Santayana, George, *The Sense of Beauty: Being the Outlines of Aesthetic Theory* (New York: Random House, 1955).

Sayeau, Michael, 'Work, Unemployment, and the Exhaustion of Fiction in "Heart of Darkness"', *Novel: A Forum on Fiction* 39.3 (Summer 2006), pp. 337–60.

Schaffer, Talia, *Romance's Rival: Familiar Marriage in Victorian Fiction* (Oxford: Oxford University Press, 2016).

Schmitt, Cannon, 'Tidal Conrad (Literally)', *Victorian Studies* 5.1 (Autumn 2012), pp. 7–29.

Schneider, Ralf, 'Blending and the Study of Narrative: An Introduction', in Ralf Schneider and Marcus Hartner (eds), *Blending and the Study of Narrative: Approaches and Applications* (Berlin: De Gruyter, 2012), pp. 1–30.

Schober, M. F., 'Speakers, Addresses, and Frames of Reference: Whose Effort is Minimized in Conversations About Locations?', *Discourse Processes* 20 (1995), pp. 219–47.

Sedgwick, Eve Kosovsky, *Between Men: English Literature and Male Homosocial Desire* (New York: Columbia University Press, 1985).
Selig, Robert L., *George Gissing*, revised edition (New York: Twayne-Macmillan, 1995).
Serres, Michel, *Genesis*, trans. Genevieve James and James Nielson (Ann Arbor: The University of Michigan Press, 1995).
Shakespeare, William, *The Oxford Shakespeare: The Complete Works*, ed. Stanley Wells et al., 2nd edn (Oxford: Oxford University Press, 2005).
Shannon, Edgar, and Christopher Ricks, '"The Charge of the Light Brigade": The Creation of a Poem', *Studies in Bibliography* 38 (1985), pp. 1–44.
Sheldon v. MGM Pictures Corp. (1936), 81 F.2d 49 (2d Cir.).
Shell, Marc, *The Economy of Literature* (Baltimore: Johns Hopkins University Press, 1978).
Shelley, Mary, *The Last Man*, ed. Anne McWhir (Peterborough: Broadview Press, 1996).
Shelley, Percy Bysshe, 'To a Skylark', in *Poetical Works*, ed. Thomas Hutchinson, corrected by G. M. Matthews (Oxford: Oxford University Press, 1991), pp. 602–3.
Skilton, David, 'The Centrality of Literary Illustration in Victorian Visual Culture: The Example of Millais and Trollope from 1860 to 1864', *Journal of Illustration Studies* (December 2007), n.p., <http://jois.uia.no/articles.php?article=30> (accessed 12 February 2019).
Slater, Michael, 'The Triumph of Humour: The *Carol* Revisited', *Dickensian* 89:3 (Winter 1993), 184–92.
Small, Helen, *Love's Madness: Medicine, the Novel, and Female Insanity, 1800–1865* (Oxford: Oxford University Press, 1996).
Smith, David Woodruff, 'Phenomenology', in Edward N. Zalta (ed.), *The Stanford Encyclopedia of Philosophy* (Winter 2016 edn), <https://plato.stanford.edu/archives/win2016/entries/phenomenology/> (accessed 12 February 2019).
Spiers, Edward M., *The Army and Society: 1815–1914* (London, New York: Longman, 1980).
Sprinker, Michael, 'Review: Terry Eagleton, *Literary Theory: An Introduction* (Minnesota, 1983) and Patricia McCallum, *Literature and Method: Toward a Critique of I. A. Richards, T. S. Eliot, and F. R. Leavis* (Humanities Press, 1983)', *Minnesota Review* 22 (Spring 1984), pp. 152–6.
'Statistics', *The London Reader: Of Literature, Science, Art and General Information*, 54.1405 (1890), pp. 575.
Stein, Gertrude, 'Portraits and Repetition', *Lectures in America* (Boston: Beacon Press, 1985).
Steiner, Joan E., 'Modern Pharisees and False Apostles: Ironic New Testament Parallels in Conrad's "Heart of Darkness"', *Nineteenth-Century Literature* 37.1 (June 1982), pp. 75–96.
Stevens, Wallace, *The Collected Poems* (New York: Vintage, 1990).
Stevens, Wallace, *Collected Poems* (London: Faber & Faber, 2006).
Stiglitz, Joseph, *The Price of Inequality: How Today's Divided Society Endangers our Future* (New York: W. W. Norton, 2013).
Strachan, Hew, *Wellington's Legacy: The Reform of the British Army 1830–54* (Manchester: Manchester University Press, 1984).

Sumner, Gordon (Sting), 'One World (Not Three)', on the Police album *Ghost in the Machine* (Santa Monica: A&M Records, 1981).
Swift, Jonathan, *A Tale of a Tub and Other Satires*, ed. Kathleen Williams (London: J. M. Dent and Sons, 1975).
Taine, H. A., *History of English Literature*, 3 vols, trans. H. Van Laun (New York: Henry Holt & Co., 1877).
Tate, Trudi, 'On Not Knowing Why: Memorializing the Light Brigade', in Helen Small and Trudi Tate (eds), *Literature, Science, Psychoanalysis, 1830–1970: Essays in Honour of Gillian Beer* (Oxford: Oxford University Press, 2003), pp. 160–80.
Tennyson, Lord Alfred, *The Princess: A Selected Edition*, ed. Christopher Ricks, revised edition (London and New York: Routledge, 2007), pp. 219–330.
Thackeray, W. M., 'Charity and Humour', in Edgar F. Harden (ed.), *English Humourists of the Eighteenth Century and Charity and Humour* (Ann Arbor: University of Michigan Press, 2007).
Thain, Marion, 'Thomas Hardy's Poetics of Touch', *Victorian Poetry* 51.2 (2013), pp. 129–45.
Therborn, Göran, *What Does the Ruling Class Do When It Rules? State Apparatuses and State Power under Feudalism, Capitalism, and Socialism* (London: New Left Books, 1978).
The Times, 'London, Monday, November 13, 1854'. Issue 21897, p. 6.
The Times, 'London, Tuesday, November 14, 1854'. Issue 21898, p. 6.
Thirlwell, A., *William and Lucy: The Other Rossettis* (New Haven: Yale University Press, 2003).
Thoreau, Henry David, *Walking* (LaVergne, TN: Watchmaker Publishing, 2010).
Toadvine, Ted, 'Thinking After the World: Deconstruction and Last Things', in Matthias Frisch, Philippe Lynes, and David Wood (eds), *Eco-deconstruction: Derrida and Environmental Philosophy* (New York: Fordham University Press, 2018).
Tönnies, Ferdinand, *Community and Civil Society*, ed. Jose Harris, trans. Jose Harris and Margaret Hollis (Cambridge: Cambridge University Press, 2001).
Trollope, Anthony, *The Life of Cicero*, 2 vols (London: Chapman and Hall, 1880).
Trollope, Anthony, *The Letters of Anthony Trollope*, ed. N. John Hall (Stanford: Stanford University Press, 1983).
Trollope, Anthony, *Framley Parsonage*, ed. Francis O'Gorman (Oxford: Oxford University Press, 2014).
Turner, Mark, *Death Is the Mother of Beauty: Mind, Metaphor, Criticism* (Chicago: University of Chicago Press, 1987).
Turner, Mark, *Reading Minds: The Study of English in the Age of Cognitive Science* (Princeton: Princeton University Press, 1991).
Turner, Mark, *The Literary Mind* (New York: Oxford University Press, 1996).
Ue, Tom, *Gissing, Shakespeare, and the Life of Writing* (Edinburgh: Edinburgh University Press, forthcoming).
Vaihinger, Hans, *The Philosophy of 'as if', a System of the Theoretical, Practical and Religious Fictions of Mankind*, trans. C. K. Ogden (New York: Harcourt, Brace and Co., [1924] 1952).
Veeser, H. Aram, ed. *The New Historicism* (London: Routledge, 1989).

Veeser, H. Aram, ed. *The New Historicism Reader* (New York: Routledge, 1994).
Venn, John, *The Logic of Chance: An essay on the foundations and province of the theory of probability, with especial reference to its logical bearings and its application to moral and social science, and to statistics* (London and New York: Macmillan and Co., 1888).
Venn, John, *Annals of a Clerical Family, being some account of the family and descendants of William Venn, Vicar of Otterton, Devon, 1600–1621* (London and New York: Macmillan and Co., 1904).
Warhol, Robyn, '"What Might Have Been Is Not What Is": Dickens's Narrative Refusals', in Dorothee Birke, Michael Butter and Tilmann Köppe, *Counterfactual Thinking – Counterfactual Writing* (Berlin: De Gruyter, 2011), pp. 227–39.
Wasserman, B., 'The Ashanti War of 1900: A Study in Cultural Conflict', *Africa: Journal of the International African Institute* 31.2 (1961), pp. 167–79.
Watt, Ian, *Conrad in the Nineteenth Century* (London: Chatto and Windus, 1980).
Watts, Cedric, *The Deceptive Text: An Introduction to Covert Plots* (Brighton: The Harvester Press, 1984).
Waugh, Evelyn, *A Handful of Dust*, ed., intro., and notes Robert Murray Davies (London: Penguin, 2000).
Weber, Samuel, *Mass Mediauras: Form, Technics, Media*, ed. Alan Cholodenko (Stanford: Stanford University Press, 1996).
Wells, H. G., 'George Gissing: An Impression', *Eclectic Magazine of Foreign Literature (1901–1907)* 143.5 (November 1904), pp. 580–7.
Whipple, Edwin P., 'Review', *Atlantic Monthly*, in Philip Collins (ed.), *Charles Dickens: The Critical Heritage* (London: Routledge, 1986), pp. 428–30.
Widdowson, Peter, 'Introduction: Tess of the d'Urbervilles Faithfully Represented By', in Peter Widdowson (ed.), *New Casebooks: Tess of the d'Urbervilles – Contemporary Critical Essays* (London: Macmillan, 1993).
Wikipedia, 'John Murphy (priest)', <https://en.wikipedia.org/wiki/John_Murphy_(priest)> (accessed 12 February 2019).
Wikipedia, 'Memoirs of Joseph Grimaldi', <https://en.wikipedia.org/wiki/Memoirs_of_Joseph_Grimaldi> (accessed 12 February 2019).
Wikipedia, 'Second Battle of Bull Run', <http://en.wikipedia.org/wiki/Second_Battle_of_Bull_Run> (accessed 12 February 2019).
Wikipedia, 'Stephen Hopkins', <http://en.wikipedia.org/wiki/Stephen_Hopkins> (accessed 12 February 2019).
Wikipedia, 'Sweet Nightingale', <http://en.wikipedia.org/wiki/Sweet_Nightingale> (accessed 12 February 2019).
Wikipedia, 'The Twa Sisters', <http://en.wikipedia.org/wiki/The_Twa_Sisters> (accessed 12 February 2019).
Wikipedia, 'William Stephen Raikes Hodson', <https://en.wikipedia.org/wiki/William_Stephen_Raikes_Hodson> (accessed 12 February 2019).
Willey, Basil, *More Nineteenth Century Studies: A Group of Honest Doubters* (New York: Columbia University Press, 1969).
Williams, Raymond, *The Country and the City* (New York: Oxford University Press, 1973).
Williams, William Carlos, *Paterson* (New York: New Directions, 1963).

Wimsatt, William K., and Cleanth Brooks, *Literary Criticism: A Short History: 2. Romantic and Modern Criticism*, 2 vols (Chicago: University of Chicago Press, 1983).

Wiskus, Jessica, *The Rhythm of Thought: Art, Literature, and Music after Merleau-Ponty* (Chicago and London: Chicago University Press, 2013).

Wolfreys, Julian, *Thomas Hardy: Critical Issues* (London and New York: Palgrave Macmillan, 2009).

Wolfreys, Julian, 'The Idea of Wessex: Subject, Place, and Memory in Thomas Hardy's Poetry', *Literature Compass* 9.11 (2012), pp. 837–47.

Wollaeger, Mark, 'Conrad's Darkness Revisited: Mediated Warfare and Modern(ist) Propaganda in *Heart of Darkness* and "The Unlighted Coast"', in Carola M. Kaplan, Peter Lancelot Mallios and Andrea White (eds), *Conrad in the Twenty-First Century: Contemporary Approaches and Perspectives* (New York: Routledge, 2005), pp. 67–82.

Woodham-Smith, Cecil, *The Reason Why* (London: Constable and Company, 1953).

Woodward, C. Vann, *The Burden of Southern History* (Baton Rouge: Louisiana State University Press, 1968).

Woolf, Virginia, 'The Novels of Thomas Hardy', *The Common Reader*, <https://ebooks.adelaide.edu.au/w/woolf/virginia/w91c2/chapter21.html> (accessed 12 February 2019).

Woolf, Virginia, *To the Lighthouse* (New York: Harcourt, Brace & World, [1927] 1955).

Wordsworth, William, 'Lines Written a Few Miles above Tintern Abbey', in *The Major Works: including the Prelude* (Oxford: Oxford University Press, 2008).

Woubshet, Dag, 'Tizita: A New World Interpretation', *English at Cornell: A Newsletter from the Department of English*; repr. in *Callaloo* 32:2 (Spring 2009), pp. 629–34.

Wright, Thomas, *The Life of Walter Pater*, 2 vols (London: Everett & Co, 1907).

Zeelenberg, Marcel, and Eric van Dijk, 'On the Comparative Nature of Regret', in David R. Mandel, Denis J. Hilton and Patrizia Catellani (eds), *The Psychology of Counterfactual Thinking* (London: Routledge, 2005), pp. 147–61.

Zunshine, Lisa, *Why We Read Fiction: Theory of Mind and the Novel* (Columbus: Ohio State University Press, 2006).

Index

Achebe, Chinua, 374, 375, 381
Albee, Edward, 299, 314
Anderson, Amanda, 322, 331
Andrews, Malcolm, 302, 314n16, 409
Anglesey, Marquess of (George Charles Henry Victor Padget), 236
Aristotle, 18, 137, 149, 241, 258, 271, 272, 273
Arkin, William M., 399
Armstrong, Paul B., 219n1
Armstrong, Tim, 80, 81n43
Arnold, Matthew, 140, 145, 146, 155, 156, 165, 167, 168, 223, 243, 244, 251, 252, 338, 339, 341
Ashton, Rosemary, 282
Asquith, Mark, 84
Atkinson, William, 227, 379, 380, 381, 420

Bagehot, Walter, 239, 302, 349, 356
Baldwin, Peter, 271
Barthes, Roland, 179, 291, 294, 296, 413
Bataille, George, 18, 279, 350
Baudelaire, Charles, 307, 389
Bazin, André, 293
Bentley, Colene, 341, 342, 345
Bergson, Henri, 133, 159, 160, 164, 166, 168, 301, 309, 314, 315
Bettinelli, Saverio, 182

Bevis, Matthew, 315
Bhabha, Homi, 356
Biagini, Eugenio, 242
Bisla, Sundeep, 355n2
Blackstone, William, 262, 279n14
Blanchot, Maurice, 18, 286, 342, 345n23
Bodenheimer, Rosemarie, 278n10, 312, 315n45
Boone, Joseph Allen, 192, 200n8
Booth, Bradford A., 241
Borges, Jorge Luis, 293
Bowen, John, 308, 315n40
Brackenbury, Henry, 377, 382n32, 382n38
Braddon, Mary, 183n13
Brook, G. L., 212
Brooks, Peter, 380n8
Bross, Addison, 381n23
Brown, Bill, 292
Browning, Robert, 158, 176, 241, 349, 354
Burgess, C. F., 380n13
Burke, Edmund, 167n16
Burke, Kenneth, 395, 411

Cardew, Francis Gordon, 373, 381n20
Carey, John, 312, 315n46
Carlisle, Janice, 217
Carlyle, Thomas, 240, 302, 314n18, 341, 363
Carroll, Lewis, 352

Casement, Roger, 372, 374, 375, 380n16
Cash, Peter, 87
Chartier, Roger, 282
Chesterton, G. K., 312
Chorley, W. H., 220
Cicero, 239–53, 281n23
Clark, Timothy, 117
Clifford, Hugh, 382n38
Clough, Arthur Hugh, 241, 352
Cohen, Tom, 117, 118, 123
Coleridge, Samuel Taylor, 80, 137, 149, 300, 314n8
Collins, Philip, 314n15
Collins, Wilkie, 217, 289, 290, 291, 405
Conrad, Joseph, 358–83
Courtney, W. L., 188, 190
Coustillas, Pierre, 184, 188, 190, 200n3
Critchley, Simon, 117

Dallas, E. S., 339, 345n19
Dalziel, Pamela, 84
Dames, Nicholas, 219n1
Davis, Lennard J., 355n3
De Man, Paul, 18, 40, 105, 263, 333, 390, 395, 397, 403, 413
Deleuze, Gilles, 18, 123, 128, 129, 130, 133, 166, 184, 346, 347, 355n1, 413
Derrida, Jacques, 1–4, 6, 8, 9, 18, 52, 62, 63, 65, 78n1, 78n6, 79n15, 80n30, 80n36, 82n76, 117, 118, 127, 130–4, 136, 140, 161, 202, 254, 257, 258, 273, 277n5, 279n15, 285, 296, 333, 347, 401, 402, 403, 413
Dickens, Charles, 85, 105, 112n6, 202–20, 284–8, 291, 292, 294, 299–315, 316, 388, 401, 402, 403, 405, 409–17
Dillon, Jacqueline, 66, 80n41, 81n42
Dollimore, Jonathan, 380n11

Eco, Umberto, 293
Eliot, George, 42, 85, 105, 254–83, 284, 285, 287, 332–45, 358, 379n2, 388, 402

Eliot, T. S., 136, 137, 140, 145, 146, 154, 155, 156, 164, 165, 166, 168n22, 301, 314n12
Empson, William, 301, 314n14, 411
Engels, Friedrich, 19, 20, 24, 44, 45, 49
Enstice, Andrew, 84
Eyre, Banning, 79n13

Farina, Jonathan, 213
Fauconnier, Gilles, 204
Felski, Rita, 135, 138, 144, 162, 165, 166n2, 167n7
Finkelstein, David, 380n17
Fleury, Gabrielle, 188, 189, 190, 193
Ford, Boris, 315n38
Forrest, Alan, 229
Forster, John, 217, 220n7, 302, 304, 305, 311, 314n19, 314n23, 314n31, 315n43
Foucault, Michel, 18, 286, 289, 290, 296, 347, 351, 404, 405
Fowler, Roger, 212, 213
Franklin, Nancy, 182n8
Freedgood, Elaine, 291, 292, 293
Freeman, Edward Augustus, 243, 244, 245
Freud, Sigmund, 136, 140, 141, 142, 160, 164, 166, 167n15, 168n23, 168n25, 202, 285, 296, 348, 349, 353, 355n3, 356n5, 401
Freundschuh, Scott, 182n6
Furbank, P. N., 87

Galef, David, 380n13
Gallagher, Catherine, 254, 257, 258, 259, 260, 261, 262, 264, 265, 266, 268, 270, 271, 272, 273, 274, 275, 276, 276n1, 278n8, 278n9, 278n11, 280n9, 280n22
Gapp, Samuel Vogt, 185, 186
Ghosh, Ranjan, 203
Gibson, James, 82n92, 85
Gide, André, 347
Girard, René, 356n8
Gissing, Alfred, 184–201
Goffman, Erving, 317, 319, 331n2
Goldhill, Simon, 245, 246, 250
Greaney, Michael, 381n28, 382n35

Greenblatt, Stephen, 254, 265, 267, 276n1, 278n11, 280n21, 280n22
Griffin, Michael, 373, 381n22
Gros, Frédéric, 170, 171, 172, 173, 177, 178, 179, 182n4
Grossman, Jonathan, 220n3
Grote George, 243
Grylls, David, 187, 198, 200n2, 201n8
Guattari, Félix, 18, 123, 129, 346

Haight, Gordon S., 345n11
Hamley, William George, 382n32
Hampson, Robert, 381n27, 382n37
Hankins, John Erskine, 81n65
Hardy, Barbara, 84, 88, 95
Hardy, Thomas, 13–51, 52–82, 83–99, 103–13, 202, 294, 337, 350
Harris, Margaret, 345n20
Hartley, Jenny, 331n3
Hartman, Geoffrey, 9n5, 136, 140, 141, 142, 149, 167n7, 168n28
Harvey, A. E., 380n7
Hauser, Arnold, 180, 182
Heffernan, Julián Jiménez, 19
Heidegger, Martin, 18, 40, 55, 68, 81n54, 88, 400
Herman, David, 212, 220n4
Hext, Kate, 247
Hogan, Patrick Colm, 206, 220n2
Hopkins, Gerard Manley, 5–8, 9n3, 9n5, 117–34, 333, 334, 345n6, 345n7, 345n8, 349
Horne, Philip, 199, 200n5, 200n6
Hughes, Kathryn, 332, 338, 344, 345
Huneker, J., 180
Husserl, Edmund, 57, 78, 81n55, 82n76, 94, 96, 160

Jaffe, Audrey, 331n4
James, Henry, 19, 112, 128, 129, 155, 203, 269, 285, 394, 405, 409, 410
Jameson, Frederic, 219n2, 224, 351
Jasanoff, Maya, 383n38
Johnson, Barbara, 82n95, 279n13
Johnson, Edgar, 217, 218
Joyce, James, 104, 112n5, 144

Kahneman, Daniel, 204, 205, 207, 208, 209, 218
Kant, Immanuel, 149, 304, 314n26
Kaplan, Fred, 218
Keats, John, 47, 85, 127, 279n14
Kendrick, Walter, 287, 288
Ketterer, David, 381n26
Kierkegaard, Søren, 346, 356n6
Kitchin, Rob, 182n6
Knowles, Owen, 359, 377, 380
Krieger, Murray, 148, 149, 151, 168n27
Kropholler, P. F., 190
Krueger, Anne O., 277n4
Kruger, Kathryn Brigger, 336, 345n13
Kumar, Krishan, 379n5
Kuriyama, Shigehisa, 163

Lacan, Jacques, 166, 202, 285, 296, 348, 349
Lacoue-Labarthe, Philippe, 361, 368, 369, 374, 380n11
Landor, Walter Savage, 183n13
Langbaum, Robert, 84, 85
Lawtoo, Nidesh, 379, 380n11, 381n25, 389n39
Ledbetter, Kathryn, 237n2
Leigh Hunt, James Henry, 311
Lindqvist, Sven, 361, 367, 369, 376
Litvak, Joseph, 265, 266, 279n18
Loesberg, Jonathan, 333, 345n4, 345n5
Lucretius, 247, 250, 251, 252, 253n1, 253n2, 253n3
Lukács, Georg, 140, 141, 167n12, 167n13, 167n14
Luxmoore, Percy Putt, 376, 378, 382n36

McAlindon, Tom, 88
McGann, Jerome, 62, 223–38
Mahlberg, Michaela, 212, 213
Maisonnat, Claude, 382n34
Manzoni, Alessandro, 175, 176
Marcus, Steven, 285, 330, 350, 351, 352
Marshall, George O., 113n20
Martin, Robert Bernard, 314n16

444   Index

Marx, Karl, 18, 19, 20, 24, 44, 45, 49, 131, 159, 160, 228, 229, 230, 271, 273, 274, 275, 282n27, 283n30, 396
May, Leila Silvana, 331n2
Meisel, Martin, 219, 220n8
Merleau-Ponty, Maurice, 84, 86, 87, 89, 97, 99, 160, 164, 166
Mill, John Stuart, 240, 241, 242, 243, 346, 349
Millar, John Hepburn, 373, 381n18
Millgate, Michael, 84
Modiano, Patrick, 52, 78n3
Moore, Gene, 377
Morris, William, 13, 15
Moynahan, Julian, 220n4

Nancy, Jean-Luc, 18, 19, 20, 21, 50, 68, 69, 81n50, 81n52, 81n53, 81n57, 81n59
Nead, Lynda, 321, 323
Nietzsche, Friedrich, 18, 136, 140, 142, 159, 160, 166, 332, 338, 345n3, 346, 347, 350, 414
Nord, Deborah Epstein, 331n5

Parry, Benita, 380n9
Pater, Walter, 6, 135–69, 239–53, 293, 347
Patmore, Coventy, 354
Paulin, Tom, 83, 84, 85
Peattie, Roger W., 176, 179
Pecora, Vincent, 379n3
Perloff, Marjorie, 224, 226, 237n1
Pettitt, Clare, 282n27
Phelan, James, 213, 214
Piketty, Thomas, 277n4
Pinion, F. B., 95
Pite, Ralph, 84
Plath, Sylvia, 100, 112n2
Plato, 18, 57, 106, 113n8, 113n10, 113n11, 137, 140, 141, 144, 159, 167n13, 168n19, 241, 273, 355n1
Poole, Adrian, 198
Poovey, Mary, 272, 273, 282n28
Prince, Gerald, 206

Ransom, John Crowe, 136, 139, 166n4, 167n9
Rapaport, Herman, 138, 143, 167n6, 167n7
Richards, I. A., 135–69, 411
Rose, Mark, 271
Rosenberg, Isaac, 217, 220n8
Rossetti, Christina, 354
Rossetti, William Michael, 170–83
Royle, Nicholas, 79n20
Russell, William Howard, 225, 227

Sachs, Jonathan, 239
Sadrin, Anny, 217, 220n8
Said, Edward, 7, 9n6, 383n39
Saint-Gelais, Richard, 205
Santayana, George, 146, 147, 163, 168n25, 168n26
Sayeau, Michael, 367
Schaffer, Talia, 192, 200n8
Schmitt, Cannon, 382n30
Schneider, Ralf, 204
Schober, M. F., 182n8
Sedgwick, Eve Kosovsky, 356n8
Selig, Robert L., 186
Serres, Michel, 334, 335, 345n9
Shakespeare, William, 16, 17, 46, 47, 64, 167n10, 190, 200n6, 281n22, 397
Shannon, Edgar, 235, 238n9
Shell, Marc, 271, 272, 273, 282n29
Shelley, Mary, 125, 171, 177, 188
Shelley, Percy Bysshe, 88, 89, 90, 113n8, 118, 119, 171, 177, 178, 288
Skilton, David, 399n2
Slater, Michael, 302, 314n20
Small, Helen, 356n3
Smith, David Woodruff, 79n23
Spiers, Edward M., 235
Sprinker, Michael, 169n34
Stein, Gertrude, 356n9
Steiner, Joan E., 380n7
Stevens, Wallace, 19, 20, 30, 85, 312, 315n47
Stiglitz, Joseph, 277n4
Strachan, Hew, 235, 237n4
Sumner, Gordon, 79n15
Swift, Jonathan, 300, 314n7

Taine, H. A., 314n22
Tate, Trudi, 224, 236, 237n2
Tennyson, Lord Alfred, 62, 223–38, 251, 252, 354, 393
Thackeray, W. M., 75, 85, 302, 304, 311, 314n17, 315n42
Thain, Marion, 84
Therborn, Göran, 238n6
Thirlwell, Angela, 176, 181
Thoreau, Henry David, 14, 15, 62, 171, 182n2, 234, 394
Toadvine, Ted, 117
Tönnies, Ferdinand, 18, 19, 34, 72
Trollope, Anthony, 20, 42, 56, 79n16, 85, 105, 239–53, 287, 288, 289, 337, 387, 388, 389, 390, 391, 393, 394, 395, 396, 398, 399n1, 402, 403
Turner, Mark, 204, 205, 208, 209, 213, 219
Tversky, Barbara, 182n8

Vaihinger, Hans, 212
Veeser, H. Aram, 277n6, 280n21, 281n22
Venn, John, 53, 65, 66, 67, 73, 74, 75, 81n66, 81n67, 82n90, 82n91

Warhol, Andy, 286
Warhol, Robyn, 205, 206, 212

Wasserman, B., 377
Watt, Ian, 379n4
Watts, Cedric, 380n12
Waugh, Evelyn, 358, 379n1
Weber, Samuel, 79n7, 79n8, 79n10
Wells, H. G., 187, 188, 190, 401
Whipple, Edwin P., 220n7
Widdowson, Peter, 109, 113n15
Willey, Basil, 244
Williams, Raymond, 13, 18, 41, 45, 169n34, 400, 401
Williams, William Carlos, 292, 405
Wimsatt, William K., 136, 146, 168n25
Wiskus, Jessica, 86
Wolfreys, Julian, 83, 85
Wollaeger, Mark, 363
Woodham-Smith, Cecil, 234, 235, 236, 238n7
Woodward, C. Vann, 32
Woolf, Virginia, 75, 98, 144, 293, 294, 295, 300, 314n3
Wordsworth, William, 15, 62, 84, 85, 120, 127, 137, 147, 149, 150, 168n28, 168n29
Woubshet, Dag, 79n13
Wright, Thomas, 246

Zunshine, Lisa, 219n1

EU representative:
Easy Access System Europe
Mustamäe tee 50, 10621 Tallinn, Estonia
Gpsr.requests@easproject.com

www.ingramcontent.com/pod-product-compliance
Lightning Source LLC
Chambersburg PA
CBHW071824230426
43672CB00013B/2756